ANTIQUE GUNS
THE COLLECTOR'S GUIDE

ANTIQUE GUNS

THE COLLECTOR'S GUIDE

Second Edition

JOHN E. TRAISTER

STOEGER PUBLISHING COMPANY

COVER DESIGN and PHOTO: Ray Wells
BACK COVER DESIGN: Charlene Cruson Step

FRONT COVER: This pair of Colt Model 1878 double-action revolvers are fitted with $7\frac{1}{2}''$ barrels in .476 caliber. Both were nickel plated at the Colt Factory. They were presented to Sir Frederick Benson and are inscribed with his initials on each trigger guard. They were shipped from the Colt factory in Hartford, Connecticut, in 1889 to the Colt London Agency.

Published by Stoeger Publishing Company
55 Ruta Court
South Hackensack, New Jersey 07606

ISBN: 0-88317-175-9
Library of Congress Catalog Card No.: 88-60403
Manufactured in the United States of America.

Distributed to the book trade and to the sporting goods trade by Stoeger Industries, 55 Ruta Court, South Hackensack, New Jersey 07606.

In Canada, distributed to the book trade and to the sporting goods trade by Stoeger Canada, Ltd., Unit 16, 1801 Wentworth Street, Whitby, Ontario L1N 8R6.

PREFACE

Antique Guns — The Collector's Guide was first published in 1989. It was the result of over 30 years of part-time research consisting of collecting old gun catalogs — both domestic and foreign, reading every publication that I could get my hands on, visiting museums from Maine to California, personally inspecting and noting the characteristics of firearms in personal collections, and finally, starting a gun collection of my own. This latter activity naturally grew into buying, selling, and trading guns.

At first, I purchased every interesting gun that I could afford. The manufacturer, model or caliber/gauge made little difference to me at the time. In fact, the less I knew about a particular firearm, the more interesting it was to me.

When an unfamiliar firearm became a part of my collection, it was thoroughly examined, each marking noted, and then the research began. I combed through the pages of each reference book in my library, looked in back issues of *American Rifleman*, and then I was off to the public library for more reference books. If all else failed, I would send a letter to the National Rifle Association with a complete description of the firearm in question. In those days, the NRA answered each and every letter — post haste! In a week or two, I would receive a letter from such experts as Julian Hatcher, Ed Brown, M.D. Waite, Elmer Keith or Phil Sharpe — either identifying the gun in question, or giving sources where more information about the model could be found. This type of research continued over the next decade.

Eventually, certain models became more intriguing to me than others. Lever-action rifles were of special interest to me — probably stemming from my youth when I spent Saturday afternoons watching the B movies starring Roy, Gene, and Hopalong. The Winchester Model 92 carbine was usually the firearm that supplemented the star's trusty "six-shooter" that fired no less than 15 or 20 shots without reloading! Yes, the Winchester Model 92 was the weapon used for long-range gun battles between the good guys and bad guys.

Whatever the reason, my interest soon turned to collecting Winchester firearms, with a few Colt handguns thrown in for good measure. Consequently, my entire gun collection took on a different form as I began trading other models for Winchesters. You might say that I started specializing in collecting Winchester firearms.

Many other collectors have taken a similar route; that is, I know of several people who collect nothing but Remington handguns of the last century. Another specializes in Kentucky flintlocks, while still another collects only Savage Model 99 rifles with perfect bores.

By-products also stem from gun collecting. For example, a box or two of ammunition sometimes accompanies a gun trade. The next gun purchase may include a few rounds of, say, .50-110 cartridges, and so on until the gun collector has a good start on a cartridge collection. Original boxes or crates in which firearms were shipped also have collector value; the same goes for price tags, instruction manuals, bullet molds, powder flasks, and the like. Even gun-cleaning items such as oil bottles and old brass or wooden cleaning rods have reached collector status. The examples are almost endless!

Gun collecting also opened up another fascinating field for me. Many times a firearm came into my possession that was incomplete or badly abused. If a part was missing, I then set out to locate an original replacement. If none could be found, I tried to obtain the original dimensions and made a replacement in my machine shop — using a small Myford lathe with a milling attachment.

During these firearm restoration sessions, I also learned the processes of casehardening, silver soldering, stock inletting, repair, and refinishing, along with the art of bluing and browning.

Many of the results obtained from my gunsmithing experiences eventually wound up in print — either in the form of magazine articles for such publications as *American Rifleman*, *Shooting Industry*, *Rifle*, *Handloader*, and others, or in several books on the subject. Then came **How to Buy and Sell Used Guns** (another Stoeger book), which was the predecessor to this one. It discusses in detail how to inspect antique (and modern) arms and determine their authenticity, firearms price trends and how to collect for investment, firearms to avoid, restoring arms and whether to do it, and how to protect your collection, among other related topics.

This title, **Antique Guns — The Collector's Guide**, covers the specific pre-1900 firearms in which most antique arms collectors are interested. It was conceived in response to the enormous demand I've encountered among collectors and shooters for a detailed guide to identifying and pricing antique firearms — a guide that is not so long and wordy that it takes hours to pour through it, nor a guide so skimpy that you can't determine exactly which item among similar models is listed.

In a concise, easy-to-follow format, I have tried to include the basics — the essential specifications necessary to make an accurate identification, some historical notes about specimens of particular interest, hundreds of photos and/or drawings for identification purposes, and a suggested monetary value — based on the average trading price. For rare items, where little or no trading has taken place in recent years — collectors, dealers and museums were consulted.

The antique arms are arranged into three broad categories: handguns, rifles and shotguns. Within those groupings, the guns are listed alphabetically by name of gunmaker or manufacturer, which ultimately makes any item relatively easy to find. At the end of the groupings are several smaller, obvious categories, such as American Kentucky Flintlock Rifles (at the end of the Rifle Section) and Confederate Handguns (at the end of Handguns). In any of my books, I've never wanted the reader to be bogged down with too much verbiage, and my objective in this title was to achieve a healthy balance between words and information.

Several other things, I believe, make this book different from a few books you may currently find in the marketplace on antique arms. One is the inclusion of guns of foreign origin. American arms are fascinating, to be sure. But our heritage, after all, is derived from many countries around the world. I have tried to give this book international scope by highlighting the craftsmanship of British gunmakers, for example, Belgian, French, Italian, Canadian, German, Chinese, and others.

Another difference from other volumes is the Blackpowder Replica Section. This is an extensive listing that encompasses contemporary reproductions of antique arms. Why is it included?

Three reasons:

- Descriptions of these guns may prevent the novice collector from getting scalped by the purchase of replicas posed as originals.

- The prices of replicas, the Colt Dragoons, for example, are more affordable than the originals— and while the "real thing" is most desirable, a replica may be a beginning for some collectors.

- No other book, to my knowledge, has such a complete, up-to-date identification/pricing guide for these models.

Another feature of this book is a detailed listing of Obsolete Cartridges, an area for some collectors that is a direct outgrowth of their collecting of antique arms. This section includes centerfire rifle cartridges, obsolete metric cartridges, rimfire cartridges, and obsolete shotshells — all well illustrated.

Finally, a complete cross-referenced index is provided to assist you in finding whatever or whomever it is you need to locate in regards to your collecting.

In a volume of this scope, it is difficult to include everything pertinent to every collector. I have endeavored to include the major U.S. gunmakers and manufacturers and a number of foreign gunmakers, as mentioned earlier, that are most often encountered in gun-trading circles. This book in no way reflects an attempt to include every model and every variation of firearm ever made prior to 1900.

In addition, the prices listed within are intended to be the average selling price as found in my "poll" throughout the country. They are not engraved in stone and can be arbitrary at times because of various contributing factors, which are discussed at length in the section "Collecting Antique Guns."

Hopefully, all collectors — aspiring or established — will discover this book as a vital reference. In addition, I hope it will prove to be a valuable resource for gunsmiths — especially those involved in repairing and restoring antique weapons — as well as museum curators, auctioneers, appraisers and insurance adjusters.

Finally, I'd like to thank Charlene Cruson Step for her enormous enthusiasm and editorial dedication on the first edition, to Robert E. Weise, Publisher, and to everyone else who was in any way involved with the project.

—John E. Traister

ACKNOWLEDGMENTS

The resources for a volume of this kind are endless. I couldn't possibly list or remember all the books and articles I've read that have helped me compile this. However, the printed sources I've used most recently are listed in the Bibliography. As far as experts I've spoken to, they have been numerous, and I would specifically like to thank Turner Kirkland of Dixie Gun Works, Fred Goodwin, Dick Reyes, and the many gun dealers all over the country whom I've consulted with at length. Also, thanks to the associations and curators of all the museums listed below who provided me with information and photographs from their collections.

I'd like to extend my thanks to all the firearms manufacturing companies who assisted in providing and clarifying information and/or supplying photographs, especially Colt Industries and Savage Arms, Beeman, CVA, Hopkins & Allen, Navy Arms, Shiloh, Thompson/Center and all the other blackpowder reproduction manufacturers.

Obtaining photographs of antique arms is a full-time pursuit in itself, and I would like to thank John Denner of North Lancaster, Ontario, Canada, for the use of hundreds of his photos; Andrew Larson of the General Robert E. Lee Museum in Gettysburg, PA, for taking photos especially for this volume; Ken Longe, the research specialist of the Union Pacific Historical Museum; Leon Wier for the loan of photos from his vast Remington handgun collection; the other museums who contributed negatives and photos; and Ray Wells for doing such a superb photography job with the cover — photographing the presentation London-cased Colts.

A deep bow of gratitude is due C. Keeler Chapman, John Karns, and Christopher Long for their untiring efforts in supplying art work in this edition, and to Ruby Updike for her able assistance in organizing and proofing the material in this book.

U.S. MUSEUMS AND ASSOCIATIONS

Antietam National Battlefield, Sharpsburg, MD
Arkansas State University, Jonesboro, AR
Arizona Historical Society, Tucson, AZ
Bangor Historical Society, Bangor, ME
Colonial National Historical Park, Yorktown, VA
DAR Museum, Washington, DC
Douglas County Historical Society, Omaha, NE
Ft. Davis Nat'l. Historic Site, Ft. Davis, TX
General Robert E. Lee Museum, Gettysburg, PA
Gettysburg Nat'l. Military Park, Gettysburg, PA
Harpers Ferry Nat'l. Historical Park, Harpers Ferry, WV
Higgins Armory Museum, Worcester, MA
Historical Society of the Militia and National Guard, Washington, DC
Hubbell Trading Post National Historic Site, Ganado, AZ
Independence Nat'l. Historical Park, Philadelphia, PA
J. M. Davis Gun Museum, Claremore, OK
Kampeska Heritage Museum, Watertown, SD
Kentucky Military History Museum, Frankfort, KY
Maine Historical Society, Portland, ME
Manassas National Battlefield Park, Manassas, VA
Maritime Philadelphia Museum, Philadelphia, PA
National Museum of American History, Washington, DC
National Museum of History and Technology, Washington, DC
National Rifle Association (NRA) Firearms Museum, Washington, DC
Naval War College, Newport, RI
New Market Battlefield Park, New Market, VA
Old Washington Historic State Park, Washington, AR
Patriots Point Development Authority, Mt. Pleasant, SC

Pendleton District Historical & Recreational
    Commission, Pendleton, SC
Petersburg National Battlefield, Petersburg, VA
Richmond National Battlefield Park,
    Richmond, VA
Rutherford B. Hayes Presidential Center,
    Fremont, OH
Shasta State Historic Park, Shasta, AR
Springfield Armory National Historic Site,
    Springfield, MA
State of Rhode Island and Providence
    Plantations, Providence, RI
The Museum of the Confederacy, Richmond, VA
U.S. Marine Corps Museum, Washington, DC
Union Pacific Historical Museum, Omaha, NE
Virginia Historical Society, Richmond, VA
Warren Rifles Confederate Museum,
    Front Royal, VA
Washington County Historical Museum,
    Ft. Calhoun, NE
West Point Museum, West Point, NY
Woolaroc Museum, Bartlesville, OK

NOTE

The term "antique" as used in this book encompasses all
firearms manufactured prior to 1900. However, the Federal
Firearms Act recognizes only firearms manufactured in
1898 or before as "antiques" under present classification.

CANADIAN MUSEUMS AND ASSOCIATIONS

F. T. Hill Museum, Rivershurst,
    Saskatchewan
Fort Howe Blockhouse, Saint John,
    New Brunswick
Fort Macleod Historical Assn., Fort Macleod,
    Alberta
Ft. Rodd Hill Nat'l. Historic Park, Victoria,
    British Columbia
Halton Region Museum, Milton, Ontario
London Historical Museums, London,
    Ontario
Montreal Military & Maritime Museum,
    Montreal, Quebec
Museum of Northern British Columbia, Prince
    Rupert, British Columbia
New Brunswick Museum, New Brunswick
Pacific National Exhibition, Vancouver,
    British Columbia
Princess Patricia's Canadian Light Infantry
    Regimental Museum, Calgary, Alberta
Regimental Museum, New Westminster,
    British Columbia

ABOUT THE AUTHOR

John Traister collected and traded antique and modern firearms ever since he was about 13 years old, living in Front Royal, Virginia. His father and uncles were accomplished hunters and outdoorsmen, and naturally John followed in their footsteps.

After attending college in Boston, Traister served a hitch in the U.S. Marine Corps that he completed in the mid-1960s. He then became involved in the building construction industry, designing and supervising the installation of electrical and mechanical systems for all types of establishments from residential to high-rise office buildings. It was during this time that he wrote his first magazine article for a trade journal, followed by a comprehensive book on the same technical subject.

Not content with writing about engineering problems, he began writing about his collecting hobby — firearms. In 1978, he turned the gun hobby into a full-fledged vocation by launching a gun-trading/gunsmithing business of his own in his present home town of Bentonville, Virginia — and continued to write about the arms as well.

To date, Traister has authored more than 100 different books, and continues to write at the rate of about three or four per year. While most of these books deal with engineering and building construction subjects, ten of these titles are aimed directly at the shooting industry — three of which are published by Stoeger Publishing Company: *How to Buy and Sell Used Guns*, *Gunsmithing at Home*, and this book, *Antique Guns — The Collector's Guide*.

Traister and an associate have also been working on a comprehensive book on firearm disassembly for the past five years. Since replacement parts for antique guns are becoming harder and harder to locate, Traister is attempting to provide working

drawings for many obsolete gun parts so that the parts may be made by any machine shop or even by hobbyists with their own lathe and milling machine. This book also contains exploded views, disassembly/assembly instructions, and complete troubleshooting charts for both popular and rare antique firearms.

"We hope to have this huge volume completed within the year," says Traister.

In the meantime, John Traister and his crew of four assistants continue tracking gun prices throughout the United States — at gunshops, gun shows, and auctions — to ensure that his books, such as this one, will be as accurate as possible.

CONTENTS

PREFACE 5
ACKNOWLEDGMENTS 7
ABOUT THE AUTHOR 9

COLLECTING ANTIQUE GUNS 13

CHAPTER 1 — HANDGUNS 19
Gunmakers A to Z 21
American Kentucky Flintlock Pistols 81
Confederate Handguns 88
U.S. Military Handguns 89

CHAPTER 2 — RIFLES 101
Gunmakers A to Z 103
American Kentucky Flintlock Rifles 171
Confederate Military Rifles 188
U.S. Military Flintlock Rifles 191
U.S. Military Cartridge Rifles and Carbines 193

CHAPTER 3 — SHOTGUNS 199
Gunmakers A to Z 201

CHAPTER 4 — BLACKPOWDER REPLICAS 229
Gunmakers A to Z 231

CHAPTER 5 — OBSOLETE CARTRIDGES 283
Centerfire Rifle Cartridges 285
Rimfire Cartridges 298
Shotshells 301

CHAPTER 6 — OBSOLETE GUN PARTS 303

BIBLIOGRAPHY 309
INDEX 311

COLLECTING ANTIQUE GUNS

Anyone engaged in buying, selling, or trading antique firearms should be and can become competent in three major areas:

- Identification of the firearm in question.
- A knowledge of the gun's characteristics in order to recognize any modifications or fakes.
- Placing a value on the firearm.

Since the beginning of the firearms industry in the 15th century, thousands of different models of rifles, muskets, shotguns and handguns have been crafted. In the earliest years, seldom did two guns ever turn out alike—even those made by the same gunmaker. This greatly complicates identification. Furthermore, markings on many older firearms were nonexistent or else are not recognizable due to aging and wear. Still, there are several characteristics to look for in any firearm, and the knowledgeable person can at least determine the approximate era of manufacture and also the approximate value from the quality of workmanship and from dealing in similar firearms.

Experts have spent the majority of their lifetimes studying old gun catalogs, museum collections and hundreds of reference books; they know not only the maker and model of a particular firearm, but can also readily identify the variations, and oftentimes pinpoint the manufacture date to within a year or two. Furthermore, they can usually tell if a particular gun has been altered, refinished or faked. Such knowledge cannot be acquired from any one book or within a short period of time. It takes years of study and experience to develop the required skills.

The term "antique" as used in this book encompasses all firearms manufactured prior to 1900. Let's take a closer look at several factors that are involved in the evaluation of any antique firearm: collector interest, scarcity and condition.

COLLECTOR INTEREST

A primary factor that influences the value of a firearm is collector interest. Was the gun made by somebody famous, owned by somebody famous, or was it fired in an important historical conflict, such as the Revolutionary War? Answers to these questions have a direct effect on the demand for any firearm. Conversely, where there is meager collector interest, demand will be low.

Although most antique firearms have collector interest to some extent, certain models are naturally more in demand than others. Few collectors will argue that Winchester and Colt firearms have been the blue chips of gun collections for the better part of this century. However, today almost any antique firearm is interesting to some collector. This situation has been brought about by the hearty increase in the number of active collectors and the correspondingly growing number of dealers who cater to them. With this growth a wide diversity in collecting interest has developed. Firearms that held little appeal a few years ago are now becoming extremely popular. Typical examples are the small-bore Stevens and Winchester rifles, single-shot pistols, the cheap cartridge revolvers; even the old single-shot, break open shotguns are fascinating to many collectors.

Specialization, however, parallels the overall popularity of gun collecting. Individual collectors will concentrate on, say, pre-1900 lever-action rifles, while others on one brand of shotgun. These specialized fields embrace the entire range of firearms development, including such accessories as loading tools, bullet molds and gunsmith's tools.

And the often-ignored rusted battlefield relics have their devotees, too. Armed with only a metal detector, many collectors enjoy hours of pleasure combing the old Civil War battlefields in search of lead bullets, buttons and other artifacts.

SCARCITY

As certain firearms become more difficult to find, their value almost always increases; an original Confederate Schneider & Glassick Revolver, for example, is almost impossible to come across casually; it will take work to obtain it for your own collection. Consequently, paying thousands of dollars for it, when found, may not be surprising.

Having established the fact that a firearm interests a particular collector, that it may or may not be a scarce commodity, the final factor to consider — and the one open to infinite debate between seller and buyer — is condition.

CONDITION

Condition is the major criterion in determining the value of an antique firearm. For example, your neighbor's grandmother discovered a Remington 1858 Army Revolver in the attic that her grandfather used during the Civil War. It did not see heavy service, so nearly 90 percent of the original finish is intact. This would command a premium price. On the other hand, if the gun had been dug up in an old garbage pit and it had a rusted barrel, heavily scratched wood grip and a missing trigger, what would you be willing to pay for it?

NRA Standards of Condition for Antique Firearms

Recognizing that the parties concerned seldom agree on the condition of a used firearm, the National Rifle Association has made available "Standards of Condition for Antique Firearms," which are probably the most popular and most often used in determining condition. They are largely based on the percentage of original finish, as follows.

Factory New: all original parts; 100% original finish; in perfect condition in every respect, in side and out. Guns packed in original boxes and/or shipping crates demand a premium. Less than 1% of all antique guns will be found in this condition.

Excellent: all original parts; over 80% original finish; sharp lettering, numerals, and design on metal and wood; unmarred wood; fine bore. Less than 5% of all antique firearms will be found in this condition.

Fine: all original parts; over 30% original finish; sharp lettering, numerals, and design on metal and wood; minor marks in wood; good bore. This is the condition of most firearms that serious collectors purchase.

Very Good: all original parts; none to 30% original finish; original metal surfaces smooth with all edges sharp; clear lettering, numerals, and design on metal; wood slightly scratched or bruised; bore disregarded for collector firearms.

Good: some minor replacement parts; metal smoothly rusted or lightly pitted in places, cleaned, or reblued; principal lettering, numerals, and design on metal legible; wood refinished, scratched, bruised, or minor cracks repaired; in good working order.

Fair: some major parts replaced; minor replacement parts may be required; metal rusted, may be lightly pitted all over, vigorously cleaned, or reblued; rounded edges of metal and wood; principal lettering, numerals, and design on metal partly obliterated; wood scratched, bruised, cracked, or repaired where broken; in fair working order or can be easily repaired and placed in working order.

Poor: major and minor parts replaced; major replacement parts required and extensive restoration needed; metal deeply pitted; principal lettering, numerals, and design obliterated, wood badly scratched, bruised, cracked, or broken; mechanically inoperative; generally undesirable as a collector firearm.

These standards, however, were compiled a number of years ago, and current dealers have found that they need to articulate the condition of a firearm even more finitely than the NRA did. Nowadays, for example, an antique arm considered in "Excellent" condition may have 95 percent original finish (not just the "over 80%" as prescribed by the NRA), and that 15 percent between the 80 and 95 would make the difference between a selling price of $500 versus $5,000. So you will find that most gun dealers today try to break down that percentage of original finish even more finely.

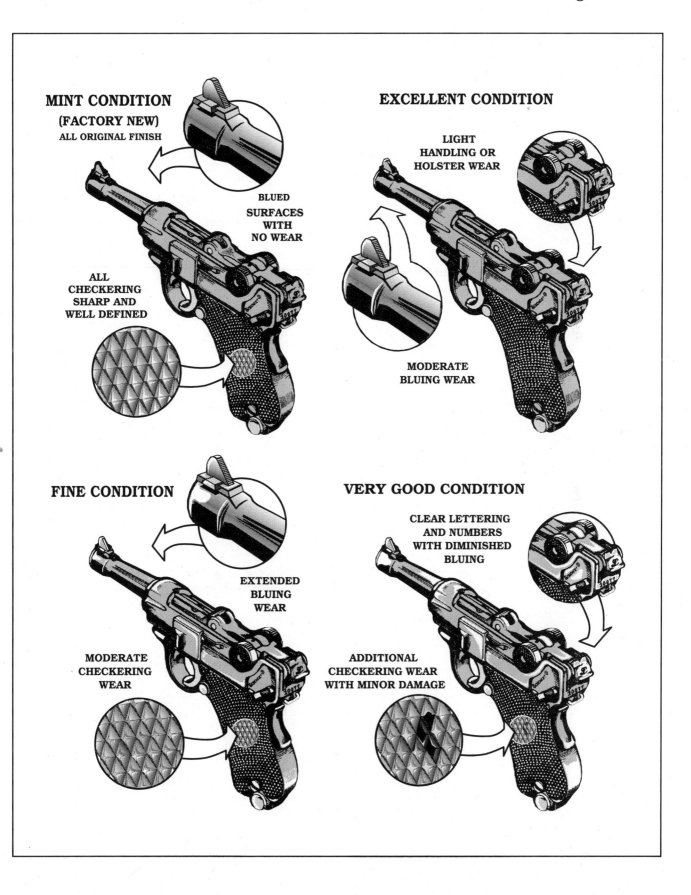

MINT CONDITION
(FACTORY NEW)
ALL ORIGINAL FINISH

BLUED
SURFACES
WITH
NO WEAR

ALL
CHECKERING
SHARP AND
WELL DEFINED

EXCELLENT CONDITION

LIGHT
HANDLING OR
HOLSTER WEAR

MODERATE
BLUING WEAR

FINE CONDITION

EXTENDED
BLUING
WEAR

MODERATE
CHECKERING
WEAR

VERY GOOD CONDITION

CLEAR LETTERING
AND NUMBERS
WITH DIMINISHED
BLUING

ADDITIONAL
CHECKERING WEAR
WITH MINOR DAMAGE

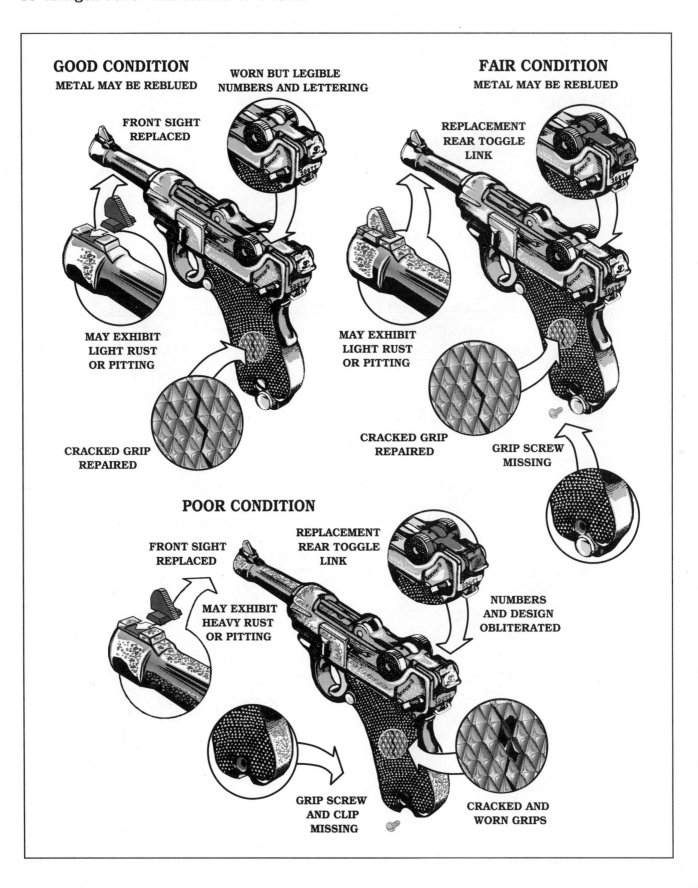

GOOD CONDITION
METAL MAY BE REBLUED

WORN BUT LEGIBLE
NUMBERS AND LETTERING

FRONT SIGHT
REPLACED

MAY EXHIBIT
LIGHT RUST
OR PITTING

CRACKED GRIP
REPAIRED

FAIR CONDITION
METAL MAY BE REBLUED

REPLACEMENT
REAR TOGGLE
LINK

MAY EXHIBIT
LIGHT RUST
OR PITTING

CRACKED GRIP
REPAIRED

GRIP SCREW
MISSING

POOR CONDITION

FRONT SIGHT
REPLACED

REPLACEMENT
REAR TOGGLE
LINK

MAY EXHIBIT
HEAVY RUST
OR PITTING

NUMBERS
AND DESIGN
OBLITERATED

GRIP SCREW
AND CLIP
MISSING

CRACKED AND
WORN GRIPS

DETERMINING GUN VALUES

While the worth of any antique firearm involves condition, relative scarcity, historical significance, and collector demand, the "true value" of any firearm is not what a collector thinks his or her gun is worth. Nor is it the price the seller asks. It is not just what the buyer is willing to pay, either. The true value is determined when the amount the seller will accept coincides with the amount the buyer is willing to pay. This, and only this, is the true value of any gun.

However, for purposes of determining the value of firearms in this book, all arms are considered to be in "Excellent" condition, as defined by the NRA Standards. If they fall below this category, then the price you might expect to receive for a particular gun will be lowered. The prices on the following pages have been established by averaging the prices polled from around the country through printed sources, gun dealers, museums, and the like.

General demand for collector firearms is constantly increasing, and any gun's worth rises and falls in proportion to the demand for it. Demand is also influenced by articles that appear in periodicals or by well-prepared gun books that describe and classify firearms of a particular maker or manufacturer.

Also remember that gun values may vary from region-to-region around the country and from dealer-to-dealer.

Even with the NRA Standards of Condition as a guide, it is difficult to appraise or evaluate the general condition and mechanical features of any firearm with precise accuracy unless you can examine it personally. It is unlikely that anyone unfamiliar with firearms would know if parts had been replaced or altered, or if a gun had been refinished, made up from two or three specimens, or was a rare variation or a transitional type. Thus, in correspondence, such points may be overlooked. Identifications or appraisals by mail may be both inaccurate and unfair to the owner or to the one being asked to identify or evaluate the gun unseen. All that can be done under the circumstances is to give a probable value of the model or type.

Keep in mind that collector values tend to rise steeply in the "Fine" and "Excellent" categories. This is particularly true of older firearms that are rarely encountered in top condition. Some of the great rarities are almost never encountered in any but worn condition, yet their values are not severely lessened by their condition.

Anyone interested in antique firearms and their values should own not only this book, **Antique Guns—The Collector's Guide,** but also read every other book you can obtain. A perusal of classified ads that appear in firearms publications such as Shotgun News, Gun List, Winchester Gun Trader, etc., will also keep you up-to-date as to value trends on specific or comparable firearms. Attending gun shows where guns are bought, sold or traded is another excellent way to acquaint you with current selling prices and trends.

It should be obvious that the serious collector must be a firearms student. Any gun worth having is worth learning about. A book for every gun used to be the policy of many successful collectors. Now it should be more like two or three books for each gun. With the wide availability of fine articles and books published today and the numerous gun shows that are held, no one need be uninformed about antique guns and their value.

CHAPTER ONE
HANDGUNS

The handgun has traditionally been a weapon of self-defense. The early smooth-bore flintlock pistols, for example, were carried by travelers to protect themselves from highwaymen or other lawless persons. The pistol also played an important role in settling disputes of the day, either in the form of duels or shootouts. There is no doubt that some shooters used their handguns to take game on occasion; sometimes they were used to finish off a wounded deer or antelope, rather than use another precious rifle cartridge. But, still, the handgun was used primarily to defend one's self or possessions.

Most of the early pistols were of single-shot design, although double-barreled varieties were also seen. As firearms evolved into the 19th century, the number of barrels multiplied into three, four or more, and became known as pepperboxes. One distinguishing feature of firearms of the 1800s is their remarkable diversity. It seemed to be a period of prolific invention, during which all types, shapes and novelties were produced: cane guns, hand cannons, saw handles, exotic wood, pearl or ivory grips, spur triggers. You name it, it was there. Many of these guns are not merely weapons, however; they are works of art and leaps of the imagination that have been preserved by and for collectors.

Samuel Colt is often credited with the first successful revolving pistol. Note the use of the term "pistol" here. You will find on the following pages many revolvers that are referred to as pistols. Remember that during this period, the revolver was a new entity, with "pistol" being a carryover from an earlier time. Nowadays, firearms aficionados easily distinguish between pistols and revolvers, but it took a while for people to make that distinction. During the last half of the century, revolvers were rapidly adopted by law enforcement personnel and, after much persuasion, by soldiers. Once accepted, they acquired great popularity with the Army and Navy as service weapons.

John S. Mosby (the "gray ghost") and his rangers of Civil War fame, probably utilized the caplock revolver more than any other outfit in military history. It was reported that each ranger wore two revolvers with another brace of holstered pistols placed across the horse's back in front of the saddle. Additional loaded cylinders were carried in the pockets for quick reloading.

In addition to Colt, manufacturers such as Remington, Harrington & Richardson, and Smith & Wesson soon followed with their own revolver models, some of which continue to be manufactured today.

For ease in locating a particular firearm, the Handgun Section is arranged in four basic groupings:

Page Number

Gunmakers A to Z. **21**

American Kentucky Flintlock Pistols. **81**

Confederate Handguns **88**

U.S. Military Handguns. **89**

  U.S. Military Handguns of Colt Mfr. **89**

  U.S. Military Pistols **92**

  U.S. Military Revolvers **97**

ADAMS REVOLVING ARMS CO.
New York, New York

Although the main office of this firm was in New York City, its percussion revolvers were actually manufactured by the Massachusetts Arms Company of Chicopee Falls, Mass. The Adams Patent Revolvers were based on English patents owned by Robert Adams (*see* separate listing) and were manufactured under license; these were undoubtedly used during the Civil War, probably by both sides, although ordnance records of the time do not substantiate their official use.

Adams Patent Percussion Revolver. . . . $395
Calibers: 36, some 31. Five-shot cylinder. Barrels: about 3, 4, or 6 inches. Solid frame. Sliding safety. Walnut grips. Blued finish. Based on the Beaumont-Adams revolver design, this was made during the late 1850s.

ROBERT ADAMS
London, England

Robert Adams (1809 – 1870) was a British gunmaker of renown. During the 1850s, his self-cocking, five-shot revolver became a chief competitor to the Colt of similar design. Service tests, in fact, were conducted comparing the two guns and, although the Adams stood up well in the testing, it was rejected in favor of the Colt because it lacked a sturdy loading ramrod. Adams solved this problem and patented the improvement in 1854 along with an improved self-cocking lock mechanism of Beaumont design (1855). This improved gun did pass British ordnance tests and replaced the Colt as a service arm. The Massachusetts Arms Co. licensed the patent designs and manufactured an Adams Patent Revolver, of different calibers, for use in the U.S.

Adams Revolver $440
Calibers: 38, 54. Barrels: 4½, 6¼, 7½ inches; octagonal. Five-shot cylinder. Solid frame. Loaded with a wadded bullet pressed in by the thumb. Manufactured by George & John Deane of London, and often called the Deane-Adams Model (1851).

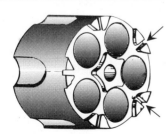

Early revolver safety. The raised sections between the chambers were grooved to provide a secure resting place for the hammer.

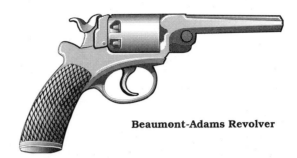

Beaumont-Adams Revolver

Beaumont-Adams Revolver $395
Calibers: 38, 54. Five-shot cylinder. Sliding safety. Cylinder-pin release. Carried the improved lock mechanism patented by Lt. F.B.E. Beaumont (1855) and an improved lever rammer patented by James Kerr (1855). Manufactured by the London Armoury Company and supplied to the British military services until about 1867.

AETNA ARMS COMPANY
New York, New York

Aetna 22 Pocket Revolver $245
Caliber: 22 RF. Seven-shot tip-up revolver. Barrel: 3⅛ inches, octagonal. Brass frame with spur trigger. Blade front sight, rear notch sight. Walnut or rosewood grips. Blued or nickel-plated finish. Made from 1880 to 1890.

Aetna 32 Pocket Revolver $225
Similar to the 22 Pocket Revolver except 32 caliber with five-shot cylinder.

Aetna No. 2 Pocket Revolver $225
Caliber: 32 Short RF. Five-shot cylinder. Single-action. Solid frame with spur trigger. Nickel finish. Checkered hard rubber grips.

Aetna No. 2½ Pocket Revolver $230
Caliber: 32 Short RF. Five-shot cylinder. Single-action. Solid frame with spur trigger. Nickel finish. Checkered hard rubber grips.

Aetna Model 1876 Single-Action Revolver $210
Calibers: 22, 32, 38 Rimfire. Seven-shot cylinder (22 caliber), Five-shot cylinder (32 and 38 caliber).

NOTE

Aetna Models No. 2, 2½, and 1876 were previously manufactured by Harrington & Richardson in Worcester, Massachusetts. Overall appearance of the Aetna revolvers closely resembles the Smith & Wesson revolvers of the day.

ALEXIA
Maker: Hopkins & Allen
Norwich, Connecticut

Alexia Single-Action Revolver
Calibers: 22, 32, 38, 41 Rimfire. Seven-shot cylinder (22 caliber), five-shot cylinder (32, 38 and 41 caliber). Solid frame with spur trigger and octagonal barrel. Also marketed as: Blue Jacket, Captain Jack, Chichester, Defender, Dictator, Mountain Eagle, Hopkins & Allen, Towers Police Safety, and Universal. Made 1868-1915.

22 Caliber Rimfire	**$160**
32 Short Rimfire	**165**
38 Short Rimfire	**180**
41 Short Rimfire	**210**

ALLEN & THURBER
Worcester, Massachusetts

Ethan Allen secured his first U.S. patent in 1837 for what eventually became the well-known pepperbox type of multiple firing pistol. He set up shop with his brother-in-law, Charles Thurber, in Grafton, Mass., from 1837 to 1842. They relocated to Norwich, Conn., from 1842 to 1847, then made a final move to Worcester, where Allen & Thurber, the company, remained until 1865. (*See* also Allen & Wheelock and Ethan Allen & Co.)

**Allen & Thurber
Center-Hammer Pistol**

Allen & Thurber Center Hammer Pistol. . $295
Caliber: 34. Center hammer. Barrel: 6 inches; half-round, half-octagonal. Made circa 1840 to 1860.

Allen & Thurber Pepperbox. $1795
Caliber: 31. Six-shot cylinder. Barrel: 3¾ inches. Engraved frame and nipple shield. Hammer stamped "ALLEN'S PATENT 1845." Made circa 1845 to 1855.

Allen & Thurber Pocket Pistol. $245
Caliber: 50. Center hammer. Barrel: half-round, half-octagonal. Trigger guard. Round walnut grip. Made circa 1840.

ALLEN & WHEELOCK
Worcester, Massachusetts

Upon Charles Thurber's retirement in 1856, Ethan Allen formed a partnership with his other brother-in-law, Thomas P. Wheelock. Under the name Allen & Wheelock, the company produced pepperbox pistols and a variety of revolvers from 1856 to 1865. In about 1865 after Wheelock's death, the company name was changed again to Ethan Allen & Co., when Allen's sons-in-law, Henry C. Wadsworth and Sullivan Forehand, became partners. (*See* also Allen & Thurber, Ethan Allen & Co., U.S. Military Revolvers.)

Allen & Wheelock Pocket Pepperbox . . $1800
Calibers: 25, 28, 31, 43. Four-, five- and six-shot cylinders. Barrels: 2½ to 4 inches, fluted. Bar hammers or hammerless, which command a premium.

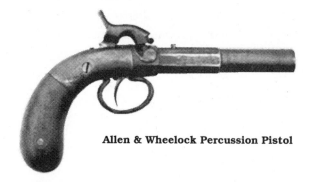

Allen & Wheelock Percussion Pistol

Allen & Wheelock Single-Shot Percussion Pistol **$395**
Calibers: 31, 36 and 38. Single-shot. Barrel: 3 to 6 inches; octagonal and half-octagonal. Fixed sights. Walnut grips. Blued finish.

ETHAN ALLEN & CO.
Worcester, Massachusetts

After their Uncle Tom Wheelock died, Sullivan Forehand and Henry Wadsworth became the "& Co." principals of Ethan Allen & Co., formerly Allen & Wheelock. Both Forehand and Wadsworth married Allen's daughters and continued the family business with their father-in-law, producing pepperboxes, underhammer pistols, revolvers and rifles. After Allen died in 1871, his sons-in-law carried on the gunmaking legacy, which endured almost until the turn of the century. (*See* also Forehand & Wadsworth, Allen & Wheelock.)

**Ethan Allen & Co.
Center Hammer Single-Shot Pistol**

E. Allen & Co. Single-Shot Pistol. **$595**
Caliber: 32 RF. Center hammer. Barrel: 4 inches, with auto ejector. Iron frame. Made from 1865 to 1871.

AMERICAN ARMS COMPANY
Boston, Massachusetts

The American Arms Company established the Boston operation in 1870 and remained there through 1901. A second operation was organized in Milwaukee, Wisconsin in 1893 which continued production until 1904. The company was acquired by Marlin Fire Arms in 1901.

**American Arms Co. Hammerless
Revolver.** **$295**
Caliber: 32. Five-shot. Top break. Barrel: ¾ inches; round, ribbed. Hard rubber grips with monogram at top. Nickel finish.

American Arms Co. Revolver (DA). **$250**
Caliber: 38 S&W. Double-action. Top break.

American Arms Co. Revolver (SA). **$265**
Caliber: 38 S&W. Five-shot cylinder. Single-action. Top break.

**American Arms Co. Wheeler Pat. O/U
Pistol (I)** **$795**
Caliber: 22 Short RF, 32 Short RF. Double-barrel. Brass frame. Spur trigger. Made from 1866 to 1878.

**American Arms Co. Wheeler Pat. O/U
Pistol (II)** **$575**
Caliber: 32 Short RF. Barrel: 3 inches, double. Brass frame. Spur trigger. Made from 1866 to 1878.

**American Arms Co. Wheeler Pat. O/U
Pistol (III)** **$775**
Caliber: 41 Short RF. Barrel: 2⅝ inches, double. Brass frame. Finger spur trigger. Square butt grips. Made from 1866 to 1878.

AMERICAN STANDARD TOOL CO.
Newark, New Jersey

American Standard Tool Co. Hero **$245**
Caliber: 34. Percussion. Screw barrel. Center hammer. Spur trigger. Made from 1865 to 1870.

American Standard Tool Co. Revolver . . **$450**
Caliber: 32 Short RF. Seven-shot cylinder. Spur trigger. Tip-up type. Made from 1865 to 1870.

ARABIAN FLINTLOCKS
Various Manufacturers

Arabian Flintlock Pistol **$495**
Caliber: ⅝-inch bore. Barrel: 13 inches, round. Overall length: 20 inches. Markings on lock plate, some inlays in stock. Brass trim.

G.H. AVELEY & WHEAKS
Great Britain

**Aveley & Wheaks
British Coat Pistol**

Aveley & Wheaks Percussion Coat Pistol . . **$515**
Calibers: various. Barrel: varied, but 5 inches common; octagonal. German silver furniture. Capbox in butt. Sterling silver escutcheon on grip, usually with initials and Scottish thistles. Made circa 1835.

BABCOCK REVOLVER
New Haven, Connecticut

Babcock Revolver. **$470**
Caliber: 32 Short RF. Five-shot cylinder. Single-action. Spur trigger. Solid frame. Made circa 1880.

BACON ARMS COMPANY
Norwich, Connecticut

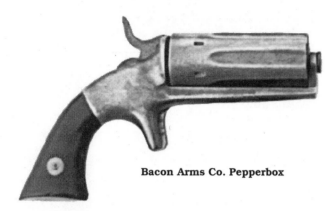

Bacon Arms Co. Pepperbox

Bacon Arms Co. Pepperbox Revolver. . . $895
Caliber: 22 RF. Six-shot cylinder. Barrel: 2½ inches, fluted. Iron frame. Spur trigger. Rosewood grips. Blued finish. Made in the early 1860s.

Bacon Arms Co. Pocket Revolver $225
Caliber: 32 Short RF. Five-shot cylinder. Barrel: 4 inches, round. Spur trigger. Rounded iron frame. Bird's-head butt with walnut grips. Blued finish. Made circa 1865.

Bacon Arms Co./GEM Pocket Revolver. . $510
Caliber: 22 Short RF. Seven-shot cylinder. Barrel: 1¼ inches, octagonal. Iron frame. Spur trigger. Plated finish. Bird's-head butt with walnut or ivory grips. Made from 1878 to 1881.

Bacon Arms Co./Governor Pocket Revolver. $190
Caliber: 22 Short RF. Seven-shot cylinder. Barrel: 3 inches, round. Spur trigger. Walnut grips. Blued finish. Made from 1869 to 1873.

BACON MANUFACTURING COMPANY
Norwich, Connecticut

This company was operational in the mid-1850s and '60s and turned out a number of prototypical 19th-century arms. Their handgun line included "boot guns," derringers, and revolvers chambered for rimfire cartridges.

Bacon Mfg. Co. "Boot Gun" Pistol $355
Caliber: 34 percussion. Barrel: half-octagonal. Underhammer.

Bacon Mfg. Co. Derringer $380
Caliber: 32 RF. Side-swing barrel. Spur trigger. Made in the early 1860s.

Bacon Mfg. Co. Navy Revolver $550
Caliber: 38 Long RF. Six-shot cylinder. Barrel: 7½ inches, octagonal. Single-action. Large-size iron frame. Spur trigger. Square butt. Blued finish with walnut grips. Made early 1860s.

Bacon Mfg. Co. Pocket Revolver. $215
Caliber: 22 Short RF. Seven-shot cylinder. Barrel: 2½ inches, octagonal. Spur trigger. Solid frame. Made in the early 1860s.

Bacon Mfg. Co. Revolver (I) $325
Caliber: 32 Short RF. Six-shot swing-out cylinder. Barrel: 4 inches, octagonal. Spur trigger. Walnut grips. Blued finish. Made 1860 to 1865.

Bacon Mfg. Co. Revolver (II) $300
Caliber: 32 Short RF. Single-action. Six-shot cylinder. Barrel: 4 inches, octagonal. Solid frame. Trigger guard. Made in the early 1860s.

C.H. BALLARD & CO.
Worcester, Massachusetts

C.H. Ballard Single-Shot Derringer $675
Caliber: 41 RF. Barrel: 2¹³/₁₆ inches; part octagonal, part round; blued or silver-plated. Brass frame with silver-plated finish. Bird's-head butt with walnut grips. Made circa 1861 to 1870.

BELGIAN HANDGUNS
Various Manufacturers

Belgian Double-Barrel Pistol. $300
Caliber: 58. Barrels: 4¾ inches. Rib engraved "CANON A DAMAS" (among others.) Clam shell-type cap box in butt. Iron furniture nicely engraved. Checkered grip. Silver escutcheons. Made circa 1850.

Belgian Over/Under Percussion Travelling Pistol $395
Caliber: 63. Barrels: about 6 inches with Damascus pattern. Double triggers — one for each barrel. Checkered European walnut grip and lightly engraved iron fittings. Fixed front sight; sighting "V" at rear of barrel. Made circa 1860.

**Belgian 7mm Pinfire
Revolver**

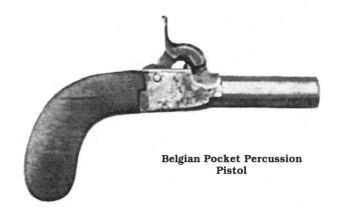

**Belgian Pocket Percussion
Pistol**

Belgian Pinfire Revolver (I) **$185**
Caliber: 7mm pinfire. Octagonal barrel. Checkered
grips.

Belgian Pocket Percussion Pistol **$165**
Caliber: 44 percussion. Flip-down trigger.

**Belgian 7mm Pinfire Revolver
Engraved**

Belgian Saloon Pistol

Belgian Pinfire Revolver (II) **$135**
Caliber: 7mm pinfire. Engraved frame.

Belgian Pocket Flintlock Pistol. **$165**
Caliber: 44. Flip-down trigger. Flintlock ignition.

Belgian Saloon Pistol **$210**
Caliber: 22. Single-shot action based on rolling-block
design. European walnut stock with checkered grip
and silver escutcheon. Blued octagonal barrel. Iron
furniture. Finger spur trigger guard. Blade front
sight; fixed "V" rear sight. Made circa 1860.

Belgian Pocket Percussion Pistol

Belgian Target Pistol

Belgian Pocket Percussion Pistol **$225**
Caliber: 45. Barrel: 3¾ inches, octagonal. Engraved
silver band around butt with silver escutcheons in
butt and on checkered grip. Engraved boxlock. Flip-
down trigger. Made circa 1850.

Belgian Target Pistol **$525**
Caliber: 44. Barrel: about 6 inches; Damascus; 20-
groove rifling. Iron furniture. Adjustable front sight.
Single-set trigger. Engraving usually dense; wood
usually shows some relief carving. Silver escutcheon
behind barrel tang.

DAVID BENTLEY
Birmingham, England

Bentley Bulldog Revolver

David Bentley Revolver **$165**
Caliber: 44. Barrel: 3 inches. Address engraved on top strap. Made circa 1880.

BERGMANN
Gaggenau, Germany

Bergmann manufactured firearms from 1892 to 1944. Re-established in 1931 under Bergmann Erben.

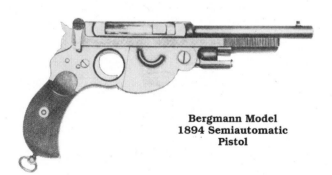

Bergmann Model 1894 Semiautomatic Pistol

Bergmann Model 1894
Caliber: 5mm or 8mm. Semiautomatic with blow-back action. Clip fed.
Caliber 5mm **$4950**
Caliber 8mm 3275

Bergmann Model 1896 No. 2. . . . . **$1550**
Caliber: 5mm. Similar to the Model 1894 except with a smaller frame.

Bergmann Model 1896 No. 3 . . . . **$1625**
Caliber: 6.5mm. Similar to the NO.2 except with 80mm barrel.

Bergmann Model 1896 No. 4 . . . . **$1675**
Caliber: 8mm. Produced under military contract.

Bergmann Model 1897 No. 5 . . . . **$1950**
Caliber: 7.8mm. Commercial manufacture.

GUILLAUME BERLEUR
Liège, Belgium

Berleur was a Belgian gunmaker who lived from 1780 to 1830.

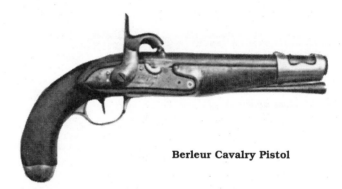

Berleur Cavalry Pistol

Berleur Austrian Cavalry Pistol **$465**
Caliber: 70. Percussion lock. Brass furniture. Lock engraved "G. BERLEUR FST. D'ARMES A LIÈGE."

BILLINGS
Address Unknown

Billings Vest Pocket Single-Shot Pistol. . **$750**
Caliber: 32 RF. Barrel: 2½ inches, round. Oversized handle with walnut grips. Blued finish. Rare. Made in the mid-1860s.

GUSTAV BITTNER
Vieprty, Bohemia, (Austria, Hungary)

Bittner Model 1893 . . . . **$3050**
Caliber: 7.7mm Bittner. Manual repeater with hand-activated mechanism. Box magazine. Checkered grips. (Limited production in 1893 circa.)

F.D. BLISS
New Haven, Connecticut

F.D. Bliss Pocket Revolver $325
Caliber: 25 RF. Six-shot cylinder. Barrel: 3¼ inches, octagonal. Spur trigger. Blued finish. Smooth walnut, rosewood, or checkered hard rubber grips. Made early to mid-1860s.

BORCHARDT
Manufactured in Germany

Originally manufactured by Ludwig Loewe with a serial number range from 1 to 1104. In 1895 manufacturing was resumed by DWM with serial number 1105 and continuing through 3000.

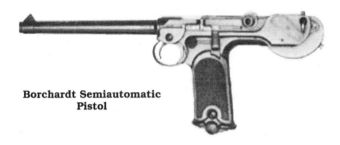

Borchardt Semiautomatic Pistol

Borchardt 1893 Semiautomatic Pistol $8250
Caliber: 7.65. Box magazine. Overall length: 14 inches.

HORACE A. BRIGGS
Norwich, Connecticut

H.A. Briggs Single-Shot Pistol $795
Caliber: 22 RF. Barrel: 4 inches; part round, part octagonal. Square butt with walnut grips. Blued finish. Made in the early 1850s.

BRITISH PISTOLS
Various Manufacturers

The following listings contain a variety of British-made flintlock and percussion pistols. They are placed together here because they are representative examples of particular types of guns and also because the specific manufacturers are unknown. In cases where a gunmaker is identified, those entries are detailed separately, by name of manufacturer/gunmaker, elsewhere in the Handgun Section.

British Flintlock Belt Pistol $560
Calibers: various. Barrel: brass; engraved "LONDON." Belt hook on left side. Brass lockplate and furniture. Made circa 1800.

British Flintlock Blunderbuss Coach Pistol $575
Caliber: ⅞-inch at muzzle. Barrel: 6½ inches, brass. Overall length: 11½ inches. Flat wood butt. Center hammer. Engraved guard that pulls back to release bayonet.

British Flintlock Holster Pistol

British Flintlock Holster Pistol $495
Calibers: various. Checkered grip. Sliding safety. Plain iron furniture. Roller on frizzen spring. Silver wedge escutcheons. Platinum touch hole. Made circa 1780.

British Flintlock Pistol $500
Calibers: various, but ⅝-inch bore common. Barrel: 2 inches, round. Overall length: 6 inches. British proofmarks on barrel.

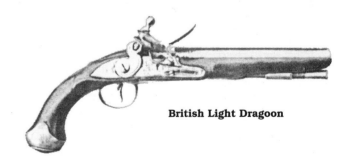

British Light Dragoon

British Light Dragoon Flintlock Pistol . . $560
Calibers: various. Made circa 1805.

British New Land Pattern Pistol $575
Calibers: various. Tower with crown and G.R. engraved on lockplate. Also called a "Horse Pistol," this was introduced circa 1790 and was the standard weapon for the cavalry.

British Overcoat Flintlock Pistol **$750**
Caliber: $^{11}/_{16}$-inch bore. Barrel: 4½ inches, round.
Overall length: 9½ inches. Swivel ramrod. Lockplate
stamped "BARNETT."

British Flintlock Trade Pistol

British Flintlock Pocket Pistol

British Pocket Flintlock Pistol **$300**
Caliber: 45. Brass trigger guard. Made circa 1750.

British Trade Flintlock Pistol **$475**
Caliber: 61. Flintlock ignition. Barrel: octagonal,
brass. Brass furniture. Top stamped "LONDON." Side
stamped "EXTRA PROOF" with proofmark. Belgian-
made lock.

British Percussion Pocket Pistol

British Percussion Trade Pistol

British Trade Percussion Pistol **$200**
Caliber: 70. Percussion ignition. Brass trigger guard
and butt cap with iron barrel band. All furniture is of
Continental pattern. Lockplate stamped "TOWER."
May have been made for the African trade circa 1850.

British Pocket Percussion Pistol (I) **$200**
Caliber: 41. Round barrel. Engraved boxlock. Checkered stock with silver escutcheon. Made circa 1850.

British Volunteer Lancer's Pistol **$450**
Caliber: 79. Percussion ignition. Lock has crown and
"TOWER" stamped on it. Brass furniture. Made circa
1840.

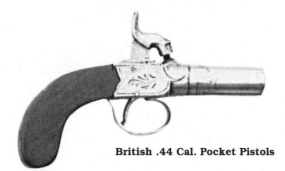

British .44 Cal. Pocket Pistols

B. BROOKE
London, England

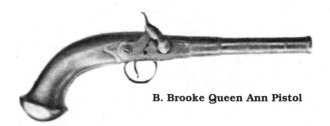

B. Brooke Queen Ann Pistol

British Pocket Percussion Pistol (II) . . . **$150**
Caliber: 44. Percussion ignition. Large oval trigger
guard. Engraved lock. Made circa 1840.

British Pocket Percussion Pistol (III) . . **$200**
Caliber: 45. Octagonal barrel. Flip-down trigger. Engraved silver band around butt with silver escutcheons in butt and on grip. Checkered grip. Engraved
boxlock. Made circa 1850.

**B. Brooke Queen Ann Pistol (Percussion
Conversion)** **$100**
Originally flintlock, but many have been converted to
percussion. The value of the flintlock should be about
50 percent higher. Made circa 1600 to 1720.

BROOKLYN ARMS CO.
Brooklyn, New York

Designed by Frank Slocum, the April 1863 patent for his front-loading revolver was one of the several attempts in the late 1850s and early 1860s to outmaneuver the Rollin White-S&W monopoly on rear-loading rimfire revolvers. The chambers in Slocum's gun can actually be opened at the sides for insertion of the cartridges.

Brooklyn Arms Co. Slocum Pocket Revolver (I) **$435**
Caliber: 32 RF. Five-shot cylinder. Barrel: 3 inches, round. Sliding chambers. Spur trigger. Engraved brass frame with silver plate. Oval-shaped butt with walnut grips. Made from 1863 to 1867.

Brooklyn Arms Co. Slocum Pocket Revolver (II) **$575**
Caliber: 32 RF. Six-shot, straight, unfluted cylinder. Barrel: 3 inches, round. Brass frame. Spur trigger. Flat butt flared at rear. Walnut grips. Made from 1863 to 1867.

BROWN MANUFACTURING CO.
Newburyport, Massachusetts

Originally made by Merrimack Arms Mfg. Co. (*see* separate listing).

Brown Mfg. Co. Southerner Derringer . . . **$375**
Caliber: 41 RF. Barrel: 2½ inches; octagonal, side swing. Brass frame, silver-plated. Spur trigger. Plated or blued iron barrel. Walnut or rosewood grips. Made 1869 to 1873.

CALDERWOOD
Dublin, Ireland

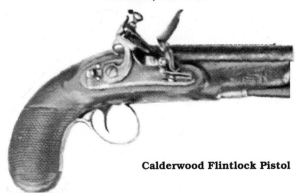
Calderwood Flintlock Pistol

Calderwood Flintlock Pistol **$700**
Calibers: various. Sliding safety on lock. Round, checkered grip. Made circa 1815.

CANADIAN PISTOLS
Various Manufacturers

Canadian P 1858 Calvary Pistol

Canadian Percussion Model 1858 Pistol . . **$750**
Calibers: various. Barrels: 4 to 7 inches, round. Lock stamped 1855 over Tower with crown and VR. Proof and inspector's marks. Termed "Cavalry Pistol." Made circa 1858. (*See* British Pistols for proofmarks.)

Canadian Webley MK III Model 1897 Presentation

Canadian Presentation Webley MK III Model 1897 . . . . **$1050**
Caliber: 455. The pistols pictured were presented to Capt. H.S. Greenwood V.D. by the citizens of Peterborough, Ontario, upon his departure for South Africa with the second Canadian contingent. Other presentation Webley pistols should have approximate same value; price shown is for the pair.

G. AND J. CHAPMAN
Philadelphia, Pennsylvania

G. & J. Chapman Pocket Revolver **$600**
Caliber: 32 RF. Seven-shot cylinder. Barrel: 4 inches, round. Brass frame. Blued barrel and cylinder. Bird's-head butt with walnut grips. Rare. Made circa 1860.

CHICAGO FIREARMS COMPANY
Chicago, Illinois

Chicago Firearms Co. Protector Palm Pistol **$625**
Caliber: 32 Extra Short RF. Squeezer-type with rotary chambers. Nickel-plated finish standard; blued finish on some. Hard rubber grip plates, although some had pearl or ivory plates.

CHINESE HANDGUNS
Various Manufacturers

Ancient Chinese Hand Cannon

Ancient Chinese Hand Cannon **$1200**
Barrel: 12 inches; diameter is 1 inch at smallest point. Overall length: 22 inches. Diameter at the breech: 1¾ inches. Barrel is supported by an additional piece of wood secured with bamboo wrappings. Swivel is intended for support against a wall or for firing from a boat.

Ancient Chinese Hand Cannon Pistol

Ancient Chinese Hand Cannon Pistol . . **$1795**
Hand-fired ancient pistol with bronze ornamentation. Overall length: 3½ inches. Very rare.

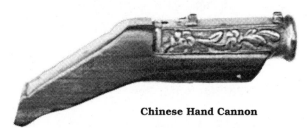

Chinese Hand Cannon

Chinese Hand Cannon **$375**
Calibers: varied, but 75 common. Bronze barrel with scroll work. Made circa 1850.

COLT'S PATENT FIRE ARMS MFG. CO.
Hartford, Connecticut

Samuel Colt whittled out the first model of a new revolving firearm, with automatic revolution and locking cylinder, while signed aboard the Brig *Corlo* on a return voyage from India. Shortly after returning to America, Colt obtained a patent on his invention, and in 1831 he commissioned a gunsmith to work on his first models. During the years between 1832 and 1836, several Colt pistols, rifles and one shotgun were produced in Albany, Baltimore and Hartford.

Colt's first factory was opened in Paterson, N.J., on March 5, 1836, in an unused section of a silk mill — calling it the Patent Arms Manufacturing Co. But due to lack of business, the Paterson operation failed and closed permanently in 1842, although valuable experience was gained in the process.

The Colt revolving system is said to be the first practical system of its kind, as it used a pawl on the hammer engaging a ratchet on the end of the cylinder to rotate the cylinder automatically during firing.

Samuel Colt died on January 10, 1862, but Colt Industries in Hartford is still producing fine firearms based on Colt's original 1830s' patents.

See also U.S. Military Handguns of Colt Manufacture and Blackpowder Replicas.

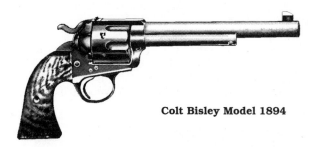

Colt Bisley Model 1894

Colt Bisley Model Single-Action Revolver
Calibers: about 18 different ones, ranging from 32 Colt to 455 Eley. Same general specifications as the Single-Action Army Model (*see* separate listing), except has longer grips with a sharper drop, lower and flatter hammer and larger trigger guard with curved trigger. Made 1894 to 1912.
Standard Bisley Model **$1675**
Flat Top Target Model **2350**

Colt Constabulary Revolver **$675**
Calibers: 38 Long & Short. Barrel: 4½ inches. Overall length: 9½ inches. Weight: 25 ounces. Checkered hard rubber grips. A 3½-inch barrel version was also manufactured without slide rod. This latter version was adopted by the Chicago police in 1892. This model was awarded the *Prize Metal of 1878* for excellence of workmanship. Made from 1877 to 1909.

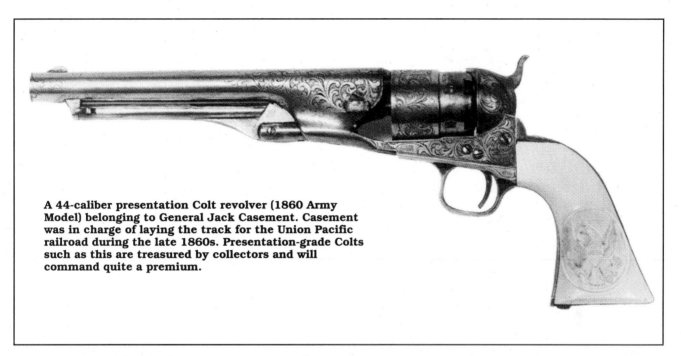

A 44-caliber presentation Colt revolver (1860 Army Model) belonging to General Jack Casement. Casement was in charge of laying the track for the Union Pacific railroad during the late 1860s. Presentation-grade Colts such as this are treasured by collectors and will command quite a premium.

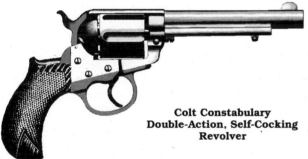

Colt Constabulary Double-Action, Self-Cocking Revolver

Colt Deringer—First Model **$1435**
Caliber: 41 RF. Single-shot. All metal. Barrel: 2¹⁄₄ inches. Overall length: 4¹⁄₄ inches. Weight: 9 ounces. Barrel turns to side to eject fired cases; thumb catch on right side of frame. Sharply curved metal butt. Lightly engraved. Originally designed by Daniel Moore and made by National Arms Co. (*see* separate listing). Made by Colt from 1870 to about 1890.

Colt First Model Deringer

Colt Deringer — Second Model **$1220**
Caliber: 41 RF. Single-shot. Barrel: 2¹⁄₂ inches, oval, flat top. Overall length: 5¹⁄₄ inches. Weight: 9 ounces. Barrel lock button on right. Lightly engraved. Bird's-head butt with wood or ivory grips. Originally made by National Arms Co., Colt manufactured it from 1870 to about 1890.

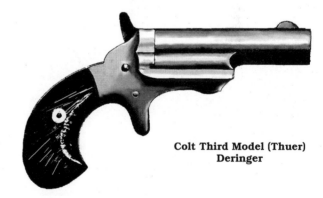

Colt Third Model (Thuer) Deringer

Colt Deringer — Third Model (Thuer)
Designed by Colt engineer F. Alexander Thuer. Caliber: 41 RF. Single-shot. Barrel: 2¹⁄₂ inches, avg., although other lengths made; round. Overall length: 4¹⁄₂ inches. Weight: 7¹⁄₂ ounces. Barrel turns to side to eject fired cases. Spur trigger. Bird's-head butt. Wood grips. Made from 1875 to about 1912.

First Issue (straight hammer spur). **$2075**
Second Issue (backward-inclining
 hammer spur) 1050
Third Issue (largest butt) 560
London Marked 1095

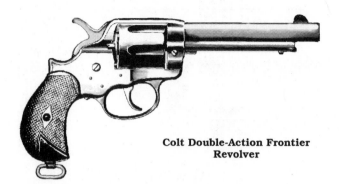

**Colt Double-Action Frontier
Revolver**

Colt Double-Action Frontier Revolver . . $1250

Model 1878 Frontier or Double-Action Army. Similar in appearance to the smaller Lightning Model, but has heavier frame of different shape, round disc on left side of frame and lanyard loop in butt. Calibers: 32-20, 38-40, 44-40 ("Frontier Six-Shooter"), 45 Colt. Six-shot cylinder. Barrels: $3\frac{1}{2}$ and 4 inches without ejector; $4\frac{3}{4}$, $5\frac{1}{2}$ and $7\frac{1}{2}$ inches w/ejector. Overall length: $12\frac{1}{2}$ inches w/$7\frac{1}{2}$-inch bbl. Weight: 39 ounces w/$7\frac{1}{2}$-inch bbl. Fixed sights. Hard rubber bird's-head grips. Blued or nickel finish. Made 1878 to 1905.

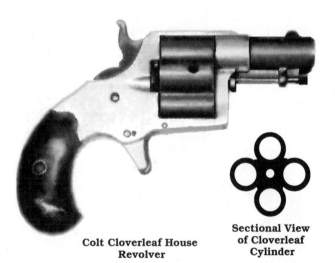

**Colt Cloverleaf House
Revolver**

**Sectional View
of Cloverleaf
Cylinder**

Colt "House Pistol"— Cloverleaf House SA Revolver

The first Colt revolver designed specifically for metallic cartridges. Caliber: 41 RF. Single-action. Four-shot cloverleaf-shaped cylinder with recessed chambers. Barrels: $1\frac{1}{2}$ inches, round or octagonal; 3 inches, round. Overall length: $5\frac{1}{4}$ inches w/$1\frac{1}{2}$-inch bbl. Weight: 14 ounces. Brass frame. Spur trigger. Straight-up hammer. Wood bird's-head grips. Rod ejector. Made 1871 to 1876.

With $1\frac{1}{2}$-inch round bbl. **$1500**
With $1\frac{1}{2}$-inch octagonal bbl. **1525**
With 3-inch round bbl. **1000**

Colt "House Pistol" SA Revolver $1050

Caliber: 41 RF. Five-shot round cylinder. No ejector. Barrel: $2\frac{5}{8}$ inches, round. Weight: 15 ounces. Made 1871 to 1876.

**Colt Model 1877 Lightning
Nickel Finish with Ivory Grips**

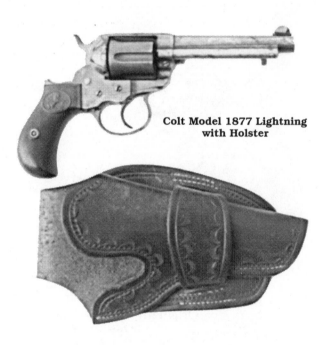

**Colt Model 1877 Lightning
with Holster**

Colt Lightning Central Fire DA Revolver . . $710

Model 1877 Lightning, the first in the line of popular double-action Colts. Interestingly, Sam Colt would not endorse the concept of double-action arms before his death, asserting that accuracy was not possible. This gun was designed by William Mason, a Colt engineer, who worked out the "bugs." Calibers: 38 and 41 centerfire (41 cal. called the "Thunderer"). Six-shot cylinder. Barrels: $1\frac{1}{2}$, $2\frac{1}{2}$, $3\frac{1}{2}$, $4\frac{1}{2}$ and 6 inches w/o ejector; $4\frac{1}{2}$, 5 and 6 to 10 inches w/ejector. Overall length: $8\frac{1}{2}$ inches w/$3\frac{1}{2}$-inch bbl. Weight: 23 ounces w/$3\frac{1}{2}$-inch bbl. Fixed sights. Hard rubber bird's-head grips. Blued or nickel finish. Made 1877 to 1909.

Colt Model 1855 Root Percussion Handgun(I) $1780

Named after Elisha King Root, Colt's old friend and superintendent/top engineer at the Colt Armory in Hartford; also called "Pocket Pistol" and "1855 Side-hammer Colt" because the hammer is on the right side of the frame. Caliber: 256 (designated 28). Five-shot, straight, round, engraved cylinder. Barrel: 3½ inches, octagonal; marked "Colt's Pat. 1855 — Address Col. Colt, Hartford, Ct. U.S.A." Overall length: 8 inches. Weight: 17 ounces. Solid, blued steel frame with spur trigger. Loading lever. No trigger guard. Made 1856 to 1861.

**Colt London Cased 31 Caliber
Model 1855 Root Percussion
Revolver**

Colt Model 1855 Root Percussion Handgun(II) $1280

A continuation of the 1855 Root (Sidehammer) series, except in 31 caliber with round or octagonal barrels of 3½ or 4½ inches. Most have full fluted cylinders, some with roll engraved scenes. Made 1861 to 1870.

Colt Model 1872 Single-Action Revolver

Also called the Open Top .44. Caliber: 44 Henry RF. Six-shot engraved cylinder. Barrel: 7½, 8 inches. Overall length: 13½ to 14 inches. No strap above cylinder. Iron or brass gripstraps. Similar to Colt 1860 Army percussion, but not a conversion. Total of approx. 7,000 made about 1872.
Army-style grip-frame $8500
Navy-style grip-frame 3000

Colt New House Single-Action Revolver . . $750

Calibers: 38 Long Colt, 41 RF, (32 rare). Five-shot cylinder with long flutes. Barrels: most 2¼ inches without ejector rod; left side stamped "COLT HOUSE" or "NEW HOUSE." Squared butt with checkered hard rubber or plain wood grips, "COLT" on upper part. One model in the "New Line Pistol" series (see below). Made 1880 to 1886.

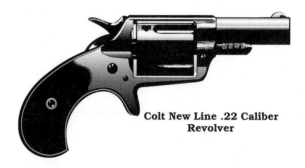

**Colt New Line .22 Caliber
Revolver**

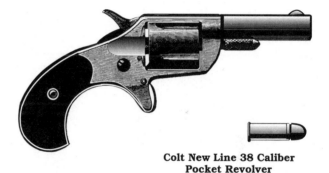

**Colt New Line 38 Caliber
Pocket Revolver**

Colt New Line Pocket Revolver $680

Calibers: 22, 30, 32, 38 and 41 RF; 32 Short Colt, 38 Short Colt, 38 Long Colt, 41 centerfire. Five-shot cylinder (7-shot in 22 cal.). Barrels: 2¼ inches to 10 inches (custom), round; 22 cal. with flat-sided barrel. Sheath trigger. Bird's-head grip. Made about 1873 to 1884.

Colt New Line Police Single-Action Revolver $625

Caliber: 38 Long Colt. Five-shot unmarked cylinder. Barrels: 4½, 5 and 6 inches, round; marked "New Police .38." Overall length: 9 inches. Side rod ejector and loading gate. Square butt with hard rubber grips. Made 1882 to 1886.

Colt New Navy Model 1889 DA Revolver . . $800

Calibers: 38 Short Colt, 38 Long Colt, 41 Short Colt, 41 Long Colt (civilian version only). Six-shot, full fluted, swing-out cylinder. Barrels: 3, 4½ and 6 inches. Overall length: 11¼ inches w/6-inch bbl. Fixed sights, knifeblade and V-notch. Walnut or hard rubber grips. Blued or nickel-plated finish. Made 1889 to 1894.

Colt New Navy Model 1892 DA Revolver . . . $695

Also known as "New Army" Models 1892, 1894, 1895, 1896, 1901 and 1903, and were improved versions of the New Navy Model 1889. Calibers: 38 and 41 Colt. Same general specifications as Colt Model 1889. Made 1892 to 1907. These were superseded in 1908 by the New Army Special revolvers, which continued the serial numbers.

**Colt New Service Double-Action
Revolver, Military Issue**

**Colt New Pocket
Double-Action Revolver**

Colt New Pocket DA Revolver $320

Calibers: 32 Short and Long Colt "central fire," 32 S&W. Double-action. Six-shot, swing-out cylinder. Small, jointless solid frame. Barrels: 2½ to 6 inches, round. Overall length: 10 inches w/6-inch bbl. Blued or nickel-plated finish. Marked "Colt's New Pocket." Made 1893 to 1905. This model replaced the S.A. New Line revolvers and, in turn, were superseded by the Pocket Positive model in 1905.

Colt New Service DA Revolver $275

The largest framed double-action with swing-out cylinder in the Colt repertoire. Calibers: 18 different, ranging from 38 Short Colt to 476 Eley. Barrel: 8 lengths, ranging from 2 to 7½ inches. Weight: 42 ounces, avg. Blued or nickel-plated finish. Lanyard loop in butt. Many variations exist. Made 1898 to 1944.

**Colt New Police
Double-Action Revolver**

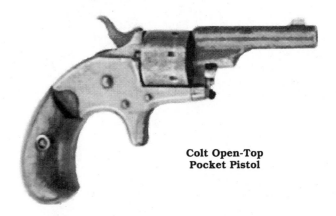

**Colt Open-Top
Pocket Pistol**

Colt New Police DA Revolver $280

Calibers: 32 Colt, 32 S&W. Six-shot swing-out cylinder. Barrels: 2½, 4, 6 inches, round. Overall length: 10½ inches w/6-inch bbl. Weight: about 19 ounces w/6-inch bbl. Blued or nickel-plated finish. Marked "Colt's New Police." In 1896, about 4500 were purchased by the New York City Police Dept., of which Theodore Roosevelt was commissioner; he was given Serial No. 1 for testing. Made 1896 to 1905.

Colt Old Line Single-Action Pocket Revolver

Also known as Open Top Pocket Pistol. Caliber: 22 RF. Seven-shot unmarked cylinder. Barrel: 2⅜ or 2⅞ inches. Overall length: 6½ inches. No strap on frame over cylinder. With or without rod ejector. Wood bird's-head grip. Made 1871 to 1877.

First Model w/ejector **$875**
Second Model w/o ejector. **475**

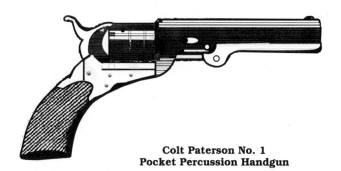

**Colt Paterson No. 1
Pocket Percussion Handgun**

Colt Paterson — "Baby" or No. 1 Pocket Percussion Handgun

Caliber: 28. Five-shot engraved cylinder with rounded cylinder stops. Barrel: length varies; octagonal. Overall length: 7 to 7⅞ inches. Smooth, straight walnut grips. This is the first handgun manufactured by Colt in Paterson, N.J., based on his original patent of Feb. 25, 1836. Made late 1836 to 1838, some altered in 1840 to include loading lever.

Without loading lever, 4-inch bbl. **$16,000**
With loading lever, 3-inch bbl. **16,900**

Colt Paterson — "Baby" Percussion

Handgun. **$16,200**
Same general specifications as above models, but with 4¼-inch barrel. Low blade front sight; rear sight on hammer nose. Two rounded bands extend around the engraved cylinder. Made between 1836 and 1838.

Colt Paterson No. 2 Belt Pistol

Caliber: 31 percussion. Five-shot engraved cylinder with square nipple separations. Barrel: avg. 4¼ to 4¾ inches, octagonal. Overall length: 8 to 8½ inches, avg. Weight: about 20 ounces. No loading lever. Straight walnut grips. Made about 1838 to 1840, some altered in 1840 to include loading lever.

Without loading lever **$17,750**
With loading lever **17,000**

Colt Paterson No. 3 Belt Pistol $19,000

Same general specifications as the Paterson No. 2 Belt Pistol, except has flared walnut grips. With the factory loading lever attached (done on some models in 1840), this is a rare item and will command a premium.

Colt Paterson No. 2 or No. 3
Belt, Cased $25,500

Same revolvers as above, except cased in original Paterson Colt mahogany case with extra cylinder, bullet mold, combination tool, cleaning rod and priming device, and combination bullet and powder flask.

Colt Single-Action Army Revolver

Dubbed "Peacemaker," "Six-Shooter," "Frontier," "Equalizer," "Sheriff's Model," and "Storekeeper's Model" to name but a few, this is by far the most famous of the Colt revolvers. It was used by such legendary figures as Gen. George Custer, Bat Masterson, Teddy Roosevelt and George S. Patton. Calibers: 30 different ones, from 22 RF to 476 Eley, those most frequently encountered 32-20, 38-40, 41, 44-40 and 45. Six-shot fluted cylinder. Barrels: 4¾ to 16⅛ inches, with ejectors; 2 to 7½ inches, often without ejectors. Solid, casehardened frame. Blued finish. Oil-finished walnut grips standard. Many variations of the S.A.A. exist, some with exquisite engravings and custom grips, etc. The Flattop Target Model, a major variation, was introduced in 1888 and the Bisley, another, was produced between 1894 and 1912 (see separate listing). In 1900, the revolvers were constructed to handle smokeless powder. Total production spanned from 1873 to 1940; production resumed in 1955 with serial number 12001SA and was discontinued in 1982. Standard model reissued in 1992, spanning approximately 120 years.

Artillery Model, 5½-inch bbl., screw-retained
   cylinder **$4750**
Flattop Target Model. **9000**
Indian Scout Model, screw-retained cylinder . **4550**
Long-barreled Models, 8- to 16-inch bbl. **5100**
Long-barreled Models w/folding rear sight. . . **4300**
Rimfire Calibers **3100**
Standard Calvary Model,
   Ser. Nos. under 15000. . . . . **4750**
Standard S.A.A. Model **3200**
Standard S.A. A. Model
   Ser. No. 1 (one). **450,000**
Storekeeper's Model (also called
   "Sheriff's Model", short bbl., no ejector **8250**

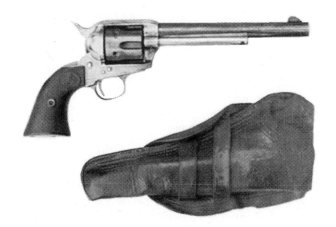

**Colt Single-Action Army
with Holster**

D. D. CONE
Washington, D. C.

D. D. Cone was allegedly a trade name used by William Uhlinger on his 1860s-produced revolvers, which were in violation of the Rollin White patent owned by S&W regarding bored-through cylinders.

D.D. Cone Revolver (I) **$295**
Caliber: 22 long RF. Six-shot cylinder. Barrel: 2¾ or 3 inches, octagonal. Spur trigger. Solid iron frame. Square butt. Blued finish. Rosewood or walnut grips. Made circa 1861 to 1865.

D.D. Cone Revolver (II) **$340**
Caliber: 32 long RF. Six-shot cylinder. Barrel: 5, 6 or 7 inches, octagonal. Single-action. Spur trigger. Solid iron frame. Plated or blued finish. Walnut or rosewood grips. Made circa 1861 to 1865.

CONNECTICUT ARMS COMPANY
Norfolk, Connecticut

One of the several attempts to produce a successful front-loading revolver in the mid-1860s. Rollin White's patent for a bored-through cylinder was still in effect. This patent was licensed to the Smith & Wesson company.

Connecticut Arms Co. Pocket Revolver . . **$295**
Caliber: 28 cup primed. Six-shot cylinder. Barrel: 3 inches, octagonal, tip-up. Spur trigger. Brass frame. Silver-plated finish. Steel parts blued. Hook-type ejector on the right side of frame, pivoting in front of the spur trigger. Square butt with walnut grips. Made circa mid-1860s.

CONNECTICUT ARMS & MFG. CO.
Naubuc, Connecticut

Connecticut Arms & Mfg. Co. Bulldog Pistol **$395**
Single-shot pivoting breechblock. Caliber: 44 and 50 RF. Barrel: 4 inches, octagonal. Spur trigger. Iron frame with casehardened finish. Blued or browned barrel. Approximately 800 of the standard 44 caliber model were manufactured between 1866 and 1868. Less than 100 of the 50 caliber model were produced.

Connecticut Arms & Mfg. Co. Bulldog Pistol (Variants) **$490**
Same general specifications as above, except with much longer barrel.

CONTINENTAL ARMS COMPANY
Norwich, Connecticut

Continental Arms Co. Continental 1 . . . **$595**
Caliber: 22 RF. Seven-shot pepperbox. Barrels: 2½ inches. Spur trigger. Solid iron frame. Square butt. Made 1866 to 1867.

Continental Arms Co. Continental 2 . . . **$645**
Caliber: 32 RF. Five-shot pepperbox. Spur trigger. Solid iron frame. Made 1866 to 1867.

JOSEPH ROCK COOPER
Birmingham, England

In 1840 J. R. Cooper patented his self-cocking, six-barreled pepperbox, the popular arm of that day. By 1850 he had established a sales outlet not only in Birmingham, but also in New York City, which imported his English-made guns.

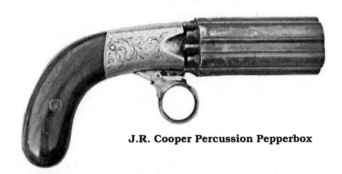

J.R. Cooper Percussion Pepperbox

J.R. Cooper Percussion Pepperbox **$785**
Caliber: 38. Six shots. Barrels: 3½ inches. Overall length: about 8 inches. Some engraved with fern design. Made from 1840 to 1853.

FRANK COPELAND
Worcester, Massachusetts

F. Copeland Pocket Revolver (I) **$245**
Caliber: 22 Short RF. Seven-shot cylinder. Barrel: 2¼ inches, octagonal. Brass frame. Spur trigger. Walnut or rosewood grips. Bird's-head butt. Made 1868 to 1874.

F. Copeland Pocket Revolver (II) **$275**
Caliber: 32 Short RF. Seven-shot cylinder. Barrel: 2¼ inches, octagonal. Brass frame. Spur trigger. Walnut or rosewood grips. Bird's-head butt. Made 1868 to 1874.

COWLES AND SON
Chicopee, Massachusetts

Cowles & Son Single-Shot Pistol...... **$265**
Calibers: 22 and 30 RF. Barrel: 3¼ inches; round, side swing, blued. Brass frame with silver-plated finish. Spur trigger. Bird's-head butt. Walnut grips. Made 1871 to 1876.

SILAS CRISPIN
New York, New York

Based on Silas Crispin's patent of 1865, the Smith Arms Co. of New York City apparently produced this revolver. It is one of the several attempts to thwart the restrictions posed by the Rollin White/S&W patent regarding rear-loading revolvers. In this version, the cylinder is split about three-quarters of the way in to allow for inserting of the unique Crispin cartridges. The cartridges themselves are prized collector items. The arm is considered scarce, and dangerous.

Silas Crispin Revolver **$9675**
Caliber: 32. Six-shot cylinder. Barrel: 5 inches, octagonal. Split cylinder. Iron frame with blued finish. Made circa late 1860s.

O. S. CUMMINGS
Lowell, Massachusetts

O.S. Cummings Pocket Revolver...... **$235**
Caliber: 22 RF. Seven-shot cylinder. Barrel: 3 inches, ribbed, inscribed with manufacturer and city (no state). Iron frame with nickel finish. Spur trigger. Rosewood or walnut grips. Bird's-head butt. Note the resemblance between this model and the S&W 1st Model revolver. Approximately 950 made in the 1870s.

GEORGE HENRY DAW
London, England

Although handguns were a part of G. H. Daw's firearms trade, shotguns were a major interest. In fact, he is credited with the first hammerless shotgun using modern-type cartridges, which he patented in 1862. His firm was active until the early 1890s.

Daw British Sea Service Pistol **$445**
Caliber: 58. Percussion ignition. Contract piece by G.H. Daw, London. Name engraved on barrel and lockplate. Belt hook on left side. Brass furniture. Lanyard ring in butt.

**Daw British Sea Service
Pistol**

HENRY DERINGER JR.
Philadelphia, Pennsylvania

Henry Deringer Jr. was born in Easton, Penn., on October 26, 1786. At age 20, he set up shop at 612 North Front Street in Philadelphia, producing flintlock pistols and muskets under Government contracts for the U. S. Army.

Deringer also catered to the civilian market with flintlock and percussion hunting rifles, along with cased dueling pistols. In 1831, he developed the percussion pistol or short-rifled barrel with heavy caliber that became the prototype of what is known as the "derringer." (Note the one "r" in the surname vs. the two in the pistol name.)

Deringer Pocket Pistol

The Deringer Pocket Pistol experienced large sales in the South, and this market spread to the Pacific Coast during the gold rush years. Deringer's pistols were copied, and even his name and trademark were stamped on the lockplate and breech of the barrel. These circumstances led to the famous lawsuit of Henry Deringer vs. A. J. Plate. Unfortunately, before the suit was settled, Deringer died in Philadelphia on February 26, 1868, in his 81st year. The damages were awarded to his estate in the final settlement.

The firm continued for a while under the direction of Dr. Jonathan Clark, a son-in-law, and other relatives (*see* Deringer Rifle & Pistol Works).

Deringer Pocket Pistol **$1345**
Calibers: 36 to 54, with 41 caliber being the most popular. Barrels: less than 1 inch to over 4 inches. Overall lengths: 3¾ to 15 inches. Lockplate was inscribed, "DERINGER PHILADELA." These pistols were not serial numbered, but the various parts were stamped with matching assembly numbers or letters. A Deringer derringer was used by John Wilkes Booth to assassinate President Abraham Lincoln.

Deringer Dueller Pistols **$2695**
Calibers: various, but 41 most common. Barrel: various lengths, from 6 to 10 inches or more. German silver mounts, cased pair. Made from 1806 to 1868.

Deringer Dueller Pistols (Gold Mounts) . . **$6200**
Same general specifications as the standard duellers, except with gold mounts rather than German silver. Made from 1806 to 1868.

Deringer Dueller Pistols (Silver Mounts) . . **$2800**
Same general specifications as standard duellers, except with Sterling silver mounts rather than German silver. Made from 1806 to 1868.

DERINGER RIFLE & PISTOL WORKS
Philadelphia, Pennsylvania

After Henry Deringer's death in 1868, relatives continued the manufacture of metallic cartridge revolvers for about 10 years.

Deringer Centennial '76 Revolver **$1400**
Caliber: 38 Long RF. Five-shot cylinder. Single-action. Spur trigger. Tip-up barrel.

Deringer Pocket Model 1 Revolver . . . **$1375**
Caliber: 22 Short RF. Seven-shot straight, unfluted, cylinder. Barrel: 3 inches; octagonal, ribbed, tip-up. Spur trigger. Walnut grips. Bird's-head butt. Made 1873 to 1879.

Deringer Pocket Model 2 Revolver . . . **$1340**
Caliber: 22 Short RF. Seven-shot, spur trigger, semi-fluted cylinder. Barrel: 3 inches; round, ribbed. Fluted sides. Spur triggers. Walnut grips. Bird's-head butt. Made 1873 to 1879.

Deringer Pocket Revolver **$1300**
Caliber: 32 Long RF. Five-shot cylinder. Barrel: 3½ inches; round, tip-up. Brass or iron frame. Silver or nickel plated. Spur trigger. Walnut grips. Bird's-head butt. Made late 1870s.

E.L. & J. DICKINSON
Springfield, Massachusetts

E. L. & J. Dickinson Pocket Pistol

E. L. & J. Dickinson Single-Shot
Pocket Pistol (I) **$450**
Caliber: 22 RF. Barrel: 3¾ inches; octagonal, pivoting, rack ejector. Brass frame, silver plated. Spur trigger. Walnut grips. Square butt. Made 1868 to 1872.

E. L. & J. Dickinson Single-Shot
Pocket Pistol (II) **$625**
All specifications the same as above model, except made in 32 rimfire caliber.

J.B. DRISCOLL
Springfield, Massachusetts

J.B. Driscoll Single-Shot
Pocket Pistol **$525**
Caliber: 22 RF. Barrel: 3½ inches; octagonal, blued, pivots downward for loading. Brass frame with silver-plated finish. Spur trigger; also has trigger-like latch release under barrel. Walnut grips. Square butt. Made circa 1870.

EAGLE ARMS COMPANY
New York, New York

Eagle Arms Co. Revolver (I) **$410**
Caliber: 28 cup primed. Six-shot cylinder. Single-action. Spur trigger. Solid frame. Made in 1865.

Eagle Arms Co. Revolver (II) **$400**
Caliber: 28 cup primed. Six-shot cylinder. Single-action. Spur trigger. Tip-up. Made in 1865.

Eagle Arms Co. Revolver (III) **$395**
Caliber: 30 cup primed. Six-shot cylinder. Barrel: 3½ inches; octagonal, ribbed. Spur trigger. Solid brass frame with silver-plated finish. Barrel and cylinder blued. Made in 1865.

Eagle Arms Co. Revolver (IV) **$425**
Same general specifications as revolver (III), above, except is tip-up model.

Eagle Arms Co. Revolver (V) **$350**
Caliber: 42 cup primed. Six-shot cylinder. Barrel: 6 inches; octagonal, ribbed. Single-action. Spur trigger. Solid frame. Made in 1865.

Eagle Arms Co. Revolver (VI) **$495**
Caliber: 42 cup primed. Six-shot cylinder. Barrel: 6 inches; octagonal, ribbed. Spur trigger. Tip-up model. Made in 1865.

DURS EGG
London, England

Durs Egg (1748 – 1831) distinguished himself as a gunmaker by handcrafting fine flintlock arms. He supplied handguns and long arms to the military service and even provided many of the guns used by British volunteers during the Revolutionary War against the "Colonies."

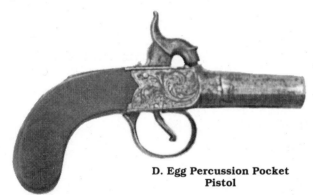

D. Egg Percussion Pocket
Pistol

Durs Egg Percussion Pocket Pistol **$285**
Caliber: 49. Engraved boxlock with silver escutcheon on grip. One of Egg's latest production pieces, this was made circa 1830.

EUROPEAN PISTOLS
Various Manufacturers

European Cavalry Flintlock **$610**
Caliber: 73. Barrel: about 6 inches, half-octagonal; stamped "EX." Inside of lock stamped "RUIZ." Brass furniture. Made circa 1800.

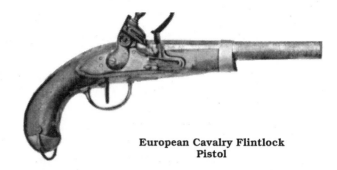

European Cavalry Flintlock
Pistol

European Percussion Pistol **$275**
Caliber: 52. Barrel: 8 inches; octagonal, engraved. Abstract rampant lion on lockplate. Captive ramrod capbox in butt. Iron-mounted. Made circa 1840.

FABRIQUE NATIONALE D'ARMES DE GUERRE
Liège, Belgium

Located in the heart of the Belgian firearms-producing area, Fabrique National is a long established arms manufacturer. It is still engaged in arms production under the name Fabrique Nationale Herstal, a suburb of Liège from which it takes its name.

FN Browning Model 1900
Pocket Auto Pistol

**FN Browning Model 1900 Pocket
Auto Pistol.** **$245**
Caliber: 32 automatic (7.65 mm). Seven-shot magazine. Barrel length: 4 inches. Overall length: 6½ inches. Weight: 22 oz. Fixed sights. Hard rubber stocks. Blued finish. Made 1899 to 1910.

FOREHAND ARMS CO.
Worcester, Massachusetts

See Forehand & Wadsworth.

FOREHAND & WADSWORTH
Worcester, Massachusetts

The Forehand & Wadsworth Company began operation in 1871, being successors and sons-in-law to Ethan Allen, who operated Ethan Allen & Co. from 1865 to 1871. In 1890, H.C. Wadsworth retired and the firm changed its name to The Forehand Arms Co. and operated under this designation from 1890 to 1902. Both firms were known primarily for their shotguns and revolvers, but the firms did produce a few rifles also.

**Forehand & Wadsworth
British Bulldog**

Forehand & Wadsworth British Bulldog (I) **$115**
Caliber: 38 S&W. Six- or seven-shot cylinder. Double-action.

Forehand & Wadsworth British Bulldog (II) **$150**
Caliber: 44 S&W. Five-shot cylinder. Double-action.

Forehand & Wadsworth Bulldog (I) **$195**
Caliber: 38 Long RF. Five-shot cylinder. Barrel: 2 inches. Double-action. Blued finish.

Forehand & Wadsworth Bulldog (II) **$160**
Caliber: 44 S&W. Five-shot cylinder. Double-action. Barrel: 2 inches.

Forehand & Wadsworth New Model Army Revolver **$575**
Caliber: 38 Long RF. Six-shot cylinder. Single-action. Barrel: 6½ inches, round. Walnut grips. Blued finish. Made late 1870s to 1880s.

Forehand & Wadsworth New Navy **$625**
Caliber: 44 Russian. Six-shot cylinder. Double-action. Barrel: 6 inches.

Forehand & Wadsworth Old Model Army **$660**
Caliber: 44 Russian. Six-shot cylinder. Single-action. Barrel: 7 inches, round. Walnut grips. Blued finish. Made in the mid-1870s.

**Forehand & Wadsworth
Pocket Model**

Forehand & Wadsworth Pocket Model . . **$120**
Caliber: 32 S&W Long. Six-shot cylinder. Double-action. Top break.

Forehand & Wadsworth Russian Model . . **$325**
Caliber: 32, 32 Short RF. Five-shot. Single-action. Spur trigger.

Forehand & Wadsworth Single-Action Revolver (I) **$240**
Caliber: 22 Short RF. Seven-shot cylinder. Barrel: 2¼ inches to 4 inches, octagonal. Side hammer. Spur trigger. Walnut grips. Bird's-head butt. Blued or nickel finish. Made in the early 1870s.

Forehand & Wadsworth Single-Action Revolver (II) **$250**
Caliber: 32 Short RF. Six-shot cylinder. Barrel: 3⅜ inches, octagonal. Rosewood or walnut grips. Bird's-head butt. Blued or nickel finish frame. Made in the early 1870s.

Forehand & Wadsworth Single-Shot (I) . . **$310**
Caliber: 22 Short RF. Spur trigger. Barrel: 2 inches; side-swing, part round/part octagonal. Iron frame with nickel or silver-plated finish. Blued or plated barrel. Bird's-head butt. Walnut grips.

Forehand & Wadsworth Single-Shot (II) . . **$450**
Caliber: 41 Short RF. Spur trigger. Barrel: 2½ inches, side-swing. Walnut grips. Bird's-head butt. Blued finish.

Forehand & Wadsworth Swamp Angel . . . **$275**
Caliber: 41 Short RF. Five-shot cylinder. Single-action. Spur trigger.

Forehand & Wadsworth Terror **$185**
Caliber: 32 Short RF. Five-shot cylinder. Single-action. Spur trigger.

AUSTIN FREEMAN
Watertown, New York

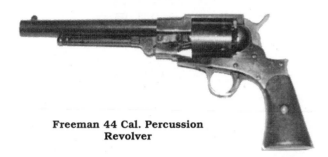

**Freeman 44 Cal. Percussion
Revolver**

Freeman Percussion Revolver **$2350**
Caliber: 44. Six-shot cylinder. Barrel: 7½ inches, rifled. Overall length: 12½ inches. Weight: 2 lbs. 13 oz. Produced at Hoard's Armory in Watertown, N.Y., this arm was patented in 1862 by Austin Freeman. It is considered a rare Civil-War-period piece, although no records have been found to substantiate its official use by the U.S. military. It was the precursor to the Rogers and Spencer Revolver, which was purchased by the U.S. Government during the Civil War (see also U.S. Military Revolvers).

FRENCH HANDGUNS
Various Manufacturers

French Charleville Flintlock Pistol . . . **$1950**
Caliber: 69. Barrel: 7¾ inches, round; marked "MRE RE de CHARLEVILLE." Overall length: 13½ inches. Lockplate is 5 inches long. Brass side plate, single brass band. Brass trigger guard, flash pan and butt. Ring for lanyard. Made from 1777 to about 1800.

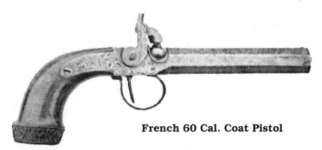

French 60 Cal. Coat Pistol

French Coat Pistol **$295**
Caliber: 60 percussion. Octagonal, Damascus barrel. Engraved box lock. Large, round trigger guard. Finely carved panel around butt of leaves. Circa 1850.

**French Coup de Poing
Pepperbox**

French Coup de Poing Pepperbox **$210**
Caliber: 7mm. Engraved checkered grips with ejector screwed into butt. "Coup de Poing" means simply a fist pistol.

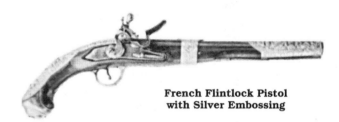

**French Flintlock Pistol
with Silver Embossing**

French Flintlock Pistol (I) **$400**
Calibers: various. Barrel: various lengths, usually round. Brass furniture with highly embossed silver overlay from muzzle to butt. The model shown has ½-inch turquoise stone on wrist.

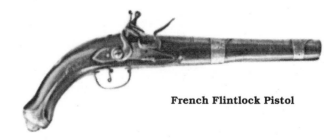

French Flintlock Pistol

French Flintlock Pistol (II) **$395**
Calibers: various. Similar to French Flintlock Pistol (I) with brass furniture, but with less embellishment.

French Flintlock Pistol (III) **$450**
Calibers: various, but ¹¹⁄₁₆-inch bore common. Barrel: 11½ inches, round. Overall length: 19 inches. Silvered butt fittings.

French Howdah Pistol. **$395**
Caliber: 16mm pinfire. Barrel: engraved, marked "ST. ETIENNE 16.0." Fitting at butt made to accept shoulder stock. Made from 1860 to 1870.

French Military Flintlock Pistol **$965**
Caliber: 65. Typical of those made by Frappier of Paris with a turn-off barrel. Octagonal section of barrel designed for wrench. Copper fittings. Circa 1793-94, French Revolutionary period.

Louis XIV Flintlock Pistol, Pair. **$3700**
Caliber: 69. Barrel: 4 inches, octagonal; etched with gold-plated designs. Overall length: 8¼ inches. Locks 3½ inches long. Silver wire inlaid grips. Round butts with plates.

GEM PISTOLS
See **Stevens Arms & Tool Co.**

GEM REVOLVERS
See **Bacon Arms Co.**

GERMAN HANDGUNS
Various Manufacturers

**German Proofed 5-Shot
Pepperbox**

German Cavalry Pistol **$310**
Calibers: various. Most were marked with the Regiment. Made circa 1851 to 1860.

German Pepperbox. **$465**
Caliber: 45. Five-shot cylinder. Nickel-plated. Made circa 1890.

GOVERNOR REVOLVERS
Various Manufacturers

See also Bacon Arms Co.

Governor Double-Action Revolver **$145**
Caliber: 32 S&W. Five-shot cylinder. Top break. Barrel: 3 inches, round.

Governor Double-Action Revolver **$150**
Caliber: 38 S&W. Five-shot cylinder. Top break. Barrel: 3 inches, round.

W.L. GRANT
Philadelphia, Pennsylvania

W.L. Grant was supposedly one of the trade names used by William Uhlinger on revolvers he produced in the 1860s. His intention, presumably, was to avert attention from himself as the manufacturer since his designs were in violation of the S&W-owned/Rollin White patent in force at the time.

W.L. Grant Revolver(I) **$275**
Caliber: 22 Long RF. Six-shot cylinder. Barrels: 2¾ or 3 inches, octagonal. Spur trigger. Solid iron frame. Square butt. Blued finish. Rosewood or walnut grips. Made circa 1861 to 1865.

W.L. Grant Revolver(II). **$295**
Caliber: 32 Long RF. Six-shot cylinder. Barrels: 5, 6 or 7 inches, octagonal. Spur trigger. Solid iron frame. Plated or blued finish. Walnut or rosewood grips. Made circa 1861 to 1865.

GROSS ARMS CO.
Tiffin, Ohio

Henry Gross operated out of Tiffin from 1841 to 1852, when his son, Charles B., joined the business. Together they operated the firm until Henry's death in 1875. The business was carried on under the name of Charles B. Gross from 1865 to 1886. Revolvers marked GROSS ARMS CO., TIFFIN, OHIO and GROSS PATENT 1861 TIFFIN, OHIO.

Gross Arms Co. Pocket Revolver (I). . . . $780
Caliber: 22 Short RF. Seven-shot cylinder. Barrel: 6 inches. Spur trigger. Tip-up. Blued finish. Walnut grips.

Gross Arms Co. Pocket Revolver (II) . . . $825
Caliber: 25 Short RF. Six-shot cylinder. Barrel: 6 inches. Spur trigger. Tip-up. Blued finish. Walnut grips.

Gross Arms Co. Pocket Revolver (III) . . $795
Caliber: 32 Short RF. Five-shot cylinder. Barrel: 6 inches. Spur trigger. Tip-up. Blued finish. Walnut grips.

JAMES HARDING
Address unknown

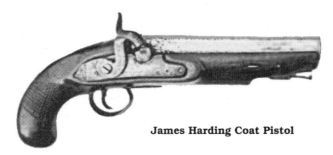

James Harding Coat Pistol

James Harding Coat Pistol (Conversion) . . $295
Caliber: 69. Originally flintlock converted to percussion. Brass furniture. Crudely checkered rounded grip. Made circa 1750 to 1815.

HARRINGTON AND RICHARDSON
Worcester, Massachusetts

Gilbert H. Harrington and William A. Richardson established the original H & R plant on Herman Street in Worcester, Mass., in 1874. Their initial enterprise consisted of producing shotguns and metallic cartridge revolvers.

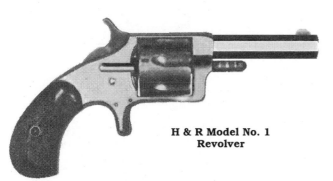

**H & R Model No. 1
Revolver**

H & R Model No. 1 Revolver (I) $250
Caliber: 32. Seven-shot cylinder. Barrel: 3 inches, octagonal. Iron frame. Spur trigger. Blade front sight; sighting rear "V" only. Bird's-head butt. Checkered hard rubber grips. Full nickel finish only.

H & R Model No. 1 Revolver (II) $275
Caliber: 38. Five-shot cylinder. Barrel: 3 inches, octagonal. Iron frame. Spur trigger. Blade front sight; sighting rear "V" only. Bird's-head butt. Checkered hard rubber grips. Full nickel finish only.

**H & R Saw-Handled Frame
Spur Trigger (I). $150**
Caliber: 32 RF. Five-shot cylinder. Barrel: 2½ inches, octagonal. Nickel finish. Blade front sight; sighting rear "V" only. Checkered hard rubber grips. Made from 1878 to 1883.

**H & R Saw-Handled Frame
Spur Trigger (II) $190**
Caliber: 32 RF. Seven-shot cylinder. Barrel: 3¼ inches, octagonal. Nickel finish. checkered hard rubber grips. Made from 1878 to 1883.

**H & R Saw-Handled Frame
Spur Trigger (III) $250**
Caliber: 38 RF. Five-shot cylinder. Barrel: 3½ inches, octagonal. Nickel finish. Blade front sight; sighting rear "V" only. Checkered hard rubber grips. Made from 1878 to 1883.

**H & R Saw-Handled Frame
Spur Trigger Model (IV)**

**H & R Saw-Handled Frame
Spur Trigger (IV) $150**
Caliber: 41 RF. Five-shot cylinder. Barrel: 2½ inches, octagonal. Nickel finish. Blade front sight; sighting rear "V" only. Checkered hard rubber grips. Made from 1878 to 1883.

HILL'S PATENT HANDGUNS
Great Britain

Hill's Patent Bull Dog

Hill's Patent Bulldog. $220
Caliber: 44 Bulldog. Five-shot cylinder. Tip-up barrel. Auto ejectors. Made circa 1880.

HENRY HOLMES
Liverpool, England

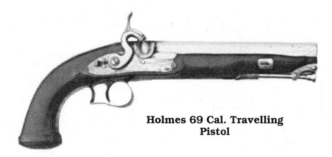

Holmes 69 Cal. Travelling
Pistol

Holmes Travelling Pistol. $415
Caliber: 69 percussion. Sliding safety on lock. Finely engraved iron furniture. Silver escutcheons on stock and silver band at breech. Made circa 1800 to 1850.

HOOD FIREARMS CO.
Norwich, Connecticut

Freeman W. Hood patented a metallic cartridge revolver in February 1875, a description of which follows.

Hood Firearms Co. Single-Action Revolver $195
Calibers: 22 Short, 32 Short and 41, all rimfire. Five-shot cylinder. Barrel: various lengths, but 3½ inches common. Spur trigger. Solid frame. Walnut grips. Blued or nickel-plated finish. Made from 1875 to 1880.

HOPKINS & ALLEN
Norwich, Connecticut

The Hopkins and Allen plant was in operation from 1868 to 1915, and turned out numerous handguns, rifles and shotguns. Many of their firearms were distributed under different names, including the revolvers made under the Merwin and Hulbert patents (*see* separate listing). The business was sold in 1915 to Marlin-Rockwell.

Allen Pocket Revolver $160
Caliber: 22 Short RF. Seven-shot cylinder. Single-action. Solid frame. Spur trigger. Made between 1880 and 1917.

Hopkins & Allen Model 1876 Revolver . . $695
Caliber: 44-40. Six-shot cylinder. Barrel: 4½, 6 or 7½ inches, round. Walnut grips with square butt. Blued or nickel finish. Made in the late 1870s to early 1880s.

Hopkins & Allen Ladies Garter Pistol . . . $195
Caliber: 22 Short RF. Single-shot. Barrel: 1¾ inches. Folding trigger; hammerless. Wooden, ivory or pearl grips. Decorative scroll engraving standard. Plated or full blued finish. Made from 1888 to 1893.

Hopkins & Allen New Model Target Pistol $400
Caliber: 22 RF. Top break. Barrel: 10 inches. Adjustable sights. Target grips.

Hopkins & Allen Ranger No. 1 . . . . $295

Hopkins & Allen Ranger No. 1
Nickel Finish

Caliber: 22 Long. Seven-shot cylinder. Nickel-plated with bluing that highlights the engraved frame and barrel. Made circa 1900.

Hopkins & Allen Ranger No. 2

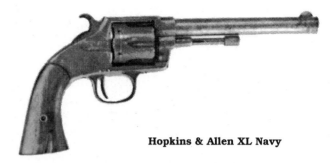

Hopkins & Allen XL Navy

Hopkins & Allen XL Navy Revolver.... $500
Caliber: 38 Short RF. Six-shot cylinder. Single-action.

WILLIAM IRVING
New York, New York

William Irving manufactured percussion revolvers, James Reid patent (*see* separate listing) metallic cartridge revolvers and single-shot derringers between 1861 and 1870.

W. Irving
Knuckle-Duster
Revolver

W. Irving Derringer $250
Calibers: 22 or 32 RF. Single-shot. Barrel: 2¾ or 3 inches; part octagonal/part round. Spur trigger. Brass frame. Wood grips. Made in the 1860s.

W. Irving SA Knuckle-Duster Revolver (I).. $450
Caliber: 22 RF. Seven-shot cylinder. Single-action. Barrel: integral part of cylinder. Silver-plated brass frame, which could be used as "knuckles" for fist fighting. Based on the Jame Reid design, this gun was made from 1869 to 1870 by Irving; from 1871 to 1884 by Reid.

W. Irving SA Knuckle-Duster
Revolver (II)..................... $450
Caliber: 32 RF. Five-shot cylinder. Silver-plated brass frame, slightly larger than the 22 cal. version; also used as "knuckles" for self-defense. Made from 1869 to 1870 by Irving; from 1871 to 1884 by Reid.

Hopkins & Allen Ranger No. 2....... $295
Caliber: 32 Long or Short RF. Single-action. Round or octagonal barrel. Spur trigger. Blued finish.

Hopkins & Allen Safety Police
DA Revolver (I) $140
Caliber: 22 RF. Barrel: various lengths. Double-action.

Hopkins & Allen Safety Police
DA Revolver (II) $175
Caliber: 32 S&W or 38 S&W. Barrel: various lengths. Double-action.

Hopkins & Allen XL 1 DA Revolver.... $150
Caliber: 22 Short RF. Double-action. Folding hammer.

Hopkins & Allen XL 3 DA Revolver.... $130
Caliber: 32 S&W. Double-action. Folding hammer.

Hopkins & Allen XL .30 Long Revolver.. $200
Caliber: 30 Long RF. Five-shot cylinder. Single-action. Spur trigger.

Hopkins & Allen XL Bulldog
Revolver (I)....................... $125
Calibers: 32 S&W, 38 S&W. Folding hammer.

Hopkins & Allen XL Bulldog
Revolver (II) $115
Caliber: 32 Short RF. Folding hammer.

Hopkins & Allen XL CR .22 Short RF
Revolver.......................... $170
Caliber: 22 Short RF. Seven-shot. Single-action. Spur trigger.

Hopkins & Allen XL Derringer....... $1030
Caliber: 41 Short RF. Single-action. Spur trigger.

Hopkins & Allen XL Double-Action
Revolver.......................... $110
Calibers: 32 S&W, 38 S&W. Folding hammer. Double-action.

W. Irving SA Pocket Revolver (I) **$395**
Caliber: 31 RF. Seven-shot cylinder. Single-action.
Barrel: 3 inches, octagonal. Solid frame. Spur trigger.

W. Irving SA Pocket Revolver (II) **$390**
Caliber: 31 RF. Seven-shot cylinder. Single-action.
Barrel: about 4½ inches; round or octagonal. Brass
or iron frame; iron frame apparently more plentiful,
but commands less. Trigger guard.

IVER JOHNSON'S ARMS & CYCLE WORKS
Massachusetts and Arkansas

This manufacturer of metallic cartridge revolvers,
shotguns and rifles was founded in 1871 in Worcester, Mass., as a partnership between Iver Johnson
and Martin Bye. Twelve years later Johnson became
the sole owner, moved the operation to Fitchburg and
renamed the company by the above designation, an
identity the firm enjoyed for almost 100 years. Modern management has abbreviated the name to Iver
Johnson's Arms, and after several changing of hands,
the company relocated to Jacksonville, Arkansas,
where today it markets primarily shotguns and rifles.

Most Iver Johnson revolvers are distinguished by
the owl-head design on the upper part of the grip and
the company name imprint. Many handguns of early
Iver Johnson manufacture, however, did not bear the
company name. Now collector's items, these carried
a spur trigger and were marketed under trade names
such as "Eclipse," "Tycoon," etc.

**Iver Johnson Safety Hammer Model
with "Perfect" Rubber Grips**

**Iver Johnson Safety Hammer Model
with Western Walnut Grips**

**Iver Johnson DA Revolver—Safety Hammer
Model** **$145**
Calibers: 22 Long Rifle, 32 S&W, 32 S&W Long, 38
S&W. Seven-shot cylinder (22 LR); 6-shot cylinder (32
S&W Long); 5-shot cylinder (32 S&W, 38 S&W). Barrel lengths: 2, 3, 3¼, 4, 5 and 6 inches. Weight: 15
to 19 oz. w/4-inch bbl., depending on caliber. Hinged
frame. Fixed sights. Checkered hard rubber stocks.
Round butt. Square butt and walnut stocks on some.
32 S&W Long and 38 S&W models built on heavy
frame. Blued or nickel finish. Made 1892 to 1950.

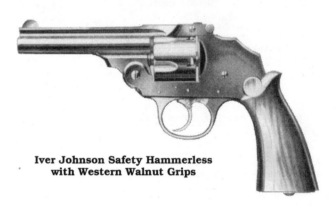

**Iver Johnson Safety Hammerless
with Western Walnut Grips**

**Iver Johnson Safety Hammerless
with Holster**

**Iver Johnson DA Revolver—Safety
Hammerless** **$135**
Same basic specifications as the Safety Hammer
Model, except in a hammerless version, with weight
ranging from 15 to 20½ oz., depending on caliber.
Made 1895 to 1950.

**Iver Johnson "Eclipse" Single-Shot
Derringer** **$150**
Caliber: 25 Short RF. Typical derringer design. Spur
trigger. Made from 1871 to 1875.

Iver Johnson "Favorite" Revolver **$325**
Caliber: 44 Short RF. Five-shot cylinder. Single-action. Spur trigger. Solid frame. Made from 1873 to 1884.

Iver Johnson "Prince" Percussion Pistol . . **$360**
Caliber: 60. Single-shot. Spur trigger. Barrel: various lengths. Made in the 1870s.

Iver Johnson "Tycoon" No. 1 Revolver. . **$180**
Caliber: 22 Short RF. Seven-shot cylinder. Barrel: various lengths. Single-action. Made from 1872 to 1887.

Iver Johnson "Tycoon" No. 2 Revolver. . **$180**
Caliber: 32 Short RF. Five-shot cylinder. Barrel: various lengths. Single-action. Made from 1872 to 1887.

Iver Johnson "Tycoon" No. 3 Revolver. . **$180**
Caliber: 22 Short RF. Five-shot cylinder. Barrel: various lengths. Single-action. Made from 1872 to 1887.

Iver Johnson "Tycoon" No. 4 Revolver. . **$180**
Caliber: 41 Short RF. Five-shot cylinder. Barrel: various lengths. Single-action. Made from 1872 to 1887.

Iver Johnson "Tycoon" No. 5 Revolver. . **$180**
Caliber: 44 Short RF. Five-shot cylinder. Barrel: various lengths. Single-action. Made from 1872 to 1887.

WILLIAM JOVER
London, England

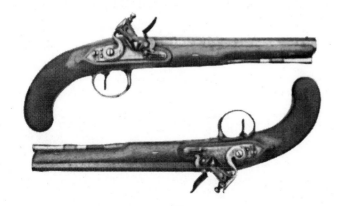

Jover 61 Cal. Duelling Pistols

Jover Duelling Pistols (Pair) **$3500**
Caliber: 61 flintlock. Barrel: about 7 inches, octagonal; blued with Damascus pattern; top flat engraved "JOVER LONDON." Lockplate also engraved with "JOVER." Sliding safety on lockplate. Single set triggers. Gold touch holes. Weatherproof pans. Roller on frizzen spring. Iron furniture with engraving. Coarse checkering on grips. Made the last half of the 18th century.

B. KITTREDGE & CO.
Cincinnati, Ohio

The Sharps Pepperbox Pistol, upon which the following handgun is patterned, was designed by Christian Sharps in 22 and 32 caliber (*see* C. Sharps & Co.). According to the Kittredge catalog of the late 1800s, he reworked it, however, by producing a more compact gun, yet in a larger caliber. After Sharps died in 1874, Kittredge bought the entire stock of this pistol and sold it as the "Sharps Triumph." Kittredge was also an agent for Sharps rifles, Colt pistols, English and Belgian shotguns.

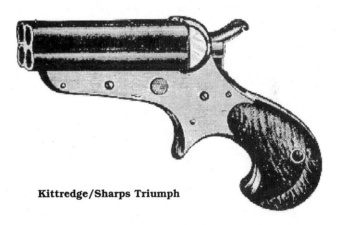

Kittredge/Sharps Triumph

Kittredge/Sharps "Triumph" **$295**
Caliber: 22 and 32 RF. Barrel: 2½ inches; four round barrels. Overall length: about 4¾ inches. Spur trigger. Bird's-head butt. Plated iron frame. Walnut grips. Some made in full plate; some with ivory grips.

NOTE

Unless indicated otherwise, all prices for the antique handguns listed in this section are for "standard" models. Engraved guns or guns with high-grade grips, etc. will always command a premium. Boxed sets of pistols will usually bring a premium of 150% more than individual guns.

HENRY LEECH
Sligo, Ireland

Henry Leech Pocket Pistol

H. Leech Pocket Pistol $695
Caliber: 45 percussion. Octagonal barrel. Sliding safety on lock. "LEECH" engraved on lockplate. German silver fittings with patchbox in butt. Silver escutcheon on wrist with Irish wolfhound engraved over initials "AC." Made circa 1820 to 1846.

EUGÈNE LEFAUCHEUX
Paris, France

Eugène Lefaucheux was the son of French gunmaker Casimir Lefaucheux, who invented the pinfire cartridge introduced in the 1840s. The first revolving pistols to use these cartridges were the popular pepperbox arms first exhibited at London's Great Exhibition of 1851. Three years later, Eugène applied for a patent using the pinfire cartridge in a breechloading revolver. The three firearms detailed below are variations of the single-shot, six-chambered pinfire revolvers bearing the Lefaucheux name.

**Lefaucheux Brevete Pinfire
Military Revolver**

Lefaucheux Brevete Military Revolver (I) $230
Caliber: 11mm pinfire. Six-shot cylinder. Octagonal barrel. Lanyard ring. Rod ejector on the right.

Lefaucheux Brevete Military Revolver (II) $310
Caliber: 11mm. Some converted from pinfire to rimfire. Six-shot cylinder. Round barrel. Finger spur trigger guard. Smooth grips.

**Lefaucheux Brevete 7mm
Military Pinfire Revolver**

Lefaucheux Pinfire Revolver $125
Caliber: 7mm pinfire. Octagonal barrel. Cylinder stamped "SYSTEME LEFAUCHEUX PERFECTIONNE." Checkered grips.

JEAN A. LeMAT
New Orleans, Louisiana

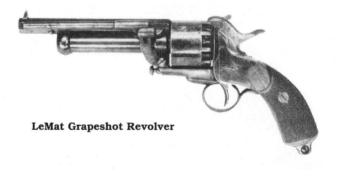

LeMat Grapeshot Revolver

LeMat Grapeshot Revolver $14,000
Caliber: 40. Nine-shot cylinder surrounding a central bore that used 16 gauge buckshot. Single-action. Barrel: about 7 inches. Finger spur trigger guard model consigned to the C.S. Army; those with plain round guards used by the Navy. Patented in 1856 by Jean Alexander Francois LeMat, a New Orleans doctor and Confederate Colonel; he received four British patents for revised models. Manufactured by partner C. Girard in France and proofed in England. Early models have half-round, half-octagonal barrels and fragile swivel loop fitted into buttframe. Later mod-

els have full octagonal barrel and heavy lanyard loop cast into buttframe. Loading lever is on the right side of early models, on the left on later models. Barrels marked, 'LeMat's Patent,'' "Col. LeMat's Patent," " Col. LeMat Bte.s.g.d.g. Paris,'' or ''Systeme LeMat Bte.s.g.d.g. Paris.'' Birmingham proofmarks. "LM" also marked on some.

LEWIS AND TOMES
London, England

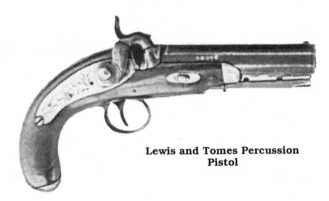

Lewis and Tomes Percussion Pistol

Lewis & Tomes Percussion Pistol $325
Caliber: 54 percussion. Octagonal barrel. German silver lock and fittings. Cap box in butt. One gold, one silver band at breech.

Lewis and Tomes Sawhandle Pistol

Lewis & Tomes Sawhandle Pistol $440
Caliber: 41 percussion. Barrel: octagonal, Dasmascus; engraved "LEWIS & TOMES LONDON." German silver frame and fittings. Belt hook on left side. Patchbox in butt.

NOTE

The majority of antique handguns will seldom have over 30% original finish. Specimens containing more than this amount will always bring a premium.

LIDDLE & KAEDING
San Francisco, California

Robert Liddle was a general gunsmith and arms dealer in San Francisco from about 1857 to 1872. After that time until about 1889, the firm name was changed to Liddle & Kaeding. It was subsequently known as the Liddle Gun Company until 1894.

Liddle & Kaeding Pocket Revolver $150
Caliber: 32 rimfire. Five-shot cylinder. Barrel: 3¼ inches, octagonal. Blued finish on metal; oil finish on walnut grips. Made for Liddle by Forehand & Wadsworth (*see* separate listing) between 1872 and 1889.

H.C. LOMBARD & CO.
Springfield, Massachusetts

H.C. Lombard made single-shot metallic cartridge pistols between 1859 and 1870.

Lombard Single-Shot Pocket Pistol $175
Caliber: 22 rimfire. Barrel: 3½ inches, octagonal; blued; pivots to load. Brass frame, silver-plated. Spur trigger. Walnut or rosewood grips, square butt on either. Made from 1859 to 1870.

T. LOVAT
Whitby, No. Yorkshire, England

T. Lovat Flintlock Pocket Pistol

T. Lovat Flintlock Pocket Pistol $395
Caliber: 43 flintlock. Sliding safety to lock pan. Lock engraved "LOVAT WHITBY." Walnut grip with diamond-shaped silver escutcheon. Made circa 1820.

LOWELL ARMS COMPANY
Lowell, Massachusetts

The Lowell Arms Company operated between 1864 and 1880, producing percussion and metallic cartridge revolvers. The firm was previously known as the Rollin White Arms Co., named after the owner of the same name, which made Smith & Wesson-marketed arms during the Civil War.

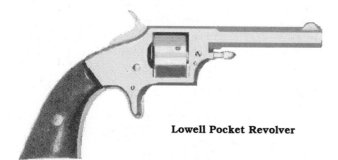

Lowell Pocket Revolver

Lowell Pocket Revolver (I) **$395**
Caliber: 22 Short RF. Seven-shot cylinder. Spur trigger. Made from 1864 to 1880.

Lowell Pocket Revolver (II) **$450**
Caliber: 32 Long RF. Six-shot cylinder. Spur trigger. Made from 1864 to 1880.

Lowell Pocket Revolver (III) **$495**
Caliber: 38 Long RF. Six-shot cylinder. Spur trigger. Made from 1864 to 1880.

JOHN P. LOWER
Denver, Colorado

John P. Lower was a general gunsmith in Philadelphia from about 1850 to the mid-1870s. At that time he moved to Denver, where he established his own business. Supposedly, his name was used on derringer pistols produced by Slotter & Co. and on revolvers made by William Uhlinger, both Philadelphia gun firms that were active in the 1860s.

J.P. Lower Single-Action Pocket Revolver (I) **$215**
Caliber: 22 Long RF. Six-shot cylinder. Barrel: various lengths. Solid iron frame. Spur trigger. Made from 1861 to 1865.

J.P. Lower Single-Action Pocket Revolver (II) **$225**
Caliber: 32 Long RF. Six-shot cylinder. Barrel: various lengths. Solid iron frame. Spur trigger. Made from 1861 to 1865.

MALTBY, HENLEY & CO.
New York, New York

From 1878 to 1890 this firm manufactured metallic cartridge revolvers, which were issued to the Metropolitan Police Force in New York City.

Maltby, Henley & Co. 22 Revolver **$195**
Caliber: 22 RF. Seven-shot cylinder. Double-action. Hammerless. Top break loading.

Maltby, Henley & Co. 32 Revolver **$250**
Caliber: 32 S&W. Five-shot cylinder. Double-action. Hammerless. Top break loading.

Maltby, Henley & Co. 38 Revolver **$265**
Caliber: 38 S&W. Five-shot cylinder. Double-action. Hammerles. Top-break loading.

MANHATTAN FIREARMS COMPANY
New York, New York

This firm initially made percussion pistols and pepperboxes, but in 1864, the firm opened offices in New York and started producing percussion revolvers similar to the Colt Navy models. They were soon forced out of business by a Colt lawsuit for infringement of patents.

Manhattan "Bar Hammer" Double Screw Barrel **$245**
Calibers: various. Single-shot.

Manhattan "Hero" Percussion Derringer **$250**
Calibers: various. Single-shot. Made from 1840 to 1864.

Manhattan Navy Percussion Revolver

Manhattan Navy Percussion Revolver . . **$795**
Series II. Caliber: 36. Single-action. Barrel length: 6½ inches.

Manhattan Percussion Pocket Revolver   **$495**
Caliber: 36. Single-action.

Manhattan Six-Shot Pepperbox. **$750**
Caliber: 28. Six-shot. Double-action.

Manhattan Three-Shot Pepperbox. **$595**
Caliber: 28. Three-shot. Double-action.

JOHN MANTON
London, England

Manton 52 Cal. Coat Pistols

Manton Coat Pistol. **$375**
Caliber: 52. Barrel: iron, octagonal; engraved, "MAN-
TON LONDON." Silver band around butt and silver
escutcheon on butt and grips. Checkered grips. Often
found in pairs worth about $750 for the pair. Made
circa 1820.

MARLIN FIRE ARMS CO.
New Haven, Connecticut

During the 19th Century, John Mahlon Marlin
manufactured rifles and metallic cartridge revolvers
in New Haven, Conn., under the names J.M. Marlin,
from 1870 to 1880, and the Marlin Fire Arms Co.,
from 1880 to 1915. The name was again changed to
the Marlin Arms Corp., 1915 to 1916; Marlin Rock-
well Corp., 1916 to 1921; and finally the Marlin
Firearms Co. from 1921 to date.

**Marlin Model 1872 XXX Standard
Revoler.** **$230**
Caliber: 30 RF. Tip-up barrel. Spur trigger.

**Marlin Model 1872 XXX Standard
Revolver** **$250**
Caliber: 30 RF. Tip-up octagonal barrel. Spur trigger.

**Marlin Model 1873 XX Standard
Revolver** **$225**
Caliber: 22 RF. Tip-up barrel. Round barrel. Spur
trigger.

**Marlin Model 1873 XX Standard
Revolver** **$230**
Caliber: 22 RF. Tip-up. Octagonal barrel. Spur trig-
ger.

Marlin Model 1875 Standard Revolver . .   **$215**
Caliber: 30 RF. Tip-up barrel. Spur trigger.

**Marlin Model 1887
Double-Action Revolver**

**Marlin Model 1887 Double-Action
Revolver** **$200**
Calibers: 32 S&W and 38 S&W. Five-shot cylinder. Top
break. Auto ejecting. Self-cocking. Barrel: 3¼ inches.
Steel frame. Rubber stock; ivory or pearl also available.
Nickel-plated or blued most common; some custom
made with engraved, full silver plating and gold trim-
mings.

WILLIAM W. MARSTON
New York, New York

Patentee and maker of the sling breech lock, William Marston also made percussion pepperboxes,
pistols and revolvers. Three-barrel pepperboxes were
also made by this firm from 1850 to about 1863.
While the firm name was changed in 1862 to Marston
& Knox, it also used the trade names of Western Arms
Co. and The Union/Arms Co. (*see* separate listing).

Marston Breech-Loader Handgun **$1500**
Caliber: 36. Barrel: half-octagonal. Single-shot. Iron or
brass frame. Blued or silver-plated finish. Engraved.

Marston Pepperbox Handgun **$495**
Caliber: 31. Double-action. Six-shot. Bat hammer.

Marston Single-Shot DA Handgun **$275**
Caliber: 36. Bar hammer. Double-action. Screw barrel.

Marston Single-Shot SA Handgun **$295**
Caliber: 36. Bar hammer. Single-action. Screw barrel.

MASSACHUSETTS ARMS COMPANY
Chicopee Falls, Massachusetts

See Adams Revolving Arms Company under Handguns.

MAUSER PISTOL
Oberndorf, Germany

Manufactured by Waffenfabrik Mauser of Mauser
Werke A .G.

**Mauser Model 1898 Military
Automatic Pistol**

**Mauser Model 1898 Military
Automatic Pistol.** **$1400**
Calibers: 7.63mm Mauser, 9mm Mauser and 9mm
Luger. Ten-shot box magazine. Barrel: 5¼ inches.
Overall length: 12 inches. Weight: 45 ounces. Adjustable rear sight. Walnut stocks. Blued finish. A number of variations exist at correspondingly higher
prices; value listed is for standard model. Made from
1898 to 1945.

MERRIMACK ARMS MFG. CO.
Newburyport, Massachusetts

For a few years beginning about 1870, the Brown
Manufacturing Co. *(see* separate listing) produced
these derringers, originally made by Merrimack in the
late 1860s.

Merrimack Southerner Handgun **$475**
Caliber: 41 Short RF. Single-shot derringer. Barrel:
short, octagonal, side swing. Brass frame. Light engraving. Stamped "SOUTHERNER."

MERWIN & BRAY
New York, New York

Joseph Merwin and Edward Bray apparently began
their partnership in Worcester, Mass., in the early
1860s. After relocating to New York City, they continued primarily as dealers and sales agents for a variety
of popular arms of the day. Known also as Merwin &
Simpkins and Merwin, Taylor & Simpkins toward the
end of the decade, they finally reorganized as Merwin
Hulbert & Co., with its own reputation as firearms
distributors *(see* separate listing).

Merwin & Bray 22 Revolver **$350**
Caliber: 22 Short RF. Seven-shot. Single-action. Spur
trigger. Solid frame.

Merwin & Bray 28 Revolver **$210**
Caliber: 28 cup primed cartridge. Six-shot. Single-action. Spur trigger. Solid frame.

Merwin & Bray 30 Cal. Revolver **$220**
Caliber: 30 cup primed cartridge. Six-shot. Single-action. Spur trigger. Solid frame.

Merwin & Bray 31 Cal. Revolver. **$195**
Caliber: 31 RF. Six-shot. Single-action. Solid frame.
Spur trigger.

Merwin & Bray 32 Cal. Revolver **$200**
Caliber: 32 Short RF. Six-shot. Single-action. Solid
frame. Spur trigger.

Merwin & Bray 42 Cal. Revolver (I) **$260**
Caliber: 42 cup primed cartridge. Six-shot. Single-action. Spur trigger. Solid frame.

**Merwin & Bray Handgun 42 Cal.
Revolver (II)** **$440**
Caliber: 42 cup primed cartridge. Six-shot. Single-ac-
tion. Barrel: 6 inches. Spur trigger. Solid frame.

Merwin & Bray Navy Revolver **$500**
Caliber: 38 Short RF. Six-shot. Single-action. Solid frame. Finger rest trigger guard.

Merwin & Bray "Original" 28 Cal. Revolver **$725**
Caliber: 28 cup primed cartridge. Six-shot. Single-action. Spur trigger. Tip-up.

Merwin & Bray "Original" 30 Cal. Revolver **$770**
Caliber: 30 cup primed cartridge. Six-shot. Single-action. Spur trigger. Tip-up.

Merwin & Bray "Original" 42 Cal. Revolver **$745**
Caliber: 42 cup primed cartridge. Six-shot. Single-action. Spur trigger. Tip-up.

Merwin & Bray "Original" Revolver . . . **$850**
Calibers: various, cup primed. Percussion.

Merwin & Bray Reynolds Revolver **$205**
Caliber: 25 Short RF. Five-shot. Single-action. Barrel: 3 inches. Spur trigger.

Merwin & Bray Single-Shot Handgun . . **$200**
Caliber: 32 RF. Barrel: 3½ inches; octagonal, side swing. Silver-plated brass frame. Blued finish. Spur trigger. Walnut grips. Square butt.

MERWIN, HULBERT & CO.
New York, New York

In 1874, this company, previously named Merwin, Taylor & Simpkins (*see* Merwin & Bray), patented an Army Model 1876 metallic cartridge revolver. These were made under Government contract at the Hopkins and Allen plant. They were also sold to foreign governments and are usually stamped "MERWIN HULBERT & CO."

Merwin, Hulbert & Co. Army Model DA Pocket Pistol **$920**
Caliber: 44-40 WCF. Barrel: 3½ inches. Six-shot. Double-action. Round butt.

Merwin, Hulbert & Co. Army Model DA Revolver **$950**
Belt pistol. Caliber: 44-40 WCF. Barrel: 7 inches. Double-action. Six-shot. Nickel-plated finish. Walnut or hard rubber grips. Round butt. With extra barrel, add **$145** to **$200**. With safety hammer, add **$40** to **$65**.

Merwin, Hulbert & Co. Army Model SA Pocket Pistol **$995**
Caliber: 44-40 WCF. Barrel: 3½ inches. Six-shot. Single-action. Square butt.

Merwin, Hulbert & Co. Army Model SA Revolver . . . . **$ 895**
Belt pistol. Caliber: 44-40 WCF. Barrel: 7 inches. Single-action. Six-shot. Nickel-plated finish standard. Walnut or hard rubber grips. Square butt.

Merwin, Hulbert & Co. Pocket Model . . . **$350**
Caliber: 32 S&W. Five-shot. Double-action.

Merwin, Hulbert & Co. Revolver (32 Cal.) **$350**
Caliber: 32 S&W. Seven-shot. Double-action. Barrel lengths: 3, 3½, 5 and 5½ inches. Automatic shell ejecting.

**Merwin, Hulbert & Co.
Automatic Shell Ejecting
Revolver**

Merwin, Hulbert & Co. Revolver (38 cal.) **$695**
Caliber: 38 S&W. Seven-shot. Double-action. Barrel lengths: 3½, 5½ inches. Automatic shell ejecting. Folding hammer or "old style." Adopted by the police in cities such as Cleveland and Cincinnati, Ohio.

MINNEAPOLIS FIREARMS CO.
Minneapolis, Minnesota

Starting in 1875, this plant made the so-called Protector Palm Metallic Cartridge Revolver. This gun was fired by holding the barrel between the index and second fingers while squeezing a lever against the frame holding the cylinder.

Minneapolis Firearms Co. "The Protector" Handgun **$695**
Caliber: 32 Extra Short RF. Nickel-plated finish.

MONARCH REVOLVER
Maker Unknown

Monarch Handgun Revolver **$295**
Caliber: 32 Short RF. Five-shot. Single-action. Spur trigger. Solid frame.

MOORE'S PATENT FIRE ARMS CO.
Brooklyn, New York

Operating from 1862 to 1865, the Moore's Patent Fire Arms Co. made Daniel Moore-patent teat cartridge single-action revolvers. They later made the Daniel Williamson-patent metallic cartridge revolvers and also all-metal derringer-type cartridge pistols. In 1865 the firm became the National Arms Company (*see* separate listing).

Moore's Front-Loading Revolver $325
Caliber: 32 TF. Barrel: 3¼ inches. Six-shot blued cylinder. Brass frame with silver-plated finish. Walnut or gutta percha grips. Bird's-head butt. Spur trigger. Single-action.

Moore's Handgun Revolver $340
Caliber: 32 TF. Barrel 3¼ inches. Six-shot blued cylinder. Single-action. Brass frame with the silver-plated finish. Walnut or gutta percha grips. Bird's-head butt. No extractor. Spur trugger.

Moore's No. 1 Derringer

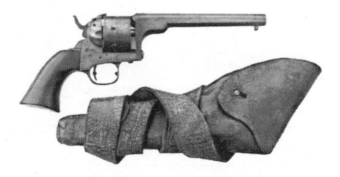

Moore's Single-Action Revolver

Moore's Single-Action Revolver $330
Caliber: 32 RF. Seven-shot cylinder. Brass frame. With holster. Made circa 1860.

Moore's Single-Shot No. 1 Derringer . . . $695
Caliber: 41 Short RF. Barrel: 2½ inches. Brass frame with silver-plated finish. Barrel either plated or blued finish.

Moore's Williamson's Patent $350
Caliber: 32 TF. Barrel: 3¼ inches. Six-shot blued cylinder. Brass frame with silver-plated finish. Walnut or gutta percha grips. Bird's head butt. Hook extractor.

MORGAN & CLAPP
New Haven, Connecticut

In operation from 1864 to 1877, Morgan & Clapp made Lucius Morgan-patent metallic cartridge revolvers.

Morgan & Clapp Single-Shot Pocket Pistol $210
Calibers: 22 and 32 RF. Barrel: 3½ inches; octagonal, side swing. Spur trigger. Blued barrel. Silver-plated brass frame. Square butt with walnut grips.

NATIONAL ARMS COMPANY
Brooklyn, New York

The National Arms Company took over the Moore Patent Fire Arms Co. and continued to manufacture Daniel Moore-patent teat cartridge revolvers as well as other types of handguns — especially the Moore Deringers — from about 1863 to 1870. See Colt handguns for further descriptions of the Moore Deringers, which were also manufactured by Colt.

**National Arms/Moore's
Front-Loading Revolver**

National Arms/Moore's Front-Loading Revolver $325

Caliber: 32 TF. Barrel: 3¼ inches. Six-shot blued cylinder. Brass frame with silver-plated finish. Walnut or gutta percha grips. Bird's-head butt. Spur trigger. Single-action. Made by National Arms Co. about 1865 to 1870.

**National Arms/Moore's
No. 2 Derringer**

National Arms/Moore's Single-Shot No. 2 Derringer $495

Caliber: 41 RF. Single-shot. Barrel: 2 or 2½ inches. Decorative scroll engraving was standard on frame and breech of barrel. Walnut grips. Patent purchased by Colt, who continued manufacturing this model under its own name. Made from 1864 to 1870 by National Arms.

National Arms Teat-Fire Revolver $1510

Caliber: 42 TF. Six-shot cylinder. Barrel: 7½ inches, half-octagonal. Silver-plated brass frame; barrel and cylinder blued. Walnut grips. Made from 1863 to 1868.

NEWBURY ARMS CO.
Albany, New York

Newbury Single-Shot Pistol. $415

Caliber: 25 RF. Barrel: 4 inches, octagonal. Silver-plated brass frame. Blued barrel. Walnut grips. Spur trigger. Made from 1856 to 1860.

HENRY NOCK
London, England

Henry Nock (1741– 1804) was a well-known and inventive English gunmaker. He produced arms for the royal families of Britain, made multi-barreled pepperbox handguns and long arms, and in 1785 devised a type of screwless lock that was used on flintlock arms of the day. This was adopted for limited use by the British Ordnance. He was also responsible for the introduction of early breech-loaders in England.

Henry Nock British Trade Pistol

Henry Nock Flintlock Trade Pistol $450

Caliber: 60 flintlock. Octagonal barrel stamped "H.N." Lockplate engraved "LONDON WARRANTED." Brass furniture. Made circa 1800.

OSGOOD GUN WORKS
Norwich, Connecticut

This firm manufactured metallic cartridge revolvers between 1870 and 1880.

Osgood Duplex Revolver $480

Calibers: 22 RF and 32 RF. Eight-shot 22 RF cylinder with 32 RF single-shot center barrel. Barrels: 2½ inches, round over/under. Blued or nickel-plated finish. Walnut grips. Made late 1870s to 1880.

JAMES PARR
Liverpool, England

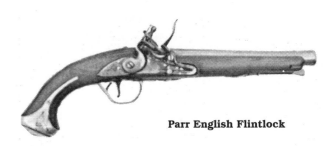

Parr English Flintlock

Parr Flintlock Pistol. $695

Caliber: 64. Barrel: brass, engraved. Brass furniture. "PARR" engraved on lockplate. Made circa 1795.

CHARLES S. PETTENGILL
New Haven, Connecticut

See also U.S. Military Revolvers.

Pettengill 36 Cal. Hammerless Revolver

Pettengill Hammerless Revolvers

Double-action. Hammerless-type frames of iron or brass. Calibers: 31, 34-36, 44. Six-shot round cylinder. Barrel: 4, 4½, 7 inches. Two-piece walnut grips. Blued finish. Made by Rogers, Spencer & Co. for Pettengill late 1850s to early 1860s.

Army Model, 7½-inch bbl., 44 cal. **$1395**
Belt or Navy Model, 4½-inch bbl. **1125**
Pocket Model, 4-inch bbl., 31 cal. **1000**

PLANT MANUFACTURING CO.
New Haven, Connecticut

E.H. and A.H. Plant manufactured metallic cartridge revolvers under the Ellis patents and the N. White patents assigned to the Plant Manufacturing Co. between 1860 and 1866. They also had a U.S. Government contract to manufacture Army revolvers.

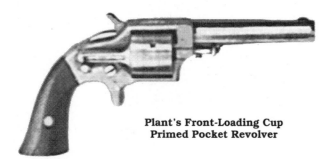

Plant's Front-Loading Cup Primed Pocket Revolver

Plant's Cup Primed Cartridge
Revolver **$245**
Calibers: 28, 30. Six-shot. Single-action. Spur trigger. Solid frame. Front loading. Made circa 1865.

Plant's "Original" Revolver (I) **$895**
Caliber: 28 cup primed cartridge. Six-shot. Single-action. Spur trigger. Tip-up.

Plant's "Original" Revolver (II) **$925**
Caliber: 30 cup primed cartridge. Six-shot. Single-action. Spur trigger. Tip-up.

Plant's "Original" Revolver (III) **$1000**
Caliber: 42 cup primed cartridge. Six-shot. Single-action. Spur trigger. Tip-up.

Plant's Revolver (I) **$725**
Caliber: 31 RF. Six-shot. Single-action. Solid frame. Spur trigger.

Plant's Revolver (II) **$750**
Caliber: 32 Short RF. Six-shot. Single-action. Solid frame. Spur trigger.

Plant's Revolver (III) **$325**
Caliber: 42 cup primed cartridge. Six-shot. Single-action. Spur trigger. Solid frame. Walnut or rosewood grips.

Plant's Revolver (IV) **$465**
Caliber: 42 cup primed cartridge. Six-shot. Single-action. Barrel: 6 inches. Spur trigger. Solid frame.

Plant's Reynold's Revolver **$230**
Caliber: 25 Short RF. Five-shot. Single-action. Barrel: 3 inches. Spur trigger.

LUCIUS W. POND
Worcester, Massachusetts

Lucius W. Pond produced top-break metallic cartridge revolvers that were declared an infringement on Smith & Wesson patents. He later made a front-loading cylinder revolver with removable steel shells.

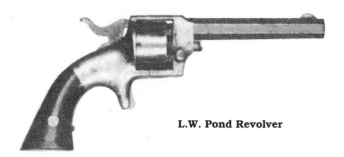

L.W. Pond Revolver

L.W. Pond Revolver **$295**
Caliber: 22. Seven-shot cylinder; front loading. Brass frame. Rosewood grips. Made from 1863 to 1870.

EDWIN A. PRESCOTT
Worcester, Massachusetts

In operation from 1860 to 1864, E.A. Prescott made metallic cartridge revolvers and had a U.S. Government contract for Navy revolvers. He was later sued by Smith and Wesson for patent infringement.

Prescott Revolver (I) **$395**
Caliber: 22 Short RF. Seven-shot. Single-action. Solid frame. Spur trigger.

Prescott Revolver (II) **$430**
Caliber: 30 RF or 32 Short RF. Six-shot. Single-action. Solid frame. Spur trigger.

Prescott Navy Revolver (I) **$595**
Caliber: 32 Short RF. Six-shot. Single-action. Solid frame. Finger rest trigger guard.

Prescott Navy Revolver (II) **$695**
Caliber: 36 RF. Six-shot cylinder. Single-action. Barrel: about 7 inches, octagonal. Solid frame. Finger rest trigger guard. Patented in 1860. Possibly used during the Civil War as perhaps a "trial" model, but no U.S. Government records substantiate its being officially purchased.

JAMES REID
Catskill, New York

James Reid patented a metallic cartridge revolver on April 28, 1863, which was initially manufactured by William Irving of New York City (*see* separate listing). Originally located in the same city, he moved his business in the mid- to late 1860s to Catskill, N.Y., where he operated until about 1884, making both percussion and metallic cartridge revolvers and derringer-type pistols. His "Knuckle-Duster" is considered to be a unique American revolver.

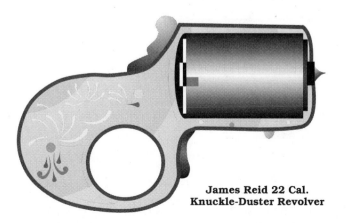

**James Reid 22 Cal.
Knuckle-Duster Revolver**

**James Reid Single-Action "Knuckle-Duster"
Revolver** **$850**
Calibers: 22 RF and 32 RF. Seven-shot cylinder. Barrel: integral part of cylinder. Silver-plated brass frame (also some blued with iron frame), which also acts as a set of knuckles for fist fighting. Made from 1869 to 1870 by Irving; from 1871 to 1884 by Reid.

James Reid Single-Action Revolver (I) . . **$395**
Caliber: 22 Short RF. Seven-shot cylinder. Spur trigger. Solid frame.

James Reid Single-Action Revolver (II) . . **$395**
Caliber: 32 Short RF. Seven-shot cylinder. Spur trigger. Solid frame.

James Reid Single-Action Revolver (III) . . **$625**
Caliber: 41 Short RF. Five-shot cylinder. Spur trigger. Solid frame.

James Reid Single-Action Revolver (IV) . . **$210**
Caliber: 41 RF. Five-shot cylinder. Barrel: 2⅞ inches, octagonal. Brass frame with silver-plated finish. Walnut grips. Made 1882 to 1884.

James Reid New Model Revolver **$545**
Caliber: 32 RF. Five-shot cylinder. Barrel: 2 inches, round. Brass frame with silver-plated finish. Walnut grips. Made 1883 to 1884. Less than 250 made.

REMINGTON ARMS CO.
Ilion, New York

Eliphalet Remington Jr., made his first rifle in 1816, and was actively engaged in the manufacture of firearms and gun parts for the next 45 years.

When Colt's revolver patent expired in February of 1856, Remington became intent on producing a handgun for commercial purposes. Colt's patent had previously effectively blocked revolver production by covering:

- Rotating the cylinder by the act of cocking the hammer, so as to bring the successive chambers in line with the barrel

- Locking the cylinder in the proper position during discharge and unlocking it by the lifting of the hammer in cocking

- Isolating each nipple and its cap from the others by means of partitions to prevent the communication of fire laterally

To produce an effective handgun, Remington needed a supervisor with knowledge of revolvers. In his search

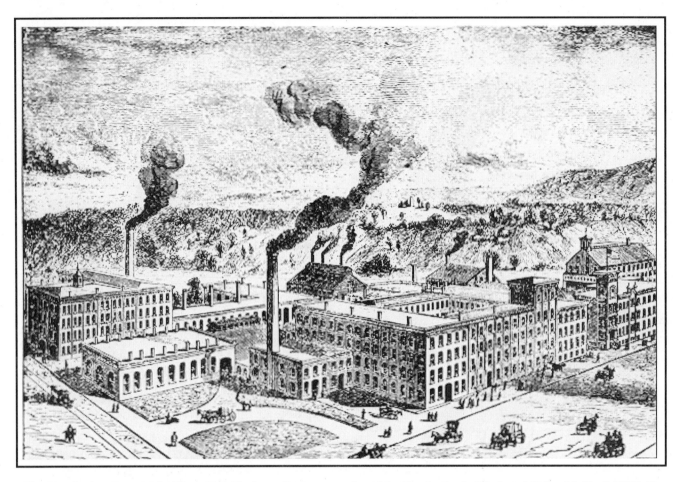

The Remington Armory in Ilion, New York, as it was reproduced in Remington's "Reduced Price List" of 1877. E. Remington & Sons at that time manufactured "military, sporting, hunting and target breechloading rifles, shotguns and pistols; also cartridges, primers, bullets, shotshells, loading implements, rifle canes, etc. etc.". . . everything to meet the shooter's needs.

for such a man, Eliphalet Remington turned to his superintendent of manufacturing — Fordyce Beals.

Beals had been with Remington since 1847. He came aboard to assist in fulfilling the government contract for the Jenks carbine. He had previously worked for the Eli Whitney firearms firm in Connecticut. In fact, Beals' earliest efforts toward revolver manufacture were in late 1854 when his patent, #11715, issued on September 26, 1854, was the basis of Whitney's Whitney-Beals revolver.

The first Beals pocket revolver incorporated new patented methods for rotating the cylinder by means of a pawl and for locking the cylinder prior to firing. These two patents gave the Beals' First Model Pocket Revolver its distinguishing characteristics — the outside pawl arm and hand for rotating the cylinder and the spring catch for locking the cylinder.

Joseph Rider was another Remington employee who did much for the development of Remington handguns. His efforts contributed to one of the first successful double-action cartridge handguns manufactured in the United States.

The partnership of E. Remington & Sons was formed in 1856 and continued as a family-run business until the organization was taken over by Hartley & Graham in 1886. At this time, the firm name was changed to Remington Arms Co. and many of the handguns were dropped from the line.

For further information, *see* U.S. Military Revolvers and also Remington Arms Co. in the Rifle and Shotgun Sections.

Remington-Beals' First Model Pocket Revolver $650
Caliber: 31; 5-shot smooth cylinder. Barrel: 3 inches, octagonal. Blued with brass or iron trigger guard. One-piece gutta percha grips. Approximately 5,000 manufactured between 1858 to 1860.

Remington-Beals' Second Model Pocket Revolver $3450
Same general specifications as Beals' First Model except has two-piece gutta percha grips. Less than 1,000 made between 1858 to 1860.

**Remington-Beals' First
Model Pocket Revolver**

Remington-Beals' Third Model Pocket Revolver $995

Caliber: 31 percussion; 5-shot, smooth cylinder. Barrel: 4 inches, octagonal. Spur trigger, blued finish, with two-piece gutta percha grips and loading lever. Slightly over 1,000 manufactured.

Remington-Beals' Navy Revolver $1950

Caliber: 36 percussion; 6-shot, smooth cylinder. Barrel: 7½ inches, octagonal. Blued finish, two-piece walnut grips — some with cartouche. Barrel inscribed, "BEALS' PATENT, SEPT. 14, 1858 – MANUFACTURED BY REMINGTONS', ILION, N.Y." Made from 1860 to 1862.

Remington-Beals' Army Revolver $2245

Caliber: 44 percussion; 6-shot, smooth cylinder. Barrel: 8 inches, octagonal with blued finish. Two-piece walnut grips. Same barrel inscription as Beals' Navy Revolver.

**Remington Model 1861
Army Revolver**

Remington Model 1861 Army Revolver . . $1450

Old Model Army. Caliber: 44 percussion; converted to 46 RF. Six-shot plain cylinder. Barrel: 8 inches, octagonal. Weight: 46 ounces. Brass trigger guard. Conversion was achieved in either of two ways: new cartridge cylinder fitted, and a metal spacer attached to standing breech, no loading gate, no ejector rod; or similar to above, except metal spacer fitted with loading gate, and ejector rod added. Smooth walnut grips. Blued finish. Made from the early 1860s to late 1870s; later factory conversions to cartridge revolvers command less.

Remington Model 1861 Navy Revolver . . $795

Old Model Navy. Caliber: 36 percussion; converted to 38 RF or CF. Six-shot round cylinder. Barrel: 7½ inches, octagonal. Single-action. Overall length: 13½ inches. Weight: 42 ounces. Blued or nickel-plated finish. Brass trigger guard. Conversion same as Remington Model 1861 Army Revolver.

**Remington Model 1865 Navy
Single-Shot Pistol**

Remington Model 1865 Navy Single-Shot Pistol $2450

First of the rolling block pistols. Caliber: 50 CF. Barrel: 8½ inches, round; blued. Casehardened frame. Spur trigger. Smooth walnut grips. Uses "Remington System" rolling block action of breechblock and hammer. Remington made a small quantity of these under contract for the Navy in 1866 and the model was soon superseded by the Model 1867 Navy, below.

Remington Model 1867 Navy Single-Shot Pistol $1795

Rolling block action. Caliber: 50 CF. Barrel: 7 inches, round; blued. Casehardened frame. Oval trigger guard. Smooth walnut stock. Made under contract with the Navy.

**Remington Model 1875 Improved
Army Revolver**

Remington Model 1875 Single-Action Army Revolver $1200

Improved or New Model Army. Calibers: 44 Rem. CF, 44-40, 45 Colt CF. Six-shot, half-fluted cylinder. Barrel: 7½ or 8 inches, round. Weight: about 32 ounces. Overall length: 13¾ inches. Web underneath ejector housing. Smooth walnut grips; offered with ivory or pearl grips. With or without lanyard ring in butt. Blued or nickel-plated finish. Made from 1875 to 1889.

Remington Model 1890 Single-Action Army Revolver $2850

Closely resembles the Colt Single-Action Army. Caliber: 44-40 CF. Six-shot, half-fluted cylinder. Barrel: 5½ or 7½ inches, round. Unlike the Remington Model 1875, the web underneath the ejector housing is cut away. Checkered hard rubber grips. Lanyard ring in butt. Nickel-plated or blued finish. Made from 1891 to 1894.

Remington Model 1891 Single-Shot Target Pistol. $1295

Rolling block action. Calibers: 22, 25 or 32 RF; 32 S&W CF or 32-20. Barrels: 8 to 12 inches; half-octagonal and round. Blade front sight in slot and adjustable V-notch rear sight. Smooth walnut grips. Blued finish. Introduced in 1891 and discontinued about 1900.

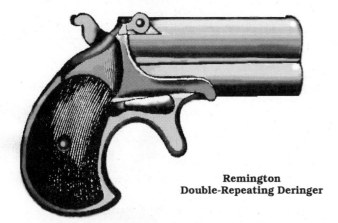

**Remington
Double-Repeating Deringer**

Remington Double Repeating Deringer. . $895

Caliber: 41 RF. Two-shot. Single-action. Barrel: 3 inches, superposed. Overall length: 4⅞ inches. Weight: 11 ounces. Sheath trigger. Walnut or checkered hard rubber grips. Finished in blue or nickel. Made from 1866 to 1935.

Remington Navy Revolver

Remington Improved Navy Revolver. . . $1950

Caliber: 38 RF or CF. Six-shot plain cylinder. Barrel: 7½ inches, octagonal. Overall length: 13¼ inches. Weight 2⅝ pounds. Web underneath ejector housing. Walnut grips; ivory and pearl also offered. Blued or nickel-plated finish. Made about 1873 to 1888.

Remington Iroquois Revolver. $345

Caliber: 22 RF. Seven-shot cylinder, plain or fluted. Single-action. Barrel: 2¼ inches, round. Top of barrel marked "IROQUOIS." Sheath trigger. No ejector. Checkered hard rubber bird's-head grip. Blued or nickel finish. Made from 1878 to 1888.

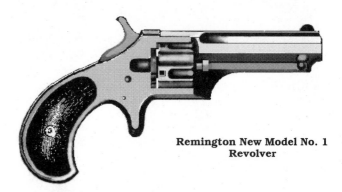

**Remington New Model No. 1
Revolver**

Remington New Model No. 1 Revolver . . $750

Based on Smoot's patent of 1873 (also referred to as New Line). Caliber: 30 RF. Five-shot cylinder. Single-action. Barrel: 2¾ inches; octagonal, integral with one-piece frame and ejector housing. Sheath trigger. Bird's-head grip of checkered hard rubber or smooth walnut. Nickel-plated or blued (less common) finish. Made from 1873 to 1888.

Remington New Model No. 2 Revolver . . $745

Same general specifications as No. 1 Smooth-Patent Revolver, except chambered for 32 Short.

Remington New Model No. 3 Revolver . . $625

Based on Smoot's patent. Caliber: 38 Short RF or CF (less common). Five-shot cylinder. Single-action. Barrel: 3¾ inches; octagonal, some ribbed. Barrel and ejector made separately from, and screwed into, two-piece frame. Sheath trigger. Checkered hard rubber grips, bird's-head or saw-handle style. Nickel-plated or blued finish. Made from 1875 to 1888.

Remington New Model No. 4 Revolver . . $545

Caliber: 38 Short or 41 Short RF or CF. Five-shot cylinder. Single-action. Barrel: 2½ inches; round, screwed into frame. Overall length: 6½ inches. Spur trigger. No ejector. Bird's-head style grip of checkered, hard rubber; pearl and ivory also offered. Nickel-plated or blued finish. Made from 1877 to 1888.

NOTE

Numbers on Remington over/under deringers were used solely for assembly purposes. The only way these pistols can be dated is by the barrel markings, and this method is only approximate.

Remington New Model No. 4
Revolver

Remington New Model Police
Revolver

Remington New Model Police Revolver . . $800
Caliber: 36 percussion; after 1873 made in 38 RF
cartridge. Five-shot plain cylinder. Barrel 3½, 4½,
5½ or 6½ inches; octagonal. Weight 21 to 24 ounces.
Overall length 8½ to 11½ inches. Walnut grips; also
offered with ivory or pearl. Finished in either blue or
nickel plate. Brass trigger guard optional. Made from
the early 1860s to the late 1890s.

Remington New Pocket Revolver

Remington New Pocket Revolver $895
Caliber: 31 percussion; later made in 32 RF cartridge
version. Five-shot plain cylinder. Single-action. Barrels: 3½ and 4½ inches; octagonal. Weight: 14 to 16
ounces. Finished in either blue or nickel plate. Spur
trigger with optional brass trigger guard. Made early
1860s to late 1890s.

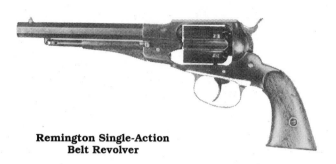

Remington Single-Action
Belt Revolver

Remington Single-Action Belt Revolver . . $825
Caliber: 36 percussion; production after 1873 in 38
RF cartridge. Six-shot plain cylinder. Barrel: 6
inches, octagonal. Some made in double-action.
Brass trigger guard. Web under ejector housing. Walnut grips; ivory and pearl also offered. Finished in
either blue or nickel plate.

Remington Vest Pocket Pistol (I) $650
Caliber: 22 RF. Single-shot. Barrel: 3 inches, round.
Overall length: 4 inches. Weight 3½ ounces. Trigger
projects from forward edge of frame. Hammer also
serves as breechblock, which is one-piece with frame.
Smooth walnut saw-handle grips. Finished in blue or
nickel plate. Also known as "Saw-handle Deringer."
Made 1865 to 1888.

Remington Vest Pocket
Pistol II

Remington Vest Pocket Pistol (II). $765
Calibers: 22, 32, 41 RF. Single-shot. Barrel: 4 inches;
part round, part octagonal. Separate split breechblock. Trigger projects from forward edge of frame.
Blued or nickel finish. Smooth walnut saw-handle
grips. Made 1865 to 1888.

Remington-Elliot Pepperbox Deringer . $1050
Calibers: 22 RF (5-shot) and 32 RF (4-shot). Double-
action. Barrels: 3 inches, fluted (22 cal.); 3⅜ inches,
ribbed (32 cal.). Barrels are stationary and firing pin
revolves. Large ring trigger. Smooth walnut or hard
rubber grips with saw handle. Finished in blue or
nickel. Based on W.H. Elliot's patents of the early
1860s, these were made from about 1863 to 1888.

**Remington-Elliot Single-Shot
Deringer**

Remington-Elliot Single-Shot Deringer . . $650

Caliber: 41RF. Single-action. Barrel: 2½ inches, round. Overall length: 4⅞ inches. Sheath trigger. Hammer also serves as breechblock. Smooth walnut bird's-head grips. Blued or nickel-plated finish or combination of both. Made late 1860s to about 1888.

**Remington-Elliot "Zig-Zag"
Deringer**

Remington-Elliot "Zig–Zag" Deringer . . $1800

Double-actio. Caliber: 22 RF. Six-shot pepperbox. Barrels: 3³⁄₁₆ inches; they rotate by means of zig-zag grooves at end of breech. Large ring trigger. Smooth hard rubber grips with saw handle. Based on W.H. Elliot patents, this unique pepperbox was produced only one year, from 1861 to 1862.

**Remington-Rider Double-Action
Pocket Pistol**

Remington-Rider DA Pocket Pistol $610

Double-action; probably one of the first of its kind produced in the U.S. and based on the Joseph Rider patents of the late 1850s. Caliber: 31 percussion; later converted to 32 RF metallic cartridge in the 1870s. Five-shot plain cylinder. Barrel: 3 inches, octagonal. Overall length: 6½ inches. Weight :10 ounces. Self-cocking. Brass trigger guard optional. Checkered hard rubber, saw-handle grips; also ivory and pearl offered. Finished in either blue or nickel plate. Made 1860s until the late 1800s.

**Remington-Rider New Model
Magazine Pistol**

Remington-Rider New Model Magazine Pistol $1200

Caliber: 32 Extra Short RF. Five-shot. Single-action. Barrel: 3 inches, octagonal. Overall length: 5¾ inches. Weight: 9 ounces. Trigger projected from forward edge of frame. Based on the 1871 patent of Joseph Rider, a tubular magazine under the barrel held five cartridges. Projection on the breechblock is pressed down, pulled back, and then released. This process must be repeated for successive shots. Smooth walnut grips; ivory or pearl also offered. Full nickel or casehardened finish. Made from 1871 to 1888.

**Remington-Rider
Single-Shot Deringer**

Remington-Rider Single-Shot Deringer . . $4375

Caliber: .170 smoothbore percussion. Barrel, frame, and right grip are machined from one piece of brass. Left grip is a removable brass plate. Less than 1,000 manufactured. Made from 1859 to 1860.

RICHARDSON
Address Unknown

Richardson Flintlock Pistol **$475**
Calibers: various, but ⅝-inch common. Barrel: 4 inches, octagonal. Overall length: 9 inches. Checkered stock. Steel trim.

JOHN RIGBY
Dublin, Ireland

Rigby 67 Cal. Dueling Pistols

Rigby Dueling Pistols (Pair). **$2750**
Caliber: 67. Gold band at breech with gold blow plugs. Engraved iron furniture. Checkered grips with silver escutcheons. Made from 1781 to 1819.

JACOB RUPERTUS
Philadelphia, Pennsylvania

Founded in 1858 and in operation until 1888, the Jacob Rupertus company started as a manufacturer of percussion pepperboxes, patented July 19, 1864. The firm later manufactured small caliber metallic cartridge revolvers.

Rupertus Double Barrel Derringer. **$740**
Caliber: 22 Short RF. Barrel: 3⅛ inches; side-by-side, round. Iron frame. Spur trigger. Walnut grips. Squared butt. Overall blued finish.

NOTE

Most Rupertus pistols are marked "RUPERTUS PAT. PISTOL MFG. CO. PHILADELPHIA," sometimes with the patent date.

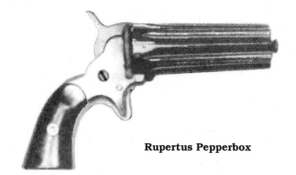

Rupertus Pepperbox

Rupertus Eight-Shot Pepperbox **$595**
Caliber: 22 Short RF. Eight shots. Barrel 2½ to 3 inches; tapered, blued finish. Spur trigger. Walnut grips.

Rupertus Revolver (I) **$395**
Caliber: 22 Short RF. Single-action. Seven-shot. Barrel: 2¾ inches, round. Spur trigger.

Rupertus Revolver (II) **$310**
Calibers: 32 Short or 38 Short RF. Five-shot cylinder. Single-action. Spur trigger. Solid frame.

Rupertus Revolver (III). **$295**
Caliber: 41 Short RF. Single-action. Barrel: 2⅞ inches, round. Semi-fluted cylinder. Spur trigger. Solid frame. Plated or blued finish.

Rupertus Singleshot Derringer (I). **$275**
Caliber: 22 Short RF. Barrel: 3 inches; part-round, part-octagonal, side-swing. Iron frame. Spur trigger. Walnut grips. Squared butt. Blued finish.

Rupertus Singleshot Derringer (II) **$225**
Caliber: 32 Short RF. Barrel: 4 or 5 inches; part-round, part-octagonal, side-swing. Iron frame. Spur trigger. Walnut grips. Squared butt.

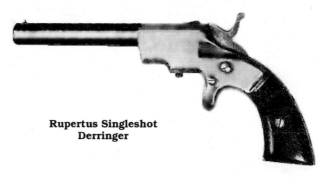

Rupertus Singleshot Derringer

Rupertus Singleshot Derringer (III). **$225**
Caliber: 38 Short RF. Barrel: 5 inches; part-round, part-octagonal, side-swing. Iron frame. Spur trigger. Walnut grips. Squared butt. Blued finish.

SAVAGE & NORTH
Middletown, Connecticut

Savage & North First Model **$7200**
Caliber: 36 percussion, 6-shot plain cylinder. Barrel: 7¹⁄₈ inches, octagonal. Round brass frame. Less than a dozen manufactured in 1856.

Savage & North First Model, Second Issue **$5100**
Same general specifications as first issue with some minor refinements. Has early type rammer assembly. Less than 300 manufactured from 1856 to 1857.

Savage & North Second Model **$4975**
Same general specifications as First Model, Second Issue except for iron frame and a more advanced rammer assembly. Approximately 100 manufactured in 1858.

Savage & North Third Model **$5000**
Caliber: 36 percussion, 6-shot plain cylinder. Barrel: 7¹⁄₈ inches, ocatagonal. Flat brass frame with rounded recoil shields. Grip modified from earlier models. Nearly 500 were manufactured in 1858.

Savage & North Fourth Model. **$5750**
Same general specifications as Third Model except for iron frame. Less than 100 were made in 1859.

SAVAGE REVOLVING FIRE-ARMS CO.
Middletown, Connecticut

**Savage Revolving Fire-Arms Co.
Navy Model Revolver**

Savage Navy Model Revolver. **$2500**
Caliber: 36 percussion, 6-shot plain cylinder. Barrel: 7¹⁄₈ inches, octagonal. Hinged-type loading lever assembly. Walnut grips. Blued finish with color case-hardened hammer and lever, trigger and trigger guard. Approximately 20,000 manufactured from 1861 to 1866.

SEGALLAS
London, England

"Segallas" was a common alias of gunmakers of the 18th century who, for sales purposes, wished to disguise their true identity. Pistols stamped with this name (spelled a variety of ways) often bore markings of "PARIS" and "DUBLIN" in addition to "LONDON." The guns were made exclusively of metal and were inexpensively produced, although to the inexperienced eye, they did appear well done on the surface. They could carry any number of barrels of the turn-off type, which allowed the shooter to screw them off for easy loading from the breech. The ball was held firmly in its breech cup when the barrel was screwed back in, thus eliminating the need for a patch. These guns were quite accurate and a good example of early breechloaders.

**Segallas Flintlock
Pocket Pistol**

Segallas Flintlock Pocket Pistol **$825**
Caliber: 31 flintlock. Double turn-off barrels. All-steel construction. Double triggers. Oversized trigger guard. Scroll engraved "LONDON" engraved on both sides. Made circa 1730 to 1750.

C. SHARPS & COMPANY
Philadelphia, Pennsylvania

Christian Sharps filed for his first patent in 1848 while living in Cincinnati, Ohio. This patent was for his famous falling breechblock used in breechloading rifles. His first plant was in Mill Creek, Penn., where his early rifles were made. In 1851 he moved to Hartford, Conn., forming the Sharps Rifle Mfg. Co., from which he received royalties on the rifles produced. After a few, short tumultuous years, he left the company in 1853 and broke relations completely.

The Hartford-based company continued to manufacture rifles and received many government contracts during the Civil War. In 1876 the operation moved to Bridgeport, Conn., where it carried on until the firm went out of business in 1881.

Meanwhile, Christian Sharps returned to Philadelphia and in 1854 formed C. Sharps & Company, which manufactured pistols only. In 1862, he formed the partnership of Sharps and Hankins, producing pepperboxes based on Sharps' patent of 1859 (*see* below) and military rifles and carbines for Civil War use. In 1866 the partnership was dissolved and Sharps went back to his former firm name, C. Sharps & Company, which it remained until his death in 1874.

Sharps Breech-Loading Single-Shot Pistol $2695
Calibers: 31, 34, and 36. Dropping-block action. Various barrel lengths. Fixed front sight. Smooth walnut grips. Made by C. Sharps & Co. 1853 to 1857.

Sharps Bryce Revolver $1165
Same general specifications as Sharps Percussion Revolver, but marked "WM BRYCE & CO."

Sharps & Hankins Four-Barrel Pepperbox—Model 3

Sharps & Hankins Four-Barrel Pepperbox—Model 1

Sharps Model 1 Four-Barrel Pepperbox Pistol. $440
Caliber: 22 RF. Barrel: 2½ inches. Rotating firing pins. Walnut grips were used most often, although gutta-percha grips were also found. Silver-plated frame and blued barrel were standard finishes. Variations exist. Made by C. Sharps & Co. and Sharps & Hankins.

Sharps Model 2 Four-Barrel Pepperbox Pistol. $395
Caliber 30 RF. Barrel: 2½ inches. Rotating firing pins. Walnut grips were used most often, but variations exist with gutta-percha grips. Silver-plated frame and blued barrel were standard finishes.

Sharps Model 3 Four-Barrel Pepperbox Pistol. $550
Caliber: 32 RF. Barrel: 3½ inches. Rotating firing pins. Smooth or checkered gutta-percha or walnut grips. Silver-plated frame and blued barrel were standard finishes. Variations exist. Sharps & Hankins.

Sharps Model 4 Four-Barrel Pepperbox Pistol $1795
Caliber: 32 RF. Barrel: 2½, 3, or 3½ inches. Smooth walnut bird's-head-style grips.

Sharps Percussion Revolver $1050
Caliber: 25. Six-shot engraved cylinder. Barrel: 3 inches; octagonal, tip-up type. Two-piece walnut grips. Blued and plated finishes. Made by C. Sharps & Co. from about 1856 to 1858.

Sharps Pistol Rifle $2760
Percussion breechloader; falling block action. Calibers: 31 and 38. Barrel: various lengths, but 28 inches standard. Silver or iron ornamentation on walnut stock. Barrel inscription: "C. SHARPS & CO. PHILADA. PA." Approximately 700 were manufactured by C. Sharps & Co. in the 1850s.

SHARPS & HANKINS
Philadelphia, Pennsylvania

Christian Sharps entered into partnership with William Hankins in 1862. The new company name was known as Sharps & Hankins which produced the four-barrel pepperboxes listed above and single-shot breechloading rifles and carbines (described in the Rifle Section). The partnership was dissolved in 1866 and Christian Sharps reverted to the C. Sharps & Company name again. The four-barrel pepperboxes continued to be manufactured under the C. Sharps name. The firm ceased to exist in 1874 upon Christian Sharps' death.

C.S. SHATTUCK
Hatfield, Massachusetts

C.S. Shattuck made metallic cartridge shotguns, pistols and revolvers from about 1880 to 1890.

Shattuck Pocket Revolver

Calibers: 22, 32, 38, 41 rimfire. Single-action. Five-shot, swing-out cylinder. Barrel: 3½ inches, octagonal. Spur trigger. Nickel finish. Slender black rubber grips with square butt. Made from about 1880 to 1890.

22 Caliber	**$325**
32 Caliber	**340**
38 Caliber	**375**
41 Caliber	**425**

SHAWK & McLANAHAN
St. Louis, Missouri

Shawk & McLanahan Navy Revolver . . **$5100**

Caliber: 36 percussion, 6-shot plain cylinder. Barrel: 8 inches, round. Two-piece walnut grips. Brass frame with remaining parts blued. Resembles the Whitney Navy revolver. Approximately 100 made in 1858.

SMITH ARMS COMPANY
New York, New York

See Silas Crispin

OTIS A. SMITH
Brook Falls, Connecticut

This firm manufactured spur-trigger and double-action metallic cartridge revolvers from about 1873 to 1890. Some models were quite cheaply made, but many were of excellent quality.

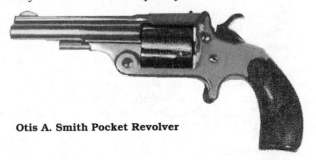

Otis A. Smith Pocket Revolver

Smith Single-Action Revolver (I) $240

Caliber: 22 RF. Seven-shot cylinder. Barrel: various lengths. Solid frame. Spur trigger.

Smith Single-Action Revolver (II)

Calibers: 32 Short, 32 S&W, 38 Short, 41 Short RF. Five-shot cylinder. Barrel: various lengths. Solid frame. Spur trigger.

32 Short	**$220**
32 S&W	**220**
38 Short	**250**
41 Short	**275**

WILLIAM SMITH
Bath, England

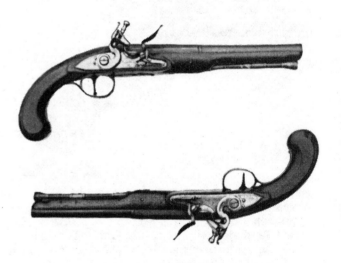

**Smith 59 Caliber Flintlock
Dueling Pistols**

Smith Dueling Pistols (Pair) $3750

Caliber: 59 flintlock. Lock engraved "SMITH." "BATH" engraved on the top of the Spanish-style half-round, half-octagonal barrels. Flat-sided butts. Brass furniture. Made circa 1791 to 1817.

NOTE

Dueling pistols are priced as a matched set or pair. Individual pistols will bring far less.

Smith Flintlock Pocket Pistol

Smith Flintlock Pocket Pistol. $435
Caliber: 45 flintlock. Engraved lock. Large trigger guard. Made circa 1800.

HORACE SMITH
FRANK B. WESSON

Horace Smith became an apprentice gunsmith at the Springfield Armory at the age of 16 and worked for this firm for the next 18 years. After leaving Springfield, he worked briefly in a number of other gun factories, including those of Charles Thurber, Eli Whitney, Allen & Thurber, Oliver Allen, and Allen, Brown & Luther.

It was while working for Allen, Brown & Luther that Smith met Daniel B. Wesson, and in 1853 the association of Smith & Wesson began. Smith began perfecting a repeating action while Wesson devoted himself to the improvement of the metallic cartridge. The firm soon began manufacturing repeating rifles and pistols, but they were forced to sell out to the Volcanic Arms Co. in 1855 and Smith retired to Springfield to operate a livery stable with his brother-in-law.

Wesson, however, continued working on a new revolver to fire metallic cartridges and in 1857 Wesson persuaded Smith to form a new partnership with him for the manufacture of the new cartridge and revolver. The new enterprise prospered as the partners worked to improve their product. Finally, in 1873, Smith, who had been executive head of the firm, sold his interests in the business to Wesson and retired to Springfield, where he became an alderman and a director of a number of industrial and commercial enterprises.

Wesson remained, carrying on the business alone until 1883 when he took his sons into a partnership with him. The Smith & Wesson firm has changed hands many times since, but the company name still remains, and along with Colt, probably appears on more handguns than any other in the world.

SMITH & WESSON, INC.
Springfield, Massachusetts

Daniel Baird Wesson and Horace Smith began manufacture of the famous Volcanic Action Repeating Pistol in Norwich, Conn., in 1854. In 1856 the Smith & Wesson patents were released to Oliver Winchester and others, resulting in the eventual formation of the Winchester Repeating Arms Co. *(See* separate history).

Manufacture of the first revolver to use self-contained ammunition began in a Market Street delivery stable in Springfield, Mass., with 25 employees. In 1859 the first building in the present location was erected. With the advent of the Civil War, Government orders expanded the business to 600 employees, and hundreds of thousands of arms were produced.

In 1870 Smith & Wesson designed the .44 Russian Model for the Russian Imperial Army and delivered huge numbers of them. Five years later, the .45 Schofield Model was adopted by the U.S., and it is reliably reported that General Custer used this model in his historical "Last Stand" at the Battle of Little Bighorn.

The year 1880 saw the introduction of the double-action type of revolver and the .44 caliber became immensely popular with Western peace officers. Near the end of that decade the Safety Hammerless revolver was brought out, making a much safer revolver that lowered the chances of accidental discharge. The firm of Smith & Wesson successfully produced firearms well into the 20th century and is still in business today.

PISTOLS

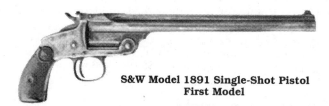

**S&W Model 1891 Single-Shot Pistol
First Model**

Smith & Wesson Model 1891 Single-Shot Target Pistol—First Model
Calibers: 22 Long Rifle, 32 S&W, 38 S&W. Barrel 6, 8 or 10 inches. Overall length: approx. 11½ inches with 8-inch bbl. Weight: about 1½ pounds. Hinged frame. Target sights, barrel catch adjustable rear sight. Squared butt. Checkered hard rubber grips. Blued finish. Offered as a combination gun with 38 caliber revolver barrel/cylinder that converts the pistol into a revolver. Made 1893 to 1905.
Single-shot pistol (22 Long Rifle) . . . . **$ 345**
Single-shot pistol (32 S&W or 38 S&W) **1050**
Combination set w/revolver cylinder/bbl. . . . **1000**

REVOLVERS

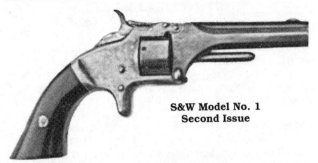

S&W Model No. 1
Second Issue

Smith & Wesson Model No. 1 Revolver

A "tip-up" revolver, this was Smith & Wesson's first metallic cartridge gun. Caliber: 22 Short RF. Seven-shot non-fluted cylinder. Barrel: 3³/₁₆ inches; octagonal, blued. Bayonet-type barrel catch. Square butt. Rosewood grips. Silver-plated brass frame.

First Issue, made 1857-1860 . . . . **$2400**
Second Issue, made 1860-1868 . . . . **450**
  (Frame had flat sides; sideplates were different shape from First Issue.)

Smith & Wesson Model 1 Revolver— Third Issue **$265**

Improved version of the First and Second issues. Caliber: 22 Short RF. Seven-shot fluted cylinder. Barrel lengths: 2¹¹/₁₆ and 3³/₁₆ inches; round ribbed. Rounded butt. Rosewood grips. Nickel-plated frame with blued barrel and cylinder, or full nickel-plating or full blued finish. Made 1868 to 1881.

Smith & Wesson Model 1 Hand Ejector Revolver—First Model **$525**

Double-action. This was the first solid-frame, swingout cylinder S&W revolver, the percussor to the current 32 Hand Ejector and Regulation Police models. Caliber: 32 S&W Long. Barrel: 3¹/₄, 4¹/₄, 6 inches. Fixed sights. No cylinder latch, and has longer top strap than that of later models. Rounded butt. Checkered hard rubber grips. Blued or nickel finish. Made 1896 to 1903.

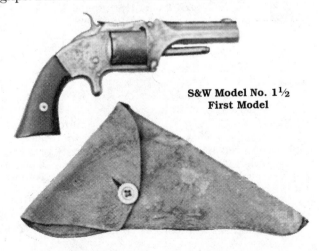

S&W Model No. 1¹/₂
First Model

Smith & Wesson Model No. 1¹/₂—First Issue **$295**

Improved version of Model No. 1. Caliber: 32 RF. Five-shot non-fluted cylinder. Barrel: 3¹/₂, 4 inches; octagonal. Rosewood grips. Squared butt. Blued or nickel-plated finish. Made 1865 to 1868.

Smith & Wesson Model No. 1¹/₂— Second Issue **$325**

Improved version of First Issue Model No. 1¹/₂ with more sleek appearance, cylinder stop in topstrap. Caliber: 32 Long RF. Five-shot fluted cylinder. Barrel: 2¹/₂, 3¹/₂ inches; round. Rosewood grips. Rounded butt. Blued or nickel-plated finish. Made 1868 to 1875.

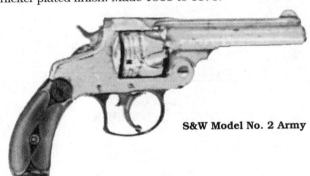

S&W Model No. 2 Army

Smith & Wesson Model No. 2 Army (Old Model). **$395**

Popular Civil War arm. Caliber: 32 Long RF. Six-shot non-fluted cylinder. Barrel: 4, 5, 6 inches; octagonal. Rosewood grips. Square butt. Blued or nickel-plated finish. Made 1861 to 1874.

Smith & Wesson No. 3 Single-Action Frontier Revolver. **$1395**

Caliber: 44-40 Win. Barrel: 4, 5, 6¹/₂ inches. Fixed or target sights. Rounded butt. Checkered hard rubber or walnut grips. Blued or nickel-plated finish. Made 1885 to 1908.

S&W No. 3 SA American Revolver
Second Model

Smith & Wesson No. 3 Single-Action Revolver

Also known as the American, this is S&W's first top-break revolver. Caliber: 44 S&W American, 44 RF Henry (rare). Six-shot fluted cylinder. Barrel: 8 inches, round. Squared butt. Walnut grips. Blued or nickel-plated finish. A number of variations exist, including shorter barreled versions, with correspondingly higher prices.

First Model American (1870–72). **$2100**
Second Model American
  (1872–74 w/steel blade front sight) **2895**

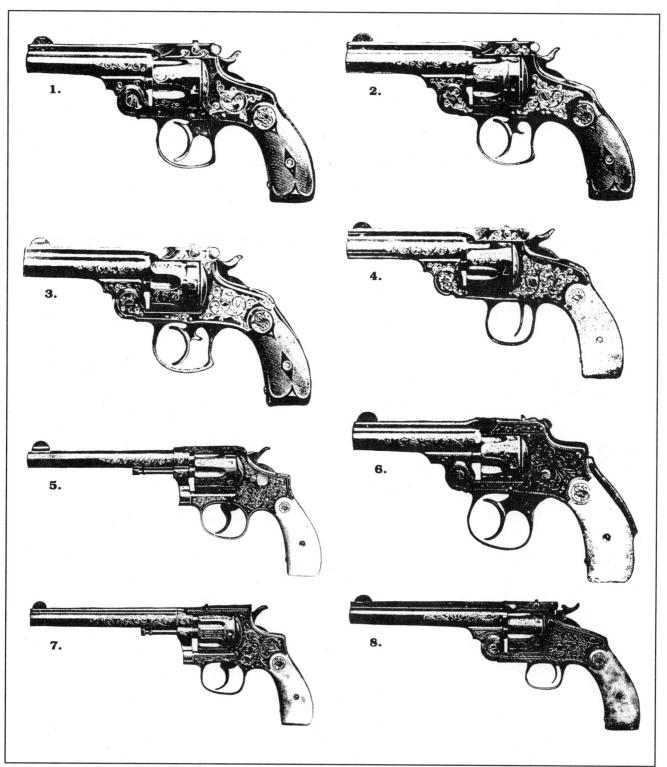

While the standard finish on pre-1900 S&W revolvers was full nickel or blue with black rubber stocks, many custom engravings, inlays and fancy pearl or ivory stocks were available. The above eight styles are examples of some of the variations that existed, which the collector may encounter. Oftentimes, guns were purchased and customized later; note that on true S&W factory-fitted pearl grips, the S&W monogram trademark would have been inserted in gold or silver as "a guarantee of quality."

Smith & Wesson No. 3 Single-Action Revolver—New Model **$1495**

Caliber: 44 S&W Russian. Six-shot cylinder. Barrel: 4 to 8 inches. Hinged frame. Fixed or target sight. Rounded butt. Checkered hard rubber or walnut grips. Blued or nickel-plated finish. A number of variations exist over the standard model listed, with correspondingly higher values. Made 1878 to 1908.

Smith & Wesson No. 3 Single-Action Russian—First Model

The Old, Old Model Russian. Basically the same as the No. 3 American, but in caliber 44 S&W Russian. Made 1871 to 1874.

Standard Commercial Model
  (6-, 7-, 8-inch bbl.) **$1475**
Russian Contract Model (8-inch bbl. w/Imp.
  Russian Eagle and Cyrillic markings). **2450**

Smith & Wesson No. 3 Single-Action Russian—Second Model

The Old Model Russian. Same as the First Model Russian, except in calibers 44 S&W Russian and 44 RF Henry with 7-inch barrels, rounded butt and spurred trigger guard. Made 1873 to 1878.

Standard Commercial Model
  (44 S&W Russian) **$1425**
Standard Commercial Model (44 Henry) **2700**
Japanese Issue (44 S&W Russian) **1100**
Russian Contract Model (44 S&W Russian w/Imp.
  Russian Eagle and Cyrillic markings). **1265**
Turkish Issue (44 Henry). **1100**

Smith & Wesson No. 3 Single-Action Russian—Third Model

New Model Russian. Basically the same as the Second Model, except with 6½-inch barrel, integral front sight, shorter extractor housing. Made 1874 to 1878.

Standard Commercial Model
  (44 S&W Russian) **1265**
Standard Commercial Model (44 Henry) **1800**
Japanese Issue (44 S&W Russian) **1650**
Russian Contract Model (44 S&W Russian w/Imp.
  Russian Eagle and Cyrillic markings). **1265**
Turkish Issue (44 Henry). **1470**

Smith & Wesson No. 3 Single-Action Target Revolver **$825**

Calibers: 32/44 S&W, 38/44 S&W Gallery & Target. Six-shot cylinder. Barrel: 6½ inches only. Hinged frame. Fixed or target sights. Rounded butt. Checkered hard rubber or walnut grips. Blued or nickel-plated finish. Made 1887 to 1910.

S&W 32 Double-Action Revolver

Smith & Wesson 32 Double-Action Revolver

Caliber: 32 S&W. Five-shot fluted cylinder. Barrel: 3, 3½ or 6 inches. Hinged frame. Fixed sights. Rounded butt. Checkered hard rubber grips. Blued or nickel-plated finish. Made 1880 to 1919.

First Issue of 1880 (rare; square sideplate,
  serial nos. 1–30). **$1625**
Standard Model **225**

Smith & Wesson 32 Single-Action Revolver **$480**

Smith & Wesson's first 32 caliber, automatic ejecting, break-open model. Caliber: 32 S&W. Five-shot fluted cylinder. Barrel: 3, 3½, 6, 8, 10 inches; round. Plain wood or checkered hard rubber grips. Rounded butt. Blued or nickel-plated finish. Made 1878 to 1892.

S&W 38 Double-Action Revolver

Smith & Wesson 38 Double-Action Revolver

Caliber: 38 S&W. Five-shot fluted cylinder. Barrel: 3¼ to 10 inches. Weight: 17 to 19 ounces. Hinged frame. Fixed sights. Hard black rubber grips. Blued or nickel-plated finish. Made 1880 to 1911.

First Issue of 1880 (squared sideplate,
  serial nos. 1 to 4000) **$685**
Third Issue (1884–5 w/8- or 10-inch bbl.) **200**
Standard Model (incl. 1st thru 4th issues) **480**

**S&W 38 Cal. Military & Police
R.A.F. Issue**

Smith & Wesson Model 38 Military & Police—First Model. $375

Also known as Model 38 Hand Ejector Double-Action Revolver or Model 1899 Army or Navy Revolver. One of the first S&W Swingout-cylinder models that resembles the Colt New Navy, minus the barrel lug and locking bolt that later S&W hand ejector models had. Caliber: 38 Long Colt. Six-shot cylinder. Barrel: 4, 5, 6 or 6½ inches. Overall length: 9 inches with 4-inch bbl. Fixed sights. Checkered walnut or hard rubber stocks. Round butt. Blued or nickel-plated finish. Made 1899 to 1902.

Smith & Wesson 38 Military & Police—Target Model $895

Same general specifications as the 38 Military & Police, except in target version with adjustable target sights. Caliber: 38 Special. Barrel: 6 inches. Weight: 32 ounces. Checkered walnut grips. Blued finish. Made 1899 to 1940.

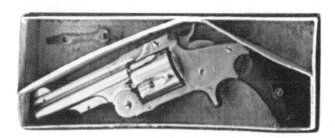

**S&W Baby Russian
First Model**

Smith & Wesson 38 Single-Action Revolver

Single-Action Model No. 2 or Baby Russian. Caliber: 38 S&W. Five-shot fluted cylinder. Top break action. Spur trigger. Barrels: 3¼, 4 inches, round (First Model); 3¼ to 10 inches, round (Second Model). Checkered hard rubber or wood grips. Blued or nickel-plated finish. Second Model has improved ejection with shorter extractor housing.

First Model (1876–77). **$425**
Second Model (1877–1981). **925**

**S&W 38 Cal. Single-Action
Revolver—Third Model**

Smith & Wesson 38 Single-Action Revolver—Third Model, or Model 1891

Caliber: 38 S&W. Five-shot fluted cylinder. Barrel: 3¼, 4, 5, or 6 inches. Weight: 17½ to about 20 ounces. Hinged frame. Fixed sights. Automatic shell extractor. Hard black rubber grips. Blued or nickel-plated finish. Available with single-shot pistol barrels of 6, 8 or 10 inches in 22, 32 or 38 caliber. Made 1891 to 1911.

Revolver only . . . . **$ 925**
Set with single-shot barrel **1400**

Smith & Wesson 38 Single-Action Mexican Model. $1750

Same as S&W Model 1891 above, except has flat-sided hammer, spur trigger assembly not integral to the frame; lacks half-cock notch on hammer.

**S&W 44 Double-Action
Frontier Model**

Smith & Wesson 44 Double-Action Revolver

Lightweight. Calibers: 44 S&W Russian, 38-40, 44-40 Win. Six-shot fluted cylinder. Barrel: 4, 5, 6 or 6½ inches. Weight: 34¼ to 37½ ounces depending on barrel length. Hinged frame. Fixed sights. Checkered hard rubber or walnut grips. Blued or nickel-plated finish. Made 1881 to 1913; Frontier Model discontinued 1910.

DA Frontier (44-40 Win.). **$1125**
Standard Model (38-40) **2500**
Standard Model (44 S&W Russian). **695**
Wesson Favorite (1882–3, 5-inch bbl.) **1800**

S&W 44 Single-Action Russian

Smith & Wesson 44 Single-Action Russian Model **$1275**

Calibers: 32-44, 38-44, 38 Win. 44 Russian, 44 Win., 450. Six-shot cylinder. Barrel: 4, 5, 6, 6½ or 8 inches (only cal. 44 Russian avail. in 8-inch). Weight: about 36 to 43 ounces. Automatic shell extractors. Checkered black rubber or wood grips.

S&W Model 1880 Single-Action Revolver

Smith & Wesson Model 1880 Single-Action Revolver **$480**

Caliber: 38 S&W. Five-shot cylinder. Barrel: 3¼, 4, 5 or 6 inches. Weight: 17¼ to 19¾ ounces. Automatic shell extractor. Black rubber stocks. Special target sights and stocks were avail. Blued or nickel-plated finish. Introduced in 1880.

Smith & Wesson Model 1891 Single-Action Revolver

See Smith & Wesson 38 Single-Action Revolver — Third Model.

S&W Bicycle Revolver

Smith & Wesson Bicycle Revolver **$265**

Safety hammerless. Caliber: 32 S&W. Five-shot cylinder. Barrel length: 2 inches. Weight: 14 ounces. Black rubber stocks. Blued or nickel-plated finish. Made late 1800s.

S&W Safety Hammerless Revolver

Smith & Wesson Safety Hammerless Revolver — New Departure Double-Action **$295**

Calibers: 32 S&W, 38 S&W. Five-shot cylinder. Barrel: 2, 3 or 3½ inches (32 cal.); 2, 3¼, 4, 5 or 6 inches (38 cal.). 7½ inches (38 cal. with 3¼-inch bbl.). Weight: 14¼ to 18¼ ounces. Hinged frame. Fixed sights. Hard rubber stocks. Blued or nickel-plated finish. Minor variations. Made 1888 to 1937 (32 cal.); 1887 to 1941 (38 cal.).

Smith & Wesson-Schofield Single-Action Revolver

Modification of S&W No. 3 by Col. G.W. Schofield's patents of 1871 and 1873. Caliber: 45 S&W. Six-shot fluted cylinder. Barrel: 5 inches; 7 inches standard. Squared butt. Walnut grips. Blued or nickel (rare) finish. Two models made; the Second Model was an improved version of the First Model with no recoil plate in frame. Both models made in the 1870s.

Commercial issue (rare) **$3650**
Standard Military issue **2400**
Wells Fargo & Co. Issue (w/5-inch bbl.) **2760**

SPANISH HANDGUNS
Various Manufacturers

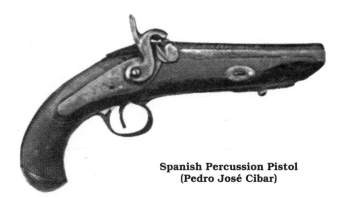

Spanish Percussion Pistol
(Pedro José Cibar)

Pedro José Cibar Percussion Pistol $235
Caliber: 68. Belt hook on left side.

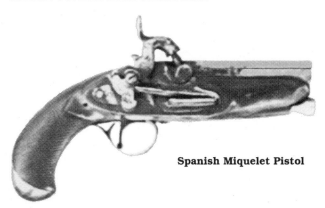

Spanish Miquelet Pistol

Spanish 65 Cal. Miquelet Pistol $360
Caliber: 65 percussion. Barrel: 3½ inches, half-octagonal. Engraved brass furniture.

Spanish 69 Cal. Miquelet Pistol $315
Caliber: 69 percussion. Iron furniture with little or no engraving. Made circa 1850.

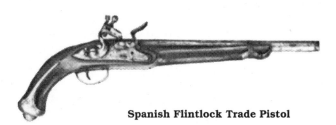

Spanish Flintlock Trade Pistol

Spanish Flintlock Trade Pistol $375
Calibers: various. Round barrel. Brass furniture. Typical of those manufactured for import to the East.

STARR ARMS COMPANY
New York, New York

Ebenezer Townsend Starr obtained Patent No. 14118 in January 1856 for a single-action percussion revolver. In December 1861, he received a second patent for a double-action revolver of the same type. Both single- and double-action revolvers were purchased under U.S. Government contracts during the Civil War and played a major part of the conflict (*see* U.S. Military Revolvers). Although New York City was home base for their offices, Starr firearms were produced at two plants, one in Yonkers and the other in Binghamton, N.Y. The firm closed in 1868.

Starr Model 1858 DA Army Revolver . . . $925
Caliber: 44. Six-shot round, plain cylinder. Barrel: 6 inches. Double-action. Blued finish. Smooth walnut grips. Made late 1850s to early 1860s.

Starr Model 1863 Single-Action
Army Revolver

Starr Model 1863 Single-Action Army
Revolver $1395
Caliber: 44. Six-shot round, plain cylinder. Barrel: 8 inches. Blued finish. Smooth walnut grips. Made mid-1860s.

J. STEVENS ARMS & TOOL CO.
Chicopee Falls, Massachusetts

Although this company is known primarily for its long arms, it did produce handguns in the early days of operation. For further background information, please turn to J. Stevens Arms & Tool Co. under Rifles.

Stevens Deringer Pistol $2375
Caliber: 41 rimfire, single-shot. Barrel: 4 inches, half-octagonal. Brass frame with blued barrel; nickel or silver plated sideplate. Walnut grips. Made circa 1875.

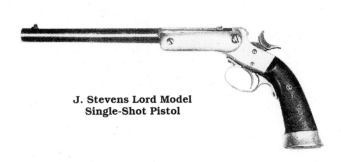

**J. Stevens Lord Model
Single-Shot Pistol**

Stevens Model 1883 Lord Gallery Pistol $725
Calibers: 22, 22 WRF, and 25 RF; 32 Short Colt, 38 Long Colt and 44 Russian centerfire. Barrel: 10 inches; half-octagonal. Large brass or iron frame with side plates. Long checkered grips with flared butt cap. Circa 1883.

Stevens No. 37 Pistol $210
Calibers: 22 or 32 Short or Long RF. Single-shot. Barrel: 10 or 12 inches, half-octagonal. Blued or nickel plated iron frame; blued barrel. Checkered walnut grips with flared and weighted butt cap. Made from 1889 to 1903.

Stevens Conlin Gallery Pistol

Stevens Conlin Gallery Pistol $895
Calibers: 22 or 32 Short or Long RF. Single-shot. Barrel: 10 or 12 inches, half-octagonal; tip-up type. Brass spur trigger frame with circular sideplate. Nickel finish with blued barrel. Checkered walnut grips with flared and weighted butt cap. Made from 1880 to 1904.

Stevens Diamond No. 43 Pistol. $290
Calibers: 22 Short, 22 LR. Single-shot. Barrel: 6 or 10 inches; half-octagonal, rust blued. Spur trigger. Nickel-plated brass frame with or without sideplates. Globe or bead front sight; peep or open adjustable rear sight. Plain walnut grips with square butt. Although this model was very lightweight, it proved to be an accurate target pistol. Made 1886 to 1896.

Stevens Diamond No. 43 Pistol—Second Issue $140
Calibers: 22 Short, 22 LR, 22 Stevens-Pope. Single-shot. Barrel: 6 or 10 inches; half-octagonal, rust blued. Spur trigger. Iron frame. Globe or bead front sight; peep or open adjustable rear sight. Full blued finish or nickel-plated frame with blued barrel. Plain walnut grips with square butt. Made from 1896 to 1916.

Stevens GEM Pocket Pistol $205
Calibers: 22 and 30 Short RF. Barrel: 3 inches; round, octagonal toward the breech, with side swing. Brass frame. Spur trigger. Blade front sight. Walnut or rose-wood grips. Bird's-head butt. Full nickel-plated finish or nickel-plated frame with blued barrel. This is the only Stevens pistol (a derringer) without a tip-up action for loading and extraction. Made 1872 to 1890.

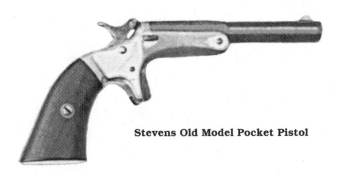

Stevens Old Model Pocket Pistol

Stevens Old Model Pocket Pistol $195
Caliber: 22 or 30 Short RF. Barrel: 3½ inches; half-octagonal. Brass frame with sideplate. Blade front sight; rear notch in hammer. Spur trigger. Rosewood grips. Full nickel-plated finish, or nickel- or silver-plated frame with blued barrel. This is one of the two original models that Joshua Stevens' 1864 patent was based on, and prior to the introduction of the GEM Pocket Pistol, this gun was known as "The Pocket Pistol." Made 1864 to 1916.

Stevens "Tip-Up" No. 41 Pistol. $225
Calibers: 22 and 30 Short RF. Single-shot. Barrel: 3½ inches, half-octagonal. Iron frame. Spur trigger. Blade front sight; rear groove in frame. Blued barrel; either blued or nickel frame. Plain walnut grips. All blued finish or nickel-plated frame with blued barrel. Made from 1896 to 1916.

CAUTION!

Several Stevens pistols were chambered for .410 and other shotshells. Such specimens are subject to the provisions (and restrictions) of the National Firearms Act.

STOCKING & COMPANY
Worcester, Massachusetts

Alexander Stocking made percussion pepperboxes and single-shot pistols. He was particularly noted for his fine-cased presentation models.

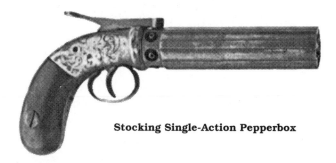

Stocking Single-Action Pepperbox

Stocking Single-Action Pepperbox $395
Caliber: 28. Barrel: 5 inches. Engraved frame. Made from 1847 to 1865.

C.D. TANNER
Hanover, Germany

**C.D. Tanner Double-Barrel
Percussion Pistol**

Tanner Double-Barrel Percussion Pistol . . . $425
Calibers: various. Rifled octagonal barrels. Double triggers. Light engraving. Iron fittings. Silver escutcheon on wrist. Made from 1846 to 1854.

WILLIAM TRANTER
Birmingham, England

William Tranter was a major manufacturer of early model percussion revolvers, some of which were based on the Robert Adams patent of 1851 (*see* separate listing). He added his own variation with a double-trigger mechanism, which he patented in 1853, and which proved quite successful with English shooters.

**Tranter Double-Trigger
Percussion Revolver**

Tranter Percussion Revolver with Case . . $1230
Calibers: varied. Removable rammer. Checkered grips with square butt. Mahogany case came complete with all accessories, including an ebony-handled nipple wrench and screwdriver, wooden cleaning rod with two brass attachments, Dixon oil bottle, Dixon brass bag flask, brass mould with Tranter's stamp, round tin containing percussion caps, etc. Made circa 1850 to 1862.

TURKISH FLINTLOCKS
Various Manufacturers

Turkish Flintlock Pistol $440
Calibers: various, but ⅝-inch bore common. Barrel: 9½ inches, round. Overall length: 16 inches. Brass butt, ramrod and ornamented barrel.

JOHN TWIGG
London, England

London gunmaker John Twigg (1732–1790) produced hand-rotated pepperboxes in the latter half of the 18th century.

Twigg Revolving Flintlock Pistol $7995
Caliber: about 32. Flintlock ignition. Barrels: 3 inches, round. Six barrels were grouped around a seventh, revolved by hand and all were numbered with proofmarks. Overall length: 9½ inches. Center hammer. Engraved frame and trigger guard.

UNION ARMS COMPANY
Hartford, Connecticut

While the plant of this firm was located in Hartford, the main office was in New York City. Union Arms made percussion pepperboxes and had U.S. Government contracts for percussion revolvers and rifles.

Union 31 Cal. Pocket Revolver

Union Arms Co. Pocket Revolver **$395**
Caliber: 31. Barrel: 3¼ inches, octagonal. Engraved frame. Made from about 1858 to 1865.

UNWIN & RODGERS
Sheffield, England

Of the unique and unusual arms that emerged in the 19th century, the knife pistol was perhaps most well known. The cutlery firm of Unwin & Rodgers, in business from about 1827 to 1868, advertised their version as early as 1839.

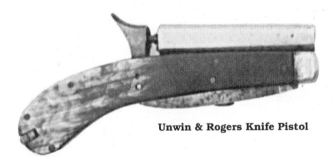

Unwin & Rogers Knife Pistol

Unwin & Rodgers Pocket Knife Pistol . . **$670**
Caliber: 31 percussion. Horn sides. Two blades. "JAMES RODGERS" marked on blades. Made circa 1845.

Unwin & Rodgers Pocket Knife Pistol . . **$395**
Caliber: 30 percussion. Two blades; one clip point, one spear point. Walnut sides. Cartridge compartment in handle. Made circa 1860s.

U.S. REVOLVER CO.
Rockfall, Connecticut

U.S. Revolver Co. Revolver **$135**
Caliber: 32. Nickel plated. Made circa 1890.

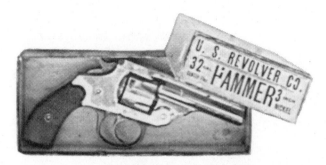

**U.S. Revolver Co. 32 Cal. Revolver
Nickel Finish**

JAMES WARNER
Springfield, Massachusetts

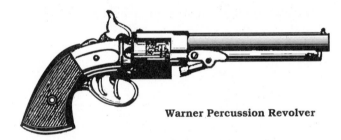

Warner Percussion Revolver

Warner Percussion Revolver. **$1540**
Caliber: 36. Patented in June 1856 by James Warner, who was a designer and manager of the Springfield Arms Co. of Springfield, Mass., which produced the gun. Engraved rolled cylinder. Double triggers, the front one revolves the cylinder and as it is drawn back, it strikes the rear trigger, which fires the gun.

WEBLEY & SCOTT LTD.
London and Birmingham, England

Webley Model 1883 Revolver **$295**
Caliber: 450. Five-shot cylinder. Barrel: 2½ inches. Marked "R.I.C." for Royal Irish Constabulary. Made circa 1880.

Webley Mark III 38 Military and Police Revolver **$275**
Caliber: 38 S&W. Six-shot half-fluted cylinder. Double-action. Hinged frame. Barrel: 3 or 4 inches. Overall length: 9½ inches with 4-inch barrel. Weight: about 1¼ pounds. Fixed sights. Checkered walnut or vulcanite grips. Blued finish. Made 1897 to 1945.

Webley & Scott 1883 R.I.C. Revolver

Webley Self-Cocking Percussion Revolver

Webley "Senior" Air Pistol $100
Caliber: 22. Plastic grips with Webley in cartouche. "WEBLEY & SCOTT LTD. BIRMINGHAM 4, WEBLEY PATENTS" stamped on right side. "THE WEBLEY SENIOR MADE IN ENGLAND" stamped on left.

Webley Mark III Revolver

Webley Wedge Frame Double-Action Revolver

Webley Wedge Frame Revolver $445
Caliber: 44. Double-action. Octagonal barrel. "BUCK. EDGEWARD ROAD LONDON" engraved on top strap.

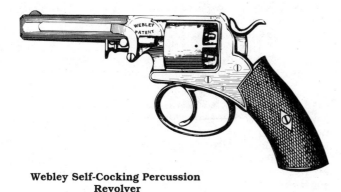

Webley Self-Cocking Percussion Revolver

Webley Self-Cocking Percussion Revolver $325
Caliber: 36 percussion. Five-shot cylinder. Octagonal barrel. Self-cocking. Open, engraved frame with "LONDON NO 40406." Checkered grips.

WESTERN ARMS COMPANY
W.W. Marston
New York City

Western Pocket Model Revolver $350
Caliber: 31 percussion, 5-shot plain cylinder. Barrel: 3¼ and 7½ inches, round and octagonal. Colt-type rammer. Walnut grips. Blued finish. Made from 1857 to 1862.

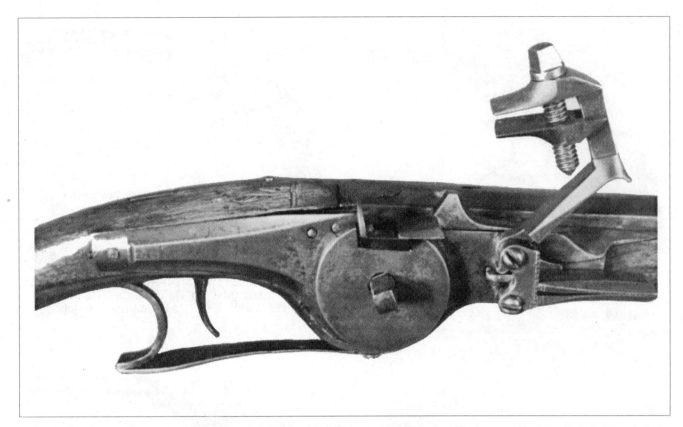

Close-up of a prototype wheellock: a French-made, 69-caliber version found at Yorktown, Virginia. It is believed that this was used by early American settlers.

WHEELLOCK PISTOLS
Various Makers

The wheel lock was invented in Nuremberg about 1517 and was used on firearms at the siege of Parma in 1521 before being taken to England circa 1530. An improvement over the earlier match lock, the mechanism consisted of a steel wheel rasped at the edge, which protruded into a priming pan, a strong spring, and a cock into which was fixed a piece of pyrite. The wheel fit on the square end of an axle or a spindle, to which the spring was connected by a chain swivel. The cock was so fitted that it could be moved backwards or forwards at will. A strong spring was connected with it to keep it in a secure position.

When the gun was to be discharged, the lock was wound up by means of a key or spanner that fit on the axle or spindle, and the cock was let down to the priming pan with the pyrite resting on the wheel. When the trigger was pressed, the wheel was released and put in motion, causing sparks to be emitted, which ignited the powder in the priming pan. The wheel lock frequently misfired, as the pyrites were of a friable nature and would sometimes break in the pan — impeding the free action of the wheel. Therefore, the old match was kept handy for use when required.

Italian Wheellock Pistol $2175
Fancy, engraved wheellock pistol with gold plating made in the Gardone area of Italy. Stamped "BORTOLO CHINELLI." This is an excellent specimen of the European wheellock and features Eastern Mediterranean influence on the style of the grip and engraved butt.

Typical Wheellock Pistol $1600
Calibers: various, but 69 common. Barrel: 17¾ inches, octagonal. Overall length: 23 inches. Seven-inch lockplate with sliding pan cover. One model marked with letter "Z" in shield. Full stock, pin fastened, straight butt with metal cap. Iron guard and iron-tipped rod.

Typical Wheellock Pistol $1600
Calibers: various, but 69 common. Barrel: 15¼ inches with makers mark. Overall length: 23 inches. Lockplate: 6¼ inches with sliding pan. Full stock, pin fastened, curved butt with iron plate. Iron trigger guard.

ROLLIN WHITE ARMS CO.
Lowell, Massachusetts

Rollin White was the patentee in 1855 of a revolver made with the cylinder bored end-to-end with a special cartridge. It was this patent that Smith & Wesson later purchased, which many firearms companies tried to duplicate or adapt, often with legal consequences. During the Civil War, however, when S&W had difficulty fulfilling government contracts for military arms because of heavy demand, Rollin White Arms was commissioned by S&W to manufacture guns. The company operated from 1861 to 1864, after which time under new management sans White, it became the Lowell Arms Company (*see* separate listing).

Rollin White 22 Cal. Revolver

Rollin White Arms Co. Revolver **$275**
Caliber: 22 RF. Seven-shot plain, round cylinder. Barrel: about 3 inches, octagonal. Spur trigger. Brass frame. With or without ejector (this version without). Walnut grips with square butt. Some marked "MADE FOR SMITH & WESSON BY ROLLIN WHITE ARMS CO. LOWELL, MASS." Made in the 1860s by both Rollin White Arms and Lowell Arms Companies.

WHITNEY ARMS COMPANY
New Haven, Connecticut

Although he did not possess the inventiveness or shrewd business sense of his father, Eli Whitney Jr. ran the Whitney Arms Company from the early 1840s to 1888, when it was purchased by Winchester Repeating Arms. During that period the firm flourished, producing handguns and long arms under government contracts, and later for the sporting market.

For further background information, *see* also Whitney Arms Company under Rifles.

**Whitney Pocket Revolver
Second Model**

**Whitney Pocket Percussion
Revolver—Second Model** **$465**
Caliber: 31 percussion. Five-shot cylinder. Barrel: 3 to 6 inches, octagonal. Five-groove rifling. Walnut grips. Blued finish. Somewhat similar to the Whitney Navy Revolver (*see* U.S. Military Revolvers). Made late 1850s to early 1860s.

WILLIAMS & POWELL
Liverpool, England

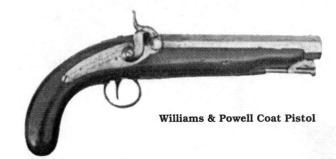

Williams & Powell Coat Pistol

Williams & Powell Coat Pistol. **$345**
Caliber: 68 percussion. Octagonal barrel. Brass furniture. Lockplate engraved "WILLIAMS & POWELL." Made circa 1840.

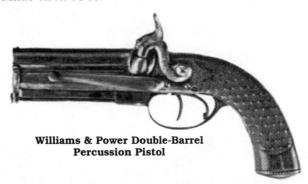

**Williams & Power Double-Barrel
Percussion Pistol**

Williams & Powell Double-Barrel Pistol. . . **$795**
Caliber: 50 percussion. Engraved with belt hook on left side. Swivel ramrod. Checkered grip with silver tacks in hatching. Minute silver floral design around butt. Capbox in butt.

WINCHESTER REPEATING ARMS CO.
New Haven, Connecticut

In the mid-1850s, Horace Smith and Daniel Wesson manufactured the first "Volcanic," an iron-frame, lever-action repeating pistol. When the firm was incorporated as the Volcanic Repeating Arms Company of Norwich, Conn., Oliver Winchester became a major investor. By 1857 production of a brass-frame Volcanic had been well under way. Unfortunately, the company met with dim financial success and Smith & Wesson sold their assets and patents to the Volcanic firm, which were, in turn, acquired by the clothing manufacturer-turned-gunmaker Winchester. Production was moved to New Haven and Volcanic Arms became New Haven Arms Company. Manufacture of the brass-frame Volcanic continued, with B. Tyler Henry at the helm. (*See* Winchester Repeating Arms Co. under Rifles for further background information.)

**Winchester/S&W Lever-Action
Volcanic Repeating Pistol**

Winchester Volcanic Repeating Pistol

Lever action. Caliber: 38. Barrel: 6, 8 or 16 inches; blued. Unfinished brass frame. Walnut grips. A few scroll engraved examples priced higher. Made by Volcanic Repeating Arms Co. 1855 to 1857.

6- or 8-inch barreled models **$2500**
16-inch barrel w/o shoulder stock (rare) **4500**
16-inch barrel with shoulder stock (rare) **6000**

**Winchester Volcanic/New Haven
Repeating Pistol**

Winchester Volcanic New Haven Repeating Pistol

Lever Action. Caliber: 30. Smaller brass frame than the 38 caliber model. Barrel: 3½ or 6 inches; octagonal, blued. Walnut grips. A few scroll engraved examples, although most are "unfinished." Made by New Haven Arms Co. 1857 to 1860.

3½-inch barreled model **$2750**
6-inch barreled model **6250**

AMERICAN KENTUCKY FLINTLOCK PISTOLS

The "Kentucky" pistol was the shorter counterpart of the famed Kentucky rifles and, like the rifle, the majority of the Kentucky pistols were manufactured in Pennsylvania. Some may be unmarked; others will have initials of the makers, while still others will have the complete name and address — although the spelling has been known to vary in some cases. Specifications for "typical" Kentucky pistols are detailed below, followed by a listing of gunmakers who were known to have produced Kentucky pistols of varying quality; approximate dates of production are indicated. Separate, additional listings appear at the end of this section, which reflect more definitive information and values about particular manufacturers' pistols.

Kentucky Flintlock Pistol. $4100
Calibers: 34 to 48. Barrel: 9 inches; octagonal, smoothbore. Overall length: 14½ inches. Kentucky-type front sight, usually no rear sight. Full maple stock with brass furniture.

Kentucky Flintlock High-Grade Pistol . . . $8970
Same general specifications as "standard" pistol, except with fancy decoration.

Kentucky Converted Pistol. $1950
Same general specifications as the original flintlock pistol, except it has been converted from flintlock to percussion.

James Angush
Lancaster, Pennsylvania, 1774 – 1775

Edward and Thomas Annely
New Jersey, 1748 – 1777

Jacob Anstadt
Kutztown, Pennsylvania, 1814 – 1815

A. and J. Ansted
Pennsylvania, circa 1810

William Antis
Frederickstown, Pennsylvania, 1775 – 1782

John Armstrong
Emmetsburg, Maryland, 1790 – 1855

R. Ashmore & Son
Lancaster County, Pennsylvania, circa 1800

Thomas Austin
Charlestown, Massachusetts, 1774 – 1778

Nathan Bailey
New London, Connecticut, 1776 – 1779

Jacob Baker
Philadelphia, Pennsylvania, 1820 – 1833

Samuel Baum
Mahoning Township, Columbia County, PA., circa 1820

Russell Bean
Jonesboro, Tennessee, circa 1770

Christopher Bechtler
Rutherford, North Carolina, 1829 – 1874

Elias Beckley
Berlin, Connecticut, 1807 – 1828

Edmund Bemis
Boston, Massachusetts, 1746 – 1785

Amos Benfer
Beaverstown, Pennsylvania, circa 1830

Peter Berry
Dauphin, Pennsylvania, circa 1800

Thomas Bicknell
Philadelphia, Pennsylvania, 1799 – 1803

Oliver Bidwell
Hartford, Connecticut, 1756 – 1812

Marmaduke Blackwood
Philadelphia, Pennsylvania, 1775 – 1777

Jonathan Blaisdel
Amesbury, Massachusetts, circa 1775

P. & E.W. Blake
New Haven, Connecticut, circa 1825

Samuel Boardlear
Boston, Massachusetts, circa 1795

Anthony Bobb
Reading, Pennsylvania, 1778 – 1781

Samuel Boone
Berks County, Pennsylvania, circa 1770

William Booth
Philadelphia, Pennsylvania, circa 1797 – 1820

Robert Boyd
New Windsor, New York, 1772 – 1778

Peter Brong
Lancaster, Pennsylvania, 1795 – 1816

John Brooke
St. Louis, Missouri, circa 1845

John Buckwalter
Lancaster County, Pennsylvania, 1771 – 1780

Elisha Buell
Marlborough, Connecticut, 1797 – 1850

Elisha Burnham
Hartford, Connecticut, 1776 – 1781

John Butler
Lancaster, Pennsylvania, 1775 – 1778

William Calderwood
Philadelphia, Pennsylvania, 1807 – 1819

George Call
Lancaster, Pennsylvania, 1775 – 1780

William Campbell
Annapolis, Maryland, circa 1780

Adam Carruth
Philadelphia, Pennsylvania, 1809 – 1821

John Carpenter
Lancaster, Pennsylvania, 1771 – 1790

Stephen Chandler
Connecticut, circa 1775

Darius Chipman
Rutland, Vermont, 1799 – 1816

Lewis Chriskey
Philadelphia, Pennsylvania, circa 1815

Jacob Christ
Lancaster, Pennsylvania, 1772 – 1780

Alexander Clagett
Hagerstown, Maryland, circa 1800

Joseph Clark
Danbury, Connecticut, circa 1800

Henry Clause
Heidelberg, Pennsylvania, circa 1820

Henry and Nathan Cobb
Norwich, Connecticut, 1795 – 1801

S. Cogswell
Albany, New York, circa 1810

Levi Coon
Ithaca, New York, 1776 – 1821

Abraham Coster
Philadelphia, Pennsylvania, 1810 – 1814

Samuel Coutty
Philadelphia, Pennsylvania, 1783 – 1795

Joseph Cowell
Boston, Massachusetts, 1745 – 1775

Thomas Crabb
Frederick Town, Maryland, 1799 – 1805

Royal Craft
Rutland, Vermont, 1799 – 1810

John Cryth
Lancaster, Pennsylvania, circa 1800

Jesse Curtis
Waterbury, Connecticut, 1776 – 1780

Richard Dalam
Hartford County, Maryland, 1775 – 1778

Jacob Dechert
Philadelphia, Pennsylvania, 1732 – 1782

Peter DeHaven
Philadelphia and Valley Forge, Penn., 1769 – 1778

Henry DeHuff
Lancaster, Pennsylvania, 1801 – 1807

Michael DeReiner
Lancaster, Pennsylvania, 1773 – 1777

John Derr
Lancaster, Pennsylvania, 1810 – 1844

John Devane
Wilmington, North Carolina, 1776 – 1832

Samuel Dewey
Hebron, Connecticut, 1775 – 1778

Jacob Dickert
Lancaster, Pennsylvania, 1762 – 1822

Jacob Doll
York, Pennsylvania, 1780 – 1805

John Douglas
Huntington, Pennsylvania, circa 1840

Christian Durr
Lancaster, Pennsylvania, circa 1840

George Dunkle
Sheppensburg, Pennsylvania, circa 1825

William Dunwicke
Chester County, Pennsylvania, 1770 – 1776

Elias Earle
Centerville, North Carolina, 1811 – 1816

Thomas Earle
Leicester, Massachusetts, 1848 – 1857

Jacob Early
Atcheson, Kansas, 1864 – 1886

John Eberly
Lancaster, Pennsylvania, 1774 – 1777

Matthew and Nathan Elliott
Kent, Connecticut, circa 1800

Henry Elwell
Liverpool, Pennsylvania, circa 1770

Martin Ely
Springfield, Massachusetts, 1770 – 1776

Jacob Ernst
Frederick, Maryland, 1780 – 1820

Brooke Evans
Evansburg, Pennsylvania, 1821 – 1825

Edward and James Evans
Evansburg, Pennsylvania, 1801 – 1818

Owen and Edward Evans
Evansburg, Pennsylvania, 1790 – 1815

Stephen Evans
Mt. Joy Forge, Pennsylvania, 1741 – 1797

William L. Evans
Evansburg, Pennsylvania, 1823 – 1833

Edward Evatt
Baltimore, Maryland, 1804 – 1818

Richard Falley
Westfield, Massachusetts, 1761 – 1808

Thomas Fancher
Waterbury, Connecticut, 1770 – 1779

Frank and Jacob Farnot
Lancaster, Pennsylvania, 1775 – 1783

William Farver
Brown County, Ohio, 1848 – 1854

Adam Faulk
Lancaster, Pennsylvania, 1830 – 1835

J. Fehr
Nazareth, Pennsylvania, 1830 – 1835

Jacob Ferree
Lancaster, Pennsylvania, 1774 – 1807

Conrad Fesig
Reading, Pennsylvania, 1779 – 1790

I. Field
Philadelphia, Pennsylvania, circa 1790

John Fitch
Bucks County, Pennsylvania, 1769 – 1796

Heinrich Fogle
Lancaster, Pennsylvania, circa 1855

Ludwig Foher
Philadelphia, Pennsylvania, circa 1775

Follecht
Lancaster, Pennsylvania, 1740 – 1770

John Ford
Harrisburg, Pennsylvania, 1800 – 1817

Jacob Fordney
Lancaster, Pennsylvania, 1837 – 1857

Melchior Fordney
Lancaster, Pennsylvania, 1823 – 1843

Franck
Lancaster, Pennsylvania, circa 1775

John Frazier
Lancaster, Pennsylvania, 1740 – 1756

Gideon Frost
Massachusetts, circa 1775

John Gall
Lancaster, Pennsylvania, circa 1850

Albert Gallatin
Fayette County, Pennsylvania, 1796 – 1808

Peter Gander
Lancaster, Pennsylvania, circa 1780

G. Gardner
Lima, Ohio, 1859 – 1865

Gaspard
Lancaster, Pennsylvania, circa 1775

Jacob George
Greenwich, Pennsylvania, circa 1800

John Gerrish
Boston, Massachusetts, circa 1710

Lewis Ghriskey
Philadelphia, Pennsylvania, 1812 – 1816

Henry Gibbs
Lancaster, Pennsylvania, 1824 – 1857

Daniel Gilbert
Brookfield, Massachusetts, 1782 – 1813

Benjamin Gill
Lancaster, Pennsylvania, 1830 – 1850

Glaze & Co.
Columbia, South Carolina, 1852 – 1865

Frederick Goetz
Philadelphia, Pennsylvania, 1806 – 1812

James Golcher
Philadelphia, Pennsylvania, 1820 – 1833

Joseph Golcher
Philadelphia, Pennsylvania, circa 1800

Peter Gonter
Lancaster, Pennsylvania, 1750 – 1818

Jonathan Goodwin
Lebanon, Connecticut, circa 1778

William Graeff
Reading, Pennsylvania, 1751 – 1784

Samuel Grant
Walpole, New Hampshire, circa 1800

J. Gresheim
Lancaster, Pennsylvania, 1775 – 1783

Samuel Grove
York, Pennsylvania, 1779 – 1783

Christopher Gumpf
Lancaster, Pennsylvania, 1791 – 1842

Nicholas Hawk
Gilbert, Pennsylvania, 1805 – 1835

J. Hillegas
Pottesville, Virginia, 1810 – 1830

Thomas Hooker
Rutland, Vermont, 1798 – 1802

James Hunter
Falmouth, Virginia, 1760 – 1775

Benjamin Hutz
Lancaster, Pennsylvania, circa 1800

Benedick Inhoff
Heidelberg, Pennsylvania, circa 1785

Christian Isch
Lancaster, Pennsylvania, 1774 – 1782

Robert James
Baltimore, Maryland, circa 1795

Stephen Jenks
Pawtucket, Rhode Island, 1795 – 1814

Robert Johnson
Middletown, Connecticut, 1822 – 1854

Charles and Robert Jones
Lancaster, Pennsylvania, 1775 – 1783

Peter Kascheline
Northampton County, Pennsylvania, circa 1775

Samuel Kearling
Bucks County, Pennsylvania, circa 1780

Sebastian and Mathias Keeley
Philadelphia, Pennsylvania, circa 1775

Jacob Keffer
Lancaster, Pennsylvania, circa 1800

David Kemmerer
Lehighton, Pennsylvania, circa 1850

Nathan Kile
Jackson County, Ohio, circa 1815

Samuel Kinder
Philadelphia, Pennsylvania, circa 1775

Adam Kinsley
Bridgewater, Massachusetts, 1795 – 1812

Daniel Kleist
Easton, Pennsylvania, 1780 – 1792

Conrad Kline
Lancaster, Pennsylvania, circa 1780

John Krider
Philadelphia, Pennsylvania, 1839 – 1870

Kunkle
Philadelphia, Pennsylvania, 1810 – 1814

Jacob Kunz
Philadelphia, Pennsylvania, 1770 – 1817

W. Larson
Harrisburg, Pennsylvania, circa 1830

George Laydendecker
Allentown, Pennsylvania, 1774 – 1783

H. Lechler
Lancaster, Pennsylvania, 1848 – 1857

Philip Lefever
Beaver Valley, Pennsylvania, 1731 – 1766

Adam and Ignatius Leitner
York, Pennsylvania, 1779 – 1810

Michael Lenz
Baltimore, Maryland, circa 1805

Eliphalet Leonard
Boston, Massachusetts, 1775 – 1780

Jacob Lether
York, Pennsylvania, 1777 – 1820

Peter Light
Berkeley County, Virginia, circa 1775

John Livingston
Walpole, New Hampshire, 1795 – 1801

Matthew Llewelyn
Lancaster, Pennsylvania, circa 1740

Loder
Lancaster, Pennsylvania, circa 1770

M. Lorney
Boalsburg, Pennsylvania, circa 1810

Longstretch & Cook
Philadelphia, Pennsylvania, circa 1770

Earl Loomis
Hamilton, New York, circa 1850

Peter Lydick
Baltimore, Maryland, 1773 – 1779

Simeon Marble
Sunderland, Vermont, circa 1850

Jacob Messersmith
Lancaster, Pennsylvania, 1779 – 1802

Samuel Messersmith
Baltimore, Maryland, 1775 – 1778

Jacob Metzger
Lancaster, Pennsylvania, 1849 – 1857

Martin Meylin
Lancaster, Pennsylvania, 1710 – 1749

Silas Merriman
Connecticut, circa 1775

Simon Miller
Hamburg, Pennsylvania, 1790 – 1820

Isaac Milnor
Philadelphia, Pennsylvania, circa 1760

Peter Moll
Hellerstown, Pennsylvania, 1791 – 1835

George Moore
Mt. Vernon, Ohio, 1885 – 1894

Joseph Morgan
Philadelphia, Pennsylvania, circa 1810

Abraham Morrow
Philadelphia, Pennsylvania, 1781 – 1798

Henry Meyer
Pennsylvania, 1771 – 1778

Robert McCormick
Philadelphia, Pennsylvania, 1796 – 1802

Alexander McRae
Richmond, Virginia, 1815 – 1821

Kester McCoy
Lancaster, Pennsylvania, circa 1770

Alexander Nelson
Philadelphia, Pennsylvania, circa 1775

John Newcomer
Lancaster, Pennsylvania, circa 1770

Peter Neihart
Lehigh County, Pennsylvania, circa 1770 – 1810

John Nicholson
Philadelphia, Pennsylvania, 1774 – 1792

Daniel Nippes
Philadelphia, Pennsylvania, 1808 – 1848

Simeon North
North Berlin, Connecticut, 1794 – 1852

Ebenezer Nutting
Falmouth, Maine, 1722 – 1745

Samuel Oakes
Philadelphia, Pennsylvania, circa 1800

Christian Oberholzer
Lancaster, Pennsylvania, 1775 – 1778

S. Odell
Natchez, Mississippi, circa 1855

John Odlin
Boston, Massachusetts, 1671 – 1685

E. Ong
Philadelphia, Pennsylvania, 1773 – 1777

Hugh Orr
Springfield, Massachusetts, 1737 – 1798

H. Osborn
Springfield, Massachusetts, 1815 – 1830

John Page
Preston, Connecticut, 1770 – 1777

Jacob Palm
Lancaster, Pennsylvania, 1759 – 1777

Jefferson Pannabecker
Lancaster, Pennsylvania, 1790 – 1810

Samuel Pannabecker
Allentown, Pennsylvania, 1780 – 1825

William Pannabecker, Jr. and Sr.
Mohnton, Pennsylvania, 1800 – 1880

James Pearson
Philadelphia, Pennsylvania, circa 1775

A. Peck
Hartford, Connecticut, circa 1800

James and Rufus Perkins
Bridgewater, Massachusetts, 1800 – 1813

Silas Phelps
Lebanaon, Connecticut, 1770 – 1777

Henry Pickel
York, Pennsylvania, 1800 – 1811

Samuel Pike
Brattleboro, Vermont, circa 1845

Lewis Prahl
Philadelphia, Pennsylvania, 1775 – 1790

Frederick Rathfong
Conestoga, Pennsylvania, 1770 – 1772

George Rathfong
Lancaster, Pennsylvania, 1774 – 1819

Reddick
Baltimore, Maryland, circa 1775

Robert Read
Chesterton, Maryland, 1775 – 1802

Francis Reynolds
New York, New York, 1844 – 1865

William Robertson
Rochester, New York, circa 1840

Peter Roesser
Lancaster, Pennsylvania, 1739 – 1782

John Roop
Allentown, Pennsylvania, 1770 – 1775

William Ruppert
Lancaster, Pennsylvania, circa 1775

Michael Rynes
Lancaster, Pennsylvania, circa 1770

Gordon Saltonstall
Connecticut, 1762 – 1775

Jacob Saylor
Bedford County, Pennsylvania, 1779 – 1790

Jacob Schley
Frederick Town, Maryland, circa 1775

Mathias Schroyer
Taney Town, Maryland, circa 1800

James Teaff
Steubenville, Ohio, 1849 – 1861

P. Valle
Philadelphia, Pennsylvania, 1826 – 1840

Peter White
Bedford County, Pennsylvania, circa 1810 – 1820

Casper Yost
Lancaster, Pennsylvania, 1773 – 1778

Frederick and George Zorger
York, Pennsylvania, 1770 – 1802

HENRY ALBRIGHT
Lancaster, Pennsylvania

Albright Kentucky Flintlock Pistol. . . . $4515
Calibers: various, but 48 smoothbore common. Barrel: 7½ inches; half-octogonal, brass. Overall length: 13½ inches. Weight: 1 lb. 12 oz. Full curly maple stock. Brass ramrod thimbles. No muzzle cap. Made from 1740 to 1792.

PETER ANGSTADT
Lancaster, Pennsylvania

Angstadt Kentucky Flintlock Pistol . . . $3900
Calibers: various, but 44 smoothbore common. Barrel: about 9 inches, half-octagonal. Overall length: 13½ inches. Weight: 1 lb. 11 oz. Full curly maple stock. Brass butt cap, trigger guard, side plate, ramrod thimbles and muzzle cap. Made from 1770 to 1777.

JOHN & PATRICK BALLANTINE
Charleston, South Carolina

Ballantine Kentucky Flintlock Pistol . . **$4450**
Calibers: various, but 48 smoothbore common. Barrel: 7½ inches; half-octagonal, brass. Overall length: about 13½ inches. Weight: 1 lb. 12 oz. Full curly maple stock, brass ramrod thimbles. No muzzle cap. Made from 1720 to 1740.

BIELRY
Philadelphia, Pennsylvania

Bielry Kentucky Flintlock Pistol **$4600**
Calibers: various, but 44 smoothbore common. Barrel: about 9 inches, half-octagonal. Overall length: 13½ inches. Weight: 1 lb. 11 oz. Full curly maple stock. Brass butt cap, trigger guard, side plate, ramrod thimbles and muzzle cap. Made from 1769 to 1770.

THOMAS P. CHERRINGTON
Cattawissa, Pennsylvania

Cherrington Kentucky Flintlock Pistol . . **$4200**
Calibers: various, but 44 smoothbore common. Barrel: about 9 inches, half-octagonal. Overall length: 13½ inches. Weight: 1 lb. 11 oz. Full curly maple stock. Brass butt cap, trigger guard, side plate, ramrod thimbles and muzzle cap. Made from 1765 to 1805.

JOHN DODD
Charleston, South Carolina

Dodd Kentucky Flintlock Pistol **$5175**
Calibers: various, but 48 smoothbore common. Barrel: 7½ inches; half-octagonal, brass. Overall length: 13½ inches. Weight: 1 lb. 12 oz. Full curly maple stock. Brass ramrod thimbles. No muzzle cap. Made from 1755 to 1762.

GILBERT FORBES
New York, New York

Forbes Kentucky Flintlock Pistol **$4435**
Calibers: various, but 44 smoothbore common. Barrel: about 9 inches, half-octagonal. Overall length: 13½ inches. Weight: 1 lb. 11 oz. Full curly maple stock. Brass butt cap, trigger guard, side plate, ramrod thimbles and muzzle cap. Made from 1767 to 1776.

ADAM FOULKE
Allentown, Pennsylvania

Foulke Kentucky Flintlock Pistol **$4125**
Calibers: various, but 44 smoothbore common. Barrel: about 9 inches, half-octagonal. Overall length: 13½ inches. Weight: 1 lb. 11 oz. Full curly maple stock. Brass butt cap, trigger guard, side plate, ramrod thimbles and muzzle cap. Made from 1773 to 1794.

DAVIE & WILLIAM GEDDY
Williamsburg, Virginia

Geddy Kentucky Flintlock Pistol **$6240**
Calibers: various, but 48 smoothbore common. Barrel: 7½ inches; half-octagonal, brass. Overall length: about 12 inches. Weight: 1 lb. 10 oz. Full curly maple stock. Brass ramrod thimbles. No muzzle cap. Made from 1748 to 1752.

JAMES & JOHN WALSH
Allentown, Pennsylvania

Walsh Kentucky Flintlock Pistol **$4500**
Calibers: various, but 44 smoothbore common. Barrel: about 9 inches, half-octagonal. Overall length: 13½ inches. Weight: 1 lb. 11 oz. Full curly maple stock. Brass butt cap, trigger guard, side plate, ramrod thimbles and muzzle cap. Made from 1760 to 1779.

CONFEDERATE HANDGUNS

The following Civil War-period handguns include only those manufactured in the South. Other guns were of course used by the Confederate States but produced elsewhere; those firearms are detailed in separate listings throughout the Handgun Section. [*See*, for example, the LeMat "Grapeshot" Revolver and the U.S. Model 1842 Percussion Pistol.]

Cofer Revolver **$21,630**
Caliber: 36 percussion. Six-shot cylinder. Barrel: 7+ inches, octagonal; marked "T.W. Cofer's Patent, Portsmouth, VA." Brass frame. Square trigger guard. Colt-type loading lever. Made in 1861.

Columbus Revolver **$11,130**
Caliber: 36 percussion. Six-shot cylinder. Barrel: 7½ inches, round; marked "Columbus Fire Arms Manuf. Col, Georgia." Octagonal breech. Brass trigger guard, front sight, handle strap.

Dance Navy Revolver **$5400**
Caliber: 36 percussion. Six-shot cylinder. Barrel: 7⅜ inches, half-octagonal. Iron frame. Made 1863–64 by the Dance Brothers—David, George and James — near Galveston, Texas.

Dance Revolver **$5775**
Caliber: 44 percussion. Six-shot cylinder. Barrel: 8 inches, round or octagonal. Iron "milled flat" frame. Brass trigger guard, backstrap, blade front sight. Made 1863–64 by the Dance Brothers; about 300 or so total Dance revolvers were supposedly produced by the time the war ended.

Fayetteville Model 1855 Pistol-Carbine . . **$3240**
Caliber: 58. Single-shot. Barrel: 12 inches. Detachable shoulder stock. Lockplate marked "Fayetteville" with spread eagle over "C.S.A." Made at the Fayetteville, N.C., armory 1861 to about 1863.

Griswold & Grier Revolver **$4150**
Also known as the Griswold & Gunnison Revolver, after Samuel Griswold and A.W. Gunnison, one of the most reliable producers of CSA guns. Caliber: 36 percussion. Six-shot cylinder. Barrel: 7½ inches, round. Later models have octagonal breech. Brass frame. Squarish trigger guard. Often called the "Brass-frame Confederate Colt." Made 1862–64 in Griswoldville, Ga.

Leech & Rigdon Revolver **$4675**
Caliber: 36 percussion. Six-shot cylinder. Barrel: 7½ inches; marked "Leech & Rigdon" or "Leech & Rigdon, C.S.A." Brass front sight, trigger guard, handle strap. Made by C.H. Rigdon and Thomas Leech in Greensboro, Ga., 1862–63.

Richmond Pistol **$3100**
Caliber: 54. Single-shot. Barrel: 10 inches, round. Brass band and butt plate. Swivel ramrod. Lockplate marked "C.S. Richmond, Va." Made at the Richmond Armory about 1861.

Rigdon & Ansley Revolver **$4300**
Caliber: 36 percussion. Six-shot cylinder. Barrel: 7½ inches, round; marked "Augusta, Ga. C.S.A." plus serial number. Twelve cylinder stops. Brass front sight, handle strap and trigger guard. Trigger guard machined and distinctly shaped — not round or square — same as on Leech & Rigdon Revolver. Made 1864–65.

Schneider & Glassick Revolver . . **$4500**
Caliber: 36 percussion. Six-shot cylinder. Barrel: 7½ inches; marked "Schneider & Glassick, Memphis, Tenn." Brass trigger guard, front sight and backstrap. Made by William S. Schneider and Frederick G. Glassick, both of Memphis. Extremely rare.

Sherrard & Taylor Revolver . . . **$10,500**
Caliber: 44 percussion. Six-shot cylinder. Barrel: 7½ inches, octagonal. Close copy of the Colt. Made by Sherrard, Taylor & Co. (Joseph Sherrard and Pleasant Taylor) of Lancaster, Texas, 1862–63.

Spiller & Burr Revolver **$4500**
Caliber: 36 percussion. Six-shot cylinder. Barrel: 7½ inches, octagonal; marked "Spiller & Burr" (later models stamped with "C.S."). Brass frame. In Nov. 1861, the C.S. War Department contracted for 15,000 S & B Navy revolvers based on Colt Navy design; problems, however, led to the manufacture of a Colt Whitney-styled gun, many of which had iron barrels because steel was not available; total production was not met. Made by Edward N. Spiller of Baltimore and David J. Burr of Richmond, Va., in Atlanta and the C.S. Armory at Macon, Ga., 1862–64.

Sutherland Pistol **$1200**
Caliber: 60 percussion. Single-shot. Barrel: 6¼ inches, octagonal. Lockplate marked "Sutherland, Richmond." Made by master gunmaker Samuel Sutherland in Virginia.

U.S. MILITARY HANDGUNS

Most of the handguns featured in the following section were contracted by the federal government for use by the military services. The Rappahannock Forge Flintlock Pistol, however, dates back to about 1775, even before the United States was officially a recognized nation; it is considered a military arm since it was used by the State of Virginia during the Revolutionary War. During the 19th century, Colt handguns were particularly popular, and a separate grouping details the pistols and revolvers of Colt manufacture that were issued to the military. The other two groupings contain U.S. Military pistols and revolvers that were produced by various manufacturers.

U.S. MILITARY HANDGUNS
Of Colt Manufacture

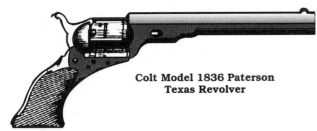

**Colt Model 1836 Paterson
Texas Revolver**

Colt Model 1836 Paterson
Texas Revolver $16,000
Calibers: 28, 31, 36. Five-shot round cylinder. Barrels: 4½ to 12 inches, octagonal. All had folding triggers with no trigger guard. Cylinder pin had a cup-shaped end that was used as a ramrod. Square-cornered butt. Made in Paterson, N.J., from 1836 to 1841.

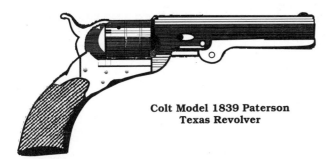

**Colt Model 1839 Paterson
Texas Revolver**

Colt Model 1839 Paterson
Texas Revolver $16,400
Caliber: 28. Later model of the 1836 Paterson. Changes were made in the shape of the handle, and was equipped with a loading lever. Made in Paterson from 1839 to 1841.

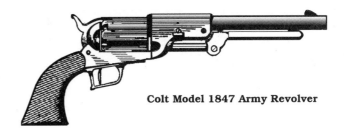

Colt Model 1847 Army Revolver

Colt Model 1847 Army Revolver . . . $148,750
Caliber: 44. Six-shot cylinder. Barrel: 9 inches, round with octagonal breech. Overall length: 15½ inches. Weight: 4 lbs. 9 oz. Straight, round cylinder that revolves to the right. Squareback trigger guard. One thousand were made in 1847 by Colt at the Eli Whitney (of cotton gin fame) Armory in Whitneyville, Conn. They had been commissioned by Captain Samuel Walker for use by the U.S. Government and were subsequently known as the "Whitneyville Walkers."

Colt Model 1848 Army Revolver $17,000
Also known as the No. 1 Dragoon or Model of 1848 Holster Pistol. Caliber: 44. Six-shot fluted cylinder. Barrel: 7½ inches, round. Overall length: 14 inches. Weight: 4 pounds. Squareback trigger guard. Made in Hartford, Conn., from 1848 to 1849.

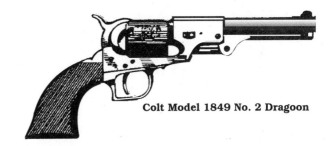

Colt Model 1849 No. 2 Dragoon

Colt Dragoon, 2nd Model $18,800
Known as No. 2 Dragoon or Old Model Army Pistol. Caliber: 44. Six-shot round, straight cylinder. Barrel: 8 inches. Overall length: 14½ inches. Weight: 4 lbs. 2 oz. Brass backstrap and squareback trigger guard. Hinged lever ramrod. Made in Hartford 1850 to 1851.

Colt Dragoon, 3rd Model $13,940
Caliber: 44. Six-shot round, straight cylinder. Barrel: 7½ inches; round with octagonal breech. Overall length: 14 inches. Hinged lever ramrod. Brass backstrap and oval trigger guard. Cut and fitted for shoulder stocks. Made in Hartford 1851 to 1860.

NOTE

The rarest of the Colt Second Model Dragoons have "V" hammer springs and no bearing wheel, and were numbered between 8,000 and 10,000.

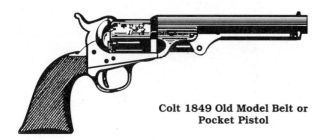

Colt 1849 Old Model Belt or Pocket Pistol

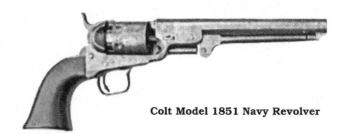

Colt Model 1851 Navy Revolver

Colt 1849 Old Model Belt or Pocket Pistol $5000

Pattern of 1849. Caliber: 31. Six-shot straight, round cylinder. Barrels: 3, 4, 5, 6 inches; octagonal. Smaller sizes were known as "Pocket" pistols. Hinged loading lever. Oval brass trigger guard. Made from 1849 to 1873.

Colt Model 1849 Wells Fargo Revolver. $7500

This is the same as the Model of 1849 Pocket Pistol without the rammer, and is often confused with the Model of 1848. Also known as the Old Model Police Pistol. Caliber: 31. Five-shot cylinder. Barrels: 3, 4, 5, 6·inches; octagonal. Made without loading lever or ramrod. Nickel-plated backstrap and oval trigger guard. Made during the 1850s.

Colt Model 1851 Navy Revolver $15,000

Called the Old Model Belt Pistol. Caliber: 36. Six-shot cylinder. Barrel: 7 inches, octagonal. Overall length: 13 inches. Weight: 2 lbs. 10 oz. Straight, round cylinder with rectangular slots and safety pins to keep the capped nipples away from the hammer. Oval, iron trigger guard. For military purposes, this arm was equipped with a Dragoon-type canteen shoulder stock and sling swivel. Introduced in 1851.

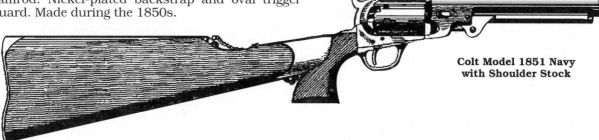

Colt Model 1851 Navy with Shoulder Stock

Colt Model 1860 Army with Shoulder Stock

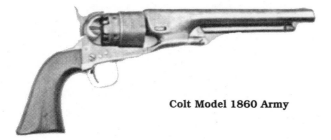

Colt Model 1860 Army

Colt Model 1860 Army Revolver. . . . $10,000

Caliber: 44. Six-shot cylinder. Barrel: 8 inches, round. Overall length: 14 inches. Weight: 2 lbs. 11 oz. Round or oval brass trigger guard. Frame and backstrap are notched for attaching a shoulder stock, for a total length of 26½ inches and weight of 5 pounds. This arm was the principal revolver of the Civil War, since about 130,000 were purchased by the U.S. Government. Made from about 1860 to 1873.

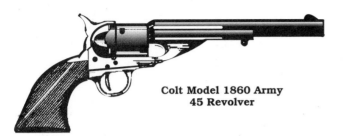

**Colt Model 1860 Army
45 Revolver**

Colt Model 1860 Army 45 Revolver . . . $7500

Altered version of Model 1860 Army for use with metallic cartridges. Caliber: 45. Six-shot cylinder. Barrel: 8 inches, round. Overall length: 14 inches. Weight: 2 lbs. 11 oz. Ramrod and lever were removed and an ejector added to the right side of the barrel. A gate was added to facilitate loading and ejecting.

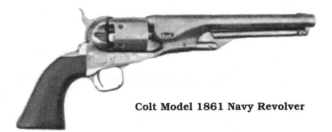

Colt Model 1861 Navy Revolver

Colt Model 1861 Navy Revolver $7200

Also called New Model Belt or Pocket Pistol. Caliber: 36. Six-shot round, straight cylinder, some fluted. Barrels: 7½ inches (also made in 4½, 5½, 6½ inches for civilian use). Weight: 2 lbs. 9 oz. Creeping lever ramrod. Brass backstrap. Oval brass trigger guard. Made from 1861 to 1873.

**Colt Model 1873 Single-Action
Army Revolver**

Colt Model 1873 Single-Action Army Revolver $3200

Caliber: 45 centerfire. Barrels: 5½, 7½ inches, round. Overall length: 11, 12½ inches, respectively. Weight: 2 lbs. 5 oz. Large steel blade front sight; V-notch rear sight. Steel frame and trigger guard. Blued barrel and cylinder. Casehardened hammer and frame. Introduced in 1873.

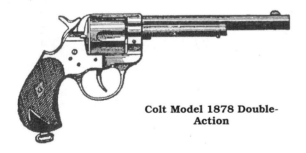

**Colt Model 1878 Double-
Action**

Colt Model 1878 Double-Action Army Revolver $1095

Caliber: 45 centerfire. Six-shot, two-thirds fluted cylinder. Barrel: 7½ inches, round. Overall length: 12½ inches. Weight: 2 lbs. 7 oz. Side rod ejector. Hard rubber bird's-head grips. This is the first heavy double-action revolver made by Colt. Last patent date is 1880. Made in Hartford from 1878 to 1905.

**Colt Model 1892 Army
(Government) Revolver**

Colt Model 1892 Army (Government) Revolver $650

Double-action. Caliber: 38. Six-shot, swing-out cylinder, the first of its type. Solid frame. Barrel: 7½ inches (Army); also 3, 4½, 6 inches; round. Overall length: 11¼ inches with 4½-inch bbl. Weight: 2 pounds. Army had checkered walnut grips, although hard rubber bird's-head grips were standard. Made 1892 to about 1907.

Colt Model 1900 38 Automatic Pistol . . $4600

Caliber: 38 ACP, 7-shot magazine. Barrel: 6 inches; 9 inches overall. Weight: 35 ounces. Fixed sights. Blued finish. Plain walnut grips. Made 1900 to 1903.

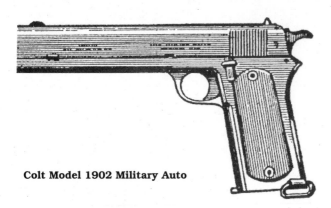

Colt Model 1902 Military Auto

Colt Model 1902 Military Automatic Pistol. $1200

Caliber: 38. Eight-shot magazine. Barrel: 6 inches. Overall length: 9 inches. Weight: 37 ounces. Fixed sights, knife-blade and V-notch. Blued finish. Checkered hard rubber stocks. Round-back hammer and later spur-type hammer. No safety. Used by the U.S. Navy until the larger caliber 45 Model 1911 superseded it. Made from 1902 to 1929.

Colt Model 1902 Phillippine Revolver

Colt Model 1902 Philippine Revolver . . $995

Enhanced version of the Double-Action Army with extremely large trigger guard and long trigger to allow for use with gloves. This arm was originally planned for U.S. troops in Alaska, but was sent instead to the Philippines where 45-caliber firepower was needed. Caliber: 45 centerfire. Six-shot fluted cylinder. Barrel: 6 inches, round. Overall length: 11 inches. Blued iron frame. Iron backstrap. Bird's-head grips. Made 1902.

U.S. MILITARY PISTOLS
Various Manufacturers

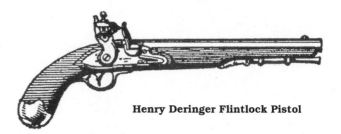

Henry Deringer Flintlock Pistol

Henry Deringer Flintlock Pistol $3700

Single-shot. Caliber: 52. Barrel: 10 inches, round. Overall length: 16½ inches. Weight: 2 lbs. 10 oz. Walnut stock with brass trigger guard, butt cap and thimbles. Made circa 1807 by Henry Deringer Sr.

Rappahannock Forge Flintlock Pistol

Rappahannock Forge Flintlock Pistol. . $3550

Single-shot. Calibers: 66 to 69. Barrel: 9 inches, average; smoothbore. Overall length: 15 inches, average. Brass mountings. Patterned after the British Light Dragoon of the period. Made circa 1775 at Rappahannock Forge, Virginia. Although contracted by the State of Virginia during the Revolutionary War, these pistols (only a few authentic ones survive) are considered by experts as the earliest "true" American military arms.

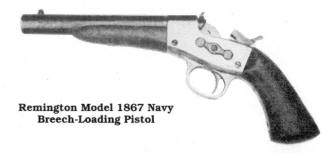

Remington Model 1867 Navy Breech-Loading Pistol

Remington Model 1867 Navy Breech-Loading Pistol $2225

Single-shot rolling block pistol. Caliber: 50 centerfire. Barrel: 7, 8½ inches. Similar to 1865 Navy Rolling Block, but with trigger guard. Walnut grips and forend. Made late 1860s to early 1870s.

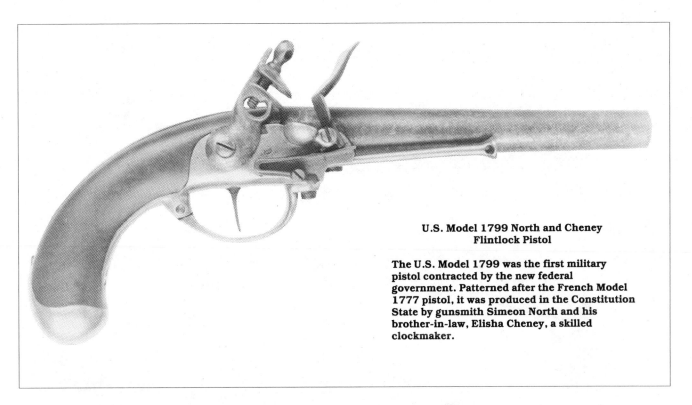

U.S. Model 1799 North and Cheney Flintlock Pistol

The U.S. Model 1799 was the first military pistol contracted by the new federal government. Patterned after the French Model 1777 pistol, it was produced in the Constitution State by gunsmith Simeon North and his brother-in-law, Elisha Cheney, a skilled clockmaker.

Remington Model 1871 Army Breech-Loading Pistol

U.S. Model 1805 Harpers Ferry Flintlock Pistol

Remington Model 1871 Army Breech-Loading Pistol. $995
Single-shot. Caliber: 50 centerfire. Barrel: 8 inches. Walnut grips and forend. Has a slight peak above the grip at rear of the frame. Made 1870s through 1880s.

U.S. Model 1799 North and Cheney Flintlock Pistol. $31,000
Single-shot. Caliber: 69. Barrel: 8½ inches; iron, smoothbore. Overall length: 14½ inches. Weight: 3 lbs. 4 oz. Brass frame, trigger guard and butt cap. Steel ramrod. One-piece walnut stock. Patterned after the French Model 1777 pistol used during the Revolutionary War. First U.S. Government pistol produced under contract. Total of 2,000 manufactured between 1799 and 1802 by Simeon North in Berlin, Conn. *See* photo, above.

U.S. Model 1805 Harpers Ferry Flintlock Pistol $3250
Single-shot. Caliber: 54. Barrel: 10½ inches; round, rifled. Overall length: 16 inches. Weight: 2 lbs. 9 oz. Walnut half-stock with brass mountings. Made 1806 to 1808 at Harpers Ferry Armory, W. Virginia. Earliest military pistol manufactured by a government armory.

U.S. Model 1808 Navy Flintlock Pistol . . $5000
Caliber: 64. Barrel: 10⅛ inches; round, iron, smoothbore. Overall length: 16¼ inches. Full walnut stock fitted with belt hook. 3,000 made between 1808 and 1810 by Simeon North. Used during the War of 1812.

U.S. Model 1811 Flintlock Pistol $875
Caliber: 69. Barrel: 8⅝ inches; round, smoothbore. Overall length: 15 inches. Brass mountings, including butt cap, trigger guard, sideplate. Manufactured by Simeon North about 1811 to 1813. Value shown is for percussion conversion; original flintlock should bring twice as much or better.

19th-CENTURY U.S. MILITARY FLINTLOCKS MANUFACTURED BY SIMEON NORTH

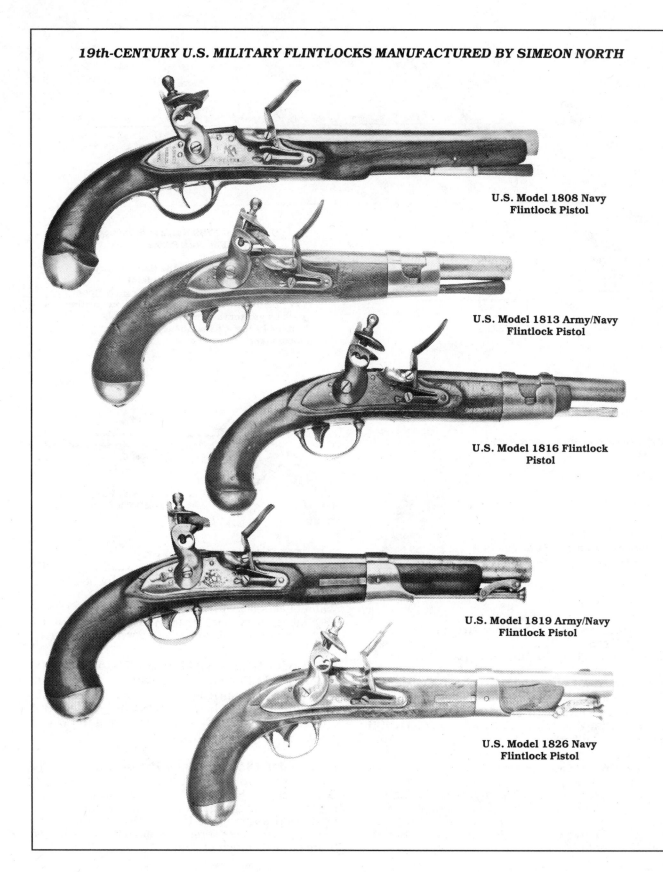

U.S. Model 1808 Navy Flintlock Pistol

U.S. Model 1813 Army/Navy Flintlock Pistol

U.S. Model 1816 Flintlock Pistol

U.S. Model 1819 Army/Navy Flintlock Pistol

U.S. Model 1826 Navy Flintlock Pistol

U.S. Model 1811 Transition Flintlock Pistol $5995

Same general specifications as U.S. Model 1811, except for iron double-strap barrel bands that secured the barrel to the stock. Value shown is for percussion conversion models.

U.S. Model 1813 Army/Navy Flintlock Pistol. $5500

Caliber: 69. Barrel: 9¹⁄₁₆ inches; round, iron, smoothbore; fitted with "Wickham" double-barrel band. Overall length: 15¼ inches. Made 1813 to 1815 by Simeon North in Middletown, Conn., under the first government arms contract specifying interchangeable parts.

U.S. Model 1816 Flintlock Pistol $1675

Calibers: 54 and 69. Single shot. Barrel: 9¹⁄₁₆ inches; iron, round, smoothbore. Overall length: 15¼ inches. Made by Simeon North 1817 to 1820. *See* photo opposite.

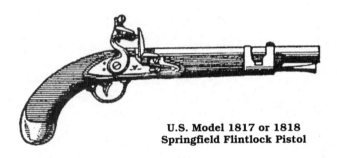

**U.S. Model 1817 or 1818
Springfield Flintlock Pistol**

U.S. Model 1817 or 1818 Springfield Flintlock Pistol. $10,000

Single-shot. Caliber: 69. Barrel: about 11 inches; round, smoothbore. Overall length: 17½ inches. Iron mountings. Double-strap barrel bands. Manufactured at Springfield Armory, Mass., some in 1807–1808 (hence the additional designation of Model 1808), but most made in and stamped 1818.

U.S. Model 1819 Army/Navy Flintlock Pistol $1750

Caliber: 54. Single-Shot. Barrels: 10 inches (Army); 8½ inches (Navy); round, iron, browned, smoothbore. Weight: 2 lbs. 10 oz. Sliding safety lock. Manufactured by Simeon North 1819 to 1823. *See* photo opposite.

U.S. Model 1826 Navy Flintlock Pistol $4775

Caliber: 54. Barrel: 8⁵⁄₈ inches; round, iron, smoothbore. Overall length: 13¼ inches. Made by Simeon North from 1826 to 1829. Value shown is for percussion conversion specimens; original flintlock commands more. *See* photo opposite.

U.S. Model 1826 Navy Flintlock Pistol (Evans). $4500

Same general specifications as the North-manufactured model, above, except for markings. Made by W.L. Evans of Valley Forge, Penn., about 1830.

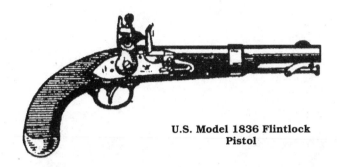

**U.S. Model 1836 Flintlock
Pistol**

U.S. Model 1836 Flintlock Pistol $1200

Single-shot. Caliber: 54. Barrel: 8½ inches; round, smoothbore. Overall length: 14¼ inches. Weight: 2 lbs. 10 oz. Made from 1836 to 1844 by A. Waters and A. H. Waters & Co., Millbury, Mass., and Robert Johnson, Middlebury, Conn. This is the last military flintlock commissioned by the government.

**U.S. Model 1842 Percussion
Pistol**

U.S. Model 1842 Percussion Pistol $2100

Single-shot. Caliber: 54. Barrel: 8½ inches; round, smoothbore. Overall length: 14 inches. Weight: 2 lbs. 12 oz. Brass mountings. Blued trigger. Made from about 1845 to 1855 by Henry Aston and Ira Johnson of Middletown, Conn. Those made by the Palmetto Armory of Columbia, S.C., were for use by the South Carolina militia and are considered Confederate arms.

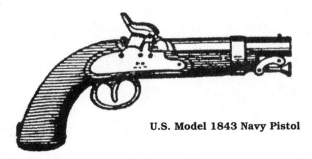

U.S. Model 1843 Navy Pistol

U.S. Model 1843 Navy Pistol. **$925**
Single-shot. Caliber: 54. Barrel: 6 inches; round,
smoothbore, browned. Overall length: 11½ inches.
Brass mountings. Casehardened box lock. Made by
N.P. Ames, Springfield, Mass., and by Henry Derin-
ger, Jr., Philadelphia, between 1842 and 1847.

**U.S. Model 1855 Springfield Pistol
Carbine** **$2150**
Single-shot. Caliber: 58. Barrel: 12 inches; round, rifled. Overall length: 17¾ inches (pistol); 28¼ inches
(with detachable stock). Weight: 3 lbs. 13 oz. (pistol);
about 5½ pounds (with stock). Walnut stock. Made by
Springfield Armory, Springfield, Mass., about 1855 to
1857.

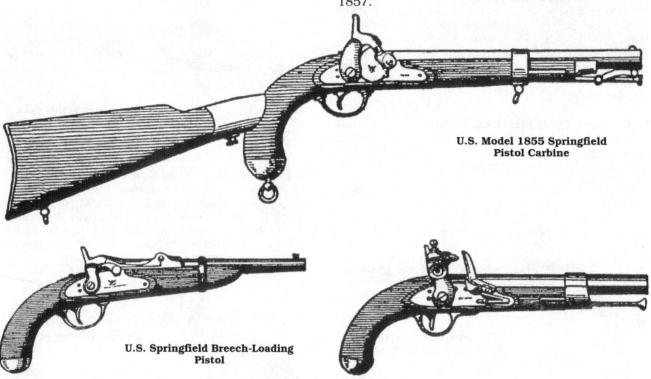

**U.S. Model 1855 Springfield
Pistol Carbine**

**U.S. Springfield Breech-Loading
Pistol**

U.S. Springfield Breech-Loading Pistol **$1200**
Single-shot. Caliber: 50. Overall length: 18½ inches.
Weight: 5 pounds. Has regulation musket lock of 1868.
None of this model was actually issued, perhaps be-
cause of the difficulty of holding it in one hand.

Valley Forge Flintlock Pistol **$4900**
Single-shot. Caliber: 69. Brass mounted. Patterned
after the French Model 1805. Made circa 1809. Very
rare.

U.S. MILITARY REVOLVERS
Various Manufacturers

The following revolvers were employed by the U.S. military services during the 19th century. While other revolvers can be cited as U.S. Government weapons, these are known to have been officially contracted, most often bear government markings and can be substantiated in ordnance records. (*See* also U.S. Military Handguns of Colt Manufacture.)

Adams Army Revolver

Adams Army Revolver **$2100**
Caliber: 44. Five-shot. Solid frame. Sliding safety. Patented in England in 1854 by Robert Adams (*see* separate listing). A small quantity were purchased by government agents for use during the Civil War. Probably manufactured by London Armoury Company. Very few Adams revolvers were made in 44 caliber.

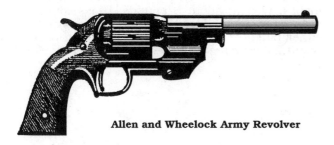

Allen and Wheelock Army Revolver

Allen and Wheelock Army Revolver . . **$2300**
Caliber: 44. Six-shot cylinder. Barrel: 7½ inches, part ocatagonal. Overall length: 13¼ inches. Weight: 2 pounds. Brass front sight, V-notch in center hammer serves as rear sight. Patent date 1857. About 500 purchased during the Civil War.

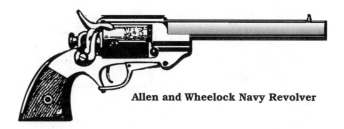

Allen and Wheelock Navy Revolver

Allen and Wheelock Navy Revolver. . . . **$1095**
Caliber: 36. Barrel: 8 inches, octagonal. Overall length: 13½ inches. Weight: 2 pounds. Cylinder engraved with animal scene. German silver blade front sight; V-notch rear sight grooved in frame. Casehardened side hammer and trigger guard. Patented in 1857.

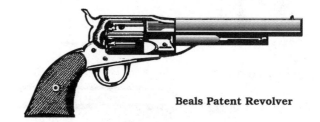

Beals Patent Revolver

Beals Patent Revolver **$2400**
Single-action Army revolver. Caliber: 44. Six-shot cylinder. Barrel: 8 inches, octagonal. Overall length: 13¾ inches. Weight: 2 lbs. 14 oz. Brass front sight; rear sight grooved in frame. Patented in 1858 by Fordyce Beals, inventor with the E. Remington & Sons Co., which manufactured the handgun. Together with the 36-caliber Navy version, about 2,800 were purchased by the U.S. Government for use during the Civil War.

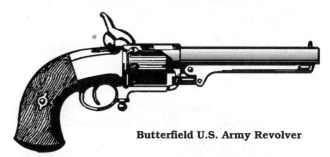

Butterfield U.S. Army Revolver

Butterfield U.S. Army. **$3470**
Caliber: about 36. Five-shot. Barrel: 7 inches. Overall length: about 14 inches. Bronze frame. Stamped "Butterfield Patent Dec. 11, 1855." A limited number were produced by Jesse Butterfield of Philadelphia in the early part of the Civil War. Rare, since the Government canceled the contract.

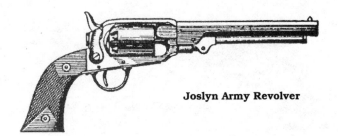

Joslyn Army Revolver

Joslyn Army Revolver **$1995**
Caliber: 44. Five-shot round cylinder. Barrel: 8 inches; octagonal, rifled. Weight: 3 pounds. Side hammer. Patented in 1858 by Benjamin Joslyn of the Joslyn Firearms Co., Stonington, Conn. The U.S. Government purchased over 1,000 during the Civil War.

Lefaucheux Army Pinfire Revolver

Lefaucheux Army Pinfire Revolver **$595**
Caliber: about 44 (12mm). Single-action. The metallic shell for the cartridge had a small pin attached at a right angle to the length and the shell could only be inserted one way. Based on the 1854 patent owned by French gunmaker Eugène Lefaucheux. Made in France and Belgium and used for a brief time in the early Civil War, but eventually discarded for American weapons; more than 12,000 were purchased, including a smaller caliber Navy revolver of the same design.

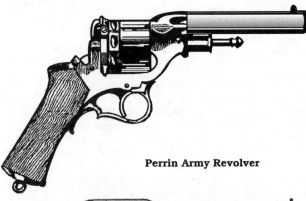

Perrin Army Revolver

Perrin Army Revolver **$815**
Caliber: about 44 (12mm). Double-action. Six-shot cylinder. Made in France, about 2,000 were purchased for use during the Civil War.

Pettingill Army Revolver

Pettingill Army Revolver **$1995**
Caliber: 44. Six-shot cylinder. Double-action. Hammerless. Barrel: 7½ inches. Overall length: 14 inches. Weight: about 3 pounds. Brass cone front sight, rear sight grooved in frame. Blued barrel and either blued or browned frame. Patented in 1856. About 2,000 were purchased during the Civil War.

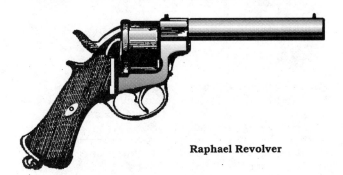

Raphael Revolver

Raphael Revolver **$825**
Caliber: about 41 centerfire. Six-shot cylinder. Double-action. Barrel: 5½ inches. Made in France, about 2,000 were purchased during the Civil War.

Remington Army Revolver **$1725**
Caliber: 44 paper cartridge. Six-shot cylinder. Barrel:
8 inches. Overall length: 13¾ inches. Weight: about
2¾ pounds. Patent dated 1858. Between 1861 and
1865 approximately 125,300 were purchased by the
Army; second only to Colt in Civil War production.

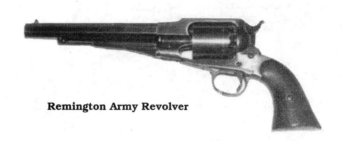

Remington Army Revolver

Remington Navy Revolver **$1925**
Same general specifications as Remington Army Revolver, except in 36 caliber paper cartridge with 7½-
inch barrel. About 5,000 were purchased by the Navy
for use in the Civil War.

Rogers and Spencer Revolver **$1625**
Caliber: 44. Six-shot cylinder. Barrel: 7 inches. About
5,000 were purchased for the Army in the latter part
of the Civil War. Apparently few saw heavy action,
since these arms are frequently found in quite good
condition. Based on the Freeman Revolver design (*see*
separate listing).

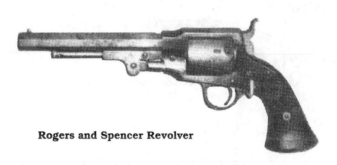

Rogers and Spencer Revolver

Savage Navy Revolver **$2500**
Caliber: 36. Overall length: 14¼ inches. This arm has
two triggers, the rear (ring) trigger to revolve the
cylinder and cock the hammer, and the front one to
fire. Patented in 1856 and made at the Savage Armory
in Middletown, Conn. More than 14,000 were purchased for use by the Navy during the Civil War.

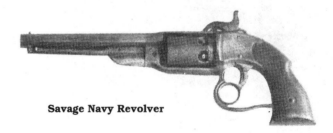

Savage Navy Revolver

Schofield/Smith and Wesson Revolver **$2400**
Caliber: 45. Barrel: 7 inches. Weight: 2½ pounds.
Modification of S&W No. 3 by Col. G.W. Schofield
who, in 1871, patented an improved latch pivoted on
the frame, rather than the barrel strap. Adopted by
the military about 1873.

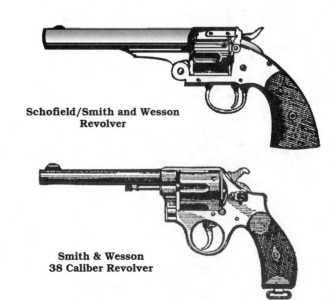

**Schofield/Smith and Wesson
Revolver**

Smith and Wesson Revolver **$545**
Caliber: 38. Barrel: 6½ inches. Overall length: 11½
inches. Used by both the Army and the Navy. Last
patent date is 1898.

**Smith & Wesson
38 Caliber Revolver**

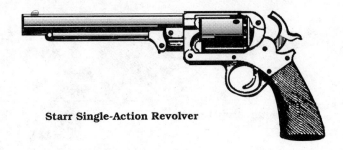

Starr Single-Action Revolver

Starr Revolvers **$925**
Caliber: 44. Six-shot cylinder. Barrel: 8 inches. Overall length: 14 inches. Weight: 3 pounds. Also made in double-action with 6-inch barrel in 36 and 44 calibers. This is a major Civil War arm, since almost 48,000 were bought between 1861 and 1865.

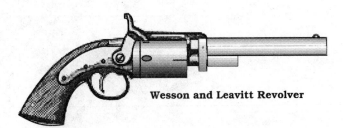

Wesson and Leavitt Revolver

Wesson and Leavitt Revolver **$2250**
Calibers: 31 and 40. Six-shot cylinder. Barrel: 6¾ inches, round. Overall length: 13¾ inches. Often referred to as a Dragoon, this was produced by the Massachusetts Arms Co. in the early 1850s. Patented in 1837 by Leavitt and in 1849 by Edwin Wesson.

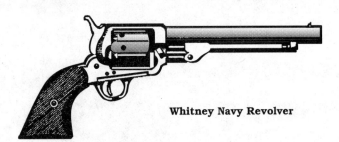

Whitney Navy Revolver

Whitney Navy Revolver **$1195**
Caliber: 36. Six-shot cylinder. Barrel: 7½ inches; octagonal, rifled. Weight: 2 lbs. 9 oz. Brass front sight, V-notch rear sight. Solid iron frame. Made under the sponsorship of Eli Whitney, Jr., in Connecticut. About 11,200 were purchased by the U.S. Government during the Civil War. This was copied at Confederate armories and made with a brass frame.

CHAPTER TWO
RIFLES

Until about 125 years ago, most long arms were muzzleloaders. They were loaded from the muzzle or mouth of the barrel with black powder and a lead projectile that was either a round ball or a conical bullet. The earliest long arms had smooth bores and, by name, were known as arquebuses and blunderbusses, muskets and fowling pieces.

Although loading from the breech or back of the barrel had been tried prior to this time, all such arms leaked powder gas at the breech, weakening the charge, and often burned the hand or face of the shooter. It was not until about 1860 that breechloaders first became practical because of fixed ammunition, that is, a cartridge with a metallic cartridge case that acted as a gas shield.

The earliest muzzleloaders were fired by a slow match applied to a "touch hole" that was located at the breech. Later the charge was set off by a shower of sparks from steel and flint, first by a wheellock wound up by a special key, and then by a more practical device called a flint lock. Thus, a gun was composed of "lock, stock, and barrel," an expression for completeness that is still frequently used today. Flintlock firearms were "primed" by fine black powder carried in a "pan" into which the sparks from the contact of flint and steel were showered. But sometimes the priming powder jarred away from the touch hole and went off with a flash that failed to set off the powder charge in the barrel. This was called a "flash in the pan."

Smoothbore muskets were far from accurate. "Don't fire until you see the whites of their eyes," was shouted at Bunker Hill for good reason. Hits beyond fifty yards became more and more unlikely as the range increased from shooter to target. Before the advent of Kentucky rifles, European gunmakers had discovered that grooves in a barrel enabled tighter fitting bullets to be rammed down the barrel easily. If the grooves were spiraled so the bullet spun, accuracy was immensely improved. This process of grooving the barrels was called "rifling," from which the word "rifle" developed.

About 1725, German gunsmiths in Pennsylvania were producing the famous "Kentucky" pattern flintlock rifles. These were light, very accurate, and being of smaller bore, were economical of lead and powder, which were scarce items along the frontier.

The next great improvement in firearms was the invention of the percussion cap in the early 1800s. The Civil War was fought mainly with percussion-cap, muzzleloading rifles using conical lead "Minie" balls. Today's primer is simply a refinement of the "cap" that fit over a "nipple" that extended into the breech. The hollow-faced hammer, on hitting the cap, shot a stream of flame through the hollow nipple into the powder charge. Bullets began to assume a conical shape, but most were of large caliber and were flatter and shorter compared to the slimmer, more elongated bullets of modern design.

Practical breechloaders began to appear at the end of the Civil War. Some were used in the Civil War, primarily by Union troops. Most notable among them were the Spencer and Henry carbines, both practical repeating rifles using the then recently invented metallic cartridge. These rifles used rimfire, coppercased cartridges of relatively low power by modern standards.

With sturdier, stronger brass cases and centerfire primers, heavier loads and the rifles to use them went hand-in-hand. Knockdown power was obtained by large caliber, heavy bullets propelled to the limit of black powder velocities, black powder being the only type of powder known at the time. Still, velocities were very low by present-day standards and the path of the bullet's flight was highly curved — limiting its range, for most shooters, to about 150 yards. If you've heard stories of the old buffalo hunters downing their game at ranges of 500 or even 1000 yards, remember, these were professional hunters who had fired hundreds of rounds through their Sharps' to be able to shoot this well.

The advent of smokeless powder brought far-reaching changes. Among these was a great increase in velocity. By reducing bullet diameter and weight, striking energy was amplified by increased velocities that were nearly double those obtained with black powder. This, in turn, meant a much flatter-shooting rifle, as the force of gravity had less time to blow the bullet off its course. Also, the target was not obscured by smoke.

On the following pages you will see all types of muskets, musketoons, carbines and rifles that span the early days until about 1900. For your ease in locating specific firearms, the section is divided into groupings:

	Page No.
Gunmakers A to Z	103
American Kentucky Flintlock Rifles	171
Confederate Military Rifles	188
U.S. Military Flintlock Rifles	191
U.S. Military Single-Shot Breechloading Carbines	193

ADIRONDACK ARMS COMPANY
Plattsburgh, New York

Orvill M. Robinson obtained a patent for a magazine-loaded repeating rifle in 1870 while living in Upper Jay, NY. Robinson, with A.S. Babbitt and others as partners, began building a rapid-firing repeating rifle in Plattsburgh, NY, shortly thereafter. In 1872, Robinson was granted a patent for a second model which was similar to the first except that a wooden forend was added and the operating mechanism was changed considerably. Following these improvements, Oliver Winchester contacted Mr. Robinson and purchased the entire Robinson operation — lock, stock, and barrel! Manufacture of the rifles was discontinued in 1874.

Adirondack Magazine-Loaded Repeating Rifle
Caliber: 38 and 44 RF. Barrel: Various lengths, but 26 inches was the most common. Brass or iron frame; later model may also be marked "A.S. Babbitt, Plattsburgh, N.Y.," Early models had finger holds on hammer.
Early model **$1750**
Late model **1675**

ARABIAN ARMS
Various Manufacturers

North African Arab Snaphaunce **$225**
Many different makers; some were made especially for the tourist trade and were not of high quality. Most, however, were very decorative

---
NOTE

The snaphaunce was one of the earliest flintlock arms, introduced about the year 1580 by the Dutch — actually by Dutch bandits called "Snaphaans," or hen snappers.

North African Arab Snaphaunce

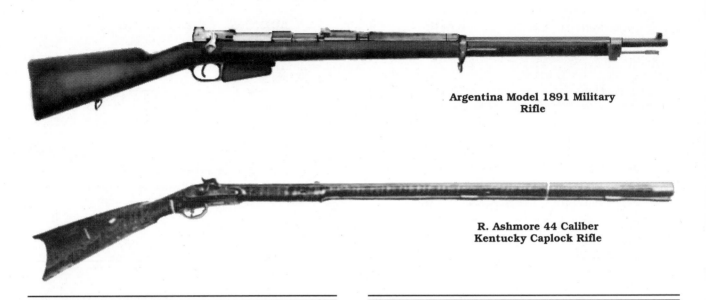

Argentina Model 1891 Military
Rifle

R. Ashmore 44 Caliber
Kentucky Caplock Rifle

ARGENTINA MILITARY
Manufactured in Germany

**Argentina Model 1891 Mauser Military
Rifle** **$100**
Bolt action. Caliber: 7.65 Belgian Mauser. Five-shot
clip loaded box magazine. Barrel: 29 inches. Weight:
about 8¾ pounds. Sights: inverted "V" front; open
rear sight. Military-type full stock. Adopted in 1891
by Argentina and several other South American
countries.

Argentina Model 1891 Mauser Carbine . . **$130**
Same general specifications as Model 1891 Rifle,
except has 17½-inch barrel and stocked to muzzle.

R. ASHMORE & SON
Lancaster County, Pennsylvania

R. Ashmore Kentucky Caplock Rifle . . **$1625**
Caliber: 44. Barrel: various lengths. Striped maple
stock, brass fittings with large patchbox. Made circa
early 1800s.

AUSTRALIAN MILITARY
Various Manufacturers

**Australian Cadet Martini B.S.A. 2nd
Pattern** **$260**
Caliber: 310 Cadet. Barrel: 29 inches, round. Weight:
9 pounds. Receiver stamped "Commonwealth of Aus-
tralia over VIC." Also same stamp on buttplate.

AUSTRIAN MILITARY
Steyr, Austria

Austrian Model 90 Mannlicher Carbine . . **$145**
Same general specifications as Model 1895 Rifle,
except has 19½-inch barrel. Weight: about 7
pounds.

Austrian Model 1867 M. Werndl Rifle . . . **$375**
Caliber: 11.2mm. Regimentally marked on butt tang.
Made 1867.

Australian Cadet Martini B.S.A.
Second Pattern

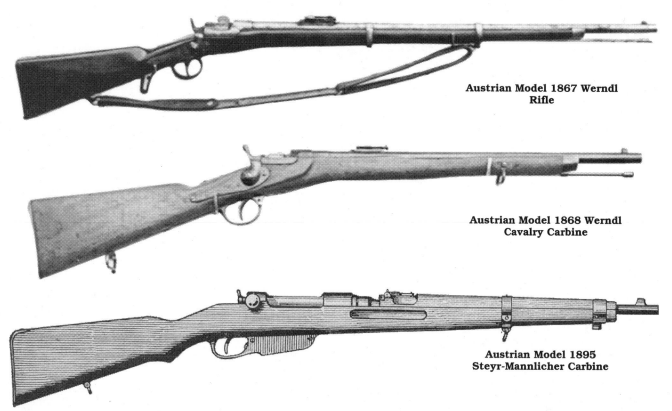

Austrian Model 1867 Werndl
Rifle

Austrian Model 1868 Werndl
Cavalry Carbine

Austrian Model 1895
Steyr-Mannlicher Carbine

Austrian Model 1868 M. Werndl Cavalry Carbine. **$325**
Caliber: 11.2mm. Barrel: 22 inches, round. Regimentally marked on butt. Made 1868.

Austrian Model 1886 Military Rifle. . . . **$115**
Caliber: 8x50R. Military-type stock. Adjustable rear sight, fixed blade front sight.

Austrian Model 1895 Steyr-Mannlicher Carbine. **$195**
Same general specifications as Model 1895 Rifle, except has 19½-inch barrel. Weight: about 7 pounds. The magazine clip with 5 cartridges is inserted from the top of the receiver. When the last cartridge has been chambered, the empty clip falls out the bottom of the rifle. Made by Steyr Armory, Steyr, Austria.

Austrian Model 1895 Steyr-Mannlicher Rifle. **$150**
Also known as Model 95. Straight-pull bolt action. Caliber: 8x50R Mannlicher (.315 bore). Five-shot projecting box magazine. Barrel: about 31 inches, round; 4 groove. 1 turn in 9.84 inches. Overall length: 48 inches. Weight: 8½ pounds with bayonet. Adjustable rear sight, blade front sight. Military full stock. Introduced in 1895. Manufactured by Steyr Armory.

BALKAN MILITARY
Various Manufacturers

Balkan Miquelet. **$595**
Iron stock with wood inlay at butt. Brass barrel bands. Usually engraved.

Balkan Miquelet

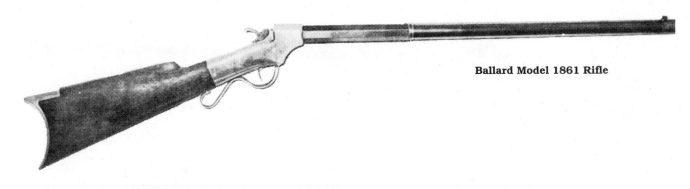

Ballard Model 1861 Rifle

BALLARD RIFLES
Massachusetts and Connecticut

The Ballard Rifle was patented by C.H. Ballard in 1861 and was used for military, sporting and target purposes for nearly thirty years. It was originally manufactured by Ball & Williams of Worcester, Mass., but by 1866, the firm was reorganized and was succeeded by the Merrimack Arms Mfg. Co. of Newburyport, Mass. (*see* separate listing). Merrimack manufactured various Ballard rifles and shotguns until they, too, went through a reorganization; in 1869 they were succeeded by the Brown Manufacturing Co. also of Newburyport.

On July 23, 1873, Brown Manufacturing was sold under foreclosure proceedings to a Mr. Daly of Schoverling & Daly. This firm then made arrangements with John M. Marlin of Marlin Firearms in Connecticut to manufacture the Ballard rifles beginning in 1875. Marlin continued to produce the Ballard rifle until 1888, when the newer repeating rifles made the Ballard unpractical for hunting purposes.

Although Ballard rifles were not manufactured after 1888, they were still used by many target shooters well into the twentieth century and had the reputation of being super-accurate target guns. These same fine guns are highly coveted today by collectors all over the world.

Ballard Model of 1861 Sporting Rifle . . $950
Single-shot, falling block. Calibers: 32, 38 Long and 44 Long RF. Barrel: 24 inches. Weight: 7 pounds. Introduced in 1861.

Ballard Model of 1862 Military Carbine $1000
Single-shot, falling block. Caliber: 54 RF (called No. 56 Ballard). Barrel: 22 inches, with markings "Merwin & Bray, Agts., N.Y.," and also "Ballard's Patent November 5, 1861." Overall length: 38 inches. Made from 1862 to 1863.

Ballard Model of 1862 Military Rifle. . . $1195
Same general specifications as Model of 1862 Carbine, except has a 30-inch barrel.

Ballard Model of 1863 "Kentucky" Rifle. $1235
Same general specifications as the Model of 1863 Military Carbine, except chambered for 46 RF, with 30-inch barrel, 45¼ inches overall length and weight of 8 pounds. Made from about 1863 to 1865.

Ballard Model of 1863 Military Carbine . . $995
Single-shot, falling block action. Caliber: 44 Long RF. Barrel: 22 inches with markings, "Ball & Williams, Worcester, Mass., Ballard's Patent November 5, 1861, Merwin & Bray, Agts., N.Y." Overall length: 37¼ inches. Weight: 6 lbs. 6 oz. Some of these rifles were made with solid breech blocks. Made from 1863 to about 1864.

Ballard Model 1864 Sporting Rifle $700
Single-shot. Falling block action. Calibers: 32 Long, 38 long, 44 Long RF. Dual ignition system, combination rimfire and percussion. Swivel striker on hammer. Patented Jan. 5, 1864.

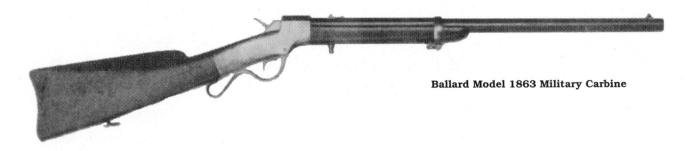

Ballard Model 1863 Military Carbine

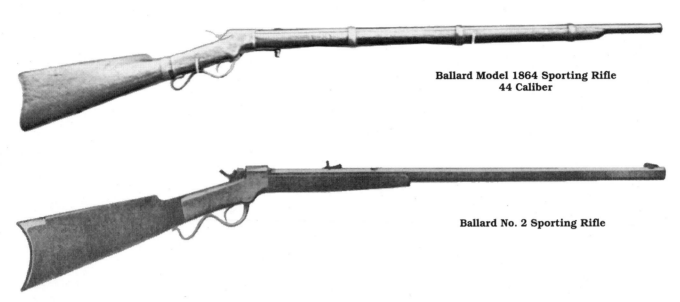

Ballard Model 1864 Sporting Rifle
44 Caliber

Ballard No. 2 Sporting Rifle

Ballard Model 1866 Carbine **$960**
Falling block, lever-operated, single-shot. Calibers: 44 Long RF and later for 56/52 Spencer. Barrel: 22 inches, marked "Merrimack Arms & Mfg. Co., Newburyport, Mass." and also "Ballard Patent Nov. 5 1861." Hammer marked, "Patented Jan. 5, 1864." Overall length: 37½ inches. Weight: 6½ pounds. Made from 1866 to 1873.

Ballard Model 1866 Sporting Rifle **$720**
Same general specifications as Model 1866 Carbine, except provided with 24- and 28-inch barrels. Calibers: 22 Long RF, 32 Long, 44 Long, 46 Long and 50 RF. Made from 1866 to 1873.

Ballard Model 1872 Military Rifle **$1145**
Falling block, lever-operated. Single-shot. Caliber: 56/52 Spencer. Barrel: 30 inches. Overall length: 35 inches. Weight: about 9 pounds. Made from 1872 to 1873.

Ballard Hunter's Rifle **$950**
Falling block, lever-operated. Single-shot. Caliber: 44 Long rimfire or centerfire. Barrel: round. Weight: about 8 pounds. Features reversible firing pin for use with either rimfire or centerfire ammunition. Made from 1875 to 1876.

Ballard Hunter's Rifle No. 1 . . . . **$950**
Falling block, lever-operated. Single-shot. Caliber: 44 Long rimfire or centerfire. Barrel: 26, 28 or 30 inches. Automatic extractor. Made from 1876 to 1880.

Ballard Hunter's Rifle No. 1½ **$1025**
Falling block, lever-operated. Single-shot. Caliber: 45-70 or 40-65-2⅜". Barrel: 28, 30 or 32 inches. Weight: about 10 pounds. Walnut stock with rifle butt. Made from 1879 to 1883.

Ballard Mid-Range Target Model. **$4000**
Falling block, lever-operated. Single-shot. Caliber: 44 Long RF. Barrel: 28 inches; extra-heavy, octagonal. Overall length: 43½ inches. Weight: about 10 pounds. Elevating peep sights. Made from 1869 to 1873. Also available in Schuetzen design; *see* illustration below.

Ballard Sporting Model No. 2 . . . . **$750**
Calibers: 32 and 38 RF or centerfire; 44 centerfire. Barrel: 26, 28 or 30 inches; octagonal. Reversible firing pin for rimfire or centerfire cartridge use. Case-hardened frame. Made by J.M. Marlin and the Marlin Firearms Company about 1876 to 1881.

Ballard Mid-Range Target Model
Schuetzen Design

BELGIAN MILITARY
Herstal, Belgium

Belgian Model 1889 Mauser Military Rifle **$175**
Caliber: 7.65 Belgian Mauser. Five-shot projecting box magazine. Barrel: 31 inches. Weight: $8\frac{1}{2}$ pounds. Straight-grip military stock. Made by Fabarique National D'Armes de Guerre from 1889 to 1935.

Belgian Model 1889 Mauser Carbine . . . **$200**
Same general specifications as Model 1889 Rifle, except has $20\frac{3}{4}$-inch barrel. Weight: about 8 pounds. Made by Fabrique National D'Armes de Guerre from 1889 to 1916.

BLAKE RIFLE COMPANY
Address Unknown

According to our reference, every catalog issued by Blake was filled with elaborate promises and heavily over-advertised with purely fictitious statements that may have contributed more or less to the failure of the firm. It is doubtful that all of the models listed in the Blake catalog were actually manufactured. Be that as it may, the Blake rifles were very strong and of excellent design and balance. The superior workmanship on all Blake rifles make them very attractive collectors' items.

Blake Grade A Sporting Rifle **$25,000**
Calibers: 30-40 Army, 30-06, 400 Blake, and others. Barrels: 18 to 30 inches long; round, octagonal, half-octagonal; or round at breech, a change to octagonal and then back to round. Weight: 6 pounds and up. Finest figured imported walnut stock with very high-grade checkering. Metal engraved with excellent workmanship and finish. The magazine was of aluminum bronze or solid silver, embossed and engraved if desired. This was practically a custom rifle made to order. Magazine hinged on left and opened on right to accept spool-type packet that holds up to seven cartridges. Made from 1895 to 1903.

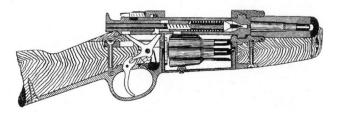

Cross-Section of Blake Hunting Rifle

Blake Grade B Hunting Rifle **$20,000**
Calibers: 30-40 Army, 30-06, 400 Blake and others. Barrels: 18 to 30 inches long; round, octagonal, half-octagonal; or round at breech, a change to octagonal, then back to round. Weight: $7\frac{1}{2}$ pounds and up. Magazine made of aluminum bronze, either blackened or plated. Fine figured imported walnut stock with straight or pistol-grip design. high-grade checkering on stock and engraving on metal parts, slightly less elaborate than the A grade. Made from 1895 to 1903.

Blake Grade C Hunting Rifle **$15,000**
Calibers: 30-40 Army, 30-06, 400 Blake, and others. Barrels: 18 to 30 inches long; round, octagonal, half-octagonal; or round at breech, a change to octagonal then back to round. Weight: $7\frac{1}{2}$ pounds and up. Magazine made of aluminum bronze, either blackened or plated. American walnut stock with straight or pistol-grip design. Made from 1895 to 1903.

Blake Grade D Hunting Rifle **$12,000**
Calibers: 30-40 Army, 30-06, 400 Blake, and others. Barrels: 18 to 30 inches long; round or octagonal. Weight $7\frac{1}{2}$ pounds and up. Magazine made of aluminum bronze, either blackened or plated. American walnut stock with straight or pistol-grip design. Made from 1895 to 1903.

BRITISH MILITARY
Various Manufacturers

The British long arms featured below are as varied and interesting as their makers. They have played a major role in the course of United States history because as Colonies of the British Crown, we purchased many of them and fought with many of them

British P. 1839 Rifle

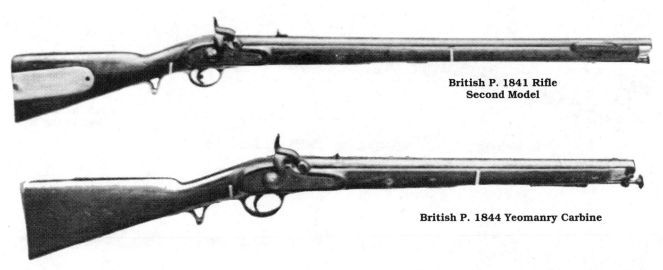

British P. 1841 Rifle
Second Model

British P. 1844 Yeomanry Carbine

in battle. The Short Land Brown Bess Musket, for example, was a particular favorite during the Revolutionary War.

British P. 1839 Rifle **$750**
Caliber: 76. Fitted with Lovell's bayonet catch. Made circa 1840.

British P. 1841 Rifle **$730**
Caliber: 704. Barrels: Damascus pattern. Made circa 1845.

British P. 1844 Yeomanry Carbine **$725**
Caliber: 66. Long side saddle ring bar with ring.

British P. 1853 Rifle **$465**
Caliber: 577. Dated 1861. Volunteer Pattern. Used by both sides in the U.S. Civil War.

British P. 1853 Rifle, 2nd Model **$545**
Caliber: 577. Dated 1857. Rare.

British P. 1856 Cavalry Carbine **$795**
Caliber: 577. Made circa 1857.

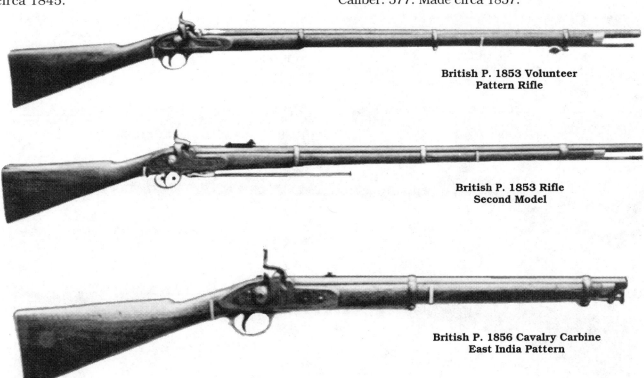

British P. 1853 Volunteer
Pattern Rifle

British P. 1853 Rifle
Second Model

British P. 1856 Cavalry Carbine
East India Pattern

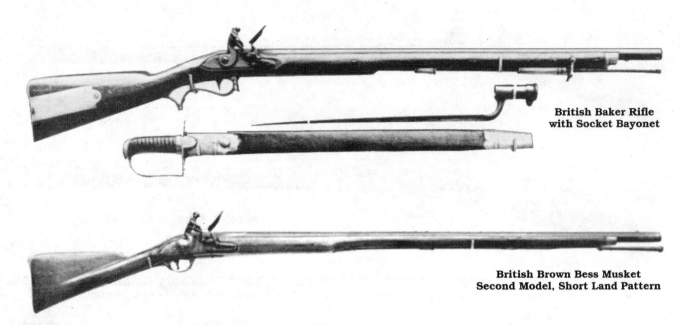

British Baker Rifle
with Socket Bayonet

British Brown Bess Musket
Second Model, Short Land Pattern

British Baker Rifle, Socket Bayonet Model **$2600**
Caliber: 65. Originally made for sword bayonet. Made 1815 to 1823.

British Brown Bess Musket, Short Land Pattern **$1750**
Caliber: about 75. Barrel: 42 inches, round. Typical Brown Bess pattern with brown stock. This model, standardized in the 1760s with 42-inch barrel, was the Second Model Brown Bess. The first was the Long Land Musket, which had a 46-inch barrel. The Short Land Pattern was a favorite during the Revolutionary War because it could be fired so rapidly. The Colonists could usually do it about 4 times per minute, while the Hessian troops were known to fire it about 6 times per minute. According to sources at Colonial Williamsburg, they used a 71 caliber bullet in the 75 caliber barrel, which facilitated loading.

British Brown Bess Musket, India Pattern **$500**
Caliber: 75. Typical Brown Bess pattern, except converted to percussion. The India Pattern was the third Brown Bess model and was cheaply made in comparison to its predecessors. Barrel: 39 inches average. Originally made 1800; converted around 1830.

British Eliott Carbine **$1595**
Caliber: 65. Dublin Castle on lock plate. Made 1760 to 1798.

British Martini Enfield Conversion **$410**
Caliber: converted to 303 British. Made from 1874 to 1899. Conversion made in 1899.

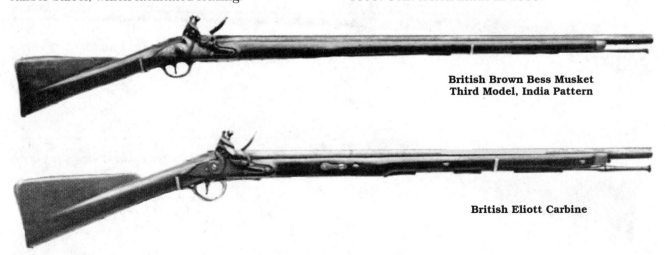

British Brown Bess Musket
Third Model, India Pattern

British Eliott Carbine

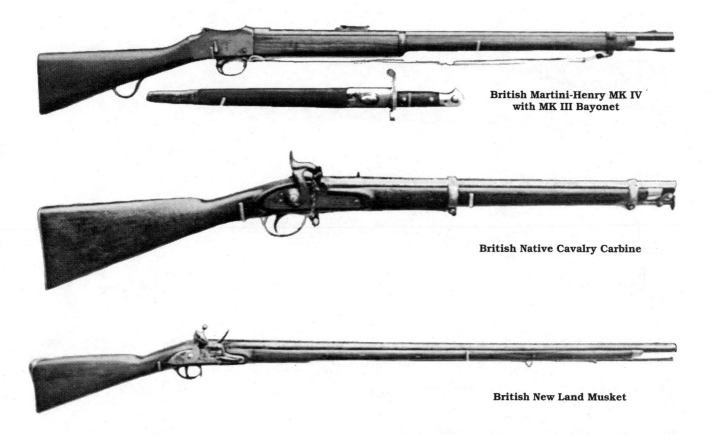

British Martini-Henry MK IV
with MK III Bayonet

British Native Cavalry Carbine

British New Land Musket

British Martini-Henry MK IV **$250**
Caliber: 450-577. Made circa 1887.

British New Land Musket **$940**
Caliber: 75. Regimentally marked on butt tang. Similar specifications as British Brown Bess. Made circa 1802.

British Double Rifle **$1300**
Caliber: 67 percussion. Seven-groove rifling, browned barrels. Walnut checkered stock. Iron furniture. Engraved.

British Native Cavalry Carbine **$545**
Caliber: 65. Barrel: smoothbore. Issued to Native Cavalry Regiments. The standard issue was 577 caliber, but the overbore ensured that the weapons could not be used against the British with their own ammunition as they would not be accurate. This proved quite useful during the Indian Mutiny. Made circa 1858.

British Paget Cavalry Carbine **$1125**
Caliber: 67. Barrel: Approximately 18 inches. Made circa 1808.

British Paget Cavalry Carbine

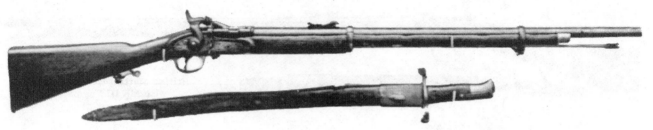

British Snider MK II

**British Snider MK III
Artillery Carbine**

British Snider MK II **$925**
Caliber: 577. Made circa 1861.

British Snider MK III Artillery Carbine . . **$695**
Caliber: 577. Made circa 1860.

British Snider MK III Percussion Rifle . . **$250**
Caliber: 577. Made circa 1871.

British Snider Target Rifle **$850**
Caliber: 45. Barrel: Damascus steel. Adjustable rear sight on barrel tang; hooded front sight. Engraved action. High-grade walnut with checkered grips and forend.

NOTE

The Snider breech action was the invention of Jacob Snider of Baltimore, Md. After the British authorities saw the repeated success of breechloaders during the U.S. Civil War, they adopted it as a means to convert their own muzzleloaders to breechloaders.

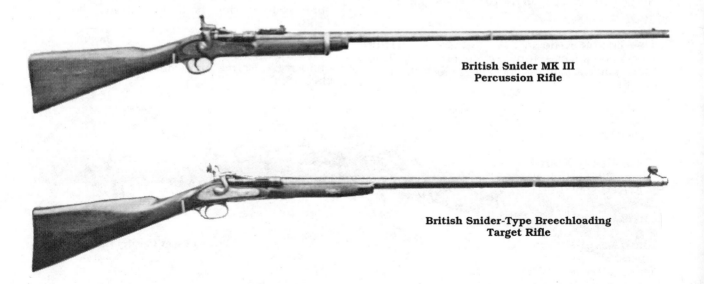

**British Snider MK III
Percussion Rifle**

**British Snider-Type Breechloading
Target Rifle**

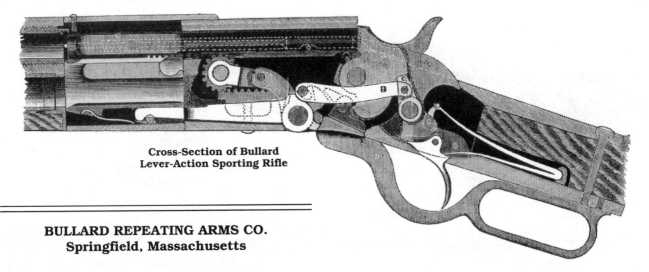

**Cross-Section of Bullard
Lever-Action Sporting Rifle**

BULLARD REPEATING ARMS CO.
Springfield, Massachusetts

The Bullard Repeating Arms Co. is best known for its development in the late 1880s of a lever-action repeating rifle, patented by former S&W mechanic and inventor, James H. Bullard. Although the gun had the general external appearance of the Winchester, the Bullard mechanism is entirely different. Before starting his own company, Bullard was responsible for inventing a simplified extractor mechanism used on the S&W No. 3 Single-Action New Model Revolver.

The Bullard company also manufactured single-shot rifles in all calibers from the .22 short to the big .50-115 Bullard—a special cartridge believed to have been adapted to no other rifle.

Bullard rifles were made of the finest forged steel of the day, utilizing the best in workmanship. Because of its excellence, it is believed that pressure was brought to bear by other manufacturers and the firm was purchased by Winchester in 1889 after being in business for only two years. The following rifles were made during that brief two-year period.

Bullard 40-90 Lever-Action Sporting Rifle **$4500**
Caliber: 40-90. Seven-shot magazine. Barrel: 28 inches; round, octagonal or half-octagonal. Weight: 10½ pounds. Full-stocked, straight grip with checkering.

Bullard Express Rifle **$5500**
Caliber: 50-95-300. Barrel: 28 inches, round. Full or half-magazine.

Bullard Heavy Frame Sporting Rifle . . **$1750**
Calibers: 40-75-258, 40-60-260, 45-85-290 and 45-70. Eleven-shot full-length magazine. Barrel: 28 inches; round, octagonal or half-octagonal. Weight: about 9½ pounds.

Bullard Lever-Action Sporting Rifle . . **$1300**
Calibers: 32-40-150 and 38-45-190. 11-shot full magazine. Barrel: 26 inches; round, octagonal or half-octagonal. Weight: 8½ pounds.

Bullard Military Lever-Action Carbine . . **$4300**
Same general specifications as the Military Lever-Action Rifle, except it has a 22-inch carbine barrel and weighs 8½ pounds.

Bullard Military Lever-Action Rifle. . . . **$4200**
Same general specifications as the Lever-Action Sporting models, except full stock with bayonet lug and open sights.

Bullard Rim Fire Hunting Rifle **$2250**
Caliber: 22 rimfire. Barrel: 26 inches. Weight: about 7½ pounds.

Bullard Schuetzen Rifle **$2520**
Calibers: various. Barrel: 30 inches most common; half-octagonal, but could be furnished in any length or weight. Weight: 12 pounds average.

Bullard Single-Shot Military Carbine **$2850**
Same general specifications as the Single-Shot Military Musket, except it had either a 24- or 26-inch round barrel, and weighed from 7 lbs. 8 oz. to 8 pounds.

Bullard Single-Shot Military Musket. . . **$2795**
Caliber: 45-70 Govt. Barrel: 32 inches with triangular bayonet lug. Weight: 8 lbs. 8 oz.

Bullard Target Rifle **$1100**
Calibers: various. Barrel: lengths of up to 28 inches in round, octagonal or half-octagonal. Regular sights included a Vernier peep rear on the tang and a wind gauge front sight.

Bullard Target and Hunting Rifle **$1050**
Calibers: various. Barrel: lengths of up to 28 inches in round, octagonal or half-octagonal style. Weight: 8 to 10 pounds.

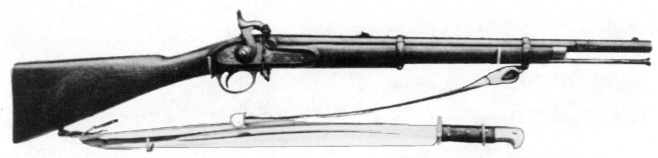

**Lower Canada P. 1853 1st Model
Artillery Carbine**

CANADIAN RIFLES
Various Manufacturers

Lower Canada P. 1853 Artillery Carbine. . . $895
Caliber: 577. Made circa 1856.

Canadian Brown Bess, India Pattern . . . $820
Caliber: 75. Typical Brown Bess pattern.

**Canadian Brown Bess, Short Land
Pattern. $1450**
Caliber: 78. Typical Brown Bess pattern. Made circa
1785.

**Canadian Lee-Enfield MK I, Bolt-Action
Rifle. $375**
Caliber: 303 British. Barrel: 25¼ inches. Weight:
8½ pounds. Walnut military stock. Bayonet lug.
Made circa 1896.

**Canadian Long Lee-Enfield MK I
Bolt-Action Rifle $375**
Same general specifications as Lee Enfield MK I,
except has 31-inch barrel.

Canadian Martini-Henry MK I Rifle $425
Caliber: 450-577. Same general specifications as the
standard Martini. Made circa 1873.

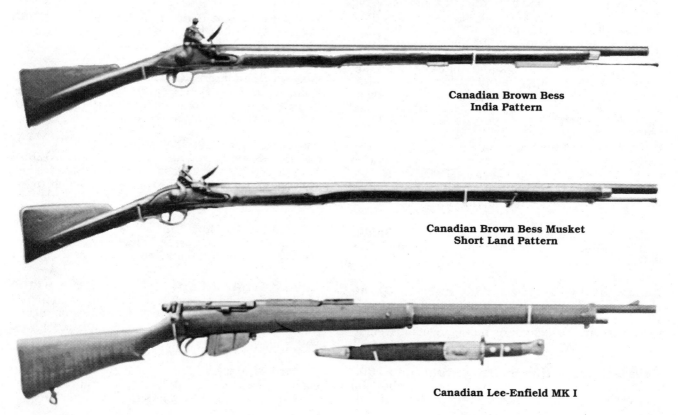

**Canadian Brown Bess
India Pattern**

**Canadian Brown Bess Musket
Short Land Pattern**

Canadian Lee-Enfield MK I

Canadian Long Lee-Enfield MK I

Canadian Martini-Henry MK I

Canadian Martini-Henry MK III Presentation Rifle

Canadian Martini-Henry MK III Presentation Rifle **$475**
Caliber: 450-577. Same general specifications as the Martini Rifle, with Henry rifling system. Sterling silver plaque in butt engraved "ROYAL SCOTS of CANADA 5th GEORGE COOK, MONTREAL, 1885." With sling, bayonet and scabbard.

Canadian Martini-Metford MK VI **$475**
Same general specifications as the Martini action. Caliber: 303. Action circa 1887, probably converted during 1890s to 303.

Canadian Newfoundland Sealing Gun . . . **$295**
Barrel: 42 inches round. The gun pictured converted from flint to percussion.

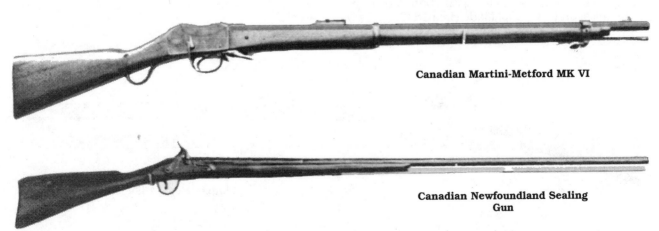

Canadian Martini-Metford MK VI

Canadian Newfoundland Sealing Gun

Canadan Snider MK II Rifle

**Canadian Snider MK III
Cavalry Carbine**

Canadian Snider MK II Rifle **$450**
Caliber: 577. Walnut stock. Iron barrel bands. Made circa 1866.

**Canadian Snider MK III Cavalry
Carbine.** **$500**
Caliber: 577. Same specifications as Snider MK II Rifle, except has short carbine barrel. Made circa 1860.

A.H. CHAPIN
Earlville, New York

Chapin Percussion Rifle **$935**
Caliber: 45. Barrel: heavy octagonal, 1-inch across flats. Lock made by Warren & Steel of Albany, N.Y. American walnut stock. Iron trigger guard. Brass buttplate, ramrod thimbles, and nose cap. Made circa 1840.

CHINESE MILITARY
Various Manufacturers

Chinese Model 1888 Mauser **$120**
Bolt action. Caliber: 8mm. Four-shot magazine. Barrel: 29 inches. Weight: 8½ pounds. Military-type stock. Introduced in 1888.

COLOMBIAN MILITARY
Various Manufacturers

**Colombian Model 1891 Mauser
Military Rifle** **$100**
Caliber: 7.65 Mauser. Five-shot box magazine. Barrel: 29 inches. Weight: about 8¾ pounds. Open rear sight, inverted "V" front sight. Military-type full stock.

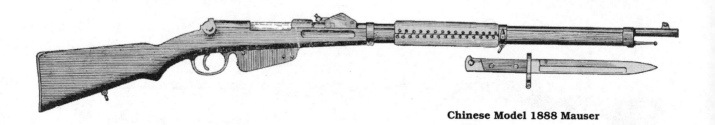

Chinese Model 1888 Mauser

**Colombian Model 1891 Mauser
Military Rifle**

COLT'S PATENT FIRE ARMS MFG. CO.
Hartford, Connecticut

The Colt's Patent Fire Arms Manufacturing Co. is known mainly for the invention and development of the first successful revolver, and therein lies Samuel Colt's personal claim to fame. However, the Colt firm also produced thousands of rifles, mostly of the revolving type, but lever-action and slide-action types as well.

It is not known exactly how many different variations of repeating rifles were turned out by the Colt factory, as researchers tend to disagree, but the following is an attempt at listing as many as could be found at this time.

For additional Colt information, *see* also the Colt sections under Handguns and Shotguns.

Colt Model 1850 Percussion Carbine . . **$12,500**
Six-shot cylinder. Apparently a revision of the Paterson Model 1839 Carbine (*see* separate listing). Barrel marked "Address Sam'l Colt, New York City." Introduced in 1850.

Colt Model 1855 Percussion Revolving Rifle
Calibers: 36, 40, 44, 50, 56 percussion. Six-shot cylinder (56 cal. is five-shot). Barrels: 24, 27 or 30 inches. Overall length: 43 inches with 24-inch barrel. Weight: ranged from 8 lbs. 12 oz. to 10 lbs. 8 oz. Introduced in 1855.

36 Caliber	**$11,250**
40 Caliber	8750
44 Caliber	8000
50 Caliber	7250
56 Caliber	7300

Colt Model 1855 Percussion Revolving Military Rifle
Calibers: 40, 44, 50, 56. Six-shot cylinder (56 cal. if five-shot). Barrel: 31⁵⁄₁₆ inches. Weight: 9 lbs. 6 oz. to 10 lbs. 4 oz. Included a full-stock barrel extending underneath the barrel itself. Introduced in 1855.

40 Caliber	**$7500**
44 Caliber	6800
50 Caliber	6500
56 Caliber	7500

**Colt Model 1855 Revolving
Carbine** **$7500**
Calibers: 36, 44 and 56 percussion. Six-shot cylinder with side hammer. Barrel: 15, 18 and 21 inches. Weight: 8 lbs. 8 oz. to 9 lbs. 8 oz. Side hammers marked "Address Col Colt, Hartford, Conn." Made from 1855 to 1866.

Colt Model 1861 Special Musket **$1750**
Single-shot muzzleloader. Caliber: 58. Barrel: 40 inches, round; three barrel bands. Iron mountings. Walnut stock. Made under U.S. Government contracts for use by Union Troops between 1861 and 1865.

**Colt New Lightning Magazine Baby
Carbine** **$10,000**
Same general specifications as standard New Lightning Carbines, except barrel was of slimmer construction. Weight: 5¼ to 8 pounds, depending on size of frame.

**Colt New Lightning Small Frame
Magazine Rifle** **$795**
Caliber: 22 Long. 15- or 16-shot magazine. Slide action. Barrel: 24 inches; round or octagonal. Weight: 5¾ pounds w/round barrel; 6 pounds w/octagonal barrel. Walnut stock. Made from 1887 to 1904.

Colt Model 1861 Special Musket

**Colt 44 Cal. New Lightning
Medium Frame Rifle**

Colt New Lightning Medium Frame Magazine Carbine $1295

Same general specifications as medium frame New Lightning Rifle, except barrel is 20 inches and full-length magazine holds 12 shots. Weight: 6¼ pounds. Made from 1894 to 1902.

Colt New Lightning Medium Frame Magazine Rifle $2800

Calibers: 32-20, 38-40, 44-40. 15-shot magazine. Slide-action. Barrel: 26 inches. Weight: about 7 pounds, unloaded. Walnut buttstock and forearm. Made 1883 to 1902.

Colt New Lightning Medium Frame Military Carbine. $3100

Differs from the medium frame rifle in that it was made in only 44-40 caliber, has shortened magazine tubes and is equipped with sling swivels, bayonet lugs and carbine-type buttplate. Made from about 1885 to 1902.

Colt New Lightning Large Frame Rifle . . $2725

Express Model. Calibers: 38-56, 40-60, 45-50, 45-85, 50-95 Express. Ten-shot magazine. Barrel: 28 inches, round or octagonal. Weight: 9¾ to 10 pounds. Walnut stock. Made from 1887 to 1894.

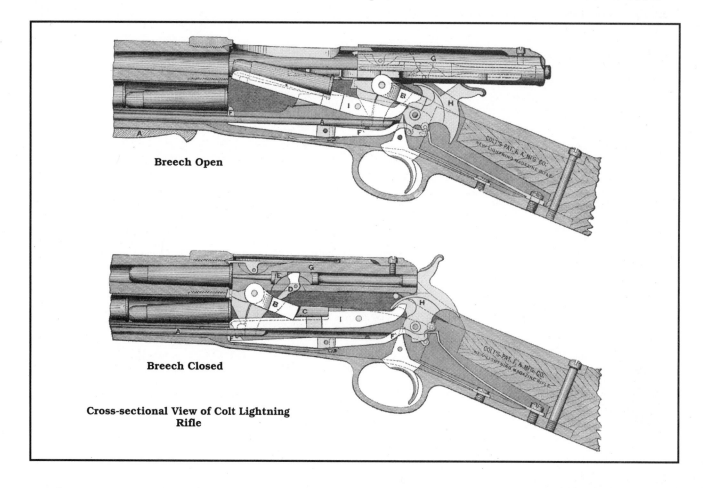

Breech Open

Breech Closed

**Cross-sectional View of Colt Lightning
Rifle**

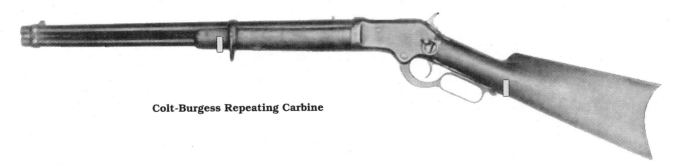

Colt-Burgess Repeating Carbine

Colt New Lightning Large Frame Carbine. **$5000**
Same general specifications as the large frame rifle, except has a 22-inch round barrel, full magazine, military-style sights and carbine-type buttplate. Weight: 9 pounds. Walnut stock. Made about 1888 to 1894.

Colt Paterson Model 1836 Percussion Rifle (34 Cal.) **$17,500**
Caliber: 34. Eight-shot fluted cylinder. Earliest models had no loading lever; it was added on later models. Barrel: 32 inches. Overall length: 50 inches. Weight: 12½ pounds. Walnut stock. Made from 1836 to 1843.

Colt Paterson Model 1836 Percussion Rifle (44 Cal.) **$16,995**
Caliber: 44. Eight-shot fluted cylinder. Earliest models had no loading lever; it was added on later models. Barrel: 24 inches. Overall length: 42 inches. Weight: 12 pounds. Walnut stock. Made from 1836 to 1843.

Colt Paterson Model 1836 Rifle (69 Cal.) **$18,000**
Hammerless. Caliber: 69 percussion. Seven-shot fluted cylinder. Earliest models had no loading lever; it was added on later models. Walnut stock. Made from 1836 to 1838.

Colt Paterson Model 1837 Percussion Rifle. **$17,225**
Caliber: 44. Eight-shot cylinder. Barrel: 24 inches. Overall length: 40 inches. Weight: 10½ pounds. Only about 20 made from 1837 to 1843.

Colt Paterson Model 1839 Carbine **$15,500**
Caliber: 47. Six-shot cylinder. Barrel: 24½ inches. Overall length: 42½ inches. Weight: 8½ pounds. Made from 1839 to 1840.

Colt-Burgess 12-Shot Repeating Carbine **$2425**
Lever action. Caliber: 44-40. 12-shot magazine. Barrel: 20 inches, round; blued finish, walnut stock. Based on a design by Andrew Burgess, only about 2600 were made from 1883 to 1885.

Colt-Burgess 15-Shot Repeating Rifle. **$2800**
Lever action. Caliber: 44-40. 15-shot magazine. Barrel: 24 to 25½ inches; round and octagonal. Blued and brown finishes with casehardened hammer and lever. Walnut stock. Based on a design by Andrew Burgess, only about 3800 were made from 1883 to 1885.

GEORGE W. CUNNINGHAM
Detroit, Michigan

Cunningham Percussion Rifle **$740**
Calibers: various. Barrel: various lengths, octagonal. Lockplate usually stamped "MOORE." Moore was a gunsmith and importer from Toronto, Ontario, Canada and imported several Cunningham rifles from the United States. Made from 1874 to 1878.

Colt-Burgess Repeating Rifle

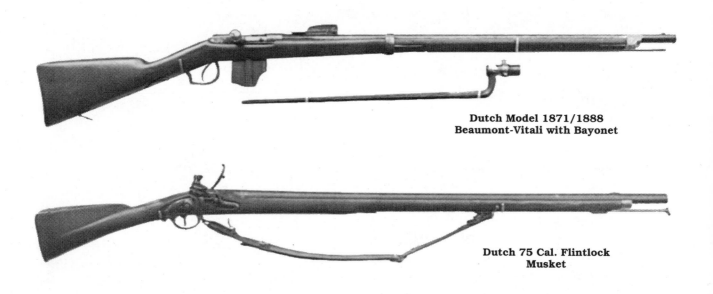

**Dutch Model 1871/1888
Beaumont-Vitali with Bayonet**

**Dutch 75 Cal. Flintlock
Musket**

CZECHOSLOVAKIAN MILITARY
Various Manufacturers

Czech Model 1898 Mauser Military Rifle . . $200
Bolt action, straight handle. Caliber: 7.9mm
(8×57mm) Mauser. Five-shot magazine. Barrel: 29
inches, stepped barrel. Weight: 9 pounds. Blade front
sight, adjustable rear sight. Military-type full-length
stock. Adopted in 1898.

DANISH MILITARY
Various Manufacturers

**Danish Model 1889 Krag-Jorgensen
Military Rifle $250**
Bolt action. Caliber: 8mmR. Five-shot magazine. Barrel: 33 inches. Weight: 9¾ pounds. Blade front sight,
adjustable rear sight. Military-type stock, straight
grip.

DUTCH MILITARY
Various Manufacturers

**Dutch Model 1871/88 Bolt Action
Beaumont-Vitali Rifle $215**
Caliber: 11mm. Marked 1873 and 91 "DELFT." Mili-
tary model with bayonet.

Dutch Flintlock Musket $675
Caliber: 75. Typical of those used during the American Revolution.

JOHN DEMUTH
Frederick Co., Maryland

Demuth Flintlock Target Rifle $2800
Caliber: 72. Barrel: Heavy octagonal with 16-groove
rifling, 1¼ inches across flats. Brass furniture. Made
from 1794 to 1796.

**John Demuth Kentucky Sporting
Target Rifle**

Ecuador Model 1891 Mauser
Military Rifle

ECUADOR MILITARY
Various Manufacturers

Ecuador Model 1891 Mauser Military Rifle **$100**
Bolt-action. Caliber: 7.65 Belgian Mauser. Five-shot box magazine, clip loaded. Barrel: 29 inches. Weight: about 8¾ pounds. Open rear sight, inverted "V" front sight. Military-type full stock. Adopted in 1891 by Argentina and several other South American countries.

EVANS RIFLE MANUFACTURING CO.
Mechanic Falls, Maine

Warren E. Evans of Thomaston, Maine, was granted patents covering his unique rifle on December 8, 1868, and again on September 18, 1871.

The Evans rifles were manufactured in two distinct models known as the "old" and the "new." Both had a special four-column fluted magazine within the butt that held a maximum of 34 cartridges—making the Evans the greatest capacity repeating rifle ever to be placed on the market. The original Evans cartridge had a 215-grain lead bullet backed with 28 grains of black powder. The new model cartridge was slightly longer, using a 280-grain bullet in front of 42 grains of black powder.

Due to financial difficulties, the Evans Rifle Company was forced out of business about 1880.

Close-up of Evans Old Model
Repeater

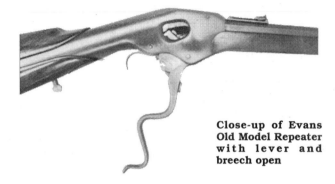

Close-up of Evans
Old Model Repeater
with lever and
breech open

Evans Old Model Military Rifle **$1050**
Essentially the same as the Old Model Sporting Rifle, except for longer forearm, provisions for bayonet, and a 30-inch barrel. Also, some of the refinements of the sporting rifle were missing.

Evans Old Model Repeating Carbine . . . **$1595**
Essentially the same as the Old Model Sporting Rifle, except for the buttplate and 22-inch barrel, which reduced the weight to 7½ pounds.

Evans Old Model Sporting Rifle **$1100**
Lever-action repeater. Special four-column fluted magazine holding 34 shots. Caliber: 44 Evans. Barrel: 26, 28 and 30 inches; octagonal. Weight: 9 lbs. 10 oz. with 26-inch barrel. Overall length: 43 inches. Various sights, but globe front sight and vernier rear were common. Two-piece walnut buttstock; walnut forend. Made from 1875 to 1877.

Evans New Model Military Repeating Rifle **$1195**
Essentially the same as the New Model Sporting Rifle, except for longer forend and bayonet provisions.

Evans New Model Repeating Carbine . . . **$900**
Essentially the same as the New Model Sporting Rifle, except for buttplate and shorter barrel. Made from 1877 to 1880.

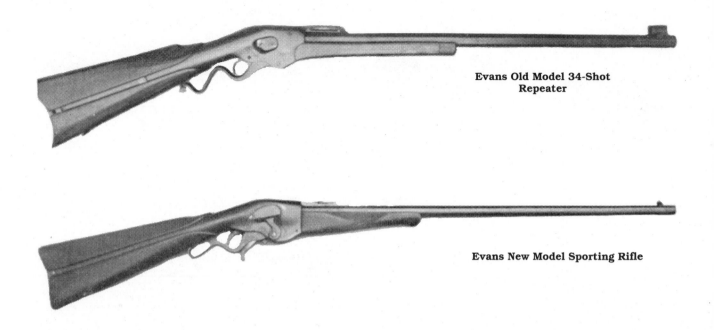

Evans Old Model 34-Shot Repeater

Evans New Model Sporting Rifle

Evans New Model Sporting Rifle **$895**
Lever-action repeater. Four-column, 26-shot, fluted magazine. Caliber: a longer version of the Old Model 44 Evans. Barrel: various lengths from 26 to 31 inches; round or octagonal. Overall length: 47½ inches. Weight: 9½ pounds. Walnut stock and forearm. Made from 1877 to 1880.

FRENCH MILITARY
Various Manufacturers

French Model 1763 Musketoon **$560**
Caliber: 73. Lock stamped "HB ST Etienne." Regimentally marked on barrel. Many original muskets were altered to musketoon style, like the one pictured.

French Model 1777 Musket **$595**
Caliber: 75. Barrel marked "MRE IMP. LE DE Versailles." Typical reconversion.

French Model 1866 Chassepot Rifle **$320**
Caliber: 11mm Needle Gun. Barrel: round with bayonet lug. Made circa 1867.

French Model 1886 Lebel Military Rifle . . **$115**
Bolt-action. Caliber: 8mm Lebel (.315). Eight-shot tubular magazine. Barrel: 31½ inches. Overall length: 49 inches. Weight: 9¼ pounds. Sights: blade front, adjustable rear. Two-piece military stock. Made with various modifications in Chatellerault, St. Étienne, France, from 1886 to about 1945.

French Model 1892 Lebel Military Carbine **$155**
Same general specifications as the Lebel Rifle, except has 17½-inch barrel and weighs 6¾ pounds.

French Flintlock Musket **$495**
Caliber: 73. Many made from surplus military pieces, so many variations exist. This musket stamped on butt "NIGER COAST PROTECTORATE FIREARMS PROTECTION."

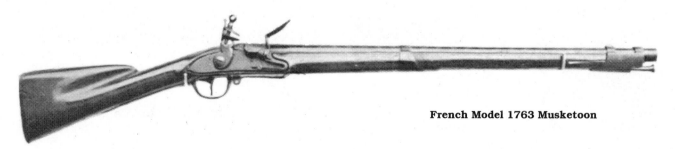

French Model 1763 Musketoon

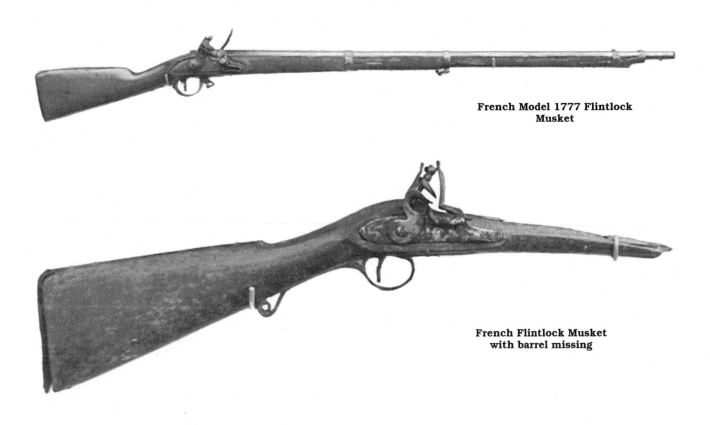

French Model 1777 Flintlock
Musket

French Flintlock Musket
with barrel missing

MAHLON J. GALLAGHER
Philadelphia, Pennsylvania

Mahlon Gallagher patented certain percussion breechloading rifle designs as well as those designed for metallic cartridges. Most were manufactured between 1860 and 1865 at the Richardson and Overman plant in Philadelphia under Mr. Gallagher's supervision.

**Gallagher Breechloading Metallic
Cartridge Rifle** **$1395**
Same general specifications as the Gallagher Percussion Rifle, except used a metallic cartridge instead of a paper cartridge.

Gallagher Percussion Carbine **$1525**
Same general specifications as the Gallagher Percussion Rifle, except had 22- or 24-inch barrel. Made from 1860 to 1865.

Gallagher Percussion Rifle **$1495**
Caliber: 54. Barrel: various lengths to 32 inches; mostly round. Color-casehardened back-lock action. Straight-grip buttstock; usually no wood forend. Combination trigger guard/lever released barrel latch for insertion of paper cartridge. Made from 1860 to 1865.

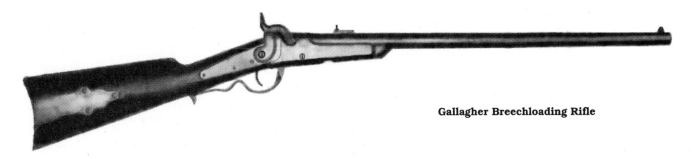

Gallagher Breechloading Rifle

German Model 1871 Rifle
with Brass Hilt Bayonet

German Model 1888 Mauser-
Mannlicher Rifle

GERMAN MILITARY
Various Manufacturers

German Model 1871 Rifle **$545**
Caliber: 11mm. Straight bolt. Barrel: musket length. Wooden stock with barrel bands. Adjustable rear sight; blade front sight. Brass hilt bayonet. This model manufactured circa 1879.

German Model 1871 Carbine **$570**
Caliber: 11mm. Barrel: round, carbine length. Wooden stock with straight grip. Turned-down bolt. Made circa 1879.

German Model 1888 Mauser-Mannlicher Carbine. **$135**
Same general specifications as the Model 1888 Rifle, except has 18-inch barrel, flat turned-down bolt handle and weighs 6¾ pounds. Manufactured by Ludwig Loewe & Co., Berlin.

German Model 1888 Mauser-Mannlicher Military Rifle **$260**
Bolt-action. Caliber: 7.9mm Mauser (8×57mm). Five-shot magazine. Barrel: 29 inches, round. Weight: 8½ pounds. Sights: adjustable rear; fixed front. Military stock. Made by Ludwig Loewe & Co., Berlin, from 1888 to 1898. The model shown is dated 1890.

German Model 1898 Mauser Military Rifle. **$245**
Bolt-action. Caliber: 7.9mm (8×57mm). Five-shot magazine. Barrel: 29 inches, stepped. Weight: about 9 pounds. Sights: blade front; adjustable rear. Military-type full stock with rounded bottom pistol grip. Adopted 1898.

German Model 1898A Mauser Carbine . . **$275**
Same general specifications as the 1898 Mauser Rifle, except has turned-down bolt handle, smaller receiver sight, 23½-inch tapered barrel and weighs about 8 pounds.

German Model 1898A Mauser Carbine

DEUTSCHE WAFFEN- UND MUNITIONSFABRIKEN, as the factory appeared in the 1890s, made most of the German military small arms of the period.

Hodges Elastic or Catapult Gun

C. G. HAENEL
Suhl, Germany

Haenel Mauser-Mannlicher Bolt-Action Sporting Rifle **$510**
Bolt-action. Calibers: 7×57, 8×57, 9×57. Five-shot Mannlicher clip-loading box magazine. Barrel: 22 or 24 inches; half or full octagonal with raised matte rib. Double-set triggers. Weight: 7½ pounds. Sights: ramp front; leaf-type open rear. Sporting walnut stock with checkered pistol grip, raised side-panels, schnabel tip and sling swivels.

Haenel Model '88 Mauser Sporter **$495**
Same general specifications as the Sporting Rifle, except has Mauser-type five-shot magazine instead of Mannlicher style.

ALEXANDER HENRY
Edinburgh, Scotland

This is the "Henry" (1819–1894) who invented the system of rifling that was combined with the Martini action to produce the Martini-Henry Rifle, officially adopted by the British government in 1869. (*See* also British and Canadian listings.)

Alexander Henry Single-Shot Rifle . . . **$2300**
Caliber: 450 black powder. Checkered pistol grip and forend. Elaborately engraved. Made circa 1862 to 1894.

R. E. HODGES
London, England

Hodges Elastic Gun **$2500**
Caliber: 44. Barrel: octagonal with "R.E. HODGES PATENTEE LONDON" engraved on top flat. Walnut stock with checkered grip and iron buttplate. Copper nosecap and two brass busts of Britannia at the muzzle. Two elastics, one on each side of barrel. The projection below the forend is a grip for the palm of the hand. Hodges believed in the power of vulcanized caouthchouc (rubber) and described his elastic gun as follows: "constructed after the manner of an ordinary fowling piece which would be well adapted for deer shooting, as it will carry a long way and be attended with neither noise nor smell." This is an unusual piece, another example of 19th-century inventiveness. Only a few hundred were ever made circa 1849.

COBOURG C .W. HOLMES
Address unknown

Holmes Percussion Rifle **$1500**
Caliber: 41. Lock by J.P. Moore of Union, N.Y. Walnut stock. Brass buttplate, trigger guard and ramrod thimbles, as well as side plate. Silver inlays.

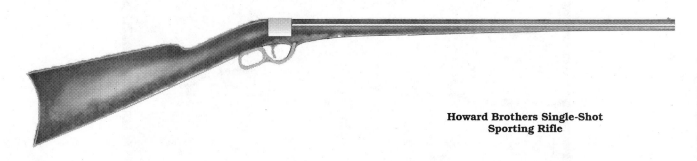

**Howard Brothers Single-Shot
Sporting Rifle**

Edwin Hunt Percussion Rifle

HOWARD BROTHERS
Whitneyville, Connecticut

Charles Howard obtained patents for a breechloading hammerless sporting rifle from September 26, 1865, to May 15, 1866. Whitney Arms Co. at Whitneyville, Conn., made most of these rifles under contract, as is stated on the barrels of many early rifles; that is, "Mf'd for Howard Brothers by Whitney Arms Co., Whitneyville, Conn."

Howard Brothers Breech-Loading Hammerless Rifle **$425**
Caliber: 38 Long rimfire. Barrel: 24 inches. Overall length: 43 inches. Weight: 6 pounds. American walnut stock. Set triggers available as extra. Made from 1866 to 1869.

Howard Brothers Single-Shot Breech-Loading Sporting Rifle **$475**
Caliber: 44 RF. Barrel: 24½ inches. Overall length: 43¾ inches. Weight: 6 pounds. American walnut stock. Set triggers available for extra cost. Made from 1866 to 1869.

EDWIN HUNT
Canada

Hunt Percussion Rifle **$795**
Caliber: 36. Barrel: part octagonal. American walnut stock with cheekpiece. Silver escutcheons. Brass buttplate, trigger guard, rear thimble and nosecap.

WALTER HUNT
New York, New York

On August 21, 1849, Walter Hunt—a 53-year old machinist and inventor—was granted U.S. Patent No. 6663 for a lever-action, breechloading, repeating rifle known as the "Volition Repeater." At the same time, Hunt was also granted U.S. Patent No. 5701 for a conical lead bullet for use in his rifle. This bullet had a cavity in the base, filled with powder and closed by a disc containing a hole in the center to admit the flame from an independent priming unit. The bullet was known as a "Rocket Ball."

This rifle was the forerunner of the Henry and Winchester actions, but mainly because of unsuitable cartridges, it was not successful.

Hunt "Volition" Repeating Rifle . . . **$90,000+**
Caliber: 54 Tubular magazine under barrel. Small-frame style with exposed ring trigger. Used "Rocketball" conical lead bullet with self-contained powder change and independent priming pill. Only one specimen is known at this time, which is in the Winchester Collection at the W.F. Cody museum in Cody, Wyoming. Made in limited numbers between 1849 and 1853.

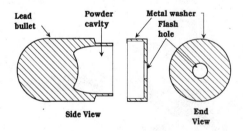

Cross-sectional view of self-contained bullet used in Hunt's rifle

Hunt Volition Repeating Rifle

Innes Scottish Hunting Musket

JAMES INNES
Edinburgh, Scotland

Innes Scottish Hunting Musket $560
Caliber: 80. Brass furniture. Adjustable single-set trigger. Walnut stock. Made 1793 to 1820; converted to percussion around 1835.

ITALIAN MILITARY
Various Manufacturers

Italian Model 1870/87/15 Vetterli $200
Caliber: 6.5×52mm. Walnut stock, full-length. Bayonet lug with bayonet and scabbard. Dated 1882 and stamped "BRESCIA."

Italian Model 1891 Mannlicher-Carcano Military Rifle $75
Bolt-action. Caliber: 6.5mm. Six-shot modified Mannlicher-style box magazine. Barrel: 30¾ inches. Weight: 9 pounds. Sights; blade front; adjustable rear. Military-style straight-grip stock. Adopted by the Italian Military Service in 1891.

Italian Model 1891 TS Cavalry Carbine . . $95
Caliber: 6.5mm. Introduced in 1891.

JAPANESE MILITARY
Various Manufacturers

Japanese Matchlock. $850
Matchlock. Calibers: various. Barrel: 39½ inches. Inlaid in silver with trees and other designs.

LEWIS JENNINGS
Windsor, Vermont

Lewis Jennings simplified and improved an earlier repeating rifle design by Walter Hunt (see separate listing), and was granted a U.S. patent on December 25, 1849. The Jennings and the Walter Hunt rifles were the basic patents for the Henry and, later, the Winchester rifles. The Jennings rifles were manufactured by Robbins & Lawrence of Windsor, Vt., and are usually so marked.

Italian Model 1870/87/15 Vetterli

Italian Model 1891 Mannlicher-Carcano

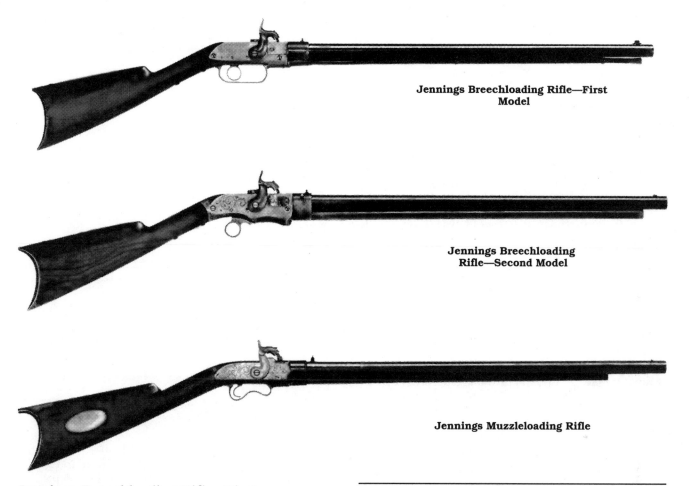

Jennings Breechloading Rifle—First
Model

Jennings Breechloading
Rifle—Second Model

Jennings Muzzleloading Rifle

Jennings Breechloading Rifle—First
Model **$2500**
Caliber: 54, with automatic priming device. Single-
shot. Straight frame with ring trigger and oval trigger
guard. Made from 1850 to 1853.

Jennings Breechloading Repeating
Rifle—Second Model **$6000**
Caliber: 54. Tubular magazine. Barrel: round with
magazine tube below. Exposed hammer. Fixed rear
and front sights. American walnut buttstock with
crescent buttplate, straight-grip. Made from 1851 to
1853.

Jennings Muzzleloading Rifle **$1250**
Caliber: 54 percussion. Single-shot. Muzzleloading
barrel with cleaning rod below. Curved trigger and
indented trigger guard. American walnut stock with
no forend. Assembled from remaining parts of the
first and second Jennings models, this was made
from 1852 to 1853.

NOTE

The Jennings rifles are considered to be the forerunners of
the famous Winchester line of repeating rifles.

BENJAMIN F. JOSLYN
Stonington, Connecticut

Benjamin Joslyn was patentee of the Joslyn
breechloading carbine, patented August 23, 1855,
and the Joslyn percussion revolver, patented May
4, 1858. Benjamin Joslyn established the Joslyn
Arms Company in 1861 and was awarded U.S.
Government contracts for both the carbines and
revolvers. These arms were also manufactured by
W.D. Freeman of Worcester, Mass., and the carbines by A.H. Waters & Co. of Millbury, Mass. The
Joslyn Arms Co. operated until 1878.

For further specifications, *see* U.S. Military Single-
Shot Breechloading Carbines at the end of the Rifle
Section.

Joslyn Breechloading
Carbine

Marlin Model 1881 Repeating Rifle
with Shotgun Butt

MARLIN FIREARMS COMPANY
North Haven, Connecticut

The Marlin Firearms Company was founded in 1870 by John Mahlon Marlin who first started producing single-shot pistols, revolvers, and the famous Ballard single-shot rifles under the brand name, "J.M. Marlin."

In 1880 the Marlin firm was incorporated as the Marlin Firearms Company and operated successfully until John Marlin died in 1900. Ownership was then carried out by the Marlin family until the business was sold in 1915 to a firm known as the Marlin Arms Corporation.

Although the Marlin Company changed owners many times, the company is still in operation at 100 Kenna Drive, North Haven, Conn.

Marlin Model 1881 Repeating Rifle $950
Calibers: 45-70, 45-85-285, 40-60, 38-55 and 32-40. Barrel lengths: 28 and 30 inches. Weight: 9½ to 11¼ pounds. Open rear sight, blade front sight. American walnut stock in either straight or pistol grip. Double-set triggers were introduced for this model in 1883, which was rather unique for a lever-action rifle. Several variations exist. Made from 1881 to 1892.

John Marlin founded the Marlin Firearms Company in 1870 and headed the organization until his death in 1900.

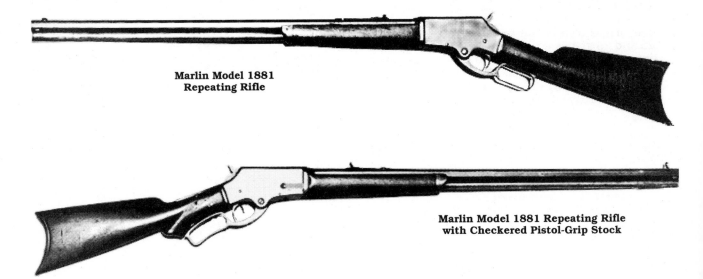

Marlin Model 1881
Repeating Rifle

Marlin Model 1881 Repeating Rifle
with Checkered Pistol-Grip Stock

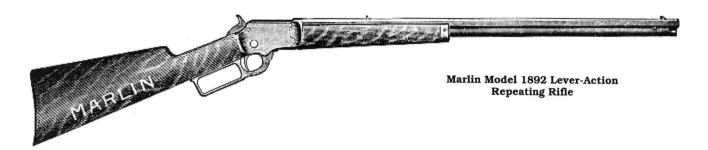

**Marlin Model 1892 Lever-Action
Repeating Rifle**

Marlin Model 1888 Repeating Rifle... $1195
Top eject. Similar to the Model 1881, except it had a shorter action for use with 32-30, 38-40 and 44-40 cartridges. Barrel lengths: 24, 26, and 28 inches; octagonal. Weight: from 6¾ pounds. Made from 1888 to 1889.

**Marlin Model 1889 Lever-Action
Repeating Carbine $590**
Same general specifications as the Model 1889 Rifle, except had a 20-inch barrel and carbine-type stock.

**Marlin Model 1889 Lever-Action
Repeating Rifle. $525**
Solid frame. Calibers: 25-20, 32-30, 38-40 and 44-40. Barrels: 24 inches; round, octagonal, or half-octagonal most common. Plain or checkered American walnut stock and forend. Made from 1889 to 1893.

**Marlin Model 1889 Lever-Action
Repeating Rifle (Fancy) $1295**
Same general specifications as Model 1889 Rifle, except had extra-fancy walnut stock and forend.

Marlin Model 1891 Repeating Rifle. . . . $525
Solid frame. Calibers: 22RF, 32 RF Long. 18-shot tubular magazine with long rifle cartridges. Barrels: 24, 25 and 26 inches average, but could be furnished in lengths of up to 32 inches; round or octagonal. Weight: 6 to 6½ pounds. American walnut stock and forend with either straight or pistol grip. Rifle-type buttplate. Made from 1891 to 1892.

**Marlin Model 1891 Fancy Repeating
Rifle. $1595**
Same general specifications as standard Model 1891 Rifle, except furnished with fancy grade walnut checkered stock and forend.

**Marlin Model 1892 Lever-Action
Repeating Rifle $530**
Calibers: 22 Short, Long, Long Rifle; 32 Short, Long (rimfire or centerfire by changing firing pin). Tubular magazines holding: 25 Short, 20 Long, 18 Long Rifle (22); 17 Short, 14 Long (32). 16-inch barrel model has shorter magazine holding 15 Short, 12 Long, 10 Long Rifle. Barrel lengths: 16 (22 cal. only), 24, 26, 28 inches; round or octagonal. Weight: 5½ pounds with 24-inch barrel. Open rear sight, blade front sight. Plain straight-grip stock and forearm. Made from 1892 to 1916.

**Marlin Model 1893 Lever-Action
Repeating Rifle $625**
Solid frame or takedown. Calibers: 25-36 Marlin, 30-30, 32 Special, 32-40, 38-55. Tubular magazine holds 10 cartridges. Barrels: 26 inches, round or octagonal standard; also made in 28-, 30- and 32-inch lengths. Weight: 7¼ pounds. Open rear sight, bead front sight. Plain straight-grip stock and forearm. Made from 1893 to 1936.

Marlin Model 93 Carbine $995
Same as Standard Model 1893 Rifle, except made in calibers 30-30 and 32 Special only. Seven-shot magazine. Barrel: 20 inches, round. Weight: 6¾ pounds. Carbine sights.

Marlin Model 1893 Rifle

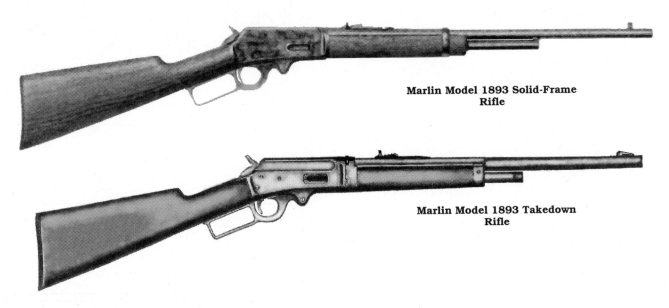

Marlin Model 1893 Solid-Frame
Rifle

Marlin Model 1893 Takedown
Rifle

Marlin Model 93 Musket **$1895**
Same as standard Model 1893 Rifle, except has
30-inch barrel, angular bayonet, ramrod under barrel, musket stock, full-length military-style forearm.
Weight: 8 pounds. Made from 1893 to 1915.

Marlin Model 93SC Sporting Carbine . . **$1250**
Same as Model 93 Carbine, except has two-thirds
magazine that holds five shots. Weight: 6½ pounds.

**Marlin Model 1894 Lever-Action
Repeating Rifle** **$900**
Solid frame or takedown. Calibers: 25-20, 32-20, 38-40,
44-40. Ten-shot tubular magazine. Barrel: 24 inches,
round or octagonal. Weight: 7 pounds. Open rear sight,
bead front sight. Plain straight-grip stock and forearm (also
available with pistol-grip stock). Made from 1894 to 1934.

**Marlin Model 1894 Lever-Action
Repeating Rifle—Fancy Grade** **$2000**
Same general specifications as standard rifle except
high-grade walnut stock, often with elaborate checkering and carving and various grades of metal engraving, silver and gold inlays, and other ornamentation.
Such custom work was readily available before 1900,
and the service continued on a limited basis until
World War II. *See* illustrations on the following two
pages.

Disassembled Marlin Model 1893 Takedown Rifle

Marlin Model 1894 Baby Carbine **$995**
Same general specifications as standard rifle except
furnished with 20-inch round barrel, half-magazine
with 6-shot capacity. Weight: 5½ pounds. Plain walnut carbine buttstock and forend.

Marlin Model 1894 Musket. **$1800**
Same general specifications as standard rifle except
furnished with 30-inch round barrel and 15-shot
magazine. Weight: 7 pounds.

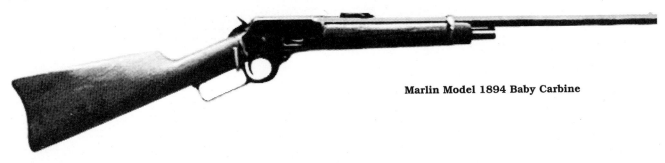

Marlin Model 1894 Baby Carbine

EARLY FORMS OF MARLIN DECORATION

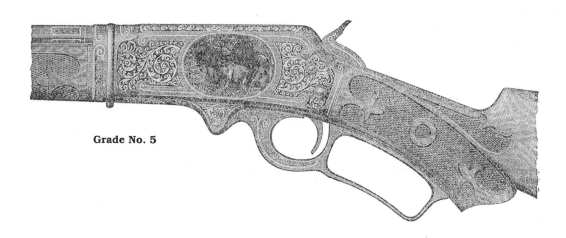

Grade No. 5

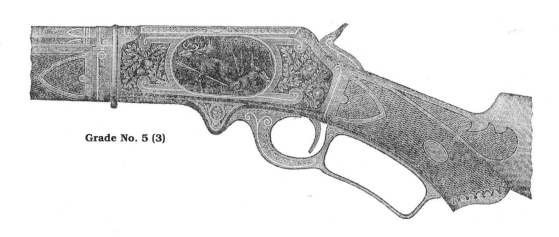

Grade No. 5 (3)

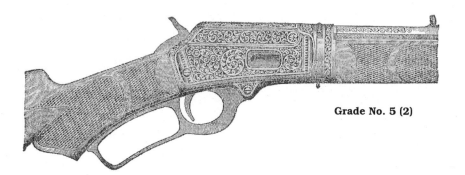

Grade No. 5 (2)

EARLY FORMS OF MARLIN DECORATION

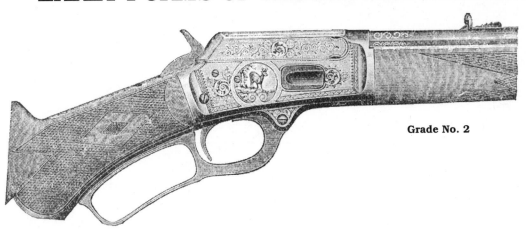

Grade No. 2

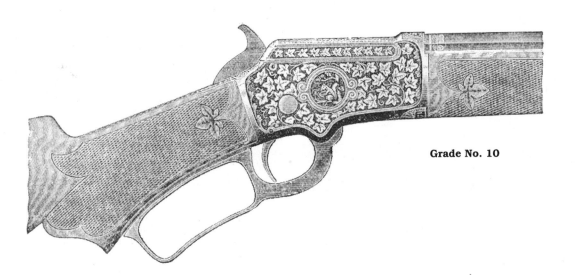

Grade No. 10

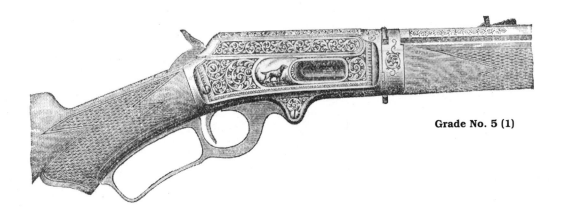

Grade No. 5 (1)

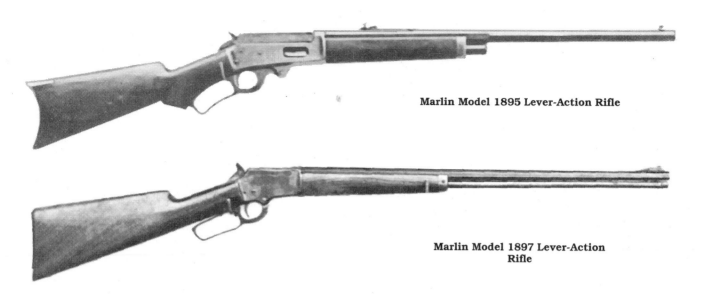

Marlin Model 1895 Lever-Action Rifle

Marlin Model 1897 Lever-Action
Rifle

**Marlin Model 1895 Lever-Action
Repeating Rifle.** **$995**
Solid frame or takedown. Calibers: 33 WCF, 38-56,
40-65, 40-70, 40-82 and 45-70. Nine-shot tubular
magazine. Barrel: 24 inches, round or octagonal
standard (other lengths available). Weight: 8 pounds.
Open rear sight, bead front sight. Plain stock and
forearm (also available with pistol-grip stock). Made
from 1895 to 1915.

Marlin Model 1895 Carbine. **$1200**
Calibers: 38-56, 40-65, 49-70, 40-82 and 45-70; 33
WCF was added later. Barrel: 15 and 22 inches.
Weight: approximately 7½ pounds. Plain walnut
carbine stock and forend. Full-length magazine with
an extra magazine-retaining band in front of the post
front sight. Most were equipped with a saddle ring on
the left side of the receiver.

Marlin Model 1895 Fancy-Grade Rifle. . **$2400**
Same general specifications as standard rifle except
high-grade walnut stock, often with elaborate checkering and carving and various grades of metal engraving, silver and gold inlays, and other ornamentation.
Such custom work was readily available before 1900,
and the service continued on a limited basis until
World War II. *See* illustrations on the preceding two
pages.

Marlin Model 1897 Lever-Action Rifle . . **$645**
Takedown. Caliber: 22 Long Rifle, Long, Short. Tubular
magazine; full length holds 25 Short, 20 Long, 18 Long
Rifle; half length holds 16 Short, 12 Long and 10 Long
Rifle. Barrel lengths: 16, 24, 26, 28 inches. Weight: 6
pounds. Open rear sight and bead front sight. Plain
straight-grip stock and forearm (also available with
pistol-grip stock). Made from 1897 to 1922.

**Marlin Model 1897 Lever-Action
Repeating Rifle** **$2650**
Same general specifications as standard rifle except
high-grade walnut stock, often with elaborate checkering and carving and various grades of metal engraving,
silver and gold inlays, and other ornamentation. Such
custom work was readily available before 1900, and the
service continued on a limited basis until World War II.
See illustrations on the preceding two pages.

MAUSER RIFLES
Various German Manufacturers

Mauser Model 1871 Rifle **$250**
Single-shot. Bolt-action. Caliber: 11mm. Barrel:
round. Had claw-type extractor on left side of bolt and
automatic cam cocking, which made it a self-cocking
arm, with safety centerfire action locked securely at
the rear. This model was an improvement over the
earlier needle-type rifle, and became very popular. It
was manufactured at various official German armories, as well as by Steyr in Austria; it was also sold to
many foreign countries.

Mauser Model 1871 Carbine. **$275**
Caliber: 11mm. Barrel: round, carbine length. Walnut stock. Made circa 1879. *See* Page 136.

Mauser-Mannlicher Model 1888 Rifle . . . **$165**
Bolt-action, straight handle. Caliber: 7.9mm, 5-shot
Mannlicher box magazine. Barrel: 29 inches, round,
step-tapered. Weight: 8½ pounds. Adjustable rear
sight; blade front sight. Rear sling swivel built into
stock. Made from 1888 to 1898. *See* Page 136.

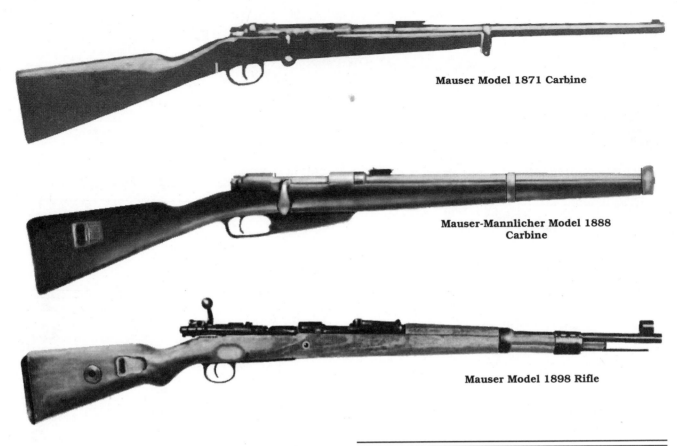

Mauser Model 1871 Carbine

Mauser-Mannlicher Model 1888
Carbine

Mauser Model 1898 Rifle

Mauser-Mannlicher Model 1888 Carbine . . $195
Same general specifications as the Model 1888 rifle
except has 18-inch round barrel, flat turned-down
bolt handle, and weighs about 6¾ pounds.

Mauser Model 1898 . . . . $245
Bolt-action, straight handle. Caliber: 7.9mm Mauser,
5-shot magazine. Barrel: 29 inches, stepped round.
Weight: 9 pounds. Adjustable rear sight; blade front
sight. Military-type full stock with semi-pistol grip.
Introduced in 1898.

MERRIMACK ARMS MFG. COMPANY
Newburyport, Massachusetts

The Merrimack Arms Mfg. Company operated in the
mid- to late 1860s, producing Ballard rifles (*see*
separate listing) as well as its own arms. At the end
of the decade, it became the Brown Mfg. Co.

Merrimack Double Barrel Rifle $1810
Calibers: various. Side-by-side. Barrel: octagonal.

MEXICAN MILITARY RIFLES
Various Manufacturers

The rifles that follow were purchased or produced
for use by the Mexican Armed Forces during the 19th
century. Prior to the introduction of these cartridge
rifles, muzzleloaders of all types were used by Mexico.
Some of the newer rifles were made by Mexican
gunsmiths, but most were imported or confiscated
from other countries.

Mexican/Mauser Model 1895 Carbine . . $245
Same general specifications as Mauser 1895 Rifle,
except has 18¼-inch barrel, overall length of 37½
inches and weight of 7½ pounds.

Mexican/Mauser Model 1895 Rifle. $210
Bolt-action. Caliber: 7mm Mauser. Barrel: 29 inches,
round. Overall length: 48½ inches. Weight: 8¾
pounds. Staggered box magazine holds 5 rounds.
inverted "V" front sight; adjustable leaf rear. Besides
German markings, top of receiver stamped with eagle
and "REPUBLICA MEXICANA."

**Mexican/Remington Model 1897
7mm Rifle**

Mexican/Mondragon Model 1893 Rifle . . $425
Straight-pull, bolt-action. Caliber: 6.5mm Mondragon. Barrel: 29 inches. Overall length: 48 inches. Weight: 7½ pounds. Box magazine holds 8 rounds. Front inverted "V" sight; adjustable leaf rear. Top tang marked, "FAB. D'ARMES, NEUHAUSEN."

Mexican/Mondragon Model 1894 Rifle . . $440
Straight-pull, bolt-action. Caliber: 5.2×68mm. Barrels: 21¾ to 34½ inches. Fixed box magazine holds 8 rounds. Inverted "V" front sight; various types of rear sights. Markings same as Model 1893 Mondragon Rifle.

**Mexican/Pieper-Nagant Model 1893
Carbine. $1800**
Revolving nine-shot cylinder. Single- and double-action. Caliber: 8mm Nagant. Barrel: 19¾ inches. Overall length: 36 inches. Weight: 6½ pounds. Plain straight-grip stock. Barleycorn front sight; adjustable leaf rear. Top of receiver marked "EJERCITO MEXICANO." Top tang marked "H. PIEPER Bte LIÈGE." Left-side plate marked "EJERCITO MEXICANO."

**Mexican/Remington Model 1871
Carbine. $725**
Same general specifications as the Remington Model 1871 Rifle, except for 20½-inch barrel, overall length of 36 inches and weight of 6¾ pounds. Also carried saddle ring on left side of receiver.

Mexican/Remington Model 1871 Rifle . . $700
Single-shot, rolling block. Caliber: 11mm Spanish. Barrel: 35 inches. Overall length: 50½ inches. Weight: 8½ pounds. Barleycorn front sight; adjustable leaf rear sight. Plain walnut stock. Top of barrel marked at breech "R. DE MEXICO" or "RM" with issue number on breech top.

**Mexican/Remington Model 1897
Carbine. $425**
Same general specifications as Remington 1897 Rifle, except has 20½-inch barrel and weighs 6¾ pounds.

Mexican/Remington Model 1897 Rifle . . $395
Single-shot, rolling block. Caliber: 7mm Mauser. Barrel: 30 inches, round. Overall length: 45½ inches. Weight 8½ pounds. Inverted "V" front sight; adjustable leaf rear. Top of receiver stamped "REPUBLICA MEXICANA."

Mexican/Spencer Model 1865 Carbine . . $995
Manually operated lever action. Caliber: 50-50. Barrel: 20 inches. Overall length: 37 inches. Weight: 8¼ pounds. Tubular magazine in buttstock holds 7 rounds. Inverted "V" front sight; adjustable leaf rear. Color casehardened receiver; balance of metal parts blued. Purchased as U.S. surplus and given Mexican ownership marks, including the letters "R.M."

Mexican/Whitney Rolling Block Carbine . . $695
Same general specifications as the Whitney Rolling Block Rifle, except has 20½-inch barrel, overall length of 36 inches and weighs about 7 pounds. Saddle ring on left side of receiver.

Mexican/Whitney Rolling Block Rifle . . . $560
Single-shot, rolling block. Caliber: 11mm Spanish. Barrel: 35 inches. Overall length: 50½ inches. Weight 9½ pounds. Barleycorn front sight; adjustable leaf rear. Serial number on lower tang; "RM" marked on top, right side of receiver.

Mexican/Winchester Model 1866 Rifle . . $6300
Manually operated lever-action. Caliber: 44 RF. Barrel: 24 inches. Overall length: 43½ inches. Weight: 9½ pounds. Tubular magazine beneath barrel holds 17 rounds. Blade front sight, adjustable leaf rear sight. Very small eagle stamped on these rifles. Serial numbers, found on tang beneath lever, should be under 20,000. Top of notch barrel marked: "HENRY'S PATENT – OCT. 16, 1860, KING'S PATENT - MARCH 29, 1866." One thousand of these rifles ordered and purchased from Winchester in late 1866.

**Mexican/Winchester Model 1894
Carbine $595**
Manually operated lever-action. Caliber: 30 WCF (30-30). Barrel: 20 inches, round. Overall length: 38 inches. Weight: 6½ pounds. Tubular magazine beneath barrel holds 6 rounds. Blade front sight; three-leaf rear sight.

Mexican Model Peabody Rifle $1625
Single-shot. Falling-block action, lever actuated. Caliber: 11mm Spanish. Barrel: 33 inches. Overall length: 52 inches. Weight: 9¾ pounds. Front inverted "V" sight; adjustable leaf rear sight. The Mexican government purchased 8,500 of these rifles between 1870 and 1872 for testing, but they were not adopted by the Mexican authorities.

**Needham Model 1861 Percussion
Rifle Rimfire Conversion**

JOSEPH NEEDHAM
London, England

Needham Model 1861 Percussion Rifle . . $450
Caliber: 58. Barrel: round. Lock stamped "BRIDES-BURG 1864." This is commonly called the Finian's Rifle as it was the rifle used by them in their attacks on Canada in 1866 and 1870.

NEW HAVEN ARMS COMPANY
New Haven, Connecticut

On April 25, 1857, the New Haven Arms Company was formally organized to take over and continue the business of the defunct Volcanic Repeating Arms Company. The New Haven Arms Company occupied the former Volcanic plant in New Haven and continued the manufacturer of the Volcanic type of firearm, both in the pistol and rifle form. The firearms were still listed as Volcanic, but were now marked NEW HAVEN CONN. PATENT FEB. 14, 1854. In 1859, the plant was moved to a new location at No. 9 Artizan Street in New Haven.

Volcanic Lever-Action Rifle $7500
Caliber: .38 RF, multi-shot magazine (the number of cartridges depended on barrel length) that ran the full length of the barrel. Barrel: 16, 20, and 24 inches. Walnut stock with crescent buttplate. No forend. Blade front sight. Made from 1858 to 1860.

NICHOLS & CHILDS
Conway, Massachusetts

**Nichols & Childs Percussion Revolving
Rifle. $7500**
Calibers: 36 and 51, six-shot cylinder. Barrel: 22 to 32 inches, round or half-octagonal. Color-casehardened frame; barrel browned. Walnut buttstock with brass or German silver patchbox, resembling those found on Kentucky flintlocks; no forearm. Made 1838 to 1839.

NORTH & SKINNER
Middletown, Connecticut

North & Skinner Revolving Rifle $3995
Calibers: 41, 44 and 45, six-shot cylinder. Barrel: approximately 24 inches, half-octagonal. Blued metal parts. Walnut buttstock; no forearm. Crescent-shaped metal buttplate. Made 1854 to 1859.

PERRY W. PORTER
New York, New York

Porter Revolving Turret Rifle $3995
Caliber: 44, 8-shot magazine. Barrel: 26 to 28 inches, round. Casehardened frame; blued barrel. Walnut stock with no forearm. Made from 1851 to 1855.

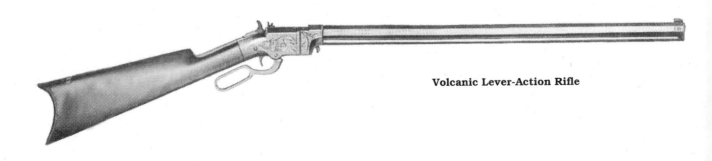

Volcanic Lever-Action Rifle

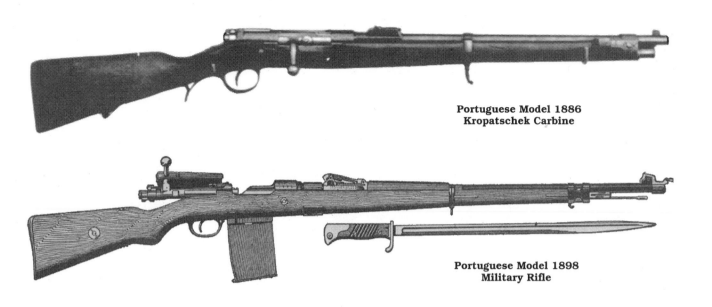

**Portuguese Model 1886
Kropatschek Carbine**

**Portuguese Model 1898
Military Rifle**

PORTUGUESE MILITARY
Various Manufacturers

**Portuguese Model 1886 Kropatschek
Carbine $100**
Caliber: 8mm. Barrel: round; shorter carbine length.
Iron furniture. Full stock, straight grip.

Portuguese Model 1898 Military Rifle . . $245
Bolt-action, straight handle. Caliber: 7.9mm Mauser,
5-shot magazine. Barrel: 29 inches, stepped round.
Weight: 9 pounds. Adjustable rear sight; blade front
sight. Military-type full stock with semi-pistol grip.
Portuguese contract crest on top of receiver. Introduced in 1898.

PRUSSIAN LONG ARMS
Various Manufacturers

Prussian Model 1839 Military Musket . . $300
Converted from the Model 1809 flintlock. Round
barrel with full-length musket stock. Brass furniture.

Prussian Flintlock Sporting Musket $500
Caliber: 72. Barrel: part octagonal; "F" stamped on
barrel ahead of touch hole. Brass furniture. Made
circa 1740.

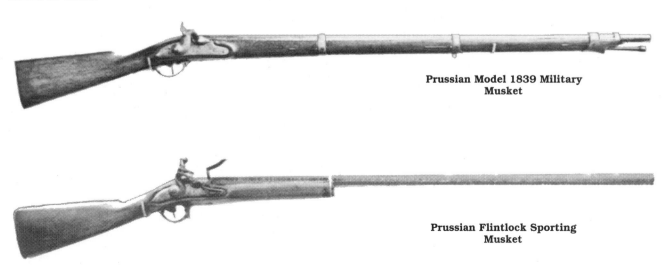

**Prussian Model 1839 Military
Musket**

**Prussian Flintlock Sporting
Musket**

Randall Percussion Rifle

JOSEPH C. RANDALL
Philadelphia, Pennsylvania

Randall Percussion Rifle **$475**
Caliber: 45. Barrel: octagonal. Pewter nose cap; silver propeller-style inlay on barrel. Double-set triggers. American walnut stock with brass and copper furniture. Made circa 1860.

REMINGTON ARMS CO.
Ilion, New York

Eliphalet Remington Jr. made his first rifle in 1816 as a young man. With his father, he produced custom rifles and gun parts at Ilion Gorge, N.Y. In 1828 they moved to a larger facility in Ilion, N.Y., to accommodate their growing business, only to be met with tragedy in the death of Eliphalet Sr. Undaunted, the son continued to expand the manufacturing operation and by 1844 he was able to take his son, Philo, into the business, changing the name to E. Remington & Son. Many U.S. Government contracts for rifles, carbines and eventually handguns were awarded to the Remingtons, so that by 1856 the volume of business was great enough for Remington to take his other two sons into the business. The partnership formed, "E. Remington & Sons" continued from 1856 to 1865, when a corporation was formed. For more than twenty years the corporation successfully produced a variety of popular guns, until 1886 when it suffered severe losses, and failed. Two years later, Hartley and Graham, partners and founders of the Union Metallic Cartridge Co. of Bridgeport, Conn., purchased controlling interest in what became the Remington Arms Company. Other investors entered into the picture from time to time, but the firm is still in operation under the same name and is now a subsidiary of the du Pont Corporation.

See also Handguns and Shotguns for additional Remington arms.

Remington No. 1 Military Rifle **$425**
Large size rolling-block action. Casehardened. Calibers: 43 (11mm), 50, 58 centerfire. With or without bayonets. Made for foreign countries from about the 1870s to 1900.

Remington No. 1 Sporting Rifle **$395**
Rolling-block, casehardened action. Calibers: 22 RF, 32 RF, 38 RF, 44 RF, 46 RF; 32-20, 32-40, 38-40 Rem., 40-45, 40-50, 40-70, 40-70 straight, 44 S&W, 44-40, 44-77 Sharps, 45-70, 50-70, 58 Govt. and others. Barrel: 20 inches round; 26 inches in round, octagonal or half-octagonal; or 30 inches octagonal. Weight: from 6½ to 15 pounds. Open sights standard. American walnut stock and forend. Made from 1869 to 1889.

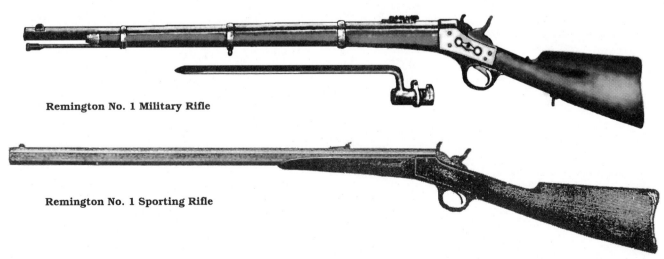

Remington No. 1 Military Rifle

Remington No. 1 Sporting Rifle

Remington No. 2 Sporting Rifle

Remington No. 1½ Sporting Rifle **$495**
Calibers: 22 Short, Long, or Extra-Long RF; 25 Stevens, 25 Long, 32 and 38 Long and Extra-Long centerfire; 32-20, 38-40, and 44-40 Winchester. Barrel: 24, 26, 28, and 30 inches; octagonal, blued. Single-shot, rolling-block, casehardened action. Sporting rear sight; bead or blade, front. Walnut stock and forearm. Made from 1869 to 1902.

Remington No. 2 Sporting Rifle
Single-shot, rolling-block action. Calibers: 22, 25, 32, 38, 44 rimfire or centerfire. Barrel: 24, 26, 28 or 30 inches. Weight: 5½ to 8 pounds. Open rear sight, bead front sight. Straight-grip sporting stock and knob-tip forearm of walnut. Made from 1873 to 1910.
Calibers 22 through 32. . . . . **$395**
Calibers 38 through 44. 495

Remington No. 3 Creedmoor and Schuetzen Rifles . . . . **$5000+**
Produced in a variety of styles and calibers, these are collectors' items and bring far higher prices than the sporting types. The Schuetzen Special, which has an under-lever action, is especially rare — perhaps less than 100 having been made.

Remington No. 3 High Power Rifle
Single-shot. Hepburn falling-block action with side lever. Calibers: 30-30, 30-40, 32 Special, 32-40, 38-55, 38-72 (high-power cartridges). Barrel: 26, 28

or 30 inches. Weight: 8 pounds. Open sporting sights. Checkered pistol-grip stock and forearm. Made from 1893 to 1907.
Calibers 30-30, 30-40, 32 Special, 32-40 . . **$1025**
Calibers 38-55, 38-72. 1150

Remington No. 3 Sporting Rifle **$975**
Single-shot. Hepburn falling-block action with side lever. Calibers: 22 WCF, 22 Extra Long, 25-20 Stevens, 25-21 Stevens, 25-25 Stevens, 32 WCF, 32-40 Ballard & Marlin, 32-40 Remington, 38 WCF, 38-40 Remington, 38-50 Remington, 38-55 Ballard & Marlin, 40-60 Ballard & Marlin, 40-60 WCF, 40-65 Remington Straight, 40-82 WCF, 45-70 Govt., 45-90 WCF; also supplied on special order in bottle-necked 40-50, 40-70, 40-90, 44-77, 44-90, 44-105, 50-70 Govt., and 50-90 Sharps Straight. Barrel: 26 inches (22, 25, 32 cal. only); 28, 30 inches; half-octagonal or full octagonal. Weight: 8 to 10 pounds, depending upon barrel length and caliber. Open rear sight, blade front sight. Checkered pistol grip stock and forearm. Made from 1880 to 1911.

Remington No. 4 Single-Shot Rifle **$295**
Rolling-block action. Solid frame or takedown. Calibers: 22 Short and Long, 22 Long Rifle, 25 Stevens RF, 32 Short and Long RF. Barrel: 22½ inches; 24 inches (32 cal. only); octagonal. Weight: 4½ pounds. Open rear sight, blade front sight. Plain walnut stock and forearm. Made from 1890 to 1933. *See* next page.

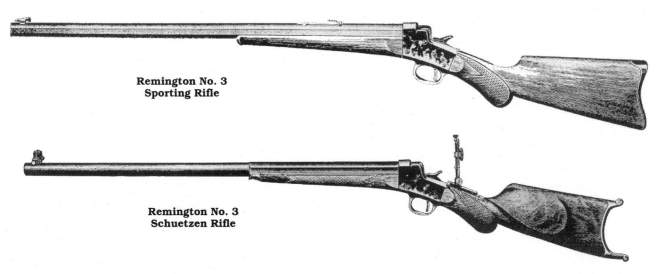

**Remington No. 3
Sporting Rifle**

**Remington No. 3
Schuetzen Rifle**

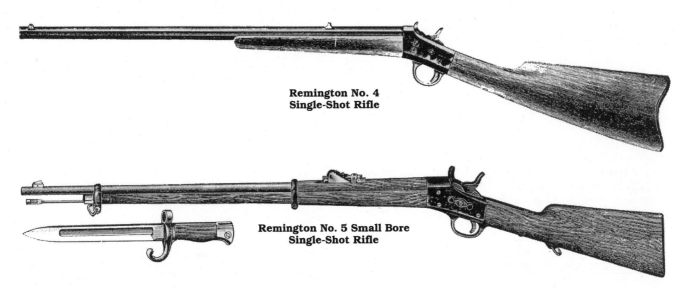

Remington No. 4
Single-Shot Rifle

Remington No. 5 Small Bore
Single-Shot Rifle

Remington No. 5 Small-Bore Rifle $495
Calibers: 7mm and 30-40 Muskets, 7mm, 30-30 and 30-40 Krag, rifles. Barrels: Lengths ranged from 20 to 30 inches depending on caliber; blued, tapered round. Weight: 8½ pounds for musket; 7¼ pounds for rifle.Blade front sight; sporting Rocky Mountain, rear on rifles. Post front sight; Military long-range, folding leaf, rear on muskets. Made from 1896 to 1906.

Remington Breechloading Carbine . . . $1425
Short, single-shot, split-breech on 56 cal. arms; longer-length, single-shot, split breech action on later 46 cal. arms. Calibers: 56-50 and 56-52 RF Spencer and 44 Gov't RF (46 Long). Barrel: 20 inches, round on 56 cal. and 20 or 22 inches on 46 cal. Weight: 6½ pounds. Pointed-blade front sight; folding-leaf, rear. Walnut straight-grip stock and forearm. Steel buttplate. Made from 1865 to 1866.

Remington Converted 1863 Musket . . $1410
Single-shot, rolling-block action. Caliber: 58 centerfire. Barrel: 39 inches, round. Weight 9 pounds. Walnut stock and forearm. Steel, carbine buttplate. Made in 1868.

Remington Converted Carbine $850
Same general specifications as previous model except has 24-inch barrel.

Remington Converted Short Rifle $795
Same general specifications as previous model except comes in 58 Roberts and has 36-inch barrel. Converted from 1863 Springfield. Made in 1868.

Remington "Creedmoor" Target Rifle. . . $825
Calibers: 44-90, 44-100, and 44-105. Barrel: 34 inches, octagonal or half-octagonal. Globe front sight; long-range Vernier peep, rear. Checkered pistol-grip walnut stock. Walnut forearm with iron cap. Steel buttplate. Made from 1873 to 1890.

Close-up of Remington Creedmoor receiver with Vernier tang sight

Remington Creedmoor Target Rifle

Remington Flintlock Rifle

Remington Danish Military Rifle $550
Single-shot, rolling-block action. Caliber: Danish 45 RF; 45 centerfire later models. Barrel: 35 inches, round; 20-inches on carbines. Weight: 9¾ pounds. Pointed-top, post front sight; military, folding leaf, rear. Walnut stock and forearm. Flanged steel carbine buttplate. Made from 1867 to 1868.

Remington Flintlock Rifle $3000
Revolutionary War style side-hammer flintlock. Calibers: 36 to 54. Barrel: 42 inches, octagonal. One-piece walnut stock and forearm; crescent iron buttplate. Blade front sight; V-notched fixed rear sight. Double-set triggers. Marked "REMINGTONS" on bottom of barrel. Made from 1816 to 1832.

Remington Jenks Carbine Conversion . . $1400
Caliber: 54. Barrel: 25 inches; converted to paper cartridge from original percussion muzzleloader. Weight: 7 pounds. Carbine front sight, folding-leaf, rear. One-piece walnut stock. Brass buttplate and patchbox. Made in 1858.

Remington Light Baby Carbine $425
Single-shot. Rolling-block action. Caliber: 44 Winchester. Barrel: 20 inches. Weight: 5¾ pounds. Open rear sight, blade front sight. Plain straight-grip carbine-stock and forearm, barrel band. Made from 1883 to 1910.

Remington Model 1877 "New York State" Rifle $710
Same general specifications as the Model 1872 "New York State" Rifle except 45-70 caliber. Made in 1877.

Remington Model 1879 Argentine Musket. . $575
Caliber: 43 Spanish. Barrel: 36 inches (20 inches for carbine), round with 2¼ inch octagon top, at breech. Weight: 9¼ pounds. Pointed-post front sights; military folding-leaf, rear. Markings include E. REMINGTON & SONS, ILION, N.Y. U.S.A PAT. MAY 3D 1864 MAY 7th June 11th NOV 12th DEC 24th 1872 on upper tang and "Modelo Argentino 1879 E.N." on octagon. Made from 1879 to 1888.

Remington "New York State" Carbine . . $695
Same general specifications as the "New York State" Rifle, except has a 22-inch carbine barrel and carbine buttplate. Made in 1872.

Remington "New York State" Rifle $600
Caliber: 50-70 centerfire. Barrel: 36 inches; round, blued. Special locking high hammer. Made in 1872.

Remington Percussion Rifle $2000
Calibers: 36 to 54 percussion. Barrel: 42 inches, octagonal. One-piece plain walnut stock without patchbox; crescent iron buttplate with upper flange. Double, adjustable set trigger. Made 1830 to 1842.

Remington Revolving Rifle $2500
Caliber: 36 percussion and 38 Long RF. Barrel: 24, 26, 28, and 30 inches; octagonal or half-octagonal. 6-shot cylinder. Plain sights on early models, folding-leaf rear on later models. Walnut stock with perch belly-bottom. Crescent-shaped buttplate with flange at top. Made from 1866 to 1880.

Remington Revolving Rifle

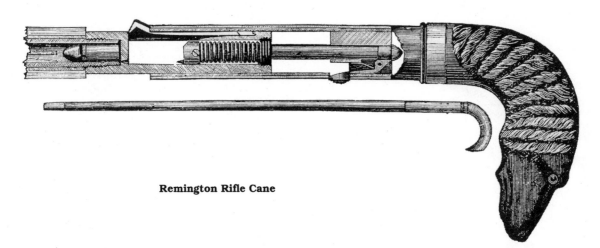

Remington Rifle Cane

Remington Single-Shot Rifle Cane . . . $3000
Caliber: 22 or 32 RF Long. Barrel: 26 inches with integral chamber which was the lower part of the cane. Metal-capped muzzle. Dull stained walnut, or varnished finish. Cane-head contained the trigger and action. Could be used as a walking stick and came with carved dogs' head handle; or rounded, wooden-handle. Remington's first cartridge-firing "long gun." Made from 1858 to 1900.

Remington "Split Breech" Carbine . . . $1195
Two-part breech system. Color-casehardened receiver. Calibers: 46 Long RF, 56-50 RF, 56-52 RF. Barrel: 20 inches, blued. Weight: about 7½ pounds. Plain carbine stock. Made from 1865 to 1867.

Remington Springfield Model Rifle $575
Casehardened rolling-block action. Caliber: 58 centerfire. Barrel: 36 inches; round, blued. Weight: about 8½ pounds. Straight-grip military walnut stock and forend. Made from 1863 to 1883.

Remington State of Masschusetts Musket $2300
Same general specifications as the previous model except lockplate was marked "S.N. & W.C.P.S. for Massachusetts, 1864".

Remington Swedish Military Rifle $550
Same general specifications as the previous model. Made from 1868 to 1872.

Remington Swiss Military Rifle $550
Same general specifications as the Danish Military Rifle except 41 caliber RF and 35-inch barrel. Made from 1869 to 1871.

Remington U.S. Model 1841 Percussion Musket. $1875
Caliber: 54 percussion. Barrel: 33 inches, round. U.S. Springfield style stock with brass barrel bands and trigger guard. Made from 1847 to 1854.

Remington U.S. Model 1842 Converted Musket. $1650
Caliber: 69 flintlock converted to percussion-cap. Barrel: 42 inches. Weight: 9½ pounds. Overall length 58 inches. Front sight on front barrel-band; folding-leaf, rear. Marked "Remington's, Ilion, N.Y.," & 1857, U.S. at rear of hammer. Made from 1855 to 1857.

Remington U.S. Model 1862 "Zouave" Percussion Rifle. $2000
Caliber: 58 percussion-cap. Barrel: 33 inches, round, blued. Weight: 9½ pounds. Post front sight; folding-leaf, rear. Full walnut stock; brass barrel bands, buttplate and patchbox. Marked with Spread Eagle forward of hammer; Date, 1863, behind hammer, and "REMINGTON'S, ILION, N.Y." Made from 1863 to 1865.

Remington U.S. 1863 Musket. $2195
Caliber: 58 percussion-cap. Barrel: 40 inches, round. Weight: 9 pounds. Full walnut stock with iron fore-arm cap and buttplate. Three barrel bands, held by bottom-screws. No band springs. Post front sight; folding, two-leaf rear. This was thte service rifle-musket for the Union Army. Made from 1864 to 1866.

Remington U.S. 1863 Musket

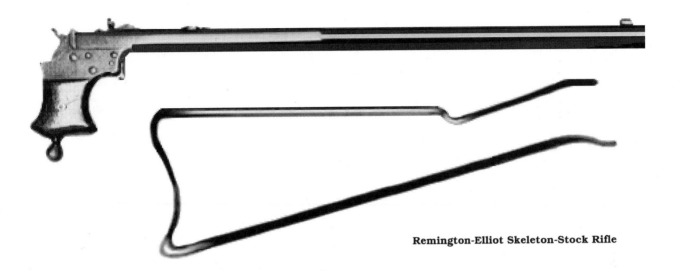

Remington-Elliot Skeleton-Stock Rifle

Remington U.S. Model 1870 Army Springfield Carbine. $1100

Similar to above rifle, except has 24-inch barrel. Made from 1870 to 1871.

Remington U.S. Model 1870 Navy Springfield Rifle $1100

Rolling-block action. Caliber: 50-70 centerfire. Barrel: 32½ inches, round. Bottom stud for Navy sabre bayonet. Springfield post, front sight; Navy musket, folding leaf, rear. Made from 1870 to 1871.

Remington Model 1871 Army Springfield Rifle $1100

Single-shot, rolling-block action. Caliber: 50-70 centerfire. Barrel: 36 inches; round, unblued. Weight: 9¼ pounds. Walnut stock and forearm. Pointed-post front sight; long-range, folding-leaf Springfield, rear. Made from 1871 to 1872.

Remington U.S. Navy Cadet Rifle $1400

Rolling-block action. Calibers: 50 Pistol Gov't and 45-70. Barrel: 32½ inches, round. Weight: 8 pounds. Musket sights. Made from 1868 to 1870.

Remington U.S. Navy Carbine $1500

Single-shot, rolling-block action. Caliber: 50-70 centerfire. Barrel: 23¼ inches, round. Weight: 7 pounds. Pointed top, post front sights; folding leaf, rear.Walnut stock. Steel buttplate. Made from 1867 to 1875.

Remington-Beals Rifle $450

Single-shot, lever-action. Calibers: 32 and 38 Long RF. Barrel: 24, 26, and 28 inches; part-octagon, blued. Weight: about 5½ pounds. Dovetail front sight; sporting, folding leaf, rear. Walnut straight-grip stock, flanged-top, crescent steel, buttlate. Some stocks were checkered, while others were plain. Made from 1866 to 1868.

Remington-Elliot Skeleton-Stock Rifle. $1850

Caliber: 22 RF. Barrel: 16 inches, part-octagonal. Barrel is on Vest-Pocket pistol frame which is modified for use with the detachable stock. The stock is a steel rod made in the shape of a rifle stock. Made circa 1877.

Remington-Keene Army or Navy Musket $495

Bolt-action. Calibers: 45-70 or 43 Spanish. Barrel: 32½-inch Army or 29¼-inch Navy; blued, round. Weight: 9 pounds. Walnut one-piece full stock. Made in 1880.

Remington-Keene Navy Musket

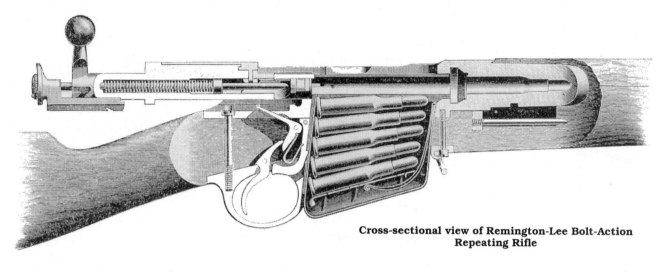

Cross-sectional view of Remington-Lee Bolt-Action Repeating Rifle

Remington-Lee Bolt-Action Sporting Rifle

Remington-Keene Magazine Gun **$525**
Calibers: 45-70 Govt, or 40-60 Marlin. Barrel: 22 inches for carbine and 24½ inches for rifle; blued. 9-shot magazine tube. Weight: approximately 8½ pounds. Post front sight; folding-leaf, V-notch military, rear. Walnut stock and forearm. Flanged, carbine, steel buttplate. Made from 1880 to 1888.

Remington-Lee Bolt-Action Sporting Rifle
Calibers: 6mm U.S.N., 30-30, 30-40, 7mm Mauser, 7.65 Mauser, 32 Rem., 32-40, 35 Rem., 38-55, 38-72, 405 Win., 43 Spanish, 44-77 Sharps, 45-70, 45-90. Detachable box magazine held 5 cartridges. Barrel: 24 or 26 inches. Weight: 7 pounds. Open rear sight, bead or blade front sight. Walnut stock with checkered pistol grip. Made from 1880 to 1906.
Standard Model **$600**
Deluxe Model **795**

RENWICH ARMS CO.
Newark, New Jersey

Renwich Single-Shot Percussion Rifle. . **$995**
Caliber: 54, Breechloading percussion. Barrel: 26 inches, half-octagonal. Plain walnut stock and forend. Lever-activated breech lock. Exposed hammer on right side of receiver. Less than 1500 rifles made between 1855 and 1862.

RUSSIAN MILITARY
Various Manufacturers

**Russian Model 1891 Mosin-Nagant
Bolt-Action Rifle** **$130**
Nagant-system bolt-action. Caliber: 7.62×54mm Russian. Five-shot box magazine. Barrel: 31½ inches, round. Weight: about 9 pounds. Open rear sight, blade front sight. Full stock with straight grip. Introduced 1891.

Russian Model 1891 Bolt-Action Rifle

SUCCESSFUL RIFLE MAGAZINES

Six basic types of magazines were successfully employed in military rifles and carbines during the last half of the 19th century and into the 20th.

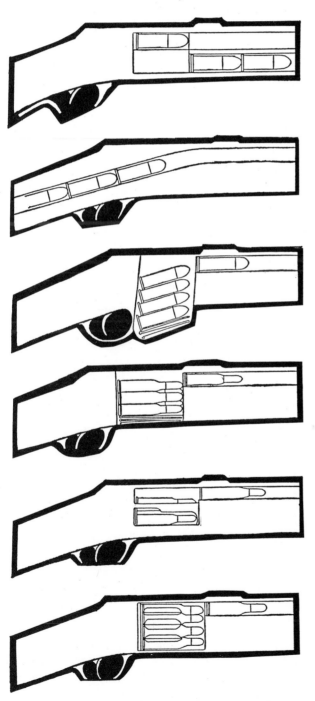

1. The first type of magazine was the invention of B. Tyler Henry, introduced in the United States with the famous lever-action Henry Rifle in 1860. In this rifle magazine, the cartridges are inserted in a tube underneath the barrel and fed into the chamber by a coiled spring. In addition to the Henry Rifle, it has been used in the Ball, U.S., 1863; the Swiss Vetterli, 1874; the French Kropatschek, 1878; the Lebel, 1886; and others.

2. The next magazine to be brought out was the Spencer type, with the feed tube in the buttstock. Christopher Spencer was the inventor in 1860. Other rifles that used this were the U.S. models Triplett and Scott, 1865; the Hotchkiss 1878 and 1883 models; the Chaffee-Reece, 1884; the Evans, 1885; the Austrian Mannlicher, 1880; and the Chinese Schulhof, 1884.

3. The third type was the invention of James P. Lee, dated 1879. This is the first of the centrally located magazines. Initially the cartridges were loaded one at a time, but later a clip was designed. Some famous guns have used this system, notably the Remington-Lee, U.S.N., 1880; the Italian Vetterli-Vitali, 1887; the Dutch Beaumont-Vitali, 1888; the Mannlicher, 1888; the Belgian Mauser, 1889; the Canadian Ross Mark III; the English Lee-Enfield, 1892–1921; the Winchester Model 1895; and the Lee Straight Pull, U.S.N., 1895; and others.

4. The fourth type is the famous Mauser design—the most successful of all rifle magazine systems. First introduced in the Spanish Model of 1893, this magazine is berthed entirely within the stock. It was also used in the U.S. Springfield 1903, and the Mausers dated 1895, 1896, 1898, 1899, 1902, 1903, 1904 and 1917.

5. The fifth system is the Krag-Jorgensen, invented by two Danish military officers. In this system, the cartridges are loaded singly and fed by a spring from the right side to the left, and then upwards into the chamber. It was introduced in the Danish Model of 1889, and used in Norway in 1894 and in the U.S. in 1892.

6. The last magazine type is the Schulhof, a product of Austria in 1888. This system revolves the cartridges on a ratchet wheel, and with a bolt, the top shell is forced into the chamber. Shells were loaded either by clip or singly in the Greek Mannlicher-Schoenauer; the U.S. Savage Mannlicher, 1887, 1888, and 1900; and the Blake Rifle, 1895.

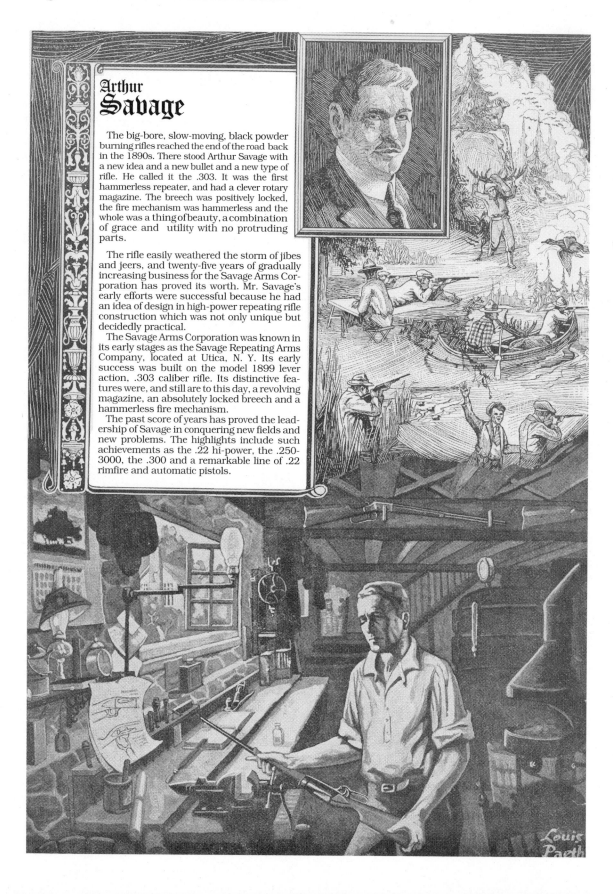

Arthur Savage

The big-bore, slow-moving, black powder burning rifles reached the end of the road back in the 1890s. There stood Arthur Savage with a new idea and a new bullet and a new type of rifle. He called it the .303. It was the first hammerless repeater, and had a clever rotary magazine. The breech was positively locked, the fire mechanism was hammerless and the whole was a thing of beauty, a combination of grace and utility with no protruding parts.

The rifle easily weathered the storm of jibes and jeers, and twenty-five years of gradually increasing business for the Savage Arms Corporation has proved its worth. Mr. Savage's early efforts were successful because he had an idea of design in high-power repeating rifle construction which was not only unique but decidedly practical.

The Savage Arms Corporation was known in its early stages as the Savage Repeating Arms Company, located at Utica, N. Y. Its early success was built on the model 1899 lever action, .303 caliber rifle. Its distinctive features were, and still are to this day, a revolving magazine, an absolutely locked breech and a hammerless fire mechanism.

The past score of years has proved the leadership of Savage in conquering new fields and new problems. The highlights include such achievements as the .22 hi-power, the .250-3000, the .300 and a remarkable line of .22 rimfire and automatic pistols.

SAVAGE REPEATING ARMS COMPANY
Utica, New York

Arthur W. Savage had experimented with a new type of lever-action rifle for military use before he incorporated his enterprise on April 5, 1894. Although the incorporation was contracted under the laws of West Virginia, the principal offices were located in Utica, N.Y. In December of 1897, the business was re-incorporated under the name of the "Savage Arms Company," under which Savage introduced and made famous the various Savage rifles, some of which are described below.

Savage's success lasted until about 1915, when the Driggs-Seabury Ordnance Co. of Sharon, Penn., bought the business. For a short time, the name was changed to the Driggs-Seabury Corporation, but in 1917 the firm became the Savage Arms Corporation, which is still in operation today in Westfield, Mass.

Savage Model 1892 Repeating Military Rifle $2595
Lever-action mechanism with rotary, 8-shot magazine. Caliber: 30-40 Krag. Barrel: 30 inches. Weight: 10 lbs. 4 oz. Made especially for military use, but was rejected by the U.S. Government in favor of the 30-40 Krag Rifle. Introduced in 1892.

Savage Model 1895 Carbine $1050
Same general specifications as the 1895 Sporting Rifle, except had a 22-inch barrel, forearm band and saddle ring. Made from 1895 to 1899 at the time of the Savage Model 1899 with an improved action of the same general design as the Model 1895.

Savage Model 1895 Repeating Military Rifle $1295
Same general specifications as the 1892 Repeating Military Rifle, except had a five-shot magazine and weighed 8¾ pounds. Made from 1895 to 1899.

Opposite Page: Savage advertisement appearing in an early issue of *Outdoor Life* magazine.

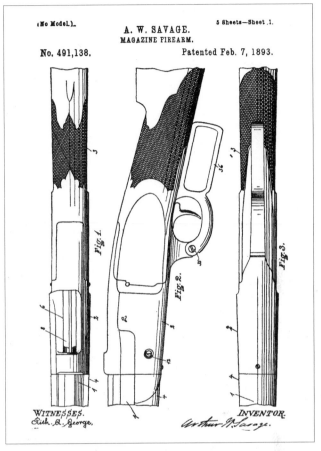

Patent drawing for Savage Model 1895 lever-action rifle. The original 8-shot magazine was later reduced to 5-shot, and the receiver was made thinner.

Savage Model 1895 Sporting Rifle $995
Caliber: 303 Savage. Five-shot rotary magazine. Barrels: 26 inches, round, half-octagonal or full-octagonal. Weight: 7 to 7¾ pounds. American walnut stock and forearm. Blade front sight, step-adjustable; open, sporting rear sight. Serial number inscribed under frame. Standard arms were manufactured in New Haven, Conn. by Marlin. Approximately 6,000 of these rifles were made between 1895 to 1899.

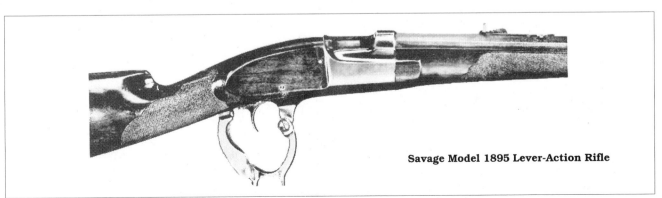

Savage Model 1895 Lever-Action Rifle

**Savage Model 1899 Sporting
Rifle (Takedown)**

**Savage Model 1899 Repeating Military
Carbine.** **$1725**
Same general specifications as the 1899 Military Rifle, except with shorter 22-inch barrel, lighter weight,
and carbine barrel band. Made from 1899 to 1908.

**Savage Model 1899 Repeating
Military Rifle** **$1150**
Same general specifications as Model 1899 Sporting
Rifle, except had a military stock, 30-inch barrel and
bayonet provisions. Made in calibers 303 Savage and
later in 30-30. Made from 1899 to 1908.

Savage Model 1899 Sporting Rifle **$495**
Hammerless solid frame or takedown. Rotary magazine. Calibers: 303 Savage, 25-35, 30-30, 32-40 and
38-55; later calibers included 22 Savage Hi-Power,
250-3000 Savage, and 300 Savage. Barrels: 22 to 26
inches; round, half-octagonal or full-octagonal.
Weight: $7\frac{3}{4}$ pounds average. American stock and
forearm with either crescent or shotgun buttplate;
also either straight or pistol grip. Made from 1899 to
date, with several variations and modifications.

OTTO SCHNEELOCK
Brooklyn, New York

Schneelock Sporting Target Rifle **$675**
Caliber: 44 percussion. Barrel: Medium-length, octagonal. American walnut stock with large cheekpiece. German silver fittings. Made 1868 to 1878.

SHARPS RIFLE COMPANY
Hartford, Connecticut

Christian Sharps founded the Sharps Rifle Manufacturing Company in Hartford, where it began operation in October 1851. After two years of problems
with "management," Sharps himself left the company
and formed another firm under his name in Philadelphia (see C. Sharps & Co. under Handguns). There
for a short time during the Civil War, he collaborated
with William Hankins, producing handguns as well
as rifles (see also Sharps & Hankins under Rifles).

The Sharps Rifle Mfg. Company in Hartford, however, continued to manufacture rifles without any
assistance or apparent contact with Christian
Sharps, and in 1874 it changed its name to simply
Sharps Rifle Company. In 1876 the operation was
transferred to Bridgeport, Conn., where it remained
until 1881, when it folded.

During the time of their manufacture, the Sharps
"Old Reliable" rifles were considered to be the strong-
est and most accurate of any available. They were
used extensively by buffalo hunters of the day for
distance shots and, as Civil War buffs know, they
were instrumental in winning the war.

Sharps 1851 Boxlock Hunting Rifle . . . **$1725**
Boxlock action. Calibers: 44 and 36. Barrel: 27 inches.
Overall length: $44\frac{1}{2}$ inches. Weight: $9\frac{3}{4}$ pounds. Some
barrels marked "Robbins & Lawrence, Windsor, Vt."
Before manufacturing was conducted in Hartford,
Sharps had arranged for Robbins & Lawrence to pro-
duce his early rifles. American walnut stock. Introduced
in 1851.

**Schneelock Sporting Target
Rifle**

Sharps 1852 Slanting Breech Carbine

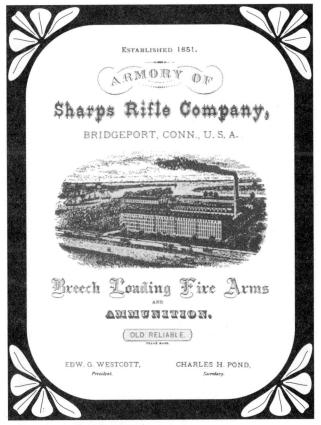

From the Sharps Catalog of 1877.

Sharps 1851 "Original" Model Breechloading Percussion Rifle $1800
Caliber; 52. Percussion, curved lockplate. Heavy barrel with ramrod beneath. American walnut stock. Introduced in 1851.

Sharps 1852 Slanting Breech Carbine . . $995
Caliber: 52 Linen. Barrel: 21½ inches. Overall length: 37¾ inches. Weight: 7¼ pounds. Barrel marked "Sharps Rifle Manufg. Co., Hartford, Conn." Tang and lockplate marked "C. Sharps, Pat. 1878." Introduced in 1852.

Sharps Model 1855 Slanting Breech Carbine $1695
Caliber: 52, with Maynard 1855 primer. Barrel: 21½ inches; six grooves. Overall length: 37¾ inches. Introduced in 1855.

Sharps Model 1859 Breechloading Percussion Carbine $895
Same general specifications as the 1859 Vertical Breech Percussion Carbine, except the patchbox was omitted and the barrel was marked, "New Model 1859." Introduced in 1859.

Sharps Model 1859 BL Percussion Military Rifle. $1600
Caliber: 52 Linen. Same general specifications as the Model 1859 Carbine, except this had a 30-inch barrel and an overall length of 47 inches. Weight: 9 pounds. This model was widely used by Berdan's Sharpshooters during the Civil War. Made from 1859 to 1862.

Sharps 1859 Vertical Breech Percussion Carbine $1050
Caliber: 52. Barrel: 22 inches, with flat brass barrel band. Overall length: 39 inches. Weight: 8 pounds. Rear sight marked "R.S. Lawrence, Patented February 15th, 1859." American walnut stock with brass buttplate and brass patchbox. A few stocks supplied for this model were equipped with a coffee mill built into the stock, which was used by military personnel to grind coffee beans in the field. Introduced in 1859.

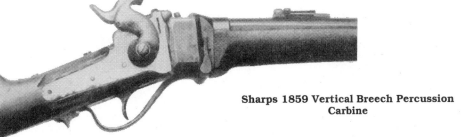

Sharps 1859 Vertical Breech Percussion Carbine

Sharps Model 1863 Percussion Carbine

Sharps Model 1863 BL Percussion Carbine. $895
Caliber: 52 Sharps Linen. Same general specifications as the Model 1859, except the barrel was marked, "New Model 1863." Serial numbers on the tang usually are preceded by the letter "C." Introduced in 1863.

Sharps Model 1863 BL Percussion Military Rifle $1625
Same general specifications as the Model 1863 Carbine, except made with full musket stock and rifle-length barrel.

Sharps Model 1867 Breechloading Carbine. $925
Caliber: 52 Sharps RF. This carbine was assembled from old percussion gun parts or with surplus parts on hand. Introduced in 1867.

Sharps Model 1868 Breechloading Sporting Rifle $2100
Calibers: 40-50, 40-70, 44-77 Sharps and 50-70 Government. Made from 1868 to 1871.

Sharps Model 1869 Breechloading Carbine. $795
Caliber: 50. Made from existing percussion carbines by replacing the breech block and relining the barrels. Introduced in 1869.

Sharps Model 1869 Breechloading Military Rifle $1195
Another alteration, chambered for the 50-70 Government centerfire cartridge. Introduced in 1869.

Sharps Model 1870 Breechloading Carbine $995
Same general specifications as the Model 1870 BL Rifle, except made in short carbine style. Chambered for the 50-70 Government cartridge.

Sharps Model 1870 Breechloading Military Rifle. $1125
Caliber: 50-70 Government. Barrel: 32½ inches. Another alteration of a percussion rifle, introduced in 1870.

Sharps Model 1873 Creedmoor Rifle . . $3000
Calibers: 44-90, 44-100, and 44-105 Sharps. Equipped with Vernier peep rear sight for 1000-yard shooting. Made from 1873 to 1874.

Sharps Model 1874 Business Rifle $2400
Caliber: 45-70 with 2$\frac{1}{10}$-inch case; 45-120 with 2$\frac{7}{8}$-inch case. Barrel: 28 inches; round; blued. Double-set trigger. Open sights. Plain wood straight stock and forend. Rifle butt. Made from 1877 to 1881.

Sharps 1874 Creedmoor Rifle #1 . . . . . $3000
Calibers: 44-77 with 2$\frac{1}{4}$-inch BN cases; 44-90 with 2$\frac{5}{8}$-inch BN case. Barrel: 32 inches; octagonal or half-octagonal; blued. Weight: just under 10 pounds. Sights: Vernier tang rear; wind-gauge front. Checkered pistol-grip stock and forend. Shotgun butt.

Sharps Model 1874 Creedmoor Rifle #2 . . . . $3000
Calibers: 44-77 with 2$\frac{1}{4}$ or 2$\frac{7}{16}$-inch BN cases; 44-90 with 2$\frac{5}{8}$-inch BN case. Barrel: 32 inches; octagonal or half-octagonal; blued. Weight: just under 10 pounds. Sights: Vernier tang rear; wind-gauge front. Straight polished stock and forend. Shotgun butt.

Sharps Model 1874 Creedmoor Rifle #1

Sharps 1874 Creedmoor Rifle #3 . . . . **$3000**
Calibers: 44-77 with $2\frac{1}{4}$-inch BN case; 44-90 with $2\frac{5}{8}$-inch BN case. Barrel: 30 inches; octagonal or half-octagonal; blued. Weight: just under 10 pounds. Sights: peep and open. Straight polished stock and forend. Shotgun butt.

Sharps 1874 Creedmoor Rifle #4 . . . . **$3500**
Same general specifications as the 1874 Creedmoor #3, except for a plainer wood rifle butt. Although the Model 1874 rifles were produced between about 1871 to 1881, this Creedmoor #4 was made only for a short time around 1875.

Sharps 1874 Military Rifle **$1695**
Caliber: 45-70 with $2\frac{1}{10}$-inch case. Barrel: 30 inches (rifle); 22 inches (carbine); round; blued. Plain straight stock and forend held by bands. Made from 1875 to 1877.

Sharps Model 1875 Rifle. **$20,000**
Only one is known to exist in an engraved version of Creedmoor pattern with extra fancy wood, and deluxe throughout. Hammer is operative like regular side hammer models.

Sharps Model 1876 BL Sporting Rifle . . **$2300**
Calibers: 40-50, 40-70, 44-77, 44-90, 50-90 Sharps and 50-70 Government. Barrel: 28 or 30 inches; octagonal. Weight: 8 to 12 pounds. Oil-finished American walnut stock. Introduced in 1876.

Sharps 1876 Long Range Rifle #1 . . . . **$2995**
Calibers: 44-90 ($2\frac{5}{8}$-inch case); 45-90 ($2\frac{4}{10}$-inch case); 45-100 ($2\frac{6}{10}$-inch case). Barrel: 34 inches standard; 32 inches rare; octagonal or half-octagonal; blued. Weight: just under 10 pounds. Sights: Vernier tang rare; spirit level wind-gauge front. Checkered pistol-grip stock and forend of extra fancy wood with sterling silver inscription plate. Made from 1876 to 1881.

Sharps 1876 Long Range Rifle #2 . . . . **$2750**
Same general specifications as the Long Range #1 Rifle, except has plainer wood without inscription plate and wind-gauge front sight is without spirit level. Made from 1876 to 1881.

Sharps 1876 Long Range Rifle #3 . . . . **$2850**
Same general specifications as Long Range #2 Rifle, except has straight, checkered stock and forend. Made from 1876 to 1881.

Sharps 1876 Mid-Range Rifle #1 . . . . . **$1995**
Caliber: 40-70 with $2\frac{1}{2}$-inch case. Barrel: 30 inches; octagonal or half-octagonal; blued. Weight: 9 pounds. Sights: Vernier tang rear; wind-gauge spirit level front. Nickel-plated rifle butt. Checkered pistol grip stock and forend. Made from 1876 to 1879.

Sharps 1876 Mid-Range Rifle #2 . . . . . **$1750**
Same general specifications as Mid-Range Rifle #1, except has plain wood straight stock and forend. Made from 1876 to 1879.

Sharps 1876 Mid-Range Rifle #3 . . . . . **$1900**
Same general specifications as Mid-Range Rifle #2, except in caliber 40-50 with $1\frac{7}{8}$-inch case; peep and globe sights. Made from 1876 to 1879.

Sharps Model 1877 Rifle **$2750**
Side hammer, fourth lock form. With the exception of the lock, these rifles were offered in three grades identical to the Long Range rifles introduced in 1876.

Sharps Model 1878 Business Rifle **$1295**
Caliber: 40-70 with $2\frac{1}{2}$-inch case; 40-90 with $2\frac{5}{8}$-inch BN case. Barrel: 28 inches; octagonal; blued. Open sights. Plain polished American walnut stock and forend. Made from 1879 to 1881.

Sharps Model 1878 Hunter's Rifle **$1495**
Caliber: 40-50 with $1\frac{7}{8}$-inch case; 40-70 with $2\frac{1}{2}$-inch case. Barrel: 26 inches; round; blued. Open sights. Plain polished American walnut stock and forend. Made from 1879 to 1881.

Sharps Model 1878 Express Rifle **$2895**
Caliber: 45-120 with $2\frac{7}{8}$-inch case, 293 gr. bullet. Barrel: 26 inches; octagonal; flat-matte top. Borchardt action. Weight: about $9\frac{1}{2}$ pounds. Sights: two-leaf rear with platinum lines; long beaded front. Sling staples. Fancy American walnut checkered pistol-grip stock and forend. Hard rubber shotgun butt. Made from 1879 to 1881.

Sharps Model 1878 Long-Range Rifle **$2650**
Caliber: 45-90 with $2\frac{4}{10}$-inch case. Barrel: 32 or 34 inches; round; blued finish. English walnut checkered pistol-grip stock and forend. Hard rubber shotgun butt. Sights: Vernier rear sight; wind-gauge spirit level front. Hard rubber or wood paneled receiver. Made from 1878 to 1881.

Sharps Model 1878 Mid-Range Rifle **$2300**
Caliber: 40-50 with $1\frac{7}{8}$-inch case; 40-70 with $2\frac{1}{2}$-inch case. Barrel: 30 inches; round; blued. Weight: about 9 pounds. Sights: Vernier tang rear; wind-gauge spirit level front and open hunting sights. Checkered pistol-grip stock and forend. Shotgun butt. Made from 1878 to 1881.

Sharps Model 1878 Military Carbine . . **$1695**
Same general specifications as Model 1878 Military Rifle except 24-inch barrel and sling ring on left side of action. *See* next page.

**Sharps Model 1878 Sporting
Rifle with Double Triggers**

Sharps Model 1878 Military Rifle $1495
Caliber: 45-70 with $2\frac{1}{10}$-inch case. Barrel: 32 inches
(rifle); 24 inches (carbine); round; blued. Sling swivel on
under side of action ahead of lever. Sling ring on left side
of action on carbine. Plain ilitary straight stock and
forend. Made from 1878 to 1881.

Sharps Model 1878 Officer's Rifle. . . . $3100
Same length, weight, and caliber as the 1878 Military
Rifle. Medium fancy American walnut stock, closely
selected barrels. Receiver inlaid with hard rubber.

Sharps Model 1878 Short-Range Rifle . $3000
Caliber: 40-50 with $1\frac{7}{8}$-inch case; 40-70 with $2\frac{1}{2}$-
inch case. Borchardt action. Sights: short Vernier
grip rear; wind-gauge front. Plain American walnut
checkered pistol-grip stock and forend. Hard rubber
shotgun butt.

Sharps Model 1878 Sporting Rifle $1325
Caliber: 45-70 with $2\frac{1}{10}$-inch case; 45-120 with
$2\frac{7}{8}$-inch case. Barrel: 30 inches; round or octagonal;
blued. Double triggers. Open sights. Plain polished
American walnut stock and forend. Made from 1879
to 1881.

Sharps Breechloading Cartridge Carbine . . $925
Caliber: 52 Sharps centerfire. Same general specifications as the Model 1863 Percussion Carbine, as the
early cartridge carbines were merely an alteration
using the old-style percussion frames. The same
breech block was used, the nipple plugged up with
the priming system milled off.

Sharps Commercial Breechloading Military Rifle. $1200
Calibers: 52-70 and 50-67-487 Sharps. Barrel: 30
inches. Overall length: 47 inches. Weight: 11 pounds.
This rifle was assembled about 1867 from recovered
percussion actions.

Sharps Model 1878 Military Carbine

**Sharps & Hankins Model 1861
Navy Rifle**

SHARPS & HANKINS
Philadelphia, Pennsylvania

Christian Sharps and William Hankins collaborated during the Civil War to produce handguns and long arms primarily for military use. Sharps had before this time organized the Sharps Rifle Manufacturing Company (*see* separate listing), which had nothing to do with the Sharps & Hankins operation in Philadelphia.

In about 1853, Sharps had left Hartford and started his own business called C. Sharps & Co. in Philadelphia. After the war, Sharps again went alone in his pursuit of producing firearms under his former name and stayed in business in the "City of Brotherly Love" until he died in 1874.

**Sharps & Hankins Model 1861 Navy
Rifle** **$1200**
Civil War breechloader based on Sharps patent of 1859. Caliber: 52 RF. Barrel: 32½ inches. Overall length: 47½ inches. Weight: 8½ pounds. Lug under barrel for saber bayonet. Walnut stock. Made in limited quantity for a short period from 1861 to 1862.

**Sharps & Hankins Model 1862 Cavalry
Carbine.** **$925**
Civil War breechloader. Caliber: 52 RF. Barrel: 19 inches. Overall length: 33⅝ inches. Weight: 7½ pounds. Walnut stock. Introduced in 1862.

SMITH ARMS
Chicopee Falls, Massachusetts

Smith carbines were manufactured by the Massachusetts Arms Co. This firm was founded by Daniel B. Wesson to manufacture percussion revolvers based on Edwin Wesson patents. The company had several U.S. Government contracts during the Civil War, making Green, Maynard and Smith percussion carbines. For further information, *see* specifications under U.S. Military Single-Shot Breechloading Carbines.

SMITH & WESSON
Springfield, Massachusetts

S&W Model .320 Caliber Revolving Rifle . . **$1500**
Double-action revolver frame, blued or nickel-plated. Caliber: 320 S&W Rifle. Barrels: 16, 18 or 20 inches. Open sights with optional tang peep sight. Weight: about 6 pounds. Circassian detachable walnut buttstock. Mottled hard rubber forend. Approximately 1,000 of these were made between 1880 and 1887.

**Sharps & Hankins Model 1862
Cavalry Carbine**

**Stevens No. 2 Single-Shot
Rifle**

J. STEVENS ARMS & TOOL CO.
Chicopee Falls, Massachusetts

Joshua Stevens started out as a toolmaker in Chester, Mass., his home town, then went to work for Cyrus Allen, a gunmaker in Springfield, Mass. For a short time he was employed by a small arms manufacturer in Hartford, Conn., before moving to Chicopee Falls, where he began working for the Massachusetts Arms Company.

At age 50, after receiving a patent on a simple breechloading single-shot pistol, Stevens decided to start his own arms-making business, J. Stevens & Company. The first plant was located in a converted grist mill along the Chicopee River and produced a small single-shot pistol in pocket and vest pocket models, based on Stevens' patent of September 6, 1864. It also turned out precision machinists' tools, which probably kept the company afloat in its early days.

In 1886, the company was incorporated as the J. Stevens Arms & Tool Company. By this time, Stevens was building target rifles and introduced many new cartridges to the shooting fraternity of a century or more ago. Of the Stevens rifle series, the Old Model Pocket rifles were among the first. These rifles were very light in weight (and strength), and eventually were followed by the heavier target rifles. The firm manufactured the Stevens Tip-Up or "Favorite" 22 single-shot rifle, a popular arm of the day. All of the Stevens rifles are choice among today's collectors.

Joshua Stevens remained with the firm until 1896 when he sold his interests in the business. The J. Stevens Arms & Tool Company became a subsidiary of Savage Arms in 1936.

Stevens No. 1 Single-Shot Rifle **$225**
Tip up, exposed hammer. Barrel: 24 to 30 inches, octagonal. Weight: about 8½ pounds. Open rear sight; blade front sight. Nickel-plated frame and buttplate. Plain straight grip, oiled walnut stock; no forend. Made from 1888 to 1902.

Stevens No. 2 Single-Shot Rifle **$195**
Tip up, exposed hammer. Same general specifications as Single-Shot No. 1 Rifle, except chambered for 22 Long Rifle RF and weight is 6½ pounds to 7½ pounds. Made from 1888 to 1902.

Stevens No. 3 Single-Shot Rifle **$200**
Tip-up action. Calibers: 32, 38 and 44RF. Barrel: 24 to 30 inches; full or half-octagonal. Weight: 6¼ to 8¼ pounds. Folding-type combination front sight with pinhead bead inside a globe and a blade for hunting; tang rear peep sight. Plain straight-grip walnut stock; no forend. Made from 1888 to 1895.

Stevens No. 4 Tip-Up Single-Shot Rifle. . **$200**
Same general specifications as the No. 3 Single-Shot Rifle, except chambered for 22 Short RF only. Half- or full-octagonal barrel.

Stevens No. 5 Tip-Up Expert Single-Shot Rifle. **$245**
Tip up, exposed hammer. Calibers: 22, 25 and 32 RF; also 32-20, 38-40 and 44-40. Barrel: 24, 26, 28 or 30 inches; half-octagonal. Weight: 5½ to 6½ pounds, depending on barrel length. Vernier peep rear sight; leaf middle sight; Beach combination front sight. Plain straight-grip stock. Finger ring rest on lower tang. Crescent buttplate; no forearm. Made from 1888 to 1902. (*See* photo, next page.)

Stevens No. 6 Tip-Up Expert Single-Shot Rifle. **$265**
Tip up, exposed hammer. Same general specifications as No. 5 Tip-Up Expert Single-Shot Rifle, except for fancy finish.

Stevens No. 7 Tip-Up Premier Single-Shot Rifle. **$250**
Tip up, exposed hammer. Calibers: 22, 25 and 32 RF; 32-20, 38-40, and 44-40. Barrel: 24, 26, 28 or 30 inches; half-octagonal. Weight: 5½ to 6¾ pounds, depending on barrel length. Vernier and open rear sights and also globe sight. Plain straight-grip stock and forend. Finger ring rest on lower tang. Swiss-type buttplate. Made from 1888 to 1902.

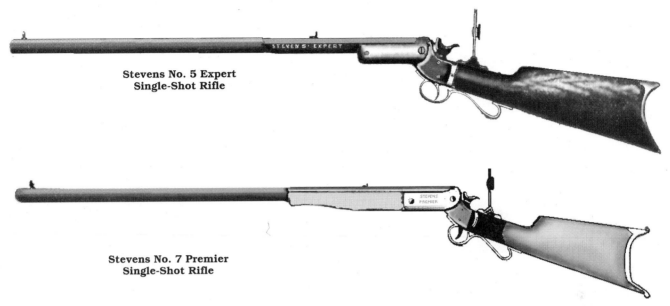

**Stevens No. 5 Expert
Single-Shot Rifle**

**Stevens No. 7 Premier
Single-Shot Rifle**

**Stevens No. 8 Tip-Up Premier Single-Shot
Rifle** **$225**
Tip up, exposed hammer model. Basically the same
specifications as the No. 7 Premier, except in fancier
grade finish.

**Stevens No. 9 Single-Shot Tip-Up Range
Model** **$195**
Tip up, exposed hammer. Calibers: 32, 38 and 44 RF
or Centerfire; 32, 38 and 44 Everlasting CF, 22-10-
45, 32-35 Stevens. Barrel: 24 to 30 inches; half-octagonal or octagonal; other lengths available up to 36
inches. Weight: 7 to 9¼ pounds. Straight-grip stock.
Schuetzen-type buttplate. Made from 1886 to 1902.

**Stevens No. 10 Single-Shot Tip-Up
Range Rifle** **$225**
Same general specifications as the No. 9 Range
Model, except for fancy stock and checkering.

Stevens No. 11 Single-Shot Ladies Rifle . . . **$200**
Same general specifications as the No. 8 and No. 9
Range Rifles, except for smaller stock, smaller fore-
arm and lighter barrel. Caliber: 22 RF and 25
Stevens. Made from 1888 to 1900.

Stevens No. 12 Single-Shot Ladies Rifle . . **$295**
Same general specifications as the No. 11 Ladies
Rifle, except for extra fancy oil-finished stock. Both
the stock and forend were checkered. Made from
1888 to about 1900.

Stevens No. 13 Single-Shot Ladies Rifle . . **$250**
Same general specifications as No. 11 Ladies Rifle,
except for Beach combination front sight and Vernier
peep rear sight mounted on upper tang. Made from
1888 to 1902.

Stevens No. 14 Single-Shot Ladies Rifle . . **$325**
Same general specifications as No. 13 Ladies Rifle,
except for fancy checkered stock and forend. Made
from about 1888 to 1895.

**Stevens No. 15 Crack Shot Single-Shot
Rifle** **$175**
Single-shot. Calibers: 22, 25, 32, 38 and 44 RF; also
25, 32, 38 and 44 centerfire. Barrel: 24, 26, 28 and
30 inches; octagonal. Weight: 6½ to 8¾ pounds.
Sights; Lyman ivory bead front sight and Lyman
combination rear sight on tang. Plain straight stock
and forend. Made from 1900 to 1938.

**Stevens No. 13 Ladies
Single-Shot Rifle**

Although today a subsidiary of Savage Arms, the J. Stevens & Co. enterprise was launched in 1864 in an old grist mill along the Chicopee River. For many years, it produced popular pocket rifles and was one of the leading arms manufacturers of its time.

Stevens No. 16 Crack Shot Single-Shot Rifle **$265**
Rolling-block action. Takedown. Calibers: 22 and 32 RF. Barrel: 20 inches, round. Weight: 3¾ pounds. Blade front sight and dovetail non-adjustable rear sight on barrel. Made from 1900 to 1913.

Stevens No. 17 Favorite Single-Shot Rifle **$325**
Swinging block, lever operated. Takedown. Calibers: 22, 25 and 32 RF. Barrel: 22 inches, half-octagonal; 24 inches, round or octagonal; other lengths were available. Weight: about 4½ pounds. Casehardened receiver; blued receiver optional. Early models were non-automatic ejecting. Open rear sight, Rocky Mountain front sight. Plain straight-grip stock, small tapered forearm. Made from 1889 to 1935.

Stevens No. 18 Favorite Single-Shot Rifle **$780**
Same general specifications as No. 17 Favorite, except has Vernier peep rear sight, left middle sight, Beach combination front sight. Made from 1895 to 1917.

Stevens No. 19 Favorite Single-Shot Rifle **$295**
Same general specifications as the No. 17 Favorite, except has Lyman combination rear sight, leaf sight, Lyman front sight. Made from 1895 to 1917.

Stevens No. 23 Sure-Shot Rifle **$750**
Single-shot takedown model. Caliber: 22 RF. Barrel: 20 inches, round. Weight: 3½ pounds. Conventional trigger. Detachable buttstock. Made in the 1890s.

Stevens No. 34 Hunters Pet Pocket Single-Shot Rifle **$1175**
Tip-up action. Calibers: all pistol cartridges ranging from 22 Short to 44 WCF. Barrel: 18, 20, 22 or 24 inches; half- or full-octagonal; other lengths available up to 36 inches. Weight: about 5¾ pounds with 18-inch barrel. Spur trigger. Sights: combination globe and blade rear; combination peep and V-notch adjustable for elevation only. Walnut grips. Detachable shoulder rest. Brass or iron nickel-plated frame. Made from 1872 to 1900.

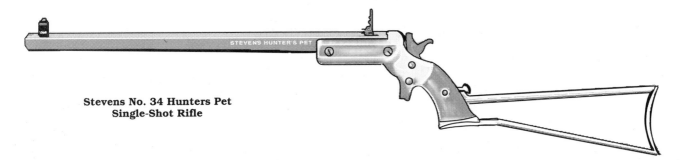

Stevens No. 34 Hunters Pet
Single-Shot Rifle

Stevens No. 40 New Model Pocket or Bicycle Rifle $525

Single-shot. Tip-up action. Calibers: 22 Long Rifle, 22 WRF, 22 Stevens-Pope, 25 Stevens, 32 Long RF or CF. Barrel: 10, 12, 15 or 18 inches; half- or full-octagonal. Iron frame nickel-plated. Sights: combination globe front and blade rear; folding combination peep and V-notch, adjustable for elevation. Conventional trigger. Walnut grips. Detachable nickel-plated shoulder stock. Made 1896 to 1916.

Stevens No. 44 Ideal Single-Shot Rifle . . $595

Rolling block, lever operated. Takedown. Calibers: 22 Long Rifle, 25 RF, 32 RF, 25-20, 32-20, 32-40, 38-40, 38-55, 44-40. Barrel: 24 and 26 inches in round, half-octagonal or full-octagonal. Weight: about 7 pounds with 26-inch round barrel. Open rear sight, Rocky Mountain front sight. Plain straight-grip stock and forearm. Made from 1894 to 1932.

Stevens No. 44½ Ideal Single-Shot Rifle $910

Falling-block, lever operated. Practically the same specifications as the Model No. 44 Ideal.

Stevens No. 45 Ideal Range Model . . . $1225

Same general specifications as the No. 44 Ideal, available in many calibers with Beach combination front and open rear sights, Vernier tang and Swiss buttplate. Made 1896 to 1916.

Stevens Central Fire Sporting Single-Shot Rifle. $380

Similar specifications to the rimfire Sporting Single-Shot Rifle, except adapted to centerfire cartridges: 38-33 Stevens, 38 Long and Extra Long special cartridges made by the Union Metallic Cartridge Co., and the UMC 44 Long or Extra Long centerfire. Made from 1875 to about 1888.

Stevens Hunters Pet Pocket Centerfire Single-Shot Rifle $575

Same general specifications as the No. 34 standard Hunters Pet, except adapted to centerfire cartridges. Made from 1877 to 1897.

Stevens Old Model Pocket Single-Shot Rifle. $510

Tip-up action. Caliber: 22 Short or 22 Long RF. Barrel: 8 or 10 inches; half-octagonal. Lightweight brass frame. Weight: about 11 ounces with 10-inch barrel. Spur trigger. Rosewood or walnut pistol-grip stock, with detachable skeleton stock either nickel-plated or Japanned finish. No forend. This was the first of the Stevens pocket rifles and is basically a long-barreled version of the Old Model Pocket Pistol. Made from 1869 to 1886.

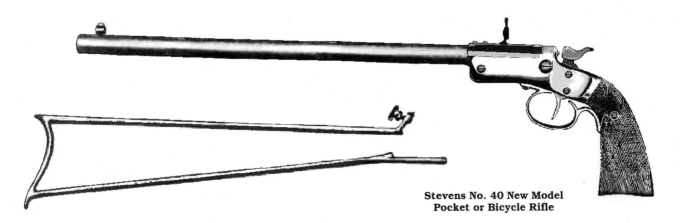

Stevens No. 40 New Model
Pocket or Bicycle Rifle

**Stevens Sporting Single-Shot
Rifle**

Stevens Sporting Single-Shot Rifle $675
Tip-up action. Calibers: 22, 32, 38 and 44 RF. Barrel:
24 to 36 inches, octagonal. Weight: 6½ pounds with
24-inch barrel. Nickel-plated frame. Standard non-
adjustable sights; adjustable sights were fitted on
special order. Made from 1872 to about 1888.

SWISS MILITARY
Various Manufacturers

**Swiss Model 1871 Vetterli Bolt-Action
Rifle $275**
Caliber: 10.5mm. Full-length military stock. Iron fur-
niture. Stamped "WAFFENFABRIK BERN."

Swiss Model 1891 Military Rifle $130
Same specifications as the Russian Mosin-Nagant.
Caliber; 7.62 × 54mm Russian. Five-shot box magazine. Barrel: 31½ inches, round. Weight: about 9
pounds. Open rear sight, blade front sight. Full stock
with straight grip. Introduced 1891.

TURKISH MILITARY
Various Manufacturers

**Turkish Mauser Model 1903 Military
Rifle $150**
Caliber: 8×57mm. Five-shot magazine. Straight bolt.
Barrel: 23½ inches, round. Weight: 8½ pounds.
Blade front sight, adjustable rear sight. Walnut, mili-
tary-type stock. Mauser trademark on receiver ring.

VOLCANIC REPEATING ARMS COMPANY
Norwich, Connecticut
New Haven, Connecticut

Courtlandt C. Palmer, Horace Smith, and Daniel B.
Wesson were the incorporators of the Volcanic Repeating Arms Company after the short-lived success,
and eventual failure, of the first Smith & Wesson
Company. Oliver F. Winchester was also a stock-
holder and this initial financial interest later led to
his presidency of the company and to his further
financial backing.

Volcanic Repeating Arms Company purchased the
assets and patent rights from the former Smith &
Wesson company. Palmer and Smith eventually
stepped out as active participants.

Volcanic pistols and rifles were first manufactured
at the old Smith & Wesson plant in Norwich with
Wesson as the shop superintendent. In February
1856, production started in a new plant located at
New Haven, Connecticut. Daniel Wesson was then
replaced by William C. Hicks as shop superintendent.

By August 1856, the Volcanic Repeating Arms Company was in financial difficulties, and production of
firearms ceased. Oliver F. Winchester then purchased a large part of the property in 1857 to cover
his loans to the company.

On April 25, 1857, the New Haven Arms Company
was formally organized to take over and continue the
business of the defunct Volcanic Repeating Arms
Company. The New Haven Arms Company occupied
the former Volcanic plant in New Haven and continued the manufacture of the Volcanic type of firearm.

See New Haven Arms Company.

**Swiss Model 1871 Vetterli
Bolt-Action Rifle**

Warner Solid-Frame Revolving Carbine

JAMES WARNER
Springfield, Massachusetts

Warner Revolving Carbine
Caliber: 40 percussion, six-shot cylinder. Barrel: 20 to 24 inches, octagonal. Walnut stock with crescent buttplate — earlier models with brass patchbox embedded into side of stock; no forearm. Made 1849 to 1850.
Retractable cylinder type **$7100**
Grooved cylinder, manually revolved
   type **4500**
Automatic revolving type **5200**

Warner Single-Shot Carbine **$3250**
Caliber: 50 RF. Barrel: 20 inches, round. Brass or iron frame; brass breech and trigger-guard assembly. Plain walnut stock and forearm with brass buttplate.

Warner Solid-Frame Revolving Carbine . . **$3000**
Caliber: 40 percussion, six-shot cylinder. Barrel: 26 to 30 inches, octagonal. Walnut stock with crescent buttplate; no patchbox or forearm. Made 1851 to 1852.

WESSON & LEAVITT
Massachusetts Arms Company
Chicopee Falls, Massachusetts

Wesson & Leavitt Revolving Rifle **$5300**
Caliber: 40 percussion, six-shot cylinder. Barrel: 16 to 24 inches, two-step round. Plain walnut stock, curved buttplate; no forearm. Made 1850 to 1851.

FRANK WESSON
Worcester, Massachusetts

Frank Wesson began his gun manufacturing career with a single-shot pistol in 1859, followed by the first of his sporting rifles chambered for the .22 Long RF. A military carbine marked "B. KITTREDGE & CO." is also described in the section titled U.S. Military Single-Shot Breechloading Carbines.

Frank Wesson Two-Trigger Rifle **$625**
Calibers: 22, 32, 38 and 44 rimfire. Barrel: 24 inches. Plain walnut stock; straight grip with crescent buttplate. Made from 1859 to 1888 in four types.

Frank Wesson Two-Trigger Rifle

Wesson & Leavitt Revolving Carbine

WHITNEY ARMS COMPANY
New Haven, Connecticut

The original Whitney firearms business was founded by Eli Whitney, born in 1763 and today well-known as the inventor of the cotton gin. Many of Whitney's patents were used by other manufacturers, but Whitney also manufactured several models under his own name.

Eli Whitney established his firearms factory in 1798 in Hampton, Conn., when he received a Government contract for 10,000 muskets to be delivered within two years. He received another contract for 15,000 muskets and a few years later, an additional contract for 3,000 more. His fourth contract called for still another 15,000 muskets.

On January 8, 1825, Whitney died in New Haven, and his two nephews, Philos and Eli Whitney Blake carried on the business. Eli Whitney Jr. came into control of the business in 1841, and the following year he was offered a Government contract for the Whitney Navy Percussion Musket, which was the first percussion arm made by the Whitney Company.

The Whitney Arms Co. continued to make muskets, rifles, carbines and revolvers for the government, as well as some sporting arms. The last rifles made were Kennedy magazine rifles, patented January 7, 1873. The Whitney plant ceased operation in 1888.

Whitney Creedmoor No. 1 Long-Range Rifle **$945**
Calibers: 44-90, 44-100 and 44-105 Sharps necked. Barrel: 32 or 34 inches; octagonal or half-octagonal. Deluxe stock with checkered pistol grip and forearm. Vernier and wind-gauge sights.

Whitney Creedmoor No. 2 Mid-Range Rifle . . **$995**
Calibers; 40-50 to 40-90 Sharps straight. Barrel: 30 or 32 inches; octagonal, half-octagonal or round. Checkered pistol-grip stock and forearm. Vernier peep rear and wind-gauge front sights.

Whitney Gallery Rifle **$725**
Caliber: 22 Short or Long RF. Barrel: 24 or 26 inches. Same general type of action as the Whitney Sporting and Target Rifle. Equipped either with inexpensive or deluxe sights. Weight: 7½ to 8½ pounds.

Whitney Light Carbine **$800**
Calibers: 44 Henry RF, 44 Short RF, 44 S&W, 46 Long RF. Barrel: 19½ inches. Weight: 5 pounds. This was widely used as a saddle weapon.

Whitney Military Carbine **$800**
Calibers: 43 Spanish Mauser centerfire, 45-70 Government and 50-70 Government. Barrel: 20½ inches, round. Overall length: 36 inches. Weight: 7 lbs. 2 oz. This model was built the same as the rifle.

Whitney Military Rifle **$1040**
Caliber: 43 Spanish Mauser centerfire, 45-70 and 50-70 Government. Barrel: 35 inches; 32½ inches in 50-70 Govt. Overall length: 50½ inches with 35-inch barrel. Weight: 9 pounds.

Whitney Phoenix Gallery Rifle **$845**
Caliber: 22 Short or Long. Barrel: 24 inches; octagonal or half-octagonal. Weight: 7 to 8½ pounds.

Whitney Phoenix Military Carbine **$945**
Calibers: same as for the Phoenix Military Rifle. Barrel: 20½ inches. Weight: 7 pounds. Half-stock with carbine-type buttplate and ring on the side of the receiver.

Whitney Phoenix Military Rifle **$1100**
Calibers: 43 Spanish Mauser centerfire, 45-70 Government and 50-70 Government. Barrel: 35 inches. Weight: 9 pounds. Full rifle stock.

Whitney Phoenix Sporting & Target Rifle . **$1000**
Calibers: 38 Long or Extra Long RF, 44 Long or Extra Long RF, 40-50 Sharps necked, 40-70 Sharps necked centerfire, 44-60 Sharps necked, 44-70 Sharps necked, 44-90, 44-100, 44-105 Sharps necked, 45-70 Government and 50-70 Government. Barrel: 26 to 30 inches; round or octagonal. Weight: 7 to 10 pounds.

Whitney Phoenix-Schuetzen Target Rifle. **$1040**
Caliber: 38 Extra Long centerfire and Sharps straight. Barrel: 30 or 32 inches; octagonal or half-octagonal. Weight: 10 to 12 pounds. Sights: Vernier peep rear; wind-gauge front. Walnut stock with checkered grip and forearm. Nickel-plated buttplate.

Whitney Sporting & Target Rifle **$625**
Calibers: 38 Long centerfire, 38-40 WCF, 44-60 Sharps, 44-77 Sharps necked, 40-50 and 40-70 Sharps straight, 40-90 Sharps straight, 44-40 WCF, 45-70 Government, 50-70 Government; 32 Short or Long RF, 32-20 WCF, 38 Long RF, and 44 Long RF. Barrel: 26 to 32 inches; round and octagonal. Weight: 7½ pounds.

Whitney-Burgess Repeating Military Carbine **$2395**
Caliber: 45-70 Government. Seven-shot tubular magazine. Barrel: 22 inches. Weight: 7½ pounds. Full stock.

Whitney-Burgess Repeating Military Rifle. **$2250**
Caliber: 45-70 Government. Barrel: 33 inches, round. Full stock with an 11-round tubular magazine enclosed in the forearm beneath the barrel. Weight: 9 pounds 1 oz.

Whitney-Kennedy Carbine

Whitney-Burgess Repeating Sporting Rifle. . $1595
Caliber: 45-70 Government. Barrel: 28 inches, round or octagonal. Nine-shot tubular magazine. Weight: 9 to 10 pounds. Introduced in 1879.

NOTE

The Burgess rifle was also manufactured by Colt under Burgess patents in .44-40 WCF caliber only and was introduced by Colt in 1883. See Colt Rifle listings.

Whitney-Kennedy Military Rifle $2400
Calibers: 44-40 WCF and 45-60 WCF. Seventeen-shot magazine for the 44-40 and thirteen-shot magazine for the 46-60. Barrel: 30 inches, round. Weight: 9 pounds. Full-length military stock enclosing the tubular magazine. Several of these models will have cut-off barrel.

Whitney-Kennedy Sporting Carbine . . $2100
Calibers: 32-20, 38-40, 40-60 WCF, 44 centerfire, 44-40, 45-60 WCF, 45-75 WCF, 50-95 Express. The magzine for the shorter cartridges held 12 shots, while the magazine for the longer ones held only 9. Barrel: 20 inches, round. Weight: 7¼ pounds.

Whitney-Kennedy Sporting Rifle. $1295
Calibers: 32-20, 38-40, 40-60 WCF, 44 centerfire, 44-40, 45-60 WCF, 45-75 WCF, 50-95 Express. 9-shot magazine for the longer cartridges; 13-shot magazine for the shorter ones. Barrel: 24, 26 or 28 inches, depending on caliber; octagonal or round. Weight: 9 to 9½ pounds, depending on shape and length of barrel.

NOTE

The major difference between the Kennedy and the Burgess lever-action rifles was the method of loading. To load the tubular magazine of the Kennedy, it was necessary to open the action whle operating the finger lever and retain it in the open position while the cartridges were inserted. The Burgess was loaded while the action was closed, similar to the Winchester lever-action rifles of the period.

Kennedy rifles were marked "Whitneyville Armory, CT. U. S. A. Kennedy .44 cal. C.F." and on the upper tang of the receiver "Patented Jan'y 7-73, Ap'l 1, May 13 and Aug. 12-79."

The first known magazine article on the Whitney-Kennedy lever-action rifles appeared in Forest & Stream, April 10, 1884, page 214.

Neither the Kennedy nor the Burgess rifles lasted very long. They were too simlar to the Winchester rifle, which had very definitely established itself as the leader in the lever-action repeating field.

O.W. WHITTIER
Enfield, New Hampshire

Whittier Percussion Revolving Rifle. . $10,000
Calibers: 41, 44 and 45. Six, nine, and ten-shot zig-zag grooved magazines. Barrel: 30, 31 or 32 inches, half- and full-octagonal. Walnut or maple stock finished with a unique dark-brown walnut stain made from walnut hulls; no forend. Brass patchbox on right side of stock. Less than 100 of these rifles produced around 1838.

Whitney-Kennedy Sporting Rifle

WINCHESTER REPEATING ARMS CO.
New Haven, Connecticut

Although Oliver F. Winchester had offered financial backing to firearms makers earlier, he did not meet with financial success until he hired an engineering genius named B. Tyler Henry. A resident of Windsor, Vt., Henry completely revolutionized the firearms industry with the .44 Henry cartridge and a complementary lever-action repeater known as the .44 Henry Rifle. This popular arm was based on U.S. Patent No. 30,466, granted to Henry on October 16, 1860, and later assigned to Oliver Winchester. In 1860, Winchester's firm, the New Haven Arms Company, concentrated on this one rifle, producing numerous grades in quality — from the plainest to the most elaborately decorated and engraved.

In 1866, with his firearms business flourishing, Winchester decided to terminate the affairs of the New Haven Arms Co. and expand the business under his own name. The Winchester Repeating Arms Company was based in Bridgeport, Conn., where it operated until 1870. At that time a new plant was built in New Haven and the firm moved back to Winchester's home town. From then on, and well into the 20th century, the Winchester Company thrived, developing many successful rifles and shotguns. At one time, it was the largest manufacturer of firearms in the world.

Winchester Model 1866 Lever-Action Carbine. $7895
Same general specifications as the Model 1866 Rifle, except manufactured with a 20-inch barrel and 13-shot magazine, barrel bands, and saddle ring on left side. Weight: 7¾ pounds.

WATCH OUT FOR REBUILT AND MODIFIED HIGH-GRADE WINCHESTERS!

Winchester Model 1866 Lever-Action Military Musket. $6000
Same general specifications as the Model 1866 Rifle, except it was fitted with a 27-inch barrel, had a 17-shot magazine, and weighed 8 lbs. 4 oz. A full-length military-type stock was attached by two barrel bands and was equipped with either triangular or saber-type bayonets. These muskets were manufactured mostly for the Turkish Government.

Winchester Model 1866 Lever-Action Rifle. $7400
The original brass-frame model was made only in 44 Henry rimfire. Barrel: 24 inches; octagonal, half-octagonal, and round. Overall length: 43 inches. Barrel marked "Winchester's Repeating Arms, Bridgeport, Conn." and later "New Haven, Conn., King's Improvement, Pat. March 29, 1866, Oct. 16, 1860." Weight: 8 lbs. 6 oz. Open, adjustable rear sights, fixed blade front sight. American walnut stock and forend with crescent buttplate. Approximately 170,100 of these rifles were made between 1866 and 1898.

Winchester Model 1873 Carbine. $3800
Same as standard Model 1873 Rifle, except has a 20-inch barrel, 12-shot magazine and weighs 7¼ pounds. A saddle ring is attached to a threaded stud that screws into the left side of the action. A knotted piece of rawhide was usually attached to this ring and then the looped rawhide was threaded over the saddle horn to secure the carbine.

Winchester Model 1873 Fancy Sporting Rifle $4100
Same general specifications as standard Model 73 Rifle, except made with casehardened receiver and trimmings, pistol-grip stock of selected walnut, octagonal barrel or half-octagonal in most cases.

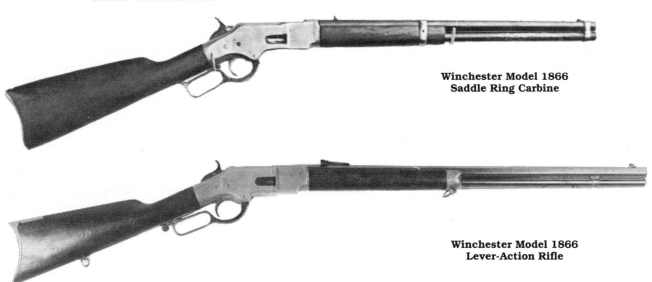

**Winchester Model 1866
Saddle Ring Carbine**

**Winchester Model 1866
Lever-Action Rifle**

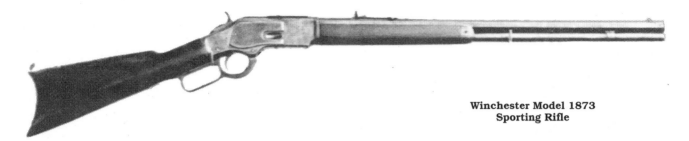

Winchester Model 1873
Sporting Rifle

Winchester Model 1873 Lever-Action Sporting Rifle $1800

Solid frame. Calibers: 22 RF; 32-20, 38-40 and 44-40. 15-shot full magazine; 6-shot half-magazine. Barrel: 24 inches; round, half-octagonal, and octagonal. Weight: about 8½ pounds. Open rear sight, bead or blade front sight. Plain straight-grip stock and forearm. 720,60 rifles of this model manufactured from 1873 to 1924.

Close-up of Model 1873 "1 of 1000" marking

Winchester Model 1873 Rifle—One of One Thousand . . . . $45,000+

During the late 1870s Winchester offered Model 73 rifles of superior accuracy and extra finish, designated "One of One Thousand" grade at a price of $100 each. These rifles are marked "1 of 1000" or "One of One Thousand." Only 136 are known to have been manufactured. This is one of the rarest of shoulder arms, and because so few have been sold in recent years, it is extremely difficult to assign a value. One such rifle—in perfect condition—was sold at a New York auction in 1981 for about $35,000. Beware of fakes!

Winchester Model 1876 Carbine. $4800

Same as standard Model 1876 Sporting Rifle, except has a 22-inch barrel, and a forend that extends almost to the muzzle.

Winchester Model 1876 Fancy Sporting Rifle $4100

Same general specifications as standard Model 76 Rifle, except made with casehardened receiver and trimmings, pistol-grip stock of selected walnut, octagonal barrel or half-octagonal in most cases.

Winchester Model 1876 Lever-Action Sporting Rifle $3650

Calibers: 40-60, 45-60, 45-75, and 50-05. Barrel: 26 to 32 inches; longer barrels were available on special order and now bring a premium. Plain walnut stock and forend. Color-casehardened or blued frame; blued barrel and magazine tube. Made from 1876 to 1897.

Winchester Model 1876 Rifle—One of One Hundred $75,000

Same general specifications as standard Model 1876 rifle except extra-fancy trimming, engraving, and wood. Only seven were made.

Winchester Model 1876 Rifle—One of One Thousand $55,000

Like the Winchester Model 1873, about 50 Model 1876 rifles were designated "One of One Thousand." Almost no trading takes place in these models and the value listed is only approximate at best. One in antique excellent condition would probably run into the six-figure bracket.

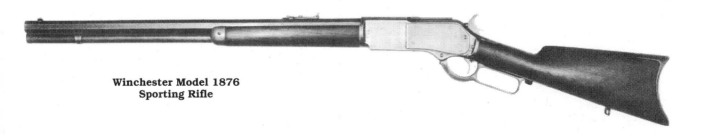

Winchester Model 1876
Sporting Rifle

During the last half of the 19th century, the Apache Indians of the American Southwest were fond of Winchester rifles. Not only did the long arms aid them in their buffalo hunts, the guns also provided them with the lethal weapons to destroy unwanted intruders in their territories. Here Apache Warrior, Nabakala, readies a Winchester 1876 Sporting Rifle.

Winchester Model 1879 Bolt-Action Rifle $1095

Caliber: 45-70; 6-shot magazine. Barrel: 26 to 32 inches. One-piece plain walnut stock. This rifle is also known as the Winchester Hotchkiss, named after its inventor. Made from 1879 to 1883.

Winchester Model 1879 Bolt-Action Carbine $1200

Same general specifications as the Model 1879 rifle except has 22-inch barrel.

Winchester Model 1883 Bolt-Action Hotchkiss Repeating Rifle $850

Same general specifications as the Model 1879 except caseharded frame and two-piece walnut stock. Made from 1883 to 1899.

Winchester Model 1885 Single-Shot Engraved Rifle . . . . $2500 to $5000

Same general specifications as standard grade 1885 Rifle, except fancy-grade American walnut stock, and various grades of metal engraving. Some furnished with set triggers and other luxuries.

Winchester Model 1885 Single-Shot Fancy Grade Rifle. $2195

Same general specifications as standard grade 1885 Rifle, except fancy grade checkered walnut stock and forearm.

Winchester Model 1885 Single-Shot Hi-Wall Rifle. $2195

Solid frame or takedown. Caliber: practically all calibers used at the time. Plain trigger, standard lever. Barrel: No. 3, No. 4, and No. 5; round, half-octagonal, or full-octagonal. Weight: 9½ pounds average. Open rear sight, blade front sight. Plain American walnut stock and forearm.

Winchester Model 1885 Single-Shot Low-Wall Rifle $1595

Solid frame. The low-wall model was used mainly for low-powered small calibers such as 22 RF, 22 Win. Centerfire, etc. Barrel: No. 1 lightweight, 28 inches round, or octagonal. Weight: 7 pounds. Open rear sight, blade front sight. Plain American walnut stock and forearm.

Winchester Model 1885 Single-Shot Musket. $595

Same general specifications as the 1885 Winder Musket, except solid-frame low-wall receiver and Lyman rear peep sight. The U.S. Government purchased a large quantity of these muskets during World War I for training purposes.

**Winchester Model 1885
Hi-Wall Single-Shot Rifle**

Winchester Model 1885 Single-Shot Schuetzen Rifle $3400

Solid frame or takedown. High-wall receiver. Calibers: various, but most common is 38-55. Double-set triggers, spur finger lever. Barrel: No. 3 weight; 30 inches, octagonal. Weight: 12 pounds. Vernier rear peep sight, wind-gauge front sight. Fancy walnut Schuetzen stock with checkered pistol grip and forearm. Schuetzen buttplate. Adjustable palm rest.

Winchester Model 1885 Single-Shot Winder Musket $595

Solid frame or takedown. High-wall receiver. Calibers: 22 Short, 22 Long Rifle. Barrel: 28 inches, round. Weight: 8½ pounds. Musket rear sight, blade front sight. Plain trigger. Standard finger lever. Military-type stock and forearm.

Winchester Model 1886 Carbine $5000

Same general specifications as standard Model 1886, except furnished with 22-inch barrel, carbine stock and forearm, and saddle ring on left-hand side of receiver. Very few of these carbines were made in the Model 1886, and it is estimated that less than 500 of these are now in circulation.

Winchester Model 1886 Fancy Sporting Rifle $2800

Same general specifications as the standard 1886 Sporting Rifle, except had fancy walnut checkered pistol-grip stock and forend.

Winchester Model 1886 Lightweight Rifle $1795

Same general specifications as the standard 1886 Sporting Rifle, except furnished with lightweight, rapid-taper barrel; 22 inches in 45-70 and 24 inches in 33 Winchester, in both solid frame and takedown. Made from about 1898 to 1935.

Winchester Model 1886 Sporting Rifle $1450

Solid frame or takedown. Caliber: (in order of introduction) 45-70, 45-90, 40-82, 40-65, 38-56, 50-110 Express, 40-70, 38-70, 50-100 and 33 WCF. Eight-shot tubular magazine; 4-shot half-magazine. Barrel: 26 inches; round, half-octagonal, and octagonal was standard. Other lengths were available on special order; odd-length barrels bring a premium price. Weight: from 7½ pounds and up. Plain walnut stock and forearm, straight grip. Crescent and shotgun buttplate. Early models had case-hardened receivers, hammer, lever, buttplate and forend cap; balance of gun blued. Made from 1886 to 1935.

Winchester Model (18)90 Slide-Action Repeater $895

Visible hammer, solid frame or takedown. Calibers: 22 Short, Long, Long Rifle, 22 WCF. Tubular magazine. Barrel: 24 inches, octagonal. Weight: 5¾ pounds. Open rear sight, bead front sight. Plain straight-grip stock, grooved slide handle. Made from 1890 to 1932.

Winchester Model (18)90 Slide-Action Repeater Fancy Grade $1095

Same general specifications as standard Model 90, except furnished with fancy-grade, walnut pistol-grip stock. Made from 1890 to 1932.

NOTE

Winchester Model 1886 rifles in .45-90, 50-110, and .50-100 calibers will command a premium. Rifles in mint, or near mint condition will also have a higher value — sometimes double the prices listed here.

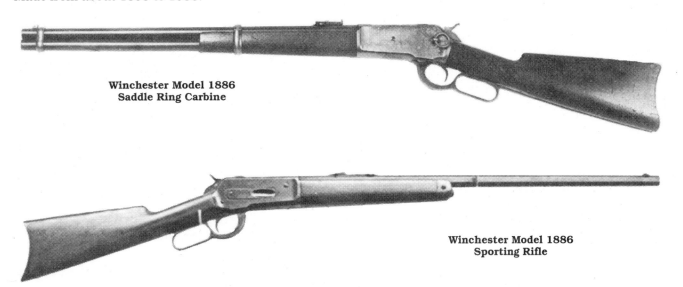

**Winchester Model 1886
Saddle Ring Carbine**

**Winchester Model 1886
Sporting Rifle**

**Winchester Model 1892
Lever-Action Sporting Rifle**

Winchester Model 1892 Carbine **$995**
Same general specifications as the standard 1892 Sporting Rifle, except had 20-inch barrel, carbine stock and forearm, barrel bands and saddle ring. Weight: about 5¾ pounds. Made from 1892 to 1941.

**Winchester Model 1892 Fancy Engraved
Models** . . . . **$2500 to $5000**
Same general specifications as standard 1892 models, except had fancy-grade walnut stock and forend with higher grades of checkering and engraved receiver parts, sometimes extending a short distance onto the barrel.

**Winchester Model 1892 Fancy Sporting
Rifle** **$1295**
Same general specifications as standard Model 1892 Sporting Rifle, except fancy walnut stock with checkered pistol grip and forend.

**Winchester Model 1892 Lever-Action
Repeating Sporting Rifle** **$895**
Solid fame or takedown. 13-shot magazine. Calibers: 25-20, 32-20, 38-40 and 44-40. Barrel: 24 inches; half-octagonal or octagonal. Weight: 6¾ pounds. Open rear sight, bead or blade front sight. American walnut, straight-grip stock and forend. 1,004,067 of these were made between 1892 and 1932.

**Winchester Model 1892 Long-Barrel
Models** **$1560**
Longer barrel lengths up to 36 inches were available at extra cost. However, this option was discontinued by the Winchester factory in 1908.

Winchester Model 1892 Musket **$7500**
Same general specifications as standard sporting rifle, except 30-inch round barrel, 17-shot magazine, and weighed 8 pounds. Musket stock and barrel bands.

**Winchester Model 1892 Short-Barrel
Model.** **$3000**
Shorter barrel lengths were available in the Model 1892; that is, 14, 15, 16 and 18 inches. These short-barreled models were sometimes called Trapper Carbines, but were used mainly by the rubber industry in South America.

Winchester Model 1894 Carbine. **$395**
Same general specifications as standard Model 94 Rifle, except furnished with 20-inch barrel, carbine-style forend (long and short), and straight-grip buttstock with shotgun buttplate. Made in 30-30, 32 Special, and 25-35 from 1894 to 1950; the 25-35 was dropped from the line in 1936, reinstated in 1940 and again dropped in 1950. Both the 30-30 and 32 Special remained until 1964 when the model went through some modifications, and only the 30-30 remained thereafter. The Winchester Model 94 was the first sporting rifle to exceed 1,000,000 in sales. Prewar Models (before 1941) bring a premium price of perhaps 25 percent more than those manufactured between 1945 and 1964.

**Winchester Model 1894 Fancy Sporting
Rifle.** **$1995**
Same general specifications as standard 1894 Rifle, except furnished with fancy-grade walnut checkered stock and forend.

**Winchester Model 1894
Lever-Action Rifle**

**Winchester Model 1895
Repeating Rifle**

Winchester Model 1894 Repeating Rifle. . . $950
Solid frame or takedown. Lever action. Calibers: 25-35, 30-30, 32 Win. Special, 32-40 and 38-55. Eight-shot magazine. Barrel: 26 inches; round, half-octagonal or octagonal. Extra length barrels up to 36 inches were also furnished at extra cost. Weight: 7½ pounds average. Plain, straight-grip stock and forend. Crescent or shotgun-type buttplates. Made from 1894 to 1936.

**Winchester Model 1894 Saddle Ring
Carbine. $995**
Same general specifications as standard Model 94, except furnished with 20-inch barrel, carbine stock and forend, barrel bands, and saddle ring on left-hand side of receiver. Made from 1894 to 1925.

Winchester Model 1895 Carbine $995
Same general specifications as standard 1895 Rifle, except had 28-inch barrel and carbine stock and forend.

**Winchester Model 1895 Fancy Sporting
Rifle $1595**
Same general specifications as standard 1895 Rifle, except with fancy-grade walnut checkered pistol-grip stock.

Winchester Model 1895 Musket $1895
Same general specifications as standard 1895 Rifle, except had 28-inch round barrel and total weight of 9¾ pounds.

Winchester Model 1895 Repeating Rifle. . . $895
Solid frame or takedown. Non-detachable six-shot box magazine. Lever action. Calibers: 30 US Army (30-40 Krag), 38-72, 40-72, 303 British, 35 Winchester, 405 Winchester, 30-03 Government, and 30-06. A number of these were also made for the Russian Government chambered for 7.63mm Russian. Barrel: 26 inches; round, half-octagonal or octagonal. Weight: 7½ pounds. Walnut stock and forend. Crescent or shotgun buttplate. 425,881 were made between 1895 and 1931, with the line continuing from already-manufactured parts until 1938.

**Winchester-Hotchkiss 1879 Bolt-Action
Repeating Rifle—First Model $1095**
Solid frame. Caliber: 45-70 Govt. Six-shot tubular magazine in buttstock. Barrel: 26 inches; round, half-octagonal and octagonal. Weight: 8½ pounds average. Plain walnut stock with crescent or shotgun buttplates. Designed by Benjamin Hotchkiss, who sold the rights to Winchester, this first model had a magazine cutoff and safety control in one unit in the form of a turn button on the right-hand side above the trigger guard. 6,419 were made between 1879 and 1880.

**Winchester-Hotchkiss 1879 Repeating
Rifle—Second Model $850**
Same general specifications as the 1879 First Model, except had the magazine cutoff on the right side, top of receiver, rear of bolt handle. Safety was on the left side of the receiver opposite the magazine cutoff. About 16,102 of these rifles were made between 1880 and 1883.

**Winchester-Hotchkiss 1883 Repeating
Rifle—Third Model. $750**
Same general specifications as Winchester-Hotchkiss 1879 Second Model Repeater, except this had a two-piece stock. 62,034 of these were made between 1883 and 1899.

Winchester-Hotchkiss Repeating Carbine
Same general specifications as the 1879 Repeating Rifle, except early models had a 24-inch round barrel, which was changed to 22½ inches around 1884. Carbine stock with barrel band. Weight: about 8¼ pounds.
First Model **$695**
Second Model **795**
Third Model **895**

Winchester-Hotchkiss Repeating Musket. . $1200
Same general specifications as the 1879 Repeating Rifle, except had a 32-inch round barrel, later changed to 28 inches (Second Model). Musket stock with barrel bands. Weight: 9 pounds.

Winchester-Lee Straight-Pull Bolt-Action Musket $695

Same general specifications as Winchester-Lee Rifle, except had a 28-inch round barrel and weight of 8½ pounds.

Winchester-Lee Straight Pull Bolt-Action Rifle. $795

Solid frame. Non-detachable five-shot magazine. Caliber: 236 or 6mm Lee Navy. Barrel: 24 inches, round. Weight: 7½ pounds. Walnut stock and forend. Designed by James Paris Lee, about 20,000 of these rifles were made from 1895 to 1900 primarily for use by the U.S. Navy. Some remained on the market until about 1916.

H.T. WOOD & CO.
Bradford, Ontario

H.T. Wood Percussion Rifle. $625

Caliber: 44. Barrel: heavy, part octagonal. Walnut stock with mounted brass. Rectangular silver escutcheon on grip. Pewter nose cap. Made circa 1830s to 1840s.

WILLIAM WURFFLEIN
Philadelphia, Pennsylvania

Wurfflein Tip-Up Rifles

Calibers: 22 and 32 RF; 32, 38, 40 and 44 centerfire. Barrel: 24 and 28 inches, octagonal and half-octagonal. Walnut stock with curved buttplate. Earlier models had no forearm. Made 1885 to 1892.

Model with no forearm . . . . $ 595
Standard models with plain stock and forearm   625
Standard model with checkered grip and
  forearm 835
Match models (target sights and Swiss
  buttplate) 2335

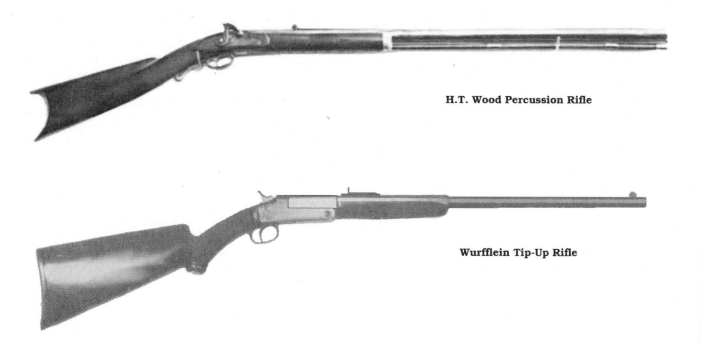

H.T. Wood Percussion Rifle

Wurfflein Tip-Up Rifle

AMERICAN KENTUCKY FLINTLOCK RIFLES

The Kentucky Rifle was America's first great contribution to firearms technology. This type of rifle was born on the frontier around 1750 and was developed by gunsmiths who were artists as well as mechanics. These accurate rifles were made well into the 1800s until the development of the percussion cap around 1830. In general, the age of the Kentucky Rifle is usually considered to be between 1750 and 1850, when it made its most important contributions to American history.

Although called "Kentucky" Rifle, the main center of its production was Pennsylvania. But regardless of its origin, it was the supreme American hunting rifle for the period—at least for the eastern half of the country. The typical rifle averaged .50 caliber, had barrels of 42 to 46 inches, with both full and half-length stocks of curly maple. The buttplate was crescent-shaped to fit the shoulder snugly, and the patchbox was usually an integral part of the buttstock. A cheekpiece was standard on most models.

The Kentucky Rifle started to decline in popularity soon after the introduction of the successful percussion lock rifles. Some rifles, however, continued to be made long after cartridge rifles came into use. Currently, many reproduction models are being manufactured for blackpowder enthusiasts. The following are some of the more well-known original Kentucky Rifle makers.

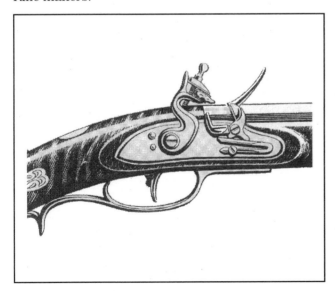

Close-up of the flintlock on a typical Pennsylvania-produced American "Kentucky" Flintlock Rifle.

ANDREW ALBRECHT
Warwick Township, Pennsylvania

Albrecht Kentucky Flintlock Rifle $1680
Lock: casehardened flintlock. Calibers: various. Barrel length: 36 inches average. Weight: 7 to 7½ pounds average. Curly maple one-piece stock, although walnut was sometimes used. Single- and double-set trigger. Brass fittings, including patchbox, ramrod ferrules, buttplate, etc. Made from 1779 to 1782.

Albrecht Fancy Grade Kentucky Flintlock. . $4500
Same general specifications as standard Albrecht Flintlock, above, except gun has some modest stock carvings, silver inlays, etc.

Albrecht Extra Fancy Grade Kentucky Flintlock Rifle $7000
Same general specifications as standard Albrecht Flintlock Rifle, except extra fancy wood, much carving, engraving on metal with gold or silver inlays.

M. ALDENDERFER
Lancaster, Pennsylvania

Aldenderfer Kentucky Flintlock Rifle. . $1680
Lock: casehardened flintlock. Calibers: various. Barrel length: 36 inches average. Weight: 7 to 7½ pounds average. Curly maple one-piece stock, although walnut was sometimes used. Single- and double-set trigger. Brass fittings, including patchbox, ramrod ferrules, buttplate, etc. Made from 1763 to 1817.

Aldenderfer Fancy Grade Kentucky Flintlock $4500
Same general specifications as standard Aldenderfer Flintlock, above, except gun has some modest stock carvings, silver inlays, etc.

Aldenderfer Extra Fancy Grade Kentucky Flintlock Rifle $7000
Same general specifications as standard Aldenderfer Flintlock Rifle, except extra fancy wood, much carving, engraving on metal with gold or silver inlays.

SILAS ALLEN
Shrewsbury, Massachusetts

Allen Flintlock Kentucky Rifle. $1680
Lock: casehardened flintlock. Calibers: various. Barrel length: 36 inches average. Weight: 7 to 7½ pounds average. Curly maple one-piece stock, although walnut was sometimes used. Single- and double-set trigger. Brass fittings, including patchbox, ramrod ferrules, buttplate, etc. Made from 1796 to 1843.

Allen Smoothbore Musket. $995
Lock: casehardened flintlock. Calibers: various. Barrel length: 41 inches average, smoothbore. American walnut or maple one-piece stock. Brass or iron fittings. Made from 1796 to 1843.

THOMAS ALLEN
New York, New York

T. Allen Flintlock Kentucky Rifle $1680
Lock: casehardened flintlock. Calibers: various. Barrel: 36 inches average. Weight: 7 to 7½ pounds average. Curly maple one-piece stock, although walnut was sometimes used. Single- and double-set trigger. Brass fittings, including patchbox, ramrod ferules, buttplate, etc. Made from 1768 to 1785.

WILLIAM ALLEN
New York, New York

W. Allen Kentucky Flintlock Rifle. . . . $1680
Lock: casehardened flintlock. Calibers: various. Barrel length: 36 inches average. Weight: 7 to 7½ pounds average. Curly maple one-piece stock, although walnut was sometimes used. Single- and double set trigger. Brass fittings, including patchbox, ramrod ferrules, buttplate, etc. Made from 1801 to 1812.

W. Allen Fancy Grade Kentucky Flintlock . . $4500
Same general specifications as standard Allen Flintlock, above, except gun has some modest stock carvings, silver inlays, etc.

W. Allen Extra Fancy Kentucky Flintlock . . $7000
Same general specifications as standard Allen Flintlock Rifle, except extra fancy wood, much carving, engraving on metal with gold or silver inlays.

PETER ANGSTADT
Lancaster, Pennsylvania

Angstadt Kentucky Flintlock Rifle. . . . $1680
Lock: casehardened flintlock. Calibers: various. Barrel length: 36 inches average. Weight: 7 to 7½ pounds average. Curly maple one-piece stock, although walnut was sometimes used. Single- and double-set trigger. Brass fittings, including patchbox, ramrod ferrules, buttplate, etc. Made from 1779 to 1782.

Angstadt Fancy Grade Kentucky Flintlock. . $4500
Same general specifications as standard Angstadt Flintlock, above, except gun has some modest stock carvings, silver inlays, etc.

Angstadt Extra Fancy Grade Kentucky Flintlock Rifle $7000
Same general specifications as standard Angstadt Flintlock Rifle, except extra fancy wood, much carving, engraving on metal with gold or silver inlays.

JAMES ANGUSH
Lancaster, Pennsylvania

Angush Kentucky Flintlock Rifle $1680
Lock: casehardened flintlock. Calibers: various. Barrel length: 36 inches average. Weight: 7 to 7½ pounds average. Curly maple one-piece stock, although walnut was sometimes used. Single- and double-set trigger. Brass fittings, including patchbox, ramrod ferrules, buttplate, etc. Made from 1775 to 1776.

Angush Fancy Grade Kentucky Flintlock. . $4500
Same general specifications as standard Angush Flintlock, above, except gun has some modest stock carvings, silver inlays, etc.

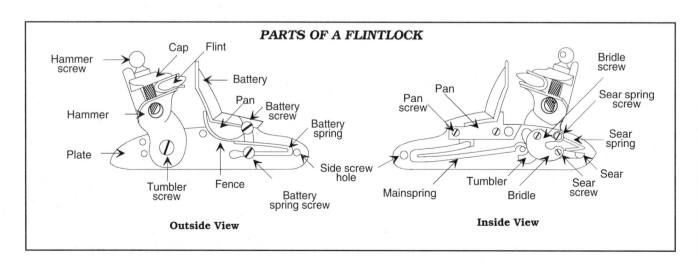

PARTS OF A FLINTLOCK

Outside View

Inside View

JACOB ANSTADT
Kutztown, Pennsylvania

Anstadt Kentucky Flintlock Rifle $1680
Lock: casehardened flintlock. Calibers: various. Barrel length: 36 inches average. Weight: 7 to 7½ pounds average. Curly maple one-piece stock although walnut was sometimes used. Single- and double-set trigger. Brass fittings, including patchbox, ramrod ferrules, buttplate, etc. Made from 1815 to 1816.

WILLIAM ANTIS
Fredericktown, Pennsylvania

Antis Kentucky Flintlock Rifle $1680
Lock: casehardened flintlock. Calibers: various. Barrel length: 36 inches average. Weight: 7 to 7½ pounds average. Curly maple one-piece stock although walnut was sometimes used. Single- and double-set trigger. Brass fittings, including patchbox, ramrod ferrules, buttplate, etc. Made from 1775 to 1782.

Antis Fancy Grade Kentucky Flintlock . . $4500
Same general specifications as standard Antis Flintlock, above, except gun has some modest stock carvings, silver inlays, etc.

Antis Extra Fancy Grade Kentucky Flintlock Rifle $7000
Same general specifications as standard Antis Flintlock Rifle, except extra fancy wood, much carving, engraving on metal with gold or silver inlays.

G. AVERY
Hamburg, Pennsylvania

Avery Kentucky Flintlock Rifle $1680
Lock: casehardened flintlock. Calibers: various. Barrel length: 36 inches average. Weight: 7 to 7½ pounds average. Curly maple one-piece stock although walnut was sometimes used. Single- and double-set trigger. Brass fittings, including patchbox, ramrod ferrules, buttplate, etc. Made from 1779 to 1782.

Avery Fancy Grade Kentucky Flintlock . . $4500
Same general specifications as standard Avery Flintlock, above, except gun has some modest stock carvings, silver inlays, etc.

NOTE

Many flintlocks were converted to percussion ignition during the 1800s. Collectors claim that such conversions lower the value of the rifles somewhat, but not a significant amount.

RICHARD BACKHOUSE
Easton, Pennsylvania

Backhouse Kentucky Flintlock Rifle . . $1450
Lock: casehardened flintlock. Calibers: various. Barrel length: 36 inches average. Weight: 7 to 7½ pounds average. Curly maple one-piece stock although walnut was sometimes used. Single- and double-set trigger. Brass fittings, including patchbox, ramrod ferrules, buttplate, etc. Made from 1774 to 1781.

Backhouse Fancy Grade Kentucky Flintlock $4400
Same general specifications as standard Backhouse Flintlock, above, except gun has some modest stock carvings, silver inlays, etc.

Backhouse Extra Fancy Grade Kentucky Flintlock Rifle $6500
Same general specifications as standard Backhouse Flintlock Rifle, except extra fancy wood, much carving, engraving on metal with gold or silver inlays.

ROBERT BAILEY
York, Pennsylvania

Bailey Kentucky Flintlock Rifle $1250
Lock: casehardened flintlock. Calibers: various. Barrel length: 36 inches average. Weight: 7 to 7½ pounds average. Curly maple one-piece stock although walnut was sometimes used. Single- and double-set trigger. Brass fittings, including patchbox, ramrod ferrules, buttplate, etc. Made from 1776 to 1777.

JACOB BAKER
Philadelphia, Pennsylvania

Baker Kentucky Flintlock Rifle $1680
Lock: casehardened flintlock. Calibers: various, usually 36 to 50. Barrel length: 36 to 41. Weight: 7 to 7½ pounds average. Curly maple one-piece stock although walnut was sometimes used. Single- and double-set trigger. Brass fittings, including patchbox, ramrod ferrules, buttplate, etc. Made from 1820 to 1833.

Baker Fancy Grade Kentucky Flintlock . . $4500
Same general specifications as standard Baker Flintlock, above, except gun has some modest stock carvings, silver inlays, etc.

Baker Extra Fancy Kentucky Flintlock . . $7000
Same general specifications as standard Baker Flintlock Rifle, except extra fancy wood, much carving, engraving on metal with gold or silver inlays.

JOHN BAKER
Newburgh, New York

Baker Kentucky Flintlock Rifle **$1680**
Lock: casehardened flintlock. Calibers: various, usually 36 to 50. Barrel length: 36 to 41 inches. Weight: 7 to 7½ pounds average. Curly maple one-piece stock although walnut was sometimes used. Single- and double-set trigger. Brass fittings, including patchbox, ramrod ferrules, buttplate, etc. Made from 1837 to 1850.

MELCHIOR BAKER
Fayette County, Pennsylvania

M. Baker Kentucky Flintlock Rifle . . . **$1680**
Lock: casehardened flintlock. Calibers: various, usually 36 to 50. Barrel length: 36 to 41 inches. Weight: 7 to 7½ pounds average. Curly maple one-piece stock although walnut was sometimes used. Single- and double-set trigger. Brass fittings, including patchbox, ramrod ferrules, buttplate, etc. Made from 1779 to 1805.

M. Baker Fancy Kentucky Flintlock . . **$4500**
Same general specifications as standard Baker Flintlock, above, except gun has some modest stock carvings, silver inlays, etc.

M. Baker Extra Fancy Grade Kentucky Flintlock Rifle **$7000**
Same general specifications as standard Baker Flintlock Rifle, except extra fancy wood, much carving, engraving on metal with gold or silver inlays.

CHRISTIAN BALSLEY
Dickinson Township, Pennsylvania

Balsley Kentucky Flintlock Rifle **$1680**
Lock: casehardened flintlock. Calibers: various, usually 36 to 50. Barrel length: 36 to 41 inches. Weight: 7 to 7½ pounds average. Curly maple one-piece stock although walnut was sometimes used. Single- and double-set trigger. Brass fittings, including patchbox, ramrod ferrules, buttplate, etc. Made from 1795 to 1796.

Balsley Fancy Kentucky Flintlock . . . **$4500**
Same general specifications as standard Balsley Flintlock, above, except gun has some modest stock carvings, silver inlays, etc.

Balsley Extra Fancy Grade Kentucky Flintlock Rifle **$7000**
Same general specifications as standard Balsley Flintlock Rifle, except extra fancy wood, much carving, engraving on metal with gold or silver inlays.

GEORGE BARNHART
Jackson, Ohio

Barnhart Kentucky Flintlock Rifle **$1680**
Lock: casehardened flintlock. Calibers: various, usually 36 to 50. Barrel length: 36 to 41 inches. Weight: 7 to 7½ pounds average. Curly maple one-piece stock although walnut was sometimes used. Single- and double-set trigger. Brass fittings, including patchbox, ramrod ferrules, buttplate, etc. Made from 1818 to 1844.

Barnhart Fancy Kentucky Flintlock . . . **$4500**
Same general specifications as standard Barnhart Flintlock, above, except gun has some modest stock carvings, silver inlays, etc.

Barnhart Extra Fancy Grade Kentucky Flintlock Rifle **$7000**
Same general specifications as standard Barnhart Flintlock Rifle, except extra fancy wood, much carving, engraving on metal with gold or silver inlays.

SAMUEL BAUM
Mahoning Township, Pennsylvania

Baum Kentucky Flintlock Rifle **$1450**
Lock: casehardened flintlock. Calibers: various, usually 36 to 50. Barrel length: 36 to 41 inches. Weight: 7 to 7½ pounds average. Curly maple one-piece stock although walnut was sometimes used. Single- and double-set trigger. Brass fittings, including patchbox, ramrod ferrules, buttplate, etc. Made from 1819 to 1821.

Baum Fancy Kentucky Flintlock Rifle . . **$4000**
Same general specifications as standard Baum Flintlock, above, except gun has some modest stock carvings, silver inlays, etc.

Baum Extra Fancy Kentucky Flintlock . . **$6500**
Same general specifications as above rifle, except has extra fancy grade wood, much wood carving, engraving on metal with gold or silver inlays.

GIDEON BECK
Lancaster, Pennsylvania

G. Beck Kentucky Flintlock Rifle **$1680**
Lock: casehardened flintlock. Calibers: various, usually 36 to 50. Barrel length: 36 to 41 inches. Weight: 7 to 7½ pounds average. Curly maple one-piece stock although walnut was sometimes used. Single- and double-set trigger. Brass fittings, including patchbox, ramrod ferrules, buttplate, etc. Made from 1780 to 1788.

G. Beck Fancy Kentucky Flintlock Rifle . . $4500
Same general specifications as standard Beck Flintlock, above, except gun has some modest stock carvings, silver inlays, minute metal engraving, etc.

G. Beck Extra Fancy Kentucky Flintlock . . $7000
Same general specifications as standard Beck Flintlock Rifle, except has extra fancy grade wood, much
wood carving, engraving on metal with gold or silver
inlays.

JOHN BECK
Lancaster, Pennsylvania

J. Beck Kentucky Flintlock Rifle $1680
Lock: casehardened flintlock. Calibers: various, usually 36 to 50. Barrel length: 36 to 41 inches. Weight:
7 to 7½ pounds average. Curly maple one-piece stock
although walnut was sometimes used. Single- and
double-set trigger. Brass fittings, including patchbox, ramrod ferrules, buttplate, etc. Made from 1772
to 1777.

J. Beck Fancy Kentucky Flintlock Rifle . . $4500
Same general specifications as above rifle, except gun
has some modest stock carvings, silver inlays, and
minute metal engraving, etc.

J. Beck Extra Fancy Kentucky Flintlock . . $7000
Same general specifications as above rifle, except
extra fancy wood, much carving, engraving on metal
with gold or silver inlays.

JOHN PHILLIP BECK
Dauphin County, Pennsylvania

J.P. Beck Kentucky Flintlock Rifle . . . $2500
Lock: casehardened flintlock. Calibers: various, usually
36 to 50. Barrel length: 36 to 41 inches. Weight: 7½
pounds average. Curly maple one-piece stock although
walnut was sometimes used. Single- and double-set
trigger. Brass fittings, including patchbox, ramrod ferrules, buttplate, etc. Made from 1785 to 1811.

J.P. Beck Fancy Kentucky Flintlock . . $6500
Same general specifications as above rifle, except gun
has some modest stock carvings, silver inlays, minute metal engraving, etc.

J.P. Beck Extra Fancy Flintlock . . . $10,000
Same general specifications as above rifle, except
extra fancy wood, much carving, engraving on metal
with gold or silver inlays. One such rifle has the
inscription "To the President George Washington AD
1791."

J. BECKER
Lebanon, Pennsylvania

Becker Kentucky Flintlock Rifle $1680
Lock: casehardened flintlock. Calibers: various, usually 36 to 50. Barrel length: 36 to 41 inches. Weight:
7½ pounds average. Curly maple one-piece stock
although walnut was sometimes used. Single- and
double-set trigger. Brass fittings, including patchbox, ramrod ferrules, buttplate, etc. Made from 1808
to 1910.

Becker Fancy Kentucky Flintlock Rifle $4500
Same general specifications as above rifle, except gun
has some modest stock carvings, silver inlays, minute metal engraving, etc.

Becker Extra Fancy Kentucky Flintlock. . $7000
Same general specifications as above rifle, except
extra fancy wood, much carving, engraving on metal
with gold or silver inlays.

S. BEIG
Lancaster County, Pennsylvania

Beig Kentucky Flintlock Rifle $1680
Lock: casehardened flintlock. Calibers: various, usually 36 to 50. Barrel length: 36 to 41 inches. Weight:
7½ pounds average. Curly maple one-piece stock
although walnut was sometimes used. Single- and
double-set trigger. Brass fittings, including patchbox, ramrod ferrules, buttplate, etc. Made from 1789
to 1790.

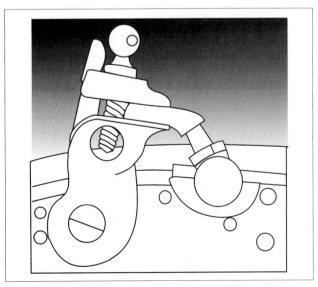

**One method to alter flintlocks to percussion was to use
the old hammer with a side lug.**

Beig Fancy Kentucky Flintlock Rifle . . $4500
Same general specifications as above rifle, except gun
has some modest stock carvings, silver inlays, minute
metal engraving, etc.

Beig Extra Fancy Kentucky Flintlock. . $7000
Same general specifications as above rifle, except
extra fancy wood, much carving, engraving on metal
with gold or silver inlays.

JOHN BELL
Carlisle, Pennsylvania

Bell Kentucky Flintlock Rifle $1550
Lock: casehardened flintlock. Calibers: various, usually 36 to 50. Barrel length: 36 to 41 inches. Weight:
7½ pounds average. Curly maple one-piece stock
although walnut was sometimes used. Single- and
double-set trigger. Brass fittings, including patchbox, ramrod ferrules, buttplate, etc. Made from 1799
to 1800.

Bell Fancy Kentucky Flintlock Rifle . . $4550
Same general specifications as above rifle, except gun
has some modest stock carvings, silver inlays, minute
metal engraving, etc.

Bell Extra Fancy Kentucky Flintlock . $7050
Same general specifications as above rifle, except
extra fancy wood, much carving, engraving on metal
with gold or silver inlays.

AMOS BENFER
Beaverstown, Pennsylvania

Benfer Kentucky Flintlock Rifle $1680
Lock: casehardened flintlock. Calibers: various,
usually 36 to 50. Barrel length: 36 to 41 inches.
Weight: 7½ pounds average. Curly maple one-piece
stock although walnut was sometimes used. Single-
and double-set trigger. Brass fittings, including
patchbox, ramrod ferrules, buttplate, etc. Made from
1814 to 1815.

**Benfer Fancy Kentucky
Flintlock Rifle $4500**
Same general specifications as above rifle, except gun
has some modest stock carvings, silver inlays, minute
metal engraving, etc.

**Benfer Extra Fancy Kentucky
Flintlock Rifle $7000**
Same general specifications as above rifle, except
extra fancy wood, much carving, engraving on metal
with gold or silver inlays.

ABRAHAM BERLIN
Easton, Pennsylvania

Berlin Kentucky Flintlock Rifle $1680
Lock: casehardened flintlock. Calibers: various, usually
36 to 50. Barrel length: 36 to 41 inches. Weight: 7½
pounds average. Curly maple one-piece stock although
walnut was sometimes used. Single- and double-set
trigger. Brass fittings, including patchbox, ramrod ferrules, buttplate, etc. Made from 1773 to 1786.

Berlin Fancy Kentucky Flintlock $4500
Same general specifications as above rifle, except gun
has some modest stock carvings, silver inlays, minute
metal engraving, etc.

Berlin Extra Fancy Kentucky Flintlock $7000
Same general specifications as above rifle, except
extra fancy wood, much carving, engraving on metal
with gold or silver inlays.

ISAAC BERLIN
Easton, Pennsylvania

I. Berlin Kentucky Flintlock Rifle $1525
Lock: casehardened flintlock. Calibers: various, usually
36 to 50. Barrel length: 36 to 41 inches. Weight: 7½
pounds average. Curly maple one-piece stock although
walnut was sometimes used. Single- and double-set
trigger. Brass fittings, including patchbox, ramrod ferrules, buttplate, etc. Made from 1781 to 1817.

I. Berlin Fancy Kentucky Flintlock . . . $4750
Same general specifications as above rifle, except gun
has some modest stock carvings, silver inlays, minute
metal engraving, etc.

I. Berlin Extra Fancy Kentucky Flintlock. . $7025
Same general specifications as above rifle, except
extra fancy wood, much carving, engraving on metal
with gold or silver inlays.

BEST
Lancaster, Pennsylvania

Best Kentucky Flintlock Rifle $1680
Lock: casehardened flintlock. Calibers: various, usually 36 to 50. Barrel length: 36 to 41 inches. Weight:
7½ pounds average. Curly maple one-piece stock
although walnut was sometimes used. Single- and
double-set trigger. Brass fittings, including patchbox, ramrod ferrules, buttplate, etc. Made from 1760
to 1775.

**Best Fancy Grade Kentucky Flintlock
Rifle** **$4500**
Same general specifications as above rifle, except gun
has some modest stock carvings, silver inlays, minute metal engraving, etc.

**Best Extra Fancy Grade Kentucky
Flintlock Rifle** **$7000**
Same general specifications as above rifle, except
extra fancy wood, much carving, engraving on metal
with gold or silver inlays.

N. BEYER
Lebanon, Pennsylvania

Beyer Kentucky Flintlock Rifle **$1680**
Lock: casehardened flintlock. Calibers: various, usually 36 to 50. Barrel length: 36 to 41 inches. Weight:
7½ pounds average. Curly maple one-piece stock
although walnut was sometimes used. Single- and
double-set trigger. Brass fittings, including patchbox, ramrod ferrules, buttplate, etc. Made from 1769
to 1770.

**Beyer Fancy Grade Kentucky Flintlock
Rifle** **$4500**
Same general specifications as above rifle, except gun
has some modest stock carvings, silver inlays, minute metal engraving, etc.

**Beyer Extra Fancy Grade Kentucky
Flintlock Rifle** **$7000**
Same general specifications as above rifle, except
extra fancy wood, much carving, engraving on metal
with gold or silver inlays.

HENRY BICKEL
York, Pennsylvania

Bickel Kentucky Flintlock Rifle **$1680**
Lock: casehardened flintlock. Calibers: various, usually 36 to 50. Barrel length: 36 to 41 inches. Weight:
7½ pounds average. Curly maple one-piece stock
although walnut was sometimes used. Single- and
double-set trigger. Brass fittings, including patchbox, ramrod ferrules, buttplate, etc. Made from 1799
to 1800.

**Bickel Fancy Grade Kentucky
Flintlock Rifle** **$4500**
Same general specifications as above rifle, except gun
has some modest stock carvings, silver inlays, minute metal engraving, etc.

**Bickel Extra Fancy Grade Kentucky
Flintlock Rifle** **$7000**
Same general specifications as above rifle, except
extra fancy wood, much carving, engraving on metal
with gold or silver inlays.

R. & W.C. BIDDLE
Philadelphia, Pennsylvania

Biddle Kentucky Flintlock Rifle **$1550**
Lock: casehardened flintlock. Calibers: various, usually 36 to 50. Barrel length: 36 to 41 inches. Weight:
7½ pounds average. Curly maple one-piece stock
although walnut was sometimes used. Single- and
double-set trigger. Brass fittings, including patchbox, ramrod ferrules, buttplate, etc. Made from 1800
to 1835.

**Biddle Fancy Grade Kentucky
Flintlock Rifle** **$4550**
Same general specifications as above rifle, except gun
has some modest stock carvings, silver inlays, minute metal engraving, etc.

**Biddle Extra Fancy Grade Kentucky
Flintlock Rifle** **$7050**
Same general specifications as above rifle, except
extra fancy wood, much carving, engraving on metal
with gold or silver inlays.

ANTHONY BOBB
Reading, Pennsylvania

Bobb Kentucky Flintlock Rifle **$1680**
Lock: casehardened flintlock. Calibers: various, usually 36 to 50. Barrel length: 36 to 41 inches. Weight:
7½ pounds average. Curly maple one-piece stock
although walnut was sometimes used. Single- and
double-set trigger. Brass fittings, including patchbox, ramrod ferrules, buttplate, etc. Made from 1778
to 1781.

**Bobb Fancy Grade Kentucky
Flintlock Rifle** **$4500**
Same general specifications as above rifle, except gun
has some modest stock carvings, silver inlays, minute metal engraving, etc.

**Bobb Extra Fancy Grade Kentucky Flintlock
Rifle.** **$7000**
Same general specifications as above rifle, except
extra fancy wood, much carving, engraving on metal
with gold or silver inlays.

SAMUEL BOONE
Berks County, Pennsylvania

Boone Kentucky Flintlock Rifle $1550
Lock: casehardened flintlock. Calibers: various, usually 36 to 50. Barrel length: 36 to 41 inches. Weight: 7½ pounds average. Curly maple one-piece stock although walnut was sometimes used. Single- and double-set trigger. Brass fittings, including patchbox, ramrod ferrules, buttplate, etc. Made from 1769 to 1770.

Boone Fancy Kentucky Flintlock $4550
Same general specifications as above rifle, except gun has some modest stock carvings, silver inlays, minute metal engraving, etc.

Boone Extra Fancy Kentucky Flintlock . . $7050
Same general specifications as above rifle, except extra fancy wood, much carving, engraving on metal with gold or silver inlays.

SAMUEL BORDER
Somerset County, Pennsylvania

Border Kentucky Flintlock Rifle. $1680
Lock: casehardened flintlock. Calibers: various, usually 36 to 50. Barrel length: 36 to 41 inches. Weight: 7½ pounds average. Curly maple one-piece stock although walnut was sometimes used. Single- and double-set trigger. Brass fittings, including patchbox, ramrod ferrules, buttplate, etc. Made from 1825 to 1861.

Border Fancy Kentucky Flintlock Rfile . . $4500
Same general specifications as above rifle, except gun has some modest stock carvings, silver inlays, minute metal engraving, etc.

Border Extra Fancy Kentucky Flintlock. . $7000
Same general specifications as above rifle, except extra fancy wood, much carving, engraving on metal with gold or silver inlays.

BOSWORTH
Lancaster, Pennsylvania

Bosworth Kentucky Flintlock Rifle . . $1680
Lock: casehardened flintlock. Calibers: various, usually 36 to 50. Barrel length: 36 to 41 inches. Weight: 7½ pounds average. Curly maple one-piece stock although walnut was sometimes used. Single- and double-set trigger. Brass fittings, including patchbox, ramrod ferrules, buttplate, etc. Made from 1760 to 1775.

Bosworth Fancy Grade Kentucky Flintlock Rifle. $4500
Same general specifications as above rifle, except gun has some modest stock carvings, silver inlays, minute metal engraving, etc.

Bosworth Extra Fancy Grade Kentucky Flintlock Rifle $7000
Same general specifications as above rifle, except extra fancy wood, much carving, engraving on metal with gold or silver inlays.

DANIEL & HENRY BOYER
Orwigsburg, Pennsylvania

Boyer Kentucky Flintlock Rifle $1525
Lock: casehardened flintlock. Calibers: various, usually 36 to 50. Barrel length: 36 to 41 inches. Weight: 7½ pounds average. Curly maple one-piece stock although walnut was sometimes used. Single- and double-set trigger. Brass fittings, including patchbox, ramrod ferrules, buttplate, etc. Made from 1790 to 1810.

Boyer Fancy Grade Kentucky Flintlock Rifle $4525
Same general specifications as above rifle, except gun has some modest stock carvings, silver inlays, minute metal engraving, etc.

Boyer Extra Fancy Grade Kentucky Flintlock Rifle. $7025
Same general specifications as above rifle, except extra fancy wood, much carving, engraving on metal with gold or silver inlays.

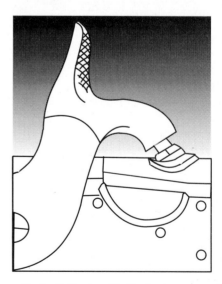

Belgian method of altering flintlocks to percussion.

GEORGE BRAMMER
Chesapeake County, Ohio

Brammer Kentucky Flintlock Rifle . . . $1680
Lock: casehardened flintlock. Calibers: various, usually 36 to 50. Barrel length: 36 to 41 inches. Weight: 7½ pounds average. Curly maple one-piece stock although walnut was sometimes used. Single- and double-set trigger. Brass fittings, including patchbox, ramrod ferrules, buttplate, etc. Made from 1795 to 1820.

Brammer Fancy Kentucky Flintlock . . $4500
Same general specifications as above rifle, except gun has some modest stock carvings, silver inlays, minute metal engraving, etc.

Brammer Extra Fancy Kentucky Flintlock . . $7000
Same general specifications as above rifle, except extra fancy wood, much carving, engraving on metal with gold or silver inlays.

JOSEPH BRONG
Lancaster, Pennsylvania

J. Brong Kentucky Flintlock Rifle . . . $1680
Lock: casehardened flintlock. Calibers: various, usually 36 to 50. Barrel length: 36 to 41 inches. Weight: 7½ pounds average. Curly maple one-piece stock although walnut was sometimes used. Single- and double-set trigger. Brass fittings, including patchbox, ramrod ferrules, buttplate, etc. Made from 1760 to 1800.

J. Brong Fancy Grade Kentucky Flintlock Rifle $4500
Same general specifications as above rifle, except gun has some modest stock carvings, silver inlays, minute metal engraving, etc.

J. Brong Extra Fancy Grade Kentucky Flintlock Rifle $7000
Same general specifications as above rifle, except extra fancy wood, much carving, engraving on metal with gold or silver inlays.

PETER BRONG
Lancaster, Pennsylvania

P. Brong Kentucky Flintlock Rifle . . . $1550
Lock: casehardened flintlock. Calibers: various, usually 36 to 50. Barrel length: 36 to 41 inches. Weight: 7½ pounds average. Curly maple one-piece stock although walnut was sometimes used. Single- and double-set trigger. Brass fittings, including patchbox, ramrod ferrules, buttplate, etc. Made from 1795 10 1816.

P. Brong Fancy Kentucky Flintlock . . . $4550
Same general specifications as above rifle, except gun has some modest stock carvings, silver inlays, minute metal engraving, etc.

P. Brong Extra Fancy Kentucky Flintlock . . $7050
Same general specifications as above rifle, except extra fancy wood, much carving, engraving on metal with gold or silver inlays.

JOHN BROOKS
Lancaster, Pennsylvania

Brooks Kentucky Flintlock Rifle $1680
Lock: casehardened flintlock. Calibers: various, usually 36 to 50. Barrel length: 36 to 41 inches. Weight: 7½ pounds average. Curly maple one-piece stock although walnut was sometimes used. Single- and double-set trigger. Brass fittings, including patchbox, ramrod ferrules, buttplate, etc. Made from 1804 to 1805.

Brooks Fancy Grade Kentucky Flintlock Rifle $4500
Same general specifications as above rifle, except gun has some modest stock carvings, silver inlays, minute metal engraving, etc.

Brooks Extra Fancy Grade Kentucky Flintlock $7000
Same general specifications as above rifle, except extra fancy wood, much carving, engraving on metal with gold or silver inlays.

JAMES BROWN
Pittsburg, Pennsylvania

Brown Kentucky Flintlock Rifle $1680
Lock: casehardened flintlock. Calibers: various, usually 36 to 50. Barrel length: 36 to 41 inches. Weight: 7½ pounds average. Curly maple one-piece stock although walnut was sometimes used. Single- and double-set trigger. Brass fittings, including patchbox, ramrod ferrules, buttplate, etc. Made from 1810 to 1848.

Brown Fancy Grade Kentucky Flintlock Rifle $4500
Same general specifications as above rifle, except gun has some modest stock carvings, silver inlays, minute metal engraving, etc.

Brown Extra Fancy Grade Kentucky Flintlock Rifle $7000
Same general specifications as above rifle, except extra fancy wood, much carving, engraving on metal with gold or silver inlays.

JAMES BRYANT
Lancaster County, Pennsylvania

Bryant Kentucky Flintlock Rifle..... $1525
Lock: casehardened flintlock. Calibers: various, usually 36 to 50. Barrel length: 36 to 41 inches. Weight: 7½ pounds average. Curly maple one-piece stock although walnut was sometimes used. Single- and double-set trigger. Brass fittings, including patchbox, ramrod ferrules, buttplate, etc. Made from 1799 to 1800.

Bryant Fancy Grade Kentucky Flintlock.. $4525
Same general specifications as above rifle, except gun has some modest stock carvings, silver inlays, minute metal engraving, etc.

Bryant Extra Fancy Grade Kentucky Flintlock Rifle $7025
Same general specifications as above rifle, except extra fancy wood, much carving, engraving on metal with gold or silver inlays.

ABRAHAM, HENRY & JOHN BUCKWALTER
Lancaster County Pennsylvania

Buckwalter Kentucky Flintlock Rifle . $1680
Lock: casehardened flintlock. Calibers: various, usually 36 to 50. Barrel length: 36 to 41 inches. Weight: 7½ pounds average. Curly maple one-piece stock although walnut was sometimes used. Single- and double-set trigger. Brass fittings, including patchbox, ramrod ferrules, buttplate, etc. Made from 1771 to 1780.

Buckwalter Fancy Kentucky Flintlock .. $4500
Same general specifications as above rifle, except gun has some modest stock carvings, silver inlays, minute metal engraving, etc.

Buckwalter Extra Fancy Grade Kentucky Flintlock $7000
Same general specifications as above rifle, except extra fancy wood, much carving, engraving on metal with gold or silver inlays.

CHARLES BULOW
Lancaster, Pennsylvania

Bulow Kentucky Flintlock Rifle $1680
Lock: casehardened flintlock. Calibers: various, usually 36 to 50. Barrel length: 36 to 41 inches. Weight: 7½ pounds average. Curly maple one-piece stock although walnut was sometimes used. Single- and double-set trigger. Brass fittings, including patchbox, ramrod ferrules, buttplate, etc. Made from 1794 to 1795.

Bulow Fancy Kentucky Flintlock Rifle.. $4500
Same general specifications as above rifle, except gun has some modest stock carvings, silver inlays, minute metal engraving, etc.

Bulow Extra Fancy Grade Kentucky Flintlock Rifle $7000
Same general specifications as above rifle, except extra fancy wood, much carving, engraving on metal with gold or silver inlays.

JOHN BURT
Donegal Township, Pennsylvania

Burt Kentucky Flintlock Rifle $1550
Lock: casehardened flintlock. Calibers: various, usually 36 to 50. Barrel length: 36 to 41 inches. Weight: 7½ pounds average. Curly maple one-piece stock although walnut was sometimes used. Single- and double-set trigger. Brass fittings, including patchbox, ramrod ferrules, buttplate, etc. Made from 1769 to 1770.

Burt Fancy Kentucky Flintlock Rifle .. $4550
Same general specifications as above rifle, except gun has some modest stock carvings, silver inlays, minute metal engraving, etc.

Burt Extra Fancy Kentucky Flintlock .. $7050
Same general specifications as above rifle, except extra fancy wood, much carving, engraving on metal with gold or silver inlays.

BUSCH
Lancaster, Pennsylvania

Busch Kentucky Flintlock Rifle $1525
Lock: casehardened flintlock. Calibers: various, usually 36 to 50. Barrel length: 36 to 41 inches. Weight: 7½ pounds average. Curly maple one-piece stock although walnut was sometimes used. Single- and double-set trigger. Brass fittings, including patchbox, ramrod ferrules, buttplate, etc. Made from 1774 to 1775.

Busch Fancy Grade Kentucky Flintlock Rifle $4525
Same general specifications as above rifle, except gun has some modest stock carvings, silver inlays, minute metal engraving, etc.

Busch Extra Fancy Grade Kentucky Flintlock Rifle........................ $7025
Same general specifications as above rifle, except extra fancy wood, much carving, engraving on metal with gold or silver inlays.

WILLIAM CALDERWOOD
Philadelphia, Pennsylvania

Calderwood Kentucky Flintlock Rifle . $1680
Lock: casehardened flintlock. Calibers: various, usually 36 to 50. Barrel length: 36 to 41 inches. Weight: 7½ pounds average. Curly maple one-piece stock although walnut was sometimes used. Single- and double-set trigger. Brass fittings, including patchbox, ramrod ferrules, buttplate, etc. Made from 1807 to 1819.

GEORGE CALL
Lancaster, Pennsylvania

Call Kentucky Flintlock Rifle $1250
Lock: casehardened flintlock. Calibers: various, usually 36 to 50. Barrel length: 36 to 41 inches. Weight: 7½ pounds average. Curly maple one-piece stock although walnut was sometimes used. Single- and double-set trigger. Brass fittings, including patchbox, ramrod ferrules, buttplate, etc. Made from 1775 to 1780.

Call Fancy Kentucky Flintlock Rifle . . $4100
Same general specifications as above rifle, except gun has some modest stock carvings, silver inlays, minute metal engraving, etc.

Call Extra Fancy Kentucky Flintlock . . $6300
Same general specifications as above rifle, except extra fancy wood, much carving, engraving on metal with gold or silver inlays.

H. CARLILE
Lancaster, Pennsylvania

Carlile Kentucky Flintlock Rifle $1680
Lock: casehardened flintlock. Calibers: various, usually 36 to 50. Barrel length: 36 to 41 inches. Weight: 7½ pounds average. Curly maple one-piece stock although walnut was sometimes used. Single- and double-set trigger. Brass fittings, including patchbox, ramrod ferrules, buttplate, etc. Made from 1779 to 1780.

THOMAS P. CHERRINGTON
Cattawissa, Pennsylvania

Cherrington Kentucky Flintlock Rifle. . $1650
Lock: casehardened flintlock. Calibers: various, usually 36 to 50. Barrel length: 36 to 41 inches. Weight: 7½ pounds average. Curly maple one-piece stock although walnut was sometimes used. Single- and double-set trigger. Made from 1765 to 1805.

Cherrington Fancy Grade Kentucky Flintlock Rifle $4650
Same general specifications as above rifle, except gun has some modest stock carvings, silver inlays, minute metal engraving, etc.

JOHN CLARK
Reading, Pennsylvania

Clark Kentucky Flintlock Rifle. $1680
Lock: casehardened flintlock. Calibers: various, usually 36 to 50. Barrel length: 36 to 41 inches. Weight: 7½ pounds average. Curly maple one-piece stock although walnut was sometimes used. Single- and double-set trigger. Brass fittings, including patchbox, ramrod ferrules, buttplate, etc. Made from 1804 to 1805.

CONESTOGA RIFLE WORKS
Lancaster, Pennsylvania

Conestoga Kentucky Flintlock Rifle. . . $1225
Lock: casehardened flintlock. Calibers: various, usually 36 to 50. Barrel length: 36 to 41 inches. Weight: 7½ pounds average. Curly maple one-piece stock although walnut was sometimes used. Single- and double-set trigger. Brass fittings, including patchbox, ramrod ferrules, buttplate, etc. Made from 1779 to 1780.

ABRAHAM COSTER
Philadelphia, Pennsylvania

Coster Kentucky Flintlock Rifle. $1680
Lock: casehardened flintlock. Calibers: various, usually 36 to 50. Barrel length: 36 to 41 inches. Weight: 7½ pounds average. Curly maple one-piece stock although walnut was sometimes used. Single- and double-set trigger. Brass fittings, including patchbox, ramrod ferrules, buttplate, etc. Made from 1810 to 1814.

Coster Fancy Grade Kentucky Flintlock Rifle $4500
Same general specifications as above rifle, except gun has some modest stock carvings, silver inlays, minute metal engraving, etc.

Coster Extra Fancy Grade Kentucky Flintlock Rifle $7000
Same general specifications as above rifle, except extra fancy wood, much carving, engraving on metal with gold or silver inlays.

GEORGE CUNKLE
Harrisburg, Pennsylvania

Cunkle Kentucky Flintlock Rifle **$1680**
Lock: casehardened flintlock. Calibers: various, usually 36 to 50. Barrel length: 36 to 41 inches. Weight: 7½ pounds average. Curly maple one-piece stock although walnut was sometimes used. Single- and double-set trigger. Brass fittings, including patchbox, ramrod ferrules, buttplate, etc. Made from 1839 to 1840.

JACOB DANNER
Canton, Ohio

Danner Kentucky Flintlock Rifle **$1680**
Lock: casehardened flintlock. Calibers: various, usually 36 to 50. Barrel length: 36 to 41 inches. Weight: 7½ pounds average. Curly maple one-piece stock although walnut was sometimes used. Single- and double-set trigger. Brass fittings, including patchbox, ramrod ferrules, buttplate, etc. Made from 1821 to 1844.

Danner Fancy Kentucky Flintlock . . . **$4500**
Same general specifications as above rifle, except gun has some modest stock carvings, silver inlays, minute metal engraving, etc.

Danner Extra Fancy Kentucky Flintlock. . **$7000**
Same general specifications as above rifle, except extra fancy wood, much carving, engraving on metal with gold or silver inlays.

H.W. DEEDS
Reading, Pennsylvania

Deeds Kentucky Flintlock Rifle **$1680**
Lock: casehardened flintlock. Calibers: various, usually 36 to 50. Barrel length: 36 to 41 inches. Weight: 7½ pounds average. Curly maple one-piece stock although walnut was sometimes used. Single- and double-set trigger. Brass fittings, including patchbox, ramrod ferrules, buttplate, etc. Made from 1774 to 1775.

JOHN DERR(E)
Lancaster, Pennsylvania

Deer(e) Kentucky Flintlock Rifle. **$6300**
Flintlock ignition system. Caliber: 42. Barrel: 42½ inches; half-octagonal. Overall length: 57½ inches. Weight: 7½ pounds. Full maple stock. Brass patchbox. Made from 1810 to 1844.

ADAM DETERER
Lancaster, Pennsylvania

Deterer Kentucky Flintlock Rifle **$1680**
Lock: casehardened flintlock. Calibers: various, usually 36 to 50. Barrel length: 36 to 41 inches. Weight: 7½ pounds average. Curly maple one-piece stock although walnut was sometimes used. Single- and double-set trigger. Brass fittings, including patchbox, ramrod ferrules, buttplate, etc. Made from 1740 to 1778.

**Deterer Fancy Grade Kentucky
Flintlock Rifle** **$4500**
Same general specifications as above rifle, except gun has some modest stock carvings, silver inlays, minute metal engraving, etc.

JACOB DOLL
York, Pennsylvania

Doll Kentucky Flintlock Rifle. **$1500**
Lock: casehardened flintlock. Calibers: various, usually 36 to 50. Barrel length: 36 to 41 inches average. Weight: 7½ pounds average. Curly maple one-piece stock, although walnut was sometimes used. Single- and double-set trigger. Brass fittings, including patchbox, ramrod ferrules, buttplate, etc. Made from 1780 to 1805.

**Doll Fancy Grade Kentucky
Flintlock Rifle** **$4500**
Same general specifications as above rifle, except gun has some modest stock carvings, silver inlays, and minute metal engraving, etc.

**Doll Extra Fancy Grade Kentucky
Flintlock Rifle** **$7000**
Same general specifications as above rifle, except extra fancy wood, much carving, engraving on metal with gold or silver inlays.

JACOB DULL
Lancaster, Pennsylvania

Dull Kentucky Flintlock Rifle **$1200**
Lock: casehardened flintlock. Calibers: various, usually 36 to 50. Barrel length: 36 to 41 inches average. Weight: 7½ pounds average. Curly maple one-piece stock, although walnut was sometimes used. Single- and double-set trigger. Brass fittings, including patchbox, ramrod ferrules, buttplate, etc. Made from 1799 to 1800.

HENRY EBERMAN
Lancaster, Pennsylvania

Eberman Kentucky Flintlock Rifle . . . $1500
Lock: casehardened flintlock. Calibers: various, usually 36 to 50. Barrel length: 36 to 41 inches average. Weight: 7½ pounds average. Curly maple one-piece stock, although walnut was sometimes used. Single- and double-set trigger. Brass fittings, including patchbox, ramrod ferrules, buttplate, etc. Made from 1819 to 1820.

Eberman Fancy Kentucky Flintlock . . $4500
Same general specifications as above rifle, except gun has some modest stock carvings, silver inlays, and minute metal engraving, etc.

Eberman Extra Fancy Grade Kentucky Flintlock Rifle $7000
Same general specifications as above rifle, except extra fancy wood, much carving, engraving on metal with gold or silver inlays.

H. EHRMS
Address Unknown

Ehrms Kentucky Flintlock Rifle $1500
Caliber: 52. Barrel: 41½ inches, full octagonal. Overall length: 56½ inches. Weight: 9 pounds. Full maple stock; all silver mountings.

H. ELWELL
Liverpool, Pennsylvania

Elwell Kentucky Flintlock Rifle $1500
Lock: casehardened flintlock. Calibers: various, usually 36 to 50. Barrel length: 36 to 41 inches average. Weight: 7½ pounds average. Curly maple one-piece stock, although walnut was sometimes used. Single- and double-set trigger. Brass fittings, including patchbox, ramrod ferrules, buttplate, etc. Made from 1769 to 1770.

FREDERICK, FRANK & JACOB FARNOT
Lancaster, Pennsylvania

Farnot Kentucky Flintlock Rifle $1500
Lock: casehardened flintlock. Calibers: various, usually 36 to 50. Barrel length: 36 to 41 inches average. Weight: 7½ pounds average. Curly maple one-piece stock, although walnut was sometimes used. Single- and double-set trigger. Brass fittings, including patchbox, ramrod ferrules, buttplate, etc. Made from 1775 to 1783.

Farnot Fancy Kentucky Flintlock Rifle . . $4500
Same general specifications as above rifle, except gun has some modest stock carvings, silver inlays, and minute metal engraving, etc.

Farnot Extra Fancy Kentucky Flintlock $7000
Same general specifications as above rifle, except extra fancy wood, much carving, engraving on metal with gold or silver inlays.

PHILIP FISHBURN
Dauphin County, Pennsylvania

Fishburn Kentucky Flintlock Rifle $1680
Lock: casehardened flintlock. Calibers: various, usually 36 to 50. Barrel length: 36 to 41 inches average. Weight: 7½ pounds average. Curly maple one-piece stock, although walnut was sometimes used. Single- and double-set trigger. Brass fittings, including patchbox, ramrod ferrules, buttplate, etc. Made from 1776 to 1795.

Fishburn Fancy Kentucky Flintlock . . . $4500
Same general specifications as above rifle, except gun has some modest stock carvings, silver inlays, and minute metal engraving, etc.

Fishburn Extra Fancy Kentucky Flintlock . . $7000
Same general specifications as above rifle, except extra fancy wood, much carving, engraving on metal with gold or silver inlays.

GEORGE FONDERSMITH
Strasburg Township, Pennsylvania

Fondersmith Kentucky Flintlock Rifle . . $1680
Lock: casehardened flintlock. Calibers: various, usually 36 to 50. Barrel length: 36 to 41 inches average. Weight: 7½ pounds average. Curly maple one-piece stock, although walnut was sometimes used. Single- and double-set trigger. Brass fittings, including patchbox, ramrod ferrules, buttplate, etc. Made from 1779 to 1780.

C. FORDNEY
Cumberland, Pennsylvania

Fordney Kentucky Flintlock Rifle $1680
Lock: casehardened flintlock. Calibers: various, usually 36 to 50. Barrel length: 36 to 41 inches average. Weight: 7½ pounds average. Curly maple one-piece stock, although walnut was sometimes used. Single- and double-set trigger. Brass fittings, including patchbox, ramrod ferrules, buttplate, etc. Made from 1800 to 1830.

**Fordney Fancy Grade Kentucky Flintlock
Rifle** **$4500**
Same general specifications as above rifle, except gun
has some modest stock carvings, silver inlays, and
minute metal engraving, etc.

**Fordney Extra Fancy Grade Kentucky
Flintlock Rifle** **$7000**
Same general specifications as above rifle, except
extra fancy wood, much carving, engraving on metal
with gold or silver inlays.

MARTIN FREY
York, Pennsylvania

Frey Kentucky Flintlock Rifle **$1680**
Lock: casehardened flintlock. Calibers: various, usually 36 to 50. Barrel length: 36 to 41 inches average.
Weight: 7½ pounds average. Curly maple one-piece
stock, although walnut was sometimes used. Single-
and double-set trigger. Brass fittings, including
patchbox, ramrod ferrules, buttplate, etc. Made from
1799 to 1800.

PETER GANDER
Lancaster, Pennsylvania

Gander Kentucky Flintlock Rifle **$1680**
Lock: casehardened flintlock. Calibers: various, usually 36 to 50. Barrel length: 36 to 41 inches average.
Weight: 7½ pounds average. Curly maple one-piece
stock, although walnut was sometimes used. Single-
and double-set trigger. Brass fittings, including
patchbox, ramrod ferrules, buttplate, etc. Made from
1779 to 1780.

JOHN GETZ
Lancaster, Pennsylvania

Getz Kentucky Flintlock Rifle **$1680**
Lock: casehardened flintlock. Calibers: various, usually 36 to 50. Barrel length: 36 to 41 inches average.
Weight: 7½ pounds average. Curly maple one-piece
stock, although walnut was sometimes used. Single-
and double-set trigger. Brass fittings, including
patchbox, ramrod ferrules, buttplate, etc. Made from
1773 to 1782.

**Getz Fancy Grade Kentucky
Flintlock Rifle** **$4500**
Same general specifications as above rifle, except gun
has some modest stock carvings, silver inlays, and
minute metal engraving, etc.

**Getz Extra Fancy Grade Kentucky Flintlock
Rifle.** **$7000**
Same general specifications as above rifle, except
extra fancy wood, much carving, engraving on metal
with gold or silver inlays.

FREDERICK GOETZ
Philadelphia, Pennsylvania

Goetz Kentucky Flintlock Rifle **$1680**
Lock: casehardened flintlock. Calibers: various, usually 36 to 50. Barrel length: 36 to 41 inches average.
Weight: 7½ pounds average. Curly maple one-piece
stock, although walnut was sometimes used. Single-
and double-set trigger. Brass fittings, including
patchbox, ramrod ferrules, buttplate, etc. Made from
1806 to 1812.

Goetz Fancy Kentucky Flintlock Rifle . . **$4500**
Same general specifications as above rifle, except gun
has some modest stock carvings, silver inlays, and
minute metal engraving, etc.

**Goetz Extra Fancy Grade Kentucky Flintlock
Rifle.** **$7000**
Same general specifications as above rifle, except
extra fancy wood, much carving, engraving on metal
with gold or silver inlays.

J. GRESHEIM
Lancaster, Pennsylvania

Gresheim Kentucky Flintlock Rifle . . . **$1680**
Lock: casehardened flintlock. Calibers: various, usually 36 to 50. Barrel length: 36 to 41 inches average.
Weight: 7½ pounds average. Curly maple one-piece
stock, although walnut was sometimes used. Single-
and double-set trigger. Brass fittings, including
patchbox, ramrod ferrules, buttplate, etc. Made from
1775 to 1783.

SAMUEL GROVE
York County, Pennsylvania

Grove Kentucky Flintlock Rifle **$1680**
Lock: casehardened flintlock. Calibers: various, usually 36 to 50. Barrel length: 36 to 41 inches average.
Weight: 7½ pounds average. Curly maple one-piece
stock, although walnut was sometimes used. Single-
and double-set trigger. Brass fittings, including
patchbox, ramrod ferrules, buttplate, etc. Made from
1779 to 1783.

Grove Fancy Kentucky Flintlock Rifle . . . $4500
Same general specifications as above rifle, except gun
has some modest stock carvings, silver inlays, and
minute metal engraving, etc.

Grove Extra Fancy Kentucky Flintlock . . $7000
Same general specifications as above rifle, except
extra fancy wood, much carving, engraving on metal
with gold or silver inlays.

CHRISTIAN GUMP
Lancaster, Pennsylvania

Gump Kentucky Flintlock Rifle $1680
Lock: casehardened flintlock. Calibers: various, usually
36 to 50. Barrel length: 36 to 41 inches average. Weight:
7½ pounds average. Curly maple one-piece stock, although walnut was sometimes used. Single- and double-
set trigger. Brass fittings, including patchbox, ramrod
ferrules, buttplate, etc. Made from 1799 to 1800.

ISAAC HAINES
Lampeter Township, Pennsylvania

Haines Kentucky Flintlock Rifle $1680
Lock: casehardened flintlock. Calibers: various, usually
36 to 50. Barrel length: 36 to 41 inches average. Weight:
7½ pounds average. Curly maple one-piece stock, although walnut was sometimes used. Single- and double-
set trigger. Brass fittings, including patchbox, ramrod
ferrules, buttplate, etc. Made from 1730 to 1775.

Haines Fancy Kentucky Flintlock Rifle . . $4500
Same general specifications as above rifle, except gun
has some modest stock carvings, silver inlays, and
minute metal engraving, etc.

Haines Extra Fancy Kentucky Flintlock . . $7000
Same general specifications as above rifle, except
extra fancy wood, much carving, engraving on metal
with gold or silver inlays.

JOHN N. HAMPTON
Hanover Township, Pennsylvania

Hampton Kentucky Flintlock Rifle . . . $1680
Lock: casehardened flintlock. Calibers: various, usually 36 to 50. Barrel length: 36 to 41 inches average.
Weight: 7½ pounds average. Curly maple one-piece
stock, although walnut was sometimes used. Single-
and double-set trigger. Brass fittings, including
patchbox, ramrod ferrules, buttplate, etc. Made from
1834 to 1835.

HENRY HARRIS
Lancaster, Pennsylvania

Harris Kentucky Flintlock Rifle $1500
Lock: casehardened flintlock. Calibers: various, usually 36 to 50. Barrel length: 36 to 41 inches average.
Weight: 7½ pounds average. Curly maple one-piece
stock, although walnut was sometimes used. Single-
and double-set trigger. Brass fittings, including
patchbox, ramrod ferrules, buttplate, etc. Made from
1834 to 184.

**Harris Fancy Grade Kentucky
Flintlock Rifle. $4500**
Same general specifications as above rifle, except gun
has some modest stock carvings, silver inlays, and
minute metal engraving, etc.

**Harris Extra Fancy Grade Kentucky Flintlock
Rifle. $7000**
Same general specifications as above rifle, except
extra fancy wood, much carving, engraving on metal
with gold or silver inlays.

PETER HENCH
Lancaster, Pennsylvania

Hench Kentucky Flintlock Rifle $1680
Lock: casehardened flintlock. Calibers: various, usually 36 to 50. Barrel length: 36 to 41 inches average.
Weight: 7½ pounds average. Curly maple one-piece
stock, although walnut was sometimes used. Single-
and double-set trigger. Brass fittings, including
patchbox, ramrod ferrules, buttplate, etc. Made from
1740 to 1775.

J. HILLEGAS
Pottsville, Pennsylvania

Hillegas Kentucky Flintlock Rifle $1680
Lock: casehardened flintlock. Calibers: various, usually 36 to 50. Barrel length: 36 to 41 inches average.
Weight: 7½ pounds average. Curly maple one-piece
stock, although walnut was sometimes used. Single-
and double-set trigger. Brass fittings, including
patchbox, ramrod ferrules, buttplate, etc. Made from
1810 to 1830.

**Hillegas Fancy Grade Kentucky Flintlock
Rifle. $4500**
Same general specifications as above rifle, except gun
has some modest stock carvings, silver inlays, and
minute metal engraving, etc.

Hillegas Extra Fancy Grade Kentucky Flintlock Rifle **$7000**
Same general specifications as above rifle, except extra fancy wood, much carving, engraving on metal with gold or silver inlays.

MATHIAS HOAK
Lancaster, Pennsylvania

Hoak Kentucky Flintlock Rifle **$1680**
Lock: casehardened flintlock. Calibers: various, usually 36 to 50. Barrel length: 36 to 41 inches average. Weight: 7½ pounds average. Curly maple one-piece stock, although walnut was sometimes used. Single- and double-set trigger. Brass fittings, including patchbox, ramrod ferrules, buttplate, etc. Made from 1799 to 1800.

MICHAEL HUMBLE
Louisville, Kentucky

Humble Kentucky Flintlock Rifle **$1995**
Lock: casehardened flintlock. Calibers: various, usually 36 to 50. Barrel length: 36 to 41 inches average. Weight: 7½ pounds average. Curly maple one-piece stock, although walnut was sometimes used. Single- and double-set trigger. Brass fittings, including patchbox, ramrod ferrules, buttplate, etc. Made from1775 to 1795.

Humble Fancy Grade Kentucky Flintlock Rifle **$4900**
Same general specifications as above rifle, except gun has some modest stock carvings, silver inlays, and minute metal engraving, etc.

Humble Extra Fancy Grade Kentucky Flintlock Rifle **$9000**
Same general specifications as above rifle, except extra fancy wood, much carving, engraving on metal with gold or silver inlays.

V. HUNTINGTON
Allentown, Pennsylvania

Huntington Kentucky Flintlock Rifle . . **$1500**
Lock: casehardened flintlock. Calibers: various, usually 36 to 50. Barrel length: 36 to 41 inches average. Weight: 7½ pounds average. Curly maple one-piece stock, although walnut was sometimes used. Single- and double-set trigger. Brass fittings, including patchbox, ramrod ferrules, buttplate, etc. Made from 1798 to 1800.

BENEDICT IMHOFF
Heidelberg Township, Pennsylvania

Imhoff Kentucky Flintlock Rifle **$1680**
Lock: casehardened flintlock. Calibers: various, usually 36 to 50. Barrel length: 36 to 41 inches average. Weight: 7½ pounds average. Curly maple one-piece stock, although walnut was sometimes used. Single- and double-set trigger. Brass fittings, including patchbox, ramrod ferrules, buttplate, etc. Made from 1784 to 1785.

Imhoff Fancy Grade Kentucky Flintlock Rifle **$4500**
Same general specifications as above rifle, except gun has some modest stock carvings, silver inlays, and minute metal engraving, etc.

Imhoff Extra Fancy Grade Kentucky Flintlock Rifle **$7000**
Same general specifications as above rifle, except extra fancy wood, much carving, engraving on metal with gold or silver inlays.

JACOB JORG
Berks County, Pennsylvania

Jorg Kentucky Flintlock Rifle **$1680**
Lock: casehardened flintlock. Calibers: various, usually 36 to 50. Barrel length: 36 to 41 inches average. Weight: 7½ pounds average. Curly maple one-piece stock, although walnut was sometimes used. Single- and double-set trigger. Brass fittings, including patchbox, ramrod ferrules, buttplate, etc. Made from 1814 to 1815.

JOHN KELLER
Carlisle, Pennsylvania

Keller Kentucky Flintlock Rifle **$1680**
Lock: casehardened flintlock. Calibers: various, usually 36 to 50. Barrel length: 36 to 41 inches average. Weight: 7½ pounds average. Curly maple one-piece stock, although walnut was sometimes used. Single- and double-set trigger. Brass fittings, including patchbox, ramrod ferrules, buttplate, etc. Made from 1823 to 1842.

Keller Fancy Grade Kentucky Flintlock Rifle **$4500**
Same general specifications as above rifle, except gun has some modest stock carvings, silver inlays, and minute metal engraving, etc.

Keller Extra Fancy Grade Kentucky Flintlock Rifle **$7000**
Same general specifications as above rifle, except extra fancy wood, much carving, engraving on metal with gold or silver inlays.

JOHN S. KINTER
Harriston County, Indiana

Kinter Kentucky Flintlock Rifle **$1680**
Lock: casehardened flintlock. Calibers: various, usually 36 to 50. Barrel length: 36 to 41 inches average. Weight: 7½ pounds average. Curly maple one-piece stock, although walnut was sometimes used. Single- and double-set trigger. Brass fittings, including patchbox, ramrod ferrules, buttplate, etc. Made from 1820 to 1851.

JOHN MAURER
Lancaster, Pennsylvania

Maurer (Mauger) Kentucky Flintlock . . **$6800**
Flintlock ignition system. Caliber: 42. Overall length: 61 inches. Weight: 9¾ pounds. Full maple stock, hand carved. Brass patchbox. Made circa 1800.

PETER NEIHARD
Whitehall Township, Pennsylvania

Neihard Kentucky Flintlock Rifle **$950**
Flintlock. Caliber: 45 most common. Barrel length: 40 inches; round and octagonal. Weight: 9 pounds. Curly maple full-length stock. Brass fittings. Made from 1785 to 1793.

CHRISTIAN OBERHOLZER
Lancaster, Pennsylvania

Oberholzer Kentucky Flintlock Musket . . . **$795**
Calibers: 45, 54 and others. Barrel: 40 inches; round and octagonal. Weight: 9 pounds. Curly maple full-length stock. Brass fittings. Made from 1775 to 1778.

JOHN PAGE
Lancaster, Pennsylvania

Page Kentucky Flintlock Rifle **$975**
Flintlock. Calibers: 36 and 45. Barrel: 40 inches; round and octagonal. Weight: 9 pounds. Curly maple full-length stock; brass fittings. Made from 1770 to 1777.

RAPPAHANNOCK FORGE
Falmouth, Virginia

Rappahannock Forge was established by Act of the Assembly of Virginia, June 1775. The forge was previously owned by the Hunter Iron Works. Rappahannock Forge was considered to have produced some of the earliest "true" American military arms.

Rappahannock Forge Flintlock Musket **$1400**
Calibers: 45, 54 and others. Barrel: 40 inches, round. Weight, 9½ pounds. American walnut stock with iron and brass fittings. Made from 1775 to 1781.

WILLIAM SCHEANER
Reading, Pennsylvania

Scheaner Kentucky Flintlock Rifle **$1725**
Calibers: 36 and 45. Barrel: 40 inches; round and octagonal. Weight: 8½ to 9¼ pounds. American walnut and curly maple stock. Mostly brass fittings. Silver inlays and wood carvings. Made from 1779 to 1790.

WELSHANTZ BROTHERS
York, Pennsylvania

Welshantz Kentucky Flintlock Rifle, Deluxe **$1425**
Caliber: 45 most common. Barrel: 40 inches; round and octagonal. Weight: 9½ pounds. Curly maple stock. Mostly brass fittings. Made from 1777 to 1811.

CONFEDERATE MILITARY RIFLES

Firearms used by the Confederacy are usually grouped into five general categories: U.S. arms already in possession of the Southern troops; U.S. arms captured by the Confederacy; arms imported from abroad; firearms manufactured by the southern states, and private firearms owned by individuals.

Rifles manufactured by the Union may be found in the section on U.S. Military Breechloading Carbines, while privately owned firearms may be found under individual listings. The firearms that follow were those most often found in use by the Confederacy and were for the most part either manufactured in the South or "adapted" by Southern armories.

C.S. & P. Rising-Breech Carbine $11,690
Caliber: 54 percussion. Barrel: 21 inches; marked "C.S.&P."

Confederate Asheville Rifle. $9000
Caplock side plate. Caliber: 58. Barrel: 32⅝ inches with bayonet lug. Overall length: 48⅝ inches. Weight: 8 lbs. 6 oz. Fixed sights. Brass buttplate, stock tip and trigger guard. Iron barrel bands. Lock plate marked "ASHEVILLE, N.C."

Confederate Austrian Rifle $3250
Caplock. Caliber: 54. Barrel: 37¼ inches. Overall length: 53 inches. Weight: approximately 9 pounds. Iron mountings. Two bands. Sling swivels attached to top band and trigger guard. "Austrian Rifle, Tyler, Tex. Cal. 54" marked on rear of hammer; some were also marked with "C.S." and the year of manufacture.

Confederate Baker Rifle $8500
Percussion, converted from flintlock. Caliber: 52. Barrel: 36 inches, with lug for sword bayonet. Overall length: 51 inches. Weight: approximately 9 pounds. Barrel marked "N. Carolina" with date on tang. "M.A. Baker, Fayetteville, N.C." marked on lock plate. "U.S." marked on buttplate tang.

Confederate Cook & Brother Artillery Rifle $7700
Percussion lock. Caliber: 58. Barrel: 24 inches. Overall length: 40 inches. Weight: approximately 7 pounds. All brass mountings. Markings include "Cook & Brother, Athens, Ga." year plus serial number on lock plate; Confederate flag rear of hammer; serial number on buttplate; "Athens, year, proved." on barrel. Black walnut stock.

Confederate Cook & Brother Infantry Rifle $9900
Percussion lock. Caliber: 58. Barrel: 33 inches. Overall length: 49 inches. Weight: approximately 8 pounds. Iron ramrod with brass cup-shaped end. Cherry stock. Other markings same as Artillery Rifle.

Confederate Cook & Brother Musketoon . . $9800
Percussion. Caliber: 58. Barrel: 21 inches. Overall length: 36½ inches. Weight: approximately 6½ pounds. Swivel ramrod with large button head end; clamping bands. Brass mountings. Other markings same as the Artillery Rifle.

Confederate Davis & Bozeman Rifle . . . $4375
Percussion. Caliber: 58. Barrel: 33 inches. Overall length; 48 inches. Weight: 8 pounds. Barrel marked "Ala. 1864." and lock plate marked "D & B Ala., 1864." Brass mountings.

Confederate Dickson, Nelson & Co. Carbine $4750
Percussion. Caliber: 58. Barrel: 24 inches. Overall length: 40 inches. Weight: approximately 6½ pounds. "Dickson, Nelson & Company, Ala., 1864" marked on lock plate. Brass furniture. Fixed rear sight. Swivel ramrod.

Confederate Dickson, Nelson & Co. Rifle. . $10,995
Percussion. Caliber: 58. Barrel: 33 inches. Overall length: 49 inches. Weight: 8 pounds. Two-leaf rear sight. Brass furniture. Lock plate marked "Dickson, Nelson & Co., C.S." in front of hammer and "Ala." plus the date behind the hammer. Barrel may also be marked "Ala." and the date. Cherry or walnut stock.

Confederate Fayetteville Rifle $6125
Percussion. Caliber: 58. Barrel: 33 inches. Overall length: 49 inches. Weight: 8¾ pounds. Markings include "V.P." with eagle head and year on barrel breech, "C.S." on buttplate tang, "Fayetteville" with spread eagle over "C.S.A." on lock plate. Made from parts and tools taken from Harper's Ferry, W.V.

Confederate Georgia Armory Rifle $4900
Percussion. Caliber: 58. Barrel: 33 inches, some equipped with saber-bayonet lug. Overall length: 49 inches. Weight: 8¾ pounds. "Ga. Armory" and the year marked on lock plate in rear of hammer. Brass furniture.

Confederate Lamb Rifle $10,500
Caplock, plain lock plate. Caliber: 58. Barrel: 33 inches; part octagonal, part round. Weight: approximately 9 pounds. yellow oak stock stamped "H.C. Lamb & Co., N.C." Serial number on breech, inside of hammer and sometimes on stock.

**Confederate Richmond
Model 1863 Carbine**

Confederate LeMat Carbine **$15,000**
Percussion, two-barrel revolving carbine; nine-shot cylinder. Caliber: 42. Barrel: 20 inches; part-round, part-octagonal. Overall length: 38¼ inches. Weight: 7½ pounds. Of French manufacture, but designed and patented by Dr. LeMat of New Orleans.

Confederate "M" Rifle. **$7000**
Percussion, caplock. Caliber: 58. Barrel 39 inches; with British proofmarks. Marked "L.S.M." on lower tang, "1862" on lock plate in front of hammer, and "M" and a spread eagle at rear of hammer.

Confederate Mendenhall, Jones & Gardner Rifle **$10,000**
Percussion. Caliber: 58. Barrel: 33 inches with sword-type bayonet lug. Weight: approximately 9 pounds. Iron buttplate and ramrod. Brass mountings. Lock plate marked "M.J. & G., N.C." forward of hammer; rear of hammer marked "C.S. 1863."

Confederate Morse Breechloading Altered Musket **$6500**
Action used metallic, self-primed cartridges. Caliber: 69. Barrel: 40½ inches with bayonet provisions. Weight: approximately 9 pounds. Lock plate marked "U.S. spread eagle, Springfield 1839."

Confederate Morse Breechloading Carbine. **$8750**
Hinged breech action. Caliber: 50. Barrel: 20 inches, round. Weight: approximately 7 pounds. Butternut stock; brass frame and mountings. Serial numbers on bottom of frame. No other markings.

Confederate Murray Cavalry Carbine . **$8550**
Same general description as Murray Carbine Musketoon, except had 23-inch barrel and weighed approximately 6¾ pounds.

Confederate Murray Carbine Musketoon. . **$8550**
Percussion. Caliber: 58. Barrel: 24 inches, round. Weight: approximately 7 pounds. Brass mountings; iron sling swivels and ramrod. Walnut stock. Lock plate marked "J.P. Murray, Columbus, GA." Breech marked "Ala 1864" and "F.C.H."

Confederate Murray Rifle **$8550**
Same general description as Murray Carbine, except had 32¾-inch barrel.

Confederate Murray Sharpshooter's Rifle. . **$9750**
Same general description as Murray Carbine, except had 29-inch heavy octagonal barrel. Caliber: 50.

Confederate "P" Breechloading Carbine. . **$7500**
Bronze-lined breech block with spiral groove to seat cartridge firmly. Caliber: 52. Barrel: 22½ inches, round. Marked "P" on breech block.

Confederate "P" Rifled Carbine (Hodgkins Carbine) **$5750**
Percussion lock. Caliber: 58. Barrel: 22 inches, round. Iron mountings except brass forearm tip. Barrel marked "P.C.S.A."; inside of lock marked "C44." Walnut stock. Sling ring mounted on rear of trigger guard bow.

Confederate Pulaski Rifle. **$2900**
Percussion lock. caliber: 58. Barrel: 32¼ inches. Brass mountings. Marking "Pulaski, T.C.S.A. 61." Walnut stock.

Confederate Richmond Carbine **$4800**
Percussion lock. Caliber: 58. Barrel: 25 inches, with two barrel bands. Weight: approximately 7½ pounds. Full walnut stock; three sling swivels. Bronze buttplate marked "C.S." Barrel marked with year and "C.S." Lock plate marked "C.S. Richmond" plus the year.

Confederate Richmond Navy Musketoon. . **$5000**
Percussion lock. Caliber: 62. Barrel: 30 inches, round. Lock plate marked "C.S. Richmond, Va." plus year.

Confederate Richmond Rifled Musket . . **$3600**
Percussion lock. Caliber: 58. Barrel: 40 inches, round. Weight: approximately 9½ pounds. Walnut stock with three barrel bands. Close copy of U.S. Model 1855. Brass buttplate. Lock plate marked "C.S. Richmond, Va." and also the year near rear of lock plate. Barrel marked with year.

Confederate Robinson-Sharps Carbine . . . $2400
Percussion breechloader. Caliber: 52. Barrel: 22 inches. Weight: approximately 7½ pounds. Lock plate marked "S.C. Robinson Arms Mfg. Co., Richmond, Va." Year plus serial number. Similar markings on barrel.

Confederate Sturdivant Rifle $2100
Percussion. Caliber: 54. Barrel: 32 inches. All brass mountings. No markings except serial number.

Confederate Tallassee Enfield Pattern Carbine $20,000
Percussion muzzleloader. Caliber: 58. Barrel: 25 inches, round; brass clamping barrel bands. Weight: approximately 7¾ pounds. Brass trigger guard and buttplate. Lock plate marked "S.C. Tallassee, Ala." Date marked at rear of hammer.

Confederate Tanner Rifle $3750
Percussion. Caliber: 54. Barrel: 33 inches, round. Serial number is the only marking. This is similar to the Mississippi Rifle.

Confederate Tarpley Carbine $43,000
Percussion breechloader. Caliber: 52. Barrel: 23 inches, round. Weight: approximately 7 pounds. Iron buttplate; brass breech.

Confederate Texas-Enfield Rifle $20,000
Percussion. Caliber: 57. Barrel: 33 inches; round, with bayonet lug. Brass mountings. Two-leafed rear sight. Lock plate marked "Texas Rifle, Tyler, Cal. 57." Barrel and buttplate marked "C.S."

Confederate Todd Rifled Musket . . . $11,500
Percussion. Caliber: 58. Barrel: 40 inches, round. Weight: approximately 9 pounds. Walnut stock. Lock plate marked "Geo. H. Todd, Montgomery, Ala."

Confederate Wallis Rifle $900
Similar to the Mississippi Rifle, except without the bayonet lug and patchbox.

Confederate Whitney-Enfield Mississippi Rifle $850
Percussion lock. Caliber: 61. Barrel: 33 inches; round, with bayonet lug. Weight: approximately 8½ pounds. Brass trigger guard; iron buttplate. Close copy of Enfield Model 1858. Lock plate marked "E. Whitney."

Confederate Whitney Rifled Musket . . . $2750
Similar to U.S. Model 1855, except has brass buttplate and no markings except "E. Whitney, New Haven" on lock plate.

Confederate Wytheville-Hall Rifle $2400
Many variations of this model exist, as all were handmade from parts captured at Harpers Ferry. One-piece brass casting was used to convert breechloader to muzzleloader.

U.S. MILITARY FLINTLOCK RIFLES

The first U.S. Military muskets were known as the "Committee of Safety" arms. In the spring of 1775 the 13 colonies, through the various "Committees," provided muskets to arm the patriots for the ensuing "Revolution." The arms were produced by about 200 different gunsmiths, so wide variations are common. Some were stamped with the maker's name; some with simply an initial, and some without any markings at all. From about 1774 to 1775, the letters "C.P."—to designate "Continental Property"—were used. After September 9, 1776, the marking "U.S." was added to most arms. The later models were of course used during other wars and some were even converted to percussion and employed during the Civil War.

Harpers Ferry Flintlock Rifle $2600
Flintlock ignition system. Caliber: 53. Barrel: 33 inches; seven-grooved rifling. Weight: 9¾ pounds. American walnut stock without barrel bands. Buttstock is provided with patchbox. Made from 1814 to 1819.

Revolutionary Flintlock Musket $9000
Flintlock ignition system. Calibers: 72 to 80. Barrel: approximately 44½ inches long; round, smoothbore, but variations exist. Weight: over 10 pounds. Stock generally without barrel bands. Made principally in Massachusetts, Rhode Island, Maryland, and Pennsylvania between 1775 and 1795.

U.S. Springfield Model 1795
Flintlock Musket $8450
Flintlock ignition system. Caliber: 70. Barrel: 45 inches; round, smoothbore. Weight: 9½ pounds. American walnut stock with barrel bands. Made from 1795 to 1808.

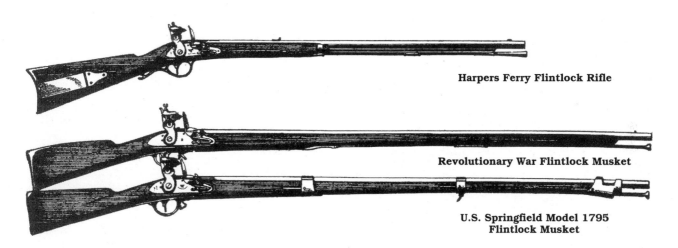

Harpers Ferry Flintlock Rifle

Revolutionary War Flintlock Musket

U.S. Springfield Model 1795
Flintlock Musket

Harpers Ferry Flintlock Musket $2700
Same general specifications as Harpers Ferry Rifle, except smoothbore with longer barrel.

U.S. Springfield Model 1809
Flintlock Carbine $12,000
Flintlock ignition system. Caliber: 56. Barrel: 19½ inches; round, smoothbore. Weight: 4¾ pounds. American walnut stock; sling swivels. No center barrel band.

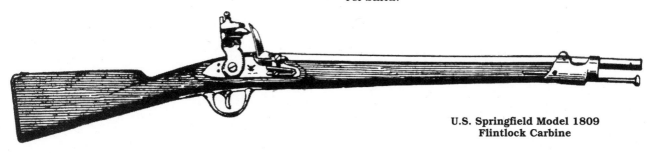

U.S. Springfield Model 1809
Flintlock Carbine

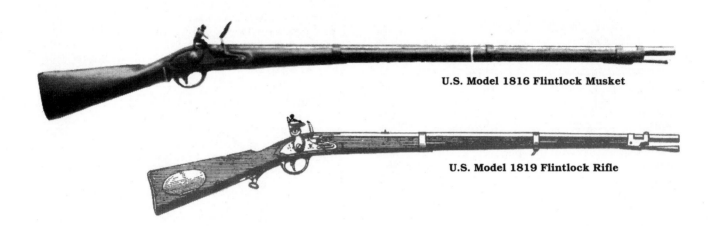

U.S. Model 1816 Flintlock Musket

U.S. Model 1819 Flintlock Rifle

U.S. Model 1816 Flintlock Musket . . . $2350
Caliber: 69. Barrel: 42 inches, smoothbore. Weight: 10 pounds with bayonet. American walnut stock with barrel bands and 16-inch bayonet. Made from about 1816 to 1840, although sources disagree.

U.S. Model of 1819 Flintlock Rifle . . . $2550
Officially known as the "Common Rifle." Caliber: 54. Barrel: 36 inches, round. Weight: 10¼ pounds. Stock with barrel bands. No bayonets provided. Made principally in Middletown, Conn., and Philadelphia.

U.S. Springfield Model 1840 Musketoon
Smoothbore $2400
Flintlock ignition. Caliber: 69. Barrel: 26 inches; round, smoothbore. Copied from the French arm of 1836. The lock and its parts are slightly smaller than the musket of the same date.

NOTE

U.S. military flintlock rifles were made by several private firms such as Whitney Arms Co., Remington and others.

U.S. Springfield Model 1840 Musketoon

U.S. MILITARY SINGLE-SHOT BREECHLOADING CARBINES

All of the carbines described below were designed just prior to and during the Civil War. They could be loaded from the breech, which made them faster to load than muzzleloaders, and most were used by the Union troops. They were, however, single-shot arms, and slower than the repeaters, like the Spencer, for example, that were very successful during the war. Other Civil War-era breechloaders can be found under the listings of the individual manufacturers.

Burnside Breechloading Carbine. $2750
Caliber: 54. During the Civil War over 56,000 of these carbines, invented by A.E. Burnside, were purchased. George P. Foster, the primary manufacturer, brought out several improvements. This carbine used the first metallic shell cartridge designed for a military arm. The tapered end was open for the purpose of igniting the powder charge by the percussion cap. Patented in 1856.

Cosmopolitan Breechloading Carbine. . $1710
Caliber: 50. Made in Hamilton, Ohio, these guns, also called "Union," consisted of three models. During the Civil War 342 were purchased. This carbine, which weighs slightly under seven pounds, has an extremely lengthy hammer caused by the fact that it spans the entire breechblock.

**Gallagher Breechloading Bolt-Action
Carbine $1295**
Caliber: 54. Made in Philadelphia by Richardson & Overman, who in 1865 altered a specimen to rimfire, calling it the Richardson, and submitted it to the Hancock Board on breechloading arms. For this particular carbine, over $212,000 was expended for cartridges. The barrel tilted up to load like a shotgun and the cartridge was linen covered. Patented in 1860.

Gibbs Breechloading Carbine $3100
Caliber: 52. W.F. Brooks of New York was given a contract in 1861 for 10,000 of these carbines, of which he completed and delivered only 1,052. The barrel slides forward and tilts up at breech to load. The gun uses a paper cartridge. Although patented in 1856, none were made until 1863.

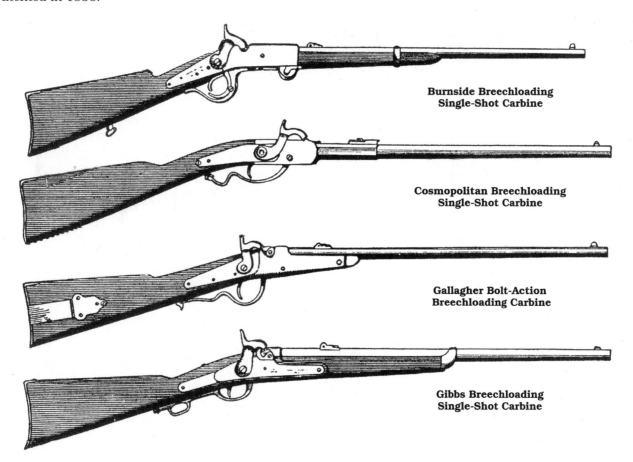

**Burnside Breechloading
Single-Shot Carbine**

**Cosmopolitan Breechloading
Single-Shot Carbine**

**Gallagher Bolt-Action
Breechloading Carbine**

**Gibbs Breechloading
Single-Shot Carbine**

Union soldier of the 22nd New York Infantry at Harpers Ferry, WV, during the Civil War.

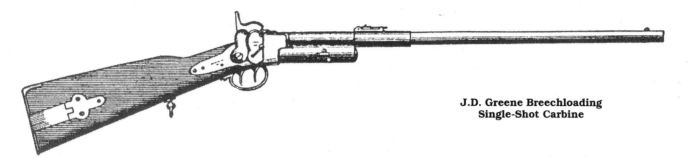

**J.D. Greene Breechloading
Single-Shot Carbine**

J.D. Greene's Breechloading Carbine . . $4150
Caliber: 53. By pulling forward on the trigger, the barrel is revolved one-quarter turn and is then pulled forward to clear the receiver. The sleeve and barrel then revolve to the right to insert the cartridge. This rare U.S. arm has the Maynard primer. In 1856–57, seven hundred of these were issued for trial. Patented in June 1854.

Joslyn Model 1864 Carbine $995
Caliber: 52 RF. Single-shot breechloader. Barrel: 22 inches average; round. Casehardened lockplate. Iron mountings. Walnut stock. Patented in 1864. Made under government contract and used at the end of the Civil War by Federal troops. Some captured arms also were used by the Confederates.

**Joslyn Model 1855 Breechloading
Single-Shot Carbine**

**Joslyn Model 1864 Civil War
Carbine**

**Joslyn Model 1855 Breechloading
Carbine. $3275**
Caliber: 54. Made by A.H. Waters of Millbury, Conn., for B.F. Joslyn, these were the first of the Joslyn systems, the rest being cartridge arms. The strap on the small of the stock lifts up and uncovers the breech when the ring on top of the butt is released. Patented in 1855. (*See* also Benjamin F. Joslyn under Rifles.)

**Maynard Breechloading Percussion
Carbine $1700**
Caliber: 50. Twenty thousand of these were purchased during the Civil War. The first few models of these carbines were equipped with the Maynard primer. The barrel tilts up to load like a shotgun, and it uses a metallic cartridge, the base of which filled the space between the barrel and breech. Patented by Dr. Edward Maynard in 1859.

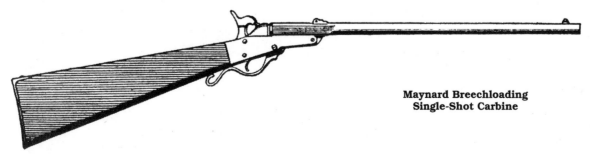

**Maynard Breechloading
Single-Shot Carbine**

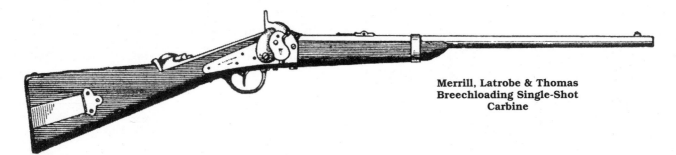

**Merrill, Latrobe & Thomas
Breechloading Single-Shot
Carbine**

Merrill, Latrobe and Thomas Breechloading Carbine $14,500

Caliber: 54. Made by Remington at Ilion, N.Y., but no records have been found as to the quantity produced, so they may be called rare. The carbine has the familiar Maynard primer, but it had an unusual method of loading, which consisted of pushing the cartridge in place with a piston worked by hand against the action of a spring. The strap along the top of the stock is brought up and forward to open the breech, which is merely a circular piece of metal with a hole extending through it. Patented in 1856.

Perry Navy Breechloading Carbine $4275

Caliber: 54. Made in Newark, N.J., 200 were purchased for trial in February, 1855, and in 1856 they were favorably commented upon by Admiral Dahlgren. This arm has a magazine primer, consisting of a tube that is inserted through the buttplate. The caps are fed by the action of a spring exactly like the cartridge in the Spencer carbines and rifles. The arm is the second model of Perry's breech action; the first is the so-called Rebel Perry. This name was applied because some of the rifles made their way to the South in the early days of the Civil War. Patented in 1855.

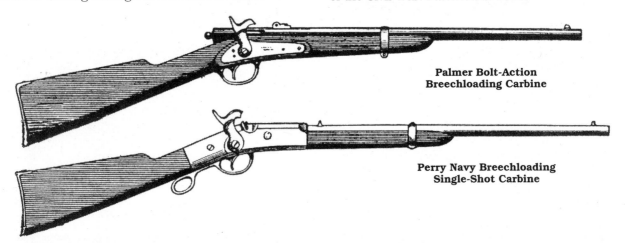

**Palmer Bolt-Action
Breechloading Carbine**

**Perry Navy Breechloading
Single-Shot Carbine**

Palmer Breechloading Bolt-Action Carbine. $1825

Caliber: 50. This was the first metallic cartridge (rimfire) bolt gun used in the U.S. One of the lightest of the Civil War guns, it weighed only 5¾ pounds. Another feature was that the sectional locking screw of the bolt was similar to the breechblocks of our modern cannon. Patented in December 1863, one thousand of these were delivered before the end of the war.

Smith Breechloading Carbine. $1750

Caliber: 52. During the Civil War 30,062 were purchased at $24.00 each. By pushing the catch in front of the trigger, the lever on top of the tang was released. This allowed the barrel to drop like a shotgun. The original cartridge used was encased in a rubber shell. Some guns were later altered to take a metallic cartridge, the invention of Silas Crispin.

**Smith Breechloading
Carbine**

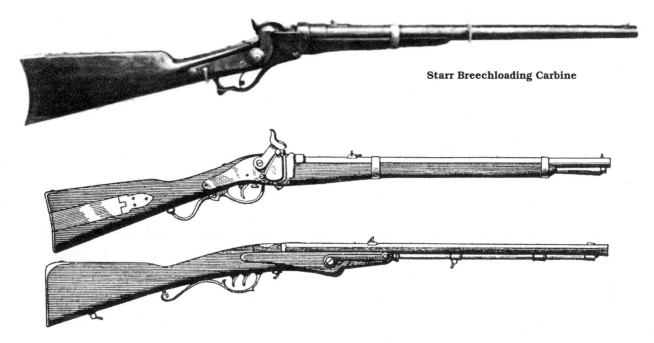

Starr Breechloading Carbine

Starr Breechloading Carbine **$975**
Caliber: 54. Patented in 1858 by E.T. Starr, inventor and manufacturer of the famous Starr revolvers, these carbines were manufactured in Yonkers, N.Y. 25,603 were purchased from 1861 to 1865.

Symmes Breechloading Carbine **$25,000**
Caliber: 54. One of the early experimental pieces, only 200 being purchased by the U.S. Government. The breechblock rotates upward and has the Maynard magazine primer. Patented in 1858.

U.S. Schroeder Carbine **$12,000**
Caliber: 53. In this needle gun, the charge is fired by a long firing pin that penetrates the powder charge and ignites the fulminate, which is at the base of the bullet in front of the cartridge. Used in 1858, these very rare guns have a sliding forward barrel with an eagle and U.S. on the tang. Several are in government collections. Patented in 1856.

Warner Breechloading Carbine **$2125**
Caliber: 50. This rimfiring carbine has a breechblock that swings to the right like the Joslyn; the extractor, however, was worked by hand. Although 4,001 of these guns were purchased during the Civil War, not many were used because of the extra movement needed to eject the shell. These guns, weighing less than seven pounds, have an extractor handle that shows at the bottom of the stock in front of the trigger guard. Patented in 1864.

Wesson Carbine **$625**
Caliber: 44. The barrel of this carbine tilts up like the Gallager and Maynard and the front trigger releases the catch holding it. The cartridge was all metal and rimfire. This gun was a great favorite with the Indians because it weighed less than six pounds. Some can be found with Indian ornamentation of brass-headed tacks on the buttstock. Invented by Frank Wesson who later became one of the founders of the firm of Smith and Wesson, this was patented in 1859. More than 150 of these breechloading arms were purchased by the U.S. during the Civil War.

Warner Breechloading Carbine

Wesson Breechloading Carbine

MAKERS OF ARMS DURING THE CIVIL WAR			
Maker	**Period**	**Model**	**Comments**
A. Jenks & Son	1861	1855	
A.M. Burt	1861	1855	
Amoskeg Mfg. Co.	1863	1861	
Bridesburg, Pa.	1863	1861	
Bridesburg, Pa.	1864	1864	
C.D. Shubarth	1863	1861	
Colt's Arms Mfg. Co.	1863	1863	Short Model
Colt's Arms Mfg. Co.	1863	1863	
E. Remington	1865	1864	
E. Robinson	1864	1861	
E. Whitney	1861		Special lock
E. Whitney	1862	1861	
Egleville A.H. Almy	1863	1861	
J. Mulholland	1862	1855	
J.D. Mowry	1861	1855	
J.T. Hodge	1861	1855	
Lamson, Goodnow & Yale	1864	1863	
Lamson, Goodnow & Yale	1863	1863	Short Model
New York Arms Co.	1863	1861	
Norfolk	1863	1861	
Norwich Arms Co.	1863	1861	
Norwich Arms Company	1865		Short Model
P.S. Justice	1864		Private
Parker Snow & Company	1863	1861	
Philadelphia	1863	1861	
Providence Tool Co.	1863	1861	
R.W. Savage	1863	1861	
S. Norris & W.T. Clement	1864	1863	For Massachusetts
Sarson & Roberts	1861		Carbines
Springfield Armory	1860	1855	
Springfield Armory	1861	1861	
Springfield Armory	1862	1861	
Springfield Armory	1863	1863	
Springfield Armory	1864	1864	
Trenton, N.J.	1864	1861	
Watertown	1863	1861	
Wm. Mason	1863	1861	
Wm. Muir & Co.	1864	1861	

SHOTGUNS

Shotguns trace their descent from the ancient bell-mouth blunderbuss. The fowling piece that developed after that was simply a shorter, lighter version of the smoothbore musket.

The slow ignition of flintlock arms limited the success of hitting birds on the wing, and fowling pieces were seldom used until the introduction of the percussion cap. With its more rapid ignition, wing shooting became more practical.

The average shooter of the 1800s found that the .69 caliber smoothbore musket, loaded with a charge of shot pellets, served well enough for sitting ducks. But rifled barrels were unsuited for shot loads. As rifled barrels started to replace the smoothbore musket and bores gradually became smaller in size, a special fowling gun was developed. This fowling piece started to be called "shotgun" and was made with both single and double barrels. It rapidly acquired the characteristics that are found in the single-shot and side-by-side double-barreled shotguns of today.

Although breechloading shotguns appeared earlier, they did not come into common usage until about 1880, when the modern shotshell evolved. Shortly after, choke boring was discovered. By constricting the bore at the muzzle, it was found that a gun would throw a narrower, denser pattern of shot, tremendously extending its effective range. Except for minor refinements in design, metallurgy and the new operating concepts, the early breechloading shotguns were very similar to the designs in use today.

Like its muzzleloading predecessor, the fowling piece, the breechloading shotgun utilized a smooth bore of relatively large size to accommodate the load of the shot pellets. The size of the bore, as the British call it, or gauge, as the Americans call it, is derived from the number of round lead balls required to make a pound. For example, a 12-gauge gun has a bore, which, if it had no choke, would accept one round ball that would fit snugly against the walls of the bore — 12 of which would weigh a pound. This antiquated means of measurement is no longer used by manufacturers, but it has stuck in the marketplace because it serves its descriptive purpose well. The smaller the number, the larger the gauge. Twelve-gauge shotguns have larger diameter bores than 16 gauge guns; 16 gauge bores are larger than 20 gauge and so on. The .410 bore is the exception; it is the actual bore diameter of .410", which is equivalent to about a 67 gauge. Since this size bore was a relative late comer, it has escaped the older nomenclature.

Shotgun ammunition in England is termed "cartridge," but "shotshell" is the common term in the United States. For information on the composition of shotshells, please turn to Shotshells in the Obsolete Cartridge Section.

Although the production and variety of 19th-century shotguns does not approximate that of either handguns or rifles, the following pages contain an assortment of shotgun makers and models, many of which are of foreign origin.

J.F. ABBEY & CO.
Chicago, Illinois

J.F. Abbey Single-Barrel Muzzle-Loading Shotgun **$275**
Percussion sidelock. Gauges: 12 to 30 bore. Barrel: 30 to 40 inches, iron. Weight: 5 to 8¾ pounds. Oil or varnished stock with checkered pistol grip. Made from 1871 to 1875.

J.F. Abbey Double-Barrel Muzzle-Loading Shotgun **$560**
Percussion back locks. Gauges: 12 to 30 bore. Barrel: 30 to 36 inches, iron. Weight: 6 to 8½ pounds. Double triggers. Oil or varnished American walnut stock with checkered pistol grip. Made from 1871 to 1875.

ACME ARMS
Chicopee Falls, Massachusetts

Acme Arms Double-Barrel Shotgun **$175**
Side-by-side. Manufactured by J.P. Stevens Arms Company of Chicopee Falls, Mass.

E.B. ALDEN
Claremont, New Hampshire

Alden Double-Barrel Muzzle-Loading Shotgun **$515**
Swivel back-action locks. Gauges: 12 and 16 standard. Barrels: 30 to 35 inches, iron. Weight: 7 to 8½ pounds. Double triggers. Oiled or varnished American walnut buttstock with shotgun buttplate and forearm with metal cap on tip. Blued and engraved steel mounting. German silver escutcheons and name plate. Made from 1863 to 1868.

ARABIAN SHOTGUNS
Various Manufacturers

Arabian DAG Blunderbuss **$450**
Flintlock. Barrel heavily engraved with Arabic inscriptions, usually prayers or religious sayings, much of it in silver inlay. Iron trigger guard. Brass wire inlay in stock. Buttplate and saddle bar on left side.

A.J. AUBREY
Meriden, Connecticut

In the 1890s, Sears, Roebuck & Co. of Chicago, Ill., established a manufacturing facility in Meriden, Conn., called the Meriden Fire Arms Company. It was designed to produce firearms for the successful Sears mail-order business. A.J. Aubrey was the manager of the Meriden plant, and many of the guns turned out there bear the name "A.J. Aubrey" as a brand name.

Firearms manufactured under the Aubrey name included hammer and hammerless single- and double-barreled shotguns, as well as hammer and hammerless revolvers of different styles.

A.J. Aubrey Standard Grade Double-Barrel Shotgun
Sidelock action. Gauge: 12. Barrels: 30 or 32 inches; armory steel, laminated steel or two-blade Damascus. Weight: 7½ to 8 pounds. Walnut stock with modest checkering.
Armory Steel Barrels **$195**
Laminated Steel Barrels 125
Two-blade Damascus Barrels 140

A.J. Aubrey Hand-Engraved Double-Barrel Shotgun **$525**
Sidelock action, modestly engraved. Gauge: 12. Barrels: 30 or 32 inches; laminated steel or two-blade Damascus. Weight: 7½ to 8 pounds. Walnut stock with modest checkering.

Arabian DAG Blunderbuss

A.J. Aubrey Highest Grade Double-Barrel
Shotgun **$775**
Sidelock action, modestly engraved. Gauge: 12. Barrels: 30 or 32 inches; laminated steel or two-blade Damascus. Weight: 7¼ to 7¾ pounds. Good grade walnut stock with nice checkering.

A.J. Aubrey Custom Grade Double-Barrel Shotgun
Sidelock action, custom engraved. Gauges: any desired. Barrels: any specified length, but usually made in 30- or 32-inch length; laminated steel or two-blade Damascus. Weight: 7 to 8¾ pounds. Any grade walnut stock with various checkering, carving, embellishments, etc. available.
Lower Grade Custom. **$750**
Medium Grade Custom. **825**
Highest Grade Custom **895**

A.J. Aubrey Hammerless Single-Shot
Shotgun **$125**
Top lever. Break-open. Single shot. Gauge: 12. Barrel: 30 or 32 inches. Weight: 6½ pounds. Walnut stock and forend with checkering on buttstock grips.

BAKER GUN & FORGING CO.
Batavia, New York

The Baker Gun & Forging Company manufactured firearms in the late 1800s and into the first third of the 1900s. They produced an extensive array of single- and double-barreled arms that differed by grade and the amount of customizing done.

Baker Batavia Leader Double-Barrel Shotgun
Standard Model. **$445**
Special Shotgun **575**
Grade C Shotgun. **250**

Baker Black Beauty Double-Barrel Shotgun
Standard Double-Barrel **$675**
Special Double-Barrel Model. **750**

Baker Deluxe Double-Barrel Shotgun
Grade H. . . . . **$ 3,800**
$300 Grade. **5,000**
$1000 Grade **15,000**

Baker Double-Barrel Shotgun
Grade A. **$375**
Grade B. **325**
Grade R. **700**
Grade S. **600**
Model 1896 . . . . **275**
Model 1897 . . . . **300**
New Model Double. **275**

Baker Paragon Double-Barrel Shotgun
With Non-automatic Ejector. **$1200**
With Automatic Ejector **1500**
Special Model **1895**

Baker Pigeon Double-Barrel Shotgun
Grade L Pigeon Grade. **$2400**

Baker Single-Shot Shotguns
Elite Model **$1295**
Sterling Model. **800**

Baker Trap Guns
N Krupp Double-Barrel Trap **$1500**
Superba Single-Shot Trap **3000**

BALLARD SHOTGUNS
Merrimack Arms & Mfg. Co.
Newburyport, Massachusetts

Ballard Single-Shot "RF" Shotgun **$900**
Guage: .58-inch bore (24-gauge rimfire). Barrel: 30 inches, round rolled steel, blued finish. Brass bead sight ½ inch from muzzle. Varnished walnut straight shotgun stock, with blued steel shotgun buttplate. Forearm capped with pointed iron cap. Made from 1867 to 1869.

BALLARD SHOTGUNS
Brown Mfg. Company
Newburyport, Massachusetts

The Merrimack Arms & Mfg. Co. factory, contents, and patents were sold to J. H. Brown of New York in 1869, and Ballard shotguns continued to be manufactured under the new firm name of Brown Mfg. Company.

Ballard Single-Shot Shotgun. **$700**
Same general specifications as the Ballard shotgun manufactured by Merrimack Arms & Mfg. Co. except stamped "BROWN MFG. CO. NEWBURYPORT, MASS—BALLARD'S PATENT—NOV. 5, 1861" and made from 1869 to 1873.

BAYARD SHOTGUNS
Herstal (Liège), Belgium

"Bayard" was the trade name of firearms produced by the well-known firm of Anciens Establissements Pieper, founded by Belgian gun manufacturer, Henri Pieper (1840–1905). Pieper contributed to the evolution of cartridge revolvers and automatic pistols in addition to making quality shotguns.

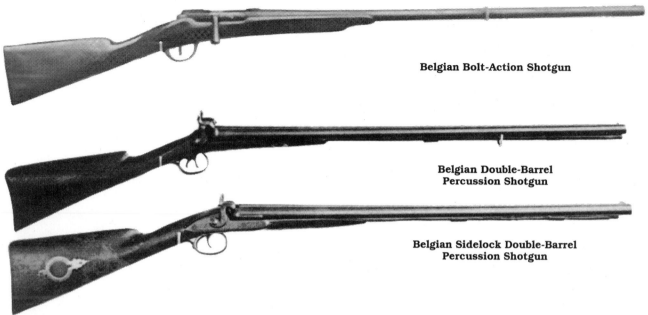

Belgian Bolt-Action Shotgun

Belgian Double-Barrel Percussion Shotgun

Belgian Sidelock Double-Barrel Percussion Shotgun

Bayard Hammer Double-Barrel Shotguns
Standard w/Damascus Barrels. **$165**
Standard w/Steel Barrels **220**
Fancy Grade **525**

Bayard Hammerless Shotgun
Standard Double-Barrel **$250**

BELGIAN SHOTGUNS
Various Manufacturers

Toward the end of the 19th century, Belgium was virtually the production center of Damascus barrels that had become so popular at that time. These barrels were imported by numerous U.S. arms manufacturers because they were in such demand. Nearly a third of all the Belgian shotguns as well sported Damascus barrels.

Belgian Bolt-Action Shotgun. $4100
Gauges: 12 and others. Barrel: 28, 30 and 32 inches, round. Half-stock with checkered grip. Made circa 1890.

Belgian Double-Barrel Shotgun $200
Gauges: 16 and others. Barrels: 28, 30 and 32 inches; side-by-side Damascus. Gold triggers and shield escutcheon in butt. High-grade walnut with checkered grip and forend.

Belgian Double-Barrel Percussion Shotgun $250
Gauges: 12 and others. Barrels: 28, 30 and 32 inches; Damascus. Fern engraving. Fine wood with checkered grip. Made circa 1850.

Belgian Sidelock Double-Barrel Percussion Shotgun. $295
Gauges: 12 and others. Barrels: 28, 30 and 32 inches; Damascus. Plain metal and wood, except for simple checkered pattern on grip.

BOND & JAMES
London, England

Bond & James Double-Barrel Percussion Shotgun. $385
Gauges: various. Barrels: various lengths, marked "LONDON FINE TWIST." Checkered grip and forend. Iron furniture. Engraved, silver escutcheon in buttstock. Made from 1868 to 1875.

BRITISH SHOTGUNS
Various Manufacturers

See also individual listings.

British Double-Barrel Percussion Shotgun . . $295
Gauges: various. Barrels: various lengths. Stocks usually checkered at grip; no checkering on forend. Several silver escutcheons. See next page.

British Double-Barrel Percussion Shotgun. $320
Gauges: 12 and others. Barrels: Damascus in various lengths. Iron furniture, usually modestly engraved. Checkered grips with silver escutcheon. Made in England circa 1840. (See next page.)

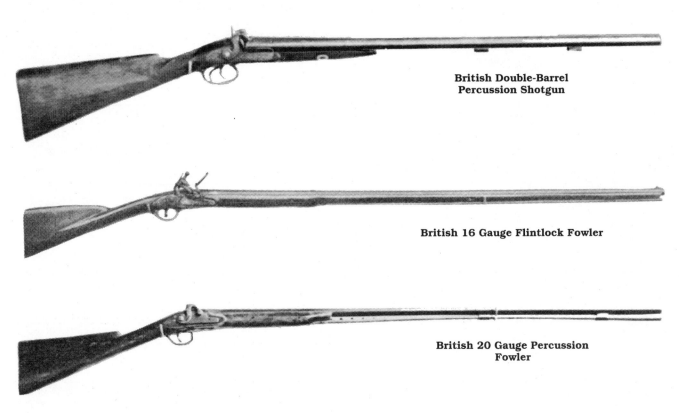

British Double-Barrel
Percussion Shotgun

British 16 Gauge Flintlock Fowler

British 20 Gauge Percussion
Fowler

British Flintlock Fowler **$1400**
Gauge: 16. Barrel: 47 inches, round. Brass furniture.
Relief carving at barrel tang, front of comb and
around lock. Large brass escutcheon on wrist. Made
in England circa 1735.

British Fowler Conversion **$1175**
Percussion lock. Gauge: 20. Barrel: 43 inches. During the early 1800s many British fowlers were converted from flintlock to percussion. Many were
unnamed, and this is one typical example of their
current value. Converted circa 1840.

**British Martini-Henry Single-Shot Military
Shotgun** **$210**

**British Milne's Patent Flintlock
Blunderbuss** **$1600**

British Percussion Fowler **$250**
Gauge: 12. Barrel: 39½ inches, round. Iron furniture, lightly engraved. Silver escutcheon on grip.

British Sea Service Boarding Blunderbuss . . **$2435**
Flintlock engraved, "TRULOCK 1757." Bore: 1 inch.
Brass furniture. Full-length plain stock. Made circa
1750s.

British Southall Blunderbuss **$1000**
Percussion lock. Brass barrel. Checkered grip. Iron
furniture, nicely engraved. Made circa 1835.

British Milne's Patent
Flintlock Blunderbuss

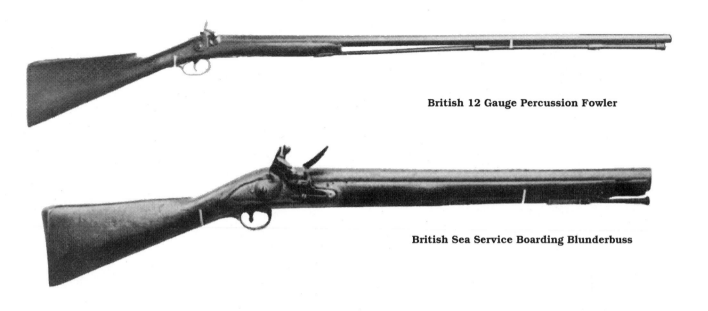

British 12 Gauge Percussion Fowler

British Sea Service Boarding Blunderbuss

ANDREW BURGESS
Oswego, New York

Burgess Slide-Action Shotgun
Gauge: 12, tubular magazine under barrel. Barrel: 28 and 30 inches (about 20 inches on folding gun). Plain or checkered walnut stock and forearm. Made 1892 to 1900 when purchased by the Winchester Repeating Arms Co.
Takedown $1425
Folding Gun 1750

WILLIAM CHANCE & SON
London, England

Wm. Chance & Son Percussion Fowler . . . $330
Gauge: 12. Barrel: various lengths. Walnut stock with iron furniture and German silver nose cap. German silver escutcheons and cap box in bottom of buttstock. Modest metal engraving. One of the better quality fowlers. Made circa 1840.

Wm. Chance & Son Double-Barrel Percussion Shotgun $365
Gauge: 12. Barrel: various lengths. Three silver bars at breech; silver patchbox with iron door. Checkered grip. Platinum blow plugs. Made from 1835 to 1845.

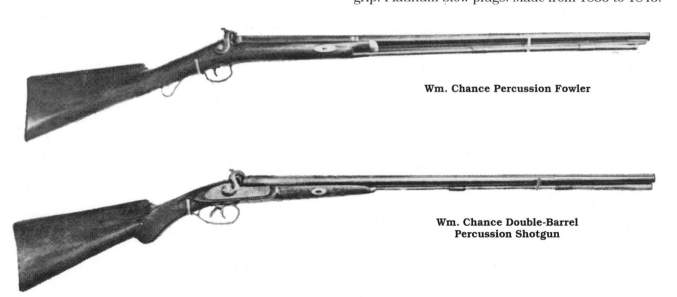

Wm. Chance Percussion Fowler

**Wm. Chance Double-Barrel
Percussion Shotgun**

CHARLES CLEMENT
Liege, Belgium

Clement Double-Barrel Hammer Shotgun
Standard Model. $225

Clement Double-Barrel Hammerless Shotgun
Damascus Barrels. $195
Steel Barrels 275

J.B. CLEMENT
Belgium

J.B. Clement Double-Barrel Shotguns
Hammer Model $210
Hammerless Model 275

COLT'S PATENT FIRE ARMS MFG. CO.
Hartford, Connecticut

Although Colt manufactured only two basic model shotguns, they became renown throughout the world for their craftsmanship and quality, as Colt's other firearms. In fact, shortly after the Model 1878 Shotgun debuted, it won a Gold Medal and Diploma of Merit at the Melbourne Exposition of 1881 and the "Highest Reward" by the Massachusetts Charitable Mechanic Association in 1881.

Colt's Model 1878 Hammer Shotgun

Colt Model 1878 Hammer Shotgun. . . . $850
Side-by-side double barrel. Gauges: 10 and 12. Barrels: 28, 30, or 32 inches; blued or brown. Weight: about 7½ pounds with 28-inch barrel. Rebounding lock. Color casehardened breech. Double triggers. Colt markings rolled on the lock plates and sometimes on the barrel rib. Semi-pistol grip standard, but English straight grip often found. Checkered English or Circassian walnut stock and forend. Available in a variety of styles with twist, fine twist, laminated or Damascus barrels, custom engravings, inlaids, etc. 22,683 guns made between 1878 and 1889.

Colt Model 1883 Hammerless Shotgun. . $900
Side-by-side double barrel. Gauges: 10 and 12. Barrel: 28, 30 or 32 inches; blued or brown. Double triggers. This was virtually a custom shotgun, similar to the Model 1878, and made in much smaller quantity, with great variation of engravings, inlaids, etc. Made from 1883 to 1895.

CRESCENT FIREARMS COMPANY
Norwich, Connecticut

The Crescent Firearms Company was founded about 1888 and operated in Norwich, Conn. It has been said that this company was the most prolific of all manufacturers of private label guns, producing not less than 100 different brand names.

In 1893, Crescent was purchased by H & D Folsom Arms Company of New York City (*see* separate listing). This firm sold guns manufactured by Crescent under a variety of names. In fact, if a certain number of the same model of gun was ordered, the buyer could have almost any label he wished stamped on the arm. For this reason, many hardware stores of the time, who always sold dozens of single- and double-barreled shotguns each year, had their own firm name stamped on the guns — providing even more confusion among gun collectors. The following shotguns were known to have been produced by the Crescent Firearms Co. and carried any of the brand names or private labels in the listing that follows them. In effect, all of the double-barreled side-by-side shotguns, for example, were identical, except for the names stamped on them, and perhaps the checkering pattern on the buttstock and forearm. The same holds true for the single-shot, breechloading shotguns.

Double-Barrel Side-by-Side Shotgun
Outside hammers. Sidelock action. Gauges: various. Barrels: 28 to 32 inches; steel or Damascus. Weight: 7½ to 9½ pounds. Checkered standard grade American walnut pistol-grip stock.
With Damascus Barrels $155
With Steel Barrels. 245

Double-Barrel Side-by-Side Hammerless Shotgun
Sidelock action. Gauges: various. Barrels: 28 to 32 inches; steel or Damascus. Weight: 7½ or 8½ pounds. Checkered standard grade American walnut pistol-grip stock.
With Steel Barrels. $260
With Damascus Barrels 165

Single-Barrel Shotgun $100
Single-shot, break-open, breechloading action. Gauges: 12, 16 and others. Barrels: 28 to 32 inches, steel. Weight: 5¾ to 6½ pounds. Plain walnut stock and forearm with light checkering on some models.

Crescent Double-Barrel Shotgun

The following "Brand Names" are those known to have been carried on Crescent Firearms Co. shotguns, but many other names exist:

Barker Gun Company
Bellmore Gun Company
Black Powder Wonder
Carolina Arms Company
Central Arms Company
Cherokee Arms Company
Chesapeake Gun Company
Columbian New York Arms Company
Comper
Cruso
Cumberland Arms Company
Elgin Arms Company
Elmira Arms Company
Empire
Empire Arms Company
Enders Oak Leaf
Enders Royal Service
Essex
Faultless
Faultless Goose Gun
F.F. Forbess
Hartford Arms Company Harvard
Hermitage Arms Company
Hermitage Gun Company
Howard Arms Company
Interstate Arms Company
Jackson Arms Company
Kingsland Special
Kingsland 10 Star
Knickerbocker
Knox-All
Lakeside
J.H. Lau & Company
Leader Gun Company
Lee Special
Lee's Munner Special
Marshwood
Massachusetts Arms Company
Metropolitan
Minnesota Arms Company
Mississippi Valley Arms Co.
Mohawk
Monitor
National Arms Company
New Rival
New York Arms Company

Not-Nac Manufacturing Co.
Occidental Arms
Oxford Arms Company
Peerless
Perfection
Piedmont
Pioneer Arms Company
Quail
Queen City
Rev-O-Noc
Charles Richter
Richmond Arms Company
Richmond Hardware & Company
Rickard Arms Company
Royal Service
Rummel
Shue's Special
Silver Shot
Southern Arms Company
Special Service
Spencer Gun Company
Sportsman
Springfield Arms Company
Square Deal
State Arms Company
Sterling
Sullivan Arms Company
U.S. Arms Company
Victor
Victor Special
Virginia Arms Company
Volunteer
Vulcan Arms Company
White Powder Wonder
Wilshire Arms Company
Winfield Arms Company
Winoca Arms Company
Wolverine Arms Company
Worthington Arms Company

W.H. DAVENPORT
Providence, Rhode Island

Davenport Shotguns

Double-Barrel Shotgun $575
Single-Shot Shotgun. 95

DAMASCUS BARRELS

The Damascus barrels that were an integral part of many 19th-century shotguns are distinctive for their often intricate pattering. The term "Damascus" is derived from the ancient Middle Eastern city of the same name, the capital of now modern Syria. In this city, swords were forged with wavy patterns, and it is from these patterns that the barrels borrow their distinction.

Damascus barrels consisted of a combination of forged iron and steel strips that were braided in different forms into a band. The band was then wound around a mandrel and welded. The manufacture proceeded gradually as the form was worked with light hammering until all the small rods or wires were joined into a solid piece. The mandrel used as the form was then removed by boring it out. Depending upon how the wires were braided and twisted, a more or less fine Damascus-like or damascened pattern would appear upon the finished barrel after browning or bluing. The finer and more regular the patterning, the greater the worth of the barrel.

Because of the construction, these barrels were lighter and usually stronger than their predecessors. Not only did these features make production cheaper. but demand for them increased considerably, because, especially with double-barreled shotguns, for example, carrying them into the field was all the more easy.

Confidence in the quality of Damascus barrels was so great before the turn of the century that even ordinary steel barrels were either painted or covered with decalcomania to imitate the real damascened patterns.

The cheaper Damascus barrels were the so-called "band" Damascus barrels. Better grades, based on the quality of the workmanship, are the "Horseshoe," "Rose," "Bernard," "Crolle," "Moire," and "Laminette." Other fine types of Damascus were the "Laminated Steel," type and "Genuine Damascus" made in England. The primary source of Damascus barrels, however, was Belgium, specifically the Liège area, and about one-third of all the Belgian shotguns produced before 1900 had Damascus barrels.

New technology in metallurgy, however, has all but made Damascus barrels obsolete in terms of use. They will take only blackpowder loads (even these are questionable) and never the modern smokeless loads of today.

Braiding strips of forged iron and steel was the first step in constructing a Damascus barrel.

Step two was wrapping the braided strips around a mandrel, then lightly hammering all the small rods or wires until the "braids" were a solid piece.

Band

Bernard

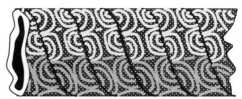

Horseshoe

Laminette

Rose

Laminated Steel

N.R. DAVIS & CO.
Freetown, Massachusetts

N.R. Davis Percussion Shotguns
Standard Model. **$595**
Percussion Shotgun No. 3 . . . . **425**

N.R. Davis Double-Barrel Hammer Shotgun
Damascus Barrels. **$230**
Steel Barrels **220**

N.R. Davis Double-Barrel Hammerless Shotgun
Damascus Barrels. **$165**
Steel Barrels **300**

JAMES DODDS
Dayton, Ohio

Dodds Double-Barrel Shotgun **$375**
Gauges: 12, 14, 16, 20 and 32. Barrels: 28 to 32 inches. Modest metal and wood decorations. Metal buttplate and forend release catch. Made 1869 to 1908.

ENTERPRISE GUN WORKS
Pittsburgh, Pennsylvania

Enterprise Double-Barrel Shotgun **$360**
Gauges: Various, but 12 most common. Barrels: 28 to 32 inches. Weight: approximately 7½ pounds. Some parts made locally while others were imported from Europe. Low to medium grade buttstock and forend. Some barrels contain foreign proof marks. Made from 1862 to 1875.

WILLIAM EVANS
London, England

Evans Double-Barrel Shotgun
Gauges: 12 and 16 noted; others were probably available. Barrels: 28 to 34 inches; steel or Damascus. Weight: 7½ pounds. Checkered walnut buttstock and forearm. Light engraving on barrels and receiver. Cased pairs always bring a premium over single guns. Damascus barrels will bring approximately 50% of the values shown.

Pistol Grip, Single Weapon **$2000**
Pistol Grip, Cased Pair **6000**
Straight Grip, Single Weapon **3000**
Straight Grip, Cased Pair **8000**

CARL AUGUST FISCHER
Lubek, Germany

Fischer Double-Barrel Percussion Shotgun. . **$775**
Percussion locks. Gauge: 14 and possibly others. Barrel: 28¾ inches, Damascus; lettered "C.A. Fischer in Lubek." Finely engraved locks. Checkered stock and forearm with carved borders. Fischer shotguns were manufactured between 1845 and 1853.

GEORGE FOGERTY
Cambridge, Massachusetts

Fogerty Double-Barrel Shotgun **$345**
Gauges: 12, 14, 16, 20 and 32. Barrels: 28 to 32 inches. Modest metal and wood decorations. Metal buttplate and forend release catch. Made 1891 to 1908.

H & D FOLSOM ARMS COMPANY
New York, New York

In about 1893, H & D Folsom purchased the Bacon Arms Company as well as Crescent Firearms Company (*see* separate listings). These two companies produced, and Folsom sold, a vast number of firearms under a host of brand names, probably around 100 different ones.

During this same period, Folsom Arms imported thousands of firearms from Europe (primarily Belgium) and sold them under a variety of private labels. Firearms manufactured in Europe are readily identifiable by the European proof marks on the underside of the barrels. The H & D Folsom Arms Co. was purchased by Savage Arms Corporation in 1931.

The following shotguns are representative of the shotguns imported by H & D Folsom Arms and may have carried any one of the brand names that are listed afterward.

Double-Barrel Side-by-Side Hammer Shotgun
Outside hammers. Sidelock action. Gauges: 12 and 16. Barrels: 28 to 32 inches; steel or Damascus. Weight: 6½ to 8½ pounds. Checkered European walnut stock with half-pistol grip and forearm. Made circa 1895.
With Damascus Barrels **$155**
With Steel Barrels. **275**

Double-Barrel Side-by-Side Hammerless Shotgun
Hammerless. Boxlock action. Gauges: 12 and 16. Barrels: 28 to 32 inches; steel or Damascus. Weight: 6½ to 8½ pounds. European walnut stock and forearm. Made circa 1895.
With Steel Barrels. **$295**
With Damascus Barrels **175**

Forehand & Wadsworth Side-by-Side Shotgun

Single-Shot Hammer Shotgun........ $115
Single-shot. Break-open, breechloading action.
Gauge: 12 most common. Barrels: 30 to 32 inches,
steel. Weight: 5¾ to 6¼ pounds. Plain European
walnut stock and forearm with light checkering on
some models. Made circa 1895.

The following "Brand Names" are those most often
found on H & D Folsom Arms Co. imported shotguns:

T. Barker
C.G. Bonehill
C.W. Franklin
Harrison Arms Company
Henry Gun Company
Hummer
Liège Arms Company
J. Manton & Company
William Moore & Company
C. Parker & Company
W. Richards
St. Louis Arms Company
Sickels Arms Company
Stanley
Ten Star
Ten Star Heavy Duty
Tiger
Warren Arms Company
Wilkinson Arms Company
Wilmont Arms Company
Wiltshire Arms Company

FOREHAND & WADSWORTH
Worcester, Massachusetts

Sullivan Forehand and Henry Wadsworth were the
sons-in-law of Ethan Allen and the successors to his
firearms interests. As the arms-producing firm of
Forehand & Wadsworth, which operated from 1871
to about 1890, they manufactured handguns and
rifles as well as shotguns (*see* separate listings).
Although they were well-built, the shotguns detailed
below have never gained much popularity as collectors' items.

**Forehand & Wadsworth Double-Barrel
Side-by-Side Shotgun............... $230**
Gauges: 10 and 12. Barrels: various lengths and
chokes to order; Belgian-twist steel. Weight: 6½ to
8½ pounds (12 Ga.); 8 to 10 pounds (10 Ga.). Color
casehardened frame. Outside hammers. Side locks.
Italian or Circassian walnut pistol-grip stock and
forend, checkered. Snap forend and extension rib.
Made from 1880 to 1890.

**Forehand & Wadsworth Hammerless
Shotgun........................ $190**
Single-shot. Top-snap action. Gauge: 12. Barrel: 30
to 36 inches; twist or Damascus steel. Weight: about
7 pounds. Automatic safety. Checkered walnut
semipistol-grip stock and forend. Made from 1880 to
1890.

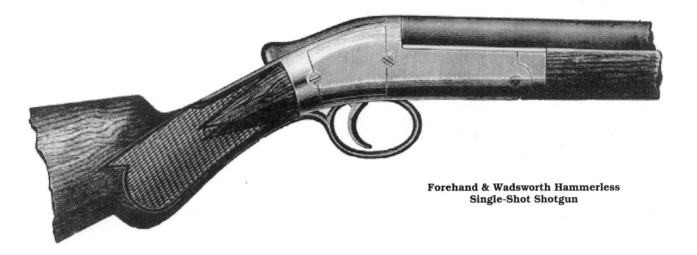

Forehand & Wadsworth Hammerless
Single-Shot Shotgun

Forehand & Wadsworth Single-Shot
Shotgun $105
Breechloading, top-snap action. Barrel: various
lengths, slightly choked. Weight: 7 to 9¾ pounds.
Plain walnut pistol-grip stock and forend. Made from
the 1870s to 1890s.

FOREHAND ARMS COMPANY
Worcester, Massachusetts

After Henry Wadsworth retired in 1890, Sullivan
Forehand continued the business they had partnered
in (*see* Forehand & Wadsworth) and changed the firm
name to simply Forehand Arms Co. The legacy of
producing fine firearms, begun by Ethan Allen in
1837, extended into the 20th century until 1902.

Forehand Arms Co. Grade No. 3
Hammerless
Side-by-Side Shotgun

Forehand Arms Co. Hammer
Side-by-Side Shotgun

Forehand Hammer Side-by-Side Shotgun . . $165
Outside hammers. Plain receiver. Gauges: 12 and 16.
Barrels: various lengths and chokes; twist or Damascus steel; extension rib, straight and matted. Weight:
7 to 8½ pounds. French or Italian half-pistol grip
stock, finely checkered. Made from about 1895 to
1902.

Forehand Hammerless Double-Barrel
Side-by-Side Shotgun
Boxlock action. Gauges: 12 and 16. Barrels: various
lengths and chokes made to order. Made from 1896
to 1902 in the following grades:

Grade No. 0: Finest Belgian twist barrels, fine walnut stock, full or half-pistol grip, well checkered;
no engraving. **$195**
Grade No. 1: Two-blade Damascus steel barrels,
full or half-pistol grip stock of French walnut,
lightly checkered and engraved **$230**
Grade No. 2: Fine three-blade or chain Damascus
steel barrels, select French walnut stock with
full or half-pistol grip, finely checkered and en-
graved. **$275**
Grade No. 3: Very fine Damascus barrels, extra fine
French walnut stock with full or half-pistol grip,
finely checkered and extra quality engraving **$395**

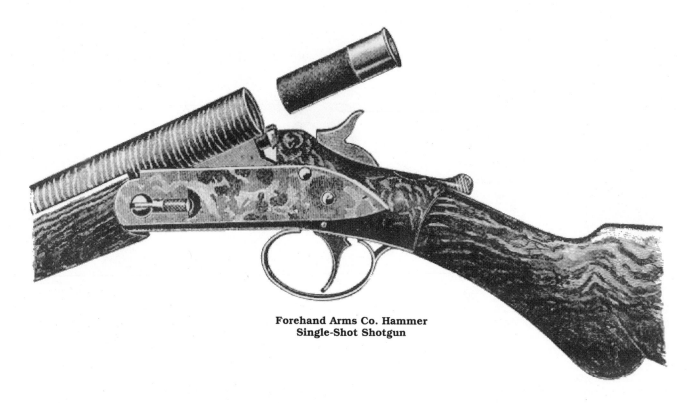

**Forehand Arms Co. Hammer
Single-Shot Shotgun**

Forehand Hammer Single-Shot Shotgun $110

Same general specifications as the Forehand &
Wadsworth Single-Shot Shotgun. Breechloading.
Top-snap action. Barrel: various lengths, slightly
choked. Weight: 7 to 9¾ pounds. Plain walnut pistol-grip stock and forend. Made from about 1890 to
1895.

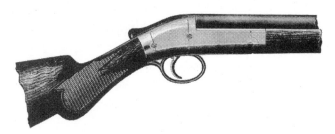

**Forehand Arms Co. Hammerless
Single-Shot Shotgun**

Forehand Hammerless Shotgun $165

Single-shot. Same general specifications as the Fore-
hand & Wadsworth Hammerless. Top-snap action.
Gauge: 12. Barrel: 30 to 36 inches; twist or Damascus
steel. Weight: about 7 pounds. Automatic safety.
Checkered semipistol-grip walnut stock and forend.
Made from 1890 to 1902.

FRENCH SHOTGUNS
Various Manufacturers

French Trade Shotgun **$2500**
Flintlock. Gauge: 10. Barrel: 47 inches. Iron furni-
ture. French proof mark on lock. Made circa 1745.
See opposite page.

JOSEPH GOLCHER
Address Unknown

Golcher locks were used on many American and
British shotguns made by different gunsmiths. The
following are two examples, but prices may vary
tremendously depending upon quality of gun and
embellishments.

American Percussion Fowler **$200**
Back-action lock. Iron furniture, silver escutcheons
on grips. See opposite page.

British Percussion Fowler **$195**
Lock marked "Joseph Golcher." Partridges also engraved on lock. Iron furniture with low-quality wood
in stock. Made circa 1850.

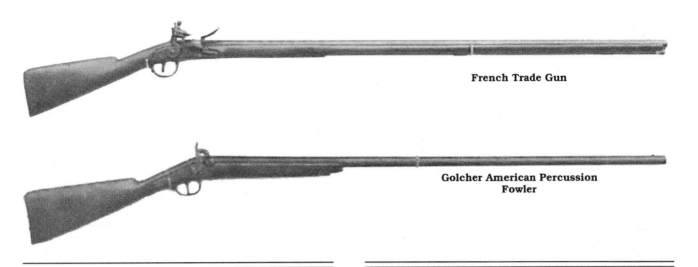

French Trade Gun

Golcher American Percussion Fowler

W.W. GREENER & SONS
Birmingham, England

Greener Hammerless Ejector Double-Barrel Shotgun
Crown Model Grade DH55	**$4500**
Jubilee Model Grade DK35	**2500**
Royal Model Grade DH75	**4000**
Sovereign Model Grade DH40	**2750**

Greener Far-Killer Model Grade FH35 Double-Barrel Shotgun
12 Gauge, Non-ejector.	**$2500**
12 Gauge, Ejector	**3200**
Deluxe, Non-ejector Model	**2300**
Deluxe Ejector Model	**2195**

Greener Single-Barrel Shotgun
General-Purpose Model. **$375**
Gauge: 12. Barrels: 28, 30, 32, and 34 inches. Weight: 6½ pounds. Medium-grade walnut buttstock and forearm. Modest checkering and some slight engraving. This was considered to be one of the best single-shot shotguns of the time.

HARRINGTON & RICHARDSON ARMS
Worcester, Massachusetts

H&R Double-Barrel Shotgun
Hammerless. Gauges: 10 and 12. Barrels: 28, 30 or 32 inches; Damascus. Casehardened frame. Checkered semipistol-grip stock. Anson & Deeley (designer) inscribed on lockplates; Harrington & Richardson markings on barrel rib and buttplate. Approximately 3500 guns were distributed by Harrington & Richardson from 1882 to 1885. Many reference books indicate that this shotgun was the first American hammerless double-barrel shotgun

A Grade: Extra select grained wood, fine Damascus barrels, fancy engraving with gold inlay plate imbedded in buttstock **$2750**

B Grade: Select grained wood, Damascus finished barrels, and high-quality engraving **$1800**

C Grade: Medium-grade wood with modest checkering; Damascus-finished barrels with some engraving on receiver and breech end of barrels **$625**

D Grade: Plain wood with little or no checkering; slight engraving on locks and barrels. **$495**

W.W. Greener Royal Grade
Hammerless Double Shotgun

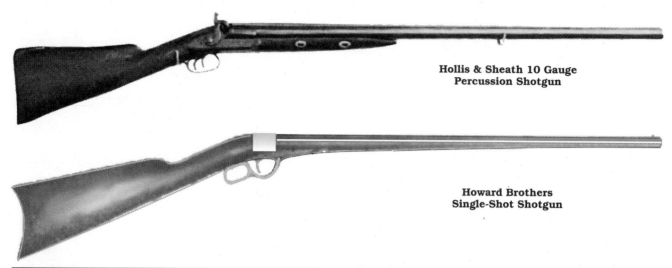

Hollis & Sheath 10 Gauge
Percussion Shotgun

Howard Brothers
Single-Shot Shotgun

HOLLENBECK GUN COMPANY
Wheeling, West Virginia

Hollenbeck Three-Barrel Gun **$995**
Gauge: 12; Caliber: 32-40 most popular. Double shotgun barrels over a single rifle barrel. Modest wood and metal decorations. Made circa 1900.

HOLLIS & SHEATH
London, England

Hollis & Sheaath 12 Gauge Percussion Shotgun **$595**
Percussion locks. Gauge: 12. Double-barrels. 30 inches; Damascus; marked "LONDON FINE STUB TWIST." Locks, hammers, short tang and trigger guard finely engraved. Checkered walnut stock with metal buttplate.

Hollis & Sheath 10 Gauge Percussion Shotgun **$265**
Gauge: 10. Massive stock and double barrels. Two wedges in forewood to hold barrels. Iron furniture.

HOWARD BROTHERS
Whitneyville, Connecticut

Charles Howard obtained patents for a breechloading hammerless action, which were applied to handguns, rifles and shotguns from September 26, 1865, to May 15, 1866. The Whitney Arms Co. of Whitneyville, Conn., made most of these arms under contract, as is stamped on the barrels of many of the early models, "Mf'd for Howard Brothers by Whitney Arms Co., Whitneyville, Conn."

Howard Brothers Single-Shot Shotgun . . **$175**
Breechloading shotgun. Gauge: 20. Barrel: 30½ inches. Overall length: 49¾ inches. Weight: 6 pounds. American walnut stock. Made from 1866 to 1869.

JAPANESE MILITARY
Various Manufacturers

Japanese Matchlock "Blunderbuss" **$955**
Matchlock. Calibers: various. Barrel: 38 inches; heavy, octagonal. Overall length: 50 inches. Two brass bands, brass outside hammer spring. Brass escutcheons, brass flower ornament at tang. Imperial seal inlaid in silver on barrel.

IVER JOHNSON'S ARMS & CYCLE WORKS
Fitchburg, Massachusetts

Iver Johnson, from Norway, and Martin Bye, from Sweden, joined efforts in 1871 to manufacture muzzleloading pistols under the firm name of Johnson, Bye and Co. The original firm, quite small, consisted of the two gunsmiths and a staff of three assistants. They occupied two rooms in a building in Worcester, Mass. However, in 1873 they purchased a five-story building and rapid expansion followed.

In 1883 after Bye retired, Johnson changed the name twice until in 1884 the company became known as Iver Johnson's Arms & Cycle Works, relocated in Fitchburg. This company produced bicycles, and it was as a bicycle manufacturer that the firm name became a household word. In addition to bicycles, however, the plant made a great assortment of revolvers and pistols (*see* Handgun Section), as well as

**Iver Johnson Single-Barrel
Top-Snap Shotgun**

single- and double-barreled shotguns. They also sold a line of police equipment, handcuffs and accessories.

Iver Johnson Single-Barrel Shotguns
Side Snap Model **$125**
Top Snap Model **135**

Iver Johnson Double-Barrel Shotgun . . **$325**
Gauges: 12, 16, 20 and 32. Barrel: 28, 30 and 32 inches, round. Walnut buttstock and forearm with modest checkering.

NICANOR KENDALL
Windsor, Vermont

Kendall Percussion Underhammer
Single-Barrel Shotgun. $440
Underhammer percussion lock. Gauges: various. Barrel: 37 inches; part round, part octagonal; marked "N. KENDALL/WINDSOR, VT./PATENT." Engraved tang and breech marked, "SMITH'S/IMPROVED/PATENT/STUD/LOCK." One-piece walnut stock.

CASIMIR LEFAUCHEUX
Paris, France

Casimir Lefaucheux (1802–1852) was a French Gunmaker who invented the pinfire cartridge in the 1830s, which was covered in the 1835 addition to his initial 1832 patent. His son, Eugene, carried on the gunmaking tradition and helped introduce pinfire cartridge revolvers to the world during the mid-19th century (*see* separate listing under Handguns). The shotgun detailed below was one of the first to use pinfire cartridges.

Lefaucheux Double-Barrel Shotgun. . . . **$175**
Highly engraved frame and lock. Outside hammers. Side locks. Gauges: various pinfire cartridges. Barrels: 30 inches standard, but other lengths made. Weight: about 6 pounds. Straight-grip, finely figured walnut stock and forend, usually checkered. Introduced in 1836.

LEFEVER ARMS CO.
Syracuse, New York

Daniel "Uncle Dan" Lefever learned his trade as a gunsmith in Rochester, New York. When the Civil War broke out in 1861, Lefever had a little gun shop in Canandaigua, N.Y., where he made superior rifles for some of the sharpshooters in the Northern Army. A few years later he moved to Auburn, where he did high-class gunsmithing and produced a few shotguns on special order. The Lefever was the first double-barrel breechloading hammerless gun made in America.

The original breechloading Lefever hammerless was cocked by a side lever, which the shooter pushed down directly after firing the gun. This motion cocked the gun so it could be loaded and fired again. A short time later, however, this design was modified to cock the hammers automatically upon opening the breech. Patents on the first Lefever hammerless were issued in 1872. (For a brief time in the 1870s, Lefever partnered with John Nichols to make Nichols & Lefever fine grade shotguns with Damascus barrels.)

From Auburn, Uncle Dan moved to Syracuse, where the Lefever Arms Company was incorporated in 1884. Lefever went into the extensive manufacture of shotguns bearing his name, and for many years he superintended the building of his famous line of hand-finished guns.

In 1901, a few years before his death, Lefever sold his interests in Lefever Arms Co. and moved to Bowling Green, Ohio. There he started another factory under the name of D.M. Lefever & Son, which produced shotguns until Lefever died in 1906.

The Syracuse company, however, operated independently a little longer, and was eventually sold to the Ithaca Gun Company of Ithaca, N.Y., in about 1915. Lefever shotguns are still coveted by collectors of fine shotguns, and continue to rise in price each year.

NOTE

Lefever shotguns are among the most desirable American made shotgun for collectors, surpassed only by the Parker.

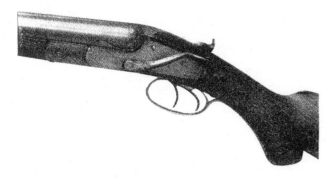

The First Lefever Shotgun

Lefever Hammerless Double-Barrel Shotguns

Hammerless, boxlock breechloader. Full "compensated" action with square-shouldered top fastener. Gauges: 10, 12, 14, 16, 20; 8 gauge was available at additional cost. Barrel: Damascus or laminated steel, tapered, with matted rib; length varies. Weight: 10 gauge, 8 to 10 lbs.; 12 gauge, 7 to 9 lbs. Auto or non-auto safety. Checkered pistol-grip stock and forend. Double triggers. In 1889, according to the Lefever catalog of that year, prices ranged from **$80** for F Grade to **$400** for Optimus Grade. Today, those prices range from **$400** to about **$3000.**

Optimus. Whitworth fluid steel or Kilby barrels; finest French walnut stock; full pistol grip with horn cap; horn or skeleton butt plate; special gold designs; highest grade of engraving, checkering and finish.

AA Grade. Finest Damascus or laminated steel barrels; finest French walnut stock; full pistol grip with horn cap; horn or skeleton butt plate; elegantly engraved, checkered and finished.

A Grade. Same as above, but differs in finish and engraving.

B Grade. Fine Damascus or laminated steel barrels; fine English walnut stock; full pistol grip with horn cap; horn heel plate; handsomely engraved and checkered.

C Grade. Fine Damascus or laminated steel barrels; choice English walnut stock; full pistol grip with horn or steel cap; rubber heel plate; richly engraved and checkered.

D Grade. Damascus or laminated steel barrels; fine English walnut stock; full pistol grip with horn cap; rubber heel plate; finely engraved and checkered.

E Grade. Damascus or laminated steel barrels; English walnut stock; full pistol grip with horn cap; horn or rubber plate; nicely engraved and checkered.

F Grade. Damascus or laminated steel barrels; English walnut stock; horn or rubber buttplate; full pistol grip; checkered and engraved.

LEWIS & TOMES
London, England

Lewis & Tomes Percussion Double-Barrel Shotgun $295

Gauges: various. Barrel: London Fine Twist Damascus. Iron buttplate and trigger guard. German silver nose cap, wedge escutcheons and cap box in buttstock. Checkered grip.

THE MARLIN FIRE ARMS CO.
New haven, Connecticut

The Marlin Firearm Co. entered the shotgun business with their Model 1898 Slide Action Shotgun, and its later variations: the Models 16, 17, 19, 21, 24, 26, 28 and 30. However, only the Model 1898 was manufactured prior to 1900; the remaining models were not produced until at least 1904, with the Model 16; 1906, with the Model 17, etc.

Marlin Model 1898 Slide-Action Repeating Shotgun

Takedown. Five-shot tubular magazine. Gauge: 12. Barrel: 26, 28, 30, or 32 inches; various chokes. Weight: 7½ pounds. Pistol-grip stock, grooved slide handle; checkering on higher grades.

Grade A: (Field) $550

Grade B: plain gun with checkered, fancy walnut and matte barrel rib 745

Grade C: same as B, except simple engraving on receiver. 1050

**Lewis & Tomes Percussion
Double-Barrel Shotgun**

**Marlin Slide-Action
Repeating Shotgun**

Grade D: European walnut, fancy checkering, engraving on receiver, gold-plated screws and trigger **$2750**

MASSACHUSETTS ARMS CO.
Chicopee Falls, Massachusetts

Founded by Daniel B. Wesson of Smith & Wesson fame, the Massachusetts Arms Company had several U.S. Government contracts for the manufacture of firearms during the Civil War. The original operation was supposedly discontinued around 1866, but the name has since been used on many inexpensive shotguns.

Mass. Arms Co. Single-Barrel Shotgun . . **$75**
Gauge: 12. Barrel: various lengths from 28 to 32 inches. Typical break-open, single-shot shotgun with barrel latch on upper tang. Made circa 1890s.

JOHN P. MOORE & CO.
Toronto, Canada

John P. Moore was an importer and wholesaler of guns; most of the shotguns that bear his name were produced in Belgium.

John P. Moore Double-Barrel Percussion Shotgun **$175**
Gauge: 12 and others. Barrel: browned Damascus. Iron furniture. Imported between 1884 and 1886.

WILLIAM MOORE & CO.
London, England

William Moore & Co. Double-Barrel Percussion Shotgun **$500**
Percussion front-action locks. Gauges: 10 and 12. Barrel: 30 inches; browned Damascus steel. Lock plates marked, "W. Moore & Co." Fine English-style checkering on walnut stock and forend.

ONION & WHEELOCK
London, England

Onion & Wheelock was one of the British manufacturers who produced percussion shotguns for export to America. This firm made a medium-quality shotgun for the sportsman who wanted a reliable weapon, but who was unwilling (or unable) to pay a great amount of money for the extras — the elaborate ornamentation, for example, that was found on such shotguns as those produced by W & C Scott and others.

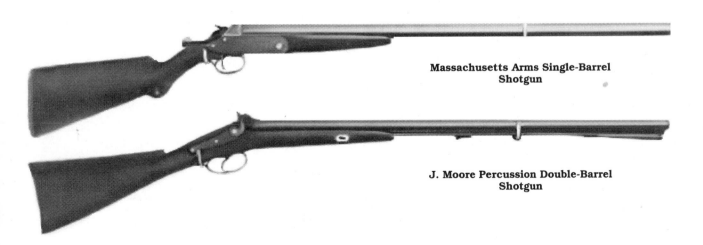

**Massachusetts Arms Single-Barrel
Shotgun**

**J. Moore Percussion Double-Barrel
Shotgun**

Onion & Wheelock Percussion Double-Barrel Shotgun **$385**
Color casehardened frame. Outside hammers. Side locks. Gauge: 12. Barrels: various lengths, but most measured approximately 30 inches; marked "Fine Damascus London Double Proof"; Damascus steel. English walnut straight-grip stock. Plain ornamentation. Wood ramrod. Made circa 1850.

F. ORGAN
Meriden, Connecticut

F. Organ Percussion Double-Barrel Shotgun . . **$345**
Percussion locks. Gauge: 12. Barrels: 30 inches; London twist steel; marked "LONDON FINE TWIST." Locks lightly engraved in coarse pattern. Walnut stock, checkered at grip; metal buttplate.

PARKER BROTHERS
Meriden, Connecticut

Under the leadership of Charles Parker, the first models of the commercial Parker Double-Barrel Shotgun were completed and marketed in 1868. It was a breechloading, 14-gauge shotgun with 29-inch barrels using outside primed ammunition, similar to the ignition system used on the Sharps carbine.

The locking mechanism on the first Parker was operated by means of a lever under the breech mechanism, which was both crude and inconvenient when compared to the later shotgun development of the 1870s. Therefore, with the help of designer Charles A. King, the Parker Shotgun was given a new streamlined locking system, using what has become known as the "doll's head" extension to the top rib of the barrel; also a hardened, tapered wedge was set into the vertical lug below the barrels. This design was so satisfactory that it remained an integral part of the Parker Shotgun until it was discontinued in the early 1940s.

Although The Parker Gun is often referred to as an "American Classic," the laminated-twist barrels were manufactured in Belgium, as were the barrels for the majority of shotguns made in the United States at the time.

Unlike some other types of antique firearms, the later Parker shotguns are worth more than the earlier models. One Parker A-1 Special in 28 gauge, for example, sold for the sum of $95,000 a few years ago at a New York auction. None of the antique varieties of the same shotgun will even approach this figure. You will find a broad range of prices in dealing with Parker shotguns, starting at $225 for the lowest grades, to about $10,000 for the highest quality with intricate engraving.

Parker Hammerless Side-by-Side Shotgun
Color casehardened boxlock action. Non-automatic ejectors. Gauges: 10, 12, and 16. Barrels: various lengths with various chokes. Weight: 6¼ to 8 pounds. Double triggers. Checkered pistol-grip stock and forend. Made from 1899 to 1912 in the following grades: AAH Pigeon, AH, BH, CH, DH, EH, GH, NH, PH and VH.

Parker Outside Hammer Double-Barrel Shotgun
Color casehardened receiver. Engraved sidelocks. Gauges: 8 to 12. Barrel: 30 to 36 inches. Weight: 7 to 13 pounds. Top lever, double bolt, rebounding locks, patent forend bolt, solid head plungers, improved check hook, and choke bore. Various grades as follows:

Quality A "Premiere": Gauge: 10. Barrels: 32 inches; finest Damascus steel. Weight: 9 to 10½ pounds. Finest imported pistol-grip walnut stock, gold shield, finest checkering and engraving combined with the best finish available.

Quality D: Gauge: 10. Barrels: 32 inches; fine Damascus steel. Weight: 9 to 10½ pounds. Fine imported pistol-grip walnut stock, silver shield, fine checkering and engraving, skeleton buttplate.

Quality 3: Same as Grade D, except made in 12 gauge with 32-inch barrels. Weight: 7 to 9 pounds.

Quality E: Gauge: 10. Barrels: 32 inches; Damascus steel. Fine figured American or imported walnut pistol-grip stock, checkered and engraved.

Quality G: Similar to Quality E, except chambered for 12 gauge and weighs 9 pounds.

Quality I: Gauge: 10. Barrels: 32 inches; fine laminated steel. Weight: 10¼ to 10½ pounds. Fine figured American walnut pistol-grip stock, checkered and engraved with rubber buttplate.

Quality 8: Gauge: 8. Barrels: 34 inches; fine laminated steel. Weight: 13 pounds. Fine figured American walnut pistol-grip stock, checkered and engraved. Rubber buttplate.

Quality R: Gauge: 10. Barrels: 32 inches; twist. Weight: 10 pounds. Pistol-grip American walnut stock and forend, lightly checkered and engraved.

Quality S: Basically the same as Quality R, except for straight grip and slightly lighter weight.

Quality T: Gauge: 12. Barrels: 32 inches; twist. Weight: 9 pounds. American walnut pistol-grip stock and forend, very lightly engraved with modest checkering.

Quality U: Basically the same as Quality T, except for straight grip and slightly lighter weight.

Parker Under Lever Side-by-Side Shotgun . . **$1295**
Outside hammers. Under-lever locked action. Gauges: various. Barrels: various lengths; laminated-twist steel. Weight: about 8½ pounds average.

WILLIAM POWELL & SON LTD.
Birmingham, England

Established in 1802, the business of William Powell has been carried on by generation after generation of Powells on the old painstaking lines, and by the personal and active participation of the members of the firm in the production of guns — all built without any possibility of deterioration by resorting to cutting of costs. Consequently, the Powell shotguns are rated among the best in the world, and many of these 100-year-old scatterguns are in use today — still functioning without a flaw.

**Powell No. 1 Best Grade
Double-Barrel Shotgun**

Powell No. 1 Best Grade Double-Barrel Shotgun **$25,000**
Sidelock. Gauges: Made to order in any gauge desired, with 12, 16, and 20 being the most common. Barrels: Made to order in any length desired, but 28 inches was the recommended length. Highest grade French walnut buttstock and forearm with fine checkering. Metal elaborately engraved.

Powell No. 2 Best Grade Double-Barrel Shotgun **$20,000**
Same general specifications as the Powell No. 1 except finished plain without engraving.

**Powell No. 6 Crown Grade
Double-Barrel Shotgun**

Powell No. 6 Crown Grade Double-Barrel Shotgun **$8000**
Boxlock. Gauges: Made to order in any gauge desired, with 12, 16, and 20 being the most common. Barrels: Made to order in any length desired, but 28 inches was the recommended length. Highest grade French walnut buttstock and forearm with fine checkering. Metal elaborately engraved. Uses Anson & Deeley locks.

**Powell No. 7 Aristocrat
Double-Barrel Shotgun**

Powell No. 7 Aristocrat Grade Double-Barrel Shotgun **$2500**
Same general specifications as the Powell No. 6 except with lower quality wood and metal engraving.

**Powell No. 2 Best Grade
Double-Barrel Shotgun**

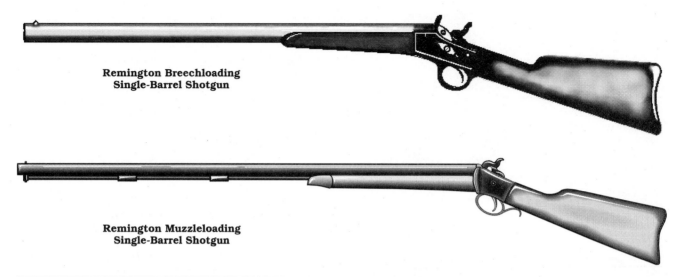

Remington Breechloading
Single-Barrel Shotgun

Remington Muzzleloading
Single-Barrel Shotgun

REMINGTON ARMS COMPANY
Ilion, New York

The Remington Arms Co., America's oldest firearms manufacturer, was one of the first successful producers of shotguns in this country.

Remington Breechloading Single-Barrel Shotgun
Single-shot, rolling-block action. Gauge: 16. Barrel: 30 or 32 inches; laminated. Overall length: 48 inches. Weight: 6½ pounds. Straight-grip walnut stock and forend; plain on standard model. Made from about 1873 to 1909.
Engraved Model. **$495**
Extra-Fancy Engraved Model **625**

Remington Muzzleloading Single-Barrel Shotgun **$395**
Hammer model. Straight-grip walnut stock. Offered in 1877.

Remington Model 1874 Side-by-Side Breechloading Shotgun . . . . **$300-$695**
Outside hammers. Sidelock action. Gauges: 10 and 12. Barrels: 28 or 30 inches; decarbonized steel, twist or Damascus. Weight: 8 to 8½ pounds. Double triggers. Stock varied from plain walnut to select and English walnut, with various grades of checkering and ornamentation. Double gun with one barrel rifle and one decarbonized steel barrel available; also double rifle with decarbonized steel barrels available, with price rising accordingly. Made in the 1870s.

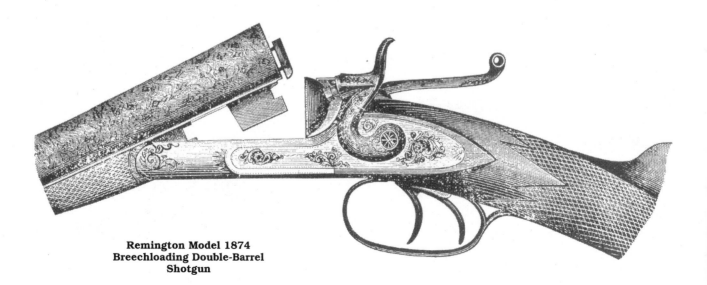

Remington Model 1874
Breechloading Double-Barrel
Shotgun

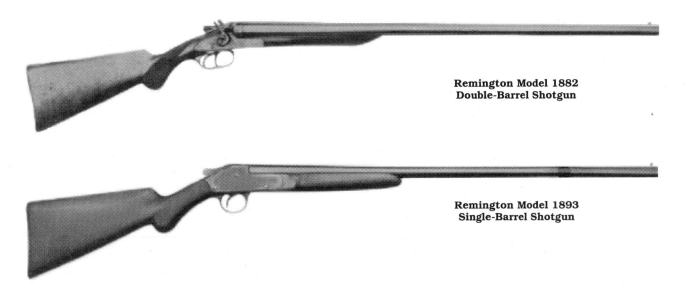

Remington Model 1882
Double-Barrel Shotgun

Remington Model 1893
Single-Barrel Shotgun

Remington New Model 1882 Double-Barrel Shotgun $1250
Outside hammers. Sidelock. Gauges: 10, 12 and 16. Barrels: 28 to 32 inches; plain or Damascus. Weight: 6¾ to 10¼ pounds. Double triggers. Checkered pistol-grip stock and forend. Made from 1882 to 1910.

Remington Model 1885 Double-Barrel Shotgun $995
Similar to the Model 1882 except locking mechanism and sighting picture was improved. Made from 1885 to 1887.

Remington Model 1887 Double-Barrel Shotgun $895
Specifications were similar to the Model 1882, but like the Model 1885 certain features were improved. Made from 1887 to 1894.

Remington Model 1889 Double-Barrel Shotgun $795
Gauges: 10, 12 and 16. Barrels: 28 to 32 inches; steel or Damascus. Weight: 7 to 10 pounds. Checkered pistol-grip stock and forend. Made from 1889 to 1908.

Remington Model 1893 Single-Barrel Shotgun $225
Also known as the Model No. 3 Rider. Gauges: 10, 12, 16, 20, 24, and 28. Barrels: 28 to 34 inches depending on gauge; blued, plain steel barrels. Weight: 5½ to 6½ pounds, depending on gauge. Casehardened, semi-hammerless, top-snap, break-open lock. Walnut half-pistol grip stock. Plain, short forend. Approximately 25,750 made from 1893 to 1906.

Remington Model 1889
Double-Barrel Shotgun

**Remington Model 1894
Double-Barrel Shotgun**

Remington Model 1894 Double-Barrel Shotgun

Boxlock. Automatic ejector. Gauges: 10, 12 and 16. Barrels: 28 to 32 inches; ordnance steel or Damascus. Weight: 7 to 10 pounds. Double triggers. Checkered stock and forend. Different grades consisted of fancier wood, elaborate checkering and engraving, and other ornamentation. Made from 1894 to 1910.

AE Grade	$ 520
AEO Grade	830
AO Grade	750
B Grade	365
BE Grade	690
BEO Grade	1150
BO Grade	775
C Grade	640
CE Grade	760
CEO Grade	1540
CO Grade	1100
D Grade	970
DE Grade	1115
DEO Grade	2240
DO Grade	2000
E Grade	1400
EE Grade	1800
EEO Grade	4200
EO Grade	3850
Special Grade	10,800

Remington Model 1900 Double-Barrel Shotgun $540

Improved version of Remington Model 1894 Shotgun. Same general specifications as above. Made from 1900 to 1910.

NOTE

Lt. Col. H.A. Gildersleeve of the American Rifle Team wrote in November 1876 that "I have just returned from the Big South Bay, where I have been gunning for ducks. I tried for the first time the Remington 10 gauge (shot)gun. My success with it was excellent. In my judgement its shooting capacity cannot be surpassed. I want no better gun, and if I did, I don't believe I could find it, even among the expensive grades of English ones." (Originally published in the 1877 Remington Catalog about the Model 1874.)

Muzzle → Breech

English-Style Choke

German-Style or Straight-Taper Choke

Swaged Choke

Convex Choke

Reversed, or Bell Choke

Muzzle → Breech

Popular choke designs used in both antique and modern shotgun barrels.

**Robertson Percussion
Double-Barrel Shotgun**

WESTLEY RICHARDS & CO. LTD.
Birmingham, England

**Westley Richards Double-Barrel
Shotgun** **$8500**
Box lock. Hammerless. Gauges: 12, 16 and 20. Barrels: lengths and boring to order; side-by-side. Weight: 5½ to 6¼ pounds, depending on gauge and barrel length. Hand-detachable locks and hinged cover plate. Selective ejectors. Double triggers or selective single trigger. Straight half-pistol grip checkered stock and forend. Although there are various grades, the price does not vary significantly. Made from 1899 to the mid-1900s.

Westley Richards Single-Barrel Shotgun **$450**
Gauge: 16. Barrel engraved "W. Richards London Fine Damascus." Lock engraved with flying geese and "W. Richards." Checkered grip and forend. Fanny gutta percha buttplate. A family of deer among trees in cartouche.

RIVERSIDE ARMS CO.
Address Unknown

Riverside Single-Shot Shotgun **$105**
Gauges: 12 and others. Barrel stamped "Electro Steel Choke Bored." Typical of inexpensive break-open, single-shot shotguns sold by hardware stores and mail-order houses of the period.

ROBERTSON
Scotland

**Robertson Double-Barrel Percussion
Shotgun** **$310**
Gauges: 12 and others. Iron furniture. Half stock. Made circa 1840.

W. & C. SCOTT & SON
London, England

**W & C Scott Double-Barrel Percussion
Shotgun** **$1050**
Bar and wood percussion locks, engraved with high-quality line drawings and maker's name. Gauges: 1 and others. Barrels: 32 inches; Damascus steel; top rib marked "W & C Scott & Sons, Makers, 10 Gt Castle St., Regent Circus London." Serial number usually marked on trigger guard. Checkered straight-grip stock with plain steel butt plate.

L. C. SMITH
Syracuse, New York

Lyman Cornelius Smith began the manufacture and sale of shotguns as early as 1877 with the Baker double- and three-barreled shotguns. The official L.C. Smith Shotgun did not debut until 1884, however, and was the exposed-hammer double-barrel, side-by-side model, manufactured in Syracuse, N.Y. In 1886, a hammerless model was introduced that established the reputation of performance and quality that the L.C. Smith shotgun still enjoys.

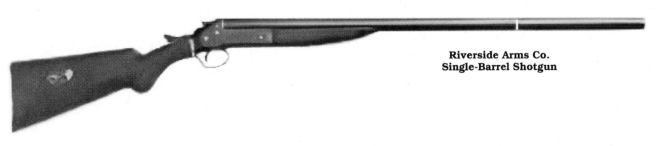

**Riverside Arms Co.
Single-Barrel Shotgun**

L.C. Smith Hammer Double-Barrel Shotgun

In 1888, John Hunter Sr. of Fulton, N.Y., purchased the Smith gun business and moved the entire operation to Fulton. The firm name was changed to Hunter Arms Co., but the name of the gun remained "The L.C. Smith Shotgun." Hunter Arms continued to manufacture L.C. Smith shotguns well into the 20th century until the Hunter holdings were sold prior to the outbreak of WWI. The L.C. Smith name maintained its appearance on newly manufactured firearms until 1971, when Marlin purchased the rights.

L.C. Smith Hammer Double-Barrel Shotguns

Back-action, double cross-bolted. Breechloading. Gauges: 10 and 12. Barrels: 26 to 32 inches; Damascus; any standard boring. Weight: 8½ to 12 pounds (10 Ga.); 7½ to 10 pounds (12 Ga.). Plain extractors. Double triggers.

A Grade: very fine. Damascus steel barrels, extra fine English walnut stock with pistol grip, extra fine checkering and engraving **$670**

B Grade: extra fine Damascus steel barrels, fine English walnut stock with pistol grip, fine checkering and engraving **$500**

C Grade: fine Damascus steel barrels, fine English walnut stock with pistol grip, fine checkering and engraving **$420**

D Grade: fine Damascus steel barrels, good English walnut stock with pistol grip, checkering, engraved metal **$320**

E Grade: Damascus steel barrels, good imported English walnut stock with pistol grip, checkering, engraved metal **$235**

F Grade: English stub twist barrels, checkered American walnut stock with pistol grip, engraved metal **$185**

L.C. Smith Hammerless Side-by-Side Shotguns (I)

Sidelock. Gauges: 10 and 12. Barrels: 30 or 32 inches; Damascus. Weight: 7½ to 12 pounds. Plain extractors. Compensating forend. Interchangeable main spring. Grades differ only in quality of workmanship, wood, style and amount of checkering and engraving, and quality of steel barrels. Manufactured by Smith in Syracuse from 1886 to 1888.

No. 2 Grade: good Damascus steel barrels, good English walnut stock and forend, half-pistol grip **$290**

No. 3 Grade: fine Damascus steel barrels, fine English walnut stock and forend with pistol grip or half-pistol grip, nicely checkered and engraved **$335**

No. 4 Grade: very fine Damascus steel barrels, very fine walnut stock and forend, full pistol grip or half-pistol grip, fine checkering and engraving **$500**

No. 5 Grade: very fine Damascus steel barrels, extra fine walnut stock and forend, full or half-pistol grip, finest checkering and engraving, extra fine finish **$675**

No. 6 Grade: finest Damascus steel barrels, finest imported English walnut stock, full or half-pistol grip, finest checkering and engraving, very finest finish **$1000**

L.C. Smith Hammerless Side-by-Side Shotguns (II)

Side lock. Gauges; 8, 10, 12, 16. Barrels: 26 to 32 inches. Weight: 6½ to 8 pounds. Automatic ejectors standard on higher grades, extra on lower grades. Checkered stock and forend; choice of straight, half- or full pistol grip. Beavertail or splinter forend. Grades differ only in quality of workmanship, wood,

L.C. Smith Hammerless Double-Barrel Shotgun

checkering, engraving, etc. Made by Hunter Arms from 1888 to 1900.

00 Grade	$ 1,295
0 Grade	1,495
1 Grade	1,675
2 Grade	1,795
3 Grade	1,995
Pigeon Grade	4,450
4 Grade	5,595
5 Grade	6,000
Monogram Grade	9,500
A1 Grade	7,000
A2 Grade	10,700
A3 Grade	15,000+

J. Stevens & Co.
Chicopee Falls, Massachusettes

Stevens New Model Pocket Shotgun

Gauge: .410. Calibers: 38-40 Shot, 44-40 Shot. Barrels: 10, 12, 15, or 18 inches, half-octagonal smoothbore. Brass frame with nickel finish; blued barrel. Rosewood or walnut grips. Detachable shoulder stock. Made 1875 to 1896.

Complete with detachable shoulder stock	**$565**
Pistol with no stock	**$350**

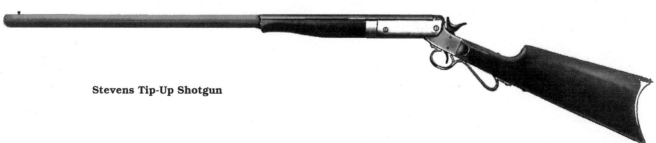

Stevens Tip-Up Shotgun

Stevens New Model Pocket Shotgun
No. 39 . . . . $495
Gauge: .410. Calibers: 38-40 Shot, 44-40 Shot. Barrels: 10, 12, 15, or 18 inches, half-octagonal smoothbore. Shotgun sights. Made from 1895 to 1906.

Stevens Tip-Up Shotgun $230
Gauges: 10, 12, 14, 16, and 20, single-shot. Barrel: 30 and 32 inches, round. Blued frame; some with nickel finish. Walnut stock and forearm. Made 1877 to 1896.

Stevens "Favorite" No. 20 Shotgun $310
Calibers: 22 and 32 Shot cartridges. Smoothbore barrel. Blade front sight; no rear sight. Made 1893 to 1939.

J. TURNEY
London, England

Turney Flintlock Fowler $695
Gauges: 12 and other. Brass furniture. High-quality fowling piece. Made from 1820 to 1832. See next page.

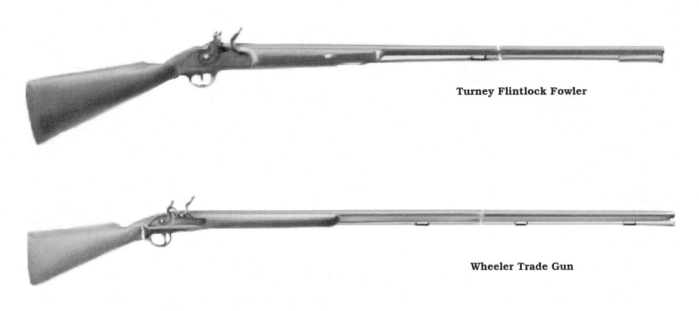

Turney Flintlock Fowler

Wheeler Trade Gun

ROBERT WHEELER
England/Canada

Robert Wheeler had a contract to produce arms for the Hudson's Bay Co. in Canada.

Wheeler Trade Shotgun. $900
Gauge: 12. Barrel: 48 inches. Plain iron furniture of typical trade gun style. Proof marks stamped on barrel. Made circa 1800.

WINCHESTER REPEATING ARMS CO.
New Haven, Connecticut

The Winchester Repeating Arms Co., prior to 1879, manufactured only repeating rifles (*see* Winchester under Rifles). In 1876 the company experimented with a few handguns, but none were ever produced for public use. Owing to the popularity of double-barreled breechloading shotguns of the time, and because there was a shortage of such weapons in the U.S., an agent from Winchester was sent to Birmingham, England, to purchase a quantity of the cheaper grade English "doubles." The first shipment of shotguns, purchased in 1878 from W.C. McEntree & Company, Richard Rodman, C.G. Bonehill, and some better grades from W.C. Scott & Sons, sold out so quickly that Winchester decided to purchase another quantity. This time it was the better grades marked with the Winchester name.

These imported shotguns bearing the Winchester name were available in five grades and were offered between 1879 and 1884, when serious consideration was given to a Winchester-manufactured line of shot-

guns. The first was the Model 1887 Lever Action, followed by the Model 1893 Pump or Slide Action Repeating Shotgun and finally an improved version of the 1893, called the Model 1897 Repeating Shotgun. These three models, offered in several grades, were the only true Winchester-produced shotguns before 1900.

Winchester Imported Side-by-Side Shotgun
Sidelock. Outside exposed hammers. Gauges: 10 and 12. Barrels: 30 and 32 inches; top rib marked "Winchester Repeating Arms Co./New Haven, Connecticut U.S.A., Class A" (or whatever class it was). Weight: 7½ to 10 pounds. Double triggers. Distributed by Winchester from 1879 to 1884.

Winchester Match Gun.	**$4000**
Winchester Class A.	**3300**
Winchester Class B.	**2750**
Winchester Class C.	**2295**
Winchester Class D	**1750**

Winchester Imported Shotgun

NOTE

The first Winchester shotguns were manufactured abroad and distributed by the Winchester firm. It was not until the Model 1887 that Winchester made a shotgun of its own.

Winchester Model 1887 Lever-Action Shotgun

Winchester Model 1887 Lever-Action Repeating Shotgun

Casehardened solid frame. Gauges: 10 and 12. Four-shot tubular magazine under barrel. Barrels: 30 or 32 inches; full choke. Weight: 8 pounds (12 Ga.); 9 pounds (10 Ga.). Pistol-grip stock and forend. Made from 1887 to 1901.

Standard Model. **$675**
Fancy Wood, Plain Stock. **600**
Fancy Wood, Checkering, Damascus Barrel . . . **995**

Winchester Model 1893 Slide-Action Repeating Shotgun

Solid frame. Five-shot tubular magazine. Gauge: 12. Barrel: 30 or 32 inches; full choke. Weight: 7¾ pounds with 30-inch barrel. Pistol-grip stock. Rounded slide handle with semicircular notches on

Winchester Model 1893 Slide-Action (cont.)

standard model. About 34,000 made from 1893 to 1897.

Standard Model **$350**
Fancy wood, Plain Stock. **425**
Fancy Wood, Checkering **575**

Winchester Model 1897 Slide-Action Repeating Shotgun

Vibible hammer. Takedown or solide frame. Gauges: 12 and 16. Five-shot tubular magazine. Barrels: 26 to 32 inches; 20 inches on riot gun. Choked full to cylinder. Weight: about 7¾ pounds. Made from 1897 to 1957.

Standard Model . . . . **$ 410**
Trap Grade **725**
Tournament Grade. **850**
Pigeon Grade **1500**

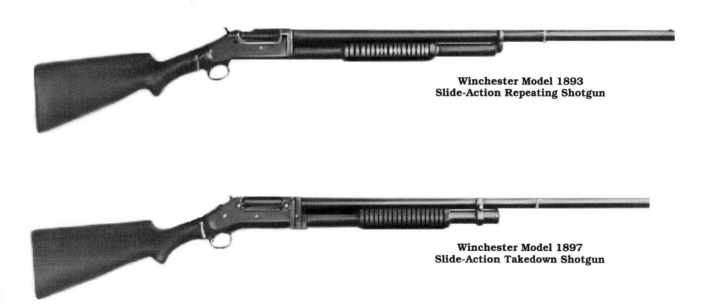

Winchester Model 1893 Slide-Action Repeating Shotgun

Winchester Model 1897 Slide-Action Takedown Shotgun

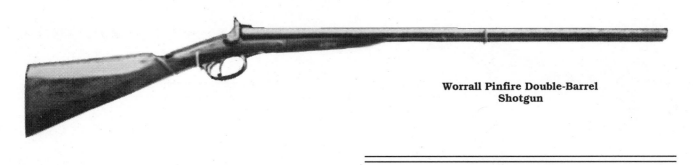

**Worrall Pinfire Double-Barrel
Shotgun**

JAMES WORRALL
Chester, England

Worrall Pinfire Double-Barrel Shotgun . . $400
Gauge: 15. Barrels: browned Damascus. High-grade walnut stock with checkered forend. Nicely engraved locks and trigger guard. Made from 1859 to 1864.

CHAPTER FOUR
BLACKPOWDER REPLICAS

During the mid-1950s, a number of black-powder buffs began importing replica arms from Europe. Although many take the credit for being the first, Turner Kirkland of Dixie Gun Works probably offered the first production replica in 1955. This was a typical Kentucky rifle manufactured to Kirkland's specifications in Belgium. Val Forgett of Navy Arms followed shortly thereafter with a basic Remington percussion revolver design manufactured in Italy.

The sale of these replica arms surpassed all expectations, and sales quickly exceeded the supply. Eventually, other models were introduced by the major importers, and soon several additional firms entered into the replica business. Custom shops also sprang up in the United States where higher quality blackpowder arms were produced on a limited basis, similar to the custom cartridge rifles made to individual specifications. It did not take long for replica arms to become big business nationwide, and even the major firearms manufacturers scrambled for a piece of the pie. Colt brought back into production several of the original Colt percussion designs; H&R came out with a replica model of the 1873 Springfield rifle chambered for the .45-70 cartridge; and Ruger introduced a replica stainless steel percussion revolver. The trend continues today.

Although replica arms are not antiques in the true sense, they are of great interest to antique collectors and shooters. Many blackpowder shooters who once utilized an original collector's item now keep their highly prized collector pieces in the gun cabinet, and use one of the replicas for their shooting requirements. Also, there is a need for trading information on replica arms since many exchange hands each year, and detailed pricing information for used models is sometimes difficult to obtain. . .especially with identifying specifications. Thus, the reason for including this section in **Antique Guns—The Collector's Guide.**

AMERICAN ARMS
N. Kansas City, Missouri

HANDGUNS

American Arms 1847 Walker Percussion Revolver **$195**
Caliber: 44. Six-shot cylinder. Barrel: 9inches, round with hinged loading lever. Overall length: 15.5 inches. Weight: 72 ounces. Engraved blued steel cylinder; color casehardened steel frame and backstrap; solid brass trigger guard; one-piece walnut grip.

American Arms 1851 Colt Navy Percussion Revolver **$100**
Caliber: 36. Six-shot cylinder. Barrel: 7.5 inches, octagonal with hinged loading lever. Overall length: 13 inches. Weight: 44 ounces. Solid brass frame, trigger guard and backstrap, one-piece walnut grip; engraved blued steel cylinder.

American Arms 1858 Remington Army Percussion Revolver **$115**
Caliber: 44. Six-shot cylinder. Barrel length: 8 inches, round tapered. Overall length: 13 inches. Weight: 38 ounces. Two-piece walnut grips.

American Arms 1858 Army Stainless Steel Target Revolver **$230**
Same general specifications as 1858 Remington Army except fitted with adjustable rear target sight and ramp blade front sight. Stainless steel frame, barrel and cylinder.

American Arms 1860 Colt Army Percussion Revolver **$105**
Caliber: 44. Six-shot cylinder. Barrel: 13.5 inches. Overall length: 13.5 inches. Weight: 44 ounces. Solid brass frame, trigger guard and backstrap; one-piece walnut grip; engraved blued steel cylinder.

LONG ARMS

American Arms Hawkeye Cap-'N-Ball Percussion Rifle
Bolt-action with ambidextrous bolt handle. Calibers: 50 and 54. Barrel: 22 inches; round, tapered. Overall length: 41.5 inches. Weight: 6.75 pounds. Adjustable trigger. Adjustable ramp-type rear sight; blade front sight.
Blued finish. **$210**
Stainless steel **$315**

ARMSPORT, INC.
Miami, Florida

HANDGUNS

Armsport Colt 1847 Walker Revolver Model 5145 . . . . **$215**
Caliber: 44. Weight: 4½ pounds.

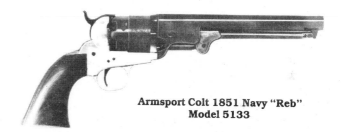

Armsport Colt 1851 Navy "Reb"
Model 5133

Armsport Colt 1851 Navy "Reb" Percussion Revolver Model 5133 . . . . **$110**
Caliber: 36. Six-shot cylinder. Barrel: 7 inches. Polished walnut grips. Finish: blued barrel and cylinder; brass frame and trigger guard.

Armsport Colt 1851 Navy "Reb" Percussion Revolver Model 5134 . . . . **$155**
Same general specifications as Model 5133, except manufactured in 44 caliber. Discontinued.

Armsport Colt 1851 Navy Percussion Revolver Model 5135 . . . . **$175**
Same general specifications as Model 5133, except with steel frame. Discontinued.

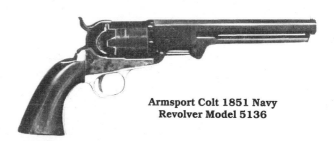

Armsport Colt 1851 Navy
Revolver Model 5136

Armsport Colt Navy 1851 Percussion Revolver Model 5136 . . . . **$140**
Caliber: 36. Six-shot engraved cylinder. Barrel: 7 inches, round. Walnut grips. Finish: blued steel frame and cylinder; polished brass trigger guard.

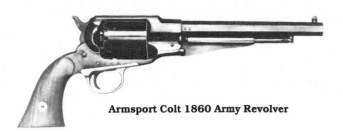

Armsport Colt 1860 Army Revolver

Armsport Colt 1860 Army Percussion Revolver Model 5139 . . . . $160

Caliber: 44. Six-shot unfluted cylinder. Barrel: 8 inches, round. Weight: about 42 ounces. Walnut grips. Finish: blued barrel and frame; polished brass trigger guard.

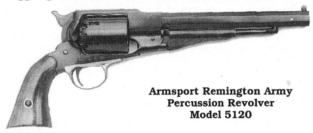

Armsport Remington Army Percussion Revolver Model 5120

Armsport Remington Army Percussion Revolver Model 5120 . . . . $160

Caliber: 44. Six-shot cylinder. Barrel: 8 inches, octagonal. Walnut grips. Finish: blued steel frame and cylinder; polished brass trigger guard.

Armsport Remington Army Stainless

Armsport Remington Army Revolver Model 5138 Stainless Steel. $275

Same general specifications as Model 5120, except made with stainless steel frame.

LONG ARMS

Armsport Hawken Rifle Model 5101 . . . . $180

Lock: color casehardened, percussion. Caliber: 45. Barrel: 28 inches, octagonal. Weight: about 7 pounds. High-luster walnut stock. Double-set triggers. Brass fittings, including patchbox, ferrules, buttplate, etc. Discontinued.

Armsport Hawken Rifle Model 5102 . . . . $180

Same general specifications as Model 5101, except available in 50 caliber. Discontinued.

Armsport Hawken Smoothbore Rifle Model 5102S $180

Same general specifications as Model 5101, except made in 50 caliber smoothbore. Discontinued.

Armsport Hawken Rifle Model 5102V . . . $180

Lock: color casehardened, percussion. Caliber: 36. Barrel: 28 inches, octagonal. Weight: about 6.75 pounds. High-luster walnut stock. Double-set triggers. Brass fittings, including patchbox, ferrules, buttplate, etc. Discontinued.

Armsport Hawken Rifle Model 5103 . . . . $180

Same general specifications as Model 5102, except manufactured in 54 caliber. Discontinued.

Armsport Hawken Rifle Model 5103C . . . $180

Same general specifications as Model 5103, except manufactured in 58 caliber. Discontinued.

Armsport Hawken Rifle Model 5103CS . . . $180

Same general specifications as Model 5103, except made with 58 caliber smoothbore barrel. Discontinued.

Armsport Hawken Rifle Model 5103S . . . $180

Same general specifications as Model 5103, except with smoothbore barrel. Discontinued.

Armsport Hawken Rifle Model 5104 . . . . . $200

Lock: color casehardened, flintlock. Caliber: 50. Barrel: 28 inches, octagonal. Weight: about 7½ pounds. Walnut stock. Double-set triggers. Brass fittings, including patchbox, ferrules, buttplate, etc. Discontinued.

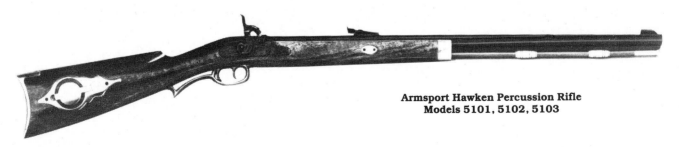

Armsport Hawken Percussion Rifle Models 5101, 5102, 5103

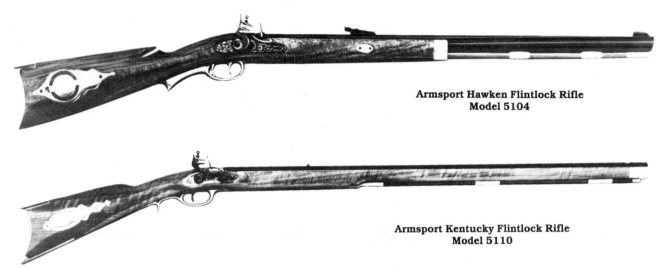

Armsport Hawken Flintlock Rifle
Model 5104

Armsport Kentucky Flintlock Rifle
Model 5110

Armsport Hawken Rifle Model 5104B . . $200
Same general specifications as Model 5104, except manufactured in 54 caliber. Discontinued.

Armsport Hawkentucky Rifle $190
Lock: color casehardened, percussion. Calibers: 36 or 50. Barrel: 28 inches, octagonal. Weight: 6 pounds. Walnut stock. Double-set triggers. Brass fittings, including patchbox, ferrules, buttplate, etc.

Armsport Kentucky Rifle Deluxe $225
Lock: color casehardened, percussion. Caliber: 45. Barrel: 28 inches, octagonal. Weight: about 7.25 pounds. Select walnut stock. Single trigger. Brass fittings, including patchbox, ferrules, buttplate, etc.

Armsport Kentucky Rifle Model 5108 . . $175
Lock: color casehardened, percussion. Caliber: 45. Barrel: 28 inches; octagonal, chrome-lined. Weight: about 7 pounds. Walnut stock. Single trigger. Brass fittings, including patchbox, ferrules, buttplate, etc.

Armsport Kentucky Rifle Model 5108V . . . $175
Same general specifications as Model 5108, except manufactured in 36 caliber without chrome-lined barrels.

Armsport Kentucky Rifle Model 5109 . . $175
Lock: color casehardened, percussion. Caliber: 50. Barrel: 28 inches; octagonal, chrome-lined. Weight: about 7 pounds. Walnut stock. Single trigger. Brass fittings, including patchbox, ferrules, buttplate, etc.

Armsport Kentucky Rifle Model 5110 . . $150
Lock: color casehardened, flintlock. Caliber: 45. Barrel: 28 inches; octagonal, chrome-lined. Weight: about 7.5 pounds. Walnut stock. Single trigger. Brass fittings, including patchbox, ferrules, buttplate, etc.

Armsport Kentucky Rifle Model 5110A . . $180
Same general specifications as Model 5110, except manufactured in 50 caliber.

Armsport Kentucky Rifle-Shotgun Combination, Model 5115 . . . . $260
Lock: color casehardened, percussion. Caliber/gauge: 50 with 20 gauge. Barrel: 28 inches, octagonal. Weight: about 7 pounds. Select-grain walnut stock. Single trigger. Brass fittings, including patchbox, ferrules, buttplate, etc.

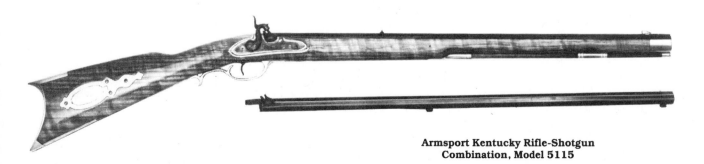

Armsport Kentucky Rifle-Shotgun
Combination, Model 5115

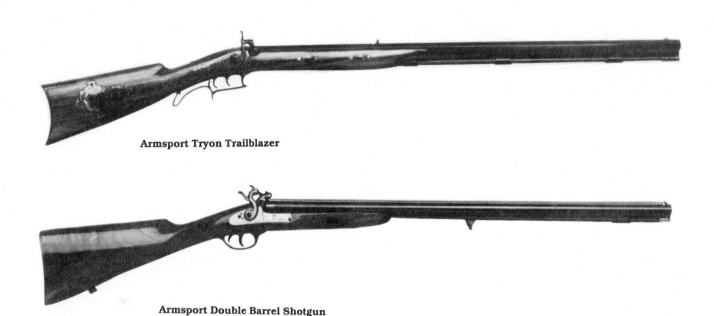

Armsport Tryon Trailblazer

Armsport Double Barrel Shotgun

**Armsport Kentucky Rifle-Shotgun
Combination, Model 5115C** **$260**
Same general specifications as Model 5115, except
made in 45 caliber.

Armsport Tryon Trailblazer Rifle **$315**
Lock: color casehardened, percussion. Calibers: 50
or 54. Barrels: 28 or 32 inches; octagonal, chrome-
lined. Weight: about 7 pounds. European walnut
stock. Double-set triggers. Brass fittings, including
patchbox, ferrules, buttplate, etc. Engraved Model
5131 commands a higher price.

**Armsport Double-Barrel Muzzleloading
Shotgun** **$340**
Lock: color casehardened, percussion. Gauges: 10 or
12. Barrel: 28 inches, octagonal. Weight: 6½ pounds.
Straight-grip, checkered stock. Double triggers.

BEEMAN PRECISION ARMS, INC.
Santa Rosa, California

Beeman Precision Arms, Inc., began operations primarily distributing high-quality air guns. During the
1980s, they created a new division that now imports
a variety of modern quality firearms and accessories
for distribution in the U.S. For their entry into the
blackpowder replica market, they have made available the following reproductions, produced by the
West German firm of Hege.

Hege Waffenschmiede im Zeughaus, located in
Uberlingen, was established by the Hebsacker family
in 1959. The owner, Frederick, is a master gunmaker
who studied at the government arms engineering
school in Austria. One of the foremost weapons dealers in Germany today, the company caters to serious
shooters and collectors and prides itself on its out-
standing craftsmanship. The family also owns one of
the largest collections of antique and modern arms
and accessories.

Beeman/Hege-Siber Single-Shot Pistol
An exact replica of the 33-caliber pistol made by Jean
Frederick Siber in the mid-1800s. A master gunmaker, engraver and medalist, Siber (1812–1898)
came from a Swiss watch-making family and lived in
the French-speaking section of Lausanne in Switzer-
land. In constant touch with exacting European
marksmen (Lord Byron was one of his clients), he
designed this pistol to satisfy the demands of small
caliber, high-precision barrel, low recoil, fast ignition
and "natural" 70-degree grip angle.

Specifications. The Siber formula: 33-3-333, or 33
caliber, .3mm groove depth, 333mm rifling twist (one
turn in 13.1 inch). Engraved, percussion, precision-
made lock. Barrel: 10 inches, octagonal. Overall
length: 15½ inches. Weight: 2.4 pounds. French-
style single-set trigger. Barleycorn dovetailed front
sight; micro-adjustable rear sight. Oil-finished hand-
checkered stock of European walnut rounded at 70-
degree angle. Tulip forend.

French Deluxe Model has rust blued barrel and
trigger guard, elaborate, original engraving, 24-carat
gold inlay on top of barrel inscribed "Siber A
Lausanne."

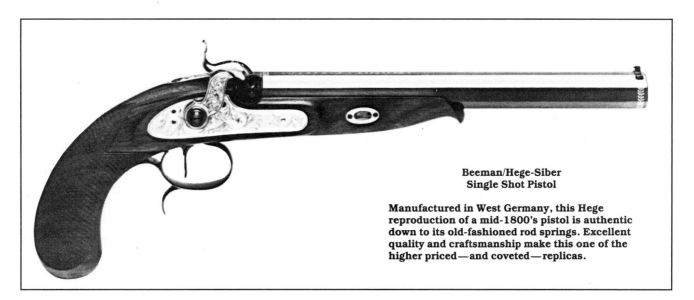

**Beeman/Hege-Siber
Single Shot Pistol**

Manufactured in West Germany, this Hege reproduction of a mid-1800's pistol is authentic down to its old-fashioned rod springs. Excellent quality and craftsmanship make this one of the higher priced—and coveted—replicas.

English Standard Model is similar to the French version, except has less elaborate engraving on lockplate and hammer; barrel and trigger guard are plum brown. Paired, cased sets available.

French Deluxe Model **$1400**
English Standard Model **830**

**Beeman/Hege-Manton Flintlock
Pistol** **$1320**
An excellent reproduction of the high-performance, highly desired flintlock pistol designed by the Man-ton brothers, John and Joseph, in the early 1800s. John held the patent for the lock and gun design, while Joseph designed the breeching. This design was considered by many to be among the top for the period.

Caliber: 44. Barrel: octagonal, rifled or smoothbore. Flintlock ignition that worked very fast because of the profile of the hammer and V-shaped pan emitting only a thin layer of powder. Rounded European walnut stock with hand-checkering. Engraved hammer and lockplate inscribed "John Manton."

CLEANING BLACKPOWDER FIREARMS

Blackpowder firearms should be cleaned as soon as possible after firing. Both blackpowder and its substitute, Pyrodex®, are highly corrosive and will cause the bore of the gun to rust if not cleaned properly.

Our ancestors relied upon warm water and homemade lye soap for cleaning their muzzleloaders, and this combination is still hard to beat. Soak a patch in warm water and some detergent. Since homemade lye soap is rare today, any commercial detergent will do. Then run the patch the full length of the bore. Replace this first patch with another saturated with the water/detergent mixture and repeat the former operation. Again, change patches and repeat until the wet patches come out clean. Then dry the bore thoroughly using clean, dry patches.

After the bore is completely dry, soak a clean patch with a good gun oil and run this in the bore several times. Wipe around the lock and hammer with a wet patch, then dry and oil all metal parts. Check the gun in several days and run another oiled patch through the bore. The gun should be further checked every week or two thereafter; more often if subjected to corrosive atmospheres.

Cap-and-ball revolvers should be disassembled and the cylinder flushed with detergent water or a detergent and water-based commercial blackpowder solvent. Clean the bore as described above.

When you run across a blackpowder bore that is extremely dirty, try the "pumping" cleaning method. Fill a two-gallon pail with warm water and about $\frac{1}{4}$ cup of dishwashing detergent. Cock the hammer and attach a piece of small-diameter rubber or flexible plastic tubing to the nipple. The tubing must be long enough to reach from the nipple, with the gun standing upright, to the bottom of the pail. It should also fit the nipple tightly so it will not easily be forced off from pumping pressure. Holding the gun in this position, attach a tight patch to your cleaning rod, insert the patch into the muzzle, and slowly push it all the way to the breech. Pull the patch back toward the muzzle, but not all the way out. This suction action will draw the detergent water into the bore through the nipple. Pushing the rod toward the breech end will discharge the water back into the pail. Keep this back-and-forth pumping motion going for about 5 to 10 minutes. Then clean, dry, and oil the bore as described previously.

COLT FIREARMS
Hartford, Connecticut

In January 1979, Colt Firearms, a division of Colt Industries, announced the introduction of an expanded range of famous Colt blackpowder revolvers to be offered to the public as part of a new program — "The Authentic Colt Blackpowder Series." In addition to the Third Model Dragoon and 1851 Navy revolvers — reintroduced in 1974 — Colt offered the 1861 Navy, 1860 Army, 1862 Pocket Navy and 1862 Pocket Police, 1847 Colt Walker, Baby Dragoon, and the First and Second Dragoons.

These Colt blackpowder handguns are authentic in every detail and continue to bear serial numbers following those stamped on earlier issues. Therefore, rather than be considered reproductions or replicas, they are a continuation of the legacy laid down by Colonel Samuel Colt and his predecessors more than 150 years ago. *See* also Colt listings in Handguns, Section One.

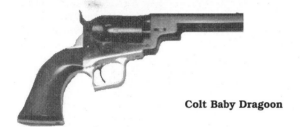

Colt Baby Dragoon

Colt Baby Dragoon Percussion Revolver. . . $360
Caliber: 31. Unfluted, straight cylinder engraved with Ranger-Indian scene. Barrel: 4 inches. Finish: color casehardened frame and hammer; blued barrel, trigger, wedge, cylinder and screws. Silver backstrap and trigger guard. Varnished grips. Made from 1979 to 1984.

Colt 1st Model Dragoon Percussion Revolver. $340
Caliber: 44. Six-shot cylinder engraved with Ranger-Indian scene. Barrel: 7½ inches, part round, part octagonal. Weight: 66 ounces. Finish: color casehardened frame, loading lever, plunger and hammer; blued barrel, cylinder, trigger and wedge. Polished brass backstrap and squareback trigger guard. One-piece, oil-finished walnut stocks. German silver front sight. Made from 1979 to 1984. (*See* photo opposite page.)

Colt 2nd Model Dragoon Percussion Revolver. $350
Caliber: 44. Six-shot cylinder engraved with Ranger-Indian scene. Barrel: 7½ inches, part round, part octagonal. Weight: 66 ounces. Finish: color casehardened frame, loading lever, plunger and hammer; blued barrel, cylinder, trigger and wedge. Polished brass backstrap and squareback trigger guard. One-piece, oil-finished walnut stocks. (*See* photo opposite page.)

Colt 3rd Model Dragoon Percussion Revolver $310
Caliber: 44. Six-shot cylinder engraved with Ranger-Indian scene. Barrel: 7½ inches, part round, part octagonal. Weight: 66 ounces. Finish: color casehardened frame, loading lever, plunger and hammer; blued barrel, cylinder, trigger and wedge. Polished brass backstrap and squareback trigger guard. One-piece, oil-finished walnut stocks. Made from 1974 to 1984. (*See* photo opposite page.)

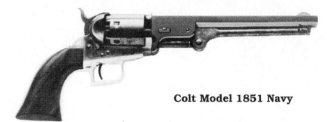

Colt Model 1851 Navy

Colt Model 1851 Navy Percussion Revolver $300
Caliber: 36. Six-shot cylinder with engraved naval scene. Barrel: 7½ inches, octagonal. Weight: 42 ounces. Finish: color casehardened frame, loading lever, plunger, hammer and latch; blued cylinder, trigger, barrel, screws and wedge. Silver-plated trigger guard and backstrap. Brass front sight. One-piece varnished walnut grips. Made from 1974 to 1984.

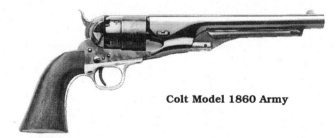

Colt Model 1860 Army

Colt Model 1860 Army Percussion Revolver $325
Caliber: 44. Six-shot unfluted cylinder with engraving of navy scene and markings "Patented Sept. 10th, 1850." Barrel: 8 inches, round. Weight: 42 ounces. Finish: color casehardened frame, loading lever, plunger, hammer and latch; brush blued cylinder, trigger, barrel, backstrap, screws and wedge. Polished brass trigger guard. German silver front sight. Oiled walnut grips. Made from 1979 to 1984.

Colt Model 1861 Navy Percussion Revolver $295
Caliber: 36. Six-shot round cylinder engraved with naval scene. Barrel: 7½ inches, round. Weight: 42 ounces. Finish: color casehardened frame, loading lever, plunger, hammer and latch; blued cylinder, trigger, barrel screws and wedge. Silver-plated trigger guard and backstrap. German silver front sight. Varnished one-piece walnut grips. Made 1979 to 1984.

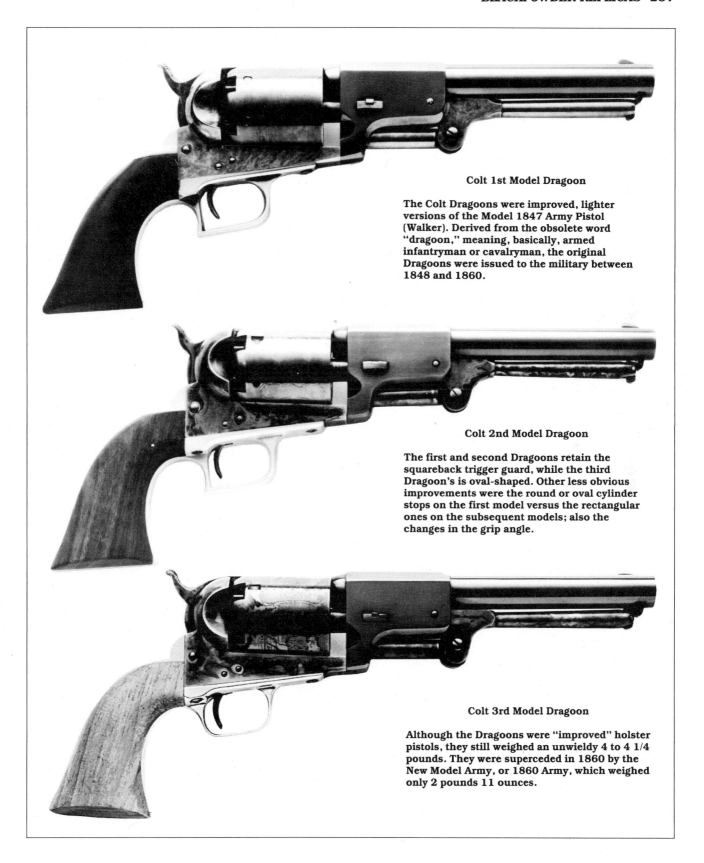

Colt 1st Model Dragoon

The Colt Dragoons were improved, lighter versions of the Model 1847 Army Pistol (Walker). Derived from the obsolete word "dragoon," meaning, basically, armed infantryman or cavalryman, the original Dragoons were issued to the military between 1848 and 1860.

Colt 2nd Model Dragoon

The first and second Dragoons retain the squareback trigger guard, while the third Dragoon's is oval-shaped. Other less obvious improvements were the round or oval cylinder stops on the first model versus the rectangular ones on the subsequent models; also the changes in the grip angle.

Colt 3rd Model Dragoon

Although the Dragoons were "improved" holster pistols, they still weighed an unwieldy 4 to 4 1/4 pounds. They were superceded in 1860 by the New Model Army, or 1860 Army, which weighed only 2 pounds 11 ounces.

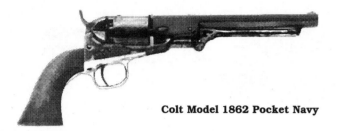

Colt Model 1862 Pocket Navy

Colt Model 1862 Pocket Navy Percussion
Revolver **$295**
Caliber: 36. Five-shot, round-rebated cylinder engraved with stage coach scene. Barrel: 5½ inches, octagonal. Weight: 27 ounces. Finish: color casehardened frame, hammer, loading lever, plunger and latch; blued barrel, wedge, cylinder, trigger guard and backstrap. Brass pin front sight. Varnished one-piece walnut grips. Made from 1979 to 1984.

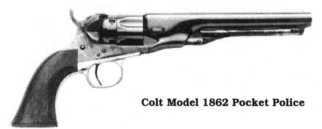

Colt Model 1862 Pocket Police

Colt Model 1862 Pocket Police Percussion
Revolver **$300**
Caliber: 36. Five-shot, rebated fluted cylinder. Barrel: 5½ inches, round. Weight: 25 ounces. Finish: color casehardened frame, hammer, loading lever, plunger and latch; blued barrel, wedge, cylinder, trigger and screws. Silver-plated trigger guard and backstrap. Brass front sight. Varnished one-piece walnut grips. Made from 1979 to 1984.

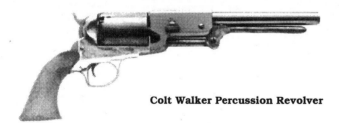

Colt Walker Percussion Revolver

Colt Walker Percussion Revolver **$325**
Caliber: 44. Six-shot cylinder with engraving of soldiers fighting Indians. Barrel: 9 inches, round. Weight: 73 ounces. Finish: color casehardened frame, hammer, loading lever and plunger; blued barrel, cylinder, backstrap, trigger and wedge. Polished brass trigger guard. German silver sight. Oil-finished walnut grips. Made from 1979 to 1984.

CVA
Norcross, Georgia

Connecticut Valley Arms, Inc. (CVA) was founded in 1971 by David Silk and was located in Haddam, Connecticut. Its chief aim was to provide the American market with an extensive line of replica arms, knives and blackpowder accessories manufactured at various European plants. Most CVA items are moderate in cost, although a few higher priced, presentation-grade models are now available. The current line-up includes flint and percussion firearms such as cap-and-ball revolvers, mountain guns, Hawken rifles, Kentucky pistols and rifles, and the like.

PISTOLS

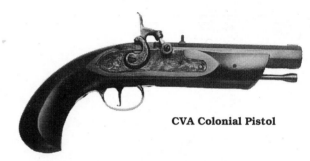

CVA Colonial Pistol

CVA Colonial Pistol **$80**
Lock: color casehardened, engraved flintlock or percussion. Caliber: 45 (.451). Barrel: 6¾ inches, octagonal. Overall length: 12¾ inches. Weight: 31 ounces. Blade front sight; fixed rear. Finish: blued barrel; brass hardware. Dark walnut-tone stock.

CVA Hawken Flintlock Pistol **$130**
Same general specifications as Hawken Percussion model, except for flintlock ignition.

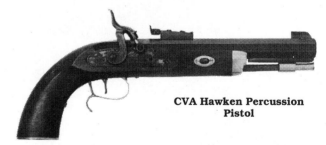

**CVA Hawken Percussion
Pistol**

CVA Hawken Percussion Pistol. **$120**
Lock: color casehardened, engraved percussion. Caliber: 50. Barrel: 9¾ inches; octagonal, 1 inch across the flats. Overall length: 16½ inches. Weight: 50 ounces. Beaded blade front sight; adjustable rear. Finish: blued barrel; brass wedge plate, nose cap, ramrod thimbles, trigger guard and grip cap. Select walnut stock.

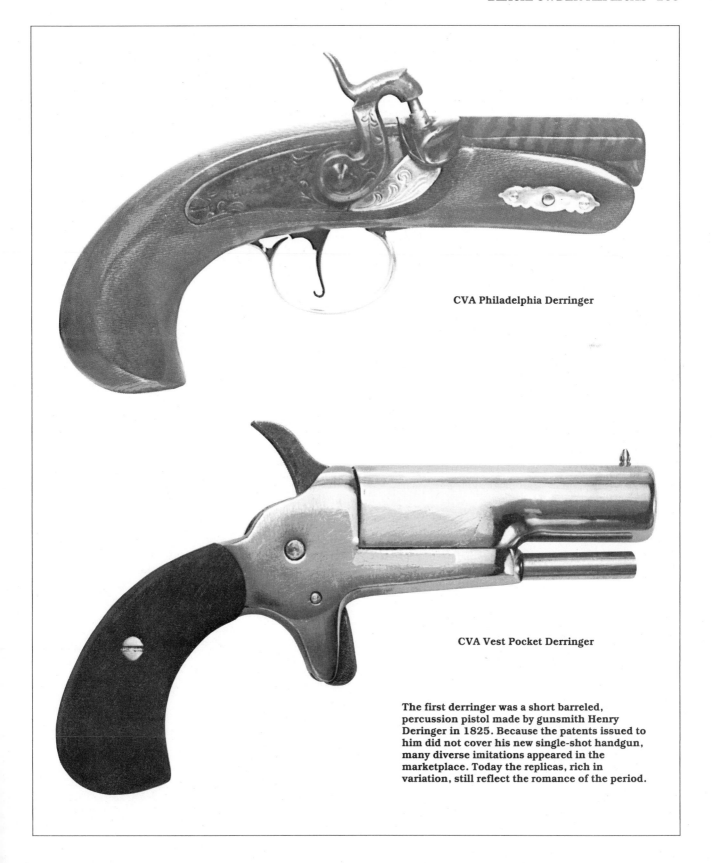

CVA Philadelphia Derringer

CVA Vest Pocket Derringer

The first derringer was a short barreled, percussion pistol made by gunsmith Henry Deringer in 1825. Because the patents issued to him did not cover his new single-shot handgun, many diverse imitations appeared in the marketplace. Today the replicas, rich in variation, still reflect the romance of the period.

CVA Kentucky Flintlock Pistol **$115**
Same general specifications as Kentucky Percussion model, except has flintlock ignition.

CVA Kentucky Percussion Pistol

CVA Kentucky Percussion Pistol. **$105**
Lock: color casehardened, engraved percussion. Caliber: 45. Barrel: 10¼ inches, octagonal. Overall length: 15¼ inches. Weight: 40 ounces. Finish: blued barrel; brass hardware. Dovetailed Kentucky front and rear sights.

CVA Mountain Flintlock Pistol **$150**
Same general specifications as Mountain Percussion model, except for flintlock ignition.

CVA Mountain Percussion Pistol

CVA Mountain Percussion Pistol. **$145**
Lock: color casehardened, engraved percussion. Caliber: 50. Barrel: 9 inches; octagonal, ¹⁵⁄₁₆ inch across flats. Overall length: 14 inches. Weight: 40 ounces. Finish: brown steel, German silver wedge plates. German silver blade front sight; fixed primitive rear. American maple stock.

CVA Philadelphia Derringer **$65**
Lock: color casehardened, engraved, coil-spring back-action percussion lock. Caliber: 45. Barrel: 3¼ inches, octagonal. Overall length: 7⅛ inches. Weight: 16 ounces. Finish: blued barrel, brass hardware. No sights. Walnut-toned stock. (*See* photo, previous page.)

CVA Pioneer Single-Shot Percussion Pistol **$80**
Lock: color casehardened, engraved percussion. Caliber: 32. Barrel: 7½ inches; octagonal, ⅞ inch across flats. Overall length: 13 inches. Weight: 14 ounces. Brass blade front sight; open rear sight.

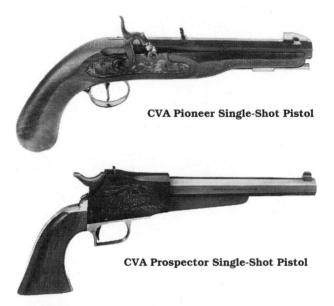

CVA Pioneer Single-Shot Pistol

CVA Prospector Single-Shot Pistol

CVA Prospector Single-Shot Pistol **$75**
Caliber: 44. Barrel: 8½ inches, tapering octagonal. Overall length: 12¾ inches. Weight: 42 ounces. Blade front sight; notch in hammer rear sight. Grips of one-piece walnut.

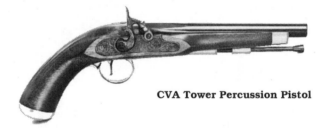

CVA Tower Percussion Pistol

CVA Tower Percussion Pistol **$115**
Lock: color casehardened, engraved percussion. Caliber: 45. Barrel: 9 inches; octagonal at breech tapering to round at muzzle. Overall length: 15¾ inches. Weight: 36 ounces. Finish: blued barrel, brass hardware. Dark-grained walnut stocks.

CVA Vest Pocket Derringer **$65**
Caliber: 31. Single-shot. Barrel: 2½ inches. Overall length: 5 inches. Weight: 16 ounces. Finish: brass frame and barrel. Two-piece walnut grips. (*See* photo, previous page.)

REVOLVERS

CVA Colt 1851 Navy Percussion Revolver . . **$75**
Caliber: 36. Six-shot engraved cylinder. Barrel: 7½ inches, octagonal. Overall length: 13 inches. Weight: 44 ounces. Post front sight; hammer notch rear. One-piece walnut grips. Hinged-style loading lever. Finish: blued barrel and cylinder; brass frame, trigger guard and backstrap; color casehardened loading lever and hammer. (*See* next page.)

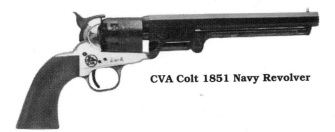

CVA Colt 1851 Navy Revolver

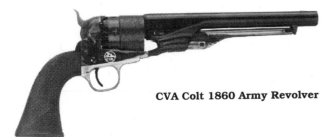

CVA Colt 1860 Army Revolver

CVA Colt 1860 Army Percussion Revolver $175

Caliber: 44. Six-shot engraved cylinder. Barrel: 7½ inches, rounded; creeping style. Weight: 44 ounces. Blade front sight; hammer notch rear. One-piece walnut grips. hinged-style loading lever. Finish: blued barrel and cylinder with color casehardened loading lever, hammer and frame; brass trigger guard.

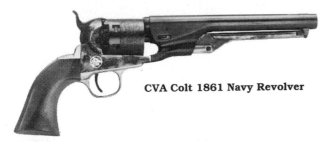

CVA Colt 1861 Navy Revolver

CVA Colt 1861 Navy Percussion Revolver $170

Caliber: 36. Six-shot engraved cylinder. Barrel: 7½ inches, rounded. Overall length: 13 inches. Weight: 44 ounces. Creeping-style loading lever. Blade front sight; hammer notch rear. Walnut grips. Finish: blued barrel and cylinder; color casehardened loading lever, hammer and frame. Brass trigger guard and backstrap.

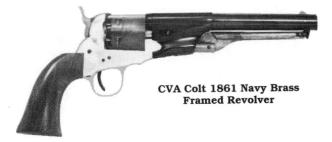

CVA Colt 1861 Navy Brass Framed Revolver

CVA Colt 1861 Navy Percussion Revolver (Brass Frame) $180

Same general specifications as blued model, except has brass frame.

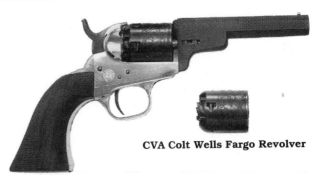

CVA Colt Wells Fargo Revolver

CVA Colt Wells Fargo Percussion Revolver $135

Caliber: 31. Five-shot engraved cylinder with extra 5-shot cylinder. Barrel: 4 inches, octagonal. Overall length: 9 inches. Weight: 28½ ounces w/extra cylinder. Post front sight; hammer notch rear sight. Finish: solid brass frame, trigger guard and backstrap. Blued steel barrel and cylinder; color casehardened hammer. One-piece walnut grip.

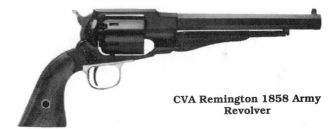

CVA Remington 1858 Army Revolver

CVA Remington 1858 Army Percussion Revolver $110

Caliber: 44. Barrel: 8 inches, octagonal. Weight: about 2½ pounds. Overall length: 13 to 14 inches. Adjustable front sight. Finish: blued frame, cylinder and barrel: brass trigger guard. Walnut stocks.

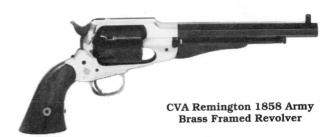

CVA Remington 1858 Army Brass Framed Revolver

CVA Remington 1858 Army Percussion Revolver (Brass Frame) $115

Same general specifications as steel frame model, except for brass frame, trigger guard and backstrap.

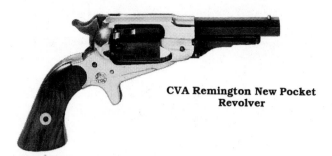

CVA Remington New Pocket Revolver

CVA Remington New Model Pocket Percussion Revolver $80

Caliber: 31. Five-shot cylinder. Barrel: 4 inches, octagonal. 7½ inches overall. Weight: 15½ ounces. Post front sight; groove in frame at rear. Finish: blued barrel, cylinder and loading lever; solid brass frame.

LONG ARMS

CVA Big Bore Mountain Flintlock Rifle . . $280

Same general specifications as Big Bore Percussion version, except has flintlock ignition system.

CVA Big Bore Mountain Percussion Rifle $290

Lock: color casehardened, engraved percussion. Calibers: 54 and 58. Barrel: 32 inches; octagonal, 1 inch across flats. Overall length: 48 inches. Weight: 8 lbs. 2 oz. Double-set triggers. German silver front sight; adjustable dovetail rear. Select hardwood stock with fully formed cheekpiece. Finish: browned steel and wedge plates; authentic pewter-type nose cap.

CVA Blazer Rifle. $115

Lightweight percussion rifle with straight-through ignition. Caliber: 50. Barrel: 28 inches; octagonal, $15/16$ inch across flats. Overall length: 43½ inches. Weight: 6 lbs. 12 oz. Select hardwood stock with pistol grip. Front brass blade sight; fixed semibuckhorn rear.

CVA Blazer II $100

Scaled-down version of the CVA Blazer Rifle. Caliber: 45 percussion. Barrel: 24½ inches; octagonal, $11/16$ inch across flats. Overall length: 38½ inches. Weight: 5 lbs. 12 oz.

CVA Big Bore Mountain Percussion Rifle

CVA Blazer Rifle

CVA Double-Barreled Express Rifle

CVA Frontier Percussion Rifle

CVA Frontier Rifle — Left Hand

CVA Hawken Percussion Rifle

CVA Express Rifle **$360**
Locks: color casehardened, engraved percussion style. Caliber: 50. Barrels: two 28-inch tapered, round. Overall length: 44¼ inches. Weight: 9 lbs. 3 oz. Select hardwood stock. Sights: dovetail, beaded blade front; adjustable, hunting-style rear. Finish: polished steel wedge plates; color casehardened hammers, double triggers and trigger guard; blued barrels. See photo on previous page.

CVA Frontier Percussion Rifle **$245**
Lock: color casehardened, engraved percussion style, bridle with fly and tumbler. Caliber: 50. Barrel: 28 inches; octagonal, ¹⁵⁄₁₆ inch across flats. Overall length: 44 inches. Weight: 6 lbs. 14 oz. Selected hardwood stock. Double-set triggers. Brass blade front sight; adjustable open rear sight. Finish: blued steel; brass wedge plates; brass nose cap, trigger guard and buttplate.

CVA Frontier Percussion Rifle, Left Hand **$250**
Same general specifications as above rifle, except lock and nipple are located on left-hand side for left-hand shooter.

CVA Hawken Percussion Rifle **$295**
Lock: color casehardened, engraved percussion style. Calibers: 50 and 54. Barrel: 28 inches; octagonal, 1 inch across flats. Overall length: 44 inches. Weight: 7 lbs. 15 oz. Selected walnut stock with fully formed beavertail cheekpiece. Double-set triggers. Dovetail, beaded blade front sight; adjustable, dovetail open rear sight. Finish: blued steel; brass patchbox, wedge plates, nose cap, ramrod thimbles, trigger guard and buttplate.

CVA Kentucky Flintlock Rifle **$230**
Same general specifications as Kentucky Percussion model, except with flintlock ignition.

CVA Kentucky Percussion Rifle **$210**
Caliber: 45. Engraved color casehardened lock. Barrel: 33½ inches; octagonal. Overall length: 48 inches. Weight: 7¼ pounds. Kentucky-style front and rear sights. Brass furniture. Blued barrel. Dark walnut-toned stock.

CVA Kentucky Flintlock Rifle

CVA Kentucky Percussion Rifle

CVA Mountain Flintlock Rifle

CVA Mountain Percussion Rifle

CVA Mountain Flintlock Rifle $280
Same general specifications as Mountain Percussion Rifle, except has flintlock ignition system.

CVA Mountain Percussion Rifle $275
Lock: color casehardened, engraved percussion. Calibers: 45 and 50. Barrel: 32 inches; octagonal, $\frac{15}{16}$ inch across flats. Overall length: 48 inches. Weight: 7 lbs. 14 oz. Select hardwood stock with fully formed cheekpiece. Double-set triggers. German silver blade front; adjustable rear. Finish: brown steel, German silver patchbox and wedge plates; pewter-type nose cap.

CVA Pennsylvania Flintlock Long Rifle . . $325
Lock: color casehardened, engraved flintlock. Caliber: 50. Barrel: 40 inches; octagonal, $\frac{7}{8}$ inch across flats. Overall length: $55\frac{3}{4}$ inches. Weight: 8 lbs. 3 oz. Double-set triggers. Fixed semibuckhorn rear sight. Selected walnut stock. Finish: brass buttplate, patchbox, trigger guard, thimbles and nose cap.

CVA Pennsylvania Percussion Long Rifle . . $295
Same general specifications as Pennsylvania Flintlock above, except made with percussion lock. Discontinued in 1984.

CVA Pennsylvania Flintlock Long Rifle

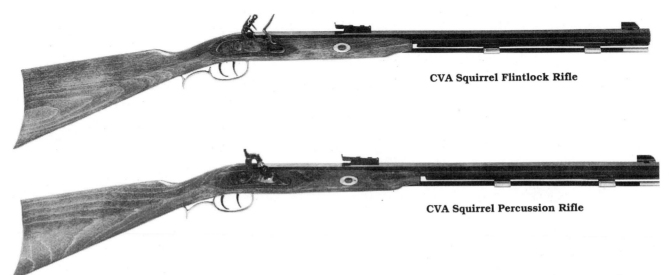

CVA Squirrel Flintlock Rifle

CVA Squirrel Percussion Rifle

CVA Squirrel Rifle **$215**
Lock: color casehardened, engraved percussion or flintlock ignition. Caliber: 32. Barrel: 25 inches; octagonal, $^{11}/_{16}$ inch across flats. Overall length: 40¾ inches. Weight: 5 lbs. 12 oz. Double-set triggers. Dovetailed, beaded blade front sight; adjustable, open hunting-style rear sight. Selected hardwood stock. Finish: blued steel; brass buttplate, trigger guard, wedge plates and thimbles.

CVA Squirrel Percussion Rifle, Left Hand . . **$200**
Same general specifications as standard Squirrel Percussion, model, except lock and nipple are on left side for left-hand shooter.

CVA St. Louis Hawken Rifle **$170**
Caliber: 50. Percussion lock. Barrel: 28 inches; octagonal, $^{15}/_{16}$ inch across flats, rifled one turn in 66 inches. Overall length: 44 inches. Weight: 7 lbs. 13 oz. Hooked breech. Double-set triggers. Adjustable pull. Dovetailed blade front sight; adjustable open hunting-style rear. Solid brass wedge plates, nose cap, ramrod thimbles, finger spur trigger guard and patchbox. Select hardwood stock with beavertail cheekpiece.

CVA Blunderbuss **$265**
Lock: engraved flintlock. Bore: .690. Barrel: 16 inches; tapered to flared muzzle. Weight: 5 lbs. 5 oz. Select hardwood stock. Finish: solid brass buttplate, ramrod thimbles, trigger, trigger guard, barrel, and engraved side plate.

CVA Double-Barrel Percussion Shotgun . . **$280**
Locks: polished steel, engraved percussion. Gauge: 12. Barrels: 28 inches; round, smoothbore. Overall length: 44½ inches. Weight: 6 lbs. 10 oz. Double triggers. Brass bead front sight. Finish: blued steel; polished steel wedge plates, trigger guard, triggers, tang. Engraved lock, hammers, tang and trigger guard. Select hardwood checkered stock.

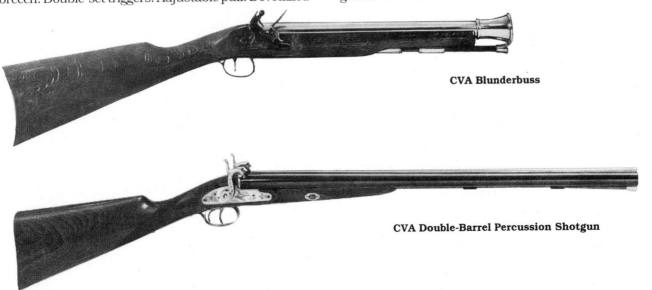

CVA Blunderbuss

CVA Double-Barrel Percussion Shotgun

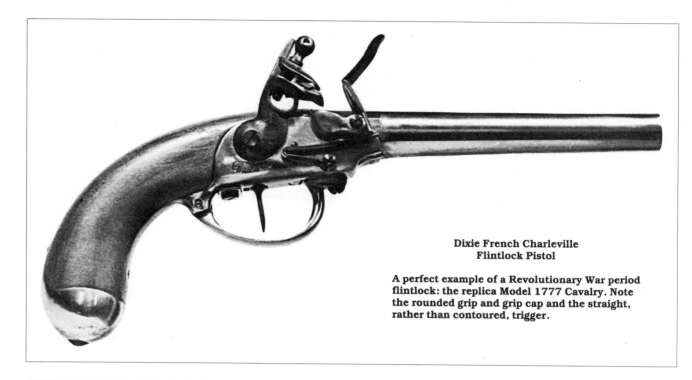

**Dixie French Charleville
Flintlock Pistol**

**A perfect example of a Revolutionary War period
flintlock: the replica Model 1777 Cavalry. Note
the rounded grip and grip cap and the straight,
rather than contoured, trigger.**

DIXIE GUN WORKS, INC.
Union City, Tennessee

Dixie Gun Works is the largest and oldest dealer of antique and replica blackpowder arms in the U.S. Under the direction of Turner Kirkland, the firm has bought, sold and traded muzzleloaders since 1954. It publishes a 500-plus-page catalog. "Blackpowder Shooting and Antique Gun Supplies" that details an inventory of more than 7,000 blackpowder-related items. Among their offering of replicas are the following.

HANDGUNS

Dixie 1848 Baby Dragoon Percussion
Revolver. $145
Caliber: 31. Five-shot cylinder. Barrel: 6 inches, octagonal. Overall length: 10½ inches. Weight: 1½ pounds. Color casehardened frame and loading lever. One-piece walnut grip. Polished brass backstrap and square bowed trigger guard.

**Dixie 1851 Navy Percussion
Revolver**

Dixie 1851 Navy Percussion
Revolver (Steel) $150
Caliber: 36. Six-shot engraved cylinder. Barrel: 7½ inches, octagonal. Overall length: 13¾ inches. Weight: 3 pounds. Color casehardened steel frame and loading lever brass backstrap and trigger guard. Blued barrel and cylinder. Italian reproduction of Civil War favorite.

**Dixie 1860 Army Percussion
Revolver**

Dixie 1860 Army Percussion Revolver . . $165
Caliber: 44. Six-shot half-fluted cylinder. Barrel: 8 inches. Overall length: 14 inches. Weight: 2¾ pounds. Cut for shoulder stock.

Dixie Abilene Derringer $60
Caliber: 41. Barrel: 2½ inches. Finish: deep blue black; casehardened frame and hammer. Walnut grips. Comes with wood presentation case.

Dixie French Charleville Flintlock Pistol . . $175
Reproduction of the Model 1777 Cavalry pistol of the Revolutionary War period. Color casehardened hammer, frizzen, and trigger. Round barrel and rounded European walnut stock. Shoots .680 ball with 40 gr. FFg powder. (*See* photo, opposite.)

Dixie LePage Percussion Dueling Pistol . . . $195
Caliber: 45. Barrel: 10 inches, octagonal. Overall length: 16 inches. Weight: 2½ pounds. Brass-bladed front sight with open rear sight dovetailed into the barrel. Polished silver-plated trigger guard and buttcap.

Dixie Lincoln Derringer $215
Caliber: 41. Barrel: 2 inches, browned.

Dixie Navy Percussion Revolver (Brass) . . . $100
Caliber: 36. Six-shot cylinder. Barrel: 7½ inches. Overall length: 12⅞ inches. Weight: 3 pounds. Brass frame with blued steel barrel and cylinder.

Dixie Pedersoli English Dueling Pistol . . $200
This is a reproduction of an English percussion dueling pistol, created by Charles Moore of London. Caliber: 45. Barrel: 11 inches, octagonal. Finish: blued barrel, color casehardened lock and trigger guard. European walnut halfstock with oil finish and checkered grip.

Dixie Pedersoli Mang Target Pistol $560
Caliber: 38. Barrel: 10⁷⁄₁₆ inches, octagonal. Overall length: 17¼ inches. Weight: 2½ pounds. Blade dovetailed front sight; rear adjustable sight is mounted on breech-plug tang.

Dixie Pennsylvania Pistol $115
Percussion or flintlock. Caliber: 44. Barrel: 10 inches, octagonal. Finish: bright blue barrel; highly polished brass trigger guard, thimbles, and nose plates. Gooseneck engraved hammer. Walnut stained stock with bird's head-type grip.

Dixie Queen Anne Pistol $145
Named for the Queen of England (1702–1714). Flintlock. Barrel: 7½ inches which tapers from rear to front with a cannon-shaped muzzle. Overall length: 13 inches. Weight: 2¼ pounds. Fluted brass trigger guard. Brass butt on walnut stock features a grotesque mask worked into it.

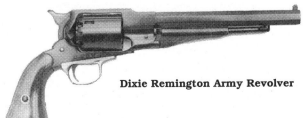

Dixie Remington Army Revolver

Dixie Remington Army Revolver $145
Caliber: 44, percussion. Six-shot cylinder. Barrel: 8 inches, octagonal. Overall length: 13½ inches. Weight: 2½ pounds. Brass trigger guard. Blued steel. Color casehardened hammer.

Dixie Screw Barrel (DSB-58) Derringer . . . $65
Overall length: 6½ inches. Finish: color casehardened frame, trigger and center-mounted hammer. European walnut, one-piece, "bag"-type grip.

Dixie Screw Barrel Pistol $70
Folding trigger. Overall length: 6½ inches. Finish: color casehardened frame, trigger, and center-mounted hammer. Fires a .445 round ball.

Dixie Spiller & Burr Brass Frame Revolver. . $70
Caliber: 36. Six-shot cylinder. Barrel: 7 inches, octagonal. Overall length: 12¾ inches. Weight: 2½ pounds. Brass frame, trigger guard and backstrap. Color casehardened loading lever, hammer and trigger.

Dixie Third Model Dragoon Percussion Revolver $135
Caliber: 44. Six-shot engraved cylinder. Barrel: 7⅜ inches. Overall length: 14 inches. Weight: 4½ pounds. Brass backstrap and trigger guard. Color casehardened steel frame. Blued barrel and cylinder.

Dixie Walker Revolver

Dixie Walker Percussion Revolver $130
Modeled after the largest Colt pistol ever made. Caliber: 44. Six-shot engraved cylinder. Barrel: 9 inches, round. Overall length: 15½ inches. Weight: 4½ pounds. Steel backstrap and brass squareback trigger guard. Walnut grips. Metal parts blued. Col. Walker of Mexican War fame suggested this style pistol instead of the Paterson, and only about 1,000 of the original were produced.

Dixie Wyatt Earp Percussion Revolver . . $100
Caliber: 45. Five-shot cylinder. Barrel: 12 inches, octagonal. Overall length: 18¼ inches. Weight: 3 pounds. Brass frame, backstrap and trigger guard. Blued barrel and cylinder. Color casehardened hammer, trigger, and loading lever.

**Dixie Brown Bess Musket
Second Model**

LONG ARMS

Dixie Brown Bess Musket, Second Model . . $330
Lock: color casehardened, flintlock. Caliber: 75. Barrel: 41¾ inches, octagonal. Weight: 9½ pounds. Walnut stock. Single trigger. Brass fittings, including patchbox, ferrules, buttplate, etc.

Dixie Buffalo Hunter. $265
Lock: color casehardened, percussion. Caliber: 58. Barrel: 26 inches, octagonal. Weight: 8¼ pounds. Walnut stock. Single trigger. Brass fittings, including patchbox, ferrules, buttplate, etc.

Dixie Deluxe Cub Rifle $240
Lock: color casehardened, percussion or flintlock. Caliber: 40. Barrel: 28 inches, octagonal. Weight: 6¾ pounds. Walnut stock. Double-set triggers. Brass fittings, including patchbox, ferrules, buttplate, etc.

Dixie Double-Barrel Magnum Shotgun
Gauges: 10 and 12. Barrels: 30 inches; choked modified and full. Finish: brown barrels with color casehardened lock, barrel tang and trigger.
10 Gauge Magnum $320
12 Gauge. $300

Dixie Enfield Model 1858 Two-Band Rifle . . $325
Lock: color casehardened, percussion. Caliber: 58. Barrel: 33 inches, octagonal. Weight: 9¼ pounds. European walnut stock. Single trigger. Brass fittings, including patchbox, ferrules, buttplate, etc.

Dixie Enfield Three-Band Rifled Musket . . $370
Lock: color casehardened, percussion. Caliber: 58. Barrel: 39 inches, octagonal. Weight: 10½ pounds. European walnut stock. Single trigger. Brass fittings, including patchbox, ferrules, buttplate, etc.

Dixie Hawken Percussion Rifle. $230
Lock: color casehardened, percussion. Calibers: 45, 50 and 54. Barrel: 28 inches, octagonal. Weight: 9 pounds. Walnut stock. Double-set triggers. Brass fittings, including patchbox, ferrules, buttplate, etc.

Dixie Indian Gun $395
Lock: color casehardened, flintlock. Caliber: 75. Barrel: 31 inches, octagonal. Weight: 8 pounds. Walnut-stained stock. Single trigger. Brass fittings, including patchbox, ferrules, buttplate, etc.

Dixie In-Line Carbine. $265
Made in Italy by D. Pedersoli. Caliber: 50 and 54. Barrel: 32¾ inches, octagonal. Overall length: 41 inches. Weight: 6½ pounds. Ramp front sight with red insert; adjustable rear. Walnut-colored wood stock with Monte Carlo comb. Black plastic buttplate. Chromed bolt and handle.

Dixie Kentuckian Carbine
Lock: color casehardened, flintlock or percussion. Caliber: 45. Barrel: 27½ inches, octagonal. Weight: 5½ pounds. European walnut stock. Single trigger. Brass fittings, including patchbox, ferrules, buttplate, etc.
Flintlock $215
Percussion **200**

Dixie Indian Flintlock Gun

Dixie Kentuckian Percussion Rifle

Dixie Mississippi Rifle

Dixie Kentuckian Rifle
Lock: color casehardened, flintlock or percussion. Caliber: 45. Barrel: 33½ inches; octagonal, ¹³⁄₁₆ inch across the flats. Overall length: 48 inches. Weight: 6¼ pounds. European walnut stock. Single trigger. Brass fittings, including patchbox, ferrules, buttplate, etc.
Flintlock $210
Percussion. 195

Dixie Mississippi Rifle $260
Lock: color casehardened, percussion. Caliber: 58. Barrel: 33½ inches, octagonal. Weight: 10 pounds. Walnut-stained stock. Single trigger. Brass fittings, including patchbox, ferrules, buttplate, etc.

Dixie Pedersoli Waadtlander Rifle. $970
Caliber: 45. Barrel: 31 inches, octagonal. Multi-lever type, double-set, adjustable triggers. Fitted post front sights; tang-mounted Swiss-type diopter rear. Color casehardened hardware. Walnut stock.

Dixie Pennsylvania Rifle $295
Lock: color casehardened, percussion or flintlock. Caliber: 45. Barrels: 41½ inches, octagonal. Weight: 8 pounds. Walnut stock. Double-set, double-phase triggers. Brass fittings, including patchbox, ferrules, buttplate, etc.

Dixie Sanfti Schuetzen Target Rifle $685
Lock: color casehardened, percussion. Caliber: 45. Barrel: 29 inches, octagonal. Weight: 10¾ pounds. Walnut stock. Single trigger. Brass fittings, including patchbox, ferrules, buttplate, etc.

Dixie Sharps Military Carbine $345
Lock: color casehardened, percussion. Caliber: 54. Barrel: 22 inches, round. Weight: 7½ pounds. Walnut stock. Single trigger. Brass fittings, including patchbox, ferrules, buttplate, etc. (*See* next page.)

Dixie Sharps Rifle $375
Lock: color casehardened, percussion. Caliber: 54. Barrel: 28½ inches, round. Weight: 8½ pounds. Walnut stock. Single trigger. Brass fittings, including patchbox, ferrules, buttplate, etc. (*See* next page.)

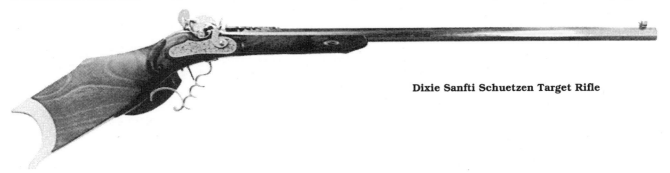

Dixie Sanfti Schuetzen Target Rifle

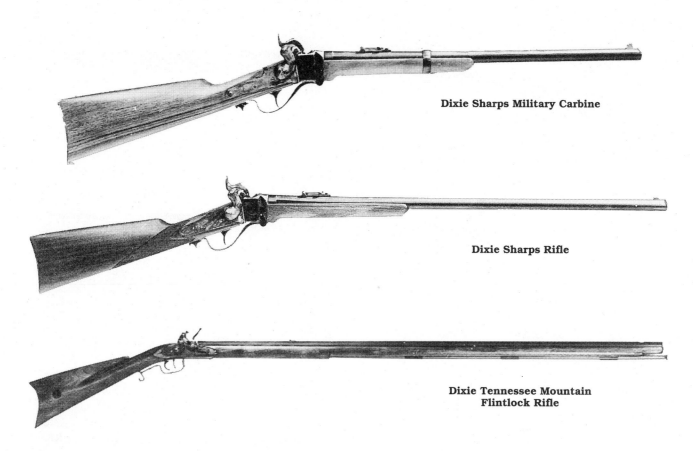

Dixie Sharps Military Carbine

Dixie Sharps Rifle

**Dixie Tennessee Mountain
Flintlock Rifle**

**Dixie Springfield Model 1863 Civil War
Musket** **$320**
Lock: color casehardened, percussion. Caliber: 58.
Barrel: 40 inches, octagonal. Weight: 9½ pounds.
Walnut-stained stock. Single trigger. Brass fittings,
including patchbox, ferrules, buttplate, etc.

Dixie Swiss Federal Target Rifle **$915**
Lock: color casehardened, percussion. Caliber: 45.
Barrel: 32 inches, octagonal. Weight: 13¼ pounds.
Walnut stock. Double-set triggers. Brass fittings, in-
cluding patchbox, ferrules, buttplate, etc.

Dixie Tennessee Mountain Rifle **$260**
Flintlock or percussion. Caliber: 50. Barrel: octagonal, ¹⁵⁄₁₆ inch across the flats. Overall length: 41½
inches.

Dixie Tennessee Squirrel Rifle **$345**
Caliber: 32. Flint or percussion. Cherry stock.

Dixie Tryon Rifle **$345**
Lock: color casehardened, percussion. Caliber: 50.
Barrels: 32 inches, octagonal. Walnut stock. Adjustable double-set triggers. Brass fittings, including
patchbox, ferrules, buttplate, etc.

Dixie Wesson Rifle **$375**
Lock: color casehardened, percussion. Caliber: 1⅛
× 50. Barrels: 28 inches, octagonal. Weight: 10¼
pounds. European walnut stock. Double-set triggers.
Brass fittings, including patchbox, ferrules,
buttplate, etc.

Dixie Wesson Percussion Rifle

Dixie 1873 Winchester Carbine

Dixie 1873 Winchester Rifle

Dixie Winchester 1873 Carbine $480
Caliber: 44/40. Barrel: 20 inches, round. Overall length: 39 inches. Weight: 7 pounds. Full tubular magazine holds 11 shots. Blade front sight; leaf rear sight. High-luster blued steel. Walnut forearm and buttstock.

Dixie Winchester 1873 Rifle $650
Caliber: 44/40. Barrel: 23½ inches, octagonal. Weight: 8 pounds. Color casehardened frame with engraving. Walnut forearm and buttstock.

Dixie York County Pennsylvania Rifle
Lock: color casehardened, percussion or flintlock. Caliber: 45. Barrels: 36 inches, octagonal. Overall length: 51½ inches. Weight: 7½ pounds. Walnut one-piece stock. Double-set triggers. Brass fittings, including patchbox, ferrules, buttplate, etc.
Flintlock $260
Percussion. **250**

Dixie U.S. Model 1816 Musket $545
Flintlock. Caliber: 69. Barrel: 42 inches, held by three barrel bands. Overall length: 56½ inches. Weight:

Dixie U. S. Model 1816 Musket (cont.)
9¾ pounds. Metal parts are finished in "National Armory Bright." Lockplate has a brass pan and marked "Harpers Ferry" behind hammer. An American eagle is in front of hammer.

Dixie U. S. Model 1861 Springfield
Rifle-Musket $340
Percussion. Caliber: 58. Barrel: 40 inches; round and tapered with three bands. Overall length: 55¹³⁄₁₆ inches. Weight: 8 pounds. Military rear sights; bayonet-attachment lug front. "1861" is marked on rear of lockplate and "U.S. Springfield" in front of hammer.

Dixie Zouave Carbine $245
Lock: color casehardened, percussion. Caliber: 58. Barrel: 26 inches, octagonal. Weight: 8½ pounds. Walnut-stained stock. Single trigger. Brass fittings, including patchbox, ferrules, buttplate, etc.

Dixie Zouave Model 1863 Rifle $290
Lock: color casehardened, percussion. Caliber: 58. Barrel: 33½ inches, octagonal. Weight: 9¾ pounds. Walnut-stained stock. Single trigger. Brass fittings, including patchbox, ferrules, buttplate, etc.

Dixie Zouave Model 1863 Rifle

EUROARMS OF AMERICA
Winchester, Virginia

HANDGUNS

Euroarms 1851 Navy Revolver $135
Model 1120. Caliber: 36 percussion; #11 cap. Barrel: 7½ inches, octagonal. Overall length: 13 inches. Weight: 42 ounces. Blued finish. Walnut grips. Brass backstrap and trigger guard.

Euroarms 1851 Navy Sheriff

Euroarms 1851 Navy Sheriff Model 1080 . . $135
Caliber: 36 percussion; #11 cap; .375 round or conical lead ball. Barrel: 5 inches, octagonal. Overall length: 11½ inches. Weight: 38 ounces. Brass cone front sight; V-notch rear sight. Blued finish. Walnut grips. Brass backstrap and trigger guard.

Euroarms 1851 Navy Sheriff Model 1090 . . $135
Same general specifications as Model 1080, except available in 44 caliber percussion with .451 round or conical ball.

Euroarms New Model Army Revolver Model 1010 . . . . $120
Caliber: 36 percussion. Barrel: 6½ inches. Weight: 34 ounces. Blued finish. Polished walnut stock. Brass trigger guard.

Euroarms New Model Army Revolver Model 1020 . . . . $140
Same general specifications as Model 1010, except caliber 44 percussion, 8-inch barrel, overall length of 14¾ inches and weight of 40 ounces. (*See* photo, opposite.)

Euroarms New Model Army Target Revolver
Caliber: 44 percussion. Barrel: 8 inches. Overall length: 14¾ inches. Weight: 41 ounces. Adjustable rear sight; ramp front sight. Polished walnut grips. Brass trigger guard.
Blued Model 1030 . . . . $180
Stainless Steel Model 1045 280

Euroarms Remington 1858 New Model Army Engraved $275
Caliber: 44 percussion. Barrel: 8 inches. Overall length: 14¾ inches. Weight: 41 ounces. Adjustable rear sight, ramp front sight. Classical 19th-century scroll engraving. Blued finish. Polished walnut grips. Brass trigger guard.

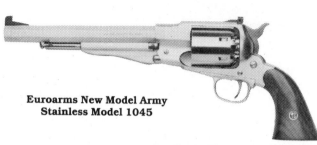

Euroarms New Model Army
Stainless Model 1045

Euroarms Remington 1858 New Model Army Stainless Revolver
Caliber: 44 percussion. Overall length with 8-inch barrel: 13¼ inches. Weight: 40 ounces. Stainless steel finish with polished walnut stock and brass trigger guard.
Model 1047 with 6½-inch barrel $205
Model 1048 with 8-inch barrel 230

Euroarms Rogers & Spencer
Revolver

Euroarms Rogers & Spencer Revolver . . $180
Model 1005. Caliber: 44 percussion; #11 cap. Barrel: 7½ inches. Overall length: 13¾ inches. Weight: 47 ounces. Blued finish with flared walnut grip.

Euroarms Rogers & Spencer
Army Revolver

Euroarms Rogers & Spencer Army Target Revolver $245
Model 1006. Caliber: 44 percussion; #11 cap. Barrel: 7½ inches. Overall length: 13¾ inches. Weight: 47 ounces. Adjustable rear sight; ramp front sight. Blued finish with flared walnut grip.

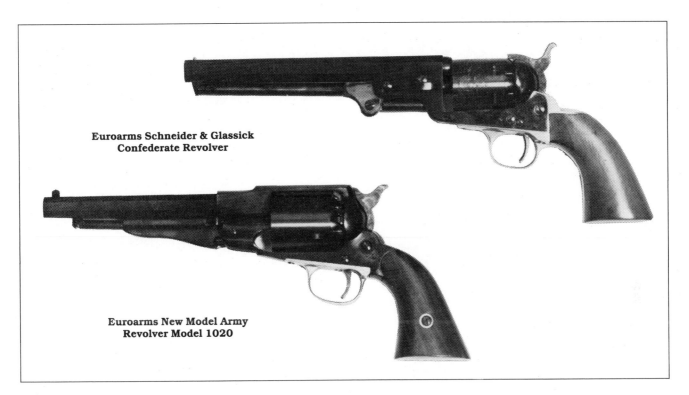

**Euroarms Schneider & Glassick
Confederate Revolver**

**Euroarms New Model Army
Revolver Model 1020**

Euroarms Rogers & Spencer London Gray Revolver

Same general specifications as Model 1005, except made with London gray finish.

Model 1007 . . . . **$210**
Engraved Model 1008 . . . . **280**

Euroarms Schneider & Glassick Confederate Revolver **$135**

Calibers: 36 and 44 percussion. Barrel: 7½ inches. Overall length: 13 inches. Weight: 40 ounces. Blued barrel. Color casehardened hammer and loading lever. Brass frame, backstrap and trigger guard. Engraved cylinder with naval battle scene. Model 1050, 36 caliber: Model 1060, 44 caliber. (*See* photo, above.)

LONG ARMS

Euroarms Cook & Brother Confederate Carbine **$345**

Model 2300. Caliber: 58 percussion. Barrel: 24 inches, round. Overall length: 40½ inches. Weight: 7½ pounds. Antique brown finish. Brass trigger guard, buttplate, barrel bands, sling swivels, nose cap.

Euroarms Hawken Rifle Model 2210A . . **$245**

Caliber: 50 percussion. Barrel: 28 inches, octagonal. Weight: about 9½ pounds. Solid one-piece walnut stock. Adjustable target rear sight; blade front sight. Double-set triggers. Polished brass mountings.

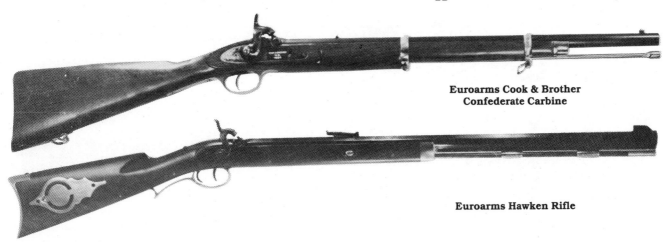

**Euroarms Cook & Brother
Confederate Carbine**

Euroarms Hawken Rifle

**Euroarms London Armory Co.
Enfield Musketoon**

**Euroarms London Armory Co.
Two-Band Enfield Musket**

**Euroarms London Armory Co.
Three-Band Enfield Musket**

Euroarms London Armory Company Enfield Musketoon **$280**
Model 2280. Caliber: 58 percussion; Minie ball. Barrel: 24 inches. Overall length: 40½ inches. Weight: 7 to 7½ pounds. Walnut stock with sling swivels. Blued finish with brass trigger guard, nose cap and buttplate.

Euroarms London Armory Company Two-Band Enfield Musket **$365**
Model 2270. Caliber: 58 percussion. Barrel: 33 inches, round and rifled. Overall length: 49 inches. Weight: about 8⅝ pounds. One-piece walnut stock. Brass buttplate, trigger guard and nose cap. Blued barrel and barrel bands.

Euroarms London Armory Company Three-Band Enfield Musket **$430**
Model 2260. Caliber: 58 percussion. Barrel: 39 inches, round and rifled. Overall length: 54 inches.

Weight: about 9⅝ pounds. Enfield folding ladder-type rear sight; inverted "V" front sight. One-piece walnut stock. Blued barrel and barrel bands. Brass buttplate, trigger guard, nose cap.

Euroarms Percussion Double-Barrel Shotgun **$430**
Model 2290. Gauge: 12. Chokes: modified/full. Weight: about 6 pounds. Checkered, English-style walnut stock. Blued barrels. Engraved sidelocks.

Euroarms Magnum Cape Gun **$345**
Model 2295. Single-barrel. Gauge: 12. Barrel: 32 inches; open choke. Overall length: 47½ inches. Weight: 7½ pounds. Classic English-styled stock of oil-finished European walnut. Blued barrel, trigger guard and buttplate. Scroll-engraved lock.

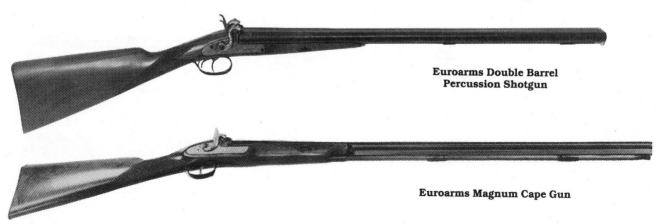

**Euroarms Double Barrel
Percussion Shotgun**

Euroarms Magnum Cape Gun

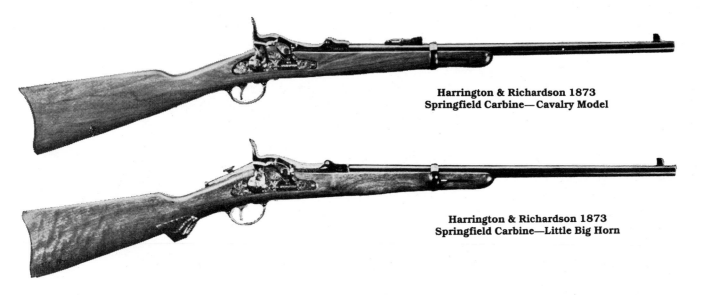

Harrington & Richardson 1873
Springfield Carbine—Cavalry Model

Harrington & Richardson 1873
Springfield Carbine—Little Big Horn

HARRINGTON & RICHARDSON, INC.
Gardner, Massachusetts

The firm of Harrington & Richardson was established by Gilbert Harrington and William Richardson in Worcester, Mass., in 1874. Originally producing shotguns and metallic cartridge revolvers, their enterprise soon expanded to many types of firearms. It was in 1986, after more than a century in business, that the company closed its doors.

H & R 1873 Springfield Carbine—Cavalry Model $340
Model 171. Trapdoor, single-shot action. Caliber: 45-70 Govt. Barrel: 22 inches. Overall length: 41 inches. Weight: 7 pounds. Blade front sight; original military-style rear. Engraved action. Blue-black finish.

H & R 1873 Springfield Carbine—Little Big Horn Commemorative $340
Model 174. Trapdoor, single-shot action. Caliber: 45-70 Govt. Barrel: 22 inches. Overall length: 41 inches. Weight: 7 lbs. 8 oz. Blade front sight; tang-mounted aperture rear. American walnut stock with metal grip adapter. Blue-black finish.

H & R 1873 Springfield Officer's Rifle . . $340
Model 173. Trapdoor, single-shot action. Caliber: 45-70 Govt. Barrel: 26 inches. Overall length: 45 inches. Weight: 8 pounds. Blade front sight; tang-mounted aperture rear. Hand-checkered American walnut stock. Blue-black finish. Color casehardened receiver.

HOPKINS & ALLEN
Hawthorne, New Jersey

The firm of Hopkins & Allen has been in the blackpowder replica business for many years. Its underhammer designs are exclusively American; they are manufactured in the U.S. and stem from 1830 New England. Some of the other replicas, particularly the handguns, are produced in Italy with German-made parts.

Hopkins & Allen 1851 Navy Revolver . . . $135
Caliber: 36 percussion. Casehardened hammer, frame and loading lever. Blued barrel. Brass square-back trigger guard and back strap. Steel frame. Engraved cylinder.

Hopkins & Allen 1860 Army Revolver . . $140
Caliber: 44 percussion. Color casehardened hammer, frame and loading lever. Roll engraved cylinder. Walnut grips.

PISTOLS

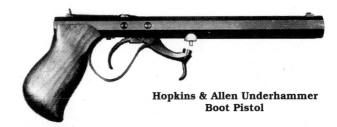

Hopkins & Allen Underhammer
Boot Pistol

Hopkins & Allen Boot Pistol $75
Underhammer percussion lock. Calibers: 36 or 45. Barrel: 6 inches, octagonal. Weight: 40 ounces. Overall length: 13 inches. Open post-type front sight; open rear sight with step elevator. Sculptured walnut pistol grip. Match trigger. Blue-black finish.

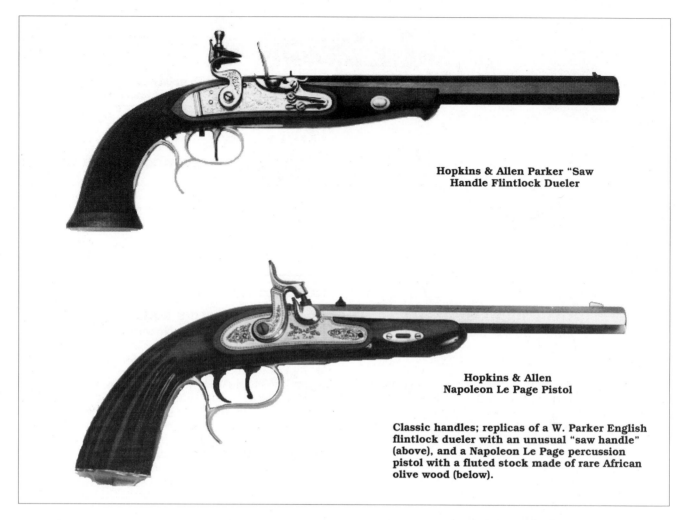

Hopkins & Allen Parker "Saw Handle Flintlock Dueler"

Hopkins & Allen Napoleon Le Page Pistol

Classic handles; replicas of a W. Parker English flintlock dueler with an unusual "saw handle" (above), and a Napoleon Le Page percussion pistol with a fluted stock made of rare African olive wood (below).

Hopkins & Allen Bounty Hunter Pistol . . $110
Caliber: 45 percussion. Barrel: 17 inches; octagonal, 13/16 inch across the flats. Overall length: 22 inches. Weight: 52 ounces. Solid brass nose cap and rib.

Hopkins & Allen J. S. Hawken Pistol. . . $200
Calibers: 50 or 54 percussion. Barrel: octagonal, 15/16 inch across the flats; German-made. Overall length: 14 inches. Weight: 36 ounces. Full hooked breech. Finger spur trigger guard. Engraved lockplate and hammer. Checkered European walnut stock. Blue-black barrel. Early models have Italian-made barrels, brass trim, no engraving.

Hopkins & Allen Kentucky Pistol $90
Model 10. Flintlock or percussion; convertible ignition system. Caliber: 44. Barrel: 10 inches; octagonal, rifled. Overall length: 15½ inches. Weight: 48 ounces.

Hopkins & Allen John Manton Pistol . . . $200
Caliber: 45 percussion. Barrel: 10 inches; octagonal, 7/8 inch across the flats; German-made, precision-rifled. Overall length: 15½ inches. Weight: 40 ounces. Two barrel wedges. Polished steel finish. Hand-checkered European walnut stock. Engraved lockplate and hammer. Early models have Italian-made barrels, no engraving and brass trim.

Hopkins & Allen Kentucky Percussion Pistol

Hopkins & Allen W. Moore Flintlock Pistol

Hopkins & Allen W. Moore Flintlock Target Pistol $195

Model 1800. Flintlock or percussion. Caliber: 45. Barrel: 10 inches; octagonal, 7/8 inch across the flats; German-made precision match, brown. Single trigger. Engraved lock in white. German silver-plated furniture. Rounded European walnut stock with checkered grip.

Hopkins & Allen Mountain Pistol $110

Caliber: 50. Color casehardened lock. Bronzed barrel. Single trigger. Checkered, engraved stock. Brass furniture, solid brass forend.

Hopkins & Allen Napoleon Le Page Pistol . . $200

Percussion dueling pistol. Caliber: 45. Barrel: 10 inches; octagonal, 7/8 inch across the flats; German-made, precision rifled. Overall length: 16 inches. Weight: 40 ounces. Double-set triggers. Fixed sights. Stock of African olive wood (rare and higher prices) has unusual fluted grip and silver-plated grip cap; some newer stocks of fluted European walnut. Engraved silver-plated lock plate and hammer. Finger spur trigger guard. (*See* photo, opposite.)

Hopkins & Allen W. Parker English Flintlock Dueling Pistol $210

Same general specifications as Parker English Percussion model, except with flintlock ignition and engraved lockplate and hammer. (See photo, opposite.)

Hopkins & Allen Parker "Saw Handle" Percussion Dueler

Hopkins & Allen W. Parker English Percussion Dueling Pistol $195

Caliber: 45. Barrel: 10 inches; octagonal, 7/8 inch across the flats; German-made precision match in brown finish. Double-set triggers. Fixed sights. Checkered "saw handle" European walnut stock with German silver inlay. Silver-plated furniture.

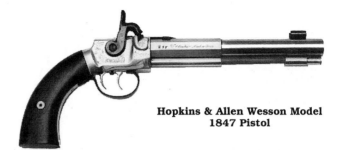

Hopkins & Allen Wesson Model 1847 Pistol

Hopkins & Allen Wesson Model 1847 Pistol $150

Reproduction of Daniel Wesson's 1847 percussion pistol. Caliber: 45 percussion. Barrel: 10 inches; half-octagonal, half-round. Overall length: 15 inches. Weight: 48 ounces. Double-set triggers. Polished steel barrel threaded to brass receiver.

LONG ARMS

Hopkins & Allen All-American Percussion Rifle. $110

Underhammer percussion rifle. Calibers: 36 and 45. Barrel: 18½ inches; half-round, half-octagonal, 8-grooved rifling. Overall length: 39 inches. Weight: 4½ pounds. Walnut-stained, one-piece stock.

Hopkins & Allen Brush Rifle. $185

Flintlock or percussion; convertible ignition system. Calibers: 36 and 45. Barrel: 25 inches; octagonal, 15/16 inch across the flats. Weight: 6½ to 7 pounds. Overall length: 40 inches. Silver blade front sight; notched rear sight. Select hardwood stock.

Hopkins & Allen Buggy Deluxe Percussion Rifle. $160

Underhammer percussion lock. Calibers: 36 and 45. Barrel: 20 inches; octagonal, 8-grooved. Weight: 6 pounds. American walnut stock and forend.

Hopkins & Allen Deerstalker Rifle $185

Underhammer percussion lock. Caliber: 58. Barrel: 28 inches; octagonal, 1⅛ inches across flats, one turn in 72 inches. Weight: 9½ pounds. American walnut stock and forearm. (*See* page 258.)

Hopkins & Allen Brush Rifle

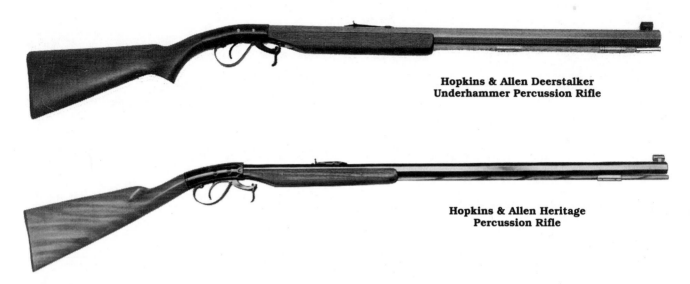

Hopkins & Allen Deerstalker
Underhammer Percussion Rifle

Hopkins & Allen Heritage
Percussion Rifle

Hopkins & Allen Heritage Percussion Rifle $170

Underhammer percussion lock. Calibers: 36, 45, 50. Barrel: 32 inches; octagonal with either uniform or grain twist rifling. Three aperture adjustable long-range rear target sights. Weight: 7½ to 8 pounds. Brass crescent-shaped buttplate, cap box and trigger guard extension. American black walnut stock and forend.

Hopkins & Allen Minuteman Brush Rifle $295

Flintlock or percussion. Calibers: 45 and 50. Barrel: 24 inches; octagonal, rifled or smoothbore. Weight: 8 pounds. Silver blade front sight; notched Kentucky rear sight. Blued finish. Maple stock. Brass patchbox, buttplate and trigger guard.

Hopkins & Allen Minuteman Rifle $275

Flintlock or percussion. Calibers: 31, 36 and 45. Barrel: 39 inches; octagonal, $^{15}/_{16}$ inch across flats, 8-grooved rifling. Overall length: 55 inches. Weight: 10½ pounds. High polished brass trimmings. Maple stock.

Hopkins & Allen Offhand Deluxe Percussion Rifle $160

Underhammer percussion lock. Calibers: 36 and 45. Barrel: 32 inches; octagonal, 8-grooved, uniform twist. Weight: 8½ pounds. American walnut stock and forend.

Hopkins & Allen Over/Under Rifle $245

Caliber: 45 percussion. Barrels: 28 inches; octagonal, each with own set of sights. Custom blued finish. Overall length: 43 inches. Weight: 8½ pounds. Crescent buttplate. American walnut stock. Introduced in 1969.

Hopkins & Allen Pennsylvania Half-Stock Rifle $310

Flintlock or percussion. Caliber: 45 or 50. Barrel: 32 inches, smoothbore or rifled. Weight: 10 pounds. Brass furniture. Maple stock.

Hopkins & Allen Pennsylvania Hawken Rifle $190

Model 29. Flintlock or percussion; convertible ignition system. Caliber: 50. Barrel: 29 inches; octagonal, $^{15}/_{17}$ inch across flats; rifled with round ball twist. Overall length: 44 inches. Weight: 7¼ pounds. Walnut stock with cheekpiece. Brass furniture.

Hopkins & Allen Pennsylvania
Hawken Percussion Rifle

**Hopkins & Allen Pennsylvania
Hawken Percussion Rifle**

**Hopkins & Allen Target
Percussion Rifle**

**Hopkins & Allen Lightweight
Percussion Shotgun**

Hopkins & Allen Target Percussion
Rifle $160
Underhammer percussion rifle. Caliber: 45. Barrel: 32 inches; octagonal, 1⅛ inches across flats, 8-grooved rifling. Weight: 11 pounds. American walnut stock. Blued barrel and receiver.

Hopkins & Allen Double-Barrel Shotgun . . . $245
Percussion. Gauge: 12. Barrels: 28 inches; choked cylinder. Weight: 6 pounds. Blued barrels. Walnut stock with checkered wrist and forearm. Engraved lockplates.

Hopkins & Allen Lightweight Shotgun . . $290
Percussion. Gauge: 12. Barrel: 28 inches, smoothbore. Weight: just under 6 pounds. Front bead sight. Blued finish. Brass furniture. Maple stock.

INTERCONTINENTAL ARMS (E.M.F.)
Santa Ana, California

Intercontinental Arms was one of the many importers that sprang up during the late 1960s and early '70s, importing replica Colt Army Single-Action revolvers and blackpowder firearms. The E.M.F. Company eventually took over the line and added a few of its own "Dakota" replicas. Although available in used gun circles, most of these are not currently being produced.

Dakota Single-Action Revolver $110
Calibers: 22LR, 22WRM, 357 Mag. and 45 Colt. Six-shot cylinder. Barrel: 4⅝ and 5½ inches. Overall length: 10¼ and 11 inches, respectively. Weights: 35 and 40 ounces, respectively. Fixed sights. Knurled hammer spur. Casehardened frame; blued barrel and cylinder; brass trigger guard and backstrap. One-piece, smooth walnut stocks.

Dakota Single-Action Revolver —Engraved $260

Same general specifications as standard model, except comes with finely engraved frame, barrel, cylinder, hammer, trigger guard and back strap.

Dakota Single-Action Revolver—Long Barrel $150

Same general specifications as regular model, except for 7½-inch barrel and weight of 42 ounces.

Intercontinental Duck's Foot Pistol . . . $110

Four-barreled percussion volley-pistol. Four, or any lesser number of loaded barrels may be fired at one time. Caliber: 36. Barrel: 3-inch tubes with 1-inch chamber. Overall length: 7 inches. Weight: 24 ounces. Walnut stock.

Intercontinental Kentucky Pistol $115

Casehardened flintlock or percussion. Caliber: 44. Barrel: 9½ inches, octagonal. Overall length: 15 inches. Weight: 40 ounces. Blued steel rifled barrel, engraved lock plate. Solid brass trigger guard, barrel cap. Dovetailed front and rear sights. Single-piece, selected walnut stock.

Intercontinental Kiwi Pocket Pistol $75

Percussion lock. Caliber: 36. Barrel: 3¾ inches, round. Weight: 9¾ ounces.

Intercontinental Kiwi Pocket Pistol— Cased Set $220

Two Kiwi Pocket Pistols in lined case with all accessories.

Intercontinental Kiwi Vest Pocket Pistol . . $75

Same general specifications as standard Kiwi Pocket Pistol, except for 1-inch barrel and weight of 6¼ pounces.

Intercontinental Renegade Double-Barrel Pistol $110

Percussion locks with engraved side plates and hammers. Calibers: 36 and 44. Barrels: 8¼ inches, round. Overall length: 13¼ inches. Weight: 31 ounces. Single-piece walnut stock.

LONG ARMS

Intercontinental Kentuckian Carbine. . . $205

Same general specifications as Kentuckian Rifle, except for 27½-inch barrel and slightly lesser weight.

Intercontinental Kentuckian Rifle $200

Flint or percussion lock. Caliber: 44. Barrel: 35 inches, octagonal. Overall length: 48 inches. Weight: 6¼ pounds. European walnut stock.

LYMAN PRODUCTS CORPORATION
Middlefield, Connecticut

Known primarily for its precision handloading tools and firearms accessories, Lyman also produces its own blackpowder replica arms. Based on tests done by in-house technicians, the company publishes a handbook as well that contains comprehensive load information for the modern blackpowder shooter.

Lyman Plains Pistol

Lyman Plains Pistol $155

Caliber: 50 or 54, percussion. Replica of mid-1800s pistol. Octagonal barrel. Authentic rib and thimble styling. Pistol-sized, coil-spring Hawken lock. Blackened iron furniture; brass trigger guard and ramrod tip. Hawken-style walnut "half" stock. Detachable belt hook.

Lyman Great Plains Rifle

Caliber: 50 or 54. Flintlock or percussion. Barrel: 32 inches; octagonal, one turn in 66 inches. Double-set triggers with Hawken-style trigger guard. Steel front sight; buckhorn adjustable or fixed primitive rear sight. Blackened steel furniture. Walnut stock.
Flintlock $335
Percussion. 325

Lyman Great Plains Rifle

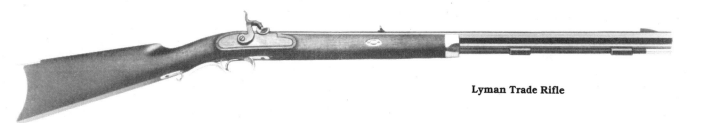

Lyman Trade Rifle

Lyman Trade Rifle
Caliber: 50 or 54. Flintlock or percussion. Barrel: 28 inches; octagonal, rifled one turn in 48 inches. Overall length: 45 inches. Spring-loaded single trigger. Hooked breech. Fixed steel sights. Steel barrel rib and ramrod ferrules. Polished brass furniture with blued steel parts. European walnut stock.
Flintlock. **$240**
Percussion **230**

W. L. MOWREY GUN WORKS
Olney, Texas

Mowrey Allen & Thurber Replica Rifle . . **$250**
Percussion. Calibers: 45, 50, 54, or 58. Barrel: 32 inches; octagonal, 8-grooved rifling. Weight: 10¼ pounds. Adjustable open sights. Walnut stock. Polished brass furniture.

Mowrey Allen & Thurber Special Rifle . . **$275**
Percussion. Calibers; 45, 50, 54, or 58. Barrel: 32 inches, octagonal. Overall length: 48 inches. Weight: 10 pounds. Walnut stock and forend. Brass furniture.

Mowrey Hawk Short Stock Rifle **$315**
Percussion lock. Calibers: 45, 50, 54, or 58. Barrel: 32 inches, octagonal. Overall length: 49 inches. Weight: 9½ pounds. Walnut sporter-type stock with cheekpiece. Fully adjustable open sights. Hawkins-type buttplate and action housing of brass. Adjustable trigger.

Mowrey Hawkins Full Stock Rifle **$375**
Percussion. Calibers: 45, 50, 54, or 58. Barrel: 27½ inches, octagonal. Overall length: 45 inches. Weight: 8¼ pounds. Blade front sight, adjustable rear. Double-set triggers. Maple stock.

Mowrey Hawkins Half-Stock Rifle **$345**
Same general specifications as full stock rifle, except for maple half stock.

Mowrey Texas Carbine **$500**
Percussion. Caliber: 58. Barrel: 24 inches, octagonal; 4-grooved. Overall length: 39 inches. Weight: 8 pounds. Adjustable front and rear sights. Maple or walnut stock. "1 of 100" inscribed on first 100 and "1 of 1000" inscribed on remaining 1000. Made from 1973 to 1974.

Mowrey Percussion Shotgun **$250**
Percussion. Gauge: 12. Barrel: 32 inches; half-octagon, half-round. Overall length: 48 inches. Weight: 7½ pounds. Bead front sight. Oil-finished maple stock. Brass furniture.

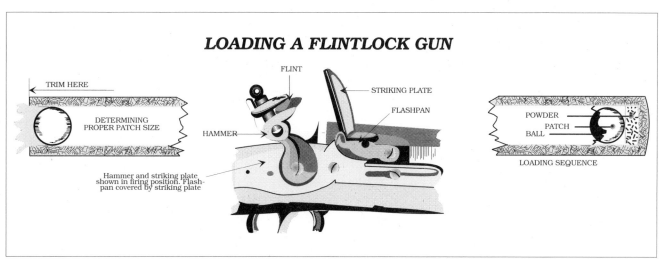

LOADING A FLINTLOCK GUN

TRIM HERE

DETERMINING PROPER PATCH SIZE

FLINT

STRIKING PLATE

FLASHPAN

HAMMER

Hammer and striking plate shown in firing position. Flashpan covered by striking plate

POWDER
PATCH
BALL

LOADING SEQUENCE

NAVY ARMS COMPANY, INC.
Ridgefield, New Jersey

Since its establishment in 1958, Navy Arms has been a forerunner in the birth and development of the muzzleloading reproduction market. The "Yank" and the "Reb" were the first replica revolvers produced to meet the needs of blackpowder shooters who wanted to preserve their original antique arms. In fact, the "Yank," based on the Colt 1851 Navy revolver, inspired the name of the firm. Under the direction of owner Val Forgett, Navy Arms has accumulated a list of "firsts" in the industry, among them using stainless steel and progressive rifling in its reproduction handguns. The company also deals in cartridge arms, military surplus and, of course, antique guns.

PISTOLS

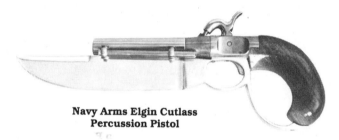

**Navy Arms Elgin Cutlass
Percussion Pistol**

Navy Arms Elgin Cutlass Percussion
Pistol $95
Caliber: 44. Combination knife and gun pistol. Overall length: 9 inches. 12-inch knife blade. Weight: 2 pounds. This was the only combination gun ever issued by the U.S. military service and one of the first percussion arms officially used by the U.S.

Navy Arms Harper's Ferry Pistol

Navy Arms Harpers Ferry Pistol $160
Caliber: 58 smoothbore. Flintlock. Barrel: 10 inches. Overall length: 16 inches. Weight: 2 lbs. 9 oz. Color casehardened lock. Brass-mounted browned barrel. Walnut stock. One of America's famous pistols, authentically reproduced.

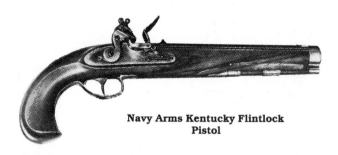

**Navy Arms Kentucky Flintlock
Pistol**

Navy Arms Kentucky Flintlock Pistol
This is a representative replica of the pistol that forged American history, dating back to the Revolution. Caliber: 45. Barrel: 10$\frac{1}{8}$ inches, octagonal. Overall length: 15$\frac{1}{2}$ inches. Weight: 2 pounds. Color casehardened lock. Brass furniture. One-piece walnut stock.
Flintlock Model. **$130**
Single-Cased Set. **210**
Double-Cased Set. **355**

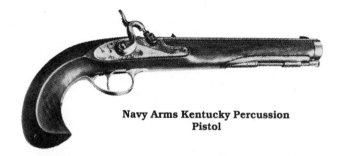

**Navy Arms Kentucky Percussion
Pistol**

Navy Arms Kentucky Percussion Pistol
Same general specifications as Kentucky Flintlock Pistol, except with percussion lock.
Percussion Model . . . . **$ 95**
Single-Cased Set. **205**
Double-Cased Set. **335**

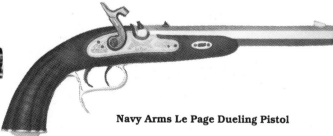

Navy Arms Le Page Dueling Pistol

Navy Arms Le Page Dueling Pistol $230
Reproduction of French percussion pistol. Caliber: 44. Barrel: 9 inches, octagonal. Overall length: 15 inches. Weight: 2 lbs. 2 oz. Engraved lock plate and hammer. Double-set triggers. Finger spur trigger guard. Fluted stock of European walnut. Discontinued 1986.

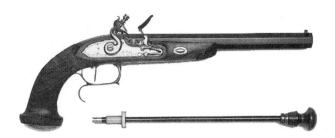

Navy Arms Le Page Flintlock Pistol

Navy Arms Le Page Flintlock Pistol

Caliber: 45. Barrel: 10½ inches, rifled or smooth-bore. Overall length: 17 inches. Weight: 2 lbs. 2 oz. Hand-checkered walnut stock with hinged buttcap and carved motif of a shell at the forward portion of the stock. Single-set trigger. Finger spur trigger guard. Brown finish.

Standard Flintlock Model $350
Single-Cased Set 505
Double-Cased Set 875

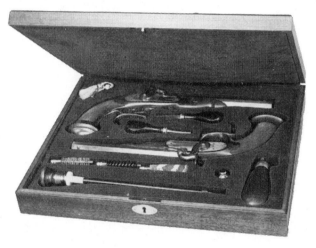

Navy Arms Le Page Percussion, Double-Cased Set

Navy Arms Le Page Percussion Pistol

Navy Arms Le Page Percussion Pistol

Caliber: 45. Barrel: 9 inches; rifled, octagonal. Overall length: 15 inches. Weight: 2 lbs. 2 oz. Adjustable single-set trigger. Boutet-style European walnut

Navy Arms Le Page Percussion Pistol (cont.)

stock. Finger spur trigger guard. Adjustable rear sight and dovetailed front sight.

Standard Pistol **$265**
Single-Cased Set **420**
Double-Cased Set **710**

Navy Arms John Manton Match Pistol

Navy Arms John Manton Match Pistol . . $210

Caliber: 45 percussion. Barrel: 10 inches, rifled. Overall length: 15½ inches. Weight: 2 lbs. 4 oz. High-polished steel barrel. Rounded, checkered European walnut stock. Brass furniture. Finger spur trigger guard. Discontinued 1986.

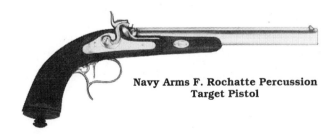

Navy Arms Moore & Patrick English Percussion Pistol

Navy Arms Moore & Patrick English Pistol

Caliber: 45. Flintlock or percussion. Barrel: 10 inches. Overall length: 14½ inches. Weight: 2 pounds.

Flintlock Model **$255**
Percussion Model **260**

Navy Arms F. Rochatte Percussion Target Pistol

Navy Arms F. Rochatte Percussion
Pistol $230

Caliber: 45 percussion. Barrel: 10 inches, round. Overall length: 16½ inches. Weight: 2 pounds. Single-set trigger. All steel furniture. Checkered European walnut half-stock. Finger spur trigger guard. Discontinued 1986.

REVOLVERS

**Navy Arms 1851 Navy "Yank"
Revolver**

Navy Arms 1851 Navy "Yank" Revolver

Calibers: 36 or 44. Six-shot. Barrel: 7½ inches, octagonal. Overall length: 14 inches. Weight: 2 lbs. 9 oz. Steel frame. Cylinder roll-engraved with naval battle scene. Brass backstrap and trigger guard. Popular with Union troops during the Civil War, this revolver was originally manufactured by Colt in the mid-1800s. Made from 1958 to date.

Standard Revolver **$115**
Single-Cased Set **200**
Double-Cased Set **325**

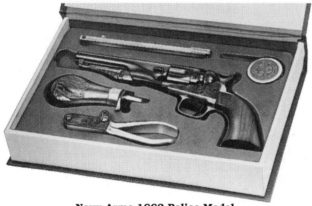

**Navy Arms 1862 Police Model
Law & Order Set**

Navy Arms 1862 Police Model Revolver

Percussion. Caliber: 36. Five-shot. Barrel: 5½ inches. Half-fluted and rebated cylinder. Brass trigger guard and backstrap. Color casehardened frame, loading lever and hammer.

Standard Revolver **$150**
Law and Order Set **205**

Navy Arms Army 60 Sheriff's Model Revolver **$85**

Calibers: 36 or 44. Six-shot. Full fluted cylinder. Barrel: 5½ inches. Shortened version of the Colt Army Model 1860 Revolver. Original snub-nose designed for quick-draw use; adopted by many police departments.

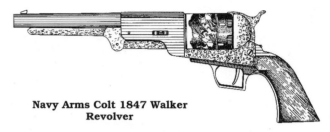

**Navy Arms Colt 1847 Walker
Revolver**

Navy Arms Colt 1847 Walker Revolver

Caliber: 44. Barrel: 9 inches. Rolled cylinder scene. Blued and color casehardened finish. Brass square-back trigger guard. Weight: 4½ pounds.

Standard Revolver **$190**
Single-Cased Set **290**

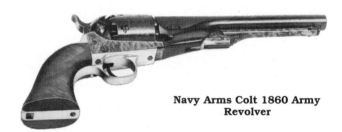

**Navy Arms Colt 1860 Army
Revolver**

Navy Arms Colt 1860 Army Revolver

Caliber: 44. Six-shot. Barrel: 8 inches, round. Overall length: 13⅝ inches. Weight: 2 lbs. 9 oz. Brass trigger guard. Steel backstrap. Color casehardened loading lever and hammer. Rebated cylinder engraved with naval scene.

Standard Revolver **$125**
Single-Cased Set **210**
Double-Cased Set **350**

Navy Arms LeMat Army Model Revolver . . **$450**

Caliber: 44. Nine-shot lightly engraved cylinder. 65-caliber single-shot lower barrel makes it a 10-shot double-barreled revolver. Barrel: 7⅚ inches. Overall length: 14 inches. Weight: 3 lbs. 7 oz. Checkered pistol grip. Blued barrels. Color casehardened hammer, trigger. Fixed lanyard loop in buttplate. This is patterned after the 42-caliber double-barreled revolver designed by New Orleans doctor Jean Francois LeMat. Originally patented in 1856, it was popular with Confederate officers. (See photo, opposite.)

Navy Arms LeMat Cavalry Model Revolver **$450**

Same general specifications as Army Model, except for finger spur trigger guard and large swivel lanyard loop at buttplate. (*See* photo, opposite.)

Navy Arms LeMat Navy Model Revolver . . **$450**

Same general specifications as Army Model, except for rear sight. (See photo, opposite.)

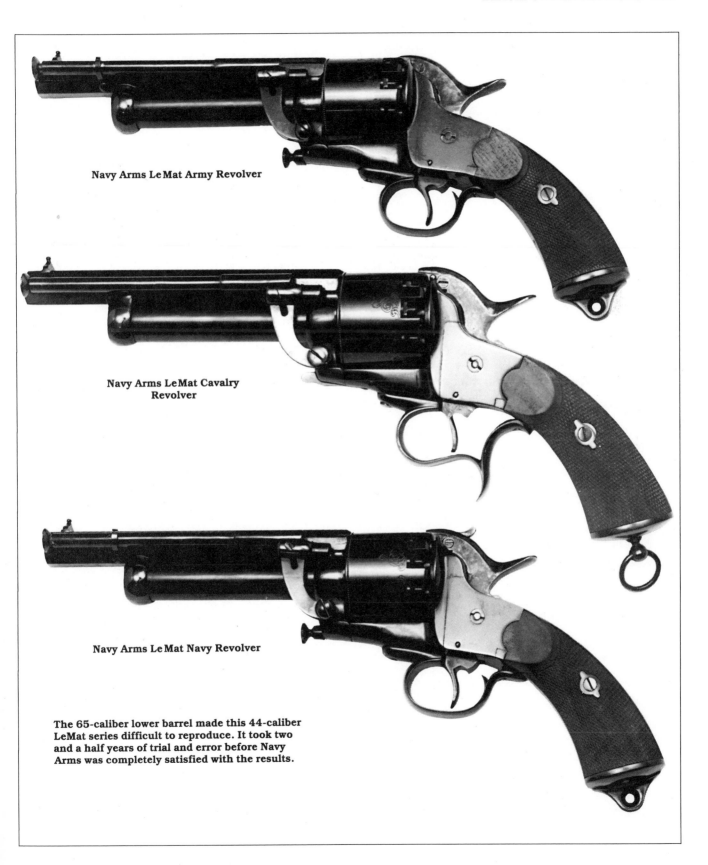

Navy Arms Le Mat Army Revolver

Navy Arms Le Mat Cavalry
Revolver

Navy Arms Le Mat Navy Revolver

The 65-caliber lower barrel made this 44-caliber LeMat series difficult to reproduce. It took two and a half years of trial and error before Navy Arms was completely satisfied with the results.

Navy Arms Reb Model 1860 Revolver

Navy Arms Reb Model 1860 Revolver

Calibers: 36 and 44. Barrel: 7¼ inches, round. Overall length: 13 inches. Brass frame, backstrap and trigger guard. Blued barrel. This is a replica of the Confederate Griswold & Gunnison Army revolver produced by Samuel Griswold from 1862 to 1864. Made by Navy Arms from 1958 to date.

Standard Revolver . . . . **$ 95**
Single-Cased Set **185**
Double-Cased Set **290**

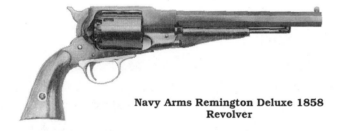

Navy Arms Remington Deluxe 1858 Revolver

Navy Arms Remington Deluxe 1858 Revolver **$230**

Caliber: 44. Barrel: 8 inches with progressive rifling. Overall length: 14¼ inches. Weight: 2 lbs. 14 oz. Adjustable front sight. Steel construction finished in charcoal blue. Walnut stocks. Brass trigger guard.

Navy Arms Remington 1858 Stainless Steel Revolver

Navy Arms Remington 1858 Stainless Steel Revolver **$205**

Same specifications as standard model, except made in all stainless steel.

Navy Arms Remington New Model Army Revolver

Calibers: 36 or 44. Barrel: 8 inches. Overall length: 13½ inches. Weight: 2 lbs. 9 oz. Blued finish. Nickel finish in 44 caliber.

Standard Revolver **$125**
Single-Cased Set **210**
Double-Cased Set **355**

Navy Arms Remington Target Model Revolver

Navy Arms Remington Target Model Revolver **$145**

Caliber: 44 percussion. Based on the Army Model, this revolver has target sights.

Navy Arms Rogers & Spencer Navy Revolver

Navy Arms Rogers & Spencer Navy Revolver **$155**

Caliber: 44. Six-shot. Barrel: 7½ inches, octagonal. Overall length: 13¾ inches. Weight: 3 pounds. Hinged-type loading lever assembly. Two-piece walnut grips. Blued finish. Casehardened hammer and lever.

LONG ARMS

Navy Arms Brown Bess Musket $335
Caliber: 75. Flintlock. Barrel: 42 inches, brown, polished. Overall length: 59 inches. Weight: 9½ pounds. Brass furniture. Patterned after the American Revolutionary favorite, this replica Brown Bess bears the Colonial Williamsburg mark of authenticity.

Navy Arms Buffalo Hunter $240
Caliber: 58 percussion. Barrel: 26 inches; precision-rifled of ordnance steel. Weight: 8 pounds. Color casehardened lock and hammer. Walnut-tone wood stock. Discontinued 1986.

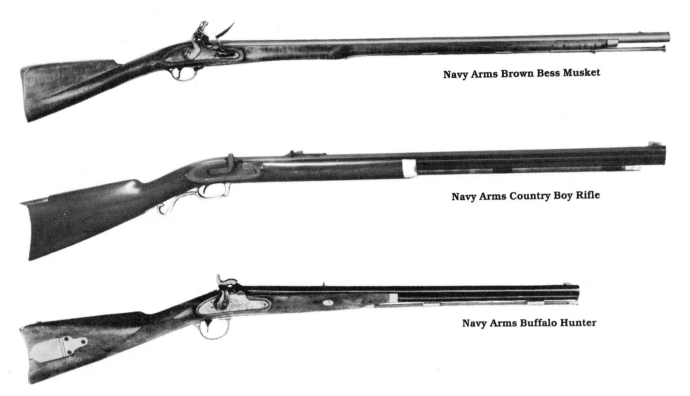

Navy Arms Brown Bess Musket

Navy Arms Country Boy Rifle

Navy Arms Buffalo Hunter

Navy Arms Country Boy Rifle $190
Calibers: 32, 36, 45, or 50. Barrel: 26 inches. Weight: 5½ pounds. Hooked breech and fully adjustable hunting sights.

Navy Arms Creedmoor No. 2 Target Rifle . . $535
Caliber: 45/70. Barrel: 30 inches, tapered. Overall length: 46 inches. Weight: 9 pounds. Color casehardened rolling block receiver. Checkered walnut stock

and forend. Blued barrel. Hooded front sight; Creedmoor tang sight.

Navy Arms Enfield 1853 Rifle Musket . . $410
Caliber: 557. Barrel: 39 inches; cold-forged with 3-grooved rifling; three-band. Overall length: 55 inches. Weight: 9 pounds. Fixed front sight; graduated rear sight. Walnut stock with brass furniture. This was popular during the Civil War on both sides of the Mason/Dixon line because of its quality and accuracy.

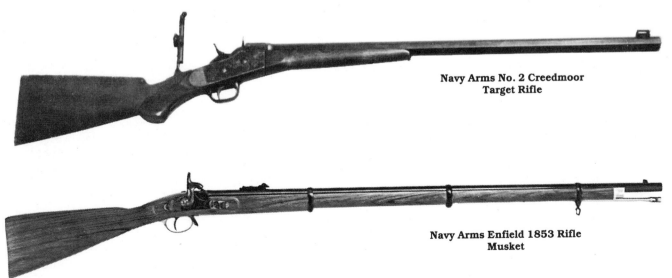

Navy Arms No. 2 Creedmoor
Target Rifle

Navy Arms Enfield 1853 Rifle
Musket

Navy Arms Enfield 1858 Rifle

Navy Arms Enfield 1861 Musketoon

Navy Arms Hawken Rifle— Left Hand

Navy Arms Enfield 1858 Rifle $370
Caliber: 557. Barrel: 33 inches, 5-grooved; progressive rifling. Overall length: 48½ inches. Weight: 8 lbs. 8 oz. Fixed front sight; graduated rear sight. Walnut stock with brass furniture. Heavy constructed rifle adopted by the British Admiralty in the late 1850s.

Navy Arms Enfield 1861 Musketoon . . . $280
Caliber: 557. Barrel 24 inches; 5-grooved, cold-forged. Overall length: 40¼ inches. Weight: 7 lbs. 8 oz. Fixed front sight; graduated rear sight. Walnut stock with brass furniture. Front and rear sling loops. Limited collector's edition, individually serial numbered.

Navy Arms Hawken Rifle—Left Hand . . $240
Percussion. Caliber: 50. Barrel: prestraightened. Black walnut stock. Brass furniture.

Navy Arms Henry Carbine
Reproduction of the arm used by the Kentucky Cavalry. Calibers: 44 rimfire or 44/40. Barrel: 23⅝ inches; octagonal. Overall length: 39 inches. Weight: 8¼ pounds. Brass frame. Blued barrel. Oil-stained American walnut stock. Limited deluxe edition of 50 has original style engraving, silver-plated frame and deluxe American walnut stock.
Henry Carbine . . . . **$ 660**
Engraved Model **1650**

Navy Arms Henry, Iron Frame Model . . . $750
Same general specifications as Henry Carbine, except with iron frame, barrel length of 24 inches, overall length of 43 inches, and weight of 9¼ pounds.

Navy Arms Iron Frame Henry

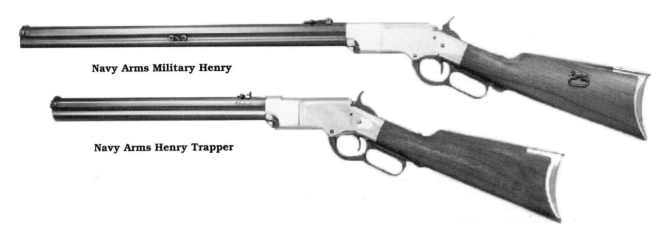

Navy Arms Military Henry

Navy Arms Henry Trapper

Navy Arms Henry, Military Model $660
Authentic replica of the original military Henry Rifle, complete with bar swivels on the barrel and stock. Calibers: 44 rimfire or 44/40. Barrel: 24 inches, octagonal. Overall length: 43 inches. Weight: 9¼ pounds. Brass frame. Blued barrel.

Navy Arms Henry Trapper. $665
Same general specifications as the Henry Carbine, except with shorter (16½ inches) barrel, overall length of 34½ inches and weight of 7¼ pounds.

Navy Arms Ithaca/Navy Hawken Rifle . . $335
Calibers: 50 or 54. Barrel: 31½ inches, octagonal. Buckhorn rear sight; blade front sight. Color casehardened percussion lock. Blued barrel and furniture, except nose cap and escutcheons. Walnut stock.

Navy Arms Kentucky Rifle
Calibers: 45 or 50. Barrel: 35 inches. Overall length: 51 inches. Weight: 6 lbs. 14 oz. Color casehardened lock. Ornate brass patchbox, brass trigger guard and stock fittings. Walnut stock.
Flintlock **$245**
Percussion **235**

Navy Arms Mark I Hawken Flintlock Rifle. $250
Calibers: 50 or 54. Barrel: 32 inches, octagonal. Overall length: 49 inches. Weight: about 9 pounds. Double-set triggers. Fancy finger spur trigger guard. Hooked breech. Hawken-style toe and buttplates. Engraved blued lock. American walnut stock. Brass furniture. Discontinued 1986.

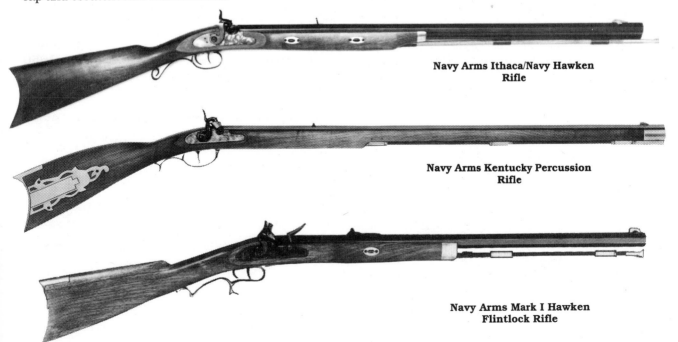

Navy Arms Ithaca/Navy Hawken Rifle

Navy Arms Kentucky Percussion Rifle

Navy Arms Mark I Hawken Flintlock Rifle

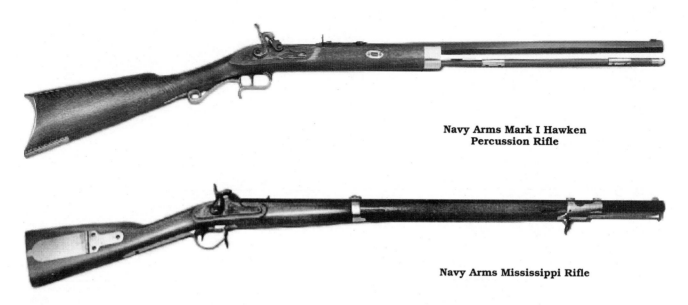

**Navy Arms Mark I Hawken
Percussion Rifle**

Navy Arms Mississippi Rifle

Navy Arms Mark I Hawken Percussion Rifle $240

Calibers: 50 or 54. Barrel: 26 inches; octagonal, precision rifled, "pre-straightened." Overall length: 43 inches. Weight: about 9 pounds. Fancy finger spur trigger guard. Blade front sight; rear sight with elevation leaf. American walnut stock. Discontinued 1986.

Navy Arms Mississippi Rifle Model 1841 . . . . $245

Caliber: 58 percussion. Barrel: 32½ inches. Overall length: 48½ inches. Weight: 9½ lbs. Walnut stock. Furnished in brass, including patchbox for tools and spare parts. Patterned after the rifle used by the Mississippi Regiment at the Battle of Buena Vista (1847) during the Mexican War.

Navy Arms Morse Muzzleloading Rifle . . $150

Calibers: 45, 50, or 58. Barrel: 26 inches; "pre-straightened" precision-rifled ordnance steel. Overall length: 41½ inches. Brass action. Oil-finished American walnut stock.

Navy Arms Parker-Hale Model 1853 Three-Band Musket $445

Caliber: 577. Barrel: 39 inches. Overall length: 55 inches. Weight: 9 pounds. Adjustable globe front and ladder-type rear sights with interchangeable leaves. Hand-checkered walnut stock.

Navy Arms Parker-Hale Model 1858 Two-Band Musket $415

Caliber: 577. Barrel: 33 inches. Overall length: 48½ inches. Weight: 8½ pounds. Globe front and ladder-type adjustable rear sights with interchangeable leaves. Hand-checkered walnut stock.

Navy Arms Parker-Hale Model 1861 Musketoon $335

Caliber: 577. Barrel: 24 inches. Overall length: 40¼ inches. Weight: 7½ pounds. Adjustable globe front and ladder-type rear sights with interchangeable leaves. Hand-checkered walnut stock.

Navy Arms Parker-Hale 451 Volunteer Rifle. $540

Caliber: 451. Barrel is rifled by the cold-forged method, making one turn in 20 inches. Weight: 9½ pounds. Sights are adjustable; globe front and ladder-type rear with interchangeable leaves. Hand-checkered walnut stock.

Navy Arms Morse Rifle

Navy Arms Parker-Hale 451 Volunteer Rifle

Navy Arms Remington-Style Rolling-Block Rifle

Navy Arms Rigby-Style Rifle

Navy Arms Remington-Style Rolling Block Rifle **$355**
Calibers: 45/70 and 50/70. Barrels: 18, 26, or 30 inches; full octagonal or half-round. Open sights. Drilled and tapped for Creedmoor sight.

Navy Arms Rigby-Style Target Rifle . . . **$450**
Caliber: 451. Barrel: 32 inches. Adjustable target front sight; adjustable vernier rear sight. Color case-hardened breech plug, hammer lock plate and escutcheons. Hand-checkered walnut stock.

Navy Arms Springfield 1863 Rifle **$410**
Caliber: 58. Barrel: 40 inches; 3-band, precision-rifled. Overall length: 56 inches. Weight: 9½ pounds. Walnut stock with polished metal lock and stock fittings. With bayonet and scabbard add $30.

Navy Arms Swiss Federal Target Rifle . . **$805**
Caliber: 45. Barrel: 31 inches. Overall length: 49 inches. Weight: 16¼ pounds. Adjustable rear peep sight. Adjustable five-lever, double-set trigger system. Walnut stock, color casehardened furniture. An exact replica of the Swiss target rifles used in European competitions during the 1880s. (*See* next page.)

Navy Arms Whitworth Military Target Rifle **$540**
Caliber: 451. Barrel: 36 inches; hexagonal bore with a pitch of 1 turn in 20 inches; cold-forged from ordnance steel. Weight: 9½ pounds. Globe front sight; open military target rifle rear sight has interchangeable blades. Walnut stock is hand-checkered.(*See* next page.)

Navy Arms Springfield 1863 Rifle

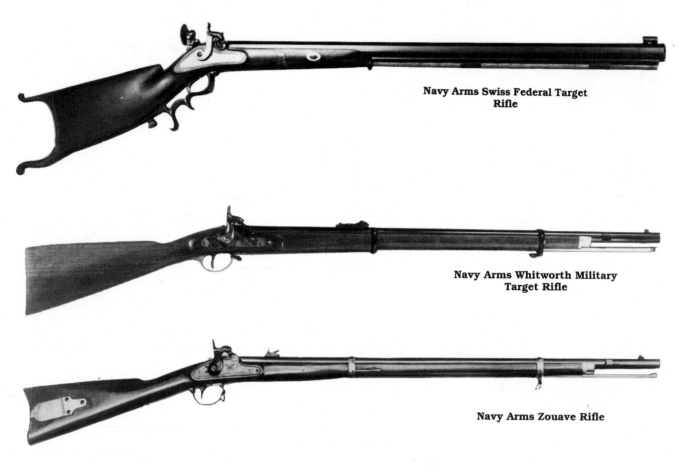

**Navy Arms Swiss Federal Target
Rifle**

**Navy Arms Whitworth Military
Target Rifle**

Navy Arms Zouave Rifle

Navy Arms Zouave Rifle **$240**
Military-style percussion rifle. Caliber: 58. Barrel:
32½ inches. Overall length: 48½ inches. Color casehardened lock. Blued barrel. Brass fitting and patchbox. Discontinued 1986.

**Navy Arms Classic Side-by-Side
Shotgun** **$325**
Gauge: 10 or 12. Barrels: 28 inches. Weight: 7 lbs. 12
oz. Color casehardened lock, plates and hammers. All
internal parts are steel. Hand-checkered walnut
stock. Blued barrel.

Navy Arms Fowler **$220**
Gauge: 12. Barrels: 28 inches; blued, cylinder bore.
Side-by-side. Overall length: 44½ inches. Weight:
7½ pounds. Bead front sight. Checkered stock, color
casehardened engraved locks.

Navy Arms Hunter Shotgun **$220**
Gauge: 20. Barrel: 28½ inches; round, chrome-lined.
Bead front sight. Walnut stock with checkering at
wrist and forend. Rubber butt pad. Engraved and
color casehardened percussion lock. Double-set triggers.

Navy Arms Fowler

Navy Arms Hunter Shotgun

Navy Arms Morse/Navy Percussion Shotgun

Navy Arms Model T & T Shotgun

Navy Arms Morse/Navy Single-Barrel Percussion Shotgun **$150**
Gauge: 12. Barrel: 26 inches. Overall length: 43 inches. Weight: 5 lbs. 12 oz. Brass receiver. Bead front sight. American walnut stock.

Navy Arms Model T & T Shotgun **$300**
Percussion. Barrels: 28 inches. Turkey and Trap side-by-side is choked full/full. Color casehardened locks. Checkered, oil-finished walnut stock.

NOTE

The Navy Arms manufacturing facilities have recently been moved to Martinsburg, West Virginia. However, they also maintain their New Jersey address.

SHILOH SHARPS
Big Timber, Montana

Originally of Farmingdale, New York, Shiloh has undergone a metamorphosis in ownership as many other companies in the firearms industry. Known for a number of years for their "Sharps Old Reliable" metallic cartridge rifles, they are now owned by C. Sharps Arms Co., Inc.

Shiloh Sharps Model 1863 Sporting Rifle. **$690**
Caliber: 54. Barrel: 30 inches; tapered octagonal. Weight: 9 pounds. Schnabel-style forend. Blade front sight; sporting rear sight with elevation leaf; optional Tang sight. Adjustable double-set triggers, curved trigger plate.

Shiloh Sharps Model 1863
Sporting Rifle

**Shiloh Sharps New Model 1863
Military Carbine**

**Shiloh Sharps New Model 1863
Military Rifle**

Shiloh Sharps New Model 1863 Military Carbine. $600
Calibers: 45, 50, and 54 (standard). Barrel: 22 inches, round. Weight: 8 lbs. 12 oz. Blade front sight; Lawrence rear sight with elevation leaf. Military forend with barrel band. Military-sight straight grip stock. Walnut finish.

Shiloh Sharps New Model 1863 Military Rifle $705
Calibers: 45, 50, and 54 (standard). Barrel: 30 inches, round, with 3 barrel bands. Weight: 8 lbs. 12 oz. Blade front sight; Lawrence rear sight with elevation leaf. Straight-grip, military-style buttstock. Steel buttplate and patchbox. Sling swivels.

Shiloh Sharps Model 1874 Business Rifle $635
Calibers: 45-70, 45-90, 45-120, 50-70, 50-90, 50-140. Barrel: 28 inches; heavy, tapered round. Weight: 9 lbs. 8 oz. Schnabel-style forend. Adjustable double-set triggers. Blade front sight; sporting rear sight with elevation leaf. Straight-grip buttstock oil-finished in American walnut. Dark blued barrel.

Shiloh Sharps Model 1874 Carbine. $650
Calibers: 45-70 and 45-90. Barrel: 24 inches, round. Weight: 8 lbs. 4 oz. Single trigger. Blade front sight; sporting rear sight. Straight-grip, oil-finished buttstock. Schnabel-style forend. Steel rifle buttplate. Dark blued barrel.

Shiloh Sharps Model 1874 Long-Range Express Sporting Rifle $810
Calibers: 45-70-2$\frac{1}{10}$", 45-90-2$\frac{4}{10}$", 45-100-2$\frac{6}{10}$", 45-110-2$\frac{7}{8}$", 45-120-3$\frac{1}{4}$", 50-110-2$\frac{1}{2}$", 50-140-3$\frac{1}{4}$". Barrel: 34 inches; medium-weight, tapered octagonal. Overall length: 51 inches. Weight: 10 lbs. 8 oz. Double-set triggers with adjustable set. Globe front sight; sporting Tang rear sight. Shotgun-style buttstock with pistol grip and cheek rest with accent line. Tapered forend with schnabel tip. Oil-finished American black walnut stock.

Shiloh Sharps Model 1874 Military Rifle . . $805
Calibers: 45-70 and 50-70. Barrel: 30 inches, round. Weight: 8 lbs. 2 oz. Blade front sight; Lawrence-style rear sight. Military-type forend with 3 barrel bands. Dark blued barrel. Oil-finished wood stock. Sling swivels.

**Shiloh Sharps Model 1874
Business Rifle**

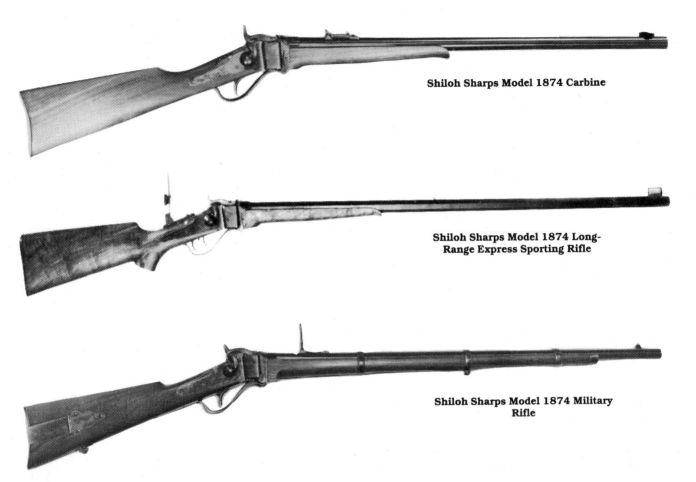

Shiloh Sharps Model 1874 Carbine

Shiloh Sharps Model 1874 Long-Range Express Sporting Rifle

Shiloh Sharps Model 1874 Military Rifle

Shiloh Sharps Model 1874 Sharps Saddle Rifle **$755**
Calibers: 45-50, 40-70 Sharps bottleneck, 45-70, 45-90. Barrel: 26 inches, tapered octagonal. Weight: 9 pounds. Double-set triggers. Blade front sight; sporting buckhorn rear sight. Straight-grip stock of select premium black walnut. Blued barrel.

Shiloh Sharps Model 1874 Sporting Rifle No. 1 . . . . **$795**
Calibers: 45-70, 45-9-, 45-120, 50-70, 50-90, 50-140. Barrel: 28 or 30 inches, tapered octagonal.

Weight: 9 lbs. 8 oz. Adjustable double-set triggers. Blade front sight; sporting rear sight with elevation leaf. Sporting schnabel-style forend. Pistol-grip shotgun-style buttstock of oil-finished American walnut. Blue-black barrel. (*See* next page.)

Shiloh Sharps Model 1874 Sporting Rifle No. 3 . . . . **$690**
Similar to the Sporting Rifle No. 1 in the same calibers. Differences are: 30-inch barrel; weight of 9 lbs. 12 oz; straight-grip stock with rifle buttplate; sporting Tang sight. (*See* next page.)

Shiloh Sharps Model 1874 Sharps Saddle Rifle

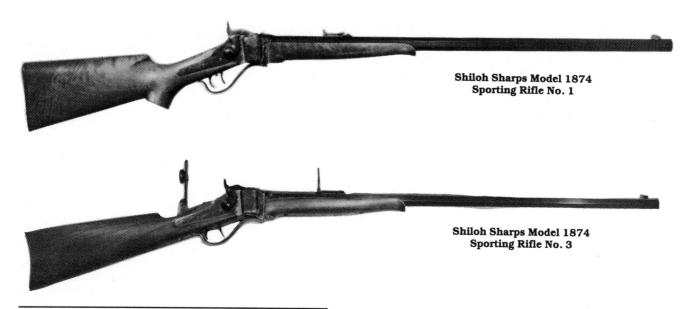

Shiloh Sharps Model 1874
Sporting Rifle No. 1

Shiloh Sharps Model 1874
Sporting Rifle No. 3

STOEGER INDUSTRIES
South Hackensack, New Jersey

Stoeger Industries began in 1918 as A. F. Stoeger, Inc., of New York City. Established by Austrian-born Alexander Stoeger, the firm distributed a wide variety of sporting arms produced by both foreign and domestic manufacturers. Stoeger for many years was the exclusive import agent of Luger pistols into the U.S. and Canada and, in fact, the company actually owns the Luger name. Stoeger's offerings expanded to include ammunition, accessories, gun parts and the famous "Stogerol," a multi-purpose solvent, cleaner and lubricant. The company became the Stoeger Arms Corporation and it publicized its wares in the "Stoeger Catalog," which first appeared in 1924. Through the years the book evolved into the best-selling Shooter's Bible, containing the same successful ingredients that has made "Stoeger" a household word among gun enthusiasts.

The company relocated several times and finally settled in northeastern New Jersey in 1962, after which time its name eventually changed to the more encompassing Stoeger Industries. As "America's Great Gun House," Stoeger was one of the first to distribute blackpowder replica arms and did so until the late 1960s.

HANDGUNS

Stoeger Brown Bess Flintlock Pistol . . . $155
Flintlock. Caliber: 65. Barrel: 9 inches, round. Overall length: 15½ inches. Weight: 2 lbs. 15 oz. Polished steel surfaces on side plates. Brass trigger guard, buttplate and ramrod brackets. Walnut-finished mahogany stock. Made during 1960s.

Stoeger Kentuckian Flintlock Pistol. . . . $190
Casehardened and engraved flintlock action. Caliber: 44. Barrel: 9½ inches, octagonal. Overall length: 15¼ inches. Weight: 40 ounces. Brass front sight; blued steel rear sight. Single-piece select walnut stock. Solid brass trigger guard and barrel cap; brass ramrod tip and ramrod holders. Made during 1960s.

Stoeger Kentuckian Percussion Pistol . . $195
Same general specifications as the Kentuckian flintlock version, except has percussion lock. Made from 1966 to 1968.

Stoeger Renegade Double-Barrel Percussion Pistol $170
Casehardened frame with engraved side plates and hammers. Calibers: 36 or 44. Barrel: 8¼ inches. Overall length: 13¼ inches. Weight: 31½ ounces. Double triggers. Engraved brass trigger guard and butt cap. Wooden ramrod with brass tip. Single-piece select walnut stock. Blued steel barrel. Made during 1960s.

LONG ARMS

Stoeger Buccaneer Gun $240
Model 4910. Flintlock. Caliber: 12 bore. Barrel: 51 inches, round. Weight: 9 lbs. 3 oz. Fixed front sight. Red-painted walnut stock. Assembled with antique locks of the Napoleonic Wars. Distributed by Stoeger from the mid-1900s to about 1968.

Stoeger Double-Barrel Flintlock Shotgun $430
Model 5033. Double flintlocks. Gauge: 14. Barrels: 31 inches. Weight: 6 lbs. 14 oz. Front bead sight. Walnut stock and forend. Distributed by Stoeger from the mid-1900s to about 1968.

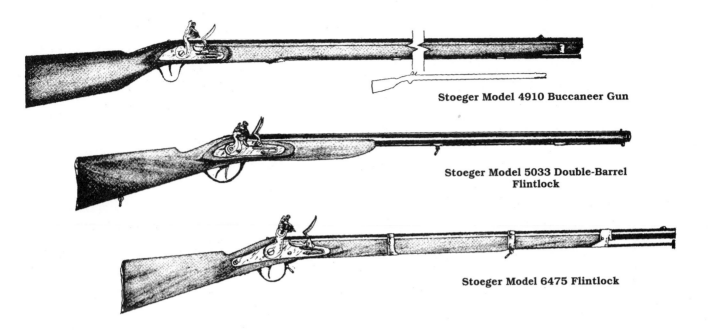

Stoeger Model 4910 Buccaneer Gun

Stoeger Model 5033 Double-Barrel Flintlock

Stoeger Model 6475 Flintlock

Stoeger Elephant Flintlock Gun **$240**
Model 6494. Flintlock. Gauge: 4. Barrel: 34 inches, round. Weight: 9 lbs. 14 oz. Distributed by Stoeger from the mid-1900s to about 1968.

Stoeger Flintlock Shotgun Model 4957B . . **$240**
Gauge: 14. Barrel: 33 inches, round. Weight: 6 pounds. Checkered walnut stock. Polished iron fittings. Distributed by Stoeger from the mid-1900s to about 1968.

**Stoeger Flintlock Shotgun
Model 6475W** **$210**
Gauge: 14. Barrel: 36 inches, round. Weight: 7 lbs. 8 oz. Checkered walnut stock. Distributed by Stoeger from the mid-1900s to about 1968.

Stoeger Single-Shot Flintlock Shotgun . . . **$200**
Model 6475. Flintlock. Gauge: 14. Barrel: 36 inches, round. Weight: $8\frac{1}{2}$ pounds. Front bead sight. Quality walnut stock. Distributed by Stoeger from the mid-1900s to about 1968.

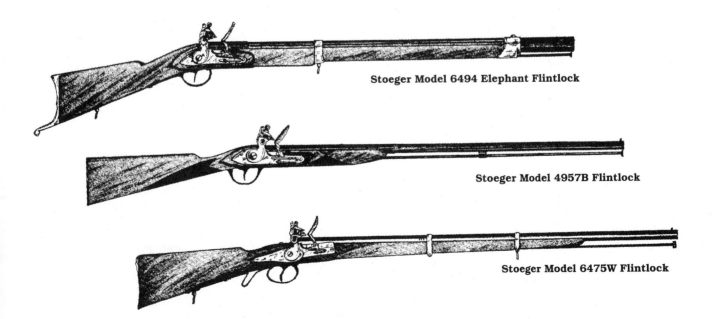

Stoeger Model 6494 Elephant Flintlock

Stoeger Model 4957B Flintlock

Stoeger Model 6475W Flintlock

STURM, RUGER & COMPANY, INC.
Southport, Connecticut

Sturm, Ruger entered into the firearms manufacturing industry shortly after World War II, and achieved remarkable success with its .22 rimfire autoloaders and single-action revolvers. With a track record of advanced design capabilities coupled with moderate pricing standards, it was no surprise that after a while they ventured into the blackpowder reproduction arena.

The Ruger Old Army Cap and Ball Revolver is an adaptation of the Ruger Black Hawk SA revolver, with the original design changed to percussion ignition and a loading lever added. It is probably the only modern-design percussion revolver in existence, and is considered to be far superior in both strength and design to any original-design replicas currently under manufacture.

**Ruger Old Army Cap & Ball
Revolver**

Ruger Old Army Cap and Ball Revolver . . $175
Percussion ignition. Caliber: 44 (.443-inch bore; .451-inch groove). Six-shot cylinder. Barrel: 7½ inches; six grooves; right twist, 1 in 16 inches. Weight: 46 ounces. Adjustable rear target sight; ramp front sight. Stainless steel nipples. American walnut grips. Finish: polished all over; blued and anodized.

**Ruger Old Army Cap & Ball
Revolver—Stainless**

**Ruger Old Army Cap and Ball Stainless
Revolver. $250**
Same general specifications as blued model, except all metal is stainless steel.

THOMPSON/CENTER ARMS
Rochester, New Hampshire

A division of the K. W. Thompson Tool Company, Inc., Thompson/Center Arms boasts its own modern investment casting foundry plus a complete gunmaking facility. The firm is well-known for its "Contender" pistol, a long-range, high-power handgun that has been popular with hunters for about 20 years. The following listing shows the quality muzzleloaders they also produce.

Thompson/Center Patriot Pistol $225
Caliber: 45 percussion. Barrel: 9 inches; octagonal, 13/16 inch across the flats. Weight: 36 ounces. Color casehardened lock with dolphin-shaped hammer. Hooked breech. Double-set triggers. Adjustable Patridge-type target rear sight. Engraved solid brass trim. Select American black walnut stock. Patterned after traditional dueling pistols. See photo, opposite.

LONG ARMS

**Thompson/Center Cherokee Caplock
Rifle. $250**
Calibers: 32, 36 or 45 percussion. Barrel: 24 inches; octagonal, 13/16 inch across the flats. Weight: about 6 pounds. Adjustable double-set triggers. Open hunting-style adjustable sights. Solid brass trim. Select American walnut stock with contoured cheekpiece on left-hand side. Patterned after an early New England hunting rifle.

Thompson/Center Cougar Hawken Rifle . . $380
Caplock percussion presentation grade. Caliber: 50. Barrel: 28 inches, octagonal. Pewter-like stainless steel furniture; hammer, lock, buttplate, double triggers, trigger guard, forend cap and thimbles. Stock of finest grade American black walnut has stainless steel medallion of cougar inletted on right side.

**Thompson/Center Hawken Caplock
Percussion Rifle. $300**
Color casehardened percussion lock. Calibers: 45, 50 or 54. Barrel: 28 inches; octagonal, 15/16 inch or 1 inch (54 cal.) across the flats. Hooked breech. Adjustable double-set triggers. Open hunting sights. Solid brass trim. Stock of select American black walnut with left-side cheekpiece. Patterned after the American rifles of the early 1800s. See photo, opposite.

**Thompson/Center Hawken Flintlock
Rifle. $315**
Same general specifications as Hawken Percussion model, except with flintlock ignition system in 50 caliber. See photo, opposite.

**Thompson/Center Patriot
Percussion Pistol**

Patterned after traditional dueling pistols, this
45-caliber Patriot — enhanced by modern
technology — retains all the character of an
authentic antique arm.

**Thompson/Center Cherokee
Caplock Rifle**

**Thompson/Center Cougar Hawken
Rifle**

**Thompson/Center Hawken
Caplock Percussion Rifle**

**Thompson/Center Renegade
Caplock Percussion Rifle**

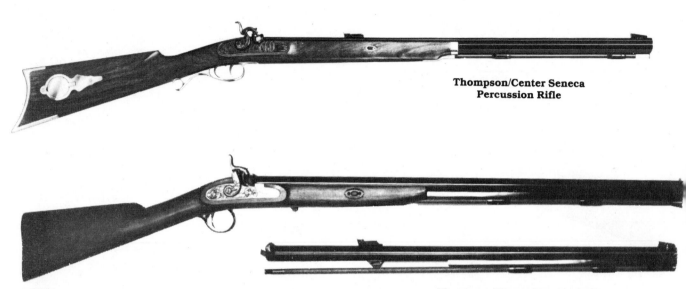

**Thompson/Center Seneca
Percussion Rifle**

**Thompson/Center New Englander
Shotgun**

Thompson/Center New Englander Percussion Rifle **$190**
Caliber: 50 percussion. Barrel: 26 inches, round; rifled one turn in 48 inches. Weight: 7 lbs. 15 oz. Adjustable iron sights. Straight-grip stock of select American black walnut. Blued barrel.

Thompson/Center Renegade Caplock Percussion Rifle **$245**
Caplock percussion rifle made of modern steel with investment cast parts. Calibers: 50 or 54. Barrel: 26 inches; octagonal, 1 inch across the flats; precision-rifled carbine-style. Weight: about 8 pounds. Hooked breech system. Coil spring lock with engraved lock plate and hammer. Double-set triggers. Adjustable Patridge-style hunting sights. Select American black walnut stock.

Thompson/Center Renegade Flintlock Rifle **$270**
Same general specifications as Renegade Percussion model, except with flintlock ignition system in 50 caliber.

Thompson/Center Renegade Musket . . **$250**
Same general specifications as Renegade Caplock Percussion Rifle, except available in 56 caliber with 26-inch smoothbore musket barrel.

Thompson/Center Renegade Single-Trigger Hunter Rifle **$230**
Same general specifications as Renegade Caplock Percussion Rifle, except available in 50 caliber with single trigger and shotgun-style trigger guard.

Thompson/Center Seneca Percussion Rifle **$290**
Patterned after early New England hunting rifles, but made with color casehardened lock. Calibers: 36 or 45 percussion. Octagonal barrel. Weight: about 6 pounds. Hooked breech. Double-set triggers. Adjustable hunting sights. Solid brass trim. Select American walnut stock.

Thompson/Center New Englander Shotgun **$190**
Gauge: 12 percussion. Barrel: 28 inches, round, with improved cylinder choke. Weight: 6 lbs. 8 oz. Hooked breech system. Color casehardened coil spring lock. Blued steel finish. Straight-grip stock of select American black walnut.

TRADITIONS, INC.
Deep River, Connecticut

In addition to muzzleloading replicas, Traditions also offers pistol and rifle kits and blackpowder accessories.

Traditions Trapper Pistol **$95**
Calibers: 36, 45 or 50. Barrel: 10 inches; octagonal, $7/8$ inch across the flats. Overall length: $14^3/4$ inches. Weight: $3^1/4$ lbs. Adjustable sear-engagement percussion lock with fly and bridle. Double-set triggers. Blade front sight; adjustable rear sight. Blued barrel. Select hardwood stock. Brass furniture, including finger spur trigger guard.

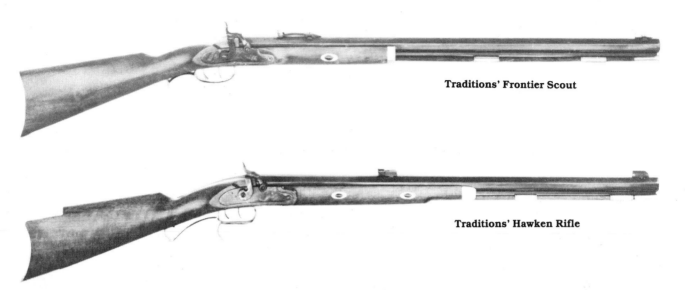

Traditions' Frontier Scout

Traditions' Hawken Rifle

LONG ARMS

Traditions Frontier Carbine

Calibers: 45 or 50. Flintlock or percussion. Barrel: octagonal, $^{15}/_{16}$ inch across the flats; rifled one turn in 66 inches. Overall length: 40 inches. Weight: 6 lbs. 7 oz. Double-set triggers. Hooked breech. Dovetailed blade front sight; Patridge-style open rear. Solid brass furniture. Blued steel. Select hardwood stock.
Flintlock **$180**
Percussion. **165**

Traditions Frontier Rifle

Same general specifications as Frontier Carbine, except overall length is 44 inches and weight is 6 lbs. 14 oz.
Flintlock **$180**
Percussion. **165**

Traditions Frontier Scout

Same general specifications as the Frontier Rifle, except has shorter trigger pull and shortened stock; barrel is 26 inches long, overall length 40 inches, weight 5 lbs. 8 oz., fully adjustable rear sight.
Flintlock **$155**
Percussion. **140**

Traditions Hawken Rifle. **$235**

Calibers: 50, 54, or 58 percussion. Barrel: $32^{1}/_{4}$ inches; octagonal, 1 inch across the flats, rifled 1 turn in 66 inches. Overall length: $49^{1}/_{2}$ inches. Weight: 9 lbs. 2 oz. Hooked breech. Double-set triggers. Authentic Hawken-style trigger guard with finger spur. Dovetailed blade front sight; Patridge-style open rear. Solid brass furniture. Blued steel. Walnut stock with beavertail cheekpiece.

Traditions Hunter Rifle **$235**

Calibers: 50 or 54. Percussion lock with adjustable sear engagement. Barrel: 28 inches; octagonal, 1 inch across the flats, rifled one turn in 66 inches. Overall length: 44 inches. Weight: 8 lbs. 10 oz. Hooked breech. Double-set triggers. Dovetailed blade front sight; Patridge-style open rear. Black-chromed brass with German silver wedge plates and stock ornaments. Walnut stock with contoured beavertail cheekpiece.

Traditions Kentucky Scout Rifle **$130**

Calibers: 45 or 50. Percussion lock with adjustable sear engagement. Barrel: 26 inches; octagonal, $^{7}/_{8}$ inch across the flats, rifled one turn in 66 inches. Overall length: 40 inches. Weight: $5^{1}/_{2}$ pounds. Double-set triggers. Blade front sight; adjustable rear sight. Solid brass furniture. Blued steel. Select hardwood stock. (*See* next page.)

Traditions' Hunter Rifle

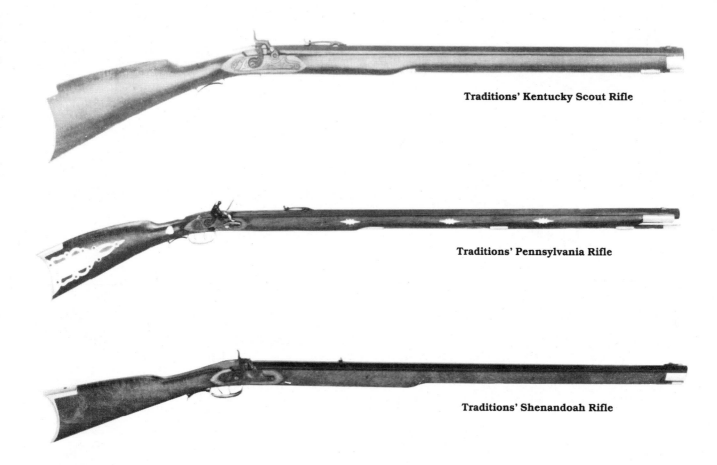

Traditions' Kentucky Scout Rifle

Traditions' Pennsylvania Rifle

Traditions' Shenandoah Rifle

Traditions Pennsylvania Rifle

A handsomely reproduced rifle, approved for Revolutionary War reenactment groups. Calibers: 45 or 50. Flintlock or percussion. Barrel: 40½ inches; octagonal, ⅞ inch across the flats, rifled one turn in 66 inches. Overall length: 57 inches. Weight: 9 lbs. 13 oz. Double-set triggers. Blade front sight; adjustable rear. Solid brass furniture, including patchbox. Blued steel. Select hardwood stock with beavertail-style cheekpiece.

Flintlock **$275**
Percussion. **265**

Traditions Shenandoah Rifle

Reproduction of the 18th-century hunting rifle. Caliber: 50. Flintlock or percussion. Barrel: 33½ inches; octagonal, ⅞ inch across the flats, rifled one turn in

66 inches. Overall length: 48 inches. Weight: 7¼ pounds. Color casehardened lock with V-type mainspring. Double-set triggers. Solid brass furniture. Blade front sight; fixed rear. One-piece, select hardwood stock.

Flintlock **$185**
Percussion **175**

Traditions Fowler Shotgun **$230**

American adaptation of the classic English fowler. Gauge: 12. Barrel: 28 or 32 inches; octagonal tapered to round. Overall length: 48¼ inches. Weight: 5 lbs. 6 oz. V-type mainspring lock with color casehardened lock plate. Brass bead front sight. German silver wedge plate. Blued trigger guard, tang and buttplate. Fine-grained walnut stock checkered at the wrist.

CHAPTER FIVE
OBSOLETE CARTRIDGES

Most antique cartridge collections probably evolved by the accumulation of odds and ends that accompanied collector firearms. For example, a collector purchases a Winchester Model 1886 Rifle chambered for .40-82 Winchester. Along with this rifle comes a partial box of original factory-loaded ammunition. Later the gun is sold or traded, but the cartridges remain. Another arm is purchased, say, a Remington Rolling Block Single-Shot Rifle chambered for the Remington .44-100-500 cartridge. Again, a few cartridges are included in the deal. Eventually, after several purchases of this nature, the collector has what might be called a cartridge collection, which grew more or less by accident. The collection continues to expand in a generalized fashion, now more deliberately, but still without much purpose or reason; anything that seems collectible is thrown into the collection.

If enough interest exists, the collector will probably start specializing in one area of cartridge collecting: for example, by brand, country of origin, caliber, or perhaps in military ammunition. The study of only one small group of cartridges will reveal all kinds of information previously unknown to the collector. He will learn facts that will help him identify headstamps, case metals, bullet shapes and designs, just to name a few.

At this point, the cartridge collector will start looking for the best ways to catalog and store the collection, build up trading stock, maintain the collection, and similar details. He or she will also be looking for methods of evaluating the worth of the collections.

Not too many years ago, obsolete cartridges of all types could be found in attics, basements, at flea markets, gun shows, and other places...all for a relatively reasonable price. However, many of the early obsolete cartridges have risen in price to the point where many beginning collectors are eliminated at the outset. The investment required to purchase and maintain such a collection can be very discouraging to the would-be collector. Still, these rare specimens will be found from time to time, and rather than collect them, the finder may wish to sell them to an established cartridge collector.

The prices that follow are based on the average value of a single cartridge of original factory loaded ammunition in good, clean condition. Fired cases also have some collector value, which is usually considered to be about 20 percent of the value shown for the loaded case of the more common cartridges, and up to 80 percent of the value shown for the more rare cases. These prices are considered to be the replacement value of each round, and also what a collector might be willing to pay for the round. However, when selling large lots of ammo or when selling to a dealer, the buyer will usually expect a discount of somewhere between 25 and 50 percent.

Full boxes of loaded factory ammunition usually command a premium, since full boxes (especially those that are sealed) are becoming more difficult to find, and also because the box itself often has collector value.

This cartridge section is grouped as follows:

	Page No.
Centerfire Rifle Cartridges	**285**
Obsolete Metric Cartridges	**298**
Rimfire Cartridges	**300**
Shotshells	**303**

CENTERFIRE RIFLE CARTRIDGES

.219 Winchester Zipper $1.75
Bullet Diameter: .224 inch
Bullet Weight: 56 grains
Muzzle Velocity: 3110 fps
Case Length: 1.94 inches
Neck Diameter: .252 inch
Shoulder Diameter: .364 inch
Base Diameter: .421 inch
Rim Diameter: .497 inch
Overall Length: 2.26 inches
Manufactured from 1936 to 1962.

.22 Savage High-Power $1.75
Bullet Diameter: .228 inch
Bullet Weight: 70 grains
Muzzle Velocity: 2800 fps
Case Length: 2.05 inches
Neck Diameter: .252 inch
Shoulder Diameter: .360 inch
Base Diameter: .416 inch
Rim Diameter: .500 inch
Overall Length: 2.51 inches
Made from 1912 to 1936. Reintroduced in recent years by Norma.

.22 Winchester Centerfire $1.25
Bullet Diameter: .228 inch
Bullet Weight: 45 grains
Muzzle Velocity: about 1500 fps
Case Length: 1.39 inches
Neck Diameter: .241 inch
Shoulder Diameter: .278 inch
Base Diameter: .295 inch
Rim Diameter: .342 inch
Overall Length: 1.61 inches
Made from 1885 to 1936.

.22 Extra Long Maynard (.22-8 Model 1882) $2.25
Bullet Diameter: .228 inch
Bullet Weight: 45 grains
Muzzle Velocity: about 1100 fps
Case Length: 1.17 inches
Neck Diameter: .252 inch
Shoulder Diameter: Straight
Base Diameter: .252 inch
Rim Diameter: .310 inch
Overall Length: 1.41 inches
Made for the Model 1882 Maynard Rifle.

.22-8 Maynard (1873) . . $20.00
Same general specifications as .22 Extra Long Maynard, above, except has large Maynard rim, typical of the 1873 cartridges.

.22-15-60 Stevens $5.25
Bullet Diameter: .226 inch
Bullet Weight: 60 grains
Muzzle Velocity: about 1150 fps
Case Length: 2.01 inches
Neck Diameter: .243 inch
Shoulder Diameter: Straight
Base Diameter: .265 inch
Rim Diameter: .342 inch
Overall Length: 2.26 inches
Introduced in 1896.

.236 Navy $10.00
Bullet Diameter: .244 inch
Bullet Weight: 112 grains
Muzzle Velocity: 2560 fps

.236 Navy (cont.)
Case Length: 2.35 inches
Neck Diameter: .278 inch
Shoulder Diameter: .402 inch
Base Diameter: .445
Rim Diameter: .448 inch
Overall Length: 3.11 inches
Manufactured 1895 to 1935.

.25 Remington . . . . . . $ 1.75
Bullet Diameter: .257 inch
Bullet Weight: 100 and 117 grains
Muzzle Velocity: 2330 and 2125 fps, respectively
Case Length: 2.04 inches
Neck Diameter: .280 inch
Shoulder Diameter: .355 inch
Base Diameter: .420 inch
Rim Diameter: .421 inch
Overall Length: 2.54 inches
Made from 1906 to about 1952.

.25-20 Single Shot $1.50
Bullet Diameter: .257 inch
Bullet Weight: 86 grains
Muzzle Velocity: 1410 fps
Case Length: 1.63 inches
Neck Diameter: .275 inch
Shoulder Diameter: .296 inch
Base Diameter: .315 inch
Rim Diameter: .378 inch
Overall Length: 1.9 inches
Made from 1882 to 1936.

.25-21 Stevens $4.25
Bullet Diameter: .257 inch
Bullet Weight: 86 grains
Muzzle Velocity: 1470 fps
Case Length: 2.05 inches
Neck Diameter: .280 inch
Shoulder Diameter: Straight
Base Diameter: .300 inch
Rim Diameter: .376 inch
Overall Length: 2.30 inches
Introduced in 1897.

.25-25 Stevens **$5.75**
Bullet Diameter: .257 inch
Bullet Weight: 86 grains
Muzzle Velocity: 1500 fps
Case Length: 2.37 inches
Neck Diameter: .282 inch
Shoulder Diameter: Straight
Base Diameter: .323 inch
Rim Diameter: .376 inch
Overall Length: 2.63 inches
Introduced about 1895.

.25-36 Marlin. **$3.50**
Bullet Diameter: .257 inch
Bullet Weight: 117 grains
Muzzle Velocity: 1855 fps
Case Length: 2.12 inches
Neck Diameter: .281 inch
Shoulder Diameter: .358 inch
Base Diameter: .416 inch
Rim Diameter: .499 inch
Overall Length: 2.50 inches
Made from 1895 to 1922.

.256 Newton **$3.95**
Bullet Diameter: .264 inch
Bullet Weight: 129 grains
Muzzle Velocity: 2760 fps
Case Length: 2.44 inches
Neck Diameter: .290 inch
Shoulder Diameter: .430 inch
Base Diameter: .469
Rim Diameter: .473 inch
Overall Length: 3.40 inches
Manufactured from 1913 to
    1938.

.275 H&H Magnum . . . **$6.50**
Bullet Diameter: .284 inch
Bullet Weight: 140 and 175 grains
Muzzle Velocity: 2660 fps
Case Length: 2.50 inches

.275 H&H Magnum (cont.)
Neck Diameter: .290 inch
Shoulder Diameter: .375 inch
Base Diameter: .513 inch
Rim Diameter: .532 inch
Overall Length: 3.30 inches
Made from 1912 to 1939.

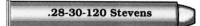

.28-30-120 Stevens . . . **$6.75**
Bullet Diameter: .285 inch
Bullet Weight: 120 grains
Muzzle Velocity: 1500 fps
Case Length: 2.51 inches
Neck Diameter: .309 inch
Shoulder Diameter: Straight
Base Diameter: .357 inch
Rim Diameter: .412 inch
Overall Length: 2.82 inches
Made from 1900 to 1918.

.30 Newton. **$4.25**
Bullet Diameter: .308 inch
Bullet Weight: 180 grains
Muzzle Velocity: 2860 fps
Case Length: 2.52 inches
Neck Diameter: .340 inch
Shoulder Diameter: .491 inch
Base Diameter: .523 inch
Rim Diameter: .525 inch
Overall Length: 3.35 inches
Made from 1913 to 1938.

.30-30 Wesson **$40.00**
Bullet Diameter: .308 inch
Bullet Weight: 165 grains
Muzzle Velocity: 1250 fps
Case Length: 1.66 inches
Neck Diameter: .329 inch
Shoulder Diameter: .330 inch
Base Diameter: .380 inch
Rim Diameter: .440 inch
Overall Length: 2.50 inches
Made from 1881 to 1917.

.30-40 Wesson **$42.00**
Bullet Diameter: .308 inch
Bullet Weight: 170 grains
Muzzle Velocity: 1700 fps
Case Length: 1.63 inch
Neck Diameter: .329 inch
Shoulder Diameter: .381 inch
Base Diameter: .377 inch
Rim Diameter: .436 inch
Overall Length: 2.39 inches
Made from 1880 to the 1890s.

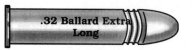

.32 Ballard Extra Long . . **$2.00**
Bullet Diameter: .317 inch
Bullet Weight: 115 grains
Muzzle Velocity: 1200 fps
Case Length: 1.24 inches
Neck Diameter: .318 inch
Shoulder Diameter: Straight
Base Diameter: .321 inch
Rim Diameter: .369 inch
Overall Length: 1.80 inches
Made from 1879 to 1920.

.32 Ideal **$2.50**
Bullet Diameter: .323 inch
Bullet Weight: 150 grains
Muzzle Velocity: 250 fps
Case Length: 1.77 inches
Neck Diameter: .344 inch
Shoulder Diameter: Straight
Base Diameter: .348 inch
Rim Diameter: .411 inches
Overall Length: 2.25 inches
Made from 1903 to 1936.

.32 Long **$7.00**
Bullet Diameter: .317 inch
Bullet Weight: 85 grains
Muzzle Velocity: 875 fps
Case Length: .82 inch
Neck Diameter: .318 inch
Shoulder Diameter: Straight
Base Diameter: .321 inch
Rim Diameter: .369 inch
Overall Length: 1.35 inches
Made from 1875 to about 1900.

.32 Remington. **$1.75**
Bullet Diameter: .320 inch
Bullet Weight: 170 grains
Muzzle Velocity: 2220 fps
Case Length: 2.04 inches
Neck Diameter: .344 inch
Shoulder Diameter: .396 inch
Base Diameter: .420 inch
Rim Diameter: .421 inch
Overall Length: 2.57 inches
Made from 1906 to the 1970s.

**.32 Winchester
Self-Loading** **$1.00**
Bullet Diameter: .320 inch
Bullet Weight: 165 grains
Muzzle Velocity: 1400 fps
Case Length: 1.28 inches
Neck Diameter: .343 inch
Shoulder Diameter: Straight
Base Diameter: .346 inch
Rim Diameter: .388 inch
Overall Length: 1.88 inches
Made from 1905 to the 1920s.

.32-30 Remington **$6.50**
Bullet Diameter: .312 inch
Bullet Weight: 125 grains
Muzzle Velocity: 1380 fps
Case Length: 1.64 inches
Neck Diameter: .332 inch
Shoulder Diameter: .357 inch
Base Diameter: .378 inch
Rim Diameter: .437 inch
Overall Length: 2.01 inches
Manufactured from 1884 to
   1912.

**.32-35 Stevens
(Maynard)** **$7.50**
Bullet Diameter: .312 inch
Bullet Weight: 165 grains
Muzzle Velocity: 1400 fps
Case Length: 1.88 inches
Neck Diameter: .339 inch
Shoulder Diameter: Straight
Base Diameter: .402 inch
Rim Diameter: .503 inch
Overall Length: 2.29 inches
Made from 1885 to 1936.

.32-40 Bullard **$6.00**
Bullet Diameter: .315 inch
Bullet Weight: 150 grains
Muzzle Velocity: 1495 fps
Case Length: 1.85 inches
Neck Diameter: .332 inch
Shoulder Diameter: .413 inch
Base Diameter: .453 inch
Rim Diameter: .510 inch
Overall Length: 2.26 inches
Made from 1886 to 1900.

.32-40 Remington **$3.50**
Bullet Diameter: .309 inch
Bullet Weight: 150 grains
Muzzle Velocity: 1350 fps
Case Length: 2.13 inches
Neck Diameter: .330 inch
Shoulder Diameter: .358 inch
Base Diameter: .453 inch
Rim Diameter: .535 inch
Overall Length: 3.25 inches
Made from 1870 to 1911.

.32-40 Winchester **$1.25**
Bullet Diameter: .320 inch
Bullet Weight: 165 grains
Muzzle Velocity: 1440 fps
Case Length: 2.13 inches

.32-40 Winchester (cont.)
Neck Diameter: .338 inch
Shoulder Diameter: Straight
Base Diameter: .424 inch
Rim Diameter: .506 inch
Overall Length: 2.59 inches
Made from 1884 to 1953.

.33 Winchester **$2.25**
Bullet Diameter: .338 inch
Bullet Weight: 200 grains
Muzzle Velocity: 2200 fps
Case Length: 2.11 inches
Neck Diameter: .365 inch
Shoulder Diameter: .443 inch
Base Diameter: .508 inch
Rim Diameter: .610 inch
Overall Length: 2.80 inches
Made from 1902 to 1940.

.35 Newton **$8.25**
Bullet Diameter: .358 inch
Bullet Weight: 250 grains
Muzzle Velocity: 2660 fps
Case Length: 2.52 inches
Neck Diameter: .383 inch
Shoulder Diameter: .498 inch
Base Diameter: .523 inch
Rim Diameter: .525 inch
Overall Length: 3.35 inches
Manufactured 1915 to 1936.

.35 Winchester **$3.50**
Bullet Diameter: .358 inch
Bullet Weight: 250 grains
Muzzle Velocity: 2200 fps
Case Length: 2.41 inches
Neck Diameter: .378 inch
Shoulder Diameter: .412 inch
Base Diameter: .457 inch
Rim Diameter: .539 inch
Overall Length: 3.16 inches
Manufactured 1903 to 1962.

.35 Winchester Self-Loading $1.60
Bullet Diameter: .351 inch
Bullet Weight: 180 grains
Muzzle Velocity: 1450 fps
Case Length: 1.14 inches
Neck Diameter: .374 inch
Shoulder Diameter: Straight
Base Diameter: .378 inch
Rim Diameter: .405 inch
Overall Length: 1.64 inches
Manufactured 1905 to 1922.

.35-30 Maynard Model 1865 . . . . $42.00
Same general specifications as Model 1873, except for rim size and ignition system.

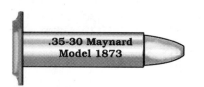

.35-30 Maynard Model 1873 . . . . $24.00
Same general specifications as Model 1882, except for large 1873 rim.

.35-30 Maynard Model 1882 . . . . $10.50
Bullet Diameter: .359 inch
Bullet Weight: 250 grains
Muzzle Velocity: 1280 fps
Case Length: 1.63 inches
Neck Diameter: .395 inch
Shoulder Diameter: Straight
Base Diameter: .400 inch
Rim Diameter: .494 inch
Overall Length: 2.03 inches
Made from 1882 to about 1900.

.35-40 Maynard Model 1873 . . . . $40.00
Bullet Diameter: .360 inch
Bullet Weight: 250 grains
Muzzle Velocity: 1200 fps
Case Length: 2.10 inches
Neck Diameter: .390 inch
Shoulder Diameter: Straight
Base Diameter: .403 inch
Rim Diameter: .764 inch
Overall Length: 2.57 inches
Made from 1873 to 1882.

.35-40 Maynard Model 1882 . . . . $20.00
Bullet Diameter: .360 inch
Bullet Weight: 250 grains
Muzzle Velocity: 1350 fps
Case Length: 2.06 inches
Neck Diameter: .395 inch
Shoulder Diameter: Straight
Base Diameter: .400
Rim Diameter: .492 inch
Overall Length: 2.53 inches
Made from 1882 to about 1900.

.38 Ballard, Extra Long . . $3.00
Bullet Diameter: .375 inch
Bullet Weight: 146 grains
Muzzle Velocity: 1275 fps
Case Length: 1.63 inches
Neck Diameter: .378 inch
Shoulder Diameter: Straight
Base Diameter: .379 inch
Rim Diameter: .441 inch
Overall Length: 2.06 inches
Introduced in 1885.

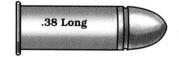

.38 Long Centerfire $1.75
Bullet Diameter: .375 inch
Bullet Weight: 150 grains
Muzzle Velocity: 1050 fps
Case Length: 1.03 inches
Neck Diameter: .378 inch
Shoulder Diameter: Straight
Base Diameter: .379 inch
Rim Diameter: .441 inch
Overall Length: 1.45 inches
Made from 1875 to 1900.

.38-35 Stevens $7.00
Bullet Diameter: .375 inch
Bullet Weight: 215 grains
Muzzle Velocity: 1255 fps
Case Length: 1.62 inches
Neck Diameter: .402 inch
Shoulder Diameter: Straight
Base Diameter: .403 inch
Rim Diameter: .492 inch
Overall Length: 2.43 inches
Manufactured from 1875 to 1890.

.38-40 Remington-Hepburn $5.25
Bullet Diameter: .372 inch
Bullet Weight: 245 grains
Muzzle Velocity: 1200 fps
Case Length: 1.77 inches
Neck Diameter: .395 inch
Shoulder Diameter: Straight
Base Diameter: .454
Rim Diameter: .537 inch
Overall Length: 2.32 inches
Introduced in 1875.

.38-45 Bullard $11.50
Bullet Diameter: .373 inch
Bullet Weight: 190 grains
Muzzle Velocity: 1390 fps
Case Length: 1.80 inches
Neck Diameter: .397 inch
Shoulder Diameter: .448 inch
Base Diameter: .454 inch
Rim Diameter: .526 inch
Overall Length: 2.26 inches
Introduced in 1887.
See top of next page.

.38-45 Stevens **$8.00**
Bullet Diameter: .363 inch
Bullet Weight: 210 grains
Muzzle Velocity: 1420 fps
Case Length: 1.76 inches
Neck Diameter: .395 inch
Shoulder Diameter: Straight
Base Diameter: .455 inch
Rim Diameter: .522 inch
Overall Length: 2.24 inches
Manufactured from 1875 to the
  1880s.

.38-50 Ballard **$8.50**
Bullet Diameter: .376 inch
Bullet Weight: 255 grains
Muzzle Velocity: 1321 fps
Case Length: 2.0 inches
Neck Diameter: .395 inch
Shoulder Diameter: Straight
Base Diameter: .425 inch
Rim Diameter: .502 inch
Overall Length: 2.72 inches
Manufactured from 1876 to
  1884.

**.38-50 Maynard
Model 1882** **$18.00**
Bullet Diameter: .375 inch
Bullet Weight: 255 grains
Muzzle Velocity: 1325 fps
Case Length: 1.97 inches
Neck Diameter: .415 inch
Shoulder Diameter: Straight
Base Diameter: .421 inch
Rim Diameter: .500 inch
Overall Length: 2.38 inches
Introduced in 1882.

**.38-50 Remington-
Hepburn** **$5.00**
Bullet Diameter: .376 inch
Bullet Weight: 255 grains
Muzzle Velocity: 1320 fps
Case Length: 2.23 inches
Neck Diameter: .392 inch
Shoulder Diameter: Straight
Base Diameter: .454 inch
Rim Diameter: .535 inch
Overall Length: 3.07 inches
Introduced in 1883.

.38-56 Winchester **$4.25**
Bullet Diameter: .376 inch
Bullet Weight: 255 grains
Muzzle Velocity: 1395 fps
Case Length: 2.10 inches
Neck Diameter: .403 inch
Shoulder Diameter: .447 inch
Base Diameter: .506 inch
Rim Diameter: .606 inch
Overall Length: 2.50 inches
Made from 1887 to 1936.

.40-50 Sharps (Necked) . . **$8.75**
Bullet Diameter: .403 inch
Bullet Weight: 265 grains
Muzzle Velocity: 1460 fps
Case Length: 1.72 inches
Neck Diameter: .424 inch
Shoulder Diameter: .489 inch
Base Diameter: .501 inch.
Rim Diameter: .580 inch
Overall Length: 2.37 inches
Introduced in 1875.

**.40-50 Sharps
(Straight)** **$8.50**
Bullet Diameter: .403 inch
Bullet Weight: 265 grains
Muzzle Velocity: 1410 fps
Case Length: 1.88 inches
Neck Diameter: .421 inch
Shoulder Diameter: Straight
Base Diameter: .454 inch
Rim Diameter: .554 inch
Overall Length: 2.63 inches
Introduced in 1880.

**.40-60 Maynard
Model 1882** **$28.00**
Bullet Diameter: .417 inch
Bullet Weight: 330 grains
Muzzle Velocity: 1370 fps
Case Length: 2.20 inches
Neck Diameter: .448 inch
Shoulder Diameter: Straight
Base Diameter: .454 inch
Rim Diameter: .533 inch
Overall Length: 2.75 inches
Introduced in 1882.

.40-60 Winchester **$6.00**
Bullet Diameter: .404 inch
Bullet Weight: 210 grains
Muzzle Velocity: 1560 fps
Case Length: 1.87 inches
Neck Diameter: .425 inch
Shoulder Diameter: .445 inch
Base Diameter: .506 inch
Rim Diameter: .630 inch
Overall Length: 2.10 inches
Manufactured from 1876 to
  1897.

.40-65 Winchester **$4.25**
Bullet Diameter: .406 inch
Bullet Weight: 260 grains
Muzzle Velocity: 1420 fps
Case Length: 2.10 inches

.40-65 Winchester (Cont.)
Neck Diameter: .423 inch
Shoulder Diameter: Straight
Base Diameter: .504 inch
Rim Diameter: .604 inch
Overall Length: 2.48 inches
Manufactured from 1887 to
    1935.

.40-70 Maynard $40.00
Bullet Diameter: .417 inch
Bullet Weight: 270 grains
Muzzle Velocity: 1645 fps
Case Length: 2.42 inches
Neck Diameter: .450 inch
Shoulder Diameter: Straight
Base Diameter: .451 inch
Rim Diameter: .535 inch
Overall Length: 2.88 inches
Manufactured from 1882 to
    1900.

.40-70 Peabody "What Cheer" $63.00
Bullet Diameter: .408 inch
Bullet Weight: 380 grains
Muzzle Velocity: 1420 fps
Case Length: 1.76 inches
Neck Diameter: .428 inch
Shoulder Diameter: .551 inch
Base Diameter: .581 inch
Rim Diameter: .662 inch
Overall Length: 2.85 inches
Manufactured from 1878 to
    1898.

.40-70 Remington . . . $10.50
Bullet Diameter: .405 inch
Bullet Weight: 330 grains
Muzzle Velocity: 1420 fps
Case Length: 2.25 inches

.40-70 Remington (cont.)
Neck Diameter: .434 inch
Shoulder Diameter: .500 inch
Base Diameter: .503 inch
Rim Diameter: .595 inch
Overall Length: 3.00 inches
Made from 1880 to 1897.

.40-70 Sharps (Necked) $17.00
Bullet Diameter: .403 inch
Bullet Weight: 330 grains
Muzzle Velocity: 1420 fps
Case Length: 2.25 inches
Neck Diameter: .426 inch
Shoulder Diameter: .500 inch
Base Diameter: .503 inch
Rim Diameter: .595 inch
Overall Length: 3.02 inches
Manufactured 1876 to 1900.

.40-70 Sharps (Straight) $12.00
Bullet Diameter: .403 inch
Bullet Weight: 330 grains
Muzzle Velocity: 1260 fps
Case Length: 2.50 inches
Neck Diameter: .420 inch
Shoulder Diameter: Straight
Base Diameter: .453 inch
Rim Diameter: .533 inch
Overall Length: 3.18 inches
Manufactured 1880 to 1900.

.40-70 Winchester $9.50
Bullet Diameter: .405 inch
Bullet Weight: 330 grains
Muzzle Velocity: 1380 fps
Case Length: 2.40 inches
Neck Diameter: .430 inch
Shoulder Diameter: .496 inch
Base Diameter: .504 inch
Rim Diameter: .604 inch
Overall Length: 2.85 inches
Manufactured 1894 to 1906.

NOTE

Fired cases for items shown on this page are worth approximately 50% of the values shown for loaded cartridges.

.40-72 Winchester . . . $14.50
Bullet Diameter: .406 inch
Bullet Weight: 330 grains
Muzzle Velocity: 1400 fps
Case Length: 2.60 inches
Neck Diameter: .431 inch
Shoulder Diameter: Straight
Base Diameter: .460 inch
Rim Diameter: .518 inch
Overall Length: 3.15 inches
Manufactured from1895 to
    approximately 1936.

.40-75 Bullard $15.00
Bullet Diameter: .413 inch
Bullet Weight: 258 grains
Muzzle Velocity: 1500 fps
Case Length: 2.09 inches
Neck Diameter: .432 inch
Shoulder Diameter: Straight
Base Diameter: .505inch
Rim Diameter: .606 inch
Overall Length: 2.54 inches
Introduced in 1887 and
    manufactured until
    about 1915.

.40-82 Winchester $4.50
Bullet Diameter: .406 inch
Bullet Weight: 260 grains
Muzzle Velocity: 1490 fps
Case Length: 2.40 inches
Neck Diameter: .428 inch
Shoulder Diameter: .448 inch
Base Diameter: .502 inch
Rim Diameter: .604 inch
Overall Length: 2.77 inches
Manufactured 1885 to 1935.

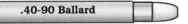

.40-85 Ballard **$15.00**
Bullet Diameter: .413 inch
Bullet Weight: 330 grains
Muzzle Velocity: 1400 fps
Case Length: 2.04 inches
Neck Diameter: .430 inch
Shoulder Diameter: .551 inch
Base Diameter: .569 inch
Rim Diameter: .622 inch
Overall Length: 2.55 inches
Manufactured from 1878 to
1900.

.40-90 Ballard **$16.00**
Bullet Diameter: .403 inch
Bullet Weight: 370 grains
Muzzle Velocity: 1425 fps
Case Length: 2.94 inches
Neck Diameter: .425 inch
Shoulder Diameter: Straight
Base Diameter: .477 inch
Rim Diameter: .545 inch
Overall Length: 3.81 inches
Introduced in 1878.

.40-90 Bullard **$17.00**
Bullet Diameter: .413 inch
Bullet Weight: 330 grains
Muzzle Velocity: 1440 fps
Case Length: 2.04 inches
Neck Diameter: .430 inch
Shoulder Diameter: .551 inch
Base Diameter: .569 inch
Rim Diameter: .622 inch
Overall Length: 2.55 inches
Manufactured from 1878 to
1900.

.40-90 Peabody
"What Cheer" **$130.00**
Bullet Diameter: .408 inch
Bullet Weight: 500 grains
Muzzle Velocity: 1250 fps
Case Length: 2.00 inches
Neck Diameter: .433 inch
Shoulder Diameter: .546 inch
Base Diameter: .596 inch
Rim Diameter: .659 inch
Overall Length: 3.37 inches
Made from 1877 to the early
1900s.

.40-90 Sharps
(Necked) **$11.00**
Bullet Diameter: .403 inch
Bullet Weight: 370 grains
Muzzle Velocity: 1475 fps
Case Length: 2.63 inches
Neck Diameter: .435 inch
Shoulder Diameter: .500 inch
Base Diameter: .506 inch
Rim Diameter: .602 inch
Overall Length: 3.44 inches
Introduced in 1876.

.40-90 Sharps
(Straight) **$20.00**
Bullet Diameter: .403 inch
Bullet Weight: 370 grains
Muzzle Velocity: 1390 fps
Case Length: 3.25 inches
Neck Diameter: .425 inch
Shoulder Diameter: Straight
Base Diameter: .477 inch
Rim Diameter: .546 inch
Overall Length: 4.06 inches
Made from 1885 to the early
1900s.

.40-110 Winchester
Express. **$35.00**
Bullet Diameter: .403 inch
Bullet Weight: 260 grains
Muzzle Velocity: 1600 fps
Case Length: 3.25 inches
Neck Diameter: .428 inch
Shoulder Diameter: .485 inch
Base Diameter: .543 inch
Rim Diameter: .651 inch
Overall Length: 3.63 inches
Made from 1886 to the early
1900s.

.401 Winchester **$2.00**
Bullet Diameter: .406 inch
Bullet Weight: 200 grains
Muzzle Velocity: 2135 fps
Case Length: 1.50 inches
Neck Diameter: .428 inch
Shoulder Diameter: Straight
Base Diameter: .429 inch
Rim Diameter: .457 inch
Overall Length: 2.0 inches
Manufactured from 1910 to
1936.

.405 Winchester **$3.00**
Bullet Diameter: .412 inch
Bullet Weight: 300 grains
Muzzle Velocity: 2200 fps
Case Length: 2.58 inches
Neck Diameter: .436 inch
Shoulder Diameter: Straight
Base Diameter: .461 inch
Rim Diameter: .543 inch
Overall Length: 3.18 inches
Manufactured from 1904
to about 1973.

.44 Ballard, Extra
Long **$15.50**
Bullet Diameter: .428 inch
Bullet Weight: 265 grains
Muzzle Velocity: 1320 fps
Case Length: 1.58 inches
Neck Diameter: .442 inch
Shoulder Diameter: .463 inch
Base Diameter: .468 inch
Rim Diameter: .515 inch
Overall Length: 1.96 inches
Made from 1876 to the early
1900s.

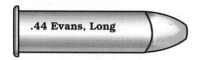

.44 Evans, Long $17.00
Bullet Diameter: .419 inch
Bullet Weight: 280 grains
Muzzle Velocity: 1200 fps
Case Length: 1.54 inches
Neck Diameter: .434 inch
Shoulder Diameter: Straight
Base Diameter: .449 inch
Rim Diameter: .509 inch
Overall Length: 2.0 inches
Made from 1877 to the early
l900s.

.44 Evans, Short $15.00
Bullet Diameter: .419 inch
Bullet Weight: 215 grains
Muzzle Velocity: 850 fps
Case Length: .99 inch
Neck Diameter: .439 inch
Shoulder Diameter: Straight
Base Diameter: .440 inch
Rim Diameter: .509 inch
Overall Length: 2.0 inches
Manufactured from 1875 to
1925.

.44 Henry $11.00
Bullet Diameter: .423 inch
Bullet Weight: 200 grains
Muzzle Velocity: 1150 fps
Case Length: .88 inch
Neck Diameter: .443 inch
Shoulder Diameter: Straight
Base Diameter: .445 inch
Rim Diameter: .523 inch
Overall Length: 1.36 inches
Manufactured from 1866 to
1900.

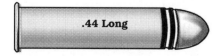

.44 Long, Centerfire . $23.00
Bullet Diameter: .439 inch
Bullet Weight: 227 grains
Muzzle Velocity: —

.44 Long, Centerfire (Cont.)
Case Length: 1.09 inches
Neck Diameter: .440 inch
Shoulder Diameter: Straight
Base Diameter: .441 inch
Rim Diameter: .506 inch
Overall Length: 1.65 inches
Manufactured from 1875 to
1898.

.44 WCF $1.25
Bullet Diameter: .427 inch
Bullet Weight: 200 grains
Muzzle Velocity: 1150 fps
Case Length: 1.31 inches
Neck Diameter: .443 inch
Shoulder Diameter: Straight
Base Diameter: .471 inch
Rim Diameter: .525 inch
Overall Length: 1.55 inches
Made from 1873 to date.

**.44 Wesson, Extra
Long. $14.00**
Bullet Diameter: .440 inch
Bullet Weight: 250 grains
Muzzle Velocity: 1340 fps
Case Length: 1.63 inches
Neck Diameter: .441
Shoulder Diameter: Straight
Base Diameter: .441 inch
Rim Diameter: .510 inch
Overall Length: 2.19 inches
Manufactured from 1876 to
1897.

.44-40 Extra Long . . . $50.00
Bullet Diameter: .428 inch
Bullet Weight: 250 grains
Muzzle Velocity: 1420 fps
Case Length: 1.575 inches
Neck Diameter: .442 inch
Shoulder Diameter: Straight
Base Diameter: .468 inch
Rim Diameter: .515 inch
Overall Length: 1.96 inches
Introduced in the late 1800s.

**.44-60 Peabody
Creedmoor $35.00**
Bullet Diameter: .447 inch
Bullet Weight: 395 grains
Muzzle Velocity: 1250 fps
Case Length: 1.89 inches
Neck Diameter: .464 inch
Shoulder Diameter: .502 inch
Base Diameter: .518 inch
Rim Diameter: .628 inch
Overall Length: 2.56 inches
Made from 1877 to the early
1900s.

**.44-60 Sharps
(Necked) $15.00**
Bullet Diameter: .447 inch
Bullet Weight: 395 grains
Muzzle Velocity: 1250 fps
Case Length: 1.88 inches
Neck Diameter: .464 inch
Shoulder Diameter: .502 inch
Base Diameter: .515 inch
Rim Diameter: .630 inch
Overall Length: 2.55 inches
Manufactured in the 1800s.

.44-60 Winchester. $7.00
Bullet Diameter: .447 inch
Bullet Weight: 395 grains
Muzzle Velocity: 1250 fps
Case Length: 1.89 inches
Neck Diameter: .464 inch
Shoulder Diameter: .502 inch
Base Diameter: .518 inch
Rim Diameter: .628 inch
Overall Length: 2.56 inches
Introduced in 1874 and made
until the beginning of World
War I.

.44-70 Maynard $70.00
Bullet Diameter: .445 inch
Bullet Weight: 430 grains
Muzzle Velocity: 1300 fps
Case Length: 2.21 inches
Neck Diameter: .466 inch
Shoulder Diameter: Straight
Base Diameter: .499 inch
Rim Diameter: .601 inch
Overall Length: 2.87 inches
Introduced in 1882.

.44-75 Ballard Everlasting $6.00
Bullet Diameter: .445 inch
Bullet Weight: 405 grains
Muzzle Velocity: 1250 fps
Case Length: 2.50 inches
Neck Diameter: .487 inch
Shoulder Diameter: Straight
Base Diameter: .497 inch
Rim Diameter: .603 inch
Overall Length: 3.0 inches
Introduced in 1876.

.44-77 Remington (or Sharps) $10.50
Bullet Diameter: .446 inch
Bullet Weight: 365 grains
Muzzle Velocity: 1460 fps
Case Length: 2.25 inches
Neck Diameter: .467 inch
Shoulder Diameter: .502 inch
Base Diameter: .516 inch
Rim Diameter: .625 inch
Overall Length: 3.05 inches
Introduced in 1875.

.44-85 Wesson $8.00
Bullet Diameter: .446 inch
Bullet Weight: 390 grains
Muzzle Velocity: 1450 fps
Case Length: 2.88 inches
Neck Diameter: —

.44-85 Wesson (Cont.)
Shoulder Diameter: Straight
Base Diameter: —
Rim Diameter: —
Overall Length: 3.31 inches
Introduced in 1881.

.44-90 Remington Special $33.00
Bullet Diameter: .442 inch
Bullet Weight: 550 grains
Muzzle Velocity: 1250 fps
Case Length: 2.44 inches
Neck Diameter: .466 inch
Shoulder Diameter: .504 inch
Base Diameter: .506 inch
Rim Diameter: .628 inch
Overall Length: 3.08 inches
Manufactured 1873 to 1910.

.44-90 Remington (Straight) $35.00
Bullet Diameter: .442 inch
Bullet Weight: 520 grains
Muzzle Velocity: 1435 fps
Case Length: 2.60 inches
Neck Diameter: .465 inch
Shoulder Diameter: Straight
Base Diameter: .506 inch
Rim Diameter: .628 inch
Overall Length: 3.08 inches
Introduced in 1880.

.44-90 Sharps (Necked). $16.00
Bullet Diameter: .446 inch
Bullet Weight: 500 grains
Muzzle Velocity: 1270
Case Length: 2.63 inches
Neck Diameter: .468 inch
Shoulder Diameter: .504 inch
Base Diameter: .517 inch
Rim Diameter: .625 inch
Overall Length: 3.30 inches
Manufactured 1873 to 1878.

.44-95 Peabody "What Cheer" $52.00
Bullet Diameter: .443 inch
Bullet Weight: 550 grains
Muzzle Velocity: 1310 fps

.44-95 Peabody "What Cheer" (cont.)
Case Length: 2.31 inches
Neck Diameter: .465 inch
Shoulder Diameter: .550 inch
Base Diameter: .580 inch
Rim Diameter: .670 inch
Overall Length: 3.32 inches
Introduced in 1875.

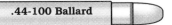

.44-100 Ballard $19.00
Bullet Diameter: .445 inch
Bullet Weight: 535 grains
Muzzle Velocity: 1400 fps
Case Length: 2.81 inches
Neck Diameter: .485 inch
Shoulder Diameter: Straight
Base Diameter: .498 inch
Rim Diameter: .597 inch
Overall Length: 3.25 inches
Manufactured 1876 to 1880.

.44-100 Remington Creedmoor $15.00
Bullet Diameter: .442 inch
Bullet Weight: 550 grains
Muzzle Velocity: 1380 fps
Case Length: 2.60 inches
Neck Diameter: .465 inch
Shoulder Diameter: Straight
Base Diameter: .503 inch
Rim Diameter: .568 inch
Overall Length: 3.97 inches
Introduced in 1880.

.44-100 Wesson $7.50
Bullet Diameter: .445 inch
Bullet Weight: 550 grains
Muzzle Velocity: 1375 fps
Case Length: 3.38 inches
Neck Diameter: —
Shoulder Diameter: Straight
Base Diameter: —
Rim Diameter: —
Overall Length: 3.85 inches
Introduced in 1881.

.45-50 Peabody (Sporting) $28.00
Bullet Diameter: .454 inch
Bullet Weight: 290 grains
Muzzle Velocity: 1300 fps
Case Length: 1.54 inches
Neck Diameter: .478 inch
Shoulder Diameter: .508 inch
Base Diameter: .516 inch
Rim Diameter: .634 inch
Overall Length: 2.08 inches
Manufactured 1873 to 1897.

.45-60 Winchester . . . $4.75
Bullet Diameter: .454 inch
Bullet Weight: 300 grains
Muzzle Velocity: 1315 fps
Case Length: 1.89 inches
Neck Diameter: .479 inch
Shoulder Diameter: Straight
Base Diameter: .508 inch
Rim Diameter: .629 inch
Overall Length: 2.15 inches
Manufactured 1879 to 1935.

.45-70 Van Choate . . . $45.00
Bullet Diameter: .457 inch
Bullet Weight: 420 grains
Muzzle Velocity: 1250 fps
Case Length: 2.25 inches
Neck Diameter: .475 inch
Shoulder Diameter: Straight
Base Diameter: .50 inch
Rim Diameter: .60 inch
Overall Length: 2.91 inches
Manufactured 1872 to 1912.

.45-75 Sharps (Straight) $17.50
Bullet Diameter: .457 inch
Bullet Weight: 400 grains
Muzzle Velocity: 1330 fps
Case Length: 2.10 inches
Neck Diameter: .453 inch

.45-75 Sharps (cont.)
Shoulder Diameter: Straight
Base Diameter: .50 inch
Rim Diameter: .60 inch
Overall Length: 2.90 inches
Introduced in 1876.

.45-75 Winchester $5.00
Bullet Diameter: .454 inch
Bullet Weight: 350 grains
Muzzle Velocity: 1383 fps
Case Length: 1.86 inches
Neck Diameter: .478 inch
Shoulder Diameter: .547 inch
Base Diameter: .559 inch
Rim Diameter: .616 inch
Overall Length: 2.25 inches
Manufactured from 1876 to 1935.

.45-82 Winchester $6.00
Bullet Diameter: .457 inch
Bullet Weight: 405 grains
Muzzle Velocity: 1468 fps
Case Length: 2.40 inches
Neck Diameter: .477 inch
Shoulder Diameter: Straight
Base Diameter: .501 inch
Rim Diameter: .597 inch
Overall Length: 2.88 inches
Introduced about 1886.

.45-85 Winchester $7.50
Bullet Diameter: .457 inch
Bullet Weight: 350 grains
Muzzle Velocity: 1510 fps
Case Length: 2.40 inches
Neck Diameter: .477 inch
Shoulder Diameter: Straight
Base Diameter: .501 inch
Rim Diameter: .597 inch
Overall Length: 2.88 inches
Introduced about 1886.

.45-90 Winchester $4.50
Bullet Diameter: .457 inch
Bullet Weight: 300 grains
Muzzle Velocity: 1554 fps

.45-90 Winchester (cont.)
Case Length: 2.40 inches
Neck Diameter: .477 inch
Shoulder Diameter: Straight
Base Diameter: .501 inch
Rim Diameter: .597 inch
Overall Length: 2.88 inches
Introduced in 1886.

.45-100 Ballard. $26.00
Bullet Diameter: .454 inch
Bullet Weight: 550 grains
Muzzle Velocity: 1370 fps
Case Length: 2.81 inches
Neck Diameter: .487 inch
Shoulder Diameter: Straight
Base Diameter: .498 inch
Rim Diameter: .597 inch
Overall Length: 3.25 inches
Made from 1878 to 1889.

.45-100 Remington . . . $14.00
Bullet Diameter: .452 inch
Bullet Weight: 500 grains
Muzzle Velocity: —
Case Length: 2.63 inches
Neck Diameter: .490 inch
Shoulder Diameter: .550 inch
Base Diameter: .558 inch
Rim Diameter: .645 inch
Overall Length: 3.26 inches
Introduced in 1880.

.45-100 Sharps (Straight). $26.00
Bullet Diameter: .453 inch
Bullet Weight: 550 grains
Muzzle Velocity: 1360 fps
Case Length: 2.40 inches
Neck Diameter: .472 inch
Shoulder Diameter: Straight
Base Diameter: .507 inch
Rim Diameter: .60 inch
Overall Length: 2.85 inches
Introduced in 1876.

**.45-120 Sharps
(3¼″ Straight)** **$34.00**
Bullet Diameter: .451 inch
Bullet Weight: 500 grains
Muzzle Velocity: 1520 fps
Case Length: 3.25 inches
Neck Diameter: .490 inch
Shoulder Diameter: Straight
Base Diameter: .506 inch
Rim Diameter: .597 inch
Overall Length: 4.16 inches
Made from 1878 to 1881.

.45-125 Winchester. . **$45.00**
Bullet Diameter: .456 inch
Bullet Weight: 300 grains
Muzzle Velocity: 1690 fps
Case Length: 3.25 inches
Neck Diameter: .470 inch
ShoulderDiameter: .521 inch
Base Diameter: .533 inch
Rim Diameter: .601 inch
Overall Length: 3.63 inches Introduced in 1886.

.50 U.S. Carbine **$8.50**
Bullet Diameter: .515 inch
Bullet Weight: 400 grains
Muzzle Velocity: 1200 fps
Case Length: —
Neck Diameter: —
Shoulder Diameter: —
Base Diameter: —
Rim Diameter: —
Overall Length: —
Introduced in 1870.

.50-50 Maynard **$9.00**
Bullet Diameter: .513 inch
Bullet Weight: 350 grains
Muzzle Velocity: 1270 fps
Case Length: 1.37 inches
Neck Diameter: .535 inch
Shoulder Diameter: Straight
Base Diameter: .563 inch
Rim Diameter: .661 inch
Overall Length: 1.91 inches
Introduced in 1882.

**.50-70 Musket
(.50 Govt)** **$15.00**
Bullet Diameter: .515 inch
Bullet Weight: 450 grains
Muzzle Velocity: 1260 fps
Case Length: 1.75 inches
Neck Diameter: .535 inch
Shoulder Diameter: Straight
Base Diameter: .565 inch
Rim Diameter: .660 inch
Overall Length: 2.25 inches
Manufactured from 1866 to
  1873.

.50-90 Sharps **$35.00**
Bullet Diameter: .509 inch
Bullet Weight: 335 grains
Muzzle Velocity: 1475 fps
Case Length: 2.50 inches
Neck Diameter: .528 inch
Shoulder Diameter: Straight
Base Diameter: .565 inch
Rim Diameter: .663 inch
Overall Length: 3.20 inches
Introduced in 1875.

.50-95 Winchester . . . **$10.50**
Bullet Diameter: .513 inch
Bullet Weight: 300 grains
Muzzle Velocity: 1557 fps
Case Length: 1.92 inches
Neck Diameter: .533 inch
Shoulder Diameter: .553 inch
Base Diameter: .562 inch
Rim Diameter: .627 inch
Overall Length: 2.26 inches
Introduced in 1879.

.50-100 Winchester. . **$10.00**
Bullet Diameter: .512 inch
Bullet Weight: 450 grains
Muzzle Velocity: 1475 fps
Case Length: 2.40 inches
Neck Diameter: .534 inch
Shoulder Diameter: Straight
Base Diameter: .551 inch
Rim Diameter: .607 inch
Overall Length: 2.75 inches
Manufactured 1899 to 1935.

.50-105 Winchester. . . **$14.00**
Bullet Diameter: .512 inch
Bullet Weight: —
Muzzle Velocity: —
Case Length: 2.40 inches
Neck Diameter: .534 inch
Shoulder Diameter: Straight
Base Diameter: .551 inch
Rim Diameter: .607 inch
Overall Length: 2.75 inches
Manufactured 1899 to 1935.

.50-110 Winchester. . . **$12.00**
Bullet Diameter: .512 inch
Bullet Weight: 300 grains
Muzzle Velocity: 1605 fps
Case Length: 2.40 inches
Neck Diameter: .534 inch
Shoulder Diameter: Straight
Base Diameter: .551 inch
Rim Diameter: .607 inch
Overall Length: 2.75 inches
Manufactured 1899 to 1935.

.50-115 Bullard **$17.00**
Bullet Diameter: .512 inch
Bullet Weight: 300 grains
Muzzle Velocity: 1539 fps
Case Length: 2.19 inches
Neck Diameter: .547 inch
Shoulder Diameter: .577 inch
Base Diameter: .585 inch
Rim Diameter: .619 inch
Overall Length: 2.56 inches
Introduced in 1886.

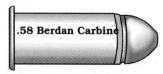

.50-140 Sharps $75.00
Bullet Diameter: .509 inch
Bullet Weight: 473 grains
Muzzle Velocity: 1580 fps
Case Length: 3.25 inches
Neck Diameter: .528 inch
Shoulder Diameter: Straight
Base Diameter: .565 inch
Rim Diameter: .665 inch
Overall Length: 3.94 inches
Manufactured from 1880 to
   1884.

.50-140 Winchester
Express $175.00
Bullet Diameter: .512 inch
Bullet Weight: 473 grains
Muzzle Velocity: 1580 fps
Case Length: 3.25 inches
Neck Diameter: .528 inch
Shoulder Diameter: Straight
Base Diameter: .551 inch
Rim Diameter: .652 inch
Overall Length: 3.95 inches
Introduced in 1887 and made
   until the early 1900s.

.55-100 Maynard $19.00
Bullet Diameter: .551 inch
Bullet Weight: 530 grains
Muzzle Velocity: 1410 fps
Case Length: 1.94 inches
Neck Diameter: .582 inch
Shoulder Diameter: Straight
Base Diameter: .590 inch
Rim Diameter: .718 inch
Overall Length: 2.56 inches
Introduced in 1882.

.58 Berdan Carbine . . $14.00
Bullet Diameter: .589 inch
Bullet Weight: 530 grains
Muzzle Velocity: 925 fps
Case Length: 1.59 inches
Neck Diameter: .625 inch
Shoulder Diameter: Straight
Base Diameter: .646 inch
Rim Diameter: .740 inch
Overall Length: 2.09 inches
Introduced in 1869.

.58 U.S. Musket
(Berdan) $32.00
Bullet Diameter: .589 inch
Bullet Weight: 530 grains
Muzzle Velocity: 1100 fps
Case Length: 1.65 inches
Neck Diameter: .625 inch
Shoulder Diameter: Straight
Base Diameter: .646 inch
Rim Diameter: .740 inch
Overall Length: 2.15 inches
Introduced in 1869 and made
   to approximately 1873.

.70-150 Winchester . $250.00
Bullet Diameter: .705 inch
Bullet Weight: —
Muzzle Velocity: —
Case Length: 2.28 inches
Neck Diameter: .725 inch
Shoulder Diameter: .790 inch
Base Diameter: .805 inch
Rim Diameter: .870 inch
Overall Length: 2.63 inches
Introduced in 1888 as an experi-
   mental cartridge. Very rare.

THE DISCOVERY AND HISTORY OF GUNPOWDER

The origin of gunpowder, the only explosive known until the middle of the 19th century, is uncertain. There is a theory that it was known in China many centuries before its first appearance in Europe, and that knowledge of it gradually worked westward. Legend goes back to the time of Alexander the Great, who, it is asserted, refused to attack the Oxydracae, a race occupying the country between the Hyphasis and the Ganges, because they "lived under the protection of the gods and overthrew their enemies with thunder and lightning, which they shot forth from their walls."

Some authorities regard Greek Fire, rather extensively used in the defense of Constantinople in the seventh century, as a form of gunpowder, but it may have been merely an incendiary mixture to which crude nitre was added to make it burn more fiercely. On the strength of passages from the works of Roger Bacon, an English monk who lived in the 13th century, he is spoken of as the inventor of gunpowder. In his late works, "Opus Tertium," "De Secretis," and "Opus Magnus," published about 1270, there is no doubt that he was acquainted with explosive mixtures of sulphur, charcoal, and nitre, the ingredients of gunpowder.

Berthold Schwartz, a monk of Freiburg, Germany, studied the writings of Bacon regarding explosives, and manufactured gunpowder while experimenting. He has commonly been credited as the inventor, and at any rate the honor is due him for making known some properties of gunpowder. Its adoption in Central Europe quickly followed his announcement, which is supposed to have taken place about 1320. It is probable that gunpowder was well known in Spain and Greece many years prior to its being used in Central and Northern Europe.

The early uses of gunpowder, however, were confined to warfare, no use being made of it for sporting purposes for several hundred years. In the late 1300s, frequent references to gunpowder were made in literature, often in a way which makes it evident that the properties of gunpowder as a propellant were widely known.

MANUFACTURING GUNPOWDER

The manufacture of gunpowder was carried out originally by the very crude method of pounding the ingredients together by hand in mortars. But edge runners were introduced toward the end of the 16th century, which greatly facilitated the incorporating or milling process. During this century, the process of "corning" or "granulating" was introduced, whereby grains of standard size are assured.

In manufacturing gunpowder, care is required in the selection of material. The potassium nitrate, or nitre, should be chemically pure. The sulphur must contain no nonvolatile matter, and must be free from sulfuric acid. The quantity of the powder depends considerably on the quality of the charcoal, so that it is customary for powder mills to prepare their own.

The composition of gunpowder varies widely with the different grades manufactured. Coarse grains are used for blasting, and fine grains for gunpowder. The composition of French military powders remained the same from 1598 until the adoption of modern smokeless powders, which developed from Schoenbein's discovery of guncotton in 1846. From this, Vielle, a French chemist, invented smokeless powder in 1886, which possesses the ability to burn without creating much smoke.

Almost all sporting powder propellants today are smokeless powders. These can be divided into two classes, the dense powders and the bulk powders, both being used in rifle shooting and in shotguns. Although smokelessness characterizes these powders, it is their superior power that is of prime importance. While black gunpowder imparts to the projectile an initial velocity of 1,700 feet per second, initial velocities of over 4,000 foot seconds have been attained with smokeless powders.

Another division of smokeless powders into types is the nitroglycerin smokeless powders and the nitrocellulose. Both nitroglycerin and nitrocellulose powders consist of colloidal masses of gelatined nitrocellulose that have been pressed into ribbons, cords, tubes, or sheets, these being frequently cut into flakes when intended for use with small arms.

Nitroglycerin was discovered in 1846 by Sobrero, an Italian chemist, but nothing was done about it until Alfred Nobel recognized its possibilities for blasting. Later, he found it was possible to mix and treat nitrocellulose dissolved in nitroglycerin, so that a hard colloid substance could be produced. This substance had all the properties that made it desirable as a rifle propellant. This led to the production in 1888 of ballistite, the first propellant of this class.

Today, nitroglycerin powders are manufactured for use in both shotguns and rifles. They usually are referred to as double-base powders, possessing the advantages of regular ballistics, and are less liable to produce back-flash than nitrocellulose powders. They keep extremely well.

RIMFIRE CARTRIDGES

.22 Extra Long. $1.75
Bullet Diameter: .223 inch
Bullet Weight: 40 grains
Muzzle Velocity: 1060 fps
Case Length: .750 inch
Neck Diameter: .225 inch
Shoulder Diameter: Straight
Base Diameter: .225 inch
Rim Diameter: .275 inch
Overall Length: 1.16 inches
Manufactured 1881 to 1935.

.22 Remington Automatic . . . . $.50
Bullet Diameter: .223 inch
Bullet Weight: 45 grains
Muzzle Velocity: 950 fps
Case Length: .663 inch
Neck Diameter: .245 inch
Shoulder Diameter: Straight
Base Diameter: .245 inch
Rim Diameter: .290 inch
Overall Length: .920 inch
Manufactured from 1914 to 1946.

.22 Remington Special . . . $.30
Bullet Diameter: .224 inch
Bullet Weight: 40 grains
Muzzle Velocity: 1440 fps
Case Length: .960 inch
Neck Diameter: .242 inch
Shoulder Diameter: Straight
Base Diameter: .243 inch
Rim Diameter: .295 inch
Overall Length: 1.17 inches
Manufactured from 1890 to date.

.22 Winchester Automatic . . . . $.45
Bullet Diameter: .222 inch
Bullet Weight: 45 grains
Muzzle Velocity: 1055 fps
Case Length: .665 inch
Neck Diameter: .250 inch
Shoulder Diameter: Straight
Base Diameter: .250 inch
Rim Diameter: .310 inch
Overall Length: .915 inch
Made from 1890 to date.

.22 Winchester Rimfire (WRF) . . . . $.30
Bullet Diameter: .224 inch
Bullet Weight: 45 grains
Muzzle Velocity: 1400 fps
Case Length: .960 inch
Neck Diameter: .242 inch
Shoulder Diameter: Straight
Base Diameter: .243 inch
Rim Diameter: .295 inch
Overall Length: 1.17 inches
Manufactured from 1891 to date.

.25 Short . . . . $.60
Bullet Diameter: .246 inch
Bullet Weight: 43 grains
Muzzle Velocity: 750 fps
Case Length: .468 inch
Neck Diameter: .245 inch
Shoulder Diameter: Straight
Base Diameter: .245 inch
Rim Diameter: .290 inch
Overall Length: .780 inch
Made from 1860 to 1921.

.25 Stevens $1.75
Bullet Diameter: .251 inch
Bullet Weight: 67 grains
Muzzle Velocity: 1200 fps
Case Length: 1.125 inches
Neck Diameter: .276 inch
Shoulder Diameter: Straight
Base Diameter: .276 inch
Rim Diameter: .333 inch
Overall Length: 1.395 inches
Manufactured 1895 to 1942.

.25 Stevens Short . . . . . $.80
Bullet Diameter: .251 inch
Bullet Weight: 65 grains
Muzzle Velocity: 950 fps
Case Length: .599 inch
Neck Diameter: .275 inch
Shoulder Diameter: Straight
Base Diameter: .276 inch
Rim Diameter: .333 inch
Overall Length: .877 inch
Manufactured 1902 to 1942.

.30 Long $2.75
Bullet Diameter: .288 inch
Bullet Weight: 75 grains
Muzzle Velocity: 750 fps
Case Length: .613 inch
Neck Diameter: .288 inch
Shoulder Diameter: Straight
Base Diameter: .288 inch
Rim Diameter: .340 inch
Overall Length: 1.020 inches
Manufactured from 1873 to 1916.

.30 Long with Merwin Base $37.00

.30 Short $4.50
Bullet Diameter: .286 inch
Bullet Weight: 58 grains
Muzzle Velocity: 700 fps
Case Length: .515 inch
Neck Diameter: .292 inch
Shoulder Diameter: Straight
Base Diameter: .292 inch
Rim Diameter: .346 inch
Overall Length: .822 inch
Manufactured from 1862 to 1920.

.32 Extra Long $10.00
Bullet Diameter: .316 inch
Bullet Weight: 90 grains
Muzzle Velocity: 1050 fps
Case Length: 1.12 inches
Neck Diameter: .317 inch
Shoulder Diameter: Straight
Base Diameter: .318 inch
Rim Diameter: .378 inch
Overall Length: 1.570 inches
Manufactured from 1875 to 1918.

.32 Extra Short . . . . . . $ 1.25
Bullet Diameter: .316 inch
Bullet Weight: 54 grains
Muzzle Velocity: 650 fps
Case Length: .398 inch
Neck Diameter: .318 inch
Shoulder Diameter: Straight
Base Diameter: .317 inch
Rim Diameter: .367 inch
Overall Length: .645 inch
Made from 1871 to 1920.

.32 Long $2.50
Bullet Diameter: .316 inch
Bullet Weight: 90 grains
Muzzle Velocity: 950 fps
Case Length: .791 inch
Neck Diameter: .318 inch
Shoulder Diameter: Straight
Base Diameter: .318 inch
Rim Diameter: .377 inch
Overall Length: 1.216 inches
Manufactured 1861 to 1975.

.32 Long Rifle $6.00
Bullet Diameter: .312 inch
Bullet Weight: 80 grains
Muzzle Velocity: 975 fps
Case Length: .937 inch
Neck Diameter: .318 inch
Shoulder Diameter: Straight
Base Diameter: .318 inch
Rim Diameter: .377 inch
Overall Length: 1.222 inches
Manufactured 1900 to 1924.

.32 Short . . . . $.80
Bullet Diameter: .316 inch
Bullet Weight: 58 grains
Muzzle Velocity: 700 fps
Case Length: .575 inch

.32 Short (cont.)
Neck Diameter: .318 inch
Shoulder Diameter: Straight
Base Diameter: .318 inch
Rim Diameter: .377 inch
Overall Length: .948 inch
Manufactured from 1861 to
   1973.

.38 Extra Long $5.25
Bullet Diameter: .375 inch
Bullet Weight: 150 grains
Muzzle Velocity: 1250 fps
Case Length: 1.480 inches
Neck Diameter: .378 inch
Shoulder Diameter: Straight
Base Diameter: .378 inch
Rim Diameter: .435 inch
Overall Length: 2.025 inches
Manufactured 1871 to 1917.

.38 Long $4.75
Bullet Diameter: .375 inch
Bullet Weight: 150 grains
Muzzle Velocity: 750 fps
Case Length: .873 inch
Neck Diameter: .376 inch
Shoulder Diameter: Straight
Base Diameter: .376 inch
Rim Diameter: .435 inch
Overall Length: 1.380 inches
Manufactured 1866 to 1932.

.38 Short $4.00
Bullet Diameter: .375 inch
Bullet Weight: 125 grains
Muzzle Velocity: 700 fps
Case Length: .768 inch
Neck Diameter: .376 inch
Shoulder Diameter: Straight
Base Diameter: .376 inch
Rim Diameter: .436 inch
Overall Length: 1.185 inches
Made from 1868 to 1941.

.41 Long $5.00
Bullet Diameter: .405 inch
Bullet Weight: 163 grains
Muzzle Velocity: 700 fps
Case Length: .635 inch
Neck Diameter: .407 inch
Shoulder Diameter: Straight
Base Diameter: .407 inch
Rim Diameter: .468 inch
Overall Length: .985 inch
Manufactured from 1873 to
   1923.

.41 Short $3.00
Bullet Diameter: .405 inch
Bullet Weight: 130 grains
Muzzle Velocity: 425 fps
Case Length: .467 inch
Neck Diameter: .406 inch
Shoulder Diameter: Straight
Base Diameter: .406 inch
Rim Diameter: .468 inch
Overall Length: .913 inch
Manufactured from 1863 to
   1942.

.41 Swiss $5.75
Bullet Diameter: .418 inch
Bullet Weight: 310 grains
Muzzle Velocity: 1325 fps
Case Length: 1.52 inches
Neck Diameter: .445 inch
Shoulder Diameter: —
Base Diameter: .539 inch
Rim Diameter: .620 inch
Overall Length: 2.205 inches
Manufactured from 1869 to
   1942.

.44 Extra Long...... $25.00
Bullet Diameter: .446 inch
Bullet Weight: 218 grains
Muzzle Velocity: 1250 fps
Case Length: 1.250 inches
Neck Diameter: .456 inch
Shoulder Diameter: Straight
Base Diameter: .457 inch
Rim Diameter: .524 inch
Overall Length: 1.843 inches
Manufactured from 1874 to
   1888.

.44 Henry Flat $7.00
Bullet Diameter: .446 inch
Bullet Weight: 200 grains
Muzzle Velocity: 1125 fps
Case Length: .875 inch
Neck Diameter: .445 inch
Shoulder Diameter: Straight
Base Diameter: .446 inch
Rim Diameter: .519 inch
Overall Length: 1.345 inches
Manufactured from 1861 to
   1934.

.44 Long $8.50
Bullet Diameter: .451 inch
Bullet Weight: 220 grains
Muzzle Velocity: 825 fps
Case Length: 1.094 inches
Neck Diameter: .455 inch
Shoulder Diameter: Straight
Base Diameter: .458 inch
Rim Diameter: .525 inch
Overall Length: 1.842 inches
Manufactured from 1862 to
   1923.

.44 Short $2.50
Bullet Diameter: .446 inch
Bullet Weight: 200 grains
Muzzle Velocity: 525 fps
Case Length: .688 inch
Neck Diameter: .445 inch
Shoulder Diameter: Straight
Base Diameter: .445 inch
Rim Diameter: .519 inch
Overall Length: 1.20 inches
Manufactured from 1865 to
   1923.

.50 Remington Navy .. $32.00
Bullet Diameter: .510 inch
Bullet Weight: 290 grains
Muzzle Velocity: 600 fps
Case Length: .860 inch
Neck Diameter: .535 inch
Shoulder Diameter: Straight
Base Diameter: .562 inch
Rim Diameter: .642 inch
Overall Length: 1.280 inches
Manufactured from 1865 to
   1880.

.56-46 Spencer...... $37.50
Bullet Diameter: .465 inch
Bullet Weight: 330 grains
Muzzle Velocity: 1200 fps
Case Length: 1.035 inches
Neck Diameter: .478 inch
Shoulder Diameter: .555 inch
Base Diameter: .558 inch
Rim Diameter: .641 inch
Overall Length: 1.595 inches
Manufactured from 1866 to
   1869.

NOTE

The largest American-made rimfire
cartridge contained a 565-grain bullet of .598 inch diameter.

.56-50 Spencer $12.00
Bullet Diameter: .512 inch
Bullet Weight: 350 grains
Muzzle Velocity: 1250 fps
Case Length: 1.156 inches
Neck Diameter: .543 inch
Shoulder Diameter: Straight
Base Diameter: .556 inch
Rim Diameter: .639 inch
Overall Length: 1.632 inches
Manufactured from 1864 to
   1920.

.56-52 Spencer $7.50
Bullet Diameter: .512 inch
Bullet Weight: 400 grains
Muzzle Velocity: 1200 fps
Case Length: 1.035 inches
Neck Diameter: .540 inch
Shoulder Diameter: Straight
Base Diameter: .559 inch
Rim Diameter: .639 inch
Overall Length: 1.50 inches
Manufactured 1866 to 1920.

.56-56 .... $11.00
Bullet Diameter: .550 inch
Bullet Weight: 350 grains
Muzzle Velocity: 1200 fps
Case Length: .875 inch
Neck Diameter: .560 inch
Shoulder Diameter: Straight
Base Diameter. .560 inch
Rim Diameter: .645 inch
Overall Length: 1.545 inches
Manufactured from 1862 to
   1920.

OBSOLETE SHOTSHELLS

Loaded Paper Shotshell

"Shotshells" or simply "shells" as they are known in the U.S. are termed "cartridges" in England. They are made of paper or plastic tubes encased within a brass head, which is flanged so it can be grasped by the extractor. Inside is a base wad which, when the brass head is crimped, binds the tube, base wad and brass head together. This prevents the backwards escape of powder gas through the shell. Both the brass head and base wad are perfo rated with a hole that accepts the primer and allows it to ignite the powder inside the case.

The shotshell, once primed, receives a powder charge over which are pressed two or more wads at considerable pressure. Many manufacturers insert a cup and wad directly over the powder charge, which effectively prevents pattern-disrupting gas leakage into the shot column. A charge of shot is next placed over the wads and the unfilled end of the tube is crimped over the shot, making the shell ready for use.

Some earlier shotshells, often referred to as "punkin balls," were loaded with round balls for deer-sized game. The rifled slug did not come into use until later in the 20th century.

Brass Shotshell

Paper and Brass Case

4 Gauge Paper Case	$ 5.00
8 Gauge Paper Case	4.75
10 Gauge	
PaperCase	1.00
BrassCase	5.00
12 Gauge	
PaperCase	1.00
BrassCase	4.00
12 Gauge Black Powder	
PaperCase	3.00
14 Gauge Brass Case	14.00
16 Gauge	
PaperCase	.75
BrassCase	1.50
20 Gauge Paper Case	.75
24 Gauge Paper Case	5.00
28 Gauge	
PaperCase	1.00
BrassCase	3.00
32 Gauge Paper Case	5.00
.410 Bore	
PaperCase	.50
BrassCase	2.00
9mm Rimfire Shotshells	
Paper	1.00
Brass	1.00

MAKING SHOT FOR SHOTSHELLS

Lead shot for muzzloading shotguns and early shotshells was made by dropping molten lead from a shot tower. Such towers dating back to the early 18th century have been recorded. A few have been restored and are now managed by the National Park Service or Department of Interior.

In general, there are two basic types of dropped shot. Early shot was made from pure lead and was therefore termed "soft shot," while most dropped shot made in the 20 century consisted of lead with antimony and tin added to make it harder. This latter type is known as "chilled shot."

The illustration on the following page shows a cross-sectional view of a typical shot tower. Although industry took advantage of steam and electrical power in later years, the operational procedures remained the same and is described as follows:

Lead was first melted down and mixed on the first floor by means of a lead-melting furnace. The resulting mixture was cast into "pigs" which were then transferred to the top floor of the tower. Here the pigs were once again melted and the molten lead was channeled through a perforated pan or sieve. The size of the perforated openings in the sieve determined the shot size. This molten lead — heated to about 700 degrees F. — then fell approximately 190 feet into a vat of water located in a pit beneath the first floor of the tower. As the lead fell toward the water, it formed into spheres. *See* the chart below for various lead shot sizes.

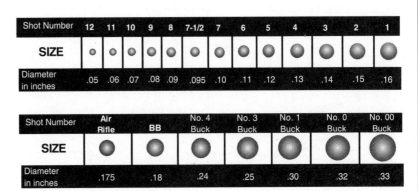

Shot Number	12	11	10	9	8	7-1/2	7	6	5	4	3	2	1
SIZE	○	○	○	○	○	○	○	○	○	○	○	○	○
Diameter in inches	.05	.06	.07	.08	.09	.095	.10	.11	.12	.13	.14	.15	.16

Shot Number	Air Rifle	BB	No. 4 Buck	No. 3 Buck	No. 1 Buck	No. 0 Buck	No. 00 Buck
SIZE	●	●	●	●	●	●	●
Diameter in inches	.175	.18	.24	.25	.30	.32	.33

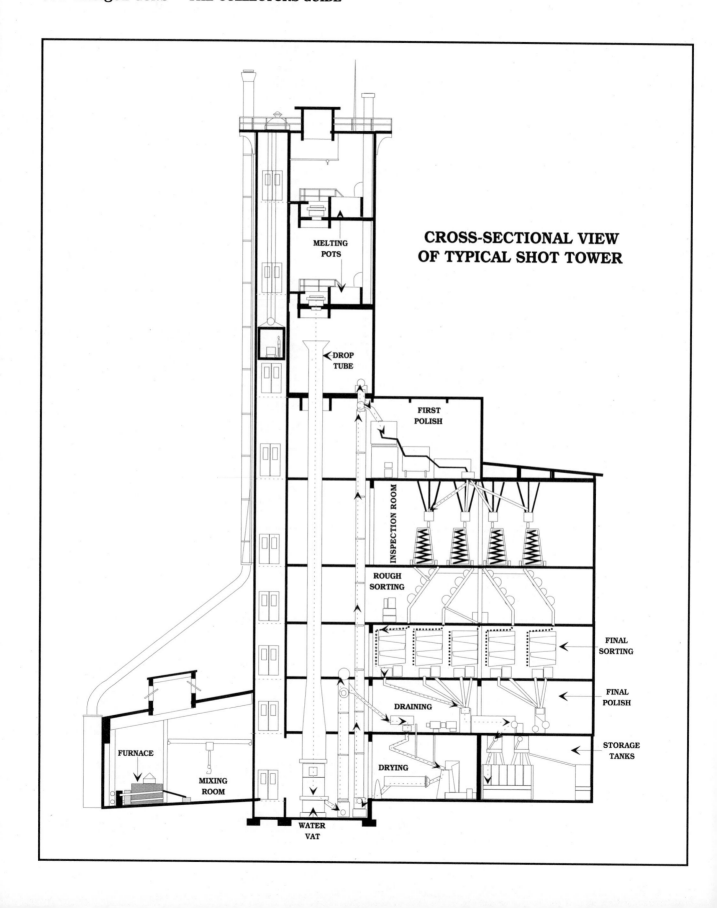

CROSS-SECTIONAL VIEW
OF TYPICAL SHOT TOWER

MELTING
POTS

DROP
TUBE

FIRST
POLISH

INSPECTION ROOM

ROUGH
SORTING

FINAL
SORTING

FINAL
POLISH

DRAINING

STORAGE
TANKS

DRYING

FURNACE

MIXING
ROOM

WATER
VAT

CHAPTER SIX
OBSOLETE
GUN PARTS

There are millions of antique guns that are incomplete or in poor repair. However, restoring antique guns can be a touchy subject — especially among collectors. Many valuable firearms have been completely ruined by hobbyists who were not aware of the guns' value and tried to "fix 'em up" a bit. A good rule-of-thumb for restoring antique firearms is to try to halt deterioration, preserve their current appearance and leave it at that.

On the other hand, there are cases where the restoration of an antique gun is warranted. Collectors prefer to have their firearms complete, so if a particular rare model is missing, say, a hammer, it would be in order to find an original hammer — preferably not a modern-made duplicate — and replace it. If the next owner of the gun frowns upon this, the replacement is easily removed without any damage to the original gun. In fact, who is to say that a 100-year-old "original" collector gun has not had a part or two replaced during its early "working" years? If, say, a broken mainspring was replaced 75 years ago with a factory replacement, it would be impossible to tell. So the firearm does not lose any collector value. By the same token, an original collector firearm that has had a broken mainspring replaced with a factory replacement seven hours ago should not lose any of its value. In fact, it should increase in value, if anything. For this reason, there has been a strong interest in all parts for obsolete guns in recent years. In many instances, disabled guns — when junked out for parts — will bring more than a complete firearm of the same model in excellent condition.

However, original replacement parts for obsolete firearms are becoming harder and harder to find. Consequently, gun parts for some antique guns have increased in value at a faster rate than the gun itself. Some parts that brought only a dollar or two a decade ago are now commanding tens of dollars or more — if the part can be found at all!

The scarcity and demand for certain gun parts have prompted some individuals and companies to offer duplicate parts for sale, but prices for these are about the same as for the originals — due to the high cost of machining.

There are thousands of different models with many more different parts, and space does not permit listing even a fraction of these in this publication. However, the Winchester Model 1894 rifle is certainly one of the most popular arms ever to come down the pike. This year marks its 100th anniversary of continuous production, although with many, many variations. Consequently, a pre-1900 Winchester Model 1894 rifle will be used to demonstrate how replacement parts are detected, priced, ordered, and installed.

DATES OF MANUFACTURE

Knowing that a certain part is missing from a particular gun may seem as simple as finding an original part and installing it. However, this is not always the case. Referring to the Model 1894, there were many changes in parts throughout the years that it has been in production. The hammer, for example, went through a number of changes in design and appearance. To restore a particular model to its original condition requires that the appropriate hammer style be purchased. While any of the styles will probably suffice to fire the rifle, it will not be authenic, and the value of the rifle will be lowered. Consequently, to obtain an authentic replacement part for most antique firearms requires knowing when the gun was manufactured. Then, a little research in one of the many reference books (and old gun catalogs) will reveal the proper part style to use.

To determine the year a particular Model 1894 rifle was manufactured, compare the serial number of the rifle to the ones in the following table. This is a condensed table that starts with the year the Model 1894 was introduced and continues to 1900.

Year	Serial Numbers	
	Beginning With	Ending With
1894	1	14759
1895	14760	44359
1896	44360	76464
1897	76465	111453
1898	111454	147684
1899	147685	183371
1900	183372	204427

If the date of manufacture cannot be determined by the serial number on other antique guns, or if no serial number is inscribed, usually each firearm will have certain characteristics that can help in dating the gun. But this may take lots of research.

IDENTIFYING THE PART

External Parts: Missing external gun parts should be readily detected. For example, a hammer (on an exposed hammer model), a front sight, buttplate, magazine tube, and similar items should be noticed immediately. However, to order a replacement part correctly requires that the part be identifed with the exact name. Let's assume that the magazine tube on your Model 1894 is hanging loose from the forearm. You notice a dovetail notch on the underside of the barrel, which you assume is for some type of holder to secure the tube, but you are not certain of the exact name of the part. Chances are, the person taking the order is not going to recognize "that little thingamajig on the bottom of the barrel near the muzzle," and if the person taking the order is not experienced with the model in question, he or she will not even recognize the part if you called it "a

magazine holder." However, if you had an exploded view of the firearm, along with a parts list as shown on pages 320 and 321, you would readily see that the part is called "magazine-tube ring" and the original Winchester part number is 12194. Such information helps to ensure that the part you need will be the one you will get.

Furthermore, by looking at the average retail price next to each part on page 325, you will know if you're getting a bargain or not. If the seller asks, say, $48.00 or even $50.00 for the hammer, the price is "in the ballpark" and you would probably go ahead and buy it. However, if the asking price was around $100, you might want to shop further.

Internal Parts: Damaged or missing interior parts from an obsolete firearm are not so easily detected. For example, let's assume that the hammer will not cock on the Model 94. The hammer is easily moved to the cocking position, and feels as though the correct spring tension is applied by the mainspring. However, it will not stay in the cocked position. If the hammer will stay in the half-cocked position, the most probable cause for this malfunction is a broken hammer notch. If the hammer will not stay in either the full- or half-cocked positions, the sear (Key No. 61 in the exploded view) is either broken or missing.

When trying to detect what hidden parts may be damaged or missing, the rifle will probably have to be disassembled to find out for certain. However, much time can be saved if some type of guide is used — such as a troubleshooting chart listing the malfunctions for a particular model along with the probable cause and corrective action. These charts can save even the seasoned professional much time when examining an unfamiliar firearm. In most cases, the entire firearm will not have to be disassembled; only the section containing the broken or missing part.

Once the problem is known, the recommended corrective action may be taken, which usually requires a replacement part or else the part must be repaired or reworked. If an authentic replacement part cannot be found, modern welding techniques can do wonders in restoring many broken parts, and if the repair involves an internal part, the repair will not be visible. If this latter route is taken, the collector value will be reduced somewhat — the exact amount depending upon the model.

Winchester Model 1894
Lever-Action Repeating Rifle

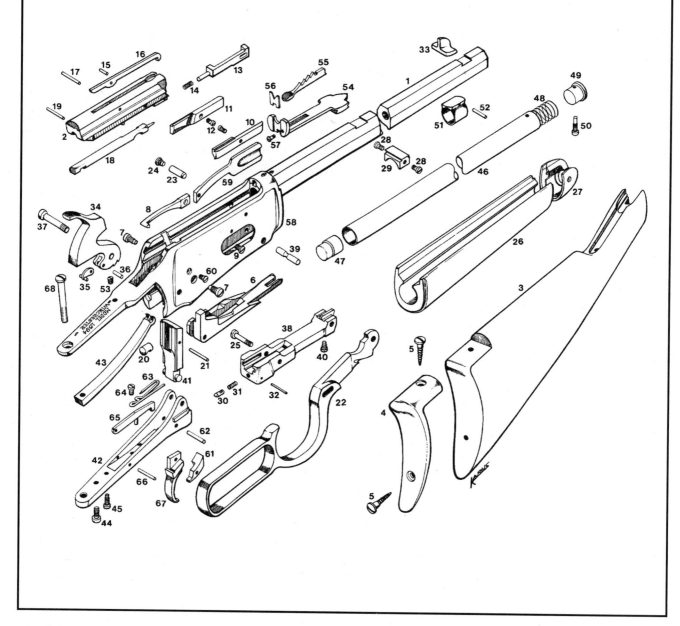

Exploded view of a pre-1900 Winchester Model 94 Sporting Rifle, with full octagonal barrel, crescent buttplate, and standard sights. A legend, identifying the parts, is shown on the facing page, along with the average value of each.

PARTS LIST

Key No.	Part No.	Part Name	Value
1	594	Barrel, 85% bore	$275.00
2	2294	Breechbolt	65.00
3	2694	Buttstock	135.00
4	4094	Buttstock Plate	40.00
5	4494	Buttstock Plate Screws (2)	3.00
6	4594	Carrier	20.00
7	4694	Carrier Screws (2)	2.00
8	4794	Carrier Spring	5.00
9	4894	Carrier-Spring Screw	2.00
10	4994	Cartridge Guide, Right	12.00
11	5094	Cartridge Guide, Left	12.00
12	5194	Cartridge-Guide Screws (2)	2.00
13	5694	Ejector	10.00
14	5894	Ejector Spring	3.00
15	5994	Ejector-Spring Stop Pin	3.00
16	5294	Extractor	16.00
17	5394	Extractor Stop Pin	3.00
18	6094	Firing Pin	18.00
19	6194	Firing-Pin Stop Pin	3.00
20	6094A	Firing-Pin Striker	6.00
21	6094B	F.P. Striker Stop Pin	3.00
22	6294	Finger Lever	30.00
23	6494	Finger-Lever Pin	5.00
24	6594	Finger-Lever Stop Screw	4.50
25	6694	Finger-Lever Link Screw	3.00
26	6794	Forearm	50.00
27	7494	Forearm Tip	25.00
28	8394	Forearm-Tip Screws (2)	3.00
29	8494	Forearm Tenon	14.00
30	8894	Friction Stud	5.00
31	8994	Friction-Stud Spring	3.00
32	9094	Friction-Stud Stop Pin	3.00
33	16994	Front Sight	30.00
34	9594	Hammer	45.00
35	9394	Hammer Stirrup	5.00
36	9494	Hammer-Stirrup Pin	3.00
37	9694	Hammer Screw	3.00
38	9794	Link	28.00
39	9894	Link Pin	3.00
40	9994	Link-Pin Stop Screw	3.00
41	10194	Locking Bolt	24.00
42	10394	Lower Tang	30.00
43	10694	Mainspring	20.00
44	10894	Mainspring Screw	4.00
45	10994	Mainspring-Strain Screw	3.00
46	12494	Magazine Tube	35.00
47	11094	Magazine Follower	8.00
48	11294	Magazine Spring	12.00
49	11394	Magazine Plug	8.00
50	11994	Magazine-Plug Screw	4.00
51	12194	Magazine-Tube Ring	12.00
52	12294	Magazine-Tube Rin Pin	3.00
53	14594	Peep-Sight Plug Screw	3.25
54	19294	Rear Sight (complete)	50.00
55	19394	Rear-Sight Elevator	12.00
56	19594	Rear-Sight Slide	20.00
57	19694	Rear-Sight Slide Screw	6.00
58	14694	Receiver	100.00
59	15394	Spring Cover	16.00
60	15494	Spring-Cover Screw	6.00
61	15694	Sear	12.00
62	15794	Sear Pin	4.00
63	15894	Sear and Safety-Catch Spring	4.00
64	15994	Sear and Safety-Catch Spring Screw	4.00
65	12094	Safety Catch	12.00
66	12294	Safety-Catch Pin	3.00
67	8794	Trigger	24.00
68	9194	Upper-Tang Screw	10.00

Once the replacement part is obtained, it is best to have the part installed by a professional gunsmith. However, if you attempt the project yourself, use caution. There are already many good gunsmithing books on the market that explain the importance of using the proper size screwdriver blade when removing gun screws and other disassembly tips, so this information will not be duplicated here. Just remember that parts for many antique guns may be brittle, and it is not uncommon to snap off a screwhead during disassembly. Again, such work is best left to the professional. Regardless of who does the replacement, the proper disassembly/assembly procedures must be followed. The following explains the basic disassembly instructions for the Winchester Model 1894 rifle.

DISASSEMBLY

Remove the tang screw and buttstock. Take out mainspring tension screw in lower tang and then remove mainspring. Remove hammer screw before removing hammer — holding up safety-catch pin while doing so; remove lower tang by backing out of frame.

Remove finger-lever stop-pin screw, then drift out finger-lever pin from right to left. Take out link-pin screw and drift out link pin (on pre '64 models.) Remove the locking block, finger lever and link. Slide out breechbolt before removing carrier screw from each side of receiver; remove carrier. Unscrew the cover screw and remove the spring cover. Remove carrier-spring screw and carrier spring.

Remove sear and safety-catch spring screw and spring. Remove safety-catch pin and safety catch. Remove trigger and sear pin along with sear and trigger.

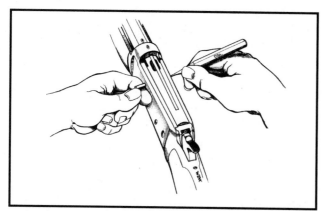

The first step in disassembling an antique is most important. Take the steps in proper order to avoid damage to a valuable firearm.

To disassemble breechbolt, first remove extractor; continue by removing the ejector stop pin, ejector and spring. The firing-pin stop pin and firing pin may then be removed.

Remove the two forend cap screws and slide cap forward away from forend. Drift out magazine ring pin, then unscrew magazine-cap screw — being careful not to let the magazine spring fly out. Carefully release the magazine cap and remove magazine spring along with its follower.

Slide magazine tube forward until it clears forend. Remove forend, then twist the magazine tube counterclockwise to remove magazine ring. Any attempt to drive out the magazine ring will result in a damaged ring or dovetail slot.

On Model 1894 carbines, the barrel-band screws are removed, followed by the barrel bands — swinging the front band upside down to clear the front sight on some models. Reassemble in reverse order.

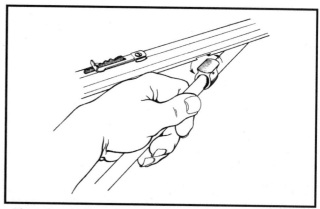

There is usually only one way in which most gun parts can correctly be removed. For example, many uninformed people will try to drive out the magazine-tube stud in an early Winchester Model 94. Doing so will damage the stud as well as the dovetail slot in the barrel. A slight twist, as shown above, is all that is required to readily remove the stud correctly.

SOURCES FOR GUN PARTS

If you are unable to locate the needed part(s) from dealers in antique gun parts, an advertisement in one of the shooting publications may bring results. Gun shows and flea markets are another possibility. If all else fails, replacement parts can be made by a machine shop, but expect to pay a pretty penny for just one or two parts. If this route is taken, exact dimensions for the part must be obtained. These can be taken from existing parts or else provided in the form of working drawings. The drawings below give the dimensions for three Winchester Model 1894 screws. Such drawings are indispensable for making accurate replacement parts for antique firearms. After shaping, most parts will have to be heat-treated to function and wear properly.

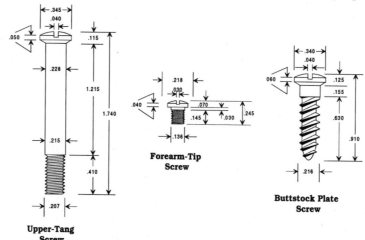

Upper-Tang Screw

Forearm-Tip Screw

Buttstock Plate Screw

BIBLIOGRAPHY

BOOKS

Baer, Larry
The Parker Gun. North Hollywood: Beinfeld Publishing Inc., 1974,1976.

Blackmore, Howard L.
British Military Firearms 1650-1850. New York: Arco Publishing Co., 1961.

Blair, Claude
Pollard's History of Firearms. New York: Macmillan Pub. Co., 1983.

Brown, M. L.
Firearms in Colonial America. Washington, D.C.: Smithsonian Institution Press, 1980.

Brownell, F. & Son
Gunsmith Kinks. Montezuma, Ia.: F. Brownell & Son, 1983.

Buchanan, Lamont
A Pictorial History of the Confederacy. New York: Crown Publishers, Inc., 1951.

Butler, David F.
The American Shotgun. New York: The Winchester Press, 1973.

Carey, A. Merwyn
English, Irish and Scottish Firearms Makers. New York: Thomas Y. Crowell Co., 1954.

Chapel, Charles E.
The Gun Collector's Handbook of Values. New York: Coward, McCann & Geoghegan, 1963 and other editions.

Cope, Kenneth L.
Stevens Pistols and Pocket Rifles. Ottawa, Ontario: Museum Restoration Service, 1971.

Datig, Fred A.
Cartridges for Collectors, Vol I. 1956.
Cartridges for Collectors, Vol. II. 1958.
Cartridges for Collectors, Vol. III. 1967.
Alhambra, Ca.: Borden Publishing Co.

Edwards, William B.
Civil War Guns. (Illus.) Harrisburg, Pa.: The Stackpole Co., 1962.

Flayderman, Norm
Flayderman's Guide to Antique American Firearms, Fifth Edition. Northfield, Ill.: DBI Books, Inc., 1983.

George, John Nigel
English Pistols & Revolvers. New York: Arco Publishing Co., 1962.

Gun Digest, 1953–1987 Editions
Northfield, Ill.: DBI Books, Inc.

Haven, Charles T., and Belden, Frank A.
A History of The Colt Revolver. New York: Bonanza Books, 1940, 1978.

House of Collectibles
The Official 1981 Price Guide to Antique & Modern Firearms. Orlando, Fla.: House of Collectibles, 1981.

Hughes, James B.
Mexican Military Arms: The Cartridge Period, 1866-1967. Houston: Deep River Armory, Inc., 1968.

Johnson, James R.
Kentucky Rifles & Pistols. Golden Age Arms Co., 1976.

Keith, Elmer
Six Guns. New York: Bonanza Books, 1955, 1961.

Kentucky Rifles and Pistols, 1750-1850
Published by Golden Age Arms Co. and James R. Johnston for the Kentucky Rifle Association, 1976.

Konig, Klaus-Peter, and Hugo, Martin
Waffen Sammein: Die Wichtigsten Pistolen und Revolver seit 1850. Stuttgart: Motorbuch Verlag Stuttgart, 1983.

Lindsay, Merrill
The Kentucky Rifle. New York: Arma Press for the York County, Pennsylvania Historical Society, 1972.

The Lure of Antique Arms
New York: David McKay, Inc., 1976.

Lord, Francis A.
Civil War Collector's Encyclopedia, (Illus.) Secaucus, N.J., Castle Books, 1965.
Uniforms of the Civil War. San Diego, Calif.: A.S. Barnes & Co., Inc., 1970.

Madis, George
The Winchester Book. Brownsboro, Tex.: George Madis, 1979.

Merino, Angel Hernandez
El Tiro Con Armas de Avancarga Hoy. Leon, Spain: Everest, S.A., 1983.

Maxwell, Samuel L., Sr.
Lever Action Magazine Rifles. Dallas: Samuel L. Maxwell Sr., 1976.

Moore, Warren
Weapons of the American Revolution...and Accoutrements. New York: Funk & Wagnalls, 1967.

Neumann, George C.
The History of Weapons of the American Revolution. New York: Harper & Row, 1967.

Nonte, George
Black Powder Guide. So. Hackensack, N.J.: Stoeger Publishing Co., 1976.

Peterson, Harold L.
A History of Firearms. New York: Charles Scribner's Sons, 1961.

Pioneer Press
Cartridge Broadsheets.
Ramagae, Kenneth
Lyman Black Powder Handbook. Middlefield, Conn.: Lyman Products Corp., 1981.
Reynolds, Major E. G. B.
The Lee-Enfield Rifle. New York: Arco Pub. Co., 1962.
Rosa, Joseph G.
Guns of the American West. New York: Exeter Books, 1988.
Rywell, Martin
American Antique Pistols and Their Current Prices. Union City, Tenn.: Pioneer Press, 1966. 17th Edition, 1974.
American Antique Rifles and Their Current Prices. Union City, Tenn.: Pioneer Press, 1975.
Confederate Guns and Their Current Prices. Union City, Tenn.: Pioneer Press, 1974.
Schroeder, Joseph J., Jr.
Gun Collector's Digest. Northfield, Ill.: DBI Books, Inc., 1983.
Rare Selections From Old Gun Catalogs.
Sellers, Frank M., and Smith, Samuel E.
American Percussion Revolvers. Ontario, Canada: Museum Restoration Service, 1971.
Sharps Firearms. Denver, Colo.: Sellers Publications, 1982.
Serven, James E.
Colt Firearms From 1836. Santa Ana, Calif.: Foundation Press, 1974.
Sharpe, Philip B.
The Rifle in America. New York: William Morrow and Co., 1938.
Shooter's Bible, Volumes 75-85.
So. Hackensack, N.J.: Stoeger Pub. Co., 1984-1988.
Shumaker, P. L.
Colt's Variations of the Old Model Pocket Pistol 1848-1872. Borden Pub. Co./Fadco Pub. Co., 1966.
Smith, James A., and Swanson, Elmer

The Antique Pistol Book. Speedwell Publishing Co., 1948.
Smith, W. H. B.
Small Arms of the World. Harrisburg, Pa.: Stackpole Pub., 1973.
Stelle & Harrison
Gunsmith's Manual. Reprint of circa 1890 Gunsmith's Manual.
The Story of American Hunting and Firearms
New York: Sunrise Books/E.P. Dutton & Company, Inc., 1959, 1976.
Time-Life Editors
The Gunfighters. New York: Time-Life Books, 1974.
Traister, John
How To Buy and Sell Used Guns.
Gunsmithing At Home. South Hackensack, N.J.: Stoeger Publishing Co., 1983.
U.S. Cartridge Co.
U.S. Cartridge Company's Collection of Firearms. Old Greenwich, Conn.: WE Inc.
Virgines, George E.
Saga of the Colt Six-Shooter and the Famous Men Who Used It. Frederick Fell, Inc., 1969.
West, Bill
Remington Arms & History. Whittier, Calif.: Bill West, 1970.
Winchester Handbook Volume I. Whittier, Calif.: Bill West, 1966.
Wilkinson, Frederick
Antique Firearms. New York: Doubleday & Co., Inc., 1969.
The World's Great Guns
New York: The Hamlyn Publishing Group Ltd., 1977.
Wilson, R. L.
The Colt Heritage: The Official History of Colt Firearms from 1836 to the Present. New York: Simon and Schuster, 1979.

ANTIQUE ARMS CATALOGS

Colt's Revolving and Breechloading Firearms, 1896.
Hartford, Conn.: Colt's Patent Fire Arms Mfg. Co.
Francis Bannerman Sons Catalogue, 1936.
New York: Francis Bannerman Sons, 1936.
Forehand Arms Company, 1896.
Stoney Creek, Ontario: Fortress Publications Inc.
Forehand & Wadsworth Illustrated Catalogue of Fire-Arms, 1880.
Stoney Creek, Ontario: Fortress Publications Inc.
Fourteen Old Gun Catalogs.
Chicago, Ill.: The Gun Digest Association, Inc., 1962.
Great Western Gun Works Illustrated Catalogue No. 40, 1888-89.
J.H. Johnston. Northfield, Ill.: Reprint by Gun Digest, 1966.
Hopkins and Allen Catalog
Ithaca Gun Catalog, 1915
Iver Johnson Firearms, Catalog No. 19A.
Iver Johnson's Arms and Cycle Works. Boston: McGrath-Sherrill Press.

Lefever Arms Co., 1889.
Stoney Creek, Ontario: Fortress Publications Inc.
Marlin Fire Arms Catalog, 1897.
New Haven, Conn.: Marlin Fire Arms Co., 1897.
Maynard Breech-Loading Firearms, 1880.
Holyoke, Mass.: Transcript Book and Job Printing House, 1880.
E.C. Meacham Arms Co., 1884.
Reprint by Gun Digest Co.
Remingtons' Illustrated Catalog and Reduced Price List, 1877.
Ilion, N..Y.: Citizen Steam Printing Establishment, 1877.
Remington Catalogs of 1885, 1902, 1906.
L.C. Smith Breech-Loading Guns, 1889.
Stoney Creek, Ontario: Fortress Publications Inc.
Smith & Wesson Catalog, 1901.
Springfield, Mass.: Smith & Wesson, 1901.
Winchester Repeating Arms Co. Catalogs of 1891, 1893, 1905.
New Haven, Conn.: Winchester Repeating Arms Co.

INDEX

Abbey, J.F. & Co.
  Single-Barrel Muzzle-Loading
    Shotgun, 201
  Double-Barrel Muzzle-Loading
    Shotgun, 201
Acme Arms Double-Barrel Shotgun, 201
Adams Revolving Arms Co. Patent
  Percussion Revolver, 21
Adams, Robert, 21, 75, 97
  Army Revolver, 97
  Beaumont-Adams Revolver, 21
  Deane-Adams Revolver, 21
Adirondack Arms Co., Magazine
  Repeating Rifle, 103
Aetna Arms Company
  Pocket Revolvers, 21
  Model 1876 Single-Action Revolver, 21
Albrecht, Andrew, Kentucky
  Flintlock Rifles, 171
Albright, Henry, Kentucky Flintlock
  Pistol, 87
Alden, E.B., Double-Barrel Muzzle-
  loading Shotgun, 201
Aldenderfer, M., Kentucky
  Flintlock Rifles, 171
Alexia, Single-Action Revolver, 22
Allen, Cyrus, 125
Allen, Ethan, 174
Allen, Ethan, & Co., Pistol, 23
Allen (Ethan) & Thurber (Charles)
  Center Hammer Pistol, 22
  Pepperbox, 22
  Pocket Pistol, 22
Allen (Ethan) and Wheelock (Thomas)
  Army Revolver, 97
  Navy Revolver, 97
  Pocket Pepperbox, 22
  Single-Shot Percussion Pistol, 22
Allen, Silas, Kentucky Flintlock
  Rifles, 171-172
Allen, Thomas, Kentucky
  Flintlock Rifles, 172
Allen, William, Kentucky
  Flintlock Rifles, 172
American Arms
  Handguns
    1847 Walker Percussion Revolver, 231
    1851 Colt Navy Revolver, 231
    1858 Remington Army Revolver, 231
    1858 Army Target Revolver, 231
    1860 Colt Army Revolver, 231
  Long Arms
    Hawkeye Cap-'N-Ball Rifle, 231
American Arms Company
  Double-Action Revolver, 23
  Hammerless Revolver, 23
  Single-Action Revolver, 23
  Wheeler Pat. O/U Pistols, 23

American Kentucky Flintlock Pistols,
  see **gunmakers,** 81-87, and also
  individual replica manufacturers
American Kentucky Flintlock Rifles,
  see **gunmakers, 138-154,** and also
  individual replica manufacturers
American Standard Tool Co.
  Hero Revolver, 23
  Seven-Shot Revolver, 23
Angstadt, Peter
  Kentucky Flintlock Pistol, 87
  Kentucky Flintlock Rifles, 172
Angush, James, Kentucky
  Flintlock Rifles, 172
Ansley, Rigdon &, Confederate
  Revolver, 88
Anstadt, Jacob, Kentucky
  Flintlock Rifles, 173
Antis, William, Kentucky Flintlock
  Rifles, 173
Arabian Firearms
  DAG Blunderbuss, 201
  Flintlock Pistol, 23
  North African Snaphaunce, 103
Argentina Military
  Model 1891 Mauser Military Rifle, 104
  Model 1891 Mauser Carbine, 104
Armsport, Inc.
  Replica Handguns
    Colt Navy 1847 Model 5145, 231
    Colt Navy 1851 "Reb" Model 5133, 231
    Colt Navy 1851 "Reb" Model 5134, 231
    Colt Navy 1851 "Reb" Model 5135, 231
    Colt Navy 1851 Model 5136, 231
    Colt 1860 Army Model 5139, 232
    Remington Army Model 5120, 232
    Remington Army Stainless Model
      5138, 232
  Replica Rifles
    Hawken Percussion Model 5101, 232
    Hawken Model 5102, 232
    Hawken Smoothbore Model 5102S,
      232
    Hawken Model 5102V, 232
    Hawken Model 5103, 232
    Hawken Model 5103C, 232
    Hawken Model 5103CS, 232
    Hawken Model 5103S, 232
    Hawken Flintlock Model 5104, 232
    Hawken Model 5104B, 233
    Hawkentucky, 233
    Kentucky Deluxe, 233
    Kentucky Model 5108, 233
    Kentucky Model 5108V, 233
    Kentucky Model 5109, 233
    Kentucky Model 5110, 233
    Kentucky Model 5110A, 233

    Kentucky Rifle/Shotgun Model 5115,
      233
    Kentucky Rifle-Shotgun Model
      5115C, 234
    Tryon Trailblazer, 234
  Replica Shotguns
    Double Muzzleloading, 234
Asheville Confederate Rifle, 188
Ashmore & Son Kentucky Caplock
  Rifle, 104
Aubrey, A.J. Shotguns
  Custom Grade Double, 202
  Hammerless Single-Shot, 202
  Hand-Engraved Double, 201
  Highest Grade Double, 202
  Standard Grade Double, 201
Australian Cadet Martini B.S.A. Rifle, 104
Austrian Firearms
  Confederate Rifle, 188
  Model 90 Mannlicher Carbine, 104
  Model 1867 M. Werndl Rifle, 104
  Model 1868 M. Werndl Cavalry
    Carbine, 105
  Model 1886 Military Rifle, 105
  Model 1895 Steyr-Mannlicher
    Carbine, 105
  Model 1895 Steyr-Mannlicher Rifle,
    105
Aveley & Wheaks Percussion
  Coat Pistol, 23
Avery, G. Kentucky
  Flintlock Rifles, 173

B

Babcock Revolver, 23
Backhouse, Richard, Kentucky
  Flintlock Rifles, 173
Bacon Arms Company, 24, 42
  GEM Pocket Revolver, 24
  Governor Pocket Revolver, 24
  Pepperbox Revolver, 24
  Pocket Revolver, 24
Bacon Manufacturing Company
  "Boot Gun" Pistol, 24
  Derringer, 24
  Navy Revolver, 24
  Pocket Revolver, 24
  Six-shot Revolvers, 24
Bailey, Robert, Kentucky
  Flintlock Rifles, 173
Baker Gun & Forging Co. Shotguns
  Batavia Leader Double, 202
  Black Beauty Double, 202
  Deluxe Double-Barrel, 202
  Double, Grades A-S, 202
  Paragon Double-Barrel, 202

Pigeon Double-Barrel, 202
Single Shot, 202
Trap Guns, 202
Baker, Jacob, Kentucky
Flintlock Rifles, 173
Baker, John, Kentucky
Flintlock Rifle, 174
Baker, M.A., Confederate Rifle, 188
Baker, Melchior, Kentucky Flintlock
Rifles, 174
Balkan Miquelet, 105
Ball & Williams, 95
Ballantine, John and Patrick, Kentucky
Flintlock Pistol, 87
Ballard, C.H., & Co., 106, 130, 136
Single-Shot Derringer, 24
Rifles
Model of 1861 Sporting Rifle, 106
Model of 1862 Military Carbine, 106
Model of 1862 Military Rifle, 106
Model of 1863 "Kentucky" Rifle, 106
Model of 1863 Military Carbine, 106
Model 1864 Sporting Rifle, 106
Model 1866 Carbine, 107
Model 1866 Sporting Rifle, 107
Hunter's Rifle, 107
Hunter's Rifle No. 1, 107
Hunter's Rifle No. 1½, 107
Mid-Range Target Model, 107
Sporting Rifle, No. 2, 107
Shotguns
Single-Shot RF Shotgun, 202
Single-Shot, 202
Balsley, Christian, Kentucky Flintlock
Rifles, 174
Barnhart, George, Kentucky Flintlock
Rifles, 174
Baum, Samuel, Kentucky Flintlock
Rifles, 174
Bayard Shotguns
Hammer Double-Barrel, 203
Hammerless Double, 203
Beals (Fordyce) Patent Revolver, 87
Beck, Gideon, Kentucky
Flintlock Rifles, 174, 175
Beck, John, Kentucky
Flintlock Rifles, 175
Beck, John Phillip, Kentucky Flintlock
Rifles, 175
Becker, J., Kentucky Flintlock Rifles, 175
Beeman Precision Arms, Inc.
Hege-Manton Flintlock Pistol, 235
Hege-Siber Single-Shot Pistol, 234
Beig, S., Kentucky Flintlock Rifles,
175-76
Belgian Firearms
Handguns
Double-Barrel Pistol, 24
O/U Percussion Travelling Pistol, 24
Pinfire Revolvers, 25
Pocket Pistols, 25
Pocket Percussion Pistol, 25
Saloon Pistol, 25
Target Pistol, 25
Rifles
Model 1889 Mauser Military Rifle,
108, 137
Model 1889 Mauser Carbine, 108
Shotguns
Bolt Action, 203
Double-Barrel, 203
Double-Barrel Percussion, 203
Double-Barrel Sidelock, 203
Bell, John, Kentucky Flintlock Rifles, 176
Benefer, Amos, Kentucky Flintlock
Rifles, 176

Bentley, David, R.I.C. Bulldog Revolver,
26
Bergman
Model 1894, 26
Model 1896 Pistols, 26
Model 1897, 26
Berleur, Guillaume, Belgian Cavalry
Pistol, 26
Berlin, Abraham, Kentucky Flintlock
Rifles, 176
Berlin, Issac, Kentucky Flintlock Rifles,
176
Best Kentucky Flintlock Rifles, 176, 177
Bielry Kentucky Flintlock Pistol, 77
Beyer, N., Kentucky Flintlock Rifles, 177
Bickel, Henry, Kentucky Flintlock Rifles,
177
Biddle, R. & W.C., Kentucky Flintlock
Rifles, 177
Billings Vest Pocket Single-Shot Pistol, 26
Bittner, Gustav
Bittner Model 1893, 26
Blake Rifle Company
Grade A Sporting Rifle, 108
Grades B, C, and D Hunting Rifle, 108
Bliss, F.D., Pocket Revolver, 27
Bobb, Anthony, Kentucky Flintlock
Rifles, 177
Bond & James Double-Barrel Percussion
Shotgun, 203
Bonehill, C. G., 174, 185
Boone, Samuel, Kentucky Flintlock
Rifles, 178
Borchardt 1893 Pistol, 27
Border, Samuel, Kentucky Flintlock
Rifles, 178
Bosworth Kentucky Flintlock Rifles, 178
Boyer, Daniel & Henry, Kentucky
Flintlock Rifles, 178
Bozeman, David &, Confederate Rifle,
155
Brammer, George, Kentucky Flintlock
Rifles, 179
Bray, Edward, Merwin &, 46
Briggs, Horace A., Single-Shot Pistol, 27
British Firearms
Pistols
Belt Pistol, 27
Blunderbuss Coach Pistol, 27
Holster Pistol, 27
Flintlock Pistol, 27
Light Dragoon Flintlock Pistol, 27
New Land Pattern Pistol, 27
Overcoat Flintlock Pistol, 28
Pocket Flintlock Pistol, 28
Pocket Percussion Pistols, 28
Trade Flintlock Pistol, 28
Trade Percussion Pistol, 28
Volunteer Lancer's Pistol, 28
Military Rifles
Baker Rifle, Socket Bayonet Model,
110
Brown Bess, India Pattern,110
Brown Bess, Short Land Pattern, 110
Eliott Carbine, 110
Double Rifle, 111
Martini-Enfield Conversion, 110
Martini-Henry MK IV, 111
Native Cavalry Carbine, 111
New Land Musket, 111
P. 1839 Rifle, 109
P. 1841 Rifle, 109
P. 1844 Yeomanry Carbine, 109
P. 1853, 109
P. 1856 Cavalry Carbine, 109
Paget Cavalry Carbine, 111
Snider MK II, 112

Snider MK III Artillery Carbine, 112
Snider MK III Percussion Rifle, 112
Snider-Type Target Rifle, 112
British Shotguns
Double-Barrel Percussion, 203
Flintlock Fowler, 204
Fowler Conversion, 204
Martini-Henry Single-Shot Military,
204
Milne's Patent Flintlock Blunderbuss,
204
Percussion Fowler, 204
Sea Service Boarding Blunderbuss,
204
Southall Blunderbuss, 204
Brooke, B., Queen Ann Pistol
Percussion Conversion, 28
Brooklyn Arms Co. Slocum Pocket
Revolvers, 29
Brong, Joseph Kentucky Flintlock Rifles,
179
Brong, Peter, Kentucky Flintlock Rifles,
179
Brooks, John, Kentucky Flintlock Rifles,
179
Brown, W.F., (Gibbs Carbine), 161
Brown Bess Muskets, See British and
Canadian Rifles, and individual
replica manufacturers
Brown, James, Kentucky Flintlock
Rifles, 179
Brown Manufacturing Co., 29, 46, 115
Southerner Derringer, 29
Bryant, James, Kentucky Flintlock
Rifles, 180
Buckwalter, Abraham, Henry & John,
Kentucky Flintlock Rifles, 180
Bullard, James H., Repeating Arms Co.,
100
Rifles
40-90 Lever Action Sporting, 113
Express Rifle, 113
Heavy Frame Sporting, 113
Lever Action Sporting (Standard),
113
Military Lever Action Carbine, 113
Military Lever Action Rifle, 113
Rim Fire Hunting Rifle, 113
Schuetzen Rifle, 113
Single-Shot Mil. Carbine, 113
Single-Shot Mil. Musket, 113
Standard Sporting Rifle, 101
Target Rifle, 113
Target and Hunting Rifle, 113
Bulow, Charles, Kentucky Flintlock
Rifles, 180
Burgess, Andrew, 105
Slide-Action Shotguns, 205
Burnside, A.E., Breech-Loading Carbine,
193
Burr, David J., and Spiller, E.N.,
Confederate Revolver, 78
Burt, John, Kentucky Flintlock Rifles,
180
Busch Kentucky Flintlock Rifles, 180
Butterfield, Jesse, U.S. Army Revolver,
87
Bye, Martin, 40, 178

C

Calderwood Flintlock Pistol, 29
Calderwood, William, Kentucky Flintlock
Rifles, 181
Call, George, Kentucky Flintlock Rifles,
181

Canadian Firearms
  Handguns
    Model 1858 Percussion Pistol, 29
    Webley MK III Model 1897, 29
  Rifles
    Brown Bess, India Pattern, 114
    Brown Bess, Short Land Pattern, 114
    Lee-Enfield MK I, 114
    Long Lee-Enfield MK I, 114
    Martini-Henry MK I, 114
    Martini-Henry MK III Presentation
      Rifle, 115
    Martini-Metford MK VI, 115
    Newfoundland Sealing Gun, 115
    P. 1853 Artillery Carbine, 114
    Snider MK II Rifle, 116
    Snider MK III Cavalry Carbine, 116
Carlile, H., Kentucky Flintlock Rifles, 181
Chance, Wm. & Son
    Percussion Fowler, 205
    Double-Barrel Percussion Shotgun,205
Chapin, A.H., Percussion Rifle, 116
Chapman, G., and J., Pocket Revolver, 29
Cheney (Elisha), North and, Model 1799
    Flintlock Pistol, 83
Cherrington, Thomas, Kentucky
    Flintlock Rifle, 181
Chicago Firearms Company Protector
    Palm Pistol, 30
Chinese Firearms
  Handguns
    Ancient Hand Cannon, 30
    Ancient Hand Cannon Pistol, 30
    Hand Cannon,30
  Military Rifles
    Model 1888 Mauser, 116
Clark, John, Kentucky Flintlock Rifles, 181
Clark, Dr. Jonathan, 33
    Double-Barrel Hammer Shotgun, 171
    Double-Barrel Hammerless
      Shotgun, 171
Clement, Charles, Double-Barrel
    Shotguns, 206
Clement, J.B., Double-Barrel Shotguns, 206
Cofer, T.W., Confederate Revolver, 78
Colombian Military, Model 1891
    Mauser, 116
**Colt Firearms, Div. of Colt
    Industries,** 194
**Colt's Patent Fire Arms
    Mfg. Co.,** 20, 30, 50
  Handguns
    Bisley Model SA Revolver, 30
    Constabulary Revolver, 30
    Deringer—First Model, 31
    Deringer—Second Model, 31
    Deringer—Third Model (Thuer), 31
    Double Action Frontier (or Army)
      Revolver, 32
    "House Pistol" (Cloverleaf)SA
      Revolver, 32
    "House Pistol" SA Revolver, 32
    Lightning Central Fire DA Revolver, 32
    Model 1855 Root Percussion
      Handguns, 33
    Model 1872 Single-Action Revolver, 33
    Model 1877 Lightning DA Revolver, 29
    Model 1878 Frontier Revolver, 28
    New House SA Revolver, 33
    New Line Pocket Revolver, 33
    New Line Police SA Revolver, 33
    New Navy Model 1889 DA Revolver, 33
    New Navy Model 1892 DA Revolver, 34
    New Pocket DA Revolver, 34
    New Police DA Revolver, 34

    New Service DA Revolver, 34
    Old Line SA Pocket Revolver, 34
    Paterson "Baby" or No. 1 Pocket
      Percussion Handgun, 35
    Paterson "Baby" Percussion, 35
    Paterson No. 2 Belt Pistol, 35
    Paterson No. 3 Belt Pistol, 35
    Paterson No. 2 or No. 3 Belt, Cased, 35
    Single-Action Army Revolver, 35
  Handgun Replicas, *See also individual*
    replica manufacturers
    Baby Dragoon, 236
    First Model Dragoon, 236
    Second Model Dragoon, 236
    Third Model Dragoon, 236
    Model 1851 Navy Percussion, 236
    Model 1860 Army Percussion, 236
    Model 1861 Navy Percussion, 236
    Model 1862 Pocket Navy Percussion, 238
    Model 1862 Pocket Police Percussion, 238
    Walker Percussion, 238
  U.S. Military Handguns
    Dragoon, 2nd & 3rd Model, 89
    Model 1836 Paterson Texas, 89
    Model 1839 Paterson Texas Revolver, 79
    Model 1847 Army Revolver, 89
    Model 1848 Army Revolver, 89
    Model 1849 Old Model Belt or Pocket
      Pistol, 90
    Model 1849 Wells Fargo Revolver, 90
    Model 1851 Navy Revolver, 90
    Model 1860 Army 45 Revolver, 91
    Model 1873 SA Army, 91
    Model 1892 Army (Govt), 91
    Modl 1900 38 Automatic, 92
    Model 1902 Mil. Auto Pistol, 92
    Model 1902 Philippine Revolver, 92
  Rifles
    Model 1850 Percussion Carbine, 117
    Model 1855 Percussion Revolving, 117
    Model 1855 Revolving Mil. Rifle, 117
    Model 1861 Special Musket, 117
    New Lightning Magazine Baby
      Carbine, 117
    New Lightning Small Frame, 117
    New Lightning Medium Frame
      Magazine Carbine, 118
    New Lightning Medium Frame, 118
    New Lightning Medium Frame Mil.
      Carbine, 118
    New Lightning Large Frame, 118
    New Lightning Large Frame Carbine, 119
    Paterson Model 1836 Percussion
      Rifles, 119
    Paterson Model 1837 Percussion, 119
    Paterson Model 1839 Carbine, 119
    Burgess 12-Shot Repeating Carbine, 119
    Burgess 15-Shot Repeating Rifle, 119
  Shotguns
    Model 1878 Hammer Double, 206
    Model 1883 hammerless Double, 206
Columbus Fire Arms Mfg. Confederate
    Revolver, 78
Cone, D.D. Revolvers, 36
Conestoga Rifle Works Kentucky
    Flintlock Rifles, 181
Confederate
    Handguns, 78
    Rifles, 188-190
Connecticut Arms Company Pocket
    Revolver, 36

Connecticut Arms Co., Pocket Revolver, 36
Connecticut Arms & Mfg. Co. Bulldog
    Pistols, 36
Connecticut Valley Arms, *See CVA*
Continental Arms Company
    Continental 1 Pepperbox, 36
    Continental 2 Pepperbox, 36
Cook & Brother
    Confederate Artillery Rifle, 188
    Confederate Infantry Rifle, 188
    Confederate Musketoon, 188
Cooper, Joseph Rock, Percussion
    Pepperbox, 36
Copeland, Frank, Pocket Revolvers, 36
Cosmopolitan Breech-Loading Carbine, 193
Coster, Abraham, Kentucky Flintlock
    Rifles, 181
Cowles and Son Single-Shot Pistol, 37
Crescent Firearms Company, 206, 209
    Side-by-Side Shotgun, 206
    Side-by-Side Hammerless Shotguns, 206
    Single Barrel Shotgun, 206
Crispin, Silas, 37, 163
    Revolver, 37
Cruso, 172
C.S. & P. Rising-Breech Carbine, 155
Cummings, O.S., Pocket Revolver, 37
Cunkle, George, Kentucky Flintlock
    Rifles, 182
Cunningham,George W., Percussion
    Rifle, 119
CVA (Connecticut Valley Arms)
  Replica Pistols
    Colonial Percussion, 238
    Hawken Flintlock, 238
    Hawken Percussion, 238
    Kentucky Flintlock, 240
    Kentucky Percussion, 240
    Mountain Flintlock & Percussion, 240
    Philadelphia Derringer, 240
    Pioneer Single-Shot Percussion, 240
    Prospector Single-Shot, 240
    Tower Percussion, 240
    Vest Pocket Derringer, 240
  Replica Revolvers
    Colt 1851 Navy Percussion, 240
    Colt 1860 Army Percussion, 241
    Colt 1861 Navy Percussion, 241
    Colt Wells Fargo Percussion, 241
    Remington 1858 Army Percussion, 241
    Remington New Model Pocket
      Percussion, 242
  CVA Replica Rifles
    Big Bore Mountain Flintlock, 242
    Big Bore Mountain Percussion, 242
    Blazer, 242
    Blazer II, 242
    Express, 243
    Frontier Percussion, 243
    Hawken Percussion, 243
    Kentucky Flintlock, 243
    Kentucky Percussion, 243
    Mountain Flintlock, 244
    Mountain Percussion, 244
    Pennsylvania Flintlock Long, 244
    Squirrel, 245
    Squirrel Percussion, Left Hand, 245
    St. Louis Hawken, 245
  Replica Shotguns
    Blunderbuss, 245
    Double-Barrel Percussion, 245
Czechoslovakian Model 1898 Mauser
    Military Rifle, 120

D

Damascus Barrels, 173
Dance, David, George and James,
  Confederate Navy Revolver, 78
  Confederate 44 Cal. Revolver, 78
Danish Model 1889 Krag-Jorgensen
  Military Rifle, 120, 147
Danner, Jacob, Kentucky Flintlock
  Rifles, 182
Davenport, W.H., Shotguns, 207
Davis & Bozeman Confederate Rifle, 188
Davis, N.R. & Co.
  Double-Barrel Hammer Shotgun, 209
  Double-Barrel Hammerless Shotgun,
  209
  Percussion Shotgun, 209
Daw, George Henry, Sea Service Pistol,
  37
Deane, George & John, Adams Model
  1851 Revolver, 19
Deeds, H.W., Kentucky Flintlock Rifles,
  182
Demuth, John, Flintlock Target Rifle, 120
Deringer, Henry, Jr., 37, 38
  Dueller Pistols, 38
  Pocket Pistol, 38
Deringer, Henry, Sr., Flintlock Pistol, 82
Deringer Rifle & Pistol Works
  Centennial '76 Revolver, 38
  Pocket Model 1 Revolver, 38
  Pocket Model 2 Revolver, 38
  Pocket Revolver, 38
Derr(e), John, Kentucky Flintlock Rifles,
  149
Deterer, Adam, Kentucky Flintlock
  Rifles, 182
Dickinson, E.L. & J., Single-Shot Pocket
  Pistols, 38
Dickson, Nelson & Co.
  Confederate Carbine, 188
  Confederate Rifle, 188
Dixie Gun Works, Inc.
  Replica Handguns
  1848 Baby Dragoon, 246
  1851 Navy Percussion, 246
  1860 Army Percussion, 246
  Abilene Derringer, 246
  French Charleville Flintlock, 247
  LePage Dueling Pistol, 247
  Lincoln Derringer, 247
  Navy Percussion (Brass), 247
  Pedersoll English Dueling Pistol, 247
  Pennsylvania Pistol, 247
  Queen Anne Pistol, 247
  Remington Army, 247
  Screw Barrel Derringer, 247
  Screw Barrel Pistol, 247
  Spiller & Burr Brass Frame, 247
  Third Model Dragoon, 247
  Walker Percussion, 247
  Wyatt Earp Percussion, 247
  Replica Long Arms
  Brown Bess Musket, Second Model,
  248
  Buffalo Hunter, 248
  Deluxe Cub Rifle, 248
  Double-Barrel Magnum Shotgun, 248
  Enfield Model 1858 Two-Band, 248
  Enfield Three-Band Rifled Musket, 248
  Hawken Percussion, 248
  Indian Gun, 248
  In-Line Carbine, 248
  Kentuckian Carbine, 248
  Kentuckian Rifle, 249
  Mississippi Rifle, 249
  Pedersoli Waadtlander Rifle, 249

  Pennsylvania Rifle, 249
  Sanftl Schuetzen Target, 249
  Sharps Military Carbine, 249
  Sharps Rifle, 249
  Springfield Model 1863 Civil War
  Musket, 250
  Swiss Federal Target, 250
  Tennessee Mountain, 250
  Tennessee Squirrel, 250
  Tryon Rifle, 250
  Wesson Rifle, 250
  Winchester 1873 Carbine, 251
  Winchester 1873 Rifle, 251
  York County Pennsylvania, 251
  U.S. Model 1816 Musket, 251
  U.S. Model 1861 Rifle-Musket, 251
  Zouave Carbine, 251
  Zouave Model 1863 Rifle, 251
Dodd, John, Kentucky Flintlock Pistol, 87
Doll, Jacob, Kentucky Flintlock Rifles,
  182
Driggs, Seabury Ordnance Co., 119
Driscoll, J.B., Single-Shot Pocket Pistol,
  38
Dull, Jacob, Kentucky Flintlock Rifles,
  182
Dutch Military Rifles
  Model 1871/88 Beaumont-Vitali, 120,
  137
  Flintlock Musket, 120

E

Eagle Arms Company Revolvers, 38, 39
Eberman, Henry, Kentucky Flintlock
  Rifles, 183
Ecuador Model 1891 Mauser Military
  Rifle, 121
Egg, Durs, Percussion Pocket Pistol, 39
Ehrms, H., Kentucky Flintlock Rifles, 183
Elliot, W.H., 62, 63
Elwell, H., Kentucky Flintlock Rifles, 183
Enterprise Double-Barrel Shotgun, 209
Euroarms of America
  Replica Handguns
  1851 Navy Revolver, 252
  1851 Navy Sheriff Model 1080, 252
  1851 Navy Sheriff Model 1090, 252
  New Model Army Model 1010, 252
  New Model Army Model 1020, 252
  New Model Army Target Revolvers, 252
  Remington 1858 New Model Army, 252
  Rogers & Spencer Revolver, 252
  Rogers & Spencer Army Target, 252
  Rogers & Spencer London Gray, 253
  Schneider & Glassick Confederate, 253
  Long Arms
  Cook & Brother Confederate Carbine,
  253
  Hawken Model 2210A, 253
  London Armory Company Enfield
  Musketoon, 254
  London Armory Company Two-Band
  Enfield Musket, 254
  London Armory Company Three-Band
  Enfield Musket, 254
  Percussion Double-Barrel, 254
  Magnum Cape Gun, 254
European Pistols
  Cavalry Flintlock, 39
  Percussion Pistol, 39
Evans (Warren) Rifle Mfg. Co.
  New Model Repeating Carbine, 121
  New Model Military Repeating Rifle,
  121
  New Model Sporting Rifle, 122
  Old Model Military Rifle, 121

  Old Model Repeating Carbine, 121
  Old Model Sporting Rifle, 121
Evans, William, Double-Barrel
  Shotguns, 209

F

Fabrique Nationale D'Armes de Guerre,
  108
  Model 1900 Pocket Auto Pistol, 39
Farnot, Frederick, Frank & Jacob,
  Kentucky Flintlock Rifles, 183
Fayetteville
  Confederate Model 1855
  Pistol-Carbine, 78
  Confederate Rifle, 188
Fischer, Carl August, Double-Barrel
  Percussion Shotgun, 209
Fishburn, Philip, Kentucky Flintlock
  Rifles, 183
Fogerty, George, Double-Barrel
  Shot-gun, 209
Folsom, H & D Company, 206, 209
  Side-by-Side Hammer Shotgun, 209
  Side-by-Side Hammerless Shotgun,
  209
  Single-Shot Hammer Shotgun, 210
Fondersmith, George, Kentucky
  Flintlock Rifles, 183
Forbes, Gilbert, Kentucky Flintlock
  Pistol, 77
Fordney, C., Kentucky Flintlock
  Rifles, 183, 184
Forehand Arms Company, 39
  Shotguns
  Hammer Side-by-Side, 211
  Hammer less Double Single-Shot, 211
  Hammer single-Shot, 212
  Hammerless Shotgun, 212
**Forehand (Sullivan) & Wadsworth
  (Henry)**
  Handguns
  British Bulldogs, 40
  Bulldogs, 40
  New Model Army Revolver, 40
  New Navy, 40
  Old Model Army, 40
  Pocket Model, 40
  Russian Model, 40
  Single-Action Revolvers, 40
  Single-Shot Revolvers, 40
  Swamp Angel, 40
  Terror Revolver, 40
  Shotguns
  Side-by-Side, 210
  Hammerless, 210
  Single-Shot, 211
Foster, George P., 193
Foulke, Adam, Kentucky Flintlock Pistol,
  77
Freeman, Austin, Percussion
  Revolver, 41, 89
Freeman, W.D., 112
French Firearms
  Handguns
  Charleville Flintlock Pistol, 41
  Coat Pistol, 41
  Coupe de Poing Pepperbox, 41
  Flintlock Pistols, 41
  Howdah Pistol, 42
  Military Flintlock Pistol, 42
  Louis XIV Flintlock Pistol, 42
  Military Rifles
  Flintlock Musket, 122
  Model 1763 Musketoon, 122
  Model 1777 Musket, 122

Model 1866 Chassepot, 122
Model 1886 Lebel, 122, 147
Model 1892 Lebel Carbine, 122
Shotguns
Flintlock Trade, 212
Frey, Martin, Kentucky Flintlock Rifles, 184

G

Gallagher, Mahlon J.
Breech-Loading Bolt-Action Carbine, 193
Breech-Loading Metallic Cartridge Rifle, 123
Percussion Carbine, 123
Percussion Rifle, 123
Gander, Peter, Kentucky Flintlock Rifles, 184
Gardner, *See* Mendenhall, Jones & Gardner
Geddy, Davie & William, Kentucky Flintlock Pistol, 77
Gem Pistols, 42, 74
Gem Revolvers, 24, 42
Georgia Armory Confederate Rifle, 188
German Firearms
Handguns
Cavalry Pistol, 42
Pepperbox, 42
Military Rifles
Model 1871 Rifle & Carbine, 124
Model 1888 Mauser-Mannlicher Carbine, 124
Model 1888 Mauser-Mannlicher, 124
Model 1898 Mauser, 124
Model 1898A Mauser Carbine, 124
Getz, John, Kentucky Flintlock Rifles, 184
Gibbs Breech-Loading Carbine, 193
Glassick (Frederick G.) & Schneider (W.S.)
Confederate Revolver, 78
Goetz, Frederick, Kentucky Rifles, 184
Goetz, John, Kentucky Flintlock Rifles, 184
Golcher, Joseph
American Percussion Fowler, 212
British Percussion Fowler, 212
Governor Double Action Revolvers, 42
Graham, Hartley &, 51, 117
Grant, W.L., Revolvers, 42
Greene's Breech-Loading Carbine, 195
Greener, W.W., & Sons
Far-Killer Grade FH35 Double-Barrel Shotgun, 213
Hammerless Ejector Double-Barrel Shotgun, 213
Single-Barrel Shotgun, 213
Gresheim, J., Kentucky Flintlock Rifles, 184
Grier. See Griswold, Samuel
Griswold (Samuel) & Grier Confederate Revolver, 78
Griswold (Samuel) & Gunnison (A.W.)
Confederate Revolver, 78
Army Revolver Replica, 222
Gross, Charles B., 38
Gross (Henry) Arms Co., Pocket Revolvers, 43
Grove, Samuel, Kentucky Flintlock Rifles, 184, 185
Gump, Christian, Kentucky Flintlock Rifle, 185
Gunnison, A.W. *See* Griswold, Samuel

Gunpowder, Discovery and History of, 297

H

Haenel, C.G.
Mauser-Mannlicher Sporting Rifle, 126
Model '88 Mauser Sporter, 126
Haines, Issac, Kentucky Flintlock Rifles, 185
Hampton, John N., Kentucky Flintlock Rifles, 185
Hankins, William, *See* Sharps & Hankins
Harding, James, Coat Pistol (Conversion), 43
Harpers Ferry
Flintlock Musket, 191
Flintlock Rifle, 191
Model 1805 Flintlock Pistol, 83
Pistol (replica), 219
Harrington & Richardson, Inc., 20,43, 255
Handguns
Model No. 1 Revolvers, 43
Saw-Handled Frame Spur Trigger Models, 43
Replica Rifles
1873 Springfield Carbine Cavalry, 255
1873 Springfield Carbine, Little Big Horn Commemorative, 255
1873 Springfield Officer's Rifle, 255
Shotguns
Double-Barrel, 213
Harris, Henry, Kentucky Flintlock Rifles, 185
Hartley & Graham, 51, 117
Hege Waffenschmiede im Zeughaus, Beeman/Hege-Siber Single-Shot Pistol (replica), 194
Hench, Peter, Kentucky Flintlock Rifle, 185
Henry, Alexander, Single-Shot Rifle, 126, *See* also Martini-Henry Rifles under British and Canadian Rifles
Hepburn, Lewis L., 118
Hillegas, J., Kentucky Flintlock Rifles, 185, 186
Hill's Patent Bulldog Revolver, 44
Hoak, Mathias, Kentucky Flintlock Rifles, 186
Hodges, R.E. Elastic Gun, 126
Hodgkins Confederate Carbine, 156
Hollis & Sheath Percussion Shotguns, 214
Holmes, Cobourg C.W., Percussion Rifle, 126
Holmes, Henry, Travelling Pistol, 44
Hollenbeck, Three-Barrel Gun, 214
Hollis & Sheath, Percussion Shotguns, 214
Hood (Freeman) Firearms Co. Single-Action Revolver, 44
Hopkins & Allen
Handguns
Pocket Revolver,44
Model 1876 Revolver, 44
Ladies Garter Pistol, 44
New Model Target Pistol, 44
Ranger No. 1, 44
Ranger No. 2, 45
Safety Police DA Revolvers, 45
XL 1 DA Revolver, 45
XL 3 DA Revolver, 45
XL .30 Long Revolver, 45
XL Bulldog Revolvers, 45
XL CR .22 Short RF, 45

XL Derringer, 45
XL Navy Revolver, 45
Replica Handguns
1851 Navy, 255
1860 Army, 255
Boot Pistol, 255
Bounty Hunter, 256
J.S. Hawken, 256
Kentucky Pistol, 256
John Manton Pistol, 256
W. Moore Target Flintlock, 257
Mountain Pistol, 257
Napoleon Le Page, 257
Parker English Flintlock Dueling, 257
Parker English Percussion Dueling, 257
Wesson Model 1847, 257
Replica Long Arms
All-American Percussion, 257
Brush Rifle, 257
Buggy Deluxe Percussion, 257
Deerstalker, 257
Heritage Percussion, 258
Minuteman, 258
Offhand Deluxe Percussion, 258
Over/Under, 258
Pennsylvania Half-Stock, 258
Pennsylvania Hawken, 258
Target Percussion, 259
Replica Shotguns
Double-Barrel, 259
Lightweight, 259
Howard Brothers
Breech-Loading Hammerless Rifle, 127
Single-Shot Shotgun, 214
Single-Shot Sporting Rifle, 110
Humble, Michael, Kentucky Flintlock Rifles, 186
Hunt Edwin, Percussion Rifle, 127
Hunt, Walter, "Volition" Repeating Rifle, 127
Hunter, John, Arms Co., 183, 185
Huntington, V., Kentucky Flintlock Rifles, 186

I

Imhoff, Benedict, Kentucky Flintlock Rifles, 186
Innes, James, Scottish Hunting Musket, 128
Intercontinental Arms (E.M.F.)
Replica Handguns
Dakota SA Revolvers, 259, 260
Duck's Foot, 260
Kentucky Pistol, 260
Kiwi Pocket Pistols, 260
Kiwi Vest Pocket, 260
Renegade Double-Barrel, 260
Replica Long Arms
Kentuckian Carbine, 260
Kentuckian Rifle, 260
Irving, William
Derringer, 45
SA Knuckle-Duster Revolvers, 45
SA Pocket Revolvers, 46
Italian Military Rifles
Model 1870/87/15 Vetterli, 128, 147
Model 1891 Mannlicher-Carcano, 128
Model 1891 TS Cavalry Carbine, 128

J

Japanese Military
Matchlock Bluderbuss, 214
Matchlock Rifle, 128

Jennings, Lewis, 128
   Breechloading Rifle First Model, 129
   Breechloading Repeating Rifle, 129
   Muzzle-Loading Rifle, 129
Johnson, Ira, 95
Johnson, Robert, 95
Johnson's, Iver, Arms & Cycle Works
  Handguns
   DA Revolver—Safety Hammer Model,
    46
   DA Revolver—Safety hammerless, 46
   "Eclipse" Single-Shot Derringer, 46
   "Favorite" Revolver, 47
   "Prince" Percussion Pistol, 47
   "Tycoon" Revolvers, 47
  Shotguns
   Side Snap Single Barrel, 215
   Top Snap Single Barrel, 215
Jones, *See* Mendenhall, Jones & Gardner
Jorg, Jacob, Kentucky Flintlock Rifles,
  186
Joslyn Arms Company
  Army Revolver, 88
  Model 1855 Breech-Loading Carbine,
   195
  Model 1864 BreechLoading Carbine,
   195
Joslyn, Benjamin F., 88, 129, 195
Jover, William, Duelling Pistols (Pair), 47

K

Kaeding, and Liddle, Pocket Revolver, 49
Keller, John, Kentucky Flintlock Rifles,
  186, 187
Kendall, Nicanor, Percussion Under-
  hammer Single Barrel Shotgun, 215
King, Charles A., 180

Kinter, John S., Kentucky Flintlock
  Rifle, 187
Kittredge, B., & Co., Sharps "Triumph",
  47
Knox, Marston &, 51

L

Lamb, H.C., Confederate Rifle, 188
Latrobe, Merrill and Thomas,
  Breech-Loading Carbine, 163
Leavitt, Wesson (Edwin) and, Revolver,
  90
Lee, James Paris, 147, 170
Lee's Munner Special, 172
Leech, Henry, Pocket Pistol, 48
Leech (Thomas) and Rigdon (C.H.),
  Revolver, 78
Lefaucheux, Casimir, 48, 215
Lefaucheux, Eugene
  Army Pinfire Revolver,88
  Brevete Military Revolvers, 48
  Pinfire Revolver, 48
  Lefever Arms Co., 178
  Hammerless Double-Barrel
   Shotguns, 215
Lefever Arms Co.,
  Lefever Hammerless Double, 216
LeMat, Dr. Jean A.
  Grapeshot Revolver, 48
  Confederate Carbine, 189
  Replica Revolvers, 222
Lewis and Tomes
  Double-Barrel Percussion Shotgun,
  216
  Percussion Pistol, 49
  Sawhandle Pistol, 49

Loewe, Ludwig, & Co., 124
Lombard, H.C., and Co., Single-Shot
  Pocket Pistol, 49
London Armoury Company, 97
Lovat, T., Flintlock Pocket Pistol, 49
Lowell Arms Company, 50, 69
  Pocket Revolvers, 50
Lower, John P., SA Pocket Revolvers, 50
Lyman Products Corporation
  Replicas
   Plains Pistol, 260
   Great Plains Rifle, 260
   Trade Rifle, 261

M

"M" Confederate Rifle, 189
Magazines, Successful Rifle, 137
Maltby, Henley & Co., Revolvers, 50
Manhattan Firearms Company
  "Bar Hammer" Double Screw
   Barrel, 50
  "Hero" Percussion Derringer, 50
  Navy Percussion Revolver, 50
  Percussion Pocket Revolver, 51
  Six-Shot Pepperbox, 51
  Three-Shot Pepperbox, 51
Manton, John, Coat Pistol, 51
  Flintlock Pistol (replica), 194
  Percussion Pistols (replicas), 214, 220
Marlin (John M.) Fire Arms Co.
  Handguns
   1872 XXX Revolvers, 51
   1873 XX Revolvers, 51
   1875 Revolver, 51
   1887 DA Revolver, 51
  Rifles
   Model 93 Carbine, 131
   Model 93 Musket, 132
   Model 93SC Sporting Carbine, 132
   Model 1881 Repeating, 130
   Model 1888 Repeating, 131
   Model 1889 Lever-Action Repeating
    Carbine, 131
   Model 1889 Rifles, 131
   Model 1891 Repeating Rifles, 131
   Model 1892 Lever-Action, 131
   Model 1893 Lever-Action, 131
   Model 1894 Lever-Action, 132
   Model 1894 Baby Carbine, 132
   Model 1894 Musket, 132
   Model 1895 Lever-Action, 135
   Model 1895 Carbine, 135
   Moel 1895 Fancy-Grade Rifle, 135
   Model 1897 Lever-Action, 135
   Model 1897 Lever-Action Repeater, 135
  Shotguns
   Model 1898 Slide-Action, 216
Marston, & Knox, 51
Marston, William W.
  Breech Loader Handgun, 52
  Pepperbox Handgun, 52
  Single-Shot DA Handgun, 52
  Single-Shot SA Handgun, 52
Massachusetts Arms Co.
  Single-Barrel Shotgun, 217
Mason, William, 32
Maurer, John, Kentucky Flintlock Rifle,
  187
Mauser Firearms, 137. *See also*
  individual military arms listings
  1898 Military Auto Pistol, 52
  Model 1871 Carbine, 135
  Model 1871 Rifle, 135
  -Mannlicher Model 1888 Rifle, 135
  -Mannlicher Model 1888 Carbine, 136

  Model 1898, 136
Maynard, Dr. Edward,
  Breech-Loading Percussion Carbine,
   156, 195
McEntree, W.C., & Company, 226
Mendenhall, Jones & Gardner
  Confederate Rifle, 189
Meriden Fire Arms Company, 201
Merrill, Latrobe and Thomas,
  Breech-Loading Carbine, 196
Merrimack Arms Mfg. Co., Southerner
  Handgun, 52
  Double-Barrel Rifle, 136
Merwin (Joseph) & Bray (Edward)
  22 Revolver, 52
  28 Revolver, 52
  30 Cal. Revolver, 52
  31 Cal. Revolver, 52
  32 Cal. Revolver, 52
  42 Cal. Revolvers, 52
  Navy Revolver, 53
  "Original" Revolvers, 53
  Reynolds Revolver, 53
  Single-Shot Handgun, 53
Merwin, Hulbert & co., 44, 53
  Army Model DA Pocket Pistol, 53
  Army Model DA Revolver, 53
  Army Model SA Pocket Pistol, 53
  Army Model SA Revolver, 53
  Pocket Model, 53
  Revolver (32 Cal.), 53
  Revolver (38 Cal.), 53
Merwin, Taylor & Simpkins, 52, 53
Mexican Military Rifles
  Mauser Model 1895 Carbine, 136
  Mauser Model 1895 Rifle, 136
  Mondragon Model 1893, 137
  Mondragon Model 1894, 137
  Pieper, Nagant Model 1893 Carbine,
   137
  Remington Model 1871 Carbine, 137
  Remington Model 1871 Rifle, 137
  Remington Model 1897 Carbine, 137
  Remington Model 1897 Rifle, 137
  Spanish Peabody, 137
  Spencer Model 1865 Carbine, 137
  Whitney Rolling Block Carbine, 137
  Whitney Rolling Block Rifle, 137
  Winchester Model 1866, 137
  Winchester Model 1894 Carbine, 137
Minneapolis Firearms Co., Protector
  Palm Metallic Cartridge Revolver, 53
Monarch Handgun Revolver, 53
Mondragon Rifles, *See* Mexican Military
  Rifles
Moore, John P., & Co., Double-Barrel
  Percussion Shotgun, 217
Moore, William, & Co., Double-Barrel
  Percussion Shotgun, 217
Moore's Patent Fire Arms Co.
  Front-loading Revolver, 54
  Handgun Revolver,54
  Single-Action Revolver,54
  No. 1 Single-Shot Derringer, 54
  Williamson's Patent Revolver, 54
Morgan (Lucius) & Clapp, Single-shot
  Pocket Pistol, 54
Morse Confederate Breech-Loading
  Musket & Carbine, 189
Mowery, W.L., Gun Works
  Replica Long Arms
   Allen & Thurber Rifle, 261
   Allen & Thurber Special, 261
   Hawk Short Stock Rifle, 261
   Hawkins Full-Stock, 261
   Hawkins Half-Stock, 261
   Texas Carbine, 261

Percussion Shotgun, 261
Murray, J.P.
    Confederate Cavalry Carbine, 189
    Confederate Carbine Musketoon, 189
    Confederate Rifle, 189
    Confederate Sharpshooter's Rifle, 189

N

National Arms Company, 30, 31, 54
    Moore's Front-loading Revolver, 55
    Moore's No. 2 Derringer, 55
    Teat-Fire Revolver, 55
Navy Arms Company, Inc.
    Replica Pistols
        Elgin Cutlass Percussion, 262
        Harpers Ferry, 262
        Kentucky Flintlock, 262
        Kentucky Percussion, 262
        Le Page Dueling, 262
        Le Page Flintlock, 263
        Le Page Percussion, 263
        John Manton Match, 263
        Moore & Patrick English, 263
        F. Rochatte Percussion, 263
    Replica Revolvers
        1851 Navy "Yank" Revolver, 264
        1862 Police Model, 264
        Army 60 Sheriff's Model, 264
        Colt 1847 Walker, 264
        Colt 1860 Army, 264
        LeMat Army Model, 264
        LeMat Cavalry Model, 264
        LeMat Navy Model, 264
        Reb Model 1860, 266
        Remington 1858 Deluxe, 266
        Remington 1858 Stainless, 266
        Remington New Model Army, 266
        Remington Target Model, 266
        Rogers & Spencer Navy, 266
    Replica Rifles
        Brown Bess Musket, 266
        Buffalo Hunter, 266
        Country Boy Rifle, 267
        Creedmoor No. 2 Target, 267
        Enfield 1853 Rifle/Musket, 267
        Enfield 1858 Rifle, 268
        Enfield 1861 Musketoon, 268
        Hawkens-Left Hand, 268
        Henry Carbine, 268
        Henry, Iron-Frame, 268
        Henry Military Model, 269
        Henry Trapper, 269
        Ithaca/Navy Hawken, 269
        Kentucky Rifle, 269
        Mark I Hawken Flintlock, 269
        Mark I Hawken Percussion, 270
        Mississippi Model 1841, 270
        Morse Muzzleloading, 270
        Parker-Hale Musketoon Model 1861, 270
        Parker-Hale Three-Band Musket Model 1853, 270
        Parker-Hale Two-Band Musket Model 1858, 270
        Parker-Hale 451 Volunteer, 270
        Remington-Style Rolling Block, 271
        Rigby-Style Target, 271
        Springfield 1863 Rifle, 271
        Swiss Federal Target, 271
        Whitworth Military Target Rifle, 271
        Zouave Rifle, 272
    Replica Shotguns
        Classic Side-by-Side, 272
        Fowler, 272
        Hunter, 272

Morse/Navy Single-Barrel Percussion, 273
    Model T & T, 273
Needham Percussion Rifle, 138
Neihard, Peter, Kentucky Flintlock Rifle, 187
New Haven Arms Co., 80, 138
    Volcanic Lever-Action Rifle, 138
Newbury, Frederick, Arms Co.,
    Single-Shot Pistol, 55
Nichols & Childs Percussion Rifle, 138
Nichols, John, 178
Nock, Henry, Trade Pistol, 55
North Simeon
    Model 1799 North & Cheney Flintlock Pistol, 83
North & Skinner, Revolving Rifle, 138

O

Oberholzer, Christian, Kentucky Flintlock Musket, 187
Onion & Wheelock, Percussion Double-Barrel Shotgun, 218
Organ, F., Percussion Double-Barrel Shotgun, 218
Osgood Gun Works, Duplex Revolver, 55

P

"P" Breechloading Carbine, 189
"P" Confederate Rifled Carbine, 189
Page, John, Kentucky Flintlock Rifle, 187
Palmer Breech-Loading Bolt Action Carbine, 196
Parker Brothers
    Hammerless Side-by-Side Shotgun, 218
    Outside Hammer Double Shotgun, 218
    Under Lever Side-by-Side Shotgun, 218
Parr, James, Flintlock Pistol, 55
Perry Navy Breech-Loading Carbine, 196
Perrin Army Revolver, 98
Pettingill, Charles S.
    Army Hammerless Revolver, 56, 98
    Belt or Navy Model Revolver, 50
    Pocket Model Revolver, 50
    Piedmont, 172
Pieper, Henri, Anciens Establissements
Pieper, 202 **See** also Mexican Military Rifles
Plant Manufacturing Co.
    Cup Primed Cartridge Revolvers, 56
    "Original" Revolvers, 56
    Six-shot Revolvers, 56
    Reynold's Revolver, 56
    Frontier Percussion, Left-hand, 202
Plate, A.J., vs. Henry Deringer, 37
Pond, Lucius W., Revolver, 56
Porter, Perry W. Revolving Turret Rifle, 138
Portuguese Military Model 1886
    Kropatschek Carbine, 139
    Model 1898 Military Rifle, 139
Powell, William & Son Ltd.
    No. 1 & 2 Best Grade Double, 219
    No. 6 Crown Grade Double, 219
    No. 7 Aristocrat Grade Double, 219
Prescott, Edwin A.
    Navy Revolvers, 57
    Revolver (I), 57
    Revolver (II), 57
Prussian Long Arms
    Flintlock Sporting Musket, 139

Model 1839 Military Musket, 139
Pulaski Confederate Rifle, 189

R

Randall, Joseph C., Percussion Rifle, 140
Raphael Revolver, 88
Rappahannock Forge
    Flintlock Musket, 187
    Flintlock Pistol, 82
Reid, James, 45, 57
    SA "Knuckle-Duster" Revolver, 57
    Single Action Revolvers, 57
Remington Arms., 20, 57, 140, 196. *See* also Mexican Military Rifles and individual replica manufacturers
    Handguns
        Model 1861 Army Revolver, 59
        Model 1861 Navy Revolver, 59
        Model 1865 Navy Pistol, 59
        Model 1867 Navy Breech-Loading, 82
        Model 1867 Navy Single-Shot, 59
        Model 1871 Army Pistol, 93
        Model 1875 SA Army Revolver, 59
        Model 1890 SA Army Revolver, 60
        Model 1891 Single-Shot Target Pistol, 60
        Army Revolver, 89
        Navy Revolver, 89
        Double Repeating Deringer, 60
        Improved Navy Revolver, 60
        Iroquois Revolver, 60
        New Models No. 1, 2 3, & 4 Revolver, 60
        New Pocket Revolver, 61
        New Model Police Revolver, 61
        SA Belt Revolver, 61
        Vest Pocket Pistols, 61
        -Beals' Model Pocket Revolvers, 58
        -Beals' Third Model Pocket Revolver, 59
        -Beals' Navy Revolver, 59
        -Beals' Army Revolver, 59
        -Elliot Pepperbox Deringer, 61
        -Elliot Single-Shot Deringer, 62
        -Elliot "Zig-Zag" Deringer, 62
        -Rider DA Pocket Pistol, 62
        -Rider New Model Magazine Pistol, 62
    Rifles
        No. 1 Military Rifle, 140
        No. 1 Sporting, 140
        No. 1½ Sporting, 141
        No. 2 Sporting, 141
        No. 3 (Hepburn) Sporting, 141
        No. 3 (Hepburn) Creedmoor and Schuetzen, 141
        No. 3 (Hepburn) High Power, 141
        No. 3 Sporting, 141
        No. 4 Single Shot, 141
        No. 5 Small-Bore Rifle, 142
        Breechloading Carbine, 142
        Converted 1863 Musket, 142
        Converted Carbine, 142
        Converted Short Rifle, 142
        Creedmoor Target Rifle, 142
        Danish Military Rifle, 143
        Flintlock Rifle, 143
        Jenks Carbine Conversion, 143
        Light Baby Carbine, 143
        Model 1877 New York State Rifle, 143
        Model 1879 Argentine Musket, 143
        New York State Carbine, 143
        New York State Rifle, 143
        Percussion Rifle, 143
        Revolving Rifle, 143
        Single-Shot Rifle Cane, 144

"Split Breech" Carbine, 144
Springfield Model Rifle, 144
State of Massachusetts Musket, 144
Swedish Military Rifle, 144
Swiss Military Rifle, 144
U.S. Model 1841 Percussion Musket, 144
U.S. Model 1842 Converted Musket, 144
U.S. Model 1862 Zouave, 144
U.S. 1863 Musket, 144
U.S. Model 1870 Army Springfield, 145
U.S. Navy Cadet, 145
U.S. Navy Carbine, 145
-Beals Rifle, 145
-Elliot Skeleton-Stock Rifle, 145
-Keene Army/Navy Musket, 145
-Keene Magazine Gun, 145
-Lee Bolt Action Sporting, 146, 147
Shotguns
Breechloading Single-Barrel, 220
Muzzleloading Single-Barrel, 220
Model 1874 Side-by-Side
Breech-Loading, 220
Model 1882 Double-Barrel, 221
Model 1885 Double-Barrel, 221
Model 1887 Double-Barrel, 221
Model 1889 Double-Barrel, 221
Model 1893 Single-Barrel, 221
Model 1894 Double-Barrel, 222
Model 1900 Double-Barrel, 222
Remington, E. (Eliphalet), & Sons Co.,
57, 97, 140
Revolutionary War Flintlock
Musket, 191
Renwick Arms Co. Single-Shot
Percussion Rifle, 146
Richards, Westley & Co., Ltd.
Side-by-Side Shotgun, 223
Single Barrel Shotgun, 223
Richardson Flintlock Pistol, 63
Richardson & Overman, 123, 193
Richmond Confederate Carbine, 189
Confederate Navy Musketoon, 189
Confederate Pistol, 78
Confederate Rifled Musket, 189
Rider, Joseph, 62
Rifle Cartridges, Obsolete Centerfire, 285
Rigby, John, Dueling Pistols, 63
Rigdon, C.H. and Leech, Thomas,
Confederate Revolver, 78
Rimfire Cartridges, Obsolete, 255
Riverside Arms Co., Single-Shot
Shotgun, 223
Robbins & Lawrence, 128, 150
Robertson Double-Barrel
Percussion Shotgun, 223
Robinson-Sharps Confederate Carbine,
190
Rodman, Richard, 226
Rogers and Spencer, 56
Army Revolver, 89
Navy Revolver Replica, 222
Root, Elisha King, 33. **See** also
Colt Handguns
Ruger, See Sturm, Ruger & Co.
Rupertus, Jacob
Double-Barrel Derringer, 63
Eight-Shot Pepperbox, 63
SA Revolvers, 63
Single-Shot Derringers, 63
Russian Military Model 1891
Mosin-Nagant Bolt Action Rifles, 146

S

Savage & North Revolvers, 64

Savage Revolving Fire-Arms Co., Navy
Model Revolver, 64
**Savage (Arthur W.) Repeating
Arms Co.,** 89, 119, 125, 126
Rifles
Model 1892 Repeating Military, 149
Model 1895 Carbine, 149
Model 1895 Repeating Mi. Rifle, 149
Model 1895 Sporting, 149
Model 1899 Repeating Mil. Carbine,
150
Model 1899 Repeating Mil. Rifle, 150
Model 1899 Sporting, 150
Scheaner, William, Kentucky
Flintlock Rifles, 187
Schneelock, Otto, Sporting Target Rifle,
150
Schofield, Col. G.W., S&W Revolvers,
63, 89
**Schneider (William S.) & Glassick
(Frederick G.),** Confederate Revolver, 78
Scott, W & C, and Son
Double-Barrel Percussion Shotgun,
223
Segallas Flintlock Pocket Pistol, 64
Sears, Roebuck & Co., 167
Sharps, C., & Company, 64. *See* also
Sharps Rifle Co.
Handguns
Breech-Loading Single-Shot Pistol, 65
Bryce Revolver, 65
Models 1, 2, 3, & 4 Four-Barrel
Pepperbox, 65
Percussion Revolver, 65
Pistol Rifle, 65
Sharps, C., Arms Co., Inc., 273
Sharps (Christian) & Hankins (William),
65, 150, 155
Model 1861 Navy Rifle, 155
Model 1862 Cavalry Carbine, 155
Pepperbox Pistols, 57
Sharps Rifle Company
Model 1851 Boxlock Hunting, 150
Model 1851 "Original" Model
Breech-Loading Percussion, 151
Model 1852 Slanting Breech
Carbine, 151
Model 1855 Slanting Breech
Carbine, 151
Model 1859 Breech-Loading
Percussion Carbine, 151
Model 1859 BL Percussion
Military, 151
Model 1859 Vertical Breech
Percussion Carbine, 151
Model 1863 BL Percussion
Carbine, 152
Model 1863 BL Percussion
Military, 152
Model 1867 BL Carbine, 152
Model 1868 BL Sporting, 152
Model 1869 BL Carbine, 152
Model 1869 BL Military, 152
Model 1870 BL Carbine, 152
Model 1870 BL Military, 152
Model 1873 Creedmoor, 152
Model 1874 Business, 152
Model 1874 Creedmoor Rifles, 152-53
Model 1874 Military, 153
Model 1875 Rifle, 153
Model 1876 BL Sporting, 153
Model 1876 Long-Range Rifles, 153
Model 1876 Mid-Range Rifles, 153
Model 1877 Rifle, 153
Model 1878 Business, 153
Model 1878 Express, 153
Model 1878 Hunter, 153

Model 1878 Long Range, 153
Model 1878 Mid Range, 153
Model 1878 Military Carbine, 153
Model 1878 Mil. Rifle, 154
Model 1878 Officer's, 154
Model 1878 Short Range, 154
Model 1878 Sporting, 154
Breech-Loading Cartridge Carbine, 154
Commercial Breech-Loading Mil., 154
Shattuck, C.S., Pocket Revolvers, 66
Shawk & McLanahan, Navy Revolver, 66
Sherrard (Joseph) & Taylor (Pleasant)
Confederate Revolver, 78
Shiloh Sharps Replicas
Model 1863 Sporting Rifle, 273
Model 1863 Military Carbine, 274
Model 1863 Military Rifle, 274
Model 1874 Business Rifle, 274
Model 1874 Carbine, 274
Model 1874 Long-Range Express
Sporting, 274
Model 1874 Military Rifle, 274
Model 1874 Sharps Saddle, 275
Model 1874 Sporting No. 1, 275
Model 1874 Sporting No. 3, 275
Shotshells, Obsolete, 303
Siber, Jean Frederick, 234
Slocum, Frank, Pocket Revolvers, 26
Slotter & Co., 50
Smith Arms, 155
Smith Arms Company, 66, 155
Smith Breech-Loading Carbine, 196
Smith, Horace, 70. **See also Smith and
Wesson, Inc.**
Smith L.C.
Hammer Double-Barrel Shotguns, 224
Hammerless Side-by-Side Shotguns
(I), 224
Hammerless Side-by-Side Shotguns
(II), 224, 225
Smith, Otis A., Single-Action Revolvers,
66
Smith, William
Duelling Pistols (Pair), 66
Flintlock Pocket Pistol, 67
Smith and Wesson, Inc., 20, 67, 79,
113, 197, 1217
Model 1891 Single-Shot Target Pistol,
67
Revolvers
Model No. 1 Revolver, 68
Model 1 Hand Ejector Revolver, 68
Model No. 1½, 68
Model No. 2 Army (Old Model), 68
No. 3 SA Frontier, 68
No. 3 SA American, 68
No. 3 SA Revolver, New Model 70
No. 3 SA Russian, 70
No. 3 SA Target, 70
32 Double Action, 70
32 Single Action, 70
38 Cal. Revolver, 89
38 Double Action, 70
38 Mil. & Police—First Model, 71
38 Mil. & Police Target, 71
38 SA Revolver, 71
38 SA Third Model or Model 1891,
71
38 SA Mexican, 71
44 Double Action, 72
44 Single-Action Russian, 72
Model 1880 SA Revolver, 72
Model 1891 SA Revolver, 72
Bicycle Revolver, 72
Revolver Styles, 60
Safety Hammerless DA, 72
-Schofield SA Revolver, 72, 99

Rifles
Model .320 Caliber Revolving, 155
Snider, Jacob, .100. See also British and Canadian Snider Rifles
Southern Arms Company, 172
Spanish Handguns
Cibar Percussion Pistol, 73
65 Cal. Miguelet Pistol, 73
69 Cal. Miguelet Pistol, 73
Flintlock Trade Pistol, 73
Spencer. See Rogers and Spencer and Mexican Military Rifles
Spiller (Edward N.) & Burr (David J.)
Confederate Revolver, 88
Springfield Armory Firearms. See U.S. Military Pistols and U.S. Military Flintlock Rifles
Starr Arms Company
Model 1858 DA Army Revolver, 73
Model 1863 Sa Army Revolver, 73
Civil War Cavalry Carbine, 197
Civil War Revolvers, 90
Starr, Ebenezer Townsend, 64, 164
Stevens, J., Arms & Tool Co., 73, 156, 201
Handguns
Conlin Gallery Pistol, 74
Deringer Pistol, 73
Model 1883 Lord Gallery Pistol, 74
No. 37 Pistol, 74
Diamond No. 43 Pistols, 74
GEM Pocket Pistol, 74
Old Model Pocket Pistol, 74
Tip-Up No. 41 Pistol, 74
Rifles
No. 1, 2, 3, & 4 Single Shot, 156
No. 5 Expert Single Shot, 156, 157
No. 6 Expert Single Shot, 156
No. 7 Premier Single Shot, 156
No. 8 Premier Single Shot, 157
No. 9 Single Shot Range, 157
No. 10 Single Shot Range, 157
No. 11 Single Shot Ladies, 157
No. 12 Single Shot Ladies, 157
No. 13 Single Shot Ladies, 157
No. 14 Single Shot Ladies, 157
No. 15 Crack Shot Single Shot, 157
No. 16 Crack Shot Single Shot, 158
No. 17 Favorite Single Shot, 158
No. 18 Favorite Single Shot, 158
No. 19 Favorite Single Shot, 158
No. 23 Sure Shot, 158
No. 34 Hunter's Pet Pocket Single Shot, 158
No. 40 New Model Pocket or Bicycle, 159
No. 44 Ideal Single shot, 159
No. 44½ Ideal Single Shot, 159
No. 45 Ideal Range, 159
Central Fire Sporting Single Shot, 159
Hunter's Pet Pocket Centerfire Single Shot, 159
Old Model Pocket Single Shot, 159
Sporting Single Shot, 160
Shotguns
New Model Pocket Shotguns, 225
Tip-Up Shotgun, 225
Favorite No. 20, 225
Steyr Armory, 105, 135
Stocking, Alexander, & Company
Single-Action Pepperbox, 75
Stoeger Industries
Replica Pistols
Brown Bess Flintlock, 276
Kentuckian Flintlock, 276
Kentuckian Percussion, 276

Renegade Double-Barrel Percussion, 276
Replica Long Arms
Buccaneer Gun, 276
Double-Barrel Flintlock Shotgun, 276
Elephant Flintlock, 276
Flintlock Shotgun Model 4957B, 276
Flintlock Shotgun Model 6475W, 276
Single Shot Flintlock Shotgun, 276
Sturdivant Confederate Rifle, 190
Sturm, Ruger & Company
Old Army Cap & Ball Revolvers, 278
Sutherland, Samuel, Confederate Pistol, 78
Swiss Military Rifles
Model 1871 Vetterli, 160
Model 1874 Vetterli, 147
Model 1891 Military, 160
Symmes Breechloading Carbine, 197

T

Tallassee Enfield-Pattern Confederate Carbine, 190
Tanner, C.D., Double-Barrel Percussion Pistol, 75
Tanner Confederate Rifle, 190
Tarpley Confederate Carbine, 190
Taylor, Pleasant, and Sherrard, J., Confederate Revolver, 78
Texas-Enfield Confederate Rifle, 190
Thomas, Merrill, Latrobe and, Breech-Loading Carbine, 163
Thompson/Center Arms
Replica Handguns
Patriot Pistol, 278
Replica Long Arms
Cherokee Caplock Rifle, 278
Cougar Hawken Rifle, 278
Hawken Caplock Percussion, 278
Hawken Flintlock, 278
New Englander Percussion Rifle, 280
New Englander Shotgun, 280
Renegade Caplock Percussion, 280
Renegade Flintlock Rifle, 280
Renegade Musket, 280
Renegade Single Trigger Hunter, 280
Seneca Percussion Rifle, 280
New Englander Shotgun, 280
Thuer, F. Alexander, Deringer, 31
Thurber, Charles, and Ethan Allen, 19, 20
Todd Confederate Rifled Musket, 190
Traditions Inc.
Replica Handguns
Trapper Pistol, 280
Replica Long Arms
Frontier Carbine, 281
Frontier Rifle, 281
Frontier Scout, 281
Hawken Rifle, 281
Hunter Rifle, 281
Kentucky Scout Rifle, 281
Pennsylvania Rifle, 282
Shenandoah Rifle, 282
Fowler Shotgun, 282
Tranter, William, Percussion Revolver, 75
Turkish Firearms
Flintlock Pistol, 75
Mauser Model 1903 Mil. Rifle, 160
Mauser Model 1903 Military Rifle, 160
Turney, J., Flintlock Fowler, 225
Twigg, John, Revolving Flintlock Pistol, 75

U

Uhlinger, William, 36, 42,50
Union Arms Company, 75
Pocket Revolver, 76
"Union" Breech-Loading Carbine. *See* Cosmopolitan
Union Metallic Cartridge Co., 140, 159
Unwin & Rodgers Pocket Knife Pistols, 76
U.S. Military Handguns of Colt Manufacture. See Colt's Patent Fire Arms Mfg. Co.
U.S. Military Pistols
Model 1799 North & Cheney Flintlock, 93
Model 1805 Harpers Ferry Flintlock, 93
Model 1808 Navy Flintlock, 93
Model 1811 Flintlock, 93
Model 1811 Transition Flintlock, 95
Model 1813 Army/Navy Flintlock, 94, 95
Model 1816 Flintlock, 94, 95
Model 1819 Army/Navy Flintlock, 94, 95
Model 1826 Navy Flintlock, 94, 95
Model 1836 Flintlock, 95
Model 1842 Percussion, 95
Model 1843 Navy, 96
Henry Deringer Flintlock, 92
Rappahannock Forge Flintlock, 92
Remington Model 1867 Navy, 92
Remington Model 1871 Army, 93
Springfield Model 1817/18 Flintlock, 95
Springfield Model 1855 Pistol Carbine, 96
Springfield Breech Loading Pistol, 96
Valley Forge Flintlock Pistol, 96
U.S. Military Revolvers
Adams Army Revolver, 97
Allen & Wheelock Army Revolver, 97
Allen & Wheelock Navy Revolver, 97
Beals Patent Revolver, 97
Butterfield U.S. Army Revolver, 97
Joslyn Army Revolver, 98
Lefaucheux Army Pinfire Revolver, 98
Perrin Army Revolver, 98
Pettingill Army Revolver, 98
Raphael Revolver, 98
Remington Army Revolver, 99
Remington Navy Revolver, 99
Rogers and Spencer Revolver, 99
Savage Navy Revolver, 99
Schofield/S&W Revolver, 99
Smith and Wesson Revolver, 99
Starr Revolvers, 100
Wesson and Leavitt Revolver, 100
Whitney Navy Revolver, 100
U.S. model 1816 Flintlock Musket, 159
U.S. Revolver Co. Revolver, 76
U.S. Schroeder Breech-Loading Carbine, 197
U.S. Springfield
Model 1795 Flintlock Musket, 191
Model 1809 Flintlock Carbine, 191
Model 1816 Flintlock Musket, 192
Model 1819 Flintlock Rifle, 192
Model 1840 Musketoon Smooth Bore, 192

V

Valley Forge Flintlock Pistol, 86

Volcanic Repeating Arms Co., 80, 160

W

Wadsworth, Henry, 22, 40, 210, 211
Waffenfabrik Mauser, Mauser-
  Werke A.G., 52
Wallis Confederate Rifle, 190
Walsh, James & John, Kentucky
  Flintlock Pistol, 77
Warner, James
  Revolving Carbine, 161
  Single-shot Carbine, 161
  Solid-Frame Revolving Carbine, 161
  Breech-Loading Carbine, 197
  Percussion Revolver,76
Waters, A.H., 85, 112, 162
Webley & Scott Ltd.
  Mark III 38 Mil./Police Revolver, 76
  Model 1883 Revolver, 76
  Self-cocking Percussion Revolver, 77
  "Senior" Air Pistol, 77
  Wedge Frame Revolver, 77
Welshantz Brothers Kentucky
  Flintlock Rifle, 187
Wesson, Daniel Baird, 80, 155, 217,
  See also Smith & Wesson, Inc.
Wesson, Edwin, and Leavitt Revolver, 90
  Revolving Rifle, 161
Wesson, Frank, Breech-Loading
  Carbine, 197
  Two-Trigger Rifle, 161
Western Arms Co., Pocket Model
  Revolver, 77
Wheeler Patent Over/Under Pistols, 221
Wheeler, Robert, Trade Shotgun, 226
Wheelock, Thomas P., 22 **See also
  Allen & Wheelock**
  Wheellock Pistols, 78
  White, N., 50
White, Rollin, Arms Co. Revolver, 79
Whitney (Eli, Jr.) Arms Co., 127, 162,
  214. *See* also **Mexican Military
  Rifles**
  Handguns
  Navy Revolver, 90
  Percussion Revolver—Second Model,
  69
  Rifles
  Confederate-Enfield Mississippi Rifle,
  190

Confederate Rifled Musket, 190
Creedmoor No. 1, 162
Creedmoor No. 2, 162
Gallery, 162
Light Carbine, 162
Military Carbine, 162
Military Rifle, 162
Phoenix Carbine, 162
Phoenix Rifles, 162
Phoenix-Schuetzen Target, 162
Sporting & Target, 162
-Burgess Carbine, 162
-Burgess Rifles, 162, 163
-Kennedy Military Rifle, 163
-Kennedy Sporting Carbine, 163
-Kennedy Sporting Rifle, 163
Whitney, Eli, Sr., 162
Whittier, O.W. Percussion Rifle, 163
Williams, Ball &, 106
Williams & Powell Coat Pistol, 79
  Double-Barrel Pistol, 79
Williamson, David, 54
Winchester, Oliver, 67. *See also*
  Winchester Repeating Arms
Winchester Repeating Arms Co.,
  See also **Mexican Military Rifles**
  Handguns
  Volcanic Repeating Pistol, 67, 80
  Volcanic New Haven Repeating
  Pistol,80
  Rifles
  Model 1866 Lever-Action Carbine, 164
  Model 1866 Lever-Action Military
  Musket, 164
  Model 1866 Lever-Action, 164
  Model 1873 Carbine, 164
  Model 1873 Fancy Sporting, 164
  Model 1873 Lever-Action Sporting, 165
  Model 1873 One of One Thousand, 165
  Model 1876 Carbine, 165
  Model 1876 Fancy Sporting Rifle, 165
  Model 1876 Lever-Action Sporting
  Rifle, 165
  Model 1876 One of One Hundred, 165
  Model 1876 One of One Thousand, 165
  Model 1879 Bolt-Action Rifle, 166
  Model 1879 Bolt-Action Carbine, 166
  Model 1883 Hotchkiss Rifle, 166
  Model 1885 Engraved Single-Shot, 166
  Model 1885 Fancy Grade Single-Shot,
  166

Model 1885 Hi-Wall Single-Shot, 166
Model 1885 Low-Wall Single-Shot, 166
Model 1885 Musket, 166
Model 1885 Schuetzen, 167
Model 1885 "Winder" Musket, 167
Model 1886 Carbine, 167
Model 1886 Lightweight, 167
Model 1886 Fancy Sporting, 167
Model 1886 Sporting, 167
Model 1890 Slide-Action Repeater, 167
Model 1890 Slide-Action Fancy, 167
Model 1892 Carbine, 168
Model 1892 Fancy Engraved Models,
  168
Model 1892 Fancy Sporting Rifle, 168
Model 1892 Lever-Action Repeating
  Sporting, 168
Model 1892 Long Barrel, 168
Model 1892 Musket, 168
Model 1892 Short Barrel, 168
Model 1894 Carbine, 168
Model 1894 Fancy Sporting, 168
Model 1894 Repeating Rifle, 169
Model 1894 Saddle Ring Carbine, 169
Model 1895 Carbine, 169
Model 1895 Fancy Sporting, 169
Model 1895 Musket, 169
Model 1895 Repeating, 169
-Hotchkiss 1879, First & Second
  Model, 169
-Hotchkiss 1883 Repeating Rifle, 169
-Hotchkiss 1883 Repeating Rifle, 169
-Hotchkiss Repeating Carbine, 169
-Hotchkiss Repeating Musket, 169
-Lee Straight-Pull Bolt-Action Musket,
  170
-Lee Straight-Pull Bolt-Action Rifle,
  170
  Shotguns
  Imported Side-by-Side, 226
  Model 1887 Lever-Action, 227
  Model 1893 Slide-Action, 227
  Model 1897 Slide-Action, 227
Wood, H.T., & Co. Percussion Rifle, 170
Worrall, James, Pinfire Double-Barrel
  Shotgun, 228
Wurfflein, William, Tip-Up Rifles, 170
Wytheville-Hall Confederate Rifle, 190